W9-BDD-267

ACCOUNTING INFORMATION SYSTEMS

ACCOUNTING INFORMATION SYSTEMS

NINTH EDITION

George H. Bodnar

Duquesne University

William S. Hopwood

Florida Atlantic University

PEARSON

Prentice
Hall

Upper Saddle River, New Jersey

Library of Congress Cataloging-in-Publication Data

Bodnar, George H.
  Accounting information systems / George H. Bodnar, William S. Hopwood.—9th ed.
    p. cm.
  Includes bibliographical information and index.
    ISBN 0-13-008205-8
      1. Accounting—Data processing. 2. Information storage and retrieval
systems—Accounting.   I. Hopwood, William S.   II. Title.
HF5679.B59 2003
657'.0285—dc21
                                                                 2003054194

Editor-in-Chief: P. J. Boardman
Acquisitions Editor: Bill Larkin
Assistant Editor: Sam Goffinet
Senior Editorial Assistant: Jane Avery
Senior Media Project Manager: Nancy Welcher
Executive Marketing Manager: Beth Toland
Marketing Assistant: Melissa Owens
Managing Editor (Production): John Roberts
Production Editor: Kelly Warsak
Production Assistant: Joe DeProspero
Permissions Supervisor: Suzanne Grappi
Manufacturing Buyer: Michelle Klein
Cover Design: Bruce Kenselaar
Cover Photo: Steve Cole/Getty Images
Project Management: Robert Runck/nSight, Inc.
Composition: LaserWords
Printer/Binder: Courier–Westford
Cover Printer: Lehigh Press

Credits and acknowledgements borrowed from other sources and reproduced, with permission, in this textbook appear on appropriate pages within the text.

Copyright © 2004, 2001 by Pearson Education, Inc., Upper Saddle River, New Jersey 07458. All rights reserved. Printed in the United States of America. This publication is protected by Copyright and permission should be obtained from the publisher prior to any prohibited reproduction, storage in a retrieval system, or transmission in any form or by any means, electronic, mechanical, photocopying, recording, or likewise. For information regarding permission(s), write to: Rights and Permissions Department.

Pearson Prentice Hall™ is a trademark of Pearson Education, Inc.
Pearson® is a registered trademark of Pearson plc
Prentice Hall® is a registered trademark of Pearson Education, Inc.

Pearson Education LTD.
Pearson Education Singapore, Pte. Ltd
Pearson Education, Canada, Ltd
Pearson Education–Japan
Pearson Education Australia PTY, Limited
Pearson Education North Asia Ltd
Pearson Educación de Mexico, S.A. de C.V.
Pearson Education Malaysia, Pte. Ltd

10 9 8 7 6 5 4 3 2 1
ISBN 0-13-008205-8

To Donna, Kendra, Andy, Debbie, Zoe, Caitlin, and Drew Bodnar

BRIEF CONTENTS

Contents

The ninth edition of *Accounting Information Systems* stresses electronic commerce applied within the context of business processes, transaction cycles, and internal control. Detailed material on business processes and internal control is central to the topical organization. The business process chapters are SAP™-oriented and rely on SAP concepts to illustrate contemporary ERP systems. However, these chapters do not require the instructor to possess technical expertise in SAP™. The detailed material on internal controls in these chapters is consistent with other, non-SAP, approaches to ERP. There is an extensive CPA examination problem set pertaining to business processes and internal controls, with complete answers and explanations in the Instructor's Manual.

The ninth edition has three fewer chapters than the eighth edition. This has been done to emphasize the textbook's core coverage of business processes, transaction cycles, and internal controls. These topics have been central to this textbook since its original publication in 1980. The recent passage of the Sarbanes-Oxley Act is a testament to the continuing importance of these topics. An understanding of business processes is fundamental to contemporary auditing, professional, and legal considerations relating to an organization's internal control processes. Each process is subject to loss exposures. Management should develop detailed control objectives for each process. Such control objectives provide a basis for analysis and audit of an organization's internal control processes as well as a basis for managing the loss exposures that are associated with an organization's dependence on information systems.

Each chapter contains the following instructional aids:
Learning Objectives
Glossary
Chapter Quiz
Review Questions

The chapters in Part I survey information technology, systems techniques, electronic commerce, internal control, and computer security. Chapter 1 surveys the relationships between accounting and information technology and thus serves as a general introduction to the text. Chapter 2 provides detailed coverage of flowcharting and other systems documentation techniques. Chapter 3 provides a comprehensive survey of the Internet, electronic commerce, and information technology. Chapters 4 and 5 provide a foundation in internal controls and computer security.

Part II, consisting of Chapters 6–9, provides comprehensive coverage of business processes, focusing on those processes most relevant to the accountant. Each process is flowcharted and explained, with a focus on applying the relevant internal controls.

Part III provides coverage of systems development in two chapters. Chapter 10 covers systems development and analysis, and Chapter 11 covers implementation.

Part IV, consisting of Chapters 12 and 13, includes applications of AIS relating to databases and auditing. Chapter 12 has been revised with a discussion of SQL. A new Internet-based, active-learning supplement allows students to run SQL against the Electric Books database which is described in the chapter.

NEW AND RETAINED FEATURES

- Updated coverage of contemporary information technology including ERP, Web-based commerce, EDI, EFT paperless accounting systems, security, and disaster planning.
- Streamlined from 16 to 13 chapters to emphasize the textbook's core coverage of business processes, transaction cycles, and internal controls.
- Extensive CPA examination problem set (multiple-choice and essay questions) pertaining to business processes and internal controls, with answers and explanations in the Instructor's Manual.
- The discussion of database technology has been revised with a discussion of SQL and includes an Internet-based, active-learning supplement that allows students to run SQL against a database which is documented in the text.

THE INSTRUCTOR'S RESOURCE AND SOLUTIONS MANUAL

This manual is a comprehensive resource, which includes chapter overviews that outline each chapter of the text and provide a strong base for planning lectures, teaching tips that introduce each chapter overview and provide helpful teaching hints, transparency masters derived from selected textbook figures, and solutions/suggested solutions for the textbook review questions, discussion questions, and problems. Available at www.prenhall.com/bodnar.

THE TEST ITEM FILE

The Test Item File includes approximately 1,600 test items that can be used as quiz and/or exam material. The Test Item File includes approximately 100 questions per chapter. Available at www.prenhall.com/bodnar.

SOFTWARE FOR TEST MANAGEMENT

TestGenEQ Testing Software is by Tamarack Software, Inc. This easy-to-use computerized testing program can create exams, evaluate, and track student results. Test items are drawn from the Test Item File.

POWERPOINT PRESENTATIONS

PowerPoint presentations are available for each chapter of the text. This resource allows instructors to offer a more interactive presentation using colorful graphics, outlines of chapter material, additional examples, and visual explanations of difficult topics. Instructors have the flexibility to add slides and/or modify the existing slides to meet the course needs. Available at www.prenhall.com/bodnar.

WEB SITE

www.prenhall.com/bodnar
This web site contains all resources for students and faculty.

ACKNOWLEDGMENTS

The authors wish to acknowledge the helpful comments of the following reviewers:

Somnath Bhattacharya	Florida Atlantic University
Timothy B. Biggart	University of North Carolina, Greensboro
Darrell Brown	Portland State University
Wede E. Brownell	Langston University
Stephanie M. Bryant	University of South Florida
Jack Cathey	University of North Carolina, Charlotte
Richard Dull	Clemson University
Ronald H. Eaton	Rhodes College
Jane Finley	Belmont University
David R. Fordham	James Madison University
George P. Geran	Florida Metropolitan University
Glenn L. Helms	University of North Carolina, Asheville
Charles Holley	Virginia Commonwealth University
Khursheed Omer	University of Houston, Downtown
Dennis L. Williams	California Polytechnic State University, San Luis Obispo
Minnie Yen	University of Alaska, Anchorage
Benny R. Zachry	Nicholls State University

G. H. B.
W. S. H.

ACCOUNTING INFORMATION SYSTEMS: AN OVERVIEW

LEARNING OBJECTIVES

Careful study of this chapter will enable you to:

❖ Understand the related concepts of transaction cycles and internal control structure.

❖ Describe the organizational structure of the information system function in organizations.

❖ Discuss applications of information technology in organizations.

❖ Characterize the development of information systems.

ACCOUNTING INFORMATION SYSTEMS AND BUSINESS ORGANIZATIONS

Organizations depend on information systems to stay competitive. Information is just as much a resource as plant and equipment. Productivity, which is crucial to staying competitive, can be increased through better information systems. Accounting, as an information system, identifies, collects, processes, and communicates economic information about an entity to a wide variety of people. Information is useful data organized such that correct decisions can be based on it. A system is a collection of resources related such that certain objectives can be achieved.

An **accounting information system (AIS)** is a collection of resources, such as people and equipment, designed to transform financial and other data into information. This information is communicated to a wide variety of decision makers. Accounting information systems perform this transformation whether they are essentially manual systems or thoroughly computerized.

INFORMATION AND DECISIONS

An organization is a collection of decision-making units that exist to pursue objectives. As a system, every organization accepts inputs and transforms them into outputs that take the form of products and services. A manufacturing firm transforms raw material, labor, and other scarce resource inputs into tangible items, such as furniture, that are subsequently sold in pursuit of the goal of profit. A university accepts a variety of inputs, such as faculty labor and student time, and transforms these inputs into a variety of outputs in pursuit of the broad goals of education and the promotion of knowledge. Conceptually, all organizational systems seek objectives through a process of resource allocation, which is accomplished through the process of managerial decision making. Information has economic value to the extent that it facilitates resource allocation decisions, thus assisting a system in its pursuit of goals. Indeed, information may be the most important organizational resource.

The users of accounting information fall into two broad groups: external and internal. External users include stockholders, investors, creditors, government agencies, customers and vendors, competitors, labor unions, and the public at large. External users receive and depend on a variety of outputs from an organization's accounting information system. Many of these outputs are of a routine nature. Accounts payable transactions with suppliers, for example, require outputs such as purchase orders and checks from an organization's accounting information system. Customers receive bills and make payments, which are processed by the accounting information system. Employees receive paychecks and other payroll-related data; stockholders receive dividend checks and routine information concerning stock transactions.

The information needs of external users are varied. The publication of general-purpose financial statements, such as balance sheets and income statements, and other nonroutine outputs, assists in meeting these needs. Stockholders, investors at large, creditors, and other external users utilize a firm's general-purpose financial statements to evaluate past performance, predict future performance, and gain other insights into an organization.

Internal users consist of managers, whose requirements depend on their level in an organization or on the particular function they perform. Figure 1.1 is a schematic of the different levels of managerial interest in information. The diagram emphasizes that there are different information needs and demands at different managerial levels in an organization. The accounting information system summarizes and filters the data available to decision makers. By processing the data, the accounting information system influences organizational decisions.

Figure 1.2 presents information characteristics relevant to lower-level, middle, and top-level managers in an organization. Top-level management generally is concerned with strategic planning and control. Accounting reports to top-level management accordingly consist largely of aggregated and summarized items such as total quarterly sales by product line or division. Middle managers need more detail, such as daily or weekly sales by product line, because their scope of control is narrower. Lower-level managers typically receive information relevant only to their particular subunit, such

FIGURE 1.1   PYRAMID OF INFORMATION LEVELS IN AN ORGANIZATION.

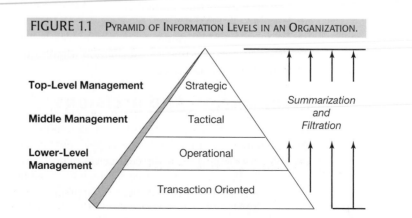

Characteristics of Information	Lower-Level Managers Operational Control	Middle Managers Management Control	Top-Level Managers Strategic Planning
Source	Largely Internal	- - - - - ->	External
Scope	Well-Defined, Narrow	- - - - - ->	Very Wide
Level of Aggregation	Detailed	- - - - - ->	Aggregate
Time Horizon	Historical	- - - - - ->	Future
Currency	Highly Current	- - - - - ->	Quite Old
Required Accuracy	High	- - - - - ->	Low
Frequency of Use	Very Frequent	- - - - - ->	Infrequent

FIGURE 1.2   INFORMATION QUALITIES.

as the total sales of Department A. Personnel in the lower levels of an organization, such as clerks processing payroll or sales transaction data, constantly interact with the detailed transaction data.

The production of useful information is constrained by the environment of an accounting information system and the cost-benefit structure inherent in users' decisions. The uncertainty of the environment in which information is developed and presented means that estimates and judgments must be made. No information system can ignore the practicality of presenting information. If information costs more to provide than it is worth to the user, it is not practical to provide this information.

From an organization's viewpoint, a distinction might be drawn between two broad classes of accounting information: mandatory and discretionary. Various government agencies, private agencies, and legislation set statutory requirements for record keeping and reports. Reports, for example, are required for federal and state income taxes, Social Security taxes, and by the Securities and Exchange Commission, Federal Trade Commission, and the like. In addition, certain basic accounting functions are essential to normal business activity. Payroll and accounts receivable are prime examples. These functions must be performed in any organization if the organization is to survive. Budgetary systems, responsibility accounting systems, and specific reports for internal management are examples of discretionary information. Conceptually, information should satisfy a cost-benefit criterion. Although the criterion theoretically applies to all the outputs of an accounting information system, the typical organization does not have control over all its information requirements. In meeting mandatory information requirements, the primary consideration is minimizing costs while meeting minimum standards of reliability and usefulness. When the provision of information is discretionary, the primary consideration is that the benefits obtained exceed the costs of production.

INFORMATION SYSTEMS

The term *information system* suggests the use of computer technology in an organization to provide information to users. A *computer-based* information system is a collection

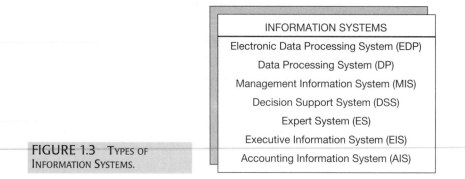

FIGURE 1.3 TYPES OF
INFORMATION SYSTEMS.

of computer hardware and software designed to transform data into useful information. As indicated in Figure 1.3, one might distinguish several types of computer-based information systems.

DATA PROCESSING

Electronic data processing (EDP) is the use of computer technology to perform an organization's transaction-oriented data processing. EDP is a fundamental accounting information system application in every organization. As computer technology has become commonplace, the term **data processing (DP)** has come to have the same meaning as EDP.

MANAGEMENT INFORMATION SYSTEMS

Management information systems (MIS) describes the use of computer technology to provide decision-oriented information to managers. An MIS provides a wide variety of information beyond that which is associated with DP in organizations. An MIS recognizes that managers within an organization use and require information in decision making and that computer-based information systems can assist in providing information to managers.

Functional MIS Subsystems   Many organizations apply the MIS concept to specific functional areas within the organization. Terms such as *marketing information system, manufacturing information system*, and *human resources information system* indicate the tailoring of the MIS concept to the development of specific information systems to support decision making in a particular, well-defined organization subunit.

A *marketing information system* is an MIS that provides information to be used by the marketing function. Much of the information is provided by the organization's accounting information system. Examples are sales summaries and cost information. Other information must be collected from the organization's environment. Examples of environmental information would include consumer preference data, customer profiles, and information on competitors' products.

A *manufacturing information system* is an MIS that provides information to be used by the manufacturing function. Much of the information is provided by the organization's accounting information system. Examples are inventory summaries and cost information. Other information must be collected from the organization's environment. Examples of environmental information would include raw materials data, potential new vendor profiles, and information on new manufacturing techniques.

A *human resource information system* is an MIS that provides information to be used by the human resource (i.e., personnel) function. Much of the information is provided by the organization's accounting information system. Examples are wage and payroll tax summaries and benefit information. Other information must be collected from the organization's environment. Examples of environmental information would include government regulation data and general labor market information.

A *financial information system* is an MIS that provides information to be used by the finance function. Much of the information is provided by the organization's accounting information system application. Examples are cash flow summaries and payment information. Other information must be collected from the organization's environment. Examples of environmental information would include interest rate data, lender profiles, and information on credit markets.

These functional information subsystems are found in many organizations. Any well-defined application area in an organization might develop its own MIS. An internal audit information system might be developed for use by the internal audit function. A corporate quality information system might be developed for use by an organization's corporate quality group.

It is important to note that functional MIS subsystems are not physically independent. They share common information system resources in an organization. In particular, they all depend on an organization's accounting information system for important inputs concerning the results of operations and other matters. Functional MIS subsystems represent a logical rather than physical way of implementing the MIS concept in organizations.

DECISION SUPPORT SYSTEMS

In a **decision support system (DSS)**, data are processed into a decision-making format for the end user. A DSS requires the use of decision models and specialized databases and differs significantly from a DP system. A DSS is directed at serving ad hoc, specific, nonroutine information requests by management. DP systems serve routine, recurring, general information needs. A DSS is designed for specific types of decisions for specific users. A familiar example is the use of spreadsheet software to perform what-if analyses of operating or budget data, such as sales forecasting by marketing personnel.

EXPERT SYSTEMS

An **expert system (ES)** is a knowledge-based information system that uses its knowledge about a specific application area to act as an expert consultant to end users. Like DSS, an ES requires the use of decision models and specialized databases. Unlike DSS, an ES also requires the development of a knowledge base—the special knowledge that an expert possesses in the decision area—and an inference engine—the process by which the expert makes a decision. An ES attempts to replicate the decisions that would be made by an expert human decision maker in the same decision situation. An ES differs from a DSS in that a DSS assists a user in making a decision, whereas an ES makes the decision.

EXECUTIVE INFORMATION SYSTEMS

An **executive information system (EIS)** is tailored to the strategic information needs of top-level management. Much of the information used by top-level management comes from sources other than an organization's information systems. Examples are meetings, memos, television, periodicals, and social activities. Some information must be processed by the organization's information systems; however, an EIS provides top-level management with easy access to selective information that has been processed by the organization's information systems. This selective information concerns the key factors that top-level management has identified as being critical to the organization's success. Actual versus projected market share for product groups and budget versus actual profit and loss data for divisions might be key success factors for a top-level executive.

ACCOUNTING INFORMATION SYSTEMS

Analogous to the preceding definitions, we might define an **accounting information system (AIS)** as a computer-based system designed to transform accounting data into information. However, we use the term *accounting information system* more broadly to include transaction processing cycles, the use of information technology, and the development of information systems.

BUSINESS PROCESSES

All financially related activities of the organization can be viewed as part of various business processes. A **business process** is an interrelated set of tasks that involve data, organizational units, and a logical time sequence. Business processes are always triggered by some economic event, and all have clearly defined starting and ending points. For example, the customer order management process might be triggered by the receipt of a customer purchase order, the process might begin with the creation of a sales order, and it might end with the collection of the customer's payment on accounts receivable.

Since most organizations experience similar types of economic events and activities, it is possible to define nine general groups of basic business processes (Fig. 1.4). These include the following:

1. Inbound sales logistics (inventory, control, returns to supplier, etc.)
2. Outbound sales logistics (sales order processing, collection, shipping, delivery, etc.)
3. Operations (machining, assembly, packaging, etc.)
4. Marketing (advertising, promotion, bidding, etc.)
5. Service (installation, repair, postsales support, etc.)
6. Procurement (purchasing, ordering, soliciting bids, etc.)
7. Technology development (resource and development)
8. Organization and human resource management (hiring, training, etc.)
9. Firm infrastructure (accounting, business planning and controlling, capital asset management, etc.)

Further, the first five of these processes can be classified as primary, and the last four processes can be classified as supporting. **Primary business processes** involve activities that directly add value to the company's products, and **supporting business processes** involve activities that indirectly add value and support the primary processes.

FIGURE 1.4   PRIMARY AND SUPPORTING BUSINESS PROCESSES.

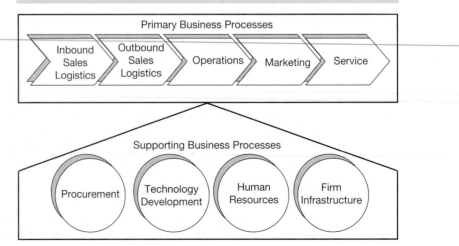

Collectively, the primary and supporting business processes comprise the entire value chain of activities. All in all, the **value chain** is simply a way of viewing the company's activities in a manner suited to analyzing its competitive advantages. The value chain breaks activities down into components that can be individually optimized in terms of the company's goals and strategies.

Both the primary and supporting business processes can be further subdivided into many subprocesses. For example, outbound sales logistics can be divided into order entry, credit checking, and so on. Subdividing processes is a helpful tool for the systems person and the accountant because it makes it possible to focus on clearly defined, specific areas of the enormous set of the company's activities.

Enterprise resource planning (ERP) consists of the company-wide integration of business processes. ERP software packages are financially oriented information systems that support and automate business processes. ERP software packages are sold by several companies, including SAP, PeopleSoft, BaaN, and Oracle.

TRANSACTION PROCESSING CYCLES

An alternative way to view the activities of the organization is through *transaction cycles*. Transaction cycles traditionally have grouped activities of a business into four common cycles of business activity:

- **Revenue cycle.** Events related to the distribution of goods and services to other entities and the collection of related payments
- **Expenditure cycle.** Events related to the acquisition of goods and services from other entities and the settlement of related obligations
- **Production cycle.** Events related to the transformation of resources into goods and services
- **Finance cycle.** Events related to the acquisition and management of capital funds, including cash

A **transaction processing cycle** consists of one or more application systems. An **application system** processes logically related transactions. An organization's revenue cycle might commonly include application systems involving customer order entry, billing, accounts receivable, and sales reporting. An expenditure cycle might commonly include application systems involving vendor selection and requisitioning, purchasing, accounts payable, and payroll. A production cycle might include application systems involving production control and reporting, product costing, inventory control, and property accounting. An organization's finance cycle might include application systems concerned with cash management and control, debt management, and the administration of employee benefit plans.

The transaction cycle model of an organization includes a fifth cycle—the **financial reporting cycle**. The financial reporting cycle is not an operating cycle. It obtains accounting and operating data from the other cycles and processes these data in such a manner that financial reports may be prepared. The preparation of financial reports in accordance with generally accepted accounting principles requires many valuation and adjusting entries that do not directly result from exchanges. Depreciation and currency translation are two common examples. Such activities are part of an organization's financial reporting cycle.

INTERNAL CONTROL PROCESS

Perhaps the most important aspect of an accounting information system is the role it plays in an organization's **internal control process**. The term *internal control process* suggests actions taken within an organization to regulate and direct the activities of the organization.

Much information needed by management to control finances and operations comes from the accounting information system. One of management's major responsibilities is stewardship. Management must protect the resources of an organization against possible losses ranging from embezzlement to careless use of supplies or productive materials, unwarranted extension of credit, failure to purchase from the lowest-cost supplier, inefficient workers, and outright theft.

Control ensures that management policies and directives are properly adhered to. Management is far removed from the scene of operations in a large organization, and personal supervision of employees is impossible. As a substitute, management must rely on various control techniques to implement its decisions and goals and to regulate the activities for which it has ultimate responsibility. Control extends over a wide range of activities, such as the maintenance of inventory quantities, the consumption of supplies in production and administration, and the payment of bills within allowed discount periods. Good internal control is a key factor in the effective management of an organization.

ELEMENTS OF INTERNAL CONTROL PROCESS

Internal control is a process designed to provide reasonable assurance regarding the achievement of objectives in (1) reliability of financial reporting, (2) effectiveness and efficiency of operations, and (3) compliance with applicable laws and regulations. An organization's internal control process consists of five elements: the control environment, risk assessment, control activities, information and communication, and monitoring. These elements are defined and discussed in Chapter 4. The present discussion seeks only to introduce the notion of internal control. The concept of internal control structure is based on two major premises, these being management's responsibility and reasonable assurance.

Internal control should require the establishment of responsibilities within an organization. A specific person should be responsible for each task or job function. The reason is twofold: Responsibilities must be clearly assigned in order to delineate problem areas and direct attention to them, and once employees have a clear understanding of the scope of their responsibilities, they tend to work harder toward controlling these responsibilities.

Internal control also calls for the maintenance of adequate records in an effort to control assets and analyze the assignment of responsibility. Good documentation means that records should be maintained by all parties involved in a transaction. Accordingly, all records should allow cross-referencing from one area of responsibility to another. Along this same line, responsibilities for related transactions should be divided. In the process, one area of responsibility will provide a check on the other, and vice versa. The people responsible for the custody of assets should not be responsible for recording the assets in the books of record. Employees are less likely to misappropriate or waste assets if they realize that others are recording their use. This does not mean that work should be duplicated, although in many cases some duplication is unavoidable. Ideally, a task can be so divided as to make job functions natural checks on each other.

For example, the inventory records maintained by an inventory application system establish accountability over goods in a store. Periodic physical inventory counts will reveal shortages or errors that may creep into the records, and the knowledge that the results of their activities will be compared gives the stock clerks and the inventory clerk an incentive to work carefully. The stock clerks will watch the accuracy of receiving room counts as goods are transferred to their custody because the receiving records will be the basis for charging the inventory records for the goods the stock clerks must account for.

SEGREGATION OF ACCOUNTING FUNCTIONS

Of primary importance is the segregation of duties so that no individual or department controls the accounting records relating to its own operation. A common violation of this principle is the delegation of both accounting and financial responsibilities to the same individual or department. Both the accounting and finance functions are concerned primarily with money, so "logical" thinking places both responsibilities under one person. The financing function of a business is just as much an operating responsibility as the manufacturing or sales function. Recognizing this fact suggests the need for segregation of the accounting and finance functions.

A common approach is to delegate the accounting function to a controller or similar office and the finance function to a treasurer. Typically, the controller and treasurer are top-management officials functioning on an equal plane with other executives who report directly to the president. The organization chart in Figure 1.5 illustrates such an arrangement.

The accounting function involves several subfunctions. In a small business, the controller is likely to handle these personally, but in a large concern, the duties ordinarily are delegated to staff assistants or department heads.

Figure 1.5 shows several normal staff positions that commonly report to the controller. The budgeting function involves the preparation of operating budgets, capital expenditure budgets, and the related forecasts and analyses used by management in planning and controlling the operations of the organization. The tax planning function concerns the administration of tax reporting and the analysis of transactions that have significant tax consequences for the organization. The accounting manager supervises the routine operating functions of the accounting department, such as posting the general ledger and preparing financial reports.

The treasurer is responsible for the finances of the business. He or she arranges to obtain the funds necessary to finance operations and is charged with securing any required funds under the best terms commensurate with the needs of the business. In addition, the treasurer is responsible for the liquid assets of the business—cash, receivables, and investments.

FIGURE 1.5 ORGANIZATION CHART.

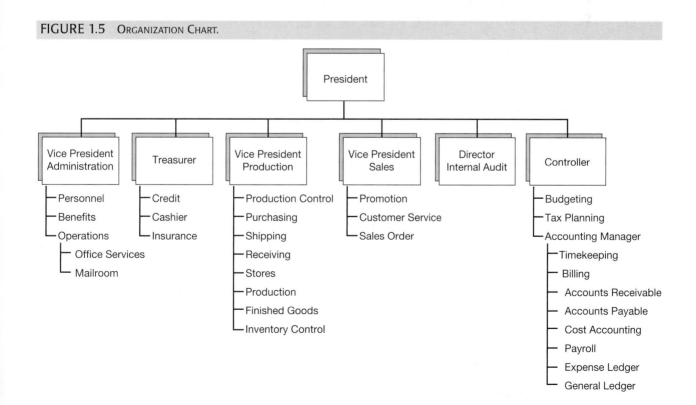

Records of these assets are maintained under the controller in order to obtain the desired segregation of accounting and operations. Under the treasurer is the credit manager, who is responsible for credit and collections, even though the original charge to accounts receivable and the accounting for receivables are both handled by the accounting department. Cash collections on these receivables are placed in the custody of a cashier, who is also responsible to the treasurer. Accountability over the cashier is established through the accounts receivable records and the general ledger record of cash. The credit to receivables that relieves the credit manager of responsibility when cash is received on an account is offset by the debit to cash that charges the cashier with the collected funds.

INTERNAL AUDIT FUNCTION

Recognizing the need for and complexity of adequate internal control in a large organization has led to the evolution of internal auditing as a control over all other internal controls. Internal audit is charged with monitoring and assessing compliance with organizational policies and procedures.

Internal audit is an independent appraisal activity within an organization. The organizational level of the internal audit function must be high enough to enable it to operate independently. Figure 1.5 shows the director of internal audit at the vice-presidential level. This placement of internal audit responsibilities is now common in large organizations because it enhances the independence of internal audit, although historically most internal audit functions have been subject to the authority of the controller or other chief accounting officer. Whatever its organizational status, the internal audit function must be segregated from the accounting function and also have neither responsibility nor authority for any operating activity.

ACCOUNTING AND INFORMATION TECHNOLOGY

The term *accounting information system* includes the use of information technology to provide information to users. Computers are used in all types of information systems. Information technology includes computers, but it also includes other technologies used to process information. Technologies such as machine-readable bar codes and scanning devices and communications protocols and standards such as ANSI X.12 are essential to office automation and quick-response systems.

THE INFORMATION SYSTEM FUNCTION

Every organization that uses computers to process transactional data has an information system function. The **information system function** is responsible for data processing (DP). DP is a fundamental accounting information system application in every organization. The information system function in organizations has evolved from simple organizational structures involving few people to complex structures involving many qualified specialists.

ORGANIZATIONAL LOCATION

Figure 1.6 shows the head of the information systems function titled as **chief information officer (CIO)** and an advisory group called a *steering committee*. Each of these functions represents a common response to the issues related to the organizational placement of responsibility for the overall information system function. The location of the information system function in the organization has become important as computer applications have become common and essential in all parts of an organization. As computer applications have crossed functions and the computer system's budget has

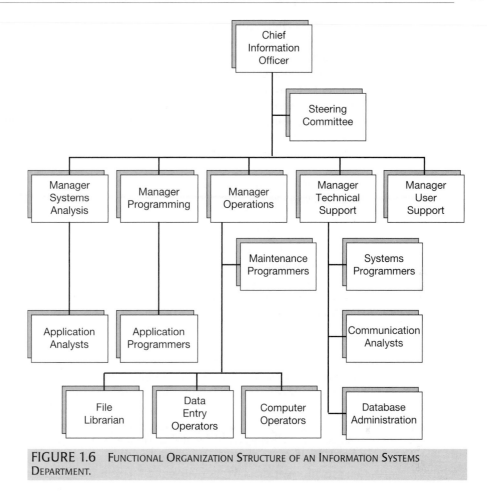

FIGURE 1.6 FUNCTIONAL ORGANIZATION STRUCTURE OF AN INFORMATION SYSTEMS DEPARTMENT.

increased in size, there has been a trend toward elevating the information system function in the organization. In many firms, the CIO reports to the firm's vice-presidential level or is in a position at the vice-presidential level. However, many information system departments still report to a senior financial officer such as the controller. This is often true in small firms and among relatively new users.

Regardless of the organizational location of the information system function, a **steering committee** or other advisory group is the means by which managers of other areas can influence the policies, budget, and planning of information services. A steering committee consists of high-level members of user functions such as manufacturing and marketing, as well as the head of the information system function and several of his or her staff. The steering committee meets periodically to set and review important policy, budget, and project decisions relating to information systems. Because the members are consumers of the product of the information system, a steering committee provides user feedback in controlling the information system function. A member of the internal audit function also might participate on the steering committee, or the audit function might advise and review the information system function through a different channel.

FUNCTIONAL SPECIALIZATIONS

The most prevalent information system departmental structure is the assignment of responsibilities and duties by area of technical specialization, that is, function. The larger the information system department, the more specialized functions are likely to be.

A large information systems department with functional organization is shown in Figure 1.6. The department is organized into five major functions: systems analysis, programming, operations, technical support, and user support. The **analysis function** focuses on identifying problems and projects for computer processing and designing systems to satisfy these problems' requirements. The **programming function** is responsible for the design, coding, testing, and debugging of computer programs necessary to implement the system designed by the analysis function. The **operations function** is charged with data preparation, operation of the equipment, and system maintenance. The **technical support function** allows specialization in areas such as operating systems and software, data management and database design, and communications technology. The **user support function** services end users, much as the technical support function services personnel of the information systems department.

Each of these major functions may be subdivided as the size and technical sophistication of the information system function increase. The analysis function might be factored into specialties concerning the identification of user information requirements (information analyst) and the translation of these needs into computer application systems (systems designer). The programming function might be subdivided into systems, application, and maintenance programming specialties. The operations function might be subdivided into computer operations, data preparation, and a librarian function responsible for program and data files.

Technical support specializations include systems programming, which concentrates on software development. This allows the systems analysis function to concentrate on identifying user information requirements and conceptual system design. Data administration as a technical support function coordinates data storage and use among system users and assumes responsibility for the integrity of the corporate database. Communication analysts specialize in data communications technology, the means by which data are transferred among networks for processing.

Specializations within the technical support function can vary greatly depending on the information system environment. This is true for the analysis, programming, operations, and user support functions as well. For example, note that in Figure 1.6 maintenance programmers report to the manager of operations rather than to the manager of programming. Assigning several maintenance programmers to the operations function often occurs in organizations that depend heavily on their computer-based information systems. The large number of programs makes maintenance a continuous activity and one on which the operation function becomes highly dependent.

The user support function is necessitated by distributed processing technology, which fosters end-user computing. The manager of user support works with the CIO to plan the supply of computing services to end users. The user support function often becomes an information center. An **information center** is a support facility for end users in an organization. It assists users in developing their own computer processing applications. An information center might provide users with equipment and software as well as with consulting support. In many organizations, the information center helps end users evaluate personal computer hardware and software for their particular computing requirements. The user support function also might serve as a place where users can make comments and suggestions concerning the operation of the information systems department.

Although the functional form of organization is prevalent, a common variation is to structure the analysis and programming functions by project. In **project organization**, analysts and programmers are assigned to specific application projects and work together to complete a project under the direction of a project leader. Project organization focuses responsibility for application projects on a single group, unlike functional organization, in which responsibility for a specific project is spread across different functional areas.

END-USER COMPUTING

In information systems terminology, an *end user* is an organizational function other than the information system function that requires computer data processing. The sales or marketing function is an end user that requires computer processing for sales reports, market analyses, sales projections, sales budgets, and so forth. The accounting function is an end user that requires computer processing support for posting of journals and preparation of reports.

End-user computing (EUC) is the hands-on use of computers by end users. Functional end users do their own information processing activities with hardware, software, and professional resources provided by the organization. A common EUC application is information retrieval from the organization's database using the query language feature of database management systems (DBMS).

For example, a user such as an accountant might access accounts receivable data from a company's centralized database, manipulate them, and then print a report. This might occur as shown in Figure 1.7. Using a networked personal computer and the query language software, the user prepares and submits a report request to the database access control software. The job is processed by the query language processor against the database, and the report is distributed to the user. As just illustrated, the end user has bypassed direct use of information systems specialists by developing his or her own data processing application and then directly implementing it with the query language software. This direct, hands-on use of computers by users to perform functions that previously had to be performed by information systems specialists is the distinguishing feature of EUC (Fig. 1.8). Prior to facilities for EUC, the end user would have had to specify his or her processing request to the organization's information systems department and then await the outcome. If the request was denied or delayed, the user might perform the task manually, if possible.

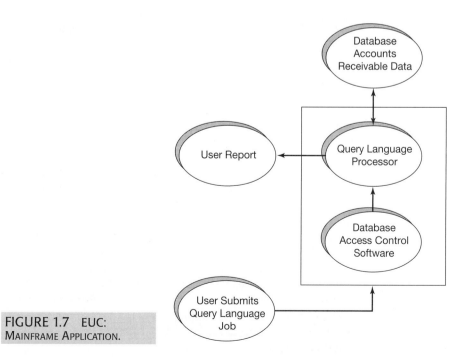

FIGURE 1.7   EUC:
MAINFRAME APPLICATION.

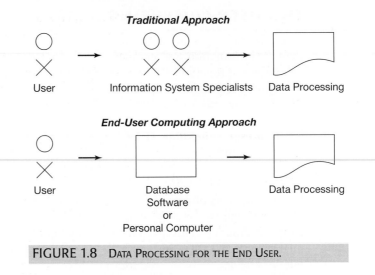

Traditional Approach

User   Information System Specialists   Data Processing

End-User Computing Approach

User   Database
              Software
              or
              Personal Computer   Data Processing

FIGURE 1.8   DATA PROCESSING FOR THE END USER.

Personal computers (PCs) give end users their own processing power. Once users have obtained data, they may perform additional processing. For example, a user might access data from a centralized database as described before but then process the data using spreadsheet software (Fig. 1.9). The significant impact of distributed information technology within organizations is this capability of end users to perform independent computer processing. End users can participate in applications development without the direct involvement of information systems specialists.

QUICK-RESPONSE TECHNOLOGY

The term *quick-response system* is seemingly self-explanatory. Certainly such systems are "quick" and "responsive." But much more is implied in the quick-response concept. Quick-response systems are essential to the **total quality performance (TQP)** movement

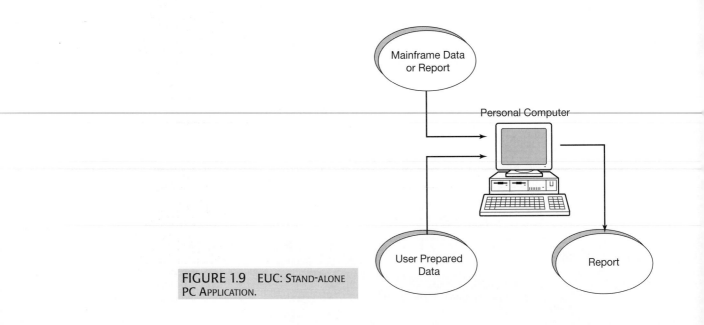

Mainframe Data
or Report

Personal Computer

User Prepared
Data

Report

FIGURE 1.9   EUC: STAND-ALONE
PC APPLICATION.

in business. TQP (also called **TQM—total quality management**) is a philosophy that one should *do the right thing right the first time*. TQP requires high-quality production, operational efficiency, and continuous improvement in operations. TQP emphasizes customer satisfaction to the point of customer obsession. In the extremely competitive environment of the business world, TQP is a strategy for survival.

Several technologies interact to make quick-response systems feasible. Hardware and software standardization and the movement toward open systems have made the interconnection of computer systems easier. **Electronic data interchange (EDI)** is essential to quick-response systems. Although EDI is essential to the "quick" in quick-response systems, it alone is not sufficient. Universal product code (UPC) bar code identification of products and scanning technology, such as point-of-sale (POS) retail terminals, are other essential technologies. The UPC bar code scanned by POS technology at the checkout counter of a retail store is the initial event in a chain of events that ends with the item, *the right item*, being quickly replenished in the store's inventory so that it can be sold again (Fig. 1.10). This is critical in retailing, where fads (i.e., customer demand for certain products) can and do change rapidly. What sold last year, last month, or maybe even last week may no longer be what the customer wants.

JUST-IN-TIME

A quick-response retail sales system is the retailing equivalent of **just-in-time (JIT)** inventory systems used in manufacturing. Purchase orders for inventory items are made on a "demand–pull" basis rather than a fixed-interval (e.g., monthly or weekly) "push" basis to restock store inventory levels.

In a non-JIT environment, process activity is intermittent. Batches of similar products are processed periodically to satisfy present and planned future needs. Setup activity costs usually are incurred every time a batch is processed, and these costs are

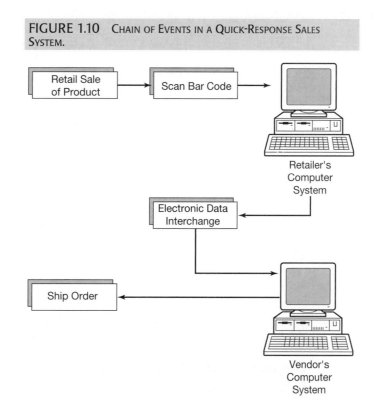

FIGURE 1.10   CHAIN OF EVENTS IN A QUICK-RESPONSE SALES SYSTEM.

typically the same regardless of the proposed size of the batch processing run. As the word *planned* indicates, a batch environment fosters a push concept of efficiency. Economic (i.e., efficient) batch size is derived by using formulas, such as those provided in EOQ (economic order quantity) models. In a non-JIT retail sales environment, for example, orders for new products are processed periodically as a batch and sent to vendors to replenish inventory stocks. Inventory stocks are kept at levels adequate to satisfy anticipated future needs. Ordering (setup) costs are minimized by applying EOQ concepts to reordering decisions.

A JIT environment is a continuous-flow environment rather than a batch-process environment. A JIT environment requires operation of a process on a continuous basis to minimize or totally eliminate inventories. JIT also advocates the elimination of waste in the manufacturing process and stresses continuous improvement in operation. JIT is similar in concept to TQM and is considered by many to be an essential aspect of TQM.

In a JIT environment, process activities occur under a pull concept. Activity (i.e., ordering new product) occurs only when it is needed to satisfy customer demand. Customer demand, as evidenced by current sales, pulls orders from the reordering process; in effect, demand causes orders to be placed to vendors. Orders to vendors are placed on the basis of actual sales to quickly replenish stocks of items that are selling. Current sales demand pulls (i.e., automatically generates) orders for inventory. Retailers can order on the basis of current buying trends.

WEB COMMERCE

Sales via the World Wide Web are an integral part of the economy. Such sales provide many benefits to both consumers and merchants. For consumers, some of the benefits are as follows:

1. There is no waiting in line for a salesperson or product information.
2. Through intelligent Web-based software, customers can find fast answers to complicated questions relating to the merchant's products.
3. Web-based transactions are normally encrypted, which provides enhanced security.

Benefits to merchants include

1. Cost savings through automated ordering.
2. Automatic electronic encoding of transaction data.
3. Low overhead. The entire Internet store can exist on a single desktop computer.
4. Worldwide availability of company's products.
5. The ability to rapidly update and disseminate new product or pricing information.

A central concern for anyone buying via the Web is security and privacy. For this reason, the American Institute of Public Accountants sponsors the **Web Trust** seal of approval that specially trained certified public accountants award to Web sites that meet the criteria.

ELECTRONIC DATA INTERCHANGE

Electronic data interchange (EDI) is the direct computer-to-computer exchange of business documents via a communications network (Fig. 1.11). EDI differs from electronic mail in that electronic mail messages are created and interpreted by humans (person to person), whereas EDI messages are created and interpreted by computers. Public EDI standards, in particular ANSI X.12, have had great impact on the development of quick-response systems. Public EDI standards provide a common architecture for data interchange and thus eliminate costly and error-prone cross-referencing of codes by parties to an EDI transaction.

An EDI link between a retailer's computer system and a vendor's computer system eliminates paper processing and allows near-instantaneous placing and processing

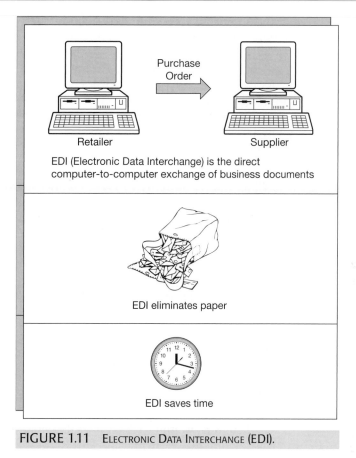

Retailer

Supplier

EDI (Electronic Data Interchange) is the direct
computer-to-computer exchange of business documents

EDI eliminates paper

EDI saves time

FIGURE 1.11   ELECTRONIC DATA INTERCHANGE (EDI).

of purchase orders, facilitating quick-response shipment. The vendor also might invoice the retailer using EDI. In some cases, **electronic funds transfer (EFT)** payment might be made by the retailer to the vendor's account. All these events, including the picking of the order from the vendor's inventory, might take place without any human intervention.

EXTENSIBLE BUSINESS REPORTING LANGUAGE

Extensible Business Reporting Language (XBRL) is a language that facilitates the exchange over the Internet of all kinds of business documents and financial statements. XBRL is in effect a broader standard than ANSI X.12 for EDI, and many feel that XBRL eventually will replace EDI.

The Securities and Exchange Commission (SEC) financial reporting requirements represent a good example of the application of XBRL. The SEC permits companies to file their financial reports electronically in XBRL format. Reports filed this way become available publically on the SEC's Web site within only minutes of their being submitted to the SEC.

COMPUTER-INTEGRATED MANUFACTURING

Computer-integrated manufacturing (CIM) is an integrated approach to the use of information technology in manufacturing enterprises. Components of a CIM system typically include computer-aided design (CAD) workstations, real-time production monitoring and control systems, and order and inventory control systems. CIM components are connected by a computer network and equipped with software systems designed to support distributed operations. CIM reduces information costs and, through EDI, brings the producer, the supplier, and the customer closer together.

Source data automation of production activities is essential to CIM, thus machine-readable bar codes and scanner technology are critical system components. If you look under the hood of a new car, you will see bar-code symbols on many parts, the bar symbol being similar to the UPC bar code that is commonplace on consumer products. The bar codes, which are as commonplace on factory goods as they are on consumer goods, allow a computer or robot to identify materials, process information, and initiate whatever procedures are necessary.

ELECTRONIC PAYMENT SYSTEMS

Electronic funds transfer (EFT) systems are electronic payment systems in which processing and communication are primarily or totally electronic. EFT systems provide electronic movement of funds between organizations based on customer instructions. Banks can interface with corporate EDI applications.

The banking and financial industry uses FedWire, Clearing House Interbank Payment System (CHIPS), and Clearing House Automated Payment System (CHAPS). FedWire is an electronic payment and communications system. Banks holding reserve accounts with the U.S. Federal Reserve Bank use FedWire to transfer funds among themselves. CHIPS is an automated clearinghouse system used for the clearing of Eurodollar payments between U.S. and non-U.S. financial institutions. CHAPS provides same-day settlement of sterling funds transfer and is used primarily by the major U.K. clearing banks and the Bank of England.

Retail EFT systems include the telephone wire transfers and telephone payment systems, preauthorized payment systems, POS applications, and automated teller machines (ATMs). Telephone wire transfer is the oldest form of funds movement and is primarily a manual system. Telephone payment systems, often referred to as *pay-by-phone applications*, are similar to wire transfers in that the telephone is the primary medium for data communications. In pay-by-phone systems, customers can call their bank and direct payments to merchants via a Touch-Tone phone. Preauthorized payment systems are used when both the creditor and customer hold accounts at one bank. Preauthorized payment systems allow automatic payment of recurring items with no manual intervention. POS systems allow the electronic approval and debiting of customer accounts at the merchant's site. POS systems can have a direct telecommunications interface with the credit and debit card databases, thus eliminating the courier costs of physically transporting receipts and totals. ATMs perform banking transaction tasks rapidly with reduced manual intervention. ATMs connect to computer networks that process financial transactions and, in the case of shared networks, provide settlement clearing functions with other banks. Common customer uses for ATMs include depositing or withdrawing cash, transferring funds from one account to another, and making payments.

THE ACCOUNTANT AND SYSTEMS DEVELOPMENT

The term *accounting information system* includes system development activities that an accountant or auditor might expect to encounter professionally. Accountants may undertake systems development activities either internally for their company or externally as consultants. Systems development activities are often encountered by internal and external auditors during reviews of information systems controls conducted as part of an audit.

THE NATURE OF SYSTEMS DEVELOPMENT

A systems development project ordinarily consists of three general phases: systems analysis, systems design, and systems implementation. Systems analysis involves formulating and evaluating solutions to systems problems. The emphasis of systems analysis is on the objectives of the entire system under consideration. Basic to this is an analysis of tradeoffs between system objectives. The general objectives of systems analysis can be summarized as follows:

- To improve the quality of information
- To improve internal control
- To minimize cost, where appropriate

These objectives are interrelated and often conflicting. Tradeoffs often must be made between such qualities as economy and usefulness or between simplicity and a realistic but complex system. Frequently, the only method of evaluating such tradeoffs is subjective because the factors involved defy quantification.

Systems design is the process of specifying the details of the solution selected by the systems analysis process. Systems design includes the evaluation of the relative effectiveness and efficiency of alternative system designs in light of the overall system requirements. Systems implementation is the process of placing the revised or newly designed procedures and methods into operation. Systems implementation includes testing the solution prior to implementation, documenting the solution, and reviewing the system when it actually begins operation to verify that the system functions according to the design specifications.

The **systems approach** is a general procedure for the administration of a systems project. Its purpose is to assist in the orderly development of effective systems. The systems approach can be viewed as a process that consists of six steps:

1. Statement of system objective(s)
2. Creation of alternatives
3. Systems analysis
4. Systems design
5. Systems implementation
6. Systems evaluation

The systems approach, like a system itself, is composed of subsystems. Thus each step in the process can itself be subjected to the systems approach. For example, the first step requires that the system objective(s) be stated. Solving this problem by the systems approach involves all six steps. A defined systems objective is the purpose being pursued. To achieve this purpose, alternatives can be created. The system might, for example, seek objective A, B, or C or some combination of them. These alternative objectives can then be analyzed, and the one that seems most suitable can be designed, implemented, and evaluated.

Executing each subsequent step in the systems approach also can be viewed as a process that involves all six steps. Figure 1.12 illustrates this with respect to the system design step. Top-down design with successive refinement is the essence of a systems approach to problem solving. Each successive refinement adds a finer level of detail to system plans, and a top-down approach to successive refinement structures this process in an orderly fashion.

BUSINESS PROCESS BLUEPRINTING

With business process **blueprinting** the company uses generic or industry standard stock blueprints rather than designing its own system. The same approach is often

Define Objectives of Design	Develop simple, clear, and precise specifications for effective and efficient systems implementation
Plan Alternative Possible Designs	Develop alternative design plans that meet design objectives
Analyze Alternative Possible Designs	This includes a. Separating plans into logical parts b. Evaluating the relative effectiveness and efficiency of alternatives against system output requirements c. Using a team approach in many cases d. Selecting the best alternative to form a design strategy
Develop Detailed Design Specifications	They should include a. Enough detail to serve as the basis for the implementation process b. Identification of system inputs c. Identification of system outputs d. Strategies for producing system outputs
Document Design Specifications	This should include specifications for every input and output data element and all circumstances for their uses
Evaluate Design Specifications	This involves testing for the desired output of the design process (specification of an effective and efficient design). The evaluation of the design should consider whether it is a. Developed according to the systems approach model b. Based on effective systems strategy produced by a careful and detailed systems analysis c. Effective, efficient, simple, clear, easy to build, easy to change, and easy to test or evaluate

FIGURE 1.12 THE SYSTEMS APPROACH TO DESIGN.

taken by builders in planned housing communities. The builder works with the home buyer in selecting a set of blueprints from a large book of blueprints. The selected set of blueprints is then adapted according to the buyer's specific needs.

Many companies prefer blueprinting because they find it more cost-effective than designing their own system from the ground up. In many cases blueprinting can save the company from having to reinvent the wheel, and the company can be free to focus more of its efforts on the processes that are key to its strategic goals and objectives.

One company that has pioneered the blueprinting approach is SAP. This company has developed a large knowledge base of many thousands of business processes that customers can readily adapt to their own needs. This approach has become increasingly popular in recent years.

It must be emphasized, however, that blueprinting is no cure-all, and virtually any problem that occurs without blueprinting can occur with blueprinting. Also, blueprinting can cost as much as or even more than the more traditional alternative.

BEHAVIORAL CONSIDERATIONS IN SYSTEMS DEVELOPMENT

Management, users, and systems personnel are necessarily involved in the design and subsequent operation of an information system. Typically, a design group or project team consisting of users, analysts, and management representatives is formed to identify needs, develop technical specifications, and implement a new system.

Technical, organizational, and project management problems are encountered in the implementation of an information system. A new information system creates new work relationships among existing personnel, changes in job content, and perhaps a change in the formal organizational structure. The related technical, behavioral, situational, and personnel factors should all be considered. Failure to do so may lead to the output of the system not being used, even if the system itself is technically sound. Furthermore, users' cooperation is continually required to operate the system (provide inputs, verify outputs) after its implementation.

The user cooperation needed to operate the system successfully should be ensured during the design of a system, not afterward. Most accounting applications are routine. To ensure adherence to production schedules, ongoing relationships between users and information system personnel are important. Schedules for inputs, reports, and other items are usually the responsibility of the systems group, but to implement and maintain these schedules, cooperation is required from users.

A philosophy of **user-oriented** design fosters a set of attitudes and an approach to systems development that consciously considers the organizational context. Users should be involved in the design of applications. Careful attention to output, both in quantity and format, in the design phase will prevent users having to rework data or request new reports once the system is in operation. Outputs should be directed toward decisions; users must understand the nature and purpose of outputs to be able to use them. Personnel training should be included in the design phase, not initiated after the system is installed. Finally, the system must be prepared to accept and make changes after operation begins. Users will usually request changes; anticipation of this possibility and the other factors mentioned is essential to a user-oriented philosophy of systems design.

❖ SUMMARY

An accounting information system is a collection of resources designed to transform data into information. This information is communicated to a wide variety of decision makers. We use the term *accounting information system* broadly to include transaction processing cycles, the use of information technology, and the development of information systems.

Most organizations experience similar types of economic events. These events generate activities that can be grouped into five primary business processes (inbound logistics, outbound logistics, operations, marketing, and service) and into four support business processes (procurement, technology development, organization and human resource management, and firm infrastructure). An internal control structure consists of the policies and procedures established to provide reasonable assurance that specific organizational objectives will be achieved. Transaction business processes offer a systemic framework for the analysis and design of information systems in that there is a similar objective for each of the various business processes. This objective is to be an integral part of an organization's internal control structure.

The information system function is responsible for data processing. The organizational structure and location of a large information systems department with functional organization were discussed, and common functions within the department were described. Office automation describes the use of electronic technology in the office or workplace. Office automation systems consist of computer-based technologies that allow processing of a variety of electronic messages and documents. Three technologies interact to make quick-response systems feasible. These technologies are EDI (electronic data interchange), UPC bar code identification, and scanning technology, such as POS (point-of-sale) retail terminals. Just-in-time (JIT), computer-integrated manufacturing (CIM), and electronic funds transfer (EFT) are also relevant to quick-response systems.

A systems development project ordinarily consists of three general phases: systems analysis, systems design, and systems implementation. The systems approach is a general procedure for the administration of a systems project. Its purpose is to assist in the orderly development of effective systems. Technical, organizational, and project management problems are encountered in the implementation of an information system. A philosophy of user-oriented design fosters a set of attitudes and an approach to systems development that consciously considers the organizational context.

❖ GLOSSARY

accounting information system (AIS): a collection of resources designed to provide data to a variety of decision makers according to their needs and entitlement.

analysis function: focuses on identifying problems and projects for computer processing and designing systems to satisfy these problems' requirements.

application system: processes logically related transactions.

blueprinting: the practice of adapting off-the-shelf system designs to suit an individual company's needs.

business process: an interrelated set of tasks that involve data, organizational units, and a logical time sequence.

chief information officer (CIO): has overall responsibility for the information system function.

computer-integrated manufacturing (CIM): an integrated approach to the use of information technology in manufacturing enterprises.

data processing (DP): the use of computers to perform an organization's transaction-oriented data processing.

decision support system (DSS): data are processed into a decision-making format for the end user.

electronic data interchange (EDI): the direct computer-to-computer exchange of business documents via a communications network.

electronic data processing (EDP): synonym for data processing.

electronic funds transfer (EFT): payment systems in which processing and communication are primarily or totally electronic.

end-user computing (EUC): the direct, hands-on use of computers by end users to perform their own data processing.

executive information system (EIS): an MIS tailored to the strategic information needs of top management.

expenditure cycle: events related to the acquisition of goods and services from other entities and the settlement of related obligations.

expert system (ES): a knowledge-based information system that uses its knowledge about a specific application area to act as an expert consultant to end users.

Extensible Business Reporting Language (XBRL): a universal formatting language for exchanging business documents, via the Internet.

finance cycle: events related to the acquisition and management of capital funds, including cash.

financial reporting cycle: obtains accounting and operating data from the other cycles and processes these data in order that financial statements can be prepared.

information center: a support facility for the computer users in an organization.

information system function: responsible for data processing (DP) and information systems in an organization.

internal control process: a process designed to provide reasonable assurance regarding the achievement of objectives in (a) reliability of financial reporting, (b) effectiveness and efficiency of operations, and (c) compliance with applicable laws and regulations.

just-in-time (JIT): a continuous flow environment that seeks to minimize or totally eliminate inventories.

management information system (MIS): the use of computers to provide decision-oriented information to managers.

operations function: charged with data preparation, operation of the data processing equipment, and system maintenance.

primary business process: involves inbound logistics, outbound logistics, operations, marketing, and service.

production cycle: events related to the transformation of resources into goods and services.

programming function: responsible for the design, coding, testing, and debugging of computer programs.

project organization: organization of analysts and programmers by application projects rather than by organizational function.

revenue cycle: events related to the distribution of goods and services to other entities and the collection of related payments.

steering committee: an advisory group consisting of high-level members of user functions that influences the policies, budget, and planning of information services.

supporting business process: involves procurement, technology development, organization and human resource management, and firm infrastructure.

systems approach: a general procedure for the administration of a systems project.

technical support function: specialists in areas of computer expertise such as software, data management, and database design.

total quality management (TQM):   synonym for TQP (total quality performance).

total quality performance (TQP):   a philosophy that one should do the right thing right the first time.

transaction processing cycle: consists of one or more application systems.

user-oriented: a philosophy of design that fosters a set of attitudes and an approach to systems development that consciously considers organizational context.

user support function: services and supports end users and end-user computing.

value chain: a way of viewing the company's activities in a manner suited to analyzing competitive advantages.

Web Trust: a seal of approval given to Web sites by certified public accountants indicating that certain standards of privacy and security have been met.

❖ CHAPTER QUIZ

Answers to the Chapter Quiz appear on page 30.

1. The term (_____) describes the use of computer technology to provide decision-oriented information to managers.
   (a) data processing
   (b) electronic data processing
   (c) expert system
   (d) management information system

2. The text groups economic events into how many basic business processes?
   (a) one
   (b) four
   (c) six
   (d) nine

3. Which of the following indicates a satisfactory situation from the viewpoint of good internal control?
   (a) The cashier reports to the treasurer.
   (b) Payroll accounting reports to the controller.
   (c) Both of the above indicate an unsatisfactory situation.
   (d) Both of the above indicate a satisfactory situation.

4. The statement "Amounts due to vendors should be accurately and promptly classified, summarized, and reported" might serve as a control objective in which of the following transaction cycles?
   (a) revenue cycle
   (b) expenditure cycle
   (c) production cycle
   (d) finance cycle

5. Which of the following information system functions is generally responsible for the design, coding, and debugging of computer programs?
   (a) technical support
   (b) programming
   (c) operations
   (d) systems analysis

6. Which of the following information system functions focuses on the identification of problems and projects for computer processing?
   (a) user support
   (b) programming
   (c) operations
   (d) systems analysis

7. Which of the following is a general term that is used to describe the use of electronic technology for business documents?
   (a) telecommuting
   (b) information system
   (c) office automation
   (d) electronic data interchange

8. (_____) is the direct computer-to-computer exchange of business documents via a communications network.
   (a) electronic data interchange
   (b) electronic funds transfer
   (c) telecommuting
   (d) e-mail

9. The three general phases of analysis, design, and implementation are part of a (_____).
   (a) system development study
   (b) systems approach
   (c) expert system
   (d) decision support system

10. (_____) is the first step in the systems approach.
   (a) systems design
   (b) stating objectives
   (c) systems analysis
   (d) systems evaluation

❖ REVIEW QUESTIONS

1. What is an accounting information system?
2. What groups need the outputs of an accounting information system?
3. Identify and describe several types of computer-based information systems.
4. Identify the four common operating cycles of business activity.
5. Characterize an organization's internal control structure.
6. Distinguish between a controller and a treasurer.
7. Describe the purpose of the internal audit function.
8. Characterize the organizational structure of the information system function.
9. Identify several functions that may be specialized areas of expertise in an information system department.
10. How does project organization differ from functional organization in an information system department?
11. What is the purpose of a steering committee?
12. Describe blueprinting.
13. Give an example of end-user computing (EUC).
14. Identify several components of quick-response technology.
15. How does EDI differ from e-mail?
16. Identify several components of computer-integrated manufacturing (CIM).
17. List the six steps in the systems approach.
18. What is meant by user-oriented systems design?

❖ DISCUSSION QUESTIONS AND PROBLEMS

19. "A credit sale is not a complete transaction." Discuss.
20. Discuss factors that should be considered in the organizational location of the internal audit function.

21. Apply the systems approach to the following objectives:
    (a) to improve the quality of an accounting information system
    (b) to improve the image of a university
    (c) to better the competition

22. Identify several accounting-related decisions that you feel might be made by the following personnel. Do the information needs of these positions differ?
    (a) president of a company
    (b) controller
    (c) accounting manager

23. Discuss briefly the importance in systems design of good communication among systems analysts, management, and systems operating personnel.

24. An internal control structure is an organizational plan to protect assets, ensure the integrity of accounting information, and promote operational efficiency. Indicate whether each of the following situations is satisfactory or unsatisfactory in a manufacturing company from the viewpoint of good internal control. If the situation is unsatisfactory, suggest an improvement.
    (a) Purchase requisitions are made verbally by departments to the purchasing agent.
    (b) The clerk who is responsible for maintaining raw material inventory records does not have access to the storeroom where the raw materials are kept.
    (c) All receiving operations related to shipments from vendors are handled by the clerks who are responsible for managing the storeroom where goods are kept.
    (d) Purchase orders are prepared by the clerks who are responsible for managing the storeroom where goods are kept.
    (e) Employees who are responsible for counting the shipments of goods received from vendors do not have access to the information concerning how many units were ordered from the vendor.
    (f) A periodic physical inventory is taken and reconciled to the materials inventory records by the same clerks who are responsible for managing the storeroom where goods are kept.
    (g) Purchase orders must be compared to receiving reports before a vendor can be paid.
    (h) Copies of purchase orders are sent to the personnel who originally requested the material.
    (i) A firm employs personnel whose only function is to move materials and supplies as needed by the production departments.

25. The accounting information system of an organization may be simple or it may be massive and complex. Accounting information systems are designed and implemented not only to maintain the ledger balances from which financial statements and reports are prepared but also to produce other types of management and operating information that are essential to the operation of a business. Regardless of how large and complex—or how simple—an organization's accounting information system is, accountants, auditors, and other parties are required to study the internal controls periodically. Without such studies it would be impractical or impossible in many cases to acquire a detailed knowledge of the processing procedures that affect all types of transactions. Simplification is not only acceptable but is both desirable and necessary.

    Business processes can be used to simplify this task. Although all entities differ, they experience similar economic events, which can be classified into one of the nine business processes discussed in the chapter. Each process should be an integral part of an organization's internal control structure.

    Required
    In periodic studies of the internal controls in an organization's accounting information system, accountants and auditors often develop control objectives for each major business process. The control objectives provide a basis for analysis. The accountants or auditors collect information to determine the extent to which control objectives are being achieved in each of the organization's major business processes.

    Each of the following statements is a control objective relating to a particular business process. Identify the relevant business process.
    (a) Vendors should be authorized in accordance with management's criteria.

(b) The prices and terms of goods and services provided should be authorized in accordance with management's criteria.

(c) All shipments of goods and services provided should result in a billing to the customer.

(d) Customers should be authorized in accordance with management's criteria.

(e) Employees should be hired in accordance with management's criteria.

(f) The production plan should be authorized in accordance with management's criteria.

(g) The amounts and timing of debt transactions should be authorized in accordance with management's criteria.

(h) Compensation rates and payroll deductions should be authorized in accordance with management's criteria.

(i) Amounts due to vendors should be accurately and promptly classified, summarized, and reported.

(j) Cost of goods manufactured should be accurately and promptly classified, summarized, and reported.

(k) Billings to customers should be accurately and promptly classified, summarized, and reported.

(l) Access to cash and securities should be permitted only in accordance with management's criteria.

(m) Access to personnel, payroll, and disbursement records should be permitted only in accordance with management's criteria.

26. The Red Wine Company manufactures wine coolers. The company began operations several years ago and has experienced rapid sales growth. The company is organized by business function, with vice presidents for manufacturing, marketing, finance, accounting, and general administration. The firm operates a medium-sized computer network, which supports a variety of batch processing applications for manufacturing, marketing, finance, accounting, and general administration. Manufacturing and marketing also use several computer applications relating to inventory control and shipment information. The manager of information systems (IS) reports to the vice president of general administration.

The company's rapid growth has strained the firm's computer resources, and the number of complaints concerning inadequate support and service from IS have increased dramatically in the past year. The vice presidents for manufacturing and marketing have taken their complaints about IS directly to the company president. Citing inadequate IS support of the on-line computer applications relating to inventory control and shipment information, manufacturing and marketing have requested that the firm purchase a minicomputer that would be used exclusively to support these systems. The president is somewhat perplexed by this request because she recently received a request from the vice president of general administration to fund a significant upgrading of the firm's mainframe computer system. The president is also aware that the finance and accounting divisions have recently purchased several microcomputers and are planning to request funds for additional purchases of microcomputer hardware in their next budget submissions. The president realizes the importance of adequate computer resources to the firm's operations, but given the recent complaints about IS support and these seemingly contradictory requests for additional computer hardware, she has begun to wonder whether there is sufficient control and adequate planning for the acquisition and use of computer resources at the Red Wine Company. The president thinks forming a steering committee might help solve these problems.

Required

What is a steering committee? Discuss the role of a steering committee in planning for the acquisition and use of computer resources at the Red Wine Company.

27. ***Robinson Industries: Organization of the EDP Function[1]***

Introduction

Robinson Industries is a loosely knit conglomerate that offers centralized data processing services to its affiliated companies. To improve the attractiveness of its services, the data

[1]Prepared by Frederick L. Neumann, Richard J. Boland, and Jeffrey Johnson; funded by The Touche Ross Foundation Aid to Accounting Education Program.

processing department this past year introduced on-line service. Several affiliates have become or are becoming users of this service. It has resulted in a reorganization of the data processing department that concerned Mat Dossey, the senior on the audit. Dick Goth, the semisenior on the engagement, reported that the client had not prepared a new organization chart but agreed to see what he could find out. His report is as follows:

Data Processing Department Organization

The data processing department now consists of 25 people reporting to the president through the director of data processing. In addition to these data processing department employees, key committees perform important roles, as do the internal and external auditors for the company. The internal auditors now report operationally to the board of directors and functionally to the president.

Committees

Selected functions of key committees that are important to the management and control of the data processing department are described briefly in the following:

Data Processing Committee

This committee, composed of three members of the board of directors, meets as required to review and evaluate major changes in the data processing area and to review approval of all pricing of services offered. Their responsibilities also include a review of major agreements with hardware and software vendors.

Audit Committee

In its oversight of the audit function, this committee of the board of directors is directly concerned with the quality of the records and reports processed by the department and the controls employed.

User Groups

These groups consist of representatives from on-line users within a specific geographic area. They meet periodically throughout the year to discuss common areas of interest, possible enhancements, and current problems related to the on-line system. The results of these group meetings are reported directly to the data processing department through a user advisory committee.

Data Processing Department

Data processing department management consists of five managers who report to the director through an assistant director. The department management meets weekly to review the status of projects, customer service levels, and any problems. Weekly status reports are then prepared and distributed to each level of line management. Formal meetings with Robinson's president are held quarterly, or more often if required, to review future plans and past performance.

The following describes the sections within the department under the direction of each of the five managers.

On-Line Services

On-Line Technical Staff

This staff conducts all user training, conversions, and parameter definitions necessary to set up a new user. Training classes are conducted at the data processing center. Conversion assistance is provided to the user prior to the initiation of on-line services. If conversion programs are required, these are defined by the on-line services section to the on-line analyst programmers for program preparation. During the first month after conversion of a new user, calls are directed to on-line services; thereafter, user calls are directed to the user liaison section.

Applications Coordinator

This person is responsible for coordinating the approval of user and data processing department project requests, assisting in the requirements definition of a systems maintenance project, monitoring ongoing projects, and approving project test results.

Operations

Data Communications Coordinator

This person monitors all service levels and response time related to the communications network and terminals. The coordinator receives all user calls regarding communications problems. The coordinator logs all calls, identifies the nature of the problem, and reports the status of the problems until they are corrected.

Computer Operators

This section consists of operators, supervisors, and librarians who execute, review, and service the daily computer production runs, special computer runs, and program compilations and tests. The operations are scheduled on a 24-hour basis for six days a week. Shift supervisors review all on-line operations and prepare written documentation of each problem encountered.

Scheduler

This person is responsible for setting up the computer job runs and adjusting them for on-line special requests.

User Liaison

This staff consists of four people who receive, log, and report all questions of potential problems, other than communications problems, by on-line users. User input is obtained through telephone calls, letters, and on-line messages over the communications network and notes from user committee meetings.

On-Line Reports Control

This staff is responsible for the distribution of all hard copy output to all users. Microfiche are sent directly to users from the outside processing vendor. Logs are maintained where appropriate to control distribution and to reconcile items such as check numbers and dividend totals.

Systems and Programming

On-Line Analyst Programmers

This staff is responsible for all the applications and system software programming required for the on-line system. Systems analysis and programming consist primarily of maintenance to existing computer programs, correction of problems, and enhancements to the current applications.

In-House Analyst Programmer

This staff is responsible for all applications and system software programming not on-line.

Research and Development

This staff evaluates and conducts preliminary investigations into new applications such as electronic funds transfers.

Marketing

This staff responds to requests for information regarding the services provided by the data processing department. Once a user signs an on-line service agreement as a new user, that member is turned over to on-line services for training and conversion.

Required

Based on Dick Goth's report, prepare an organization chart of the data processing department and of its relationships to the rest of the organization affecting it.

28. The Fishco Company is a regional fish distributor that sells fish to restaurants in southern Florida. It purchases all its fish from small boats at the local docks, and it pays only with cash.

To simplify its operations, Fishco takes orders only via its Web site, at *www.fishisgoodforyou.com.* All orders are delivered by a third-party contractor, and all sales are made on account. This very simple system allows the entire business to be operated only by Mr. and Mrs. Fishco. Mrs. Fishco does the Web programming, answers the telephone, and provides replacement fish when a customer is dissatisfied. Mr. Fishco does everything else, including all accounting and the handling of collections.

Required

(a) Identify all the major business processes for Fishco.

(b) Specify which business processes are probably the most important to Fishco's strategic goals and objectives.

(c) How would Fishco's business processes change if it became larger and more complicated?

(d) How would Fishco's major business processes change if it began selling shrimp in addition to fish?

29. Assume that the GreenLeaf Tea Company has decided to focus its information system development efforts on its procurement business process. At present, GreenLeaf purchases all its tea directly from tea-leaf farms, but soon it has plans to begin purchasing at spot market prices offered on overseas commodity exchanges.

Required

(a) Generate a rough sketch of GreenLeaf's procurement process.

(b) Indicate changes in the purchasing process that might occur as a result of GreenLeaf's move to purchase in the spot market.

(c) Identify at least four subprocesses for the procurement process.

30. All business processes have at least three common components: a starting point, an ending point, and a triggering event. For each business process below, give all three components.

(a) customer order management process

(b) inventory management process

(c) product delivery management process

(d) production order process

(e) payroll process

31. Luxdale is a large Internet-only vitamin store that sells retail to the public. Over the years, the business has grown steadily to the point that it now processes 15,000 orders per day from sales worldwide.

Recently Luxdale has run into a serious problem through no fault of its own. Only one week ago all the major financial newspapers carried a story about one of Luxdale's major competitors, HealthVite. The problem was that some consumer organization discovered that HealthVite had sold its entire mailing list, along with telephone numbers, to SlabM, a company that sells burial insurance. SlabM then launched a highly aggressive telephone campaign and called every one of HealthVite's customers with offers for discount burial insurance. To make things worse, the salespersons made all the calls around the evening meal hour, a time that most people are in their homes but most likely to be angered by a call from a salesperson.

HealthVite's customers were furious, and the whole affair made all the television talk shows, with many people complaining that one should never trust Internet-based companies with their personal information. Sales for HealthVite dried up overnight, and the CEO quickly resigned before the creditors began moving the armies of lawyers and accountants.

The problem for Luxdale was that its sales suddenly dropped 50%, even though it was in no way affiliated with HealthVite. Robert Baker, the CEO for Luxdale, held a series of press conferences to assure its customers and the public that his company was an innocent casualty, but the more he talked to the press, the worse the problems grew. In general, the press was very hostile, and the overall atmosphere in the industry became one of mistrust and recriminations.

Required

(a) Was Luxdale in any way responsible for its problems?

(b) What things could Luxdale have done before the problem arose to protect itself?

(c) What things could Luxdale have done after the problem arose to protect itself?

32. RoundSoft produces and markets an accounting system for small retail business. The system contains all the usual modules, such as those for accounts receivables, payables, inventory, payroll, general ledger, and so on. In addition, the RoundSoft system includes special modules for sales analysis and prediction.

The core logic for the sales analysis and prediction modules is based on a patented artificial intelligence technique that is so effective that the system can predict actual sales, by product, up to 6 months in advance with an accuracy rate exceeding 98%. There exists no other product this effective in the industry. As a result, RoundSoft enjoys robust sales and has grown 10,000% in the previous 2 years.

The main problem facing RoundSoft is its accounting system. The volume of sales orders from authorized resellers has grown so large that the accounting system can no longer handle all the transactions in a timely manner. Software deliveries and installations are backed up by a full three weeks, and many angry customers are seeking other software solutions to their accounting problems. If something is not done soon, RoundSoft's reputation will likely be damaged seriously, and a permanent loss of market share may follow.

Barbara Conta is RoundSoft's controller, and she is presently considering various options. Her assistant, Bob Blake, argues that RoundSoft needs to develop a completely new accounting system from the ground up. Blake's arguments in favor of his position include the following.

(a) The present accounting system was designed for a company one-tenth the company's present size. It is nearly impossible to adapt such a system to the present environment.

(b) The original accounting system did not include modules to record contracts for installations of the software. Over time, RoundSoft has found it very profitable to install and service installations for large regional companies. To accommodate this growing line of business, RoundSoft developed a separate software system for processing these transactions. Keeping a separate system has caused many problems, however, and has complicated the end-of-quarter process of producing financial statements.

Barbara Conta, however, has a great deal of experience in systems development and knows how painful it can be to develop an entirely new system. Recognizing Blake's arguments, she is seriously considering the option of developing the new system based on a blueprint from SysQuick, a national systems consultant that specializes in business systems blueprinting.

The salesperson from SysQuick claims that by using their blueprint method an entire new system can be implemented for RoundSoft in only 4 weeks for only a quarter of the cost required to develop a new system from the ground up. However, Bob Blake is skeptical about using a stock blueprint. "No two systems are alike," he said. "How can you just take a stock system and force it on our company? Something is bound to go wrong."

Barbara Conta is very worried about the decision. She knows that a bad decision could seriously damage her entire career. After all, who wants to hire a controller who managed the development of a failed system? On the other hand, a good decision would put her in a position to become the controller for one of the many large, sought-after high-tech companies in her area, with a salary twice as large as her present salary.

Required

(a) Describe arguments both for and against the blueprint option.

ANSWERS TO CHAPTER QUIZ

1. d	4. b	7. d	10. b
2. d	5. b	8. a	
3. d	6. d	9. a	

CHAPTER 2

SYSTEMS TECHNIQUES AND DOCUMENTATION

LEARNING OBJECTIVES

Careful study of this chapter will enable you to:

❖ Characterize the use of systems techniques by auditors and systems development personnel.

❖ Describe the use of flowcharting techniques in the analysis of information processing systems.

❖ Define common systems techniques, such as HIPO charts, systems flowcharts, and logical data flow diagrams.

USERS OF SYSTEMS TECHNIQUES

Systems techniques are tools used in the analysis, design, and documentation of system and subsystem relationships. They are largely graphic (pictorial) in nature. Systems techniques are essential to both internal and external auditors and are indispensable to systems personnel in the development of information systems. Systems techniques are also used by accountants who do systems work, either internally for their company or externally as consultants.

USE OF SYSTEMS TECHNIQUES IN AUDITING

Most audits are divided into two basic components. The first component, usually called the *interim audit*, has the objective of establishing the degree to which the organization's internal control structure can be relied on. This usually requires some type of compliance testing. The purpose of compliance testing is to confirm the existence, assess the effectiveness, and check the continuity of operation of internal controls on which reliance is to be placed.

The second component of an audit, usually called the *financial statement audit*, involves substantive testing. Substantive testing is the direct verification of financial statement figures, placing such reliance on internal control as the results of the interim audit warrant. For example, substantive testing of cash would involve direct confirmation

31

of bank balances. Substantive testing of receivables would involve direct confirmation of balances with customers. Both compliance testing and substantive testing might be undertaken by both internal and external auditors.

INTERNAL CONTROL EVALUATION

As indicated earlier, auditors are often involved in the evaluation of internal controls. As such, auditors typically are concerned with the flow of processing and distribution of documents within an application system. Because segregation and division of duties is an important aspect of internal control, the auditor needs techniques that structure the system to distribute documents and divide processing duties among personnel and/or departments. Analytic flowcharts, document flowcharts, and forms-distribution charts may be used by auditors to analyze distribution of documents. These charts are organized into columns to group the processing functions performed by each entity. Several other system techniques, such as questionnaires and matrix methods, also might be used to evaluate internal controls.

COMPLIANCE TESTING

Auditors undertake compliance testing to confirm the existence, assess the effectiveness, and check the continuity of internal controls. When these controls to be tested are components of an organization's information system, the auditor also must consider the technology employed by the information system. This requires understanding the systems techniques commonly used to document information systems, such as Input-process-output (IPO) and hierarchy plus input-process-output (HIPO) charts, program flowcharts, logical data flow diagrams (DFDs), branching and decision tables, and matrix methods. Auditors will encounter these techniques frequently as they review systems documentation. This is why familiarity with such techniques is desirable. However, auditors usually have little need to prepare such instruments in the course of an audit because these techniques are useful primarily in planning or designing a system. The usual focus of an audit is to review an existing system rather than to design a new system.

WORKING PAPERS

Working papers are the records kept by an auditor of the procedures and tests applied, the information obtained, and the conclusions drawn during an audit. The auditor is required by professional standards to maintain working papers, and these constitute the principal record of work done.

Auditors use systems techniques to document and analyze the content of working papers. Internal control questionnaires, analytic flowcharts, and system flowcharts appear frequently in working papers because they are used commonly by auditors in the evaluation of internal controls. DFDs, HIPO charts, program flowcharts, branching and decision tables, and matrix methods might appear in working papers if they are part of the documentation of a system that is being reviewed.

USE OF SYSTEMS TECHNIQUES IN SYSTEMS DEVELOPMENT

A systems development project generally consists of three phases: systems analysis, systems design, and systems implementation. Systems development personnel include systems analysts, systems designers, and programmers. Systems analysis involves formulating and evaluating solutions to systems problems. Systems design is the process of specifying the details of the solution selected by the systems analysis process. Systems design includes the evaluation of the relative effectiveness and efficiency of alternative system designs in light of the overall system requirements. Systems implementation is the process of placing the revised or newly designed procedures and methods into operation.

Systems implementation includes testing the solution prior to implementation, documenting the solution, and reviewing the system when it actually begins operation to verify that the system functions according to the design specifications.

SYSTEMS ANALYSIS

Much of a systems analyst's job involves collecting and organizing facts, using interviewing techniques, questionnaires, document reviews, and observation. Formal techniques for organizing facts include work measurement analysis, work distribution analysis, and other matrix techniques. Information flow analysis is also an important part of systems analysis. Many systems techniques are useful for this kind of analysis. Logical DFDs and analytic flowcharts can be helpful in giving an overall picture of transaction processing within the organization.

SYSTEMS DESIGN

Systems design must formulate a blueprint for a completed system. Just as an artist needs special tools for painting, the designer needs certain tools to assist in the design process. These include such techniques as input/output (matrix) analysis, systems flowcharting, and DFDs. Many design problems concern information-systems design, such as forms design for input documents, and database design. IPO and HIPO charts, program flowcharts, branching and decision tables, and other systems techniques are used extensively in documenting information systems design.

SYSTEMS IMPLEMENTATION

Systems implementation involves actually carrying out the design plan. Typical activities include selecting and training personnel, installing new computer equipment, detailed systems design, writing and testing computer programs, system testing, standards development, documentation, and file conversion.

Documentation is one of the most important parts of systems implementation. Computer programs in particular should be documented adequately. Systems techniques such as program flowcharts and decision tables serve as documentation tools as well as tools used for analysis by programmers. Good documentation, a result of the use of systems techniques in analysis and design, assists in training new employees and generally assists in ensuring that systems design specifications are met.

SYSTEMS TECHNIQUES

Flowcharts are probably the most commonly used systems technique. A **flowchart** is a symbolic diagram that shows the data flow and sequence of operations in a system.

FLOWCHARTING SYMBOLS

Flowcharts are used by both auditors and systems personnel. Flowcharts became widespread when business data-processing became computerized, giving rise to the need for standard symbols and usage conventions. In the United States, this need was filled largely by the publication of *American National Standard Flowchart Symbols and Their Usage in Information Processing*. ANSI X3.5-1970 is the current version.[1]

ANSI X3.5 defines four groups of flowchart symbols—basic symbols, specialized input/output symbols, specialized process symbols, and additional symbols—defines the shape of each symbol but not its size, and illustrates conventions governing their use.

---

[1]ANSI X3.5-1970. *American National Standard Flowchart Symbols and Their Usage in Information Processing*. New York: American National Standards Institute, 1971.

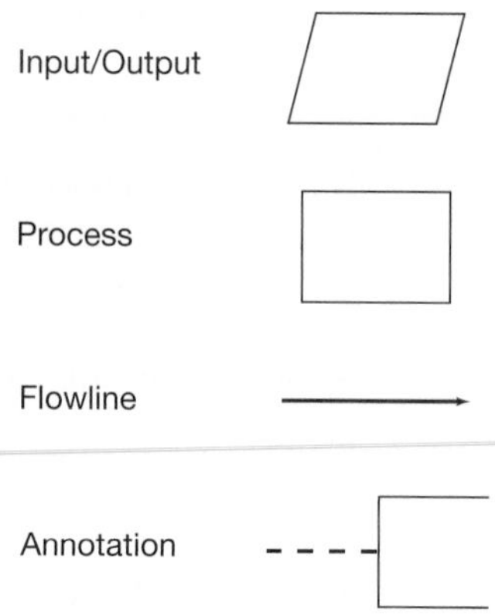

Input/Output

Process

Flowline

Annotation

FIGURE 2.1   BASIC SYMBOLS.

The **basic symbols** (Fig. 2.1) include the input/output symbol, the process symbol, the flowline symbol, and the annotation (comment) symbol. These correspond to the basic data processing functions and can always be used to represent these functions. A specialized symbol may be used in place of a basic symbol to give additional information.

The input/output symbol represents an input/output (I/O) function, that is, making data available for processing (input) or recording processed information (output). For example, a keyboard or magnetic disk may be used to input data for processing; the processed data may be output to paper or to another magnetic disk. The process symbol represents any kind of processing function; for example, executing a defined operation or group of operations resulting in a change of value, form, or location of information or in determining which of several flow directions is to be followed.

The flowline symbol is used to link other symbols. Flowlines indicate the sequence of available information and executable operations. Flowlines may cross or form a junction. A crossing of flowlines means that they have no logical relation. A junction of flowlines occurs when two or more flowlines join with one outgoing flowline. Every flowline entering or leaving a junction should have arrowheads near the junction point.

The annotation (comment) symbol represents the addition of descriptive comments or explanatory notes as clarification. The broken (dashed) line is connected to any symbol where the annotation is meaningful by extending the broken line in whatever fashion is appropriate. A brace (connected to a symbol by a broken line) also may be used to indicate an annotation or comment.

Specialized input/ output symbols (Fig. 2.2) may represent the I/O function and, in addition, denote the medium on which the information is recorded or the manner of handling the information, or both. If no special symbol exists, the basic I/O symbol is used.

The punched-card symbol represents an I/O function in which the medium is punched cards, including mark-sense cards, stub cards, deck of cards, file of cards, and so forth. The on-line storage symbol represents an I/O function using any type of on-line storage; for example, magnetic disk or optical disk. The magnetic tape symbol, the punched tape symbol, the magnetic drum symbol, the magnetic disk symbol, and the document symbol each represent an I/O function using a particular medium.

The manual input symbol represents an input function in which the information is entered manually at the time of processing, for example, by means of online keyboards, switch settings, or touch screens. The display symbol represents an I/O function in which the information is displayed for human use at the time of processing by means of video devices, console printers, plotters, and so forth. The communication link symbol represents a function in which information is transmitted by a telecommunications

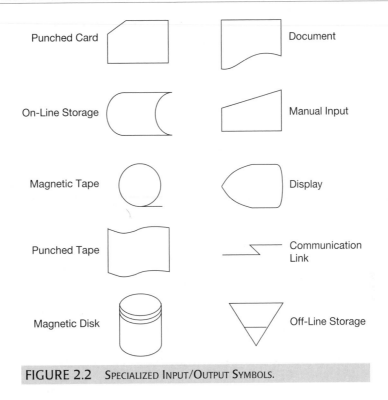

Punched Card

Document

On-Line Storage

Manual Input

Magnetic Tape

Display

Punched Tape

Communication Link

Magnetic Disk

Off-Line Storage

FIGURE 2.2   SPECIALIZED INPUT/OUTPUT SYMBOLS.

link. The offline storage symbol represents the function of storing information offline, regardless of the medium on which the information is recorded.

Specialized process symbols (Fig. 2.3) may represent the processing function and, in addition, identify the specific type of operation to be performed on the information. If no specialized symbol exists, the basic process symbol is used.

The decision symbol represents a decision or switching type of operation that determines which of a number of alternative paths is to be followed. The predefined process symbol represents a named procedure consisting of one or more operations or program steps that are not specified within this set of flowcharts. The preparation symbol represents modification of an instruction or group of instructions that change the program itself, for example, to set a switch, modify an index register, or initialize a routine.

The manual operation symbol represents any off-line process geared to the speed of a human being without using mechanical aid. The auxiliary operation symbol represents an off-line operation performed on equipment not under direct control of the central processing unit. The merge, extract, sort, and collate symbols may each be used to represent the associated specific type of processing function.

The **additional symbols** (see Fig. 2.3) may be used to clarify a flowchart or to make the flowcharting of a complete process more convenient. The connector symbol represents an exit to or an entry from another part of the flowchart. A set of two connectors is used to represent a continued flow direction when the flow is broken by any space or stylistic limitation. The terminal symbol represents a terminal point in a flowchart; for example, start, stop, halt, or interrupt. The parallel mode symbol represents the beginning or end of two or more simultaneous operations. The off-page connector symbol is not in the ANSI X3.5 standard but is used commonly to represent an exit to or entry from another page of a flowchart. The transmittal tape symbol is used commonly to represent a manually prepared batch control total.

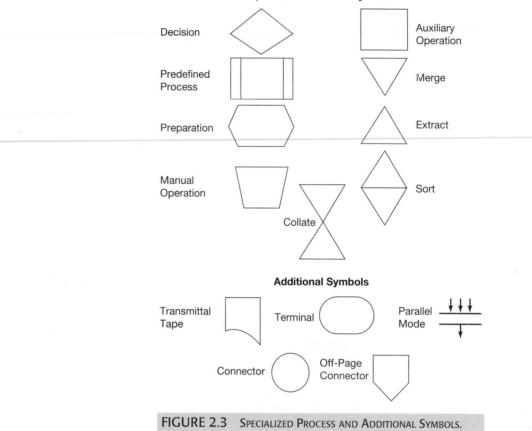

FIGURE 2.3   SPECIALIZED PROCESS AND ADDITIONAL SYMBOLS.

SYMBOL USE IN FLOWCHARTING

Symbols are used in a flowchart to represent the functions of an information or other type of system. Flow direction is represented by lines drawn between symbols. Normal direction of flow is from left to right and top to bottom. When the flow direction is not left to right or top to bottom, open arrowheads should be placed on flowlines to show that direction is reversed. To increase clarity, open arrowheads can be placed on normal-direction flowlines. When flowlines are broken by page limits, connector symbols should be used to indicate the break. When flow is bidirectional, it can be shown by either single or double lines, but open arrowheads should be used to indicate both normal-direction flow and reverse-direction flow.

Figure 2.4 contains four illustrations that correctly use symbols, flowlines, arrowheads, and the connector symbol. In the first illustration, notice that the document symbol is used for an invoice, which is shown as input to a manual operation symbol. The text inside the manual operation symbol indicates that the invoice is to be reviewed and approved. The approved invoice is output from this process. Because the direction of flow is normal in this illustration (left to right and top to bottom), no arrowheads are necessary.

The next illustration is a different flowchart for the same process of approving an invoice. In this case, the reverse flow of the approved invoice is indicated with arrowheads.

The third illustration shows how the connector symbol is used to flowchart the transmission of a requisition from the stores department to the purchasing department. The connector symbol is used instead of a flowline to indicate this transmission.

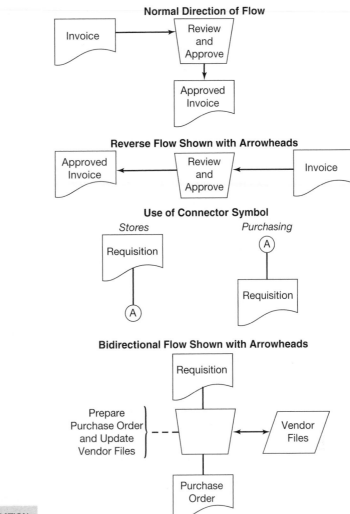

FIGURE 2.4   SYMBOL USAGE ILLUSTRATION.

The fourth illustration shows the manual preparation of a purchase order. The document symbol is used to represent the requisition, which is shown as input to a manual operation symbol. Notice that the annotation (comment) symbol is used to indicate operations that are manual. The annotation symbol is used here because all the text necessary for a complete description will not fit within the manual operation symbol.

The basic input/output symbol is used to represent vendor files. Assuming that the files were on paper or cards, it also would be correct to represent the vendor files with the document symbol. It is always correct to use the basic input/output symbol for any input or output regardless of its physical form. Notice that arrowheads are used to indicate the bidirectional (both normal and reverse) flow between the manual operation and the vendor files. This indicates that the vendor files are both used in the operation and modified (updated) by the operation. The document symbol is used to represent the purchase order that is output from the manual operation.

IPO AND HIPO CHARTS

IPO and HIPO charts are used primarily by systems development personnel to distinguish the level of system detail described in a flowchart. At the most general level of

Author: Mr. Foxx Chart Number: 3.1	System: Payroll Description: Calculate Gross Pay	Date: 6/9/0X
Input	Process	Output
Payroll job record Payroll master file	Accumulate hours worked Find correct pay rate Compute gross pay	Gross pay records Payroll master file Error messages

FIGURE 2.5   IPO Chart.

analysis, only the basic input–process–output relations in a system are of concern. An input–process–output (IPO), chart (Fig. 2.5) may be used to provide a narrative description of the inputs needed to generate desired system outputs. An **IPO chart** provides very little detail concerning the processing function but is a useful technique for analyzing overall information requirements. Additional processing detail is provided by hierarchy plus input–process–output (HIPO) charts (Fig. 2.6). A HIPO consists of a series of charts that represent systems at increasing levels of detail, where the level of detail depends on the needs of users.

A **HIPO chart** contains two segments: the hierarchy chart that factors the processing task into various modules or subtasks, and an IPO chart to describe the input–process–output requirements of each module. The hierarchy chart describes the overall system and provides a "table of contents" for the detailed IPO charts, usually through a numbering scheme, as shown in Figure 2.6. The IPO part of a HIPO chart is usually in narrative form, as shown in Figure 2.5, but other descriptive techniques may be used as well. In a complex system, the initial HIPO chart is factored into a set of HIPO rather than IPO charts, and then each separate sub-HIPO chart is factored into IPO diagrams. The progression of charts is always from the general to the specific; thus HIPO structures a top-down strategy in structured systems analysis and design.

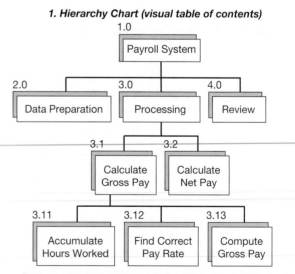

1. Hierarchy Chart (visual table of contents)

Each numbered module would be detailed in an IPO chart.

2. IPO Charts (one for each module)

HEADER

| INPUT | PROCESS | OUTPUT |

FIGURE 2.6   HIPO Illustration.

HIPO charts are a design aid and a documentation tool. They are useful for identifying what is to be done in a problem; they are limited, however, for specifying how or when processing is to be accomplished. Graphic flowcharts using the symbols discussed previously are better suited to specifying information system functions and processing logic.

SYSTEMS AND PROGRAM FLOWCHARTS

Systems flowcharts are used by both auditors and systems personnel. A **systems flowchart** identifies the overall or broad flow of operations in a system. A systems flowchart shows where inputs originate, the sequence and mode (manual or machine) of processing, and the disposition of outputs. The focus of systems flowcharting is on media and processing functions rather than the detailed logic of individual processing functions.

Program flowcharts are used primarily by systems development personnel. A **program flowchart** (also called a **block flowchart**) is more detailed concerning individual processing functions than a systems flowchart. Each of the processing functions depicted in a systems flowchart is further detailed in a program flowchart, similar to the successive layering of IPO charts in HIPO charts.

Systems flowcharts are associated with the analysis phase of a systems project, and program flowcharts, with the design phase. A program flowchart is the design step between overall system design and coding the system for computer processing.

LOGICAL DATA FLOW DIAGRAMS

Logical data flow diagrams or **data flow diagrams** (both abbreviated as DFD) are used primarily by systems development personnel in systems analysis. A systems analyst often acts as the communication link between a user who desires some type of computer-based processing and the programmers/systems support staff who actually will prepare the physical design of a system to satisfy the user's need. Explicit documentation of the user–systems analyst interface is a major systems-development-control concern. DFDs are used by systems analysts to document the logical design of a system that meets user requirements. The DFD provides the user with a picture of the systems analyst's conception of the user's problem.

The emphasis here is on the word *logical*. The intent of using DFDs is to separate clearly the logical process of systems analysis from the physical process of systems design. The systems analyst provides a logical description to the systems designer/programmer, who then designs the physical specifications.

Table 2.1 illustrates the DFD symbols that will be used in this book. Although the symbology of DFDs is simple, a complete standardization of usage does not exist. This, of course, is also the case with traditional flowcharting symbols.

TABLE 2.1	Logical Data Flow Diagram Symbols	
Name	*Symbol*	*Meaning*
Terminator		Represents sources and destinations of data
Process		Task or function being done
Data store		A repository of data
Data flow	⟶	Communication channel

There are four DFD symbols. The *terminator* is used to indicate a source or a destination of data. The *process* indicates a process that transforms data. The *data store* is used to indicate a store of data. The *data flow* is used to indicate a flow of data. Although these terms and symbols are representative, many variations exist.

Note here the similarity between the four DFD symbols and the four basic flowcharting symbols, which can be used to prepare any type of flowchart. Although a DFD reasonably could be drawn with the four basic flowcharting symbols, the DFD symbols serve two purposes. The first is to emphasize the analysis of data flows. The second is to emphasize logical rather than physical design. Many of the traditional flowcharting symbols represent data-processing operations or physical media. The use of such symbols by a systems analyst necessarily causes a blurring of the separation of logical analysis from physical design. This is not quite true if only the four basic flowcharting symbols are used. Nevertheless, this reasoning is the major argument offered by those who support the use of DFDs.

LOGICAL DATA-FLOW DIAGRAMS AND STRUCTURED ANALYSIS

This section illustrates the construction of DFDs and their role in structured systems analysis. As indicated earlier, structured systems analysis is characterized by top-down design and successive refinement. We will illustrate these ideas in the context of a payroll application system.

Figure 2.7 shows a DFD for a top-level view of a payroll system that is a very general description of the system. Payroll data supplied by timekeeping are processed against a store or file of payroll data to generate paychecks for employees. The arrowhead flowlines indicate the flow of data. Notice that the store of payroll data is both used in the payroll process (the flowline payroll details) and updated by the payroll process (the flowline payroll data).

Several points about the construction of a DFD as illustrated in Figure 2.7 can be made:

- The DFD should consist solely of DFD symbols.
- Each symbol in the DFD, including each arrowhead flowline, should be labeled.
- The flow of logic should be clear, with all sources and destinations of data indicated on the DFD.

Successive refinement of the payroll DFD in Figure 2.7 is required to attain a more meaningful description of the system. Figure 2.8 illustrates an *expansion* of the initial payroll DFD to incorporate more detail. Note that the source and destination are the same as in Figure 2.7. However, a new store—employee data—has been added, and the process payroll data in Figure 2.8 has been factored into two processes: "verify payroll

FIGURE 2.7   DFD FOR PAYROLL PROCESSING.

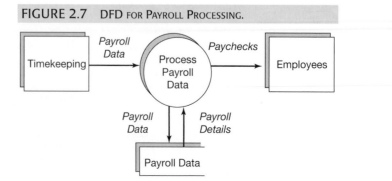

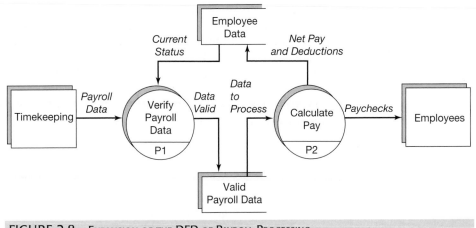

FIGURE 2.8   EXPANSION OF THE DFD OF PAYROLL PROCESSING.

data" and "calculate pay." Each of these processes has been numbered so that it may be referenced easily.

When the analyst is satisfied that all major modules have been identified, structured analysis proceeds with successive refinement of each of the major processing modules. Figure 2.9 illustrates the *explosion* of P2 in Figure 2.8. This explosion adds more detail. Notice the new stores of data and the new processing modules. Explosion of each of these new modules may then be undertaken as necessary to complete the description of the system.

The expansion and explosion process just described is conceptually identical to that used in the HIPO charts discussed earlier in this chapter. Expansion and explosion

FIGURE 2.9   EXPLOSION OF PROCESS P2.

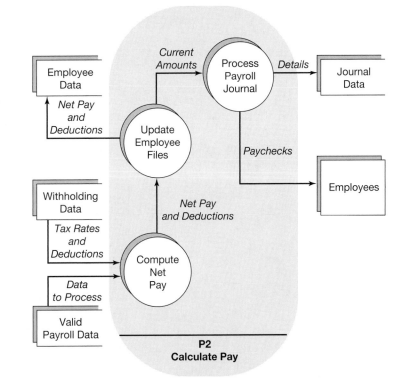

of modules generate a hierarchical collection of processing modules that is very useful in providing a description of a proposed or existing system. An important aspect of DFDs, however, is that they concentrate on stores of data and decision logic. When the DFD is complete, the systems analyst can proceed to analyze the stores of data identified as required for the application.

ANALYTIC, DOCUMENT, AND FORMS DISTRIBUTION FLOWCHARTS

Auditors often are concerned more with the flow and distribution of documents in an application system than with the mode of processing, particularly when evaluating the internal controls in an existing or proposed system. Because the segregation and division of duties is an important element of internal control, the auditor needs techniques that structure the system to distribute processing duties among personnel and/or departments.

Analytic flowcharts, document flowcharts, and forms-distribution charts may be used to analyze the distribution of documents in a system. These charts are organized into columns to group the processing functions performed by each entity. Flowcharting across the separate columns, which represent the entities in the system, is an effective way to evaluate segregation of duties. This form of flowcharting also highlights the interfaces between entities. These interfaces—such as sending a document from one department to another—are important control points in an application system.

An **analytic flowchart** (Fig. 2.10) is similar to a systems flowchart in level of detail and technique. The flow of processing is depicted using symbols connected with flowlines.

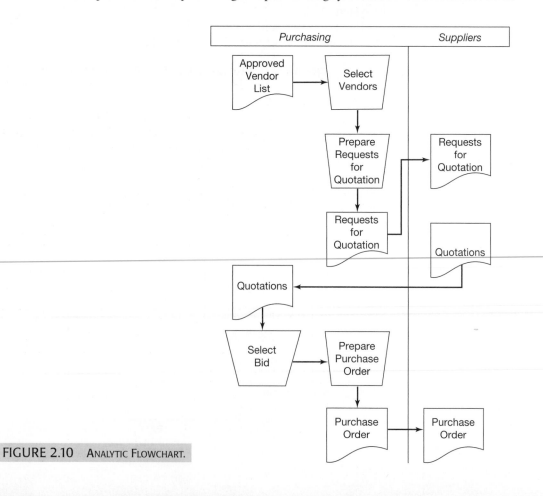

FIGURE 2.10   ANALYTIC FLOWCHART.

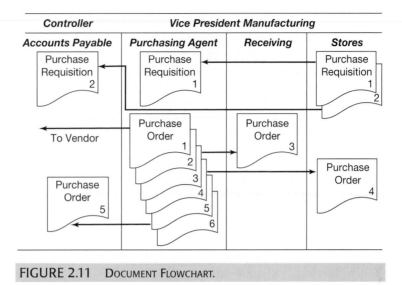

FIGURE 2.11   DOCUMENT FLOWCHART.

An analytic flowchart identifies all significant processing in an application, emphasizing processing tasks that apply controls. Note the organization of the chart by columns. All the activities of the purchasing department are collected in one column so titled.

A **document flowchart** (Fig. 2.11) is similar in format to an analytic flowchart but contains less detail about the processing functions of each entity shown on the chart. Strictly speaking, the only symbol used in a document flowchart is the document symbol. However, other symbols may be used as necessary for clarity. The intent is to take each document used in an application system and identify its points of origin, distribution, and ultimate disposition. Comments should be added as necessary to clarify the illustration. Each document symbol generally represents a batch of documents rather than a single document.

Closely related to the document flowchart is the **forms-distribution chart** (Fig. 2.12). A forms-distribution chart illustrates the distribution of multiple-copy forms within an organization. The emphasis is on who gets what forms rather than on how these forms

FIGURE 2.12   FORMS-DISTRIBUTION CHART FOR A PURCHASE ORDER.

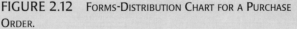
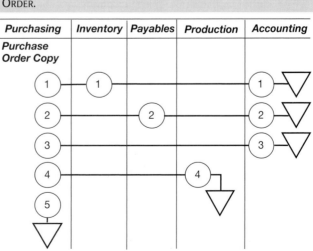

are processed. Forms may be represented by symbols, reduced photos of the forms themselves, or simply word descriptions. The form is pictured or designated on the left side of the chart and usually progresses horizontally through the various columns allotted to organizational units. Analysis may be directed toward eliminating unnecessary copies, unnecessary filing of copies, unauthorized distribution, and so on.

These techniques structure application-systems data in a format suitable for analyzing the segregation of duties within the system and the controls administered at the interfaces between various entities. It is these features that the analyst is interested in when reviewing the internal controls in a system.

ANALYTIC FLOWCHARTING ILLUSTRATION

The objective of this section is to illustrate the preparation of an analytic flowchart for a transaction-processing system. We wish to flowchart the following system:

> The cashier opens the mail containing cash payments and remittance advices that have been forwarded by customers as payments on their accounts. The cashier prepares a batch control total of the mail receipts and sends this document to the general ledger clerk for posting to the general ledger. The remittance advices are sent to the accounts receivable clerk for posting to the accounts receivable ledger. The cashier then prepares two copies of a deposit slip, deposits the cash at the bank, and files the second copy of the deposit slip, which has been validated at the bank, by date.
>
> The general ledger clerk posts the batch control total to the general ledger and then files the batch control total by date. The accounts receivable clerk posts the remittance advices to the accounts receivable ledger and then files the remittance advices by date.

PLANNING THE FLOWCHART

First, the necessary resources must be obtained. An appropriate software application is required when using a computer. If the chart is to be drawn on paper, then a flowcharting

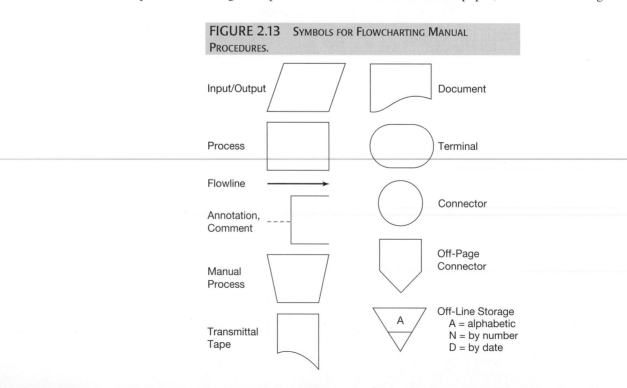

FIGURE 2.13   SYMBOLS FOR FLOWCHARTING MANUAL PROCEDURES.

Input/Output   Document

Process   Terminal

Flowline

Annotation, Comment   Connector

Manual Process   Off-Page Connector

Transmittal Tape   Off-Line Storage
A = alphabetic
N = by number
D = by date

template and suitable instruments are necessary. It is then necessary to select which type of flowchart should be drawn, determined by the intended purpose of the flowchart. Here we draw an analytic flowchart.

SYMBOL SELECTION

After determining which type of chart is required, it is necessary to determine which symbols will be used in chart construction. ANSI X3.5 standard symbols, as discussed and illustrated in this chapter, are recommended, but in some cases organizations have their own symbol definitions, which should then be used.

Figure 2.13 illustrates several flowchart symbols used commonly in preparing analytic flowcharts that depict manual processing operations. All the symbols illustrated in Figure 2.13 have been defined in this chapter and are reproduced here to emphasize their importance in preparing analytic flowcharts. Auditors and accountants frequently prepare such flowcharts for the purpose of analyzing internal controls in a system.

Figure 2.13 contains the basic flowcharting symbols—manual process, transmittal tape, document, terminal, connector, and offline storage. Note the letter *A* inside the offline storage symbol included to indicate the manner in which documents are filed. *A* indicates that documents are filed alphabetically. *N* indicates that documents are filed by number. *D* indicates that documents are filed by date.

SYSTEM ANALYSIS

In preparing any type of flowchart, it is important to review the material to be charted carefully to obtain a good understanding of the description of the system. In preparing an analytic flowchart, it is necessary to determine what entities will be represented as separate columns—usually only entities for which some detailed processing activities are described. Analyzing the system to be charted here reveals three such entities: the cashier, the general ledger clerk, and the accounts receivable clerk. Because no processing activities are described for the other two entities—customers and the bank—they will be represented in ways, discussed below.

The next step in the analysis is to identify the documents involved in the system. There are six: cash payments, remittance advices, batch control total, deposit slip, general ledger, and accounts receivable ledger. Each of these should appear in the flowchart as appropriate.

DRAWING THE FLOWCHART

Our intent here is to chart the flow of documents in the system using appropriate flowchart symbols flowlines, and style. The first step described is opening mail that contains cash payments and remittance advices by the cashier. This is a manual operation and may be charted as in Figure 2.14. The terminal symbol is used to indicate the source of the mail (customers). It also indicates the starting point in the flowchart. The mail is represented by a document symbol. The basic input/output symbol also could be used here. The manual operation symbol is used to represent the "open mail" process. The basic process symbol also could be used to represent this process. In both cases, a specialized symbol was selected because it clearly describes the system. For the same reason, the

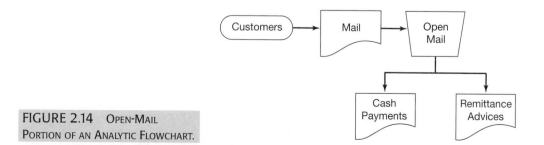

FIGURE 2.14   OPEN-MAIL PORTION OF AN ANALYTIC FLOWCHART.

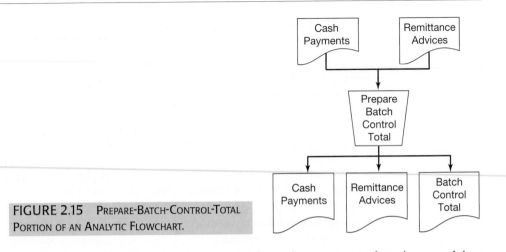

FIGURE 2.15   PREPARE-BATCH-CONTROL-TOTAL PORTION OF AN ANALYTIC FLOWCHART.

special document symbol is used to represent the cash payments and remittance advices. Although cash payments (cash and/or checks) are not documents in the same sense as remittance advices, they are important in this transaction-processing system and should be clearly identified in the flowchart. Flowlines are used to indicate the flow of action. This portion of the flowchart would be placed in a column labeled "Cashier" because the cashier is performing this process.

The next step described is the preparation of a batch control total of the mail receipts. This also is a manual operation and may be charted as in Figure 2.15. The manual operation system is used to represent the "prepare batch control total" process, and the document symbol is used to represent the cash payments and the remittance advices. The document symbol also has been selected to represent the batch control total. The transmittal tape symbol shown in Figure 2.13 also could be used to represent the batch control total. This portion of the flowchart also would be placed in the column labeled "Cashier" because it is a continuation of the flowchart of the cashier's activities.

SANDWICH RULE

Notice the similarity of construction between the two portions of the flowchart that have been described. In both cases, inputs (documents) flow into a process symbol, and outputs (documents) flow out of the process symbol. Every process symbol should have its inputs and outputs clearly specified. This has been called the **sandwich rule**: every process symbol should be "sandwiched" between an input symbol and an output symbol.

USING THE CONNECTOR SYMBOL

The cashier forwards the batch control total to the general ledger clerk and the remittance advices to the accounts receivable clerk. This may be flowcharted as in Figure 2.16. Connector symbols are used here to eliminate long flowlines. The matching connector symbols appear in the columns for the general ledger clerk and the accounts receivable clerk in the complete flowchart, which is shown in Figure 2.18.

Using connector symbols is a question of style that affects the overall appearance and clarity of a flowchart. One important advantage connector symbols have over long

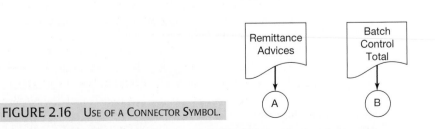

FIGURE 2.16   USE OF A CONNECTOR SYMBOL.

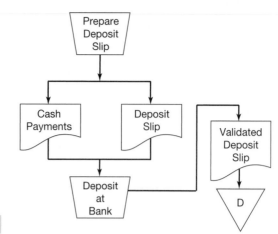

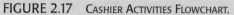

FIGURE 2.17   CASHIER ACTIVITIES FLOWCHART.

flowlines that cross over columns of a flowchart is that they add flexibility by making a flowchart modular. Notice that the absence of long flowlines crossing over columns of the flowchart in Figure 2.18 makes it possible to add or move columns without affecting the logical clarity or actual physical construction of the flowchart, or erasing and redrawing flowlines. This feature is especially useful when making changes to an existing flowchart.

ENTITY-COLUMN RELATIONS

The cashier prepares two copies of a deposit slip, deposits the cash at the bank, and files the second copy of the deposit slip, which has been validated by the bank, by date. This may be charted as in Figure 2.17. The manual operation system is used to represent the "prepare deposit slip" process, and the document symbol is used to represent the cash payments and the deposit slips. This portion of the flowchart also would be placed in the "Cashier" column because it is a continuation of the flowchart of the cashier's activities.

The bank is a separate entity, yet the process of depositing the cash payments at the bank is shown as a manual operation in the "Cashier" column of the flowchart. The bank could be shown as a separate column, and the flow of the deposit slip to and from the bank could be charted. The method shown was chosen because the narrative description being charted does not contain any discussion of processing at the bank. This is a question of style that affects the overall appearance and clarity of the flowchart. This same point is true for customers, who are also separate entities. The terminal symbol rather than a separate column was used to indicate the source of the mail (customers) because the narrative description being charted does not contain any discussion of customer processing.

Because the narrative contains a description of the processing by the general ledger clerk and the accounts receivable clerk, both these entities are shown as separate columns. The charting of the manual processing activities performed by the general ledger clerk and the accounts receivable clerk is very similar to that of the cashier's activities. The completed flowchart is shown in Figure 2.18. Notice that the basic input/output symbol has been used to represent the general ledger and the accounts receivable ledger. The document symbol or off-line storage (file) symbol could be used in either case. The basic input/output symbol has been used to emphasize that it is always correct to represent input or output with this symbol.

The preceding points have been discussed to emphasize that many choices must be made when preparing a flowchart. The result should be clear in appearance and should effectively convey the functioning of the system. Five general guidelines are as follows:

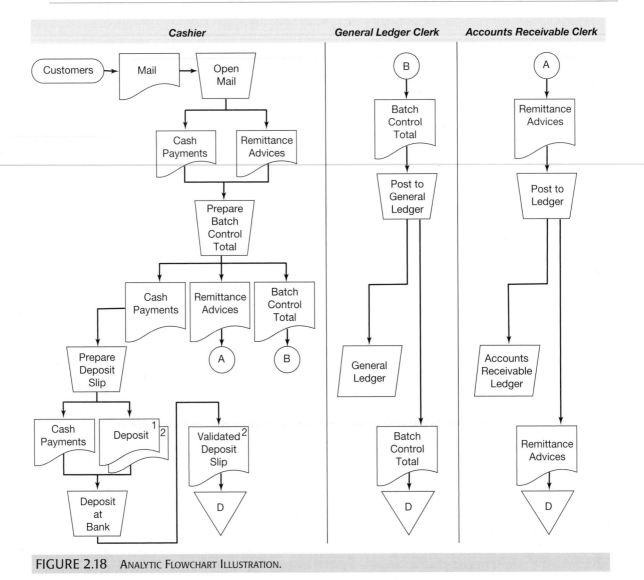

FIGURE 2.18 ANALYTIC FLOWCHART ILLUSTRATION.

1. Analyze the system to identify entities and documents, as done in this illustration.
2. Select the symbols to be used in accordance with the general guidelines described in this chapter.
3. Sketch a rough first draft of the system to organize the entity columns and flow of documents.
4. Review the sketch for major omissions or errors.
5. Finalize the flowchart, making sure that comments are added as necessary to clarify the flowchart.

NARRATIVE TECHNIQUES

Narrative techniques are often useful, particularly in the fact-finding stage of systems analysis. Interviews are useful for familiarizing the analyst with individual decision makers and their problems. In-depth interviews allow the systems analyst to establish a personal working relationship with the manager. Structured interviews might be used to answer a specific set of questions.

Open-ended questionnaires are a fact-gathering technique where people provide written answers to general rather than specific questions. Open-ended questionnaires serve the same purpose as in-depth interviews, asking very general questions such as, "Do you have any suggestions for improving the system? Please explain." Closed-ended questionnaires are a useful technique for gathering answers to a large number of questions. They require considerably less time on the part of the systems analyst. Such questionnaires are very effective in many situations, including collecting information about internal control.

Narrative techniques include document reviews. Often a large number of documents are available for review by the analyst or auditor, such as flowcharts, organization charts, procedure manuals, operation manuals, reference manuals, and historical records. These documents can assist the analyst or auditor in gaining an overall understanding of the organization.

RESOURCE UTILIZATION ANALYSIS

The techniques we have discussed assume an existing or proposed flow or structure of operations and do not directly address the question of system resource-utilization requirements. For example, assume that you had prepared flowcharts for a particular procedure, identified the changes necessary to accomplish the task at hand, and obtained approval to prepare (design) the detailed plan of operation and/or implement the newly designed procedure. Clearly, further analysis would be required to match the resources at hand with the task at hand. How many clerks or machines will be required to process the data? What type or size of machine is required? And who gets what task?

Resource utilization analysis always must be considered by systems development personnel in implementing systems. Auditors should consider resource utilization when they plan an audit. Tasks such as assigning staff to particular audit functions can be facilitated with systems techniques. Thus systems techniques for resource utilization analysis may be used by both auditors and systems personnel.

WORK MEASUREMENT

Work measurement is based on a simple premise: Quantitative measurement is essential to the design of efficient procedures. **Work measurement** includes the variety of techniques used to model, measure, or estimate clerical or other activities in a production framework. In an accounting framework, work measurement is similar to the concept employed in standard cost systems. The essential ingredient is the development of a standard, a yardstick, that may be used to gauge the efficiency of actual operation.

Work measurement involves four basic steps:

1. Identify the tasks.
2. Obtain time estimates for performing the tasks using time and motion studies, test runs, historical data, or some other source.
3. Adjust the time estimates for idle time and similar considerations.
4. Analyze requirements based on these data.

The following are general examples of step 4:

$$(\text{Average time/ unit} + \text{idle time/unit}) \times \text{average volume} = \text{total task time}$$
$$\text{Total time available/ Total task time} = \text{capacity utilization}$$

To illustrate the general idea, consider the following excerpt from an actual systems analysis:

Our desire to evaluate the relative costs associated with various operating configurations for the CVU Unit led to the programming of a computational model of the CVU operation. The model is essentially a personnel cost model. A constant volume is passed through the CVU operation under certain assumptions as to operating configuration. Costs are accumulated and reported. Costs are calculated in terms of the work hours needed to perform a given operation. A standard computation would appear as follows:

$$Y = C(X/R)$$

where

X = volume to be processed
R = processing rate (volume/hour)
C = average hourly personnel cost for this processing rate
Y = resulting cost

This standard includes such operations as counting, bundle and strap counts, verification, and destruction. In most cases, certain fixed costs are added, such as the cost of observers. Since several days are used in processing a given lot, the assumption of a constant volume allows us to calculate the cost per lot. The constant volume used is the average daily volume for the preceding year.

Work measurement techniques have two major areas of application in systems work. The first is in evaluating the technical feasibility or technical requirements of a system design. Examples of this are determining the number of magnetic disks needed to store a specific number of documents, the size of computer system necessary to process a proposed work load, and the number of clerks necessary to input data.

The second major area of application is in performance evaluation of system-related tasks such as computer programming and project development. Performance evaluation requires the definition of performance standards in terms of some directly measurable criterion such as "number of lines coded" or "hours of project work," so that actual performance may be quantified and evaluated with respect to managerial expectations for the task.

WORK DISTRIBUTION ANALYSIS

After the operational characteristics of a system have been identified and selected through some form of work measurement, a **work distribution analysis** must be undertaken to assign specific tasks to employees. This analysis may take several forms, but conceptually, the problem may be represented as a matrix. Table 2.2 illustrates a work distribution table.

A work distribution analysis requires detailed information about the functions and responsibilities of all employees involved in the analysis. A task list is used to record

TABLE 2.2   Sample Work Distribution Table

Task	Estimated Hours per Day	Lola	Dale	Neil
	Assignment to Employees			
Open mail	2	1	1	0
Sort advices	6	2	2	2
Batch control	2	0	0	2
File advices	8	4	4	0

each separate item of work performed by an individual, and the average number of hours spent on each task per week. The detail of tasks considered depends on the level of work measurement analysis. Table 2.2 shows the assignment of several tasks (left-hand column). Each employee (or department, and so on) is represented by a column; the work assignments are spread across the table. The method of assignment should be rational; that is, employee qualifications, internal control, scheduling, timing of events, and so forth, should be considered. The method of assignment is the choice of the analyst. Formal techniques using mathematical programming or similar algorithms may be found in management science and industrial engineering literature.

DECISION ANALYSIS TECHNIQUES

BRANCHING AND DECISION TABLES

Branching and decision tables are used primarily by systems development personnel. The decision logic required in a computer program is usually too complex to use a standard decision flowcharting symbol. In such cases, a **branching table** may be used to depict a decision function. The table is composed of a statement of the decision to be made, a list of the conditions that can occur, and the path to be followed for each condition. The "Go to" section contains either an inconnector (connector symbol) reference or a single flowline exiting to another symbol. Examples of branching table formats are shown in Figure 2.19.

A **decision table** is a tabular representation of a decision-making process (Fig. 2.20). It is similar to a branching table but more complex in that it incorporates multiple decision criteria. Decision tables are constructed on an IF–THEN premise and appear as a two-dimensional matrix in general form. The table is divided into four areas: the condition stub, the condition entries, the action stub, and the action entries. Conditions are listed on horizontal rows in the condition stub area and are read as "IF condition 1 And condition 2 … And condition N, THEN Action 1, Action 2, Action N." Rules are

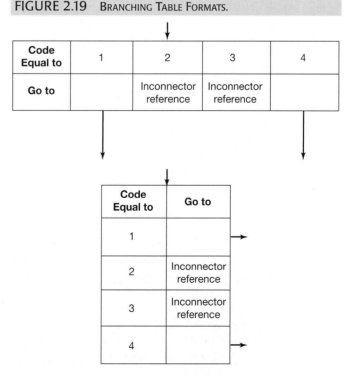

FIGURE 2.19   BRANCHING TABLE FORMATS.

Table Title		Rules				
		1	2	3	· · ·	N
If: Condition stub		Condition entry				
Then: Action stub		Action entry				

FIGURE 2.20   DECISION TABLE FORMAT.

numbered horizontally across the top of the table and represent the logical combinations of condition entries and action entries that constitute the decision process. There is one vertical row for each combination.

A decision table example is shown in Figure 2.21. As the figure shows, condition entries are usually limited to Y (for "true"), N (for "false"), or – (for "not applicable"). Action entries are listed as applicable or not applicable—the presence or absence of an x in Figure 2.21. The interpretation of rule 1 in Figure 2.21 is "IF conditions 1, 2, and 3 are Y, then take Actions 10, 11, 12, and 14." The other rules are interpreted in the same manner.

The type of decision table just discussed is called a *limited-entry table* because condition and action entries are restricted to Y, N, or not applicable. An *extended-entry decision* table also might be used, where the entries indicate specific types of actions to be taken, specific conditions, or references to other decision tables. Decision tables might

FIGURE 2.21   DECISION TABLE.

Organization   ABC Company   Page   1   Of   1

System   Labor Distribution   Project No.   123

Program Name   Labor Dist. Print   No.   LD01   Revision Date   3/26

Prepared by   W. Smith   Date   2/26   Approved by   J. Jones

Table Name:

	Line	Condition Action Rule →	1	2	3	4	5	6	7	8		
IF	1	15 Regular Hours	Y	–	–	–	N					
	2	15 Overtime Hours	Y	–	N	–	Y	–	N			
	3	15 Shift Bonus Hours	Y	N	Y	N	Y	N	Y	N		
THEN	10	Regular Dollars = Reg. Hours x (Hourly + .115)	x	x	x	x						
	11	Overtime Dollars = Overtime Hrs. 150%	x	x								
	12	Shift Dollars = Shift Bonus Hours = $10 x .10	x		x							
	13	Error No Shift or OT without Reg. Hours					x	x	x			
	14	Next Record	x	x	x	x	x	x	x			

Go to - F (Function); R (Rule, Same Table); T (Table)

Notes: The error message at line 13 should be displayed in the "Dollars"
area of the report, to the right of a dump of the 501 Record.

Condition   Y = True   Action
Entries   N = False   Entry   x = Take Action
("If")   – = Not applicable   ("Then")

be used in lieu of program flowcharts to analyze and document the logic of an application program. The tabular structure of a decision table is an important advantage compared with graphic flowcharts as the complexity of a decision process increases.

MATRIX METHODS

Matrix methods are used by both auditors and systems personnel. A decision table is essentially a matrix presentation. Matrices and array forms of presentation have many uses in systems work because they are a convenient method for analyzing and displaying a large volume of data. The work- or spreadsheets used in accounting systems to spread or distribute account balances through different subclassifications or to facilitate the closing process are common examples of matrix techniques. The essential analytic feature of matrix techniques is the spreading of row entries through various column entries. This ensures that each row/column combination is explicitly analyzed and documented.

In an application control matrix, the row entries are controls, and the column entries are processing actions. This technique may be used systematically to evaluate the internal controls in an application system. In a data control matrix, the row entries are data elements, and the column entries are forms or reports. Analysis may be directed toward the elimination of redundant data on a set of forms or to the commonality of data on a set of reports.

❖ SUMMARY

Systems techniques are used by both auditors and systems personnel as tools for analysis and documentation. Table 2.3 summarizes the many techniques described in

TABLE 2.3	Primary Users of Systems Techniques	
Analytic flowchart	Charts the flow of documents and processing between different entities, which are represented by separate columns in the chart	Auditor Systems analyst
Block flowchart	Synonym for program flowchart	Systems designer Programmer
Branching table	A tabular technique used to represent a decision function in a flowchart	Systems designer Programmer
Data flow diagram	A charting technique used to document the logical design of a system	Systems analyst Systems designer
Decision table	Used to supplement or replace the preparation of flowcharts when there are a large number of alternative decision paths	Systems designer Programmer
Document flowchart	A flowchart of document flow in which the only symbol used is the document symbol	Auditor Systems analyst
Flowchart	A symbolic diagram that shows the data flow and sequence of operations in a system	Auditor Systems analyst Systems designer Programmer
Forms distribution chart	Illustrates the distribution of multiple-copy documents within an organization	Auditor Systems analyst Systems designer
HIPO chart (hierarchy plus input-process-output)	An organized collection of IPO charts	Systems analyst Systems designer

TABLE 2.3	*(Cont.)*	
IPO chart (input-process-output)	Describes the inputs necessary to produce certain outputs, and generally provides very little detail concerning the required processing	Systems analyst Systems designer
Logical data flow diagram	Synonym for data flow diagram	Systems analyst Systems designer
Program flowchart	A flowchart indicating detailed processing functions	Systems designer Programmer
Systems flowchart	A pictorial or graphical representation of the overall flow of work, documents, and operations in an application system	Auditor Systems analyst Systems designer
Work measurement	Techniques used to measure activities in a production framework	Systems analyst Systems designer
Work distribution analysis	Techniques used to rationally assign work to entities	Auditor Systems analyst System designer

this chapter and indicates the primary users of each technique. Systems techniques are necessary to a structured systems approach to the analysis and design of information systems. One popular and widely used system technique is flowcharting. Several different types of flowcharts may be used, incorporating standard flowcharting symbols. Even though standard symbols are in widespread use, flowcharting is more art than science.

Many other system techniques are used in addition to flowcharts. Logical data flow diagrams (DFDs) are used frequently in systems analysis and design. DFDs may be used to successively refine the design of a system. Branching and decision tables, IPO and HIPO charts, and matrix methods also are used in systems analysis and design.

Techniques used in resource utilization analysis and decision analysis include flowcharts, DFDs, and other graphic techniques. Although very useful, these techniques do not consider system resource use. Work measurement techniques are necessary to address how much or how many resources will be required for the operation of a system.

❖ GLOSSARY

additional symbols: a group of flowchart symbols in ANSI X3.5 consisting of miscellaneous symbols that make flowcharting more convenient

analytic flowchart: charts the flow of documents and processing between different entities—which are represented by separate columns in the chart—in a system

basic symbols: one of the four groups of flowchart symbols in ANSI X3.5 consisting of symbols that correspond to the basic data processing functions

block flowchart: synonym for *program flowchart*

branching table: a tabular technique used to represent a decision function in a flowchart

data flow diagram(DFD): a charting technique used to document the logical design of a system

decision table: used to supplement or replace the preparation of flowcharts when there are a large number of alternative decision paths

document flowchart: a flowchart of document flow in a system in which the only symbol used is the document symbol

forms-distribution chart: illustrates the distribution of multiple-copy documents within an organization

HIPO (hierarchy plus input-process-output) chart: an organized collection of IPO charts

IPO (input-process-output) chart: describes the inputs necessary to produce certain outputs and generally provides very little detail concerning the required processing

logical data flow diagram: synonym for *data flow diagram*

program flowchart: a flowchart indicating detailed processing functions

sandwich rule: the flowcharting principle that every process symbol should be "sandwiched" between an input symbol and an output symbol

specialized input/output symbols: a group of flowchart symbols in ANSI X3.5 consisting of symbols that may be used to represent input/output and also the medium on which the information is recorded

specialized process symbols: a group of flowchart symbols in ANSI X3.5 consisting of symbols that may be used to represent processing and, in addition, identify the specific type of operation to be performed

systems flowchart: a pictorial or graphical representation of the overall flow of work, documents, and operations in an application system

systems techniques: tools used in the analysis, design, and documentation of systems

work distribution analysis: techniques used to rationally assign work to entities

work measurement: techniques used to measure activities in a production framework

❖ CHAPTER QUIZ

Answers to the Chapter Quiz appear on page 67.

1. The group concerned with establishing standards for flowchart symbols is (_____).
   - (a) ASCII
   - (b) EBCDIC
   - (c) ANSI
   - (d) AICPA

2. A pictorial or graphic representation of the overall flow of work, documents, and operations in an application system is shown in a(n) (_____).
   - (a) IPO chart
   - (b) forms distribution chart
   - (c) systems flowchart
   - (d) process chart

3. Which type of diagram emphasizes the physical description of a system?
   - (a) analytic flowchart
   - (b) logical data flow diagram (DFD)
   - (c) HIPO chart
   - (d) IPO chart

4. ANSI X3.5-1970—the information system flowcharting standard published by the American National Standards Institute—defines four groups of flowchart symbols and illustrates conventions regarding their use. Which of the following is *not* one of these groups?
   - (a) specialized input/output symbols
   - (b) specialized processing symbols
   - (c) branching and decision table symbols
   - (d) basic symbols

5. Structured systems analysis can best be referred to as (_____).
   - (a) a process of increasingly complex sets of controls
   - (b) a process of successive refinement
   - (c) a procedure for documenting process logic
   - (d) a statement of decision tables

6. An important omission from flowcharts and matrix techniques is (_____).
   - (a) the ability to represent decisions
   - (b) the ability to include internal control considerations
   - (c) the ability to incorporate error conditions
   - (d) the ability to specify systems resource requirements

7. Which of the following items would be most useful in analyzing the separation of duties and functions in an application system?
   (a) document flowchart
   (b) program flowchart
   (c) HIPO chart
   (d) source document

8. In the preparation of a logical data flow diagram for a payroll processing application, which of the following symbols should be used to indicate the payroll data?
   (a) terminator symbol
   (b) data store symbol
   (c) process symbol
   (d) input/output symbol

FIGURE 2.22   SOLUTION TO REVIEW PROBLEM.

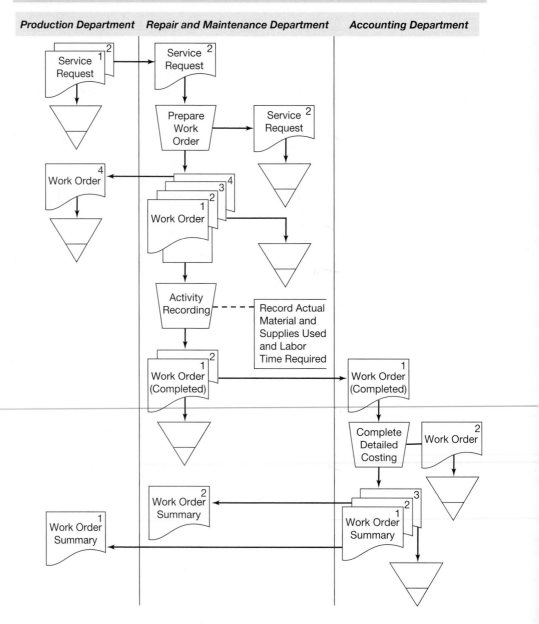

9. In the preparation of an analytic flowchart for a payroll processing application, which of the following symbols could be used to indicate the payroll data?
   (a) connector symbol
   (b) decision symbol
   (c) process symbol
   (d) input/output symbol

10. In the preparation of an analytic flowchart, which of the following symbols should be used when flowlines are broken due to a page limitation?
    (a) terminal symbol
    (b) connector symbol
    (c) manual operation symbol
    (d) input/output symbol

❖ REVIEW PROBLEM

This review problem involves a manual system. A service request form (two copies) is prepared in the production department. Copy 2 is forwarded to the repair and maintenance department. Copy 1 is filed in the production department.

In the repair and maintenance department, copy 2 of the service request is used to manually prepare a four-part work order form. Copy 2 of the service request form is then filed in the repair and maintenance department. Copy 4 of the work order form is forwarded to the production department to acknowledge the service request. Copy 3 of the work order form is filed in the repair and maintenance department. Clerks in the repair and maintenance department manually record actual materials and supplies used and labor time required onto copies 1 and 2 of the work order. When the work order is completed, copy 1 is filed in the repair and maintenance department, and copy 2 is forwarded to the accounting department.

Clerks in the accounting department manually complete a detailed costing of copy 2 of the work order and prepare a work order summary report (three copies). Copy 2 of the work order is filed in the accounting department. Copy 1 of the work order summary is forwarded to the production department. Copy 2 of the work order summary is forwarded to the repair and maintenance department. Copy 3 of the work order summary is filed in the accounting department.

Required
Prepare an analytic flowchart of the preceding procedures. (See Figure 2.22 for the solution.)

❖ REVIEW QUESTIONS

1. Define flowcharting.
2. List and draw the basic flowchart symbols.
3. Flowchart symbols represent what aspect of a system?
4. Distinguish between IPO and HIPO charts.
5. What is the difference between a systems flowchart and an analytic flowchart?
6. A logical data flow diagram can be used to document what aspect of a system?
7. Why do auditors prepare analytic flowcharts of processing systems?
8. What important feature is common to analytic, document, and forms distribution charts?
9. Identify the symbols that are used to construct logical data flow diagrams.
10. Is flowcharting useful in analyzing the resources required to implement a system?
11. Relate the concept of work measurement to the system implementation process.
12. Outline the steps involved in a work distribution analysis.

❖ DISCUSSION QUESTIONS AND PROBLEMS

Questions 13 through 15 are based on the section of a system flowchart for a payroll application shown in Figure 2.23.

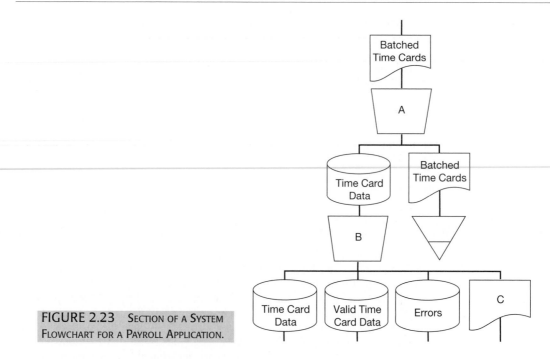

FIGURE 2.23   SECTION OF A SYSTEM FLOWCHART FOR A PAYROLL APPLICATION.

13. Symbol A could represent (_____).
    (a) computation of gross pay
    (b) input of payroll data
    (c) preparation of paychecks
    (d) verification of pay rates
14. Symbol B could represent (_____).
    (a) computation of net pay
    (b) separation of erroneous time cards
    (c) validation of payroll data
    (d) preparation of the payroll register
15. Symbol C could represent (_____).
    (a) batched time cards
    (b) unclaimed payroll checks
    (c) erroneous time cards
    (d) an error report

(CPA)

16. Which of the symbolic representations in Figure 2.24 indicates that a sales invoice has been filed?

(CPA)

17. During the review of an electronic data processing (EDP) internal control system, an auditor may review decision tables prepared by the client. A decision table is usually prepared by a client to supplement or replace the preparation of (_____).
    (a) an internal control questionnaire when the number of alternative responses is large
    (b) a narrative description of a system where transactions are not processed in batches
    (c) flowcharts when the number of alternatives is large
    (d) an internal control questionnaire not specifically designed for an EDP installation

(CPA)

18. Which of the symbolic representations in Figure 2.25 indicate that a file has been consulted?

(CPA)

19. The XYZ Company distributes three product lines to seven customers. Sales are recorded manually on invoices. Separate invoices are always used to record sales of product line number 1. Sales of the other two product lines are always recorded together on a single invoice.

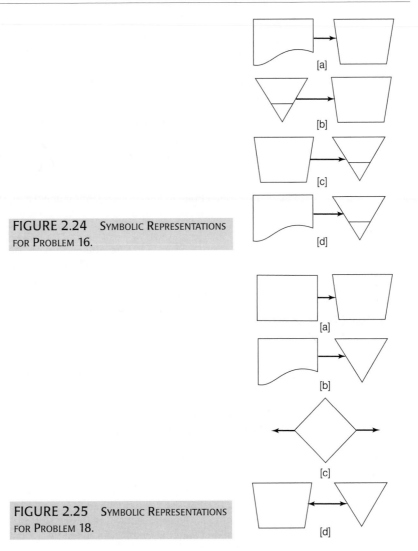

FIGURE 2.24 SYMBOLIC REPRESENTATIONS FOR PROBLEM 16.

FIGURE 2.25 SYMBOLIC REPRESENTATIONS FOR PROBLEM 18.

The manager would like to know the total daily sales of each product line in dollars and also the daily sales total for each product line sold to each customer.

To develop this information manually, the manager will collect all the invoices at the end of each day. A separate worksheet will be used to record the daily sales total for each product line. Each worksheet will have seven columns with separate headings—one for each customer. The manager will record each day's sales totals on a separate line of each worksheet.

Design a system with the specific steps necessary to develop and record the desired information from the daily batch of sales invoices.

20. The HRZ Company maintains a perpetual inventory system. Clerks in the accounting department post the data manually from receiving reports, materials requisition forms, copies of purchase orders, and other transactions, such as returns and adjustments to the inventory records. The source documents are filed by posting date. The inventory records are analyzed after each posting to determine if the item should be reordered. If an item needs to be reordered, a purchase requisition (one copy) is prepared and sent to the purchasing department. There, clerks select a vendor from a master vendor file, prepare a purchase order (four copies), and update the vendor file to reflect the order. The purchase order is approved and distributed as follows: original copy to the vendor; copy 2 is filed numerically with the corresponding purchase requisition attached; copy 3 is forwarded to the receiving department; copy 4 is sent to the accounting department.

Required

(a) Prepare an analytic flowchart of the preceding procedures.

(b) Prepare a logical data flow diagram of the preceding procedures.

21. As part of an audit engagement, you have been assigned the task of documenting the internal control system for the BrownSole Shoe Store. The business is operated by a single owner, who operates the store daily with only two additional employees who help out in everything, from stocking new shoes, to helping customers, to bill paying and accounting.

    The owner, Marjorie Renalwald, is a very stubborn person with little business education. She very much needs a set of audited financial statements in order to obtain a loan, but at the same time she seems very irritable and not especially interested in working with you.

    Your first experience with her was a 10:00 A.M. appointment with her the other day. You sat in the back of the store, in a small storage room, and waited for one hour while she talked on the telephone to her daughter in London. Then, after allowing you to ask her only one or two questions, she abruptly told you that she was late for a hair appointment.

    Required

    Describe the approach you will take in dealing with Marjorie Renalwald. Which systems techniques will you use, and what order will you use them in?

22. A systems analyst has asked you for advice concerning the construction of a logical data flow diagram for the process of validating a user ID, which is input from a data terminal, to request access to a computer system. Criticize the DFD that has been prepared by the systems analyst (see Figure 2.26).

23. You are reviewing audit work papers containing a narrative description of the Tenney Corporation's factory payroll system. A portion of that narrative is as follows:

    Factory employees punch time clock cards each day when entering or leaving the shop. At the end of each week, the timekeeping department collects the time cards and prepares duplicate batch-control slips by department showing total hours and number of employees. The time cards and original batch-control slips are sent to the payroll accounting section. The second copies of the batch-control slips are filed by date.

    In the payroll accounting section, payroll transaction records are input from the information on the time cards, and a batch total record for each batch is input from the batch-control slip. These records are input to magnetic disk. The time cards and batch-control slips are then filed by batch for possible reference. The payroll transaction file is sent to data processing, where it is sorted by employee number within batch. Each batch is edited by a computer program, which checks

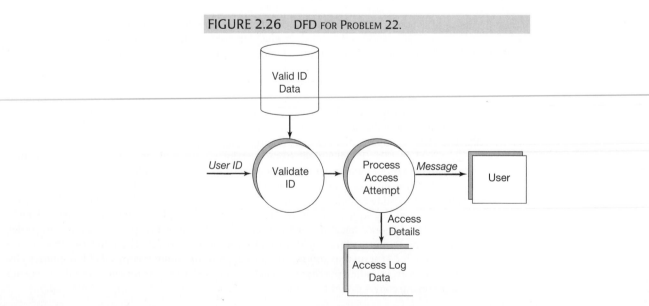

FIGURE 2.26   DFD FOR PROBLEM 22.

the validity of employee number against a master employee disk file and the total hours and number of employees against the batch total record. A detailed printout by batch and employee number is produced, which indicates batches that do not balance and invalid employee numbers. This printout is returned to payroll accounting to resolve all differences.

In searching for documentation you found a flowchart (Fig. 2.27) of the payroll system, which included all appropriate symbols (American National Standards Institute) but was only partially labeled.

Required
(a) Number your answer 1 through 16. Next to the corresponding number, supply the appropriate labeling (document name, process description, or file order) applicable to each numbered symbol on the flowchart.
(b) Flowcharts are one of the aids an auditor may use to determine and evaluate a client's internal control system. List advantages of using flowcharts in this context.

(CPA)

24. Harvard Square Software Company uses a manual sales order processing system. Sales order forms (three copies) are prepared by the sales department and forwarded to the accounting department. In the accounting department, an invoice (three copies) and a shipping order (four copies) are prepared manually on the basis of the sales order. One copy each of the sales order, the invoice, and the shipping order is forwarded to the sales department. A copy of the sales order is attached to two copies of the shipping order and then

FIGURE 2.27   FLOWCHART FOR PROBLEM 23.

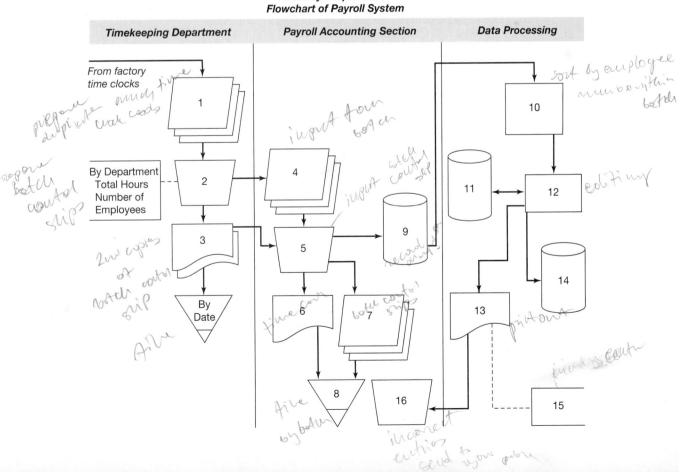

forwarded to the shipping department. One copy of the invoice is forwarded to the customer. The remaining documents are attached to each other and then filed in the accounting department by sales order number.

Required

Prepare an analytic flowchart of the previous procedures.

25. Batches of customer payments on account are processed manually in the cashier's office. Clerks open the payments, separate the checks and the remittance advices, and prepare a batch-control total (two copies) of the remittances. The checks are processed manually to prepare a deposit slip (two copies). Copy 1 of the deposit slip and the batch of checks are forwarded for deposit at the bank. Copy 2 of the deposit slip is verified to copy 1 of the batch-control total, attached to it, and then filed in the cashier's office by date. Copy 2 of the batch-control total is forwarded to the general ledger department. The remittance advices are forwarded to the accounts receivable department.

   Clerks in the accounts receivable department manually post the remittance advices to the accounts receivable ledger. The remittance advices are then filed in the accounts receivable department by customer number.

Required

Prepare an analytic flowchart of the previous procedures.

26. Production workers prepare materials requisition forms (four copies) and forward them to the production supervisor for approval. The materials requisition form is then forwarded to stores. In stores, the order is filled, and the materials requisition form is signed by a clerk. The clerk then returns copy 1 of the materials requisition form along with the materials to the production workers. Copy 2 of the materials requisition form is forwarded to the production supervisor. Copy 4 is forwarded to the cost accounting department. Copy 3 of the materials requisition form is used in stores to manually post the materials that were issued to the perpetual inventory records. Copy 4 is then filed in stores by number.

Required

Prepare an analytic flowchart of the previous procedures.

27. Collateral Deposit (part 1).[2] (This case is continued as Problem 59 in Chapter 4.)

   Dan Matt, a junior auditor for Kramp and Company, was assigned the responsibility of conducting a preliminary application review of a client bank's loan department operations.

   Dan had completed his flowchart and explanation of the loan process and turned it over to his senior. He was writing up his assessment of the process from his notes when his senior interrupted and asked what happened to the collateral received on loans. Dan recognized the significance of this omission and agreed to check it out right away.

   Collateral can be anything of value acceptable to the bank but is typically some type of security. Dan found that customers turn over any collateral to their loan officer, who prepares and signs the next in sequence of a prenumbered four-part form that describes the collateral and serves as a receipt. Each copy of the form is a different color to facilitate identification. The customer receives the original of the collateral receipt form, which is pink. The second, or white, copy of the form is sent directly to the collateral records clerk, who logs it in. The loan officer takes the blue, or third, copy to the vault custodian along with the collateral. The final, or yellow, copy is cancelled and discarded. The vault custodian compares the blue copy of the receipt with the collateral in the loan officer's presence. If they agree, the vault custodian signs the blue copy. The vault custodian then attaches a tag to the collateral and carries it and the blue copy of the collateral receipt to the vault attendant. The vault attendant also compares the description on the blue copy with the tagged collateral. If they match, the vault attendant opens the vault and jointly with the vault custodian deposits the collateral within. The vault attendant notes the location on the blue copy and signs it. The completed blue copy is then taken by the vault attendant to the collateral clerk. Until the blue copy is received, the collateral clerk keeps the unmatched white copy, filed numerically in a suspense file as a reminder for follow-up purposes.

[2]Prepared by Frederick L. Neumann, Richard J. Boland, and Jeffrey Johnson; funded by the Touche Ross Foundation Aid to Accounting Education Program.

On receiving the blue copy from the vault attendant, the collateral clerk compares it to the white copy previously received directly from the loan officer. If the blue and white copies match, the collateral clerk completes the entry in the collateral register in numerical order. The white copy and the blue copy of the collateral receipt are placed in a permanent file by name. Any differences are resolved with the loan officer's assistance.

List of Procedures

Customer
1. Brings in collateral to loan officer
2. Receives receipt for collateral

Loan Officer
3. Receives collateral from customer
4. Removes prenumbered four-part form from file
5. Completes form describing collateral and signs it
6. Gives pink copy to customer
7. Sends white copy to collateral clerk
8. Takes blue copy to vault custodian
9. Cancels and discards yellow copy
10. Takes collateral in sealed bag to vault custodian

Vault Custodian
11. Receives blue copy of collateral receipt from loan officer
12. Receives collateral from loan officer
13. Reads description and instructions regarding collateral on blue copy
14. Compares collateral with blue copy
15. Signs blue copy
16. Gives blue copy to vault attendant
17. Opens vault jointly with vault attendant
18. Deposits collateral in vault

Vault Attendant
19. Receives blue copy from vault custodian
20. Compares blue copy to collateral being deposited
21. Assists vault custodian in opening vault
22. Signs blue copy upon witnessing deposit of collateral
23. Takes blue copy to collateral clerk

Collateral Clerk
24. Receives white copy from loan officer
25. Makes entry in numerical sequence in log book
26. Holds white copy until later receipt of blue copy
27. Matches blue copy when received to white copy and notes appropriate signatures
28. Records deposit of collateral in collateral register
29. Files collateral receipt copies in permanent file

Required
Prepare a flowchart of the collateral receipt process and cross-reference it to the list of procedures provided.

28. A partially completed charge sales systems flowchart is shown in Figure 2.28. The flowchart depicts the charge sales activities of the Bottom Manufacturing Corporation.

A customer's purchase order is received and a six-part sales order is prepared from it. The six copies are initially distributed as follows:

Copy 1: Billing copy—to billing department
Copy 2: Shipping copy—to shipping department
Copy 3: Credit copy—to credit department
Copy 4: Stock request copy—to credit department
Copy 5: Customer copy—to customer
Copy 6: Sales order copy—file in sales order department

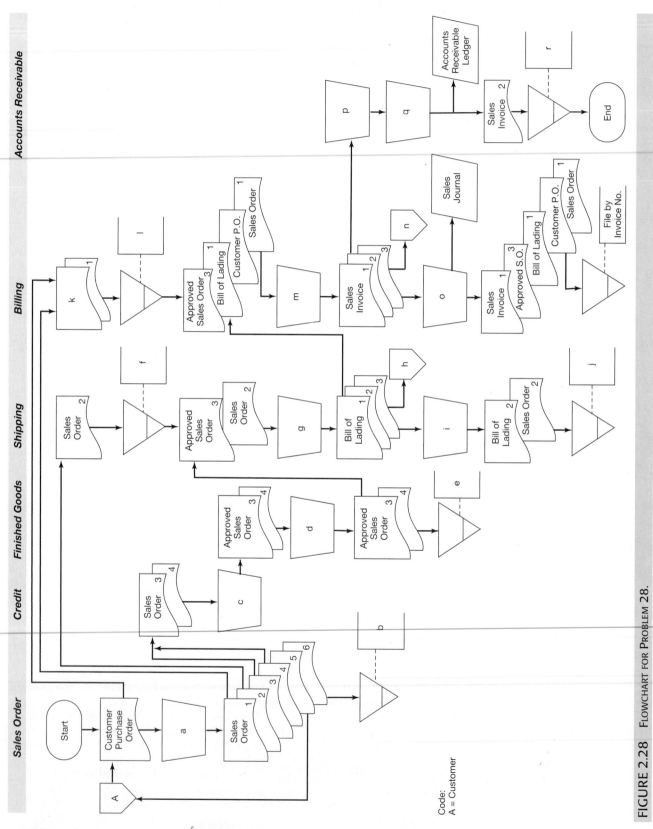

Code:
A = Customer

FIGURE 2.28 FLOWCHART FOR PROBLEM 28.

When each copy of the sales order reaches the applicable department or destination, it calls for specific internal control procedures and related documents. Some of the procedures and related documents are indicated on the flowchart. Other procedures and documents are labeled letters *a* to *r*.

Required

List the procedures or the internal documents that are labeled letters *c* to *r* in the flowchart of Bottom Manufacturing Corporation's charge sales system.

Organize your answer as follows (an explanation of the letters *a* and *b*, which appear in the flowchart, are entered as examples):

Flowchart Symbol Letter	Procedures or Internal Document
a	Prepare six-part sales order
b	File by order number

(CPA)

29. Figure 2.29 illustrates a manual system for executing purchases and cash disbursements transactions.

Required

Indicate what each of the letters A through L represents.

(CPA)

30. An analyst wishes to prepare a decision table for purchase order procedures. First, there is a credit check of the customer. If credit is approved, the order is accepted. If the order calls for 0 to 25 units, there is no discount on the order. If the order calls for 26 to 55 units, it is eligible for a 5 percent discount; if more than 55 units are ordered, the discount is 10 percent.

Required

(a) Prepare a limited-entry decision table.
(b) Prepare an extended-entry decision table.

31. An analyst wishes to document credit card purchase authorization procedures in a decision table. A purchase under $50 is approved automatically. Purchases between $50 and $100 are given an authorization number. For purchases over $100, a "hold" is placed on the customer's account in addition to an authorization number being assigned to the purchase.

Required

(a) Prepare a limited-entry decision table.
(b) Prepare an extended-entry decision table.

32. Analyze the following data incident to machine posting of checks drawn by bank depositors:

Number of checks posted	570
Total elapsed minutes	480
Rest period minutes	20
Interruption and delay minutes	20

Develop a standard time per check. In terms of percentage, what is the rest and delay allowance?

33. The Big Plastic Company manufactures a variety of plastic utensils, employing approximately 400 factory workers. Supervisors are paid a salary for a 40-hour week but receive overtime for hours worked in excess of 40. Supervisors record hours worked on a weekly time card, clocking in and out at the beginning and end of each day.

Factory workers are paid on an hourly basis. Activity rates are assigned to the operation of various machines in the factory; a worker assigned to a machine is paid the higher of either the machine's activity rate or the standard hourly pay rate. Workers clock in and out of each assigned activity on a daily basis. Supervisors record the activity code and elapsed

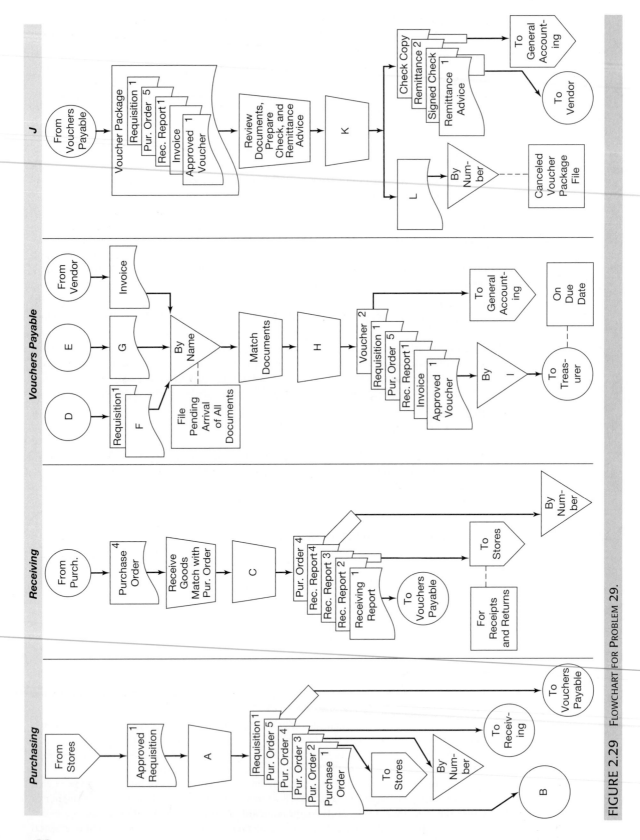

FIGURE 2.29 FLOWCHART FOR PROBLEM 29.

time for each entry on a machine operator's daily time card. Supervisors maintain a record of machine operator overtime. All workers must account for 8 hours a day and receive time-and-a-half for hours worked in excess of 8 hours per day.

A timekeeper collects time cards on a daily basis. Supervisors' time cards are collected at the end of each week. Time cards are compared to an authorized employee list, initialed by the timekeeper, and forwarded to the payroll department.

In the payroll department, a clerk verifies the timekeeper initials, batches the cards in groups of 40 or fewer cards, and prepares a prenumbered batch-control form for each batch. This form contains total regular hours, overtime hours, date, and number of documents in the batch. The payroll clerk transcribes the contents of each batch-control form onto an input batch-control log to record and maintain control of each batch. The time cards are then submitted to the computer processing department, where they are key-transcribed, verified, and processed by a payroll system edit program to produce a detailed listing of the input items. At the end of the listing, control totals are printed for the valid and rejected items. If any item in a batch is rejected, then all items in the batch are rejected to maintain batch integrity. The payroll clerk corrects rejected items, prepares a new batch-control form using the original batch number plus a suffix to identify the batch as a correction batch, and resubmits the batch to the computer processing department. This procedure is repeated throughout the week until all errors have been corrected.

The payroll is processed weekly to produce an updated payroll master file, employee checks, and payroll register. These reports are distributed to the payroll department, where a reconciliation with the input controls is performed.

Required

Flowchart the preceding payroll procedure.

34. Prepare a program flowchart for the following application. This application calculates straight-line depreciation for a file of fixed assets. The fixed-asset file consists of the following record types:

(a) A header record, which contains the file ID number and a hash total of all the record ID (key) values.

(b) A record for each fixed asset. Each record contains the following fields: ID number, a location code, original cost, useful life in months, depreciation taken to date, and salvage value.

The program should read each fixed-asset record, compute the amount of depreciation for the year (12 months), update the necessary fields, and write the updated record. End-of-job processing should print the number of assets processed, print the total depreciation computed, and verify the hash total for this run.

35. Modify the preceding problem to compute depreciation by the double-declining-balance method.

❖ ANSWERS TO CHAPTER QUIZ

1. c	4. c	7. a	10. b
2. c	5. b	8. b	
3. a	6. d	9. d	

CHAPTER 3

ELECTRONIC COMMERCE

LEARNING OBJECTIVES

Careful study of this chapter will enable you to:

❖ Explain the history of the Internet and how it works.

❖ Describe intranets and explain how they are made secure.

❖ Explain client-server technology and how it applies to electronic financial transactions.

❖ Describe various approaches to securing electronic financial transactions.

ELECTRONIC COMMERCE

ELECTRONIC NETWORKS

A great many of the business transactions in today's business environment are transmitted over some type of electronic network. The network may be very small and involve only a handful of computers within a single business, or it may be so large that it encompasses the entire globe. Either way, **electronic networks** are groups of computers that are connected together electronically. They make it possible for companies to conveniently assemble transaction data and distribute information across multiple physical locations.

LANs, MANs, AND WANs

Networks are sometimes classified according to the distance they span. **Local area networks (LANs)** are networks that span a single site, such as a building or a group of buildings that are in close proximity to one another. **Metropolitan area networks (MANs)** are networks that span a single city or metropolitan area, and finally, **wide area networks (WANs)** are networks of computers that span at least two metropolitan areas. From a practical point of view, the main difference between these three types of networks is the rate at which data flow through them. Due to hardware technology, data flow the fastest through local area networks and the slowest through wide area networks. But from the standpoint of the processing of accounting transactions, these differences in the rates of data flow are not usually critical because individual account-ing transactions involve only small amounts of data. For example, the data in a typical sales order might amount to only a couple of hundred characters. Accordingly, in less than 1 second the typical sales transaction can just as easily move from one state to the next as it can from one building to the next.

In the past, each of the three types of networks used its own hardware and soft-ware standards, and in practice, such standards even varied from one computer vendor to the next. The result was an environment in which companies more often chose to communicate with each other via the U.S. mail rather than by computer. But the Internet has brought universal standards of communication to all networks, and with today's technology, it is possible for any type of computer in any type of network to conveniently exchange information with any other computer in the world.

THE INTERNET

The **Internet** is an electronic highway consisting of various standards and protocols that allows computers everywhere to communicate with each other. The best way to fully explain the Internet is to explain some of its history. The roots of the Internet go all the way back to the 1960s during the cold war era when the U.S. government was in search of a means of maintaining military communications in the event of a nuclear war.

The government's problem was tackled by the RAND Corporation, which came up with two amazing suggestions: (1) The network should have no central command-and-control center, and (2) the network should be able to operate in tatters from the very beginning. These goals were achieved by making every node (i.e., computer) in the network operate independently. Furthermore, the physical path connecting one computer to another was considered unimportant. Specifically, computers in Boston and New York could communicate directly with each other, or alternatively, they could just as easily communicate with each other through an intermediate computer in, say, Chicago, Los Angeles, or Miami. This way, if one link in the network were de-stroyed, the computers in the network could continue to communicate with each other through the remaining links. Therefore, the network would be able to withstand a nuclear attack.

The earliest practical version of the Internet was created in the early 1970s by the Pentagon's Advanced Research Projects Agency (ARPA); it was called ARPANET. Originally, this network was used to allow the military to spread its computing tasks across several computers, but soon something unexpected happened: Users of the net-work began sending each other electronic mail containing news and personal messages.

While ARPANET grew, other networks (such as Bitnet, MILnet, and NSFnet) sprung up. Eventually they adopted a common set of communications protocols called TCP/IP (Transmission Control Protocol/Internet Protocol). TCP is a protocol for di-viding electronic messages into "packets" of information and then reassembling these packets at the receiving end. IP, on the other hand, is an addressing protocol that as-signs a unique address to each computer on the Internet. The TCP/IP protocols soon spread throughout the entire world and now constitute the universal standard for vir-tually all long-distance Internet communications.

Despite the universality of its communication protocols, the Internet has developed very much into the type of network that the RAND Corporation envisioned decades ago. That is, the Internet has no central command-and-control structure, and it operates more or less under the principle of anarchy. There is no "Internet Corporation" or "Internet Agency." Rather, the Internet operates more like a public park, where anyone can come and talk to anyone else in the park using any language he or she chooses.

Still, many groups of individuals have found it desirable to adopt their own special technologies for communicating across the Internet. Some of these technologies are discussed later. First, some basics of Internet addresses are discussed.

Internet Addresses   Every computer or user on the Internet needs an **IP (Internet Protocol) address** to communicate with other computers on the Internet. The IP address consists of a long number separated by periods. For example, a typical IP address will look something like 207.49.159.2. IP addresses are typically obtained from an organization such as InterNIC, which manages and distributes them to the general public. Most organizations obtain a group of IP addresses that they in turn allocate to their individual users. In some cases, organizations permanently allocate each user a personal IP address. From the user's standpoint, his or her IP address always remains the same. Such an IP address is called a **fixed IP address**. Fixed IP addresses are generally necessary for users whose computers are connected to the Internet 24 hours per day or for very long periods of time. On the other hand, some organizations only temporarily allocate IP addresses to users. This is helpful when an organization has, say, 100 users and only 10 IP addresses to allocate. In this case the organization will allocate IP addresses to users only while they are accessing the Internet. When an individual user disconnects from the Internet, his or her IP address is returned to the pool for someone else to use. This type of IP address is called a **dynamic IP address**, which is one that is assigned temporarily to a user while he or she is accessing the Internet.

Since IP addresses are long and difficult to remember, procedures have been created whereby easy-to-remember alias names can be used instead. For example, the name *www.bodhop.ais.com* might be used in place of 131.91.120.68. This name, *www.bodhop.ais*, is called the **domain name**, which is simply an alias name that can be used in place of the IP number. Domain names and their corresponding IP addresses are kept in electronic "phone books" at many sites on the Internet. These electronic phone books are called **domain name servers (DNSs)**.

Most Internet-related software allows the user to address another computer by its domain name. The user's software then automatically contacts a nearby DNS and finds the related IP number, which is then used to complete the user's request. This whole lookup process normally takes only a fraction of a second and the user rarely needs to be concerned with it.

INTRANETS

The various protocols and technologies relating to the Internet have become so popular that many companies have adopted them for in-house communications over local area networks. This phenomenon has given rise to self-contained, in-house internets, or **intranets**.

For those inside the organization, the intranet may appear to be part of the Internet. That is, employees of the organization may access the company's repositories of information in the same way they access similar resources anywhere on the Internet. The only difference is that the entire intranet may be completely invisible or unavailable to outsiders. Alternatively, all or part of the intranet may be available to outsiders only after they are properly authenticated.

A variation on the intranet is the extranet. Extranets exist when the intranets of two or more companies are linked together. Typical extranets involve the linking of a company's intranet with the intranets of its suppliers or customers.

Intranet Security Issues   Needless to say, intranets pose considerable security risks by potentially exposing the organization's sensitive information to everyone on the Internet. For this reason, many companies use combinations of hardware and software called *firewalls* to limit access from outsiders. **Firewalls** (Fig. 3.1) limit access to information on

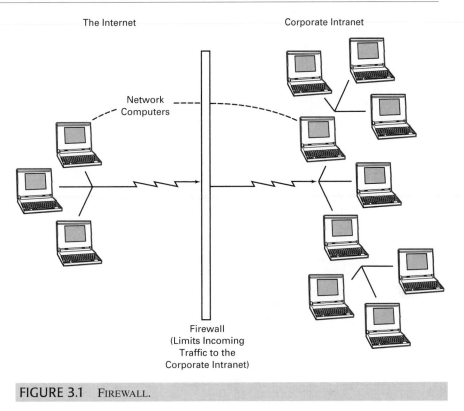

FIGURE 3.1 FIREWALL.

the company's servers from the rest of the world. Specifically, in the typical situation, the only way an outsider can access information in the company's intranet is through a single point guarded by a firewall.

Firewalls typically filter each packet of incoming information to ensure that it has originated from an authorized source. One common approach to such packet filtering is IP filtering, which blocks out incoming packets that do not originate from preauthorized IP addresses. The list of preauthorized IP addresses is an example of an **access control list**. This list is normally maintained by network administrators.

Firewalls also can filter packets based on their content or destination. Unfortunately, like all security measures, filtering-type firewalls can be defeated. For example, outsiders with the right combination of hardware and software can **spoof** an IP address. That is, they can send incoming information requests that falsely appear to come from an authorized IP address. For this reason, firewalls should serve only as the first line of defense in a system of layered defenses. The additional layers normally will include encryption and access limits through password control.

Another type of security device used with intranets is the proxy server. **Proxy servers** typically are used on the inside of the company's firewall and serve as filters for all outgoing requests for information. Specifically, all requested accesses to addresses outside the company are sent to the proxy server. The proxy server then analyzes each request and determines if it is being made by an authorized individual to an authorized site on the Internet. (The list of authorized individuals and sites is maintained on an access control list.) If the request is valid, it is then passed through the proxy server; otherwise, the request is blocked. For example, consider the situation in which a company employee requests a Web page located at *www.games.fun*. If the company does not want its employees playing games, the proxy server can block the request, and the employee will receive an error message indicating that the requested Internet address is not available.

Proxy servers also can operate in reverse, filtering incoming requests, thus preventing access to specific locations inside the organization. Reverse proxying provides a type of firewall. As compared with firewalls, proxy servers tend to be more sophisticated and support features such as password authentication and sophisticated transaction logging.

Proxy servers are useful not only for security but also for efficiency because proxy servers can store frequently requested information in a cache. This allows the proxy server to quickly supply information that is already in the cache; there is no need for the server to forward the request to the destination site on the Internet. One major Internet service provider (ISP) uses a proxy server for all its subscribers, and about 50% of all requests for information come from the proxy server's cache.

COMMERCE ON THE INTERNET

CLIENT-SERVER TECHNOLOGY

The Internet can be used to transmit almost any kind of information between two points. However, certain important patterns of usage have emerged that evolved around client-server technology. A **server** is a robot-type program that constantly runs on some computer and exchanges information with users who request it. Users' programs that access and exchange information with servers are called **clients**.

A great many of the business transactions that occur on the Internet take place in client-server environments. There are several reasons for this:

1. Being robots, servers do not get paid by the hour and do not require fringe benefits.
2. Servers can, in some cases, deal with hundreds or even thousands of users (clients) at one time. Most humans, on the other hand, can deal with only one user at a time.
3. Servers can be accessed at any time of day, anywhere in the world, with no per-minute communication charges.

There are many kinds of servers on the Internet, including mail servers, file servers, Web servers, and commerce servers. Each of these types is discussed.

TYPES OF SERVERS

Mail servers act as electronic mailboxes that hold incoming electronic mail until the user's client program requests it. They also serve as relay stations for outgoing mail, holding it until the intended recipient's mail server is able to receive it (Fig. 3.2). The most common type of mail server on the Internet uses the POP protocol, and for this reason it is often referred to as a POP server. Most POP servers are accessed by clients

FIGURE 3.2 MAIL SERVER.

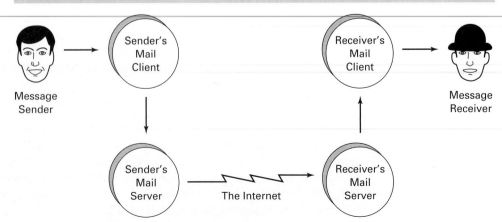

with an account name and password. The server hands over any new incoming mail to the client and then picks up outgoing mail.

Electronic mail (e-mail) messages are normally addressed according to the following form: username@domain_name. For example, one might use the address President@Whitehouse.Gov. The last three letters of the domain name provide information regarding the type of organization to which the message is being sent. "Gov" obviously refers to the government. Similarly, "Mil" refers to the military, "Com" refers to a commerical enterprise, and "Edu" refers to an educational institution. Various other suffixes also exist.

A second type of server is a file server. File servers exist mainly as repositories of files. That is, **file servers** allow authorized clients to retrieve files from libraries of files that exist on remote computers. For example, a company might use a file server to make copies of its annual report available over the Internet to the public. File servers also can receive files. For example, salespersons throughout the United States might prepare daily sales reports and then transfer them to headquarters through the company's file server.

The most common protocol for file servers is called *FTP*, and a file server that uses this protocol is called an **FTP server**. Because many client programs have the FTP protocol built into them, actual use of the protocol may be transparent to the user.

A third type of server is called a *Web server*, and this type of server is by far the one that is used most often on the Internet. A **Web server** is a server that allows a user (client) to access documents and run computer programs that reside on remote computers. Web servers are the engines that run the World Wide Web, which consists of all the documents, files, and software on the Internet that are available through Web servers. The clients that access Web servers are called *Web browsers*. Microsoft Internal Explorer and Netscape Navigator are examples of Web browsers.

As with many other things on the Internet, there exists a protocol that specifies the format of documents on the World Wide Web, namely **HTML** (hypertext markup language). All Web clients automatically read and interpret HTML and convert the remote documents into a format that is easily readable by the user.

One thing that makes HTML (and its variants such as XML) especially important is that it provides for the embedding of hyperlinks in Web documents. **Hyperlinks** are pointers to other documents that may be either on the same Web server or any other Web server on the Internet (Fig. 3.3). With most Web clients, pointing the mouse at a

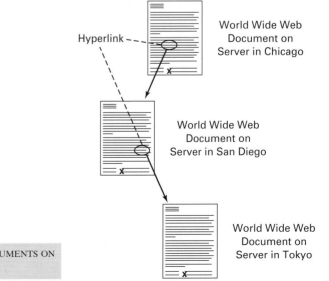

Hyperlink

World Wide Web Document on Server in Chicago

World Wide Web Document on Server in San Diego

World Wide Web Document on Server in Tokyo

FIGURE 3.3 HYPERLINKED DOCUMENTS ON THE WORLD WIDE WEB.

hyperlink causes the related document to be displayed on the computer screen. And of course, the related document also may contain additional hyperlinks of its own.

A Web document is normally located by a combination of the domain name associated with the server and the document file name. For example, a document with the file name index.html on the server with domain name *www.bodhop.ais.com* might be located with the name *http://www.bodhop.ais.com/index.html*. This name for a Web document's location is called the **URL (uniform resource locator)**.

A Web site is a collection of related documents, files, and programs that falls under the control of one individual, the Web master. A given Web server is therefore capable of hosting many different Web sites, with each individual Web site being managed by its own Web master. Similarly, one FTP server is capable of hosting more than one FTP site. But many Web servers have FTP capabilities, and separate Web and FTP servers are often unnecessary.

Commerce servers are specialized types of Web servers with various commerce-related features (Fig. 3.4). Such special features may include

1. Support for the **Secure Electronic Transaction (SET) protocol.** This protocol involves encrypting all communications between the client and the server, thus ensuring that transactions are private and free from outside manipulation.
2. Support for specialized types of client and server authentication, such as digital certificates, which positively ensures both the client and the server of each other's identity.

FIGURE 3.4   Commerce Server.

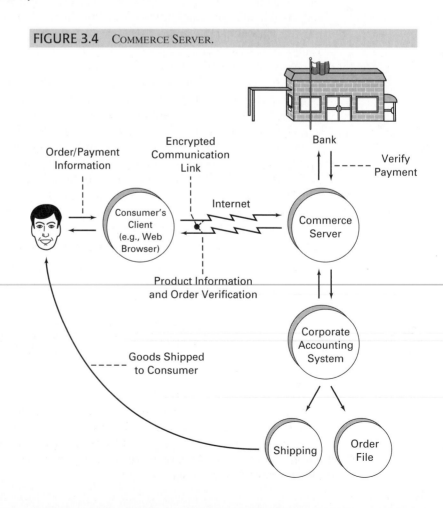

3. Support for interfacing with "external" programs. This type of support makes it possible for the client to use exchange information with accounting programs and databases that may reside on the server's computer. Examples of external program support include the **CGI (Common Gateway Interface), JAVA**, and **ActiveX** languages. CGI is a means for the client to run programs on the server system. On the other hand, JAVA is more sophisticated and allows the server to pass programs to the client for execution on the client machine.
4. Enhanced security features such as multilevel security access and detailed transaction logging.
5. On-line credit card or bank verification.

ELECTRONIC PAYMENT SYSTEMS

The Internet has created demand for specialized types of payment systems. Several of these are discussed.

Traditional Electronic Bill Payment Systems   In these types of systems, the payer sends electronic instructions to his or her bank. The instructions detail who is to be paid, when the payment is to be made, and the amount of the payment. The bank then makes the payment either electronically or by mail.

Traditional Credit Card Systems   In these types of systems, the payer transmits a credit card number to a secure server. (A **secure server** is one in which the communications link between the client and server is protected by encryption.) The payee then presents the credit card information to a bank for collection, probably through a secure credit card network.

Secure Electronic Transaction (SET) Systems   SET is a protocol established by MasterCard and Visa for consumer-based electronic payments on the Internet. The MasterCard/Visa system works in conjunction with an Internet Web browser and an electronic wallet. The electronic wallet contains encrypted credit card information and a digital certificate. (**Digital certificates**, the electronic counterparts to driver licenses, passports, and membership cards, serve as proof of identity. They are discussed in detail later.)

The consumer then makes an SET purchase by presenting the digital certificate and encrypted credit card to the merchant, who then forwards it to a participating bank for approval. Interestingly, the merchant never learns the credit card number because it is encrypted. The entire process, including obtaining the bank's approval, may only take a second or two. The process is also simple because SET is integrated into most Web browsers, which automatically handle all the details. SET is a broad standard that can be used in a wide range of electronic payment systems.

Virtual Cash Systems   There is a wide range of virtual cash systems. These are discussed later in a separate section.

SECURITY FOR ELECTRONIC TRANSACTIONS

INTRODUCTION

Encryption technology is essential for electronic commerce. **Encryption** involves using a password or digital key to scramble a readable (plaintext) message into an unreadable (ciphertext) message. The intended recipient of the message then uses the same or another digital key (depending on the encryption method) to convert the ciphertext message back into plaintext.

Consider, for example, how it might be possible to encrypt the plaintext word *ACE*. Assume that each letter of the alphabet is associated with a number so that *A* is associated with 1, *B* with 2, *C* with 3, and so on. Then in numerical terms *ACE* would be 135. Now assume that this number is to be encrypted using a key value of 2. One simple way to do this would be to add the number 2 to each digit in the number 135. This would produce the new number 357, which when converted back to the alphabet yields the ciphertext word *CEG*. This process could easily be reversed by anyone who knows the secret key.

TYPES OF ENCRYPTION SYSTEMS

SECRET-KEY ENCRYPTION

The preceding encryption example demonstrates the use of secret-key encryption. With **secret-key encryption** (Fig. 3.5), the same key is used for both encrypting and decrypting a message. The obvious difficulty with this method is that the secret key must be communicated to the receiver of an encrypted message. This means that the secret key may be vulnerable to interception.

PUBLIC-KEY ENCRYPTION

The most commonly used encryption method is public-key encryption. **Public-key encryption** uses two keys in association with each encrypted message, one key to encrypt the message and another key to decrypt it. Either key can decrypt what the other key encrypts. But the key that encrypts the message cannot be used to decrypt it. Only the other key can decrypt the message.

In practice, the sender of a message keeps one key private and makes the other public. Hence one key is called the *public key* and the other the *private key*. The advantage of public-key encryption is that the sender of a message only needs to know the recipient's public key. Neither the sender nor the receiver needs to know the other's private key.

To send someone a secret message (Fig. 3.6), all one has to do is to encrypt the message with the recipient's public key. The recipient then decrypts the message with his or her private key. Thus, if Company A wants to send Company B a secure message, then Company A uses Company B's public key to encrypt the message. Company B then uses its private key to decrypt the message.

What happens if someone intercepts the encrypted message? Can the person intercepting the message decrypt it? The answer is no; only Company B's private key can do that. The public key is worthless in decrypting the message, even though it is used to encrypt it.

FIGURE 3.5   SECRET-KEY ENCRYPTION.

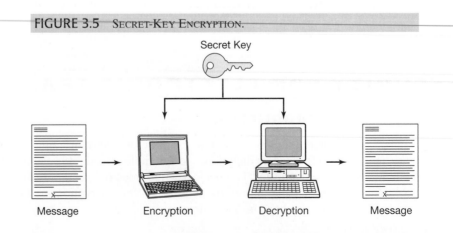

Secret Key

Message   Encryption   Decryption   Message

Recipient's Public Key   Recipient's Private Key

Message   Encryption   Ciphertext   Decryption   Message

FIGURE 3.6   PUBLIC-KEY ENCRYPTION.

HYBRID SYSTEMS AND DIGITAL ENVELOPES

In general, secret-key encryption requires fewer computations than public-key encryption. Thus, for large messages, secret-key encryption may be considerably faster.

Digital envelopes involve using both public-key and secret-key encryption (Figs. 3.7 and 3.8). This is accomplished through the following procedure:

1. The sender of the message generates a single random key.
2. The sender of the message uses this secret key to encrypt the message, using a fast secret-key encryption system.
3. The sender uses the recipient's public key to encrypt the randomly generated secret key. This encryption is done using a public-key encryption system.
4. The sender transmits both the encrypted key and the encrypted message. Together these two items constitute a digital envelope.
5. The recipient uses his or her private key to decrypt the randomly generated secret key.
6. The recipient uses the secret key to decrypt the message.

The method behind digital envelopes is sometimes referred to as double-key encryption.

FIGURE 3.7   DOUBLE-KEY ENCRYPTION.

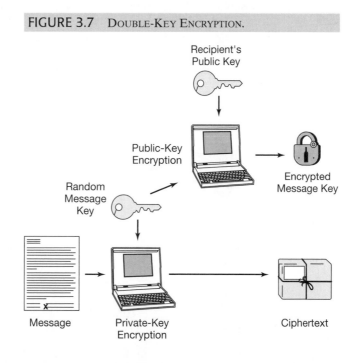

Recipient's
Public Key

Public-Key
Encryption

Encrypted
Message Key

Random
Message
Key

Message   Private-Key   Ciphertext
                Encryption

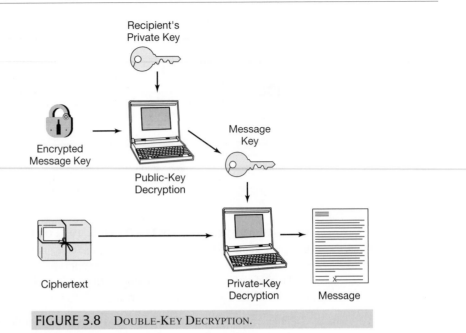

FIGURE 3.8 DOUBLE-KEY DECRYPTION.

DIGITAL SIGNATURES

Public-key encryption also can be put to another very interesting use. Consider what would happen if Company A uses its private key to encrypt a message. Then anyone, anywhere, with the related public key can decrypt it. This is important because anyone can test the message to see if Company A's public key will successfully decrypt it. If Company A's public key successfully decrypts the message, then one can be certain that the message was written and encrypted by Company A. The result is that the message can be said to be digitally signed by Company A, for no one else could have encrypted the message except Company A. A digital signature occurs when someone encrypts a message with his or her own private key (Fig. 3.9). Anyone can then use that person's public key to verify that it was in fact encrypted by that person (Fig. 3.10).

FIGURE 3.9 DIGITAL SIGNATURE CREATION.

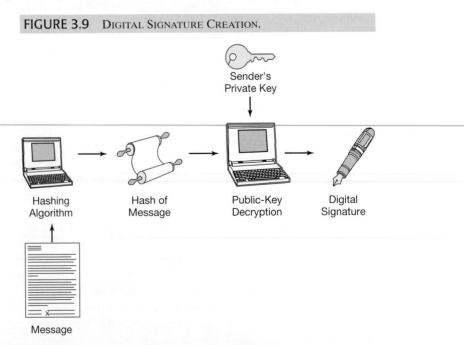

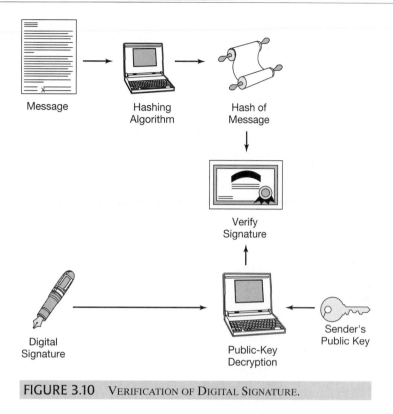

Message   Hashing   Hash of
                 Algorithm   Message

Verify
Signature

Digital   Public-Key   Sender's
Signature   Decryption   Public Key

FIGURE 3.10   VERIFICATION OF DIGITAL SIGNATURE.

There are many cases in which the sender of a message does not want to encrypt the message but does want to attach a digital signature to it. One obvious way to accomplish this is for the sender of the message to transmit both a plaintext copy and a ciphertext copy of the same message, with the encryption being based on the sender's private key. This way, anyone wanting to verify the digital signature needs only to use the sender's public key to decrypt the ciphertext message. This decrypted message is compared with the plaintext message and, if the two match, the sender's identity is certain. The only drawback to this approach is that two full copies of the message must be transmitted, both the plaintext and ciphertext versions.

An alternative approach exists in which it is not necessary to send two full copies of the message. This is accomplished by using a hashing function to create a digest of the message to be digitally signed. The **message digest** is much shorter than the message itself, and it is the digest that is encrypted with the sender's private key and attached to the plaintext message as a signature. To verify the signature, one uses the sender's public key to decrypt the digital signature. Next, one applies the same hashing function to the plaintext message to produce a message digest. Finally, one compares the resulting digest with what was obtained from decrypting the digital signature with the sender's public key.

There are many standard hashing functions available. A hashing function takes a long variable-length string of characters and converts it into a short, fixed-length string. For example, the preceding paragraph might be hashed into a message digest that might look something like "%^&ae#a5O2Ht." Similarly, the entire chapter you are now reading might be hashed into the following message digest: "TSCH4(&&!te0)." Note that both these digests are the same length (i.e., 13 characters), and each represents a unique (or nearly unique) digital fingerprint for the text being digested.

Digital signatures can be broken by attacking either the encryption or the hashing function. In practice, however, hashing functions that produce long digests are difficult to break. As a rule, it is desirable to use a digest function that produces message digests that are about the same length as the user's public and private keys. Using a longer message digest produces no additional security because an attacker can be expected to attack the public-key encryption if it is the weakest link.

Many believe that digital signatures are more secure than conventional handwritten signatures. Whereas handwritten signatures are relatively easy to forge, digital signatures are next to impossible to forge. Furthermore, digital signatures prove not only the identity of the message's signer but also that the signed message has not been altered in any way. This is so because if a digitally signed message is altered, its digest will no longer match the decrypted signature.

Digital signatures have many interesting applications. For example, a university could issue a digitally signed diploma showing the name of the graduate, the graduate's major, the date of the degree, and so on. Anyone could readily verify the authenticity of the diploma simply by using the university's public key to decrypt the signature and compare the result to a digital digest of the diploma.

Similarly, a company could transmit a digitally signed purchase order over the Internet. The receiving company could then readily verify the authenticity of the purchase order. Another company might want to issue employees digital credentials (such as identification cards) with digital signatures.

The Legality of Digital Signatures   The question arises as to whether or not digital signatures are legally binding. This issue in law is still at the formative stage, and some companies sidestep any problems by entering into a conventional written contract with others, with all parties agreeing to be bound by their digital signatures.

Digital Time-Stamping   In order to ensure the validity of electronic documents over time, there needs to be some way to attach trusted dates to them. This can be accomplished by a **digital time-stamping service (DTS)**, an organization that adds digital time-stamps to documents.

The message to be digitally time-stamped is digested, and the digest is sent to a DTS (Fig. 3.11). The DTS attaches a time-stamp to the digest and then adds its digital signature to the two. Anyone can verify the date by decrypting the digital signature of the DTS using its public key (Fig. 3.12). Note that with this method the DTS time-stamps the message without learning its contents.

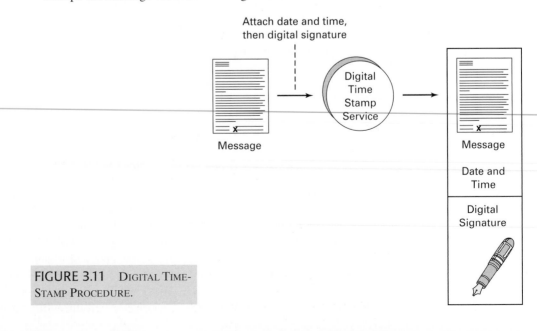

FIGURE 3.11   DIGITAL TIME-STAMP PROCEDURE.

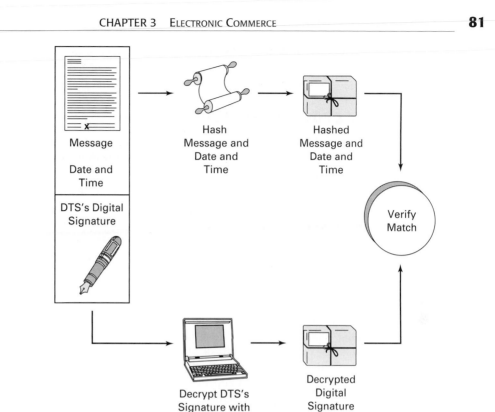

FIGURE 3.12   VERIFICATION OF DIGITAL TIME-STAMP.

SECURITY ISSUES FOR PUBLIC-KEY ENCRYPTION SYSTEMS

As with any encryption system, public-key encryption is potentially vulnerable to various types of attacks. These include cryptanalysis attacks and factoring attacks.

CRYPTANALYSIS ATTACKS

Cryptanalysis involves various techniques for analyzing encrypted messages for purposes of decoding them without legitimate access to the keys. The simplest possible attack on a message encrypted with public-key encryption is the **guessed plaintext attack**. This works if the attacker can guess the contents of a message. For example, the attacker might intercept an encrypted message and guess that it consists of the words "Secret project approved." To see if this guess is correct, the attacker would use the recipient's public key to encrypt "Secret project approved." The resulting encrypted message would be compared with the encrypted message that was intercepted. If these two encrypted messages match, then the attacker's guess is correct. This attack can be defeated simply by adding some random numbers to the end of the message.

Other more sophisticated cryptanalysis attacks exist, but most of them seem unlikely to prevail against a sufficiently long key. Furthermore, since any attack takes time, the risk against attack can be minimized by frequently changing keys. In some cases new public and private keys may be generated for each financial transaction. Obviously, it would be very difficult for an attacker to guess a private key that is used only long enough to transmit a single financial transaction over the Internet. In that case, the attacker would have to guess the key in 1 or 2 seconds. Furthermore, the decoded key would not be useful in attacking other transactions.

FACTORING ATTACKS

In practice, the public key is typically based on the product of two large prime numbers. Prime numbers are numbers that are only divisible by themselves or by 1. For example, the numbers 3, 5, 7, and 11 are all prime numbers. Therefore, 35 would be the product of two prime numbers, for its two factors are 5 and 7.

The problem is that the private key can be obtained from factoring what is essentially the public key. Thus the whole security of public-key encryption depends on the assumption that an attacker cannot factor the product of two large prime numbers.

Fortunately, factoring such long products of prime numbers is next to impossible, even with the help of the fastest computers. For example, with a supercomputer it might take hundreds or even thousands of years to factor a product of two prime numbers that is 1,000 bits long.

How difficult it would be to simply guess prime number factors can be seen from the prime number theorem. According to this theorem, the number of prime numbers having a length of 512 bits or more exceeds the number of atoms in the universe!

Still, even though products of prime numbers are difficult to factor, mathematicians have not proved conclusively that no fast shortcuts exist for such factoring. On the other hand, mathematicians do not believe that any such shortcuts will ever be discovered, at least in the foreseeable future.

KEY MANAGEMENT

Most attacks against public-key systems are likely to be made at the key-management level. Specifically, attackers are likely to attempt to break into the locations where private keys are stored. Once an attacker obtains the private key, he or she can easily decrypt any messages encrypted with the related public key. For this reason, any well-designed control system must place considerable emphasis on protecting private keys.

CREATING AND DISTRIBUTING KEYS
Each user should create his or her own public and private keys. Using a central office or authority to create and distribute keys is not recommended because any key distribution system is subject to attack and simply adds an unnecessary layer of vulnerability to the system.

Personal computers that contain sensitive keys should be protected by three methods. First, possible physical access to such machines should be limited through locked doors, security guards, and so on. Second, such machines should be set to require password access at boot-up time. Third, the keys themselves should be protected by passwords.

The longer the life of the key and the more critical it is, the more the security that must be applied to protect it. For example, assume that a company uses one public/private pair of keys for all its financial transactions. Further assume that this pair of keys has a life of, say, two years. In this case extreme caution must be exercised because any attacker who obtains the private key would be able to wreak havoc on all the company's financial transactions.

VERIFICATION OF PUBLIC KEYS THROUGH DIGITAL CERTIFICATES
Digital certificates (or *digital IDs*) are digital documents that attest to the fact that a particular public key belongs to a particular individual or organization. For all practical purposes, digital certificates serve as electronic proof of identity.

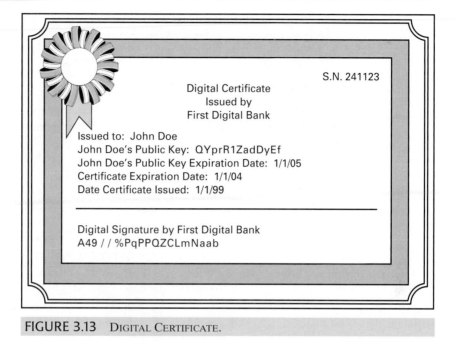

S.N. 241123

Digital Certificate
Issued by
First Digital Bank

Issued to: John Doe
John Doe's Public Key: QYprR1ZadDyEf
John Doe's Public Key Expiration Date: 1/1/05
Certificate Expiration Date: 1/1/04
Date Certificate Issued: 1/1/99

Digital Signature by First Digital Bank
A49 / / %PqPPQZCLmNaab

FIGURE 3.13   DIGITAL CERTIFICATE.

Digital certificates are issued by some **certifying authority (CA)**. For example, an employer might issue digital certificates to its employees, a bank to its customers, or a club to its members. The certificates could be stored on individuals' computers for use over the Internet. They also could be encoded onto machine-readable identification cards that could be used for various types of access privileges.

The CA creates a digital certificate by digitally signing a document that includes the name of the person being certified and the expiration data of the certificate. Other information such as a serial number also might be included (Fig. 3.13). Anyone can verify the certificate by checking the digital signature to make sure that it belongs to the certifying authority.

For a digital certificate to be useful, every relevant person must recognize and know the public key of the CA. For this reason, the public keys of CAs are often widely published over the Internet and are available from many sources. They are so widely published that they become common knowledge, and there is never any question as to whom they belong.

A digital certificate allows some trusted organization (the CA) to in effect vouch for the ownership of the public key listed in the certificate. This works because one knows and trusts the CA's digital signature. In many situations the exchange of digital certificates might only be necessary the first time two individuals do business with each other. After that time both parties may be certain of each other's public keys.

Certificate Revocation List (CRLs)   A **certificate revocation list (CRL)** is a list of public keys that have been revoked before their expiration dates. Keys might be revoked because they have been compromised or because they are no longer applicable. For example, Jane Doe's key might be stolen. Or maybe she is fired and no longer works for XYZ Company, in which case the ABC division would revoke her certificate. The keys of fired employees should immediately be placed on the appropriate CRL associated with the CA that originally issued it.

Certificate Chains   In some cases digital certificates can be linked together in chains (Fig. 3.14). For example, a well-known CA company, say, The Good Key Company,

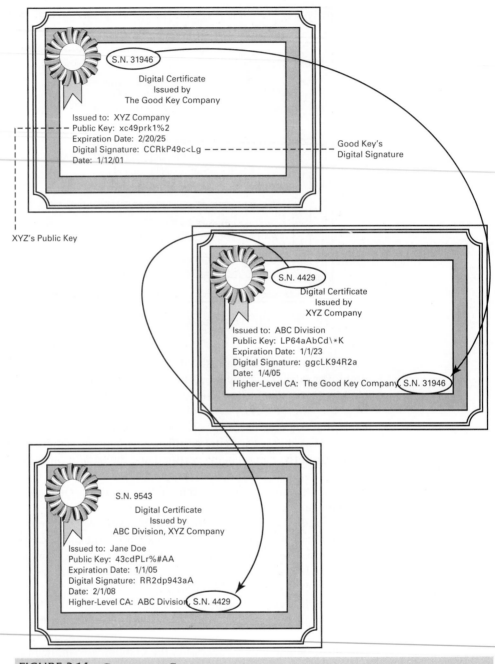

FIGURE 3.14   CERTIFICATE CHAINS.

might issue a digital certificate for XYZ Company. XYZ Company might then in turn issue another digital certificate for one of its divisions, say, the ABC division. The ABC division might then issue still another certificate to one of its employees, say, Jane Doe.

Someone interested in verifying Jane Doe's public key and her association with XYZ Company would first check the digital certificate issued by the division. This certificate would contain a reference to the certificate issued by XYZ Company, and so that certificate would be checked next. The certificate issued by XYZ Company would in turn include a reference to the one issued by The Good Key Company, which would then be checked.

Certificate-Signing Units   The private keys of CAs deserve the highest possible level of security. This is so because an attacker gaining access to the CA's private key could produce an unlimited number of forged digital certificates, and the corresponding results could be disastrous. For this reason, it is important that the CA's private keys be stored in a completely secure manner.

One approach to securely storing keys is by placing them in a **certificate-signing unit (CSU)**. A CSU is a tamperproof box for storing private keys. It should be shielded from all outside electromagnetic radiation and should be such that its contents will be destroyed automatically in the event of tampering. Moreover, it should be built around secret-sharing technology so that the private keys of several employees are required to open it. Finally, there should be a method for authorized employees to use the stored private key without knowing what it actually is.

Various CSUs are available on the market. For example, RSA Data Security sells a full-fledged certificate-issuing system based on a CSU developed by Bolt, Baranek, and Newman. The important thing is that some secure system be adopted for protecting important private keys.

KEY EXPIRATIONS

In general, all keys should have an associated expiration date. First, the longer a key is in the public domain, the more time that possible attackers have to perform cryptanalysis and factoring attacks. Furthermore, the power of computers increases over time, making factoring attacks more possible for keys with long lives.

Of course, keys with longer lives should be correspondingly long. For example, a key that is 128 bits long might be perfectly adequate for use in a single transaction that takes place over a 1-minute time span. But a key over 1,000 bits long might be desirable if it is to be used for years. It is widely believed that 1,000-bit keys will not be vulnerable for many years. Still, it is best to change keys regularly.

When keys expire, it is sometimes desirable to replace them with new, longer keys. Doing so compensates for any increased vulnerability due to increases in the speed of computers. However, if the length of a key is still considered acceptable when it expires, the same key might be recertified by the issuance of a new digital certificate.

APPLICATIONS OF ELECTRONIC COMMERCE AND ENCRYPTION TECHNOLOGY

This section discusses various applications of the concepts discussed thus far in the chapter.

VIRTUAL CASH SYSTEMS

DIGITAL CASH

Cryptographic techniques have given rise to whole new payment systems based on digital cash. **Digital cash** (or *e-cash* or *electronic money*) is typically created when a bank attaches its digital signature to a note promising to pay the bearer some amount of money (Fig. 3.15). For example, the Electronic Bank of America might digitally sign a message that contains the following information:

1. The bank's name and address
2. The dollar value of the bank note being created
3. A unique serial number
4. The date the note is created
5. A possible expiration date

Furthermore, a digital certificate from some large CA might be attached.

Bank's Digital Signature
Normally Used for $1 Notes

FIGURE 3.15   DIGITAL CASH.

Anyone can verify the authenticity of the digital cash by verifying the bank's digital signature. The only problem, however, is the possibility that the note might have been spent once before. This is so because, unlike real currency, digital cash can be copied easily.

A typical way to prevent double spending is to verify with the bank that the digital cash has not been spent already. This can be done by electronically transmitting the digital cash's serial number to the bank. If the serial number has not been presented previously, then the bank verifies the validity of the transaction. It then records the note as having been spent.

In practice, banks will use a different digital signature for each denomination. For example, one digital signature might be used for a $1 note, another for a $2 note, and so on. Digital signatures also can be issued for coins, thus allowing for the making of small change.

Note that anyone can issue his or her own digital notes. Such notes could be accepted and processed in the same way that paper checks are now.

PRIVACY ISSUES

Privacy is a major issue in electronic transactions. Most electronic transactions are traceable, and this may be true even with encryption. For example, assume that the ABC Soft Drink Company manufactures a soft drink based on a secret formula. Further assume that ABC deals with its vendors electronically using the best encryption available.

An attacker interested in discovering ABC's secret formula might monitor the flow of ABC's incoming and outgoing messages over the Internet. This might in turn lead the attacker to discover that ABC frequently communicates with XYZ Company, which specializes in the sale of rare coffees. The result is that the hacker deduces that the secret ingredient is a rare coffee sold by XYZ Company.

There are presently no good defenses to attacks of this sort. Therefore, the Internet should not be used for communications if the IP address of one of the parties in a transaction needs to remain fully anonymous.

Another risk may come from a company using the same public key for many of its transactions. In this case each transaction would leave a digital record, and at some point in time it would be possible to link all the company's transactions together to form a dossier on all the company's activities. This especially may be a problem with digital cash because when the bank verifies the serial number on the digital note, it immediately discovers to whom it originally issued the note. Thus the bank knows both the payer and the payee in the transaction.

BLINDED DIGITAL CASH

The technique of **blinding** permits a bank to issue digital cash so that it is unable to link the payer to the payee. This is accomplished by the bank signing the note with a **blinded digital signature**, which works as follows, assuming that Alice is the payer and that she wishes to create a $1 digital note (see Fig. 3.16):

1. Alice creates a digital note that contains only a unique serial number.
2. Alice in essence multiplies the serial number by another number called the *blinding factor*.
3. Alice digitally signs the note.
4. Alice sends the note (with the multiplied serial number) to the bank and requests that the bank digitally sign it with the digital signature it uses exclusively for its $1 notes.
5. The bank deducts $1 from Alice's account and digitally signs the note.
6. Alice uses a special technique to remove the blinding factor from the note's serial number without affecting the validity of the bank's digital signature.
7. Alice gives the note to Joe for payment of goods.

FIGURE 3.16   BLINDED DIGITAL SIGNATURE.

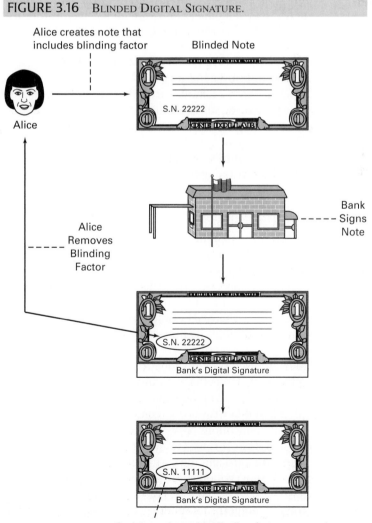

Serial number with blinding factor removed
(Bank's digital signature is still intact and valid)

8. Joe presents the note to the bank. The bank does not recognize the note number because it originally signed the note in its blinded form, but it recognizes its digital signature for $1 and therefore credits Joe accordingly.

9. The bank keeps a list of note numbers on deposits received so that it does not pay the same note twice.

In this case the bank is unable to link Alice and Joe together. When it receives the note from Joe, it has no way of knowing that it was the same note that it had issued to Alice.

COMPUTER SOFTWARE AND COMPUTER CARD SYSTEMS

The cryptographic techniques are such that virtual cash payments can be made either on a PC or a stand-alone electronic wallet-sized (smart) card. Both approaches are discussed.

VIRTUAL CASH ON THE PC

Most electronic cash systems on PCs are based on the concept of an electronic wallet. An **electronic wallet** is essentially a computer program that keeps track of the various keys, digital certificates, and items of information associated with electronic money. The user acquires digital cash (from a financial institution), which is then stored in the electronic wallet. Money is then received or spent by transferring it in or out of the wallet.

VIRTUAL CASH IN ELECTRONIC CARDS

Smart cards are hand-held electronic cards that are used for payments. There are four types of cards: memory cards, shared-key cards, signature-transporting cards, and signature-creating cards. Each type of card is discussed.

Memory cards contain microchips that are only capable of storing information. They also contain the hardware that provides PIN (personal identification number) access to the card's contents. Memory cards possess very weak security and should be used only for the simplest applications where the amount of money is small and security is not of much concern.

An example of a memory card might be a card that allows a small number of employees to purchase lunch in the company cafeteria. Employees would use the cards by inserting them in the cash register at the end of the cafeteria line, followed by PIN verification. The register would deduct the balance of cash stored in the cards according to the employee purchases.

A memory card can be defeated easily by inserting a small computer between it and the cash register the first time the card is used. The small computer would record all the information exchanged between the card and the cash register. The cash register could then be defeated simply by replaying the same information back for all future transactions.

ATM cards are a form of memory card, but they are not really smart cards because they are used only for identification rather than payment per se. The user inserts the ATM card, enters the PIN, and then requests money from the bank. All the money balances are stored in the bank's computer.

Shared-key cards overcome the weakness of memory cards by using encryption for all communications between the card and the cash register (or other point-of-payment device). Thus it is useless for an attacker to intercept and record communications between the card and the cash register.

The encryption is carried out with both the card and the cash register using (sharing) the same secret key. For this to work securely, both the card and the register must contain tamperproof modules that will protect the keys from hardware hackers.

The biggest weakness of shared-key cards is that massive fraud is possible if an attacker manages to discover the secret key. Another problem is that the cash register must maintain a list of keys for use with every vendor with which it communicates. This can become complicated and cumbersome.

Signature-transporting cards carry essentially the same hardware as shared-key cards. The main difference is the software: Signature-transporting cards allow the user to spend digital cash notes. These notes are transferred to the cash register on payment. The cash register can immediately (or later) verify the notes via an on-line link to the bank. In the case of immediate verification, no tamperproof module is required. Alternatively, the card can contain a tamperproof module that prevents the notes from being spent twice, thus avoiding the need for on-line verification.

Finally, **signature-creating cards** are similar to signature-transporting cards but are capable of generating their own digital signatures. This type of card might be used to write electronic "checks" that bear the digital signature of the cardholder. Of the four card types, the signature-transporting card shows the most promise for wide-scale use in retail transactions in the foreseeable future.

THE INTERNET STORE

This section describes the typical Internet store and brings together many of the concepts discussed in this chapter.

A typical sales transaction follows the pattern described in Figure 3.17. The major functions performed in this diagram are discussed individually.

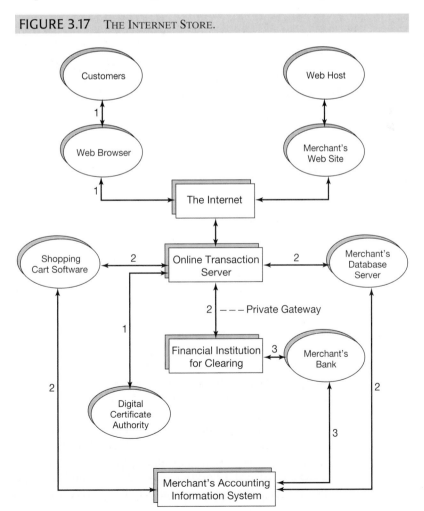

FIGURE 3.17   THE INTERNET STORE.

1. The customer uses a Web browser to access the merchant's Web site via the Internet. The Web browser may perform important functions, such as opening an encrypted (SSL) communication session. If the browser is "wallet enabled," it might pass customer information to the Web site, including the name, address, and credit card information. Further, the browser might assist in authenticating both the customer and merchant to each other. This authentication typically would be completed via an exchange of digital certificates, with the assistance of a certificate server from a third-party digital certificate authority.

2. The merchant's on-line Web transaction server will perform several key functions. First, it will communicate with "shopping cart" software that will display current items available for sale and current prices. It also will relay the customer payment information to a financial institution for clearing the transaction. The clearing institution might be any type of financial institution that processes electronic payments. Finally, the transaction server will send the purchase information to the merchant's database/accounting server for further processing and order fulfillment.

3. The financial institution that clears the payment will then electronically remit the funds, less any processing fees, to the merchant's bank. The merchant's bank in turn will send an electronic advice to the merchant's accounting system. The accounting software will reconcile sales transactions with bank receipts.

Note that the entire system is fully automated with no human intervention. Further, systems such as this can be set up in as little as 24 hours if the accounts with the financial institutions are already in place. Such rapid deployment can be accomplished by using turnkey storefront software solutions that are readily available for sale on the Internet. These solutions can be implemented even if one does not have a merchant account with a financial institution because there are companies who supply reseller agreements in which they collect funds using their own merchant accounts.

VIRTUAL PRIVATE NETWORKS

The **virtual private network (VPN)** represents one important application of encryption technology combined with Internet communications. VPNs allow remote users belonging to a private network to communicate securely over a public network such as the Internet.

Normally, in VPNs all communications involving remote users first pass through some type of hardware or software gateway that automatically encrypts and decrypts data. Other requirements include the following:

1. One or more security servers that assist in the exchange of public keys
2. Authentication techniques
3. Certification (by some certifying authority) of remote users

The process of sending and receiving encrypted data over VPNs is sometimes called tunneling. The tunnel represents the conduit for the transmission of secure information.

Although many protocols are possible for exchanging secure information in VPNs, one protocol that is frequently used is IPSec (Internet Protocol Security Protocol).

There exist a large number of VPN vendors on the market. Many offer turnkey solutions so that remote users simply access the private network by supplying a user ID and/or a password. Everything else, the exchanging of public keys, authentication, certification, and encryption, are all handled automatically in the background.

TRUST IN E-COMMERCE: PRIVACY, BUSINESS PRACTICES, AND TRANSACTION INTEGRITY

Electronic commerce has opened up previously un-thought-of problems with consumers' privacy. Most Web browsers support the use of **cookies**, small pieces of information that the electronic merchant can place on the user's computer. One problem with cookies is that any merchant who knows how can view and analyze all cookies on a user's computer, including those placed there by other merchants.

The result is that it is possible for a Web site to capture all of a person's cookies and immediately discover every other Web site that the user has visited and received a cookie from. Further, given a telephone number, address, or birth date, it also might be possible for a marketer to cross-reference the cookie information with additional information in public databases, such as driver's license information, court records, property records, and so on.

To complicate things even further, many Web merchants collect extensive amounts of information on their customers' private lives, such as income, number of children, and so on. In many cases these merchants publish statements of what protections they provide for the privacy of information collected, but all too often such statements, when studied carefully, indicate that the merchants share the private information with others. Too often customers do not carefully read merchants' privacy statements.

Some of the adverse results of privacy problems include large volumes of spam (unsolicited e-mail), telephone solicitations, credit card fraud, and even identity theft. By some estimates, the rate of credit card fraud on the Internet is as high as 30%.

It is usually very much in the merchant's best interest to assure its customers that it will protect their privacy. This is usually accomplished by the merchant obtaining some third-party seal of approval, audit, or limited endorsement. One example of such a program is the AICPA's **Web Trust** attestation program, by which specially trained CPAs provide a seal of assurance after a special audit. Assurances are made along three lines: information protection, business practice disclosure, and transaction integrity.

Regarding information protection, the CPA examines all important control, policies, and procedures relevant to protecting the customer's private information. Thus even a merchant with a strict privacy policy might not obtain the Web Trust seal if there are weak controls in place to ensure that the policy is enforced.

Business practice disclosure simply requires that the merchant adequately disclose its business practices.

Finally, transaction integrity involves proper user identification, validation, data accuracy, completeness, and timeliness, as well as complete disclosure of all terms relating to billing and shipping.

❖ SUMMARY

Today many business transactions are conducted over electronic networks, that is, over groups of computers linked together electronically. Networks can be classified according to the distance they span. Hence networks can be classified as local, metropolitan, or wide area. The Internet is the largest wide area network available today.

The Internet allows many different computers to communicate via the TCP/IP protocols. Each computer on the Internet is assigned a unique address called the IP number. IP numbers can be either dynamic or fixed. Dynamic addresses are normally assigned for temporary use, that is, for a single communications session. Fixed addresses are assigned for permanent use.

Intranets are basically in-house miniature versions of the Internet. They are typically protected from the outside world by firewalls, which restrict access to authorized individuals and are used for authorized business. Proxy servers, on the other hand, limit the outgoing access to the Internet.

Client-server technology serves as the basic technology for many types of business communications on the Internet. Servers are robot-type programs that automate various kinds of information exchanges. Clients are programs that communicate with servers. Major types of servers include mail servers, file servers, FTP servers, Web servers, and commerce servers. Commerce servers typically communicate with clients for the purposes of engaging in secure financial transactions.

Various types of electronic payment systems exist on the Internet. These include traditional bill payment systems, traditional credit card systems, Secure Electronic Transaction (SET) systems, and virtual cash systems.

On the Internet, information security is achieved in part through encryption technology. Secret-key encryption is sometimes used to encrypt messages, but it does not provide a way for the secret key to be sent from the sender of a message to the receiver. Public-key encryption, however, allows messages to be sent using only public keys. The recipient's public key is used to encrypt a message. That person's private key is then used for decryption.

Digital signatures are a means of positively guaranteeing the identity of the sender of a message without requiring that the message be encrypted. To create a digital signature the sender of the message uses a hash function to create a digest of the message. The sender then encrypts the digest with his or her private key. The result is the digital signature, which is attached to the original message. Any recipient of the message can verify the signature by using the sender's public key to decrypt the signature. This would then be compared to a digest of the message created by the recipient, using the same digest function used by the sender.

Digital signatures might not be legal in some situations, but they may sometimes be made legal by all parties agreeing to honor them through a traditional written contract. The dates on digitally signed documents can be established by a digital time-stamping service.

Public-key encryption schemes are subject to cryptanalysis and factoring attacks. The best way to prevent both these attacks is to use very long keys. In practice, public-key encryption systems are most likely to be attacked at the key-management level. Users should create and manage their own keys. The central distribution of keys simply adds an additional layer of vulnerability. Access to keys must be strictly limited.

Individuals' public keys can be verified through the use of digital certificates, which are digital documents that associate a particular person or organization with a given public key and are signed with the private key of some trusted certifying authority.

Critical private keys must be assigned the highest level of protection. One approach to protecting private keys is the certificates-signing unit. This device is a tamperproof box for storing private keys. Authorized individuals should be able to use the protected keys without being able to see them. Finally, keys should have expiration dates, and it may be desirable to replace them with new, longer keys on their expiration. The longer keys may compensate for any improvements in hacker technology that may have occurred during the keys' lifetime.

Digital cash is an important application of encryption technology. It is created when a bank (or other institution) digitally signs a financial note. Banks typically use a different digital signature for each denomination.

One privacy-related limitation of digital cash is that it may be traceable so that the bank can match up the payer and payee. One way to solve this problem is through the use of blinded digital signatures. Blinded digital signatures make it impossible for the bank to link the payer and the payee.

In practice, digital cash is implemented on both PCs and smart cards. On PCs, the digital wallet is used to receive and pay money. On smart cards, however, the money value may be stored on wallet-sized electronic cards. Digital cash also can be integrated into a wide range of programs.

Four types of smart cards exist: memory cards, shared-key cards, signature-transporting cards, and signature-creating cards. Memory cards are the least secure. Shared-key cards are more secure, but they use secret keys that may be subject to attack, and catastrophic losses may occur if a secret key is breached. On the other hand, signature-transporting cards carry digital cash that is based on public-key encryption, thus making them less vulnerable. Finally, smart cards actually create their own digital signatures. One of their uses might be to carry the digital signature of the card's owner. This would allow the cardholder to digitally sign transactions.

❖ GLOSSARY

access control list: for a proxy server, the list of IP addresses authorized to access the server.

ActiveX: Microsoft's alternative to JAVA.

blinded digital signature: a digital signature and related digital cash that have been issued with blinding.

blinding: a technique in which a bank issues digital cash in such a way that it is unable to link the payer to the payee.

certificate revocation list: a list of public keys that have been revoked before their expiration dates.

certificate-signing unit (CSU):   a tamperproof box for storing private keys.

certifying authority: individual or organization that issues digital certificates.

CGI: Common Gateway Interface, software that helps Web clients communicate with programs (such as accounting to database programs) linked to the server.

client: a program that accesses and exchanges information with a server.

commerce server: a specialized type of Web server with various commerce-related features.

cookies: small amounts of information placed on a user's computer by a Web site.

cryptanalysis: various techniques for analyzing encrypted messages for purposes of decoding them without legitimate authorization.

digital cash: money created when a bank attaches its digital signature to a note promising to pay the bearer some amount of money.

digital certificate: a digitally signed document issued by a certification authority that attests to the ownership of a public key by a particular individual or organization.

digital envelope: an encryption method in which the message is encrypted with a secret key, and the secret key is encrypted with the recipient's public key.

digital time-stamping service (DTS):   an organization that adds digital time-stamps to documents.

domain name: an alias name that can be used in place of the IP address.

domain name server (DNS):   electronic phone book that associates domain names with IP addresses.

electronic networks: groups of computers that are connected together electronically.

electronic wallet: a computer program that keeps track of the various keys and items of information associated with digital money.

encryption: uses a password or digital key to scramble a readable (plaintext) message into an unreadable (ciphertext) message. The intended recipient of the message then uses the same or another digital key (depending on the encryption method) to convert the ciphertext message back into plaintext.

file server: allows authorized clients to retrieve files from libraries of files.

firewall: limits access to information on the company's servers from the rest of the world.

fixed IP address: an IP address that is permanently assigned to an individual, client, or server.

FTP server: a file server that uses the FTP protocol, the most commonly used protocol for file servers.

guessed plaintext attack: the simplest possible attack on a message encrypted with public-key encryption.

HTML: Hypertext Markup Language, a protocol that specifies the format of documents on the World Wide Web.

hyperlinks: pointers to other documents that may be either on the same Web server or any other Web server.

Internet: an electronic highway consisting of various standards and protocols that allows computers everywhere to communicate with each other.

intranet: a self-contained in-house internet.

IP address (or IP number):   address for an individual computer, client, or server on the Internet.

JAVA: software that extends the functionality of Web clients by allowing the server to transfer software to the client for execution on the client computer.

local area networks: networks that span a single site, such as a building or a group of buildings that are in close proximity to one another.

mail server: acts as an electronic mailbox that holds incoming electronic mail until the user's client program requests it.

memory card: a type of smart card that contains microchips only capable of storing information.

message digest: used with digital signatures, a meaningless fixed-length hash of a message that is much shorter than the message itself.

metropolitan area networks: networks that span a single city or metropolitan area.

proxy servers: typically used on the inside of the company's firewall and serve as filters for all outgoing requests for information.

public-key encryption: an encryption method that uses two keys in association with each encrypted message, one key to encrypt the message and another key to decrypt it.

secret-key encryption: an encryption method in which the same key is used for both encrypting and decrypting a message.

Secure Electronic Transactions (SET) protocol: a protocol that involves encrypting all communications between the client and the server, thus assuring that transactions are private and free from outside manipulation.

secure server: a server in which the communications link between the client and server is protected by encryption.

server: a robot-type program that constantly runs on some computer and exchanges information with clients.

shared-key card: a type of smart card that uses encryption for all communications between the card and the cash register (or other point-of-payment device).

signature-creating card: a type of smart card that is capable of generating its own digital signatures.

signature-transporting card: a type of smart card that stores digital cash.

smart card: a wallet-sized electronic card that is used for payments.

spoof: a type of hacker attack in which the attacker assumes a false identity such as a false IP address.

URL: uniform resource locator, the name for a Web document's location.

virtual private network (VPN):   a private network that uses a public network such as the Internet as its communication medium, with privacy being obtained through encryption and other means.

Web server: a server that allows a user (client) to access documents and run computer programs that reside on remote computers.

Web Trust: An AICPA-sponsored attestation program that provides assurances in three areas for on-line merchants: information protection, business practice disclosure, and transaction integrity.

wide area networks: networks of computers that span at least two metropolitan areas.

❖ CHAPTER QUIZ

Answers to the Chapter Quiz appear on page 101.

1. Which of the following best describes the Internet?
    (a) developed by Microsoft and IBM
    (b) highly centralized
    (c) highly decentralized
    (d) none of the above

2. Which of the following is true?
    (a) The Internet is faster than most local area networks.
    (b) Most metropolitan networks are faster than the Internet.
    (c) The speed of the Internet is usually critical in processing single accounting transactions.
    (d) None of the above.

3. TCP/IP is (_____).
    (a) an approach to networking developed by the RAND Corporation
    (b) the standard for virtually all long-distance Internet communications
    (c) the standard protocol for the formatting of Web documents
    (d) none of the above

4. Spoofing would be most applicable to (_____).
    (a) a hacker attack
    (b) a failure in a proxy server
    (c) the elimination of an access control list
    (d) none of the above

5. An FTP server is an example of a (_____).
   (a) Web server
   (b) mail server
   (c) commerce server
   (d) none of the above

6. The SET protocol would be most applicable to (_____).
   (a) a commerce server
   (b) a Web server
   (c) a mail server
   (d) an FTP server

7. Which approach to encryption is the most secure for a server that deals with many unknown clients?
   (a) public-key encryption
   (b) secret-key encryption
   (c) anonymous encryption
   (d) none of the above

8. Which of the following statements is true regarding digital signatures?
   (a) They require the related message to be encrypted
   (b) They do not require the related message to be encrypted
   (c) They require the use of message digests
   (d) None of the above

9. Encryption keys should be created and distributed at the (_____).
   (a) workstation level
   (b) department level
   (c) organization level
   (d) security office level

10. Which of the following is used to store digital cash on a personal computer?
    (a) electronic digest
    (b) digital-signing unit
    (c) virtual cash transporting system
    (d) none of the above

❖ REVIEW QUESTIONS

1. Describe the different types of electronic networks and contrast the differences between them.
2. Summarize the development of the Internet.
3. Explain the security risks inherent in any intranet.
4. Explain how addressing works on the Internet.
5. Summarize any differences between firewalls and proxy servers. In what situations would both be used?
6. How might EDI (electronic data interchange) be implemented on a commerce server?
7. Define and describe several different types of servers used in electronic commerce.
8. Discuss one or two different types of hacker attacks that might be made against a commerce server.
9. If two companies did electronic business with each other on a regular basis, would they need to exchange digital certificates with each new transaction? Why or why not?
10. Summarize any advantages of public-key encryption over secret-key encryption.
11. What would a hacker have to do to forge a digital signature? How can such an attack be prevented?
12. Why do message digests normally have a fixed length?
13. Why might the message digesting function be the target of an attack for a hacker?
14. Discuss the relative advantages and disadvantages of digital signatures versus traditional signatures.
15. What security issues might exist in maintaining a certificate revocation list?

❖ DISCUSSION QUESTIONS AND PROBLEMS

16. The Yacht Company in Chicago manages several divisions around the United States, including the Arco Division. Arco produces sailboats and spans a 100-acre site near the Port of Miami, in Miami, Florida. All of Arco's personal computers are presently linked together over a local area network. Specifically, sales records are kept on a personal computer at the dockside warehouse, and all other records are kept in the main building, where most of top management is also located. The only exception is payroll, which is kept on a personal computer in the maintenance building.

    Arco has recently hired Betty Brill, a new information systems manager. At her first staff meeting Betty informed Brad Wilson, the controller, that she wanted to develop a virtual private network to link all the company's computers together.

    Brad's initial response was negative. He said the following:

    > Our present systems work fine. As it now stands the sales and payroll departments are translating their accounting files into ASCII text and sending them over the local area network to the main building. When the text files arrive in the main building, we then run a program that converts them into a format compatible with our main computer system.

    Betty interrupted:

    > Brad, that's an archaic system. We're using all kinds of incompatible formats, and on top of that we're wasting a lot of effort by expressing mailing disks of our payroll files to Chicago every week so that they can handle the taxes and write the paychecks. What we really need is our own intranet with an outside link to the Internet. That will help us make the transition to compatible file formats. We can also set up a server so that the people in Chicago can access any of the accounting data any time they need them. There will be no need to send them disks all the time.

    Brad responded:

    > That's really dumb, Betty. Our present system works fine. But your plan will probably cost a lot of money, generate a lot of hassle, and it will even open us to potential hackers. The results could be a major disaster.

    Betty concluded her argument:

    > Brad, I don't appreciate your calling my ideas dumb. Yours are even dumber. You need to go back to school and learn about today's technology. Everyone is switching to intranets and wiring up to the Internet. When you get right down to it, we don't have any choice but to keep up with the times.
    >
    > What I suggest we do is put our entire accounting system on our own private Web site. This way any of us can access the system from either here or Chicago, and I'm not worried about hackers. We can require passwords to access anything on this Web.

    ### Required
    (a) Select one side of the argument and defend your position.
    (b) Assume that Arco has decided to implement Betty's plan. What would be some important considerations relevant to the implementation?

17. The HZP Company operates in Chicago, where it designs and manufactures its own line of specialized women's clothing. The company maintains a Web presence and recently started accepting orders through a commerce server that it developed in-house. The problem is that the commerce server stores incoming orders in a format that is not consistent with the format used by the accounting system. In fact, the problem is so bad that all incoming data require a considerable amount of manual editing in a word processor before they can be read into the accounting system.

    ### Required
    Sketch out a general solution to HZP's problem.

18. Comway Corporation is a medium-sized shoe wholesaler whose sales territory includes Illinois, Michigan, and Indiana. Every day the sales managers for these states collect orders from retail stores. They then use local Internet service providers to connect to the Internet

and enter the order information. In each case the sales manager uses a Web-browser client to enter the information into a Web server dedicated to collecting orders.

A problem has arisen recently with deliveries to some of Comway's retail customers. For example, one customer, Brown Shoe Store, complained that it never received delivery of a $6,000 order that it had recently made. In order to investigate the matter, Sandra Hill, Comway's controller, looked at the order files and concluded that the shoes were in fact shipped to a warehouse several blocks from Brown Shoe Store. Brown, however, said that it had never authorized a shipment to anywhere but directly to its store.

Puzzled, Sandra Hill checked with Brown's sales manager, who immediately produced a printed copy of the order. The sales manager had printed out the contents of the computer screen at the time he had entered the order, and sure enough he had set the shipment up for normal delivery right at Brown's store.

To further investigate, Sandra Hill checks the logs of the Web server used to collect orders from the sales managers. However, everything seemed in order, and it appeared the sales manager had used his proper password to access the Web server.

Required

Analyze the problem and make suggestions as to its possible cause. What additional information would you need to complete Sandra Hill's investigation? What additional security measure should be taken, if any?

19. ACE Company is a small start-up company that intends to publish electronic documents on the World Wide Web. It does not intend to engage in publishing any printed materials.

   Janet Thompson, the president of ACE, has decided that a Web commerce server will be set up to take all orders. The server also will be required to take payments and distribute documents to customers.

Required

Design and specify the requirements for the desired commerce server. Your design should include all relevant considerations, including the following:
   (a) information collected by the server
   (b) means for organizing electronic documents (Assume that ACE's catalog will consist of approximately 2,000 documents.)
   (c) security issues
   (d) payment methods
   (e) the overall structure of ACE's Web site and any necessary and related hyperlinks

20. For each of the following electronic payment systems, give an example of a company for which it might be applicable:
   (a) traditional electronic bill payment system
   (b) traditional credit card system
   (c) secure Electronic Transaction system
   (d) virtual cash system.

21. Tireco is a medium-sized firm that manufactures and distributes specialty tires. The company has good separation of duties, and at the top of the organization chart is the president, controller, vice president of manufacturing, vice president of marketing, and the finance officer. Under the vice president of manufacturing are four departments.

   The company has decided to do all its business over the Internet using a whole array of commerce servers, each with a JAVA or CGI interface to the central accounting system. The commerce servers are set up to process secure EDI-based orders with customers and vendors.

   The president, a recent accounting graduate, has insisted that the company use digital certificates in all its transactions. Furthermore, the company has informed all its vendors that it will not be responsible for the payment of any invoices, electronic or paper, that are not supported by a digital certificate issued by Tireco.

Required

Assuming that Tireco elects to use public-key encryption, design a system for managing the company's keys and digital certificates. Your design should consider at least the following:
   (a) the number of keys that will be needed, and the number of departments that will need them

   (b) who will issue keys

   (c) the expiration dates to be used for keys

   (d) who will have the authority to issue digital certificates

   (e) the structure of the company's certificate chains

   (f) the security measures that will need to be adopted

22. All Clear Company is a large manufacturer of custom draperies. In all, the company has seven divisions spread out across the country. Furthermore, the company has adopted a policy of issuing digital certificates for all company transactions, and it has even decided to issue digital credentials for all key employees. The typical employee's credentials contain the employee's social security number, name, position in the company, public key, and any special authorizations to act on the company's behalf. For example, the purchasing officers all contain credentials that contain the words "Authorized Purchasing Officer." All credentials are digitally signed using the company's general private key.

A dispute has arisen between management, accounting, and finance regarding the proper procedures for issuing the digital credentials. Accounting argues that a major control issue is at stake and that it should process all credentials. Management sees no need for accounting's involvement and argues that it alone should do the processing. Finance, on the other hand, argues that digital credentials are like the keys to the safety deposit box, or to the signature-signing machine. Therefore, finance feels that it should assume sole responsibility for processing the digital credentials.

Required

1. Which function (accounting, finance, or management) should process the digital credentials? In formulating your answer, keep in mind at least the following considerations:

   (a) segregation of duties

   (b) the types of credentialing that might be done

   (c) the ability of the function to handle the type of work required

2. What procedures should be followed in issuing the digital credentials?

23. Given the information in the previous question, analyze and criticize the information that is issued with the purchasing officer's credentials.

24. GGG Company has entered into a contract with its financial institution that would allow it to issue its own digital cash. GGG would create sequenced notes that would be digitally signed with one of several private keys. The exact keys used would depend on the denominations of the individual notes.

GGG would then electronically transmit the signed notes to its suppliers, who in turn would either use them somewhere else as cash or present them to GGG's bank for collection.

Required

How well would GGG's payment system work? What problems might arise?

25. Ramco Company sells gift items and flowers through its Internet store. In the past it has accepted traditional credit card payments through its secure commerce server. However, the company has recently decided to accept digital cash.

The company's head of finance feels that digital cash would save the company a considerable amount of money in bank processing fees, as compared to credit card transactions. The only problem is that if digital cash is accepted, many customers may elect to pay with blinded digital notes.

Ramco's vice president of marketing is against accepting blinded digital cash because it will allow customers to order and pay with pseudonyms, that is, fake names designed to protect the customers' identities. The result is that the marketing department will not be able to build its usual database of information for customers paying with the blinded notes. That in turn will prevent marketing from soliciting those customers for repeat business.

John Carlos, Ramco's controller, is more concerned about the potential for fraud. Specifically, he is concerned that the company may end up accepting counterfeit digital money. Furthermore, due to cost considerations Ramco does not have the resources for online verification of each note of digital cash. He estimates that in most cases approximately two days will elapse before a note can be determined to be counterfeit. The problem is that flowers are normally shipped same day the order is taken.

Required

Present the arguments for and against implementing the acceptance of digital cash. What changes might be made to make the system more workable?

26. Roadco Company has been hired to collect tolls for the Blue Ocean toll road. Robert Asphalt, the controller of Roadco, has been analyzing the situation and has come up with the following pieces of information:
    (a) During rush hour, commuters must presently wait in line for approximately 40 minutes at the main exit from the toll road.
    (b) Estimates show that during the rush hour 95% of all cars on the toll road are driven by regular commuters.
    (c) The technology is available for the inexpensive creation of electronic smart cards that are capable of radio-controlled communications directly with the toll booths.

Required

Design a smart card for collecting tolls from regular commuters. Your design should include the following:
    (a) procedures for issuing and accounting for cards
    (b) procedures for accounting for card usage
    (c) security measures
    (d) specifications for the types of smart cards to be used
    (e) procedures for communicating between the tollbooth and the central office

27. The following facts pertain to the e-commerce Web site for WCEComp, a personal computer manufacturer and seller.

Privacy Statement

    (a) All information collected on this Web site will be used only for legitimate business purposes. We do not give away or rent any information to third parties.
    (b) We will only contact you for legitimate business purposes, possibly from time to time, as needed. Please be 100% assured that all transactions between you and us are held in the strictest confidence.

Disclosure of Business Practices, Shipping, and Billing

    (a) All items will be shipped at the earliest possible date.
    (b) You are not required to accept items that you did not order.
    (c) All invoices are generated on the first day of the month.
    (d) In the event that you are accidentally billed twice for the same item, you will immediately be issued a refund.

Transaction Integrity

    (a) We thoroughly audit at least 10% of all transactions for accuracy and integrity. This ensures that our system is working properly.
    (b) All transactions are encrypted by the latest encryption standards.

Required

Evaluate these statements in terms of how well the stated policies promote customer trust and confidence in WCEComp's on-line business.

28. The Tinjin Company is in the process of developing a Web site to market fine linens. Some of the basic business considerations are as follows:
    (a) Tinjin is new and without much capital. Therefore, obtaining a merchant account from any of the major credit card companies seems unlikely.
    (b) Tinjin has a small storefront in the city, but business there is too slow to make enough money to survive. It is hoped that Internet sales will make the business a success.
    (c) The owners of Tinjin do not have enough capital to hire any professional consultants, but they have some basic knowledge of personal computers and the Internet.

Required

Draft a plan for a solution to Tinjin's problems described here.
    (a) Describe at least two options for Tinjin to set up its Web site.

   (b) Describe options for Tinjin to collect funds from customers.
   (c) What problems might Tinjin encounter in integrating its Web site with its accounting system?

29. Ramwood Company is a large distributor in the candy business with offices in Miami, Florida. The company accepts only very large orders from wholesalers, and the controller has a strict policy that orders will only be filled on the basis of an encrypted electronic purchase order from the customer.

   Ramwood has recently had some serious problems with its Web site,

   www.ramwoodcandy.com.

   The problem is that someone has spoofed its domain name and has been intercepting its business. In other words, many recent orders have gone to a competitor with offices in the Cayman Islands, who just happens to operate under a similar legal name, namely, Ramwood Candy.

   The CEO checked with the company's outside attorney and found out that there was little that could be done about another company using a similar name, and given that the competitor was offshore it would even be difficult to do anything about the domain name spoofing.

   The controller spent her nights without sleep, thinking about the problem. Finally, she concluded that they needed to add something to their Web site that the competitor could not counterfeit, some sort of token or something that the customer could look for to be assured that it was dealing with the real

   www.ramwoodcandy.com.

   Required
   (a) How would you suggest that Ramwood solve its problem?
   (b) Design a complete system that can protect Ramwood from imposters.

30. *www.WhiteFlowers4You.com* sells flower arrangements over the Internet. Recently the company has been experimenting with accepting digital cash. At first, the introduction of digital cash brought an immediate 10% increase in sales, and everyone in the company was pleased.

   Problems began to occur, however, with some of the digital cash notes received. In one day, a week ago, 20 notes, each denominated in the amount of $20, turned out to be counterfeit. The bad notes were received from different customers, but in each case the flowers were being sent to someone as a gift. Further, in every case the flowers were shipped the same day that the order was placed. It was not until the next day that the bank refused to pay the digital notes.

   To make things worse, all the notes turned out to be blinded digital cash, so the bank could not provide any information on the maker. Further verification showed that in every case the customer had entered a false name, address, and telephone number. In short, there was no easy way to find out who had perpetrated the frauds.

   The controller argued strongly for contacting the recipients of the flowers to ask questions about who had made the false purchases. But the CEO was against this, as she felt that to make an issue of it would produce bad customer relations and possibly bad press. The last thing the company needed was bad press.

   While the controller and CEO were debating what to do, the treasurer popped in and said that they had just discovered another 120 bad notes for $20 from only the day before.

Required
(a) What should *www.WhiteFlowers4You.com* do about its problem with bad digital notes? Design a solution to the problem.
(b) Should the company contact the recipients of the fraudulent orders? Explain why they should or should not.

❖ ANSWERS TO CHAPTER QUIZ

1. c	4. a	7. a	10. d
2. b	5. d	8. b	
3. b	6. a	9. a	

TRANSACTION PROCESSING AND THE INTERNAL CONTROL PROCESS

LEARNING OBJECTIVES

Careful study of this chapter will enable you to:

❖ Understand the nature of control exposures.

❖ Discuss the concept of the internal control process.

❖ Identify general and application processing controls.

❖ Discuss the behavioral assumptions inherent in traditional internal control practices.

❖ Describe the techniques used to analyze internal control systems.

THE NECESSITY FOR CONTROLS

CONTROLS AND EXPOSURES

Controls are needed to reduce exposures. An organization is subject to a variety of exposures that can have an adverse effect on its operations or even its very existence as a viable going concern. An **exposure** consists of the potential financial effect of an event multiplied by its probability of occurrence. The term **risk** is synonymous with *probability of occurrence*. Thus an exposure is a risk times its financial consequences.

Undesirable events such as floods or thefts are not themselves exposures. An organization's exposure to these types of events is the organization's potential financial loss times the probability of the occurrence of these events. Exposures do not arise simply due to a lack of controls. Controls tend to reduce exposures, but controls rarely affect the causes of exposures. Exposures are inherent in the operation of any organization and may result from a variety of causes (Fig. 4.1).

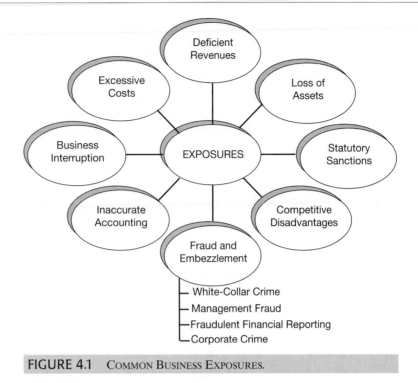

FIGURE 4.1   COMMON BUSINESS EXPOSURES.

COMMON EXPOSURES

EXCESSIVE COSTS

Excessive costs reduce profits. Every expenditure made by an organization is potentially excessive. Prices paid for goods purchased for use in the organization may be excessive. Paychecks may be distributed for work that was ineffective, inefficient, or both. Production may be inefficient, causing the purchase and use of excessive materials and labor. Excessive assets may be purchased. Excessive expenses for advertising and travel expense may be incurred. Bills or taxes may be paid late, causing penalty fees and interest expense to be incurred.

DEFICIENT REVENUES

Deficient revenues reduce profits. Bad debt expense on credit sales may be excessive. Sales may be shipped to customers but not recorded and thus not collected. Customers may be incorrectly billed for smaller amounts than they should. Bills may be lost or incorrectly summarized as receivables. Sales may be returned or cancelled due to late shipment of orders, shipment of unacceptable quality, or incorrect shipment of items ordered. Excessive sales allowances may be incurred for similar reasons.

LOSS OF ASSETS

Assets may be lost due to theft, acts of violence, or natural disaster. An organization has custody of a large quantity of assets, all of which are subject to loss. Assets may be lost unintentionally. Cash, materials, or equipment may be accidentally misplaced or damaged by careless employees or even careful employees. Cash, materials, or equipment also may be intentionally misplaced or damaged by employees, including management.

INACCURATE ACCOUNTING

Accounting policies and procedures may be error-prone, inappropriate, or significantly different from those that are considered to be generally acceptable. Errors may include valuation, timing, or classification of transactions. Errors in record keeping may be unintentional or intentional. Errors can result in inaccurate information for management decisions and materially misleading financial statements.

BUSINESS INTERRUPTION

Business interruption may consist of a temporary suspension of operations or ultimately the termination of operations and end of the organization. Business interruption may result from excessive operating exposures, from physical acts of violence, or from natural disaster.

STATUTORY SANCTIONS

Statutory sanctions include any penalties that may arise from judicial or regulatory authorities who have jurisdiction over an organization and its operations. An organization must ensure that its activities are in compliance with a variety of laws and regulations. Interruption of normal business operations might result as a penalty imposed by regulatory agencies when corporate crime has been committed.

COMPETITIVE DISADVANTAGE

Competitive disadvantage is the inability of an organization to remain viable in the marketplace. Competitive disadvantage might result from any combination of the previous exposures and also might result from ineffective management decisions.

FRAUD AND EMBEZZLEMENT

Fraud is the intentional perversion of truth in order to induce another to part with something of value or to surrender a legal right. Embezzlement occurs when assets are fraudulently appropriated to one's own use. Fraud and embezzlement may be perpetrated by outsiders against an organization or by insiders within the organization. Excessive costs, deficient revenues, loss of assets, inaccurate accounting, business interruption, statutory sanctions, and competitive disadvantage may all result from fraud and embezzlement.

FRAUD AND WHITE-COLLAR CRIME

The term **white-collar crime** describes a grouping of illegal activities that are differentiated from other illegal activities in that they occur as part of the occupation of the offender. White-collar crime occurs when assets are deceitfully diverted from proper use or deceitfully misrepresented by an act or series of acts that are nonviolent in nature. White-collar crime often involves the entry of fictitious (i.e., fraudulent) transactions into an accounting system.

Three basic forms of theft occur in white-collar crime. Employee theft involves diversion of assets by an employee for personal gain. Employee-outsider theft involves diversion of assets by an employee in collusion with an outsider (i.e., nonemployee) for personal gain. Management fraud concerns diversion of assets or misrepresentation of assets by management. **Management fraud** may involve diversion or misrepresentation of assets from either employees or third-party outsiders, or both. Management is responsible for the establishment of controls in an organization and is thus not subject to these controls to the extent that other employees are. Irregularities by management are less likely to be detected than are irregularities committed by other employees.

White-collar crime may result in fraudulent financial reporting. **Fraudulent financial reporting** is intentional or reckless conduct, whether by purposeful act or by omission, that results in materially misleading financial statements. Employees at any level of the organization might be involved. Fraudulent financial reporting might involve fictitious transactions processed by an accounting system, falsified valuation of assets such as inventories, or misapplication of accounting principles. No organization of any size is immune from the possibility that fraudulent financial reporting might occur.

Corporate crime is white-collar crime that benefits a company or organization rather than the individuals who perpetrate the fraud. Such individuals may benefit indirectly. Examples of corporate crime include defense contract cost overages charged to the federal government by defense contractors, publicized charges for reimbursement for non-contract-related expenses by universities, and bidding improprieties at auctions for government securities by major brokerage firms.

The fascinating aspect of white-collar crime is that it often seems to be victimless. Crimes such as embezzlement, tax fraud, fraudulent financial statements, unemployment insurance fraud, and the like require some sort of procedural analysis (a physical examination and analysis of transaction records, documentation, inventories, and so on) as a prerequisite to discovering and proving that a crime has been committed. In one publicized case of corporate crime, a major brokerage firm was convicted of mail and wire fraud concerning bank deposits that it processed. During the investigation, most of the banks that had been victims of the fraud were surprised to learn that they had in fact been robbed. They were unaware of this until they were contacted by investigators, which was well after the crimes had occurred.

FORENSIC ACCOUNTING

Forensic accounting is concerned with the prevention and detection of fraud and white-collar crime. **Forensic accounting** is one of several terms that is used to describe the activities of persons who are concerned with preventing and detecting fraud. The terms *fraud examiner, fraud auditor*, and *loss-prevention professional* are also descriptive of this type of activity.

The National Association of Certified Fraud Examiners (NACFE) is a professional organization that was established as a response to the increased concern for fraud in business and government. The mission of NACFE is to reduce the incidence of fraud and white-collar crime and to assist its membership in its detection and deterrence. NACFE provides bona fide qualifications for certified fraud examiners (CFEs) through administration of the Uniform CFE Examination. Certified fraud examiners have expertise to resolve allegations of fraud, obtain evidence, take statements and write reports, testify to findings, and assist in the prevention and detection of fraud and white-collar crime. Typical CFEs include fraud auditors and investigators, forensic accountants, public accountants, law enforcement personnel, loss-prevention professionals, and academicians. All CFEs must exemplify high moral and ethical standards and must abide by a code of professional ethics.

Fraud examination draws on the fields of accounting, law, and criminology. A knowledge of accounting is necessary to understand the nature of fraudulent transactions. There are many legal aspects involved in fraud examination; thus an understanding of related law is essential. The basics of criminology are essential to understand the behavior of criminals. Principles of legal investigation are also central to fraud examination. Fraud examiners must know how to legally gather evidence related to fraud—how to obtain documentation, interview witnesses, take lawful statements, and write unbiased reports. Fraud examination has to adhere to investigation standards acceptable to a court of law.

SERIOUSNESS OF FRAUD

Fraud is a serious problem. KPMG Peat Marwick conducted a survey of 2,000 of the largest companies in the United States.[1] Companies were asked questions pertaining to overall awareness of fraud, perceptions of fraud in American business, specific instances of fraud, procedures to prevent fraud, and vulnerability to fraud. More than half the 330 respondents had gross revenue/assets between $1 billion and $4.9 billion.

---

[1] *Fraud Survey Results 1993.* KPMG Peat Marwick, 1993.

The survey results leave no doubt that fraud is a significant problem for business. More than 75% of the 330 respondents experienced fraud during the past year, with 23% reporting losses of $1 million or more. More than half these respondents (58%) experienced up to 5 incidents of fraud; 25% observed more than 21 cases of fraud. The three most expensive types of fraud were patent infringement, credit card fraud, and false financial statements, each totaling more than $1 million per company involved. The most frequent type of fraud was misappropriation of funds—accounting for 20% of all acts of fraud reported. This was followed by check forgery (19%), credit card fraud (15%), false invoices (15%), and theft (12%). Other types of fraud reported include accounts receivable manipulation, false financial statements, diversion of service, phantom vendors, purchase for personal use, diversion of sales, unnecessary purchases, vandalism, and sabotage.

Internal controls were cited most frequently as the reason frauds are discovered (59% of respondents). Internal auditor review and specific investigation by management were the next two most frequently mentioned methods of discovering fraud. Poor internal controls were identified as the most frequent reason that frauds occurred (56% of respondents). Collusion between employees and third parties was an important factor in 44% of reported cases. Management overrode existing controls in 40% of the cases. Forty-eight percent of respondents indicated that there were "red flags"— such as changes in an employee's lifestyle or spending habits—that pointed to the possibility of fraud(s), but these red flags were either ignored or not acted on quickly enough by personnel or management.

COMPUTER PROCESSING AND EXPOSURES

Many aspects of computer processing tend to significantly increase an organization's exposure to undesirable events. Some aspects of computer processing increase either the risk and/or potential dollar loss of exposures that would exist in an organization regardless of whether or not computer processing was employed. Other aspects of computer processing create their own types of exposures.

Mechanical processing of data, mechanical data storage, and complexity of processing are aspects of computer processing that can increase either the risk and/or potential dollar loss of exposures that would exist in an organization regardless of whether computer processing was employed. Concentrated processing, concentrated data storage, and the data processing assets themselves are aspects of computer processing that create their own types of exposures.

DATA PROCESSING ASSETS

The data processing assets must be protected, as must any other asset in the organization. Mainframe computer equipment can be quite expensive and often requires a special environment for efficient operation. Restricted access is a major consideration. There should be few entrances to the computer system location. Only individuals with proper validation should be permitted to enter. There are a number of approaches to restricting access. These include programmable locks (which can be programmed to reject particular keys), security guards, and closed-circuit television monitors.

CONTROL OBJECTIVES AND TRANSACTION CYCLES

Controls act to reduce exposures. The analysis of exposures in an organization is often related to the transaction cycle concept. Although no two organizations are identical, most organizations experience the same types of economic events. These events generate transactions that may be grouped according to four common cycles of business activity:

- **Revenue cycle:** Events related to the distribution of goods and services to other entities and the collection of related payments

- **Expenditure cycle:** Events related to the acquisition of goods and services from other entities and the settlement of related obligations
- **Production cycle:** Events related to the transformation of resources into goods and services
- **Finance cycle:** Events related to the acquisition and management of capital funds, including cash

Each transaction cycle will have exposures. Management should develop detailed control objectives for each transaction cycle. These control objectives provide a basis for analysis. Once control objectives have been stated, management may collect information to determine the extent to which control objectives are being achieved in each of the organization's transaction cycles.

Figure 4.2 lists representative control objectives for each transaction cycle. Control objectives such as those illustrated are drawn from the concept of an internal control

FIGURE 4.2 REPRESENTATIVE CONTROL OBJECTIVES.

Representative Control Objectives	
Revenue Cycle	Customers should be authorized in accordance with management's criteria.
	The prices and terms of goods and services provided should be authorized in accordance with management's criteria.
	All shipments of goods and services provided should result in a billing to the customer.
	Billings to customers should be accurately and promptly classified, summarized, and reported.
Expenditure Cycle	Vendors should be authorized in accordance with management's criteria.
	Employees should be hired in accordance with management's criteria.
	Access to personnel, payroll, and disbursement records should be permitted only in accordance with management's criteria.
	Compensation rates and payroll deductions should be authorized in accordance with management's criteria.
	Amounts due to vendors should be accurately and promptly classified, summarized, and reported.
Production Cycle	The production plan should be authorized in accordance with management's criteria.
	Cost of goods manufactured should be accurately and promptly classified, summarized, and reported.
Finance Cycle	The amounts and timing of debt transactions should be authorized in accordance with management's criteria.
	Access to cash and securities should be permitted only in accordance with management's criteria.

structure. Management must first develop an internal control structure. This structure can then be applied to transaction cycles by developing specific control objectives for each cycle.

COMPONENTS OF THE INTERNAL CONTROL PROCESS

Internal control is a process—affected by an entity's board of directors, management, and other personnel—designed to provide reasonable assurance regarding the achievement of objectives in the following categories: (1) reliability of financial reporting, (2) effectiveness and efficiency of operations, and (3) compliance with applicable laws and regulations.

An organization's **internal control process** consists of five elements: the control environment, risk assessment, control activities, information and communication, and monitoring (Fig. 4.3). The concept of internal control is based on two major premises: responsibility and reasonable assurance.

The first premise, **responsibility**, has to do with management and the board of directors being responsible for establishing and maintaining the internal control process. While specific responsibilities for controls may be delegated to subordinates, final responsibility remains with management and the board of directors. External auditors, internal auditors, and other parties may be concerned directly with an organization's internal control process, but the ultimate responsibility for the control remains with management and the board of directors.

The second premise, **reasonable assurance**, has to do with the relative costs and benefits of controls. Prudent management should not spend more on controls than the benefits to be received from the controls. For example, suppose that purchasing a credit check report for new customers costs $35. The credit check would tend to reduce bad debt expense for new customers (i.e., reduce the probability or risk of its occurring) and thus would reduce the organization's exposure in this area. If sales to new customers average only $25, however, then the cost of this control would exceed its expected benefits. It would not be rational to implement this control.

Quite often management's consideration of the relative costs and benefits of controls necessarily will be subjective in nature. It is often difficult to measure costs and benefits when intangible factors such as the reputation of the company or the morale effects of controls on employees are major considerations. Management must exercise its judgment to attain reasonable assurance that its control objectives are being met.

FIGURE 4.3 INTERNAL CONTROL STRUCTURE.

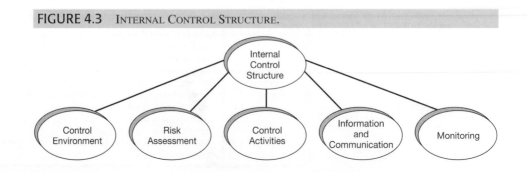

EXTERNAL INFLUENCES CONCERNING AN ENTITY AND INTERNAL CONTROL

Many organizations are subject to specific statutory requirements that are issued by judicial or regulatory authorities. An organization must ensure that its activities are in compliance with laws and regulations issued by those who have jurisdiction over an organization and its operations. The Securities and Exchange Commission (SEC) is active in the area of financial accounting, as is the Financial Accounting Standards Board (FASB). Laws, regulations, and pronouncements from such agencies are a major factor in an organization's internal control process.

The Federal Foreign Corrupt Practices Act of 1977 (FCPA) is a specific legal requirement that concerns many organizations. Failure to comply with this law could result in fines and imprisonment.

Section 102 of the FCPA requires all companies who are subject to the Securities Exchange Act of 1934 to

A. Make and keep books, records, and accounts, which, in reasonable detail, accurately and fairly reflect the transactions and dispositions of the assets of the issuer;
B. Devise and maintain a system of internal accounting controls sufficient to provide reasonable assurances that

   1. Transactions are executed in accordance with management's general or specific authorization;
   2. Transactions are recorded as necessary (i) to permit preparation of financial statements in conformity with generally accepted accounting principles or any other criteria applicable to such statements and (ii) to maintain accountability for assets;
   3. Access to assets is permitted only in accordance with management's general or specific authorization;
   4. The recorded accountability for assets is compared with the existing assets at reasonable intervals and appropriate action is taken with respect to any differences.

Noncompliance with these provisions could result in fines up to $10,000 for both the corporation and its officials along with 5 years' imprisonment for those executives involved.

A section of the Omnibus Trade and Competitiveness Act of 1988 (OTCA) amends both the accounting and antibribery provisions of the FCPA. The FCPA requires registrants to keep records in "reasonable detail" and to maintain systems of internal accounting control that provide "reasonable assurances" that specified goals are met. As originally passed, the act did not contain definitions of either *reasonable detail* or *reasonable assurances*. A new subsection added by the OTCA defines the terms *reasonable detail* and *reasonable assurances* to mean a level that would satisfy prudent officials in the conduct of their own affairs. Another amendment to the accounting provisions limits criminal liability to intentional actions taken to circumvent the internal accounting control systems or to falsify company records. The OTCA also includes several amendments that clarify or modify the antibribery provisions of the FCPA and increase penalties for violation of the antibribery provisions.

THE SARBANES-OXLEY ACT

For public companies, the Sarbanes-Oxley Act of 2002 (SOA) imposes certain requirements and restrictions on management, auditors, and company audit committees. Severe financial and criminal penalties may apply.

The act establishes the five-member Public Company Accounting Oversight Board (PCAOB), whose responsibilities are directed primarily toward regulating the conduct of auditors but with important implications for management in all publicly traded companies. The SOA grants the PCAOB powers to make up rules and impose sanctions, subject to SEC review. Violations of PCAOB rules are deemed to be violations of the 1934 Securities Act.

The SOA also substantially increases criminal penalties for various types of white-collar crimes. It increases the maximum penalties for violations of the 1934 Securities Act from $1 million and 10 years in prison to $5 million and 20 years in prison. The maximum jail time for mail fraud is increased from 5 to 20 years. Similarly, the maximum jail time for violating the reporting and disclosure portions of the Employee Retirement Income Security Act of 1974 is increased from 1 to 10 years.

The act greatly expands the scope of laws relating to obstruction of justice. Under the SOA, any acts of obstruction that are merely done in *contemplation of a future investigation* may subject the perpetrator to imprisonment for up to 20 years. (Prior to the SOA, obstruction of justice was limited to ongoing investigations.) Under the SOA, acts of obstruction include knowingly altering, destroying, or falsifying documents with the intent to impede, obstruct, or influence any federal investigation or bankruptcy proceeding. It is also illegal to attempt to improperly influence or impede an audit firm in the course of its duties.

Special provisions in the act provide whistleblower protection to employees who disclose private employer information in certain judicial proceedings involving claims of fraud against the company. Whistleblowers may collect attorneys' fees and damages from the company.

Restrictions on Nonaudit Services   The SOA severely restricts the nonaudit services that auditors can provide to their clients. Barred services include (1) bookkeeping or other services related to the accounting records or financial statements of the audit client, (2) financial information systems design and implementation, (3) appraisal or valuation services, fairness opinions, or contribution-in-kind reports, (4) actuarial services, (5) internal audit outsourcing services, (6) management functions or human resources, (7) broker or dealer, investment adviser, or investment banking services, (8) legal services and expert services unrelated to the audit, and (9) any other service that the board determines, by regulation, is impermissible.

Other nonaudit services are permissible with prior approval of the company's audit committee. Such prior approval is not required if the nonaudit services constitute less than 5% of the audit fees.

Role of the Audit Committee   The SOA legislates the importance of the audit committee. The company must maintain a properly funded audit committee (as part of the board of directors) that is composed of independent members who do not receive any compensation from the company (or its subsidiaries) for work other than service on the board of directors.

The auditor is required to report all audit-relevant information to this committee, and the audit committee has sole responsibility for selecting, hiring, and overseeing the auditor.

Conflicts of Interest   The chief executive officer (CEO), controller, chief financial officer (CFO), chief accounting officer, or person in an equivalent position cannot have been employed by the company's audit firm during the 1-year period preceding the audit.

Corporate Responsibility for Financial Reports   The CEO and CFO must prepare a statement to accompany the audit report to certify the "appropriateness of the financial statements and disclosures contained in the periodic report and that those financial statements and disclosures fairly present, in all material respects, the operations and financial condition of the issuer." An intentionally false certification may result in penalties as large as a $5 million fine and 20 years in prison.

Insider Trades During Pension Fund Blackout Periods Prohibited   The SOA prohibits the purchase or sale of stock by officers and directors and other insiders during blackout periods. Such blackout periods typically exist in pension plans, for example, at times when employees are not permitted to sell their shares in the company.

Prohibition on Personal Loans to Executives and Directors   Companies are barred from lending money to directors or executive officers.

Code of Ethics   Companies are required to disclose whether they have adopted a code of ethics for senior financial officers, and they also must disclose the content of the code.

Management Assessment of Internal Controls   The SOA requires the annual report to contain an internal control report that (1) states the responsibility of management for establishing and maintaining an adequate internal control structure and procedures for financial reporting and (2) contains an assessment, as of the end of the company's fiscal year, of the effectiveness of the internal control structure and procedures of the company for financial reporting.

The auditor shall attest to and report on the assessment. An attestation made under this section shall be in accordance with standards for attestation engagements issued or adopted by the PCAOB.

THE IMPACT OF THE BUSINESS ENVIRONMENT ON INTERNAL CONTROL

Another important consideration is that an entity's internal control process will vary depending on the context of its size; organizational structure; ownership characteristics; methods of transmitting, processing, maintaining, and assessing information; legal and regulatory requirements; and the diversity and complexity of its operations.

For example, in small organizations there may not be a large enough number of employees to achieve the same degree of separation of duties that might be expected in a large company. This situation often can be dealt with by involving the owner in various aspects of transactions, such as signing checks, approving invoices, and record keeping. Furthermore, procedure manuals, policy manuals, organization charts, and many other types of documentation, as well as policies and procedures, may prove infeasible for the small organization.

CONTROL ENVIRONMENT

An organization's control environment, the first of the five components of internal control, is the foundation of all other components of the control system. The **control environment** is the collective effect of various factors on establishing, enhancing, or mitigating the effectiveness of specific policies and procedures. In other words, the control environment sets the overall tone of the organization and influences the control consciousness of the employees.

Factors included in the control environment are as follows:

- Integrity and ethical values
- Commitment to competence
- Management philosophy and operating style
- Organizational structure
- Attention and direction provided by the board of directors and its committees
- Manner of assigning authority and responsibility
- Human resource policies and procedures

Corporate Ethics Breaches
Marketing executives of Anheuser-Busch were accused of taking kickbacks from a supplier, Hanely Wordwide, Inc. It was alleged that this supplier contributed $13,500 toward the purchase of a Porsche automobile by Anheuser-Busch's director of promotions.
Chrysler Corporation was charged in a 16-count indictment. The allegations stated executives of the company drove Chrysler automobiles with their odometers disconnected. The automobiles were then allegedly sold as new.
General Dynamics, a large defense contractor, was suspended from doing business for defrauding the Pentagon. Investigators alleged that General Dynamics was guilty of fraudulently billing the government.
General Electric and Rockwell were found guilty of fraudulently billing the federal government.
E. F. Hutton & Company pleaded guilty to 2,000 counts of mail and wire fraud.

FIGURE 4.4   CORPORATE ETHICS BREACHES.

INTEGRITY AND ETHICAL VALUES

Potential ethical violations present a significant loss exposure for the corporation (Fig. 4.4). Such exposures include the possibility of large fines or criminal prosecution against both the company and its executives. For example, E. F. Hutton was fined $12 million when it pleaded guilty to allegations relating to wire and mail fraud. In another case, Film Recovery Systems, which used cyanide to extract silver from film, was accused of knowingly creating a dangerous work environment that led to the death of an employee. Three of the company's executives were charged and convicted of murder. They were subsequently sentenced to 25 years in prison. In another case, Manville Corporation was driven into bankruptcy by problems relating to health hazards associated with asbestos, its primary product. Court testimony indicated that for years the company knew and intentionally overlooked severe damage to the health of company employees by asbestos.

Ethics and Corporate Culture   Many companies have adopted ethics codes of conduct that specify guidelines for conducting business in an ethical manner. Similarly, many professional organizations, such as the American Institute of Certified Public Accountants, have adopted codes of conduct. The code of conduct is often written in legal-style language that focuses on laws that might be broken. Accordingly, such codes have been criticized sometimes as being devoid of general ethical values such as "diligently looking out for the safety of employees" or "always telling the truth when dealing with customers."

Many have argued that every corporation has its own corporate culture and that it is this corporate culture that either promotes or hinders ethical behavior. The corporate culture pertains to the general beliefs, practices, and attitudes of employees. It does not matter how good a code of conduct is if there are significant problems in the corporate culture. For example, some companies have an excessively inward focus. A company that focuses too much internally and not enough on the outside world is more likely to get into trouble. Examples of excessive internal focus would include overemphasis on sales quotas, making unreasonable deadlines, pleasing the boss, and so on. For example, if construction employees were told to either complete a building by a certain date or be fired, they might be tempted to cut corners and compromise safety. An excessive short-run focus also may be a problem. A company that focuses too much on the short run might be more inclined not to worry about the long-term consequences of its actions. In the case of Manville Company, the long-run health hazards of asbestos were overlooked to the point that the company was destroyed. Morale can be a problem. Unhappy employees can be dangerous. One such case involved a disgruntled employee of a company that produced an accounting software package. The employee made changes to the software that scrambled up the records of those companies who used the accounting system. Some companies have an excessively autocratic organizational structure. Highly autocratic managers are relatively unlikely to accept criticism, and the employees of such managers may fear pointing out ethics problems.

Producing a corporate culture supportive of ethical behavior can be difficult and certainly cannot be accomplished without education, training, and compliance. Some companies use seminars to educate and train their employees. Compliance is achieved by giving ethics a formal place in the organization chart. Each division should have an ethics director. The ethics director should be readily available to employees for consultations. All employees should be trained in how and when to contact the ethics director. Employees should be advised of penalties for ethics violations. The ethics director should be contacted whenever an employee observes an ethics violation or is ordered to commit an ethics violation or whenever an employee needs advice on any problem involving ethics. Employees should be able to report problems anonymously. Some companies have "squeal systems" that reward employees for reporting ethical violations.

For any ethics program to work, the company should have a cultural audit of its culture and ethical behavior. Ethical problems can exist in many areas. Some of the areas that must be dealt with relate to safety, equal opportunity employment, sexual harassment, product and service quality, privacy, honesty in business dealings, conflicts of interest, and respect for intellectual property.

Ethical Considerations in Job Design   Consider the following job description:

> The person who accepts the treasurer's position shall be entirely responsible for the company's securities transactions. The position entails keeping the supporting records, exclusive control over the safe deposit box, and complete discretion over buying and selling of securities.

Would you accept this job?

Many readers will recognize several violations of conventional internal control principles in the preceding job description. Is this job offering an invitation to fraud? That is, does the lack of conventional controls over the treasurer's duties constitute the equivalent of an invitation to steal? What is an organization's responsibility for the integrity of its employees?

These questions raise issues that should be considered in the design of business systems. The need for an adequate system of internal control can be viewed ethically as well as from the view of efficient management. The following quotation is representative of this often expressed view:

> I can recall a sizable industrial concern which was headed by a president who was perhaps more interested in his avocation of preaching than in running his business. Attempts to improve internal control in his corporation were constantly rebuffed because he believed that people were fundamentally honest, that his employees could be trusted, and therefore that there was no need for any system of checks and balances. The accountant became increasingly concerned with the company's exposure of its assets to possible defalcation. Finally, he went to the company president and said, "As a good Christian, you have a moral obligation to remove temptation from your employees!" This

ethical appeal succeeded where an appeal to good business judgment alone failed, and the company's system of internal control was improved after all.[2]

Organizations should have sufficient controls to deter fraudulent actions, if only through reducing temptation by the threat of being caught. On the other hand, overly rigid controls hamper the actions and decisions of individuals, artificially limiting an employee's response to the variety of her or his task. Accountability and pressures for performance may boomerang. Rigid control systems may create or stimulate the types of actions that the controls were designed to prevent.

COMMITMENT TO COMPETENCE

Competence in employees is essential to the proper functioning of any process of internal control. In the final analysis, it is the quality and competence of the employees that ensure the ability to carry out the control process. No control process can function adequately without competent employees.

MANAGEMENT PHILOSOPHY AND OPERATING STYLE

Effective control in an organization begins with and ultimately rests with management philosophy. If management believes that controls are important, then it will see to it that effective control policies and procedures are implemented.

This control-conscious attitude will be communicated to subordinates through management's operating style. If, on the other hand, management pays only "lip service" to the need for controls, it is very likely that subordinates will sense management's true attitude and control objectives will not be achieved.

ORGANIZATIONAL STRUCTURE

An organization's structure is defined by the patterns of authority and responsibility that exist within the organization. The formal organization structure is often denoted by an organization chart, such as Figure 4.5. As shown, the billing function is directly

FIGURE 4.5 ORGANIZATION CHART.

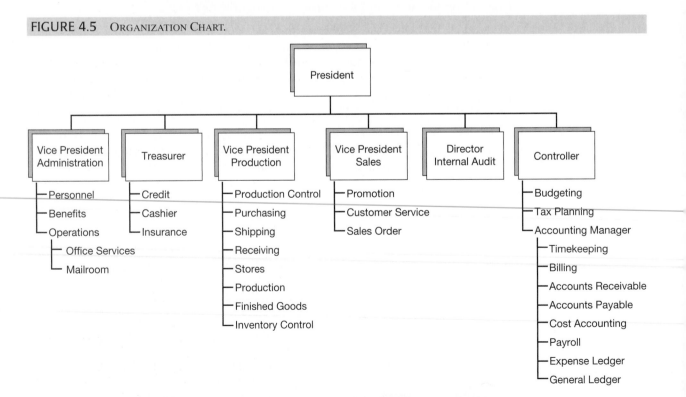

---

[2]"Business Ethics." *Review*. New York: Price Waterhouse, 1977.

responsible to the accounting manager. At the next higher level in the chart, the accounting manager is responsible to the controller. The controller is, in turn, responsible to the president.

An organization chart indicates the formal communication patterns within an organization. In Figure 4.5, for example, one would not normally expect the billing function to communicate the results of its operations to the vice president of production. As indicated in the chart, billing is not directly responsible to the vice president of production. An informal organization structure exists when regular communication patterns do not follow the lines indicated by the formal organization structure.

FUNCTIONS OF THE BOARD OF DIRECTORS AND ITS COMMITTEES

An organization's board of directors is the interface between the stockholders who own the organization and the organization's operating management. Stockholders exercise control over management through the functions of the board of directors and its committees. If the board consists entirely of members of management, or if the board meets infrequently, then stockholder control over operating management is likely to be weak or nonexistent.

Audit Committee   Typically a board of directors delegates specific functions to various operating committees. All public companies whose stock is traded on the New York Stock Exchange are required to have an audit committee composed of outside directors. Many other companies also have audit committees.

The audit committee should be independent of an organization's management, composed primarily of outside members of the board of directors (Fig. 4.6). The audit committee is usually charged with overall responsibility for the organization's financial reports, including compliance with existing laws and regulations. The audit committee nominates public accountants, discusses the scope and nature of audits with public accountants, and reviews and evaluates reports prepared by the organization's public accountants. Audit committees should be charged with reviewing management's reaction to public accountants' reports on the organization's internal control process.

To be effective, the audit committee must maintain communication with an organization's internal audit function as well as with the organization's external auditors (i.e., public accountants). As shown in Figure 4.6, an internal audit should report to the audit committee of the board of directors to maintain independence of internal auditing from other functions.

MANNER OF ASSIGNING AUTHORITY AND RESPONSIBILITY

The methods of assigning authority and responsibility within an organization are indicative of management's philosophy and operating style. If only verbal or informal methods exist, control is likely to be weak or nonexistent.

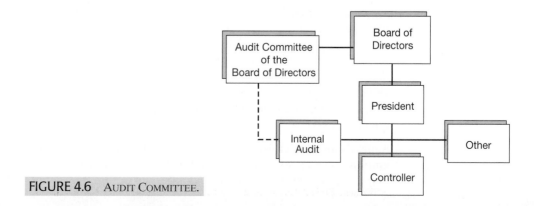

FIGURE 4.6   AUDIT COMMITTEE.

A formal organization chart, a written document, is often used to indicate the overall assignment of authority and responsibility in an organization. The organization chart is often accompanied by formal job descriptions and statements of work assignments. Written memoranda, policy manuals, and procedure manuals are other common means used to formally assign authority and responsibility within an organization.

Budgeting   Budgeting is the process of preparing budgets. Budgeting is a major management activity. Budgets are generally set for the entire organization as well as for each subunit. The budget for the entire organization is usually called the *master budget*. The master budget is often presented as a set of pro forma financial statements. Pro forma financial statements are forecasted statements—such as a balance sheet and income statement—that represent the predicted financial results of management's plan of operation for the coming budget period. The master budget is the accumulated result of all the detailed budgets that are prepared for the organizational subunits. Detailed operating budgets are prepared for subunits to evidence management's plan concerning operation of each subunit and to serve as the device by which management's plans are communicated to subunits. In addition to operating budgets, other types of budgets may be prepared as necessary to help management plan and control the activities of the firm. A common example is the capital expenditure budget, which is used to plan capital expenditures. Budgets generally are prepared on both a monthly and a yearly basis; frequently, a 5- or 10-year long-term budget is prepared as well.

Budgeting data are used to plan and control the activities within a firm. Control is established by comparing the results of activity to the budget for each activity. A budget is a control that sets forth a financial plan and/or an authorized amount of resources that may be used by a subunit in performing its functions. Budgets are set in advance of organizational activity and serve as the control by which management authorizes the transactional activity that the organization will undertake.

HUMAN RESOURCE POLICIES AND PRACTICES

Personnel should be competent and have capabilities and/or training commensurate with their duties. In the final analysis, personnel are the key components in any control system. The qualifications established for each job position in a company should reflect the degree of responsibility associated with the position. Qualifications may include experience, intelligence, character, dedication, and leadership ability. Fidelity bonding is common for employees who are directly responsible for the custody of assets. A **fidelity bond** is a contract with an insurance company that provides a financial guarantee of the honesty of the individual who is named in the bond contract. The insurance company usually will investigate the background of a person who is to be bonded. Thus fidelity bonding helps ensure that an organization is hiring reliable personnel.

Segregation of Duties   Responsibility for specific tasks in an organization should be clearly designated by manuals, job descriptions, or other documentation. Effective **segregation of duties** depends to a considerable extent on the precise and detailed planning of all procedures and the careful assignment of functions to various people in the organization. The details of the procedures should be set forth in memoranda that also show explicit assignment of duties to individual departments or employees. Written procedures, instructions, and assignments of duties will prevent duplication of work, overlapping of functions, omission of important functions, misunderstandings, and other situations that might weaken the internal accounting controls. Such notes typically form the basis for a formal manual on procedures and policy.

Supervision   **Supervision** is the direct monitoring of personnel performance by an employee who is so charged. In addition to properly selecting and adequately training employees, proper supervision is necessary to ensure that duties are being carried out as assigned. Supervision becomes very important in a small firm or in other situations where segregation of duties is not possible.

Job Rotation and Forced Vacations   Job rotation and forced vacations allow employees to check or verify the operations of other employees by performing their duties for a period of time. Several advantages may be gained by these techniques.

Irregularities that may have been committed by an employee may be disclosed while the employee is on vacation and her or his duties are assumed by another employee. Job rotation allows more than one employee to become familiar with certain duties and procedures so that the replacement of employees in cases of emergency is less difficult. Job rotation frequently serves as a general check on the efficiency of the employee on vacation or who has been rotated to another job. Finally, job rotation broadens the training of the personnel in general.

Dual Control   Closely related to direct supervision is the concept of **dual control**—the assignment of two individuals to perform the same work task in unison. The intent of dual control is not work reduction but work redundancy. Each individual is assumed to check the work of the other constantly. Responsibility for the custody of high-valued securities, for example, is frequently delegated to two or more people working in unison. Multiple control involves three or more people in unison. Dual or multiple control differs from supervision in that a supervisor is expected to supervise several people or operations simultaneously and, therefore, may effectively supervise a particular operation or employee less than 100% of the time. Dual control is essentially "dedicated" supervision; that is, one employee constantly checks the work of another, and vice versa.

RISK ASSESSMENT

Risk assessment, the second of the five components of internal control, is the process of identifying, analyzing, and managing risks that affect the company's objectives. Probably the most critical step in risk assessment is identifying internal and external changing conditions and related actions that may be necessary. Examples of risks relevant to the financial reporting process include changes in the organization's operating environment, changes in personnel, changes in the information system, new technology, major industry changes, new product lines, and new rules, laws, or accounting pronouncements.

CONTROL ACTIVITIES

Control activities, comprising the third component of internal control, are the policies and procedures established to help ensure that management directives are carried out. There are many potential control activities that may be used by organizations. These include accounting controls designed to provide reasonable assurance that the following specific control objectives are met for every significant application system within an organization:

- The plan of organization includes segregation of duties to reduce opportunities to allow any person to be in a position to both perpetrate and conceal errors or irregularities in the normal course of his or her duties.
- Procedures include the design and use of adequate documents and records to help ensure the proper recording of transactions and events.
- Access to assets is permitted only in accordance with management's authorization.
- Independent checks and reviews are made on the accountability of assets and performance.
- Information processing controls are applied to check the proper authorization, accuracy, and completeness of individual transactions.

Each of these specific control objectives is discussed in turn.

SEGREGATION OF DUTIES

Segregation of duties is necessary to reduce opportunities to allow any person to be in a position to both perpetrate and conceal errors or irregularities in the normal course of his or her duties. Segregation of duties is implemented by assigning to different people the responsibilities of authorizing transactions, recording transactions, and maintaining custody of assets. To achieve segregation of duties, the responsibilities of authorizing transactions, recording transactions, and maintaining custody of assets should be performed by independent functions.

Segregation of Authorization from Recording of Transactions   Segregation of authorization of transactions from recording of transactions reduces opportunities for errors and irregularities by establishing independent accountability for authorization functions. If each function in an organization kept its own records, there would be no accountability. There would be no basis for an independent reconciliation and analysis of a function's activities because there would be no assurances that all transactions have been recorded. In order to ensure unbiased information, record-keeping functions are usually centralized in a separate function headed by the controller.

For example, in a sales order application, the sales manager authorizes credit sales. A copy of the sales order form is sent to the warehouse to authorize the shipment of goods. If notice of the shipment is subsequently sent only to the sales manager, then the sales manager is accountable for his or her own performance. The sales manager is thus in a position to perpetrate errors and irregularities in the normal course of his or her duties. Perhaps he or she has authorized a shipment to a relative or friend. When notice of the shipment is received, the sales manager simply may destroy it or ignore it rather than forward it to billing for collection.

Segregation of Authorization from Custody of Assets   Segregation of authorization of transactions from custody of assets reduces opportunities for errors and irregularities by establishing independent accountability for the use (custody) of assets. Authorization of activities is communicated to those who have custody of assets and simultaneously communicated to the record-keeping function (i.e., accounting). Those charged with the custody of assets subsequently communicate the results of activity (i.e., transactions) to the record-keeping function. Reconciliation of these data with the authorizations that were received from an independent function provides accountability for both the authorization and the subsequent use of assets.

For example, in a sales order application, the sales manager authorizes credit sales. A copy of the sales order form is sent to the warehouse to authorize the shipment of goods. Another copy of the sales order form is sent to accounting. Notice of the shipment is subsequently sent to accounting. Reconciliation of shipment data with the authorizations that were received from an independent function provides accountability for both the authorization and the subsequent use of assets. Notice of shipment without a matching authorization indicates unauthorized shipments. Notice of authorization without subsequent shipment indicates ineffectiveness or inefficiency in completing sales transactions.

Segregation of Recording Transactions from Custody of Assets   Segregation of recording transactions from custody of assets reduces opportunities for errors and irregularities by establishing independent accountability for the use of assets. Authorization of activities is communicated to those who have custody of assets and simultaneously communicated to the record-keeping function (i.e., accounting). Those charged with the custody of assets subsequently communicate the results of activity (i.e., transactions) to the record-keeping function. Reconciliation of these data with the authorizations that were received from an independent function provides accountability for both the authorization and the subsequent use of assets.

If there is no segregation of duties between recording transactions from custody of assets, then those charged with the custody of assets are accountable for their own performance. There would be no basis for an independent reconciliation and analysis of a function's activities because there would be no assurances that all transactions have been recorded. The persons charged with the custody of assets are in a position to perpetrate errors and irregularities in the normal course of their duties by omitting records or falsifying entries into the records. In the preceding sales example, goods may be shipped by those who have custody of assets without authorization and without recording the shipment because there is no independent accountability for shipments.

ADEQUATE DOCUMENTS AND RECORDS

Procedures should include the design and use of adequate documents and records to help ensure the proper recording of transactions and events. Documents and records are the physical media used to store information. They may take many different forms, ranging from common paper documents such as sales orders and purchase orders to magnetic and optical storage media such as magnetic tape and optical disk.

Certain control practices are relevant to any type of documents and records. Items should be prenumbered in sequential order to facilitate accountability. Items should be easy to use and clearly understood by those who use them. Forms should provide specific space for the indication of necessary authorizations and approvals.

RESTRICTED ACCESS TO ASSETS

Access to assets should be permitted only in accordance with management's authorization. This requires adequate physical controls and safeguards over access to and use of assets and records, such as secured facilities and authorization for access to computer programs and data files.

It is well documented that physical theft and embezzlement are substantial threats to the solvency of business organizations. Physical controls are directed at reducing the opportunities for theft and embezzlement. Safeguarding of assets such as cash, securities, and inventory is accomplished by close supervision, physical protection devices, and segregation of duties. Common examples of physical controls include the following:

- Cash registers and lock boxes
- Locks, vaults, and limited-access areas
- Security forces
- Closed-circuit TV monitors
- Alarm systems

No physical control or safeguard in and of itself can protect assets; it is the procedures surrounding the use of physical controls that dictate whether or not the controls are effective. For example, every lock has a key; therefore, a lock is only as effective as is access to the key. TV monitors are effective only if they are being watched constantly or, alternatively, if personnel believe they are being watched. Limited-access areas are effective only if access is truly limited. The effectiveness of physical controls depends largely on the measures surrounding their use, not on the mere existence of the devices.

INDEPENDENT ACCOUNTABILITY CHECKS AND REVIEWS OF PERFORMANCE

The recorded accountability for assets should be compared with the existing assets at reasonable intervals and appropriate action taken with respect to any difference. This reconciliation function should be performed by someone who is independent of authorization, record keeping, and custody of the assets in question. Examples of independent checks on performance and proper valuation of recorded amounts include clerical checks, reconciliations, comparison of assets with recorded accountability, computer-programmed controls, management review of reports that summarize the detail of account balances (e.g., an aged trial balance of accounts receivable), and user review of computer-generated reports.

Budgets and general performance reviews are also an important means for assessing performance. These reviews are accomplished by comparing actual results with budgets, forecasts, standards, and prior-period performance.

INFORMATION PROCESSING CONTROLS

Information processing controls ensure the proper authorization, accuracy, and completeness of individual transactions.

Authorization limits the initiation of a transaction or performance of an activity to selected individuals. Authorization prevents unauthorized transactions and unauthorized activities. Proper authorization of transactions and activities is necessary if management is to obtain reasonable assurance that its control objectives are achieved.

Management's authorization may be general or specific in nature. Specific authorization pertains to individual transactions. Setting automatic reorder points for inventory items is an example of general authorization because no specific transaction is involved. Approval of a construction budget for a (specific) warehouse is an example of specific authorization. Establishment of general requirements to be met in determining customers' credit limits is an example of general authorization because no specific transaction (i.e., customer) is involved. Establishment of sales prices for products to be sold to any customer is another example of general authorization.

Approval is the acceptance of a transaction for processing after it is initiated. Approval comes after authorization and is used to detect unauthorized transactions and unauthorized activities. Approval is necessary to ensure that employees are operating within the realm of their authority.

Completeness and accuracy ensure the integrity of the data and information in the accounting system. Both completeness and accuracy are necessary to ensure a system whose information can be relied on. A wide range of transaction controls enhances completeness and reliability. Transaction controls are discussed later in a separate section.

INFORMATION AND COMMUNICATION

Information and communication comprise the fourth component of internal control. *Information* refers to the organization's **accounting system**, which consists of the methods and records established to identify, assemble, analyze, classify, record, and report the organization's transactions and to maintain accountability for the related assets and liabilities. The accounting system of an organization may be simple, or it may be complex. Many organizations have systems that are able to process huge numbers of various types of transactions. Information systems are designed and installed not only to produce the ledger balances from which financial statements are prepared but also to produce management control and operational information. Thus accounting systems and operational control are closely related in an organization.

DOCUMENTATION OF THE ACCOUNTING SYSTEM

Documentation of the accounting system is essential. Accounting procedures should be set forth in accounting procedure manuals so that policies and instructions may be known explicitly and applied uniformly. Well-designed forms should be used to report transactions. Subsidiary ledgers should be used to accumulate detailed information that is summarized in the general ledger. A chart of accounts containing detailed descriptions of the meanings and uses of accounts in the general ledger should be maintained and revised as necessary. A chart of accounts will aid in the consistent application of accounting policies, ensure proper recording of transactions, and facilitate the preparation of financial statements. Control accounts should be used extensively because they are a proof of accuracy between the account balances of duly segregated employees in a double-entry system of accounting.

DOUBLE-ENTRY SYSTEM OF ACCOUNTING

An accounting system should contain features that readily confirm or question the reliability of recorded data. Double-entry systems of accounting should not be underestimated as a device that will produce a balanced set of records. To conceal an irregularity under a double-entry system, it is necessary to omit from the accounts both sides of the transaction or to record entries offsetting the amount of the irregularity. Errors can be made under a double-entry system, however; the system alone will not prove omission, incorrect entry, or dishonesty.

Audit Trail   The term *audit trail* originates with the concept of an external auditor who is asked to express an opinion on the financial statements of an organization. An **audit trail** exists if a financial total that appears in a general ledger account can be supported by evidence concerning all the individual transactions that comprise that total and vice versa. If an audit trail exists, the auditor can be confident that the accounting information system and related financial statements are very reliable; that is, the system and its outputs are accurate. If an audit trail does not exist, then the reliability of the accounting information system must be suspect.

The audit trail concept is basic to the design and audit of an accounting information system and is relevant to internal auditors, management, systems analysts, and other parties involved in the operation of an accounting information system. An audit trail consists of the documentary evidence of the various control techniques that a transaction was subject to during its processing. Each transaction should be subjected to a set of control techniques that in total provides a sufficient degree of assurance that the transaction was processed accurately and reliably. The nature of the documentary evidence that comprises the audit trail will depend on the technology of the system and also on the design of the system. Audit trails do not have an independent existence—they are a consideration that must be included in the design of an accounting information system. That is particularly true in computer-based systems.

COMMUNICATION

Communication relates to providing a clear understanding regarding all policies and procedures relating to controls. Good communication requires effective oral communication, adequate procedure manuals, policy manuals, and other types of documentation.

Effective communication also requires an adequate upstream flow of information in the organization. Such information is used for performance reviews, exception reports, and so on.

MONITORING

Monitoring, the fifth component of internal control, involves the ongoing process of assessing the quality of internal controls over time and taking corrective actions when necessary. The quality of controls might be adversely affected in various ways, including a lack of compliance, changing conditions, or even misunderstandings.

Monitoring is accomplished through ongoing activities, separate evaluations, or some combination of the two. Ongoing activities would include management supervisory activities and other actions that personnel might take to ensure an ongoing effective internal control process.

An internal audit function is common in large organizations to monitor and evaluate controls on an ongoing basis. The expanded span of control and the growth in the volume of transactions associated with large organizations were factors in the emergence of the internal audit function. The increased reliance on accounting data that is necessary in management of a large organization, coupled with the increased possibilities of defalcations and improperly maintained accounting records in a large organization, has created the need for continuous auditing. The objective of the internal audit function is to serve management by furnishing management with the results of analysis and appraisals of such activities and systems as

- The organization's information systems
- The organization's internal control structure
- The extent of compliance to operating policies, procedures, and plans
- The quality of performance by company personnel

As indicated, the scope of auditing activity undertaken by a modern internal audit function is broader than just the financial activities of the organization. The terms **management audit** and **operational audit** describe internal audit services to management that extend beyond the financial activities of the organization. The existence of an effective internal audit function does not substitute for the external auditor, although internal audit may be of assistance to the external auditor in arranging and accumulating audit evidence.

The internal audit function has no less of a need for independence than the external auditor, but the nature of independence is different. The external auditor must be independent of the organization, for his or her opinion is given to third parties (e.g., banks, stockholders, etc.). The internal auditor cannot be independent of the organization, but he or she must be independent from management of the activities being reviewed. This can be accomplished by having the internal audit function report to the organization's audit committee.

External auditors may participate in monitoring controls. For example, it is common practice for external auditors to provide lists of specific recommendations for management to improve internal control.

TRANSACTION PROCESSING CONTROLS

Transaction processing controls are procedures designed to ensure that elements of an organization's internal control process are implemented in the specific applications systems contained within each of an organization's transaction cycles. Transaction processing controls consist of general controls and application controls. **General controls** affect all transaction processing. **Application controls** are specific to individual applications.

GENERAL CONTROLS

General controls concern the overall environment of transaction processing. General controls comprise the following:

- The plan of data processing organization
- General operating procedures
- Equipment control features
- Equipment and data-access controls

General controls are not a substitute for application controls. It is possible to have relatively strong general controls with relatively weak or nonexistent application controls.

General controls thus may be seen as necessary but not sufficient for adequate control of transaction processing.

A plan of organization for data processing includes provision for segregation of duties within data processing and the organizational segregation of data processing from other operations. General operating procedures include written manuals and other documentation that specify procedures to be followed. Equipment control features are those that are installed in computers to identify incorrect data handling or erroneous operation of the equipment. Equipment and data-access controls involve procedures related to physical access to the computer system and data. There should be adequate procedures to protect equipment and data files from damage or theft.

THE PLAN OF DATA PROCESSING ORGANIZATION AND OPERATION

Segregation of Duties   Responsibility for authorization, custody, and record keeping for handling and processing of transactions are separated.

EXAMPLE: The computer librarian function maintains a depository of computer programs and documentation but does not have access to or authority to operate the computer processing equipment.

Segregation of Duties in Data Processing   Computer data processing functions should be centralized. Computer data processing should have neither custody nor authority over any assets other than the data processing assets.

EXAMPLE: Departments that are responsible for the custody of inventories should not report to the vice president of computer data processing.

It is also desirable to segregate the following personnel functions associated with computer processing within the data processing department.

- *Systems analysts.*   Systems analysts are responsible for development of the general design of computer system applications. Systems analysts work with users to define their specific information requirements.
- *Programmers.*   Computer programmers develop the programs that produce computer output. They design and code newly developed computer programs based on specifications provided by systems analysts.
- *Computer operators.*   Computer operators operate the mainframe computer equipment. They should not have access to detailed program listings in order to maintain a segregation of functions between programming and operations.
- *Librarian.*   The librarian function maintains a depository of computer programs and documentation. This function is responsible for the custody of information assets.
- *Data control clerks.*   Data control clerks establish control over jobs and input data for processing. This includes consideration of the quality of input, the completeness of processing, and the reasonableness of output.

General Operating Procedures

Definition of Responsibilities: Descriptions of tasks for each job function within a transaction processing system. Beginning and termination points for each job function should be clearly indicated, as should the relationship of job functions to each other.

Example: The computer operator has restricted access to programs and data files.

Reliability of Personnel: Personnel performing the processing may be relied on to function in a consistent manner.

Example: The supervisor of computer operations has a good attendance record and a good performance record.

Training of Personnel: Personnel are provided explicit instructions and tested on their understanding before being assigned new duties.

Example: All new programmers attend a 5-day training seminar before beginning duties.

Competence of Personnel: Persons assigned to processing or supervisory roles in transaction processing systems have the technical knowledge necessary to perform their functions.

Example: The director of data processing is an MBA.

Rotation of Duties: Jobs assigned to people are rotated periodically at irregularly scheduled times, if possible, for key processing functions.

Example: Responsibility for the destruction of sensitive data is rotated among clerical personnel.

Forms Design: Forms are constructed to be self-explanatory, understandable, and concise and to gather all necessary information with a minimum of effort.

Example: The form to authorize a purchase has clear and concise instructions for each field in which data are to be entered.

Prenumbered Forms: Sequential numbers on individual forms are printed in advance to allow subsequent detection of loss or misplacement.

Example: Checks are prenumbered.

Preprinted Forms: Fixed elements of information are entered on forms in advance and sometimes in a format that permits direct machine processing to prevent errors in entry of repetitive data.

Example: MICR account encoding on checks and deposit tickets.

Simultaneous Preparation: The one-time recording of a transaction for all further processing, using multiple copies, as appropriate, to prevent transcription errors.

Example: A one-write system is used to prepare a receiving report form and receiving register simultaneously.

Turnaround Document: A computer-produced document that is intended for resubmission into the system.

Example: The part of a utility bill that the customer returns with payment.

Documentation: Written records for the purpose of providing communication.

Example: Standard journal entries communicate the accounting data to be supplied by various operating departments.

Labeling: The identification of transactions, files, or other items for control purposes.

Example: All computer files have an external label.

Equipment Control Features

Backup and Recovery: Backup consists of file equipment and procedures that are available if the originals are destroyed or out of service. Recovery is the ability to re-create master files using prior files and transactions.

Example: Master files and transaction files are maintained after the creation of an updated master file in case the current master file is corrupted.

Transaction Trail: The availability of a manual or machine-readable means for tracing the status and contents of an individual transaction record backward or forward and between output, processing, and source.

Example: A list of changes to on-line computer files is stored on magnetic tape to provide a transaction trail.

Error-source Statistics: Accumulation of information on the type of error and origin. This is used to determine the nature of remedial efforts needed to reduce the number of errors.

Example: The data input supervisor collects and reviews statistics on input errors made by clerks.

Equipment and Data-Access Controls

Secure Custody: Information assets are provided security similar to tangible assets such as cash, negotiable securities, and the like.

Example: The general ledger master file is locked in a safe each night.

Dual Access/Dual Control: Two independent, simultaneous actions or conditions are required before processing is permitted.

Example: A safe deposit box for sensitive computer files requires two keys to open it.

APPLICATION CONTROLS

Application controls are specific to individual applications. Application controls are categorized into input, processing, and output controls. These categories correspond to the basic steps in the data processing cycle.

INPUT CONTROLS

Input controls are designed to prevent or detect errors in the input stage of data processing. When computers are used for processing, the input stage involves the conversion of transaction data into a machine-readable format. Typical input controls include the following items:

Authorization: Limits the initiation of a transaction or performance of a process to selected individuals.

Example: Only the timekeeper may submit payroll hours data for processing.

Approval: The acceptance of a transaction for processing after it is initiated.

Example: An officer of the company approves the payroll before it is distributed to employees.

Formatted Input: Automatic spacing and format shifting of data fields during data input to a recording device.

Example: The computer automatically inserts commas into the numbers that are input by clerks using data terminals.

Endorsement: The marking of a form or document to direct or restrict its further processing.

Example: Checks are restrictively endorsed "Pay only to the order of ABC Company" immediately on receipt.

Cancellation: Identifies transaction documents in order to prevent their further or repeated use after they have performed their function.

Example: Marking bills as "paid" to prevent duplicate payment.

Exception Input: Processing proceeds in a predefined manner unless specific input transactions are received that indicate special processing with different values or in a different sequence.

Example: Overtime hours are input on special forms.

Passwords: The authorization to allow access to data or processing by providing a code or signal known only by authorized individuals.

Example: An automatic bank terminal requires that a user enter his or her password before processing is initiated.

Anticipation: The expectation of a given transaction or event at a particular time.

Example: Daily cash deposits are always made at 3:00 P.M.

Transmittal Document (Batch Control Ticket): The medium for communicating control totals over movement of data, particularly from source to processing point or between processing points.

Example: Daily cash deposits are accompanied by a deposit slip that indicates the total amount of the deposit.

Batch Serial Numbers (Batch Sequence): Batches of transaction documents are numbered consecutively and accounted for.

Example: Sales tickets are batched daily, numbered, and filed by date.

Control Register (Batch Control Log): A log or register indicating the disposition and control values of batches of transactions.

Example: A register is used to record the time and batch control number of express mail that is picked up by courier services.

Amount Control Total: Totals of homogeneous amounts for a group of transactions or records, usually dollars or quantities.

Example: Total net pay is an amount control total for a payroll processing application.

Document Control Total: A count of the number of individual documents.

Example: A count of the number of time cards is a document control total for a payroll application.

Line Control Count: A count of the number of lines of data on one or more documents.

Example: A count of the number of individual products sold (i.e., a line) on invoices is a line control count for a sales order application.

Hash Total: A meaningless total that is useful for control purposes only.

Example: Total department number of all paychecks processed is a meaningless total that is useful for control purposes only.

Batch Control (Batch Totals): Any type of control total or count applied to a specific number of transaction documents or to the transaction documents that arrive within a specific period of time.

Example: Total sales dollars is a batch control total for a billing application.

Visual Verification: The visual scanning of documents for general reasonableness and propriety.

Example: Clerks visually scan each invoice before submitting the document for further processing.

Sequence Checking: A verification of the alphanumeric sequence of the "key" field in items to be processed.

Example: Prenumbered checks are sorted in sequence for further processing.

Overflow Checks: A limit check on the capacity of a field, file, or device.

Example: The number 12345 cannot be entered into a four-digit, numeric field.

Format Check: Determination that data are entered in proper mode—numeric or alphabetic—in fields.

Example: Vendor number is checked to ensure that all characters in the field are numeric.

Completeness Check: A test that ensures that fields cannot be processed in a blank state.

Example: A voucher will not be processed if the "vendor number" field is blank.

Check Digit: A digit that is a function of the other digits within a record or number used for testing an accurate transcription.

Example: An account number contains a check digit that is validated during processing.

Reasonableness Test: Tests applied to various fields of data through comparison with other information available within the transaction or master records.

Example: A male patient should not be billed for services by the gynecology department of a hospital.

Limit Check: A test to ensure that only data within predetermined limits will be entered into and accepted by the system.

Example: A test ensures that rate per hour cannot be lower than the minimum set by law or higher than the maximum set by union contract.

Validity Check: The characters in a coded field are either matched to an acceptable set of values in a table or examined for a defined pattern of format, legitimate subcodes, or character values, using logic and arithmetic other than tables.

Example: All Social Security numbers should have nine numeric digits.

Readback: Immediate return of input information to the sender for comparison and approval.

Example: A computer echoes messages received from a data terminal back to the terminal for visual verification.

Dating: The recording of calendar dates for purposes of later comparison or expiration testing.

Example: Customer remittances are stamped with the date received.

Expiration: A limit check based on a comparison of current date with the date recorded on a transaction, record, or file.

Example: Checks to vendors are dated and marked "void after 60 days."

Key Verification: Reentry of transaction data with machine comparison of the initial entry to the second entry to detect errors.

Example: A second clerk keys payroll into a computer. The computer compares this input, character by character (i.e., key by key) to the initial input of the data by the first clerk and reports differences.

PROCESSING CONTROLS

Processing controls are designed to provide assurances that processing has occurred according to intended specifications and that no transactions have been lost or incorrectly inserted into the processing stream. Typical processing controls include the following items.

Mechanization: Consistency is provided by mechanical or electronic processing.

Example: Cash deposits are totaled by adding machine.

Standardization: Uniform, structured, and consistent procedures are developed for all processing.

Example: A chart of accounts documents the normal debits and credits to each account.

Default Option: The automatic use of a pre-defined value in situations where input transactions have certain values left blank.

Example: Salaried employees receive pay for 40 hours each week.

Batch Balancing: A comparison of the items or documents actually processed against a predetermined control total.

Example: The cashier batch balances deposit tickets to control totals of cash remittances.

Run-to-Run Totals: The use of output control totals resulting from one process as input control totals over subsequent processing. The control totals are used as links in a chain to tie one process to another in a sequence of processes over a period of time.

Example: Beginning accounts payable balance less payments plus net purchases should equal ending accounts payable balance.

Balancing: A test for equality between the values of two equivalent sets of items or one set of items and a control total. Any difference indicates an error.

Example: The balance of the accounts receivable subsidiary ledger should equal the balance of the general ledger control account.

Matching: Matching items with other items received from independent sources to control the processing of transactions.

Example: The accounts payable clerk matches vendor invoices to purchase orders and receiving reports.

Clearing Account: An amount that results from the processing of independent items of equivalent value. Net control value should equal zero.

Example: The imprest payroll checking account has a zero balance after all paychecks have been cashed.

Tickler File: A control file consisting of items sequenced by age for processing or follow-up purposes.

Example: Invoices are filed by due date.

Redundant Processing: A repetition of processing and an accompanying comparison of individual results for equality.

Example: A second payroll clerk computes the gross and net pay of each employee for comparison purposes.

Summary Processing: A redundant process using a summarized amount. This is compared for equality with a control total from the processing of the detailed items.

Example: Total overhead applied to production is recomputed by applying the overhead rate to the total amount of direct labor cost charged for all jobs.

Trailer Label: A record providing a control total for comparison with accumulated counts or values of records processed.

Example: The last record of an inventory file contains a record count of the number of records in the file.

Automated Error Correction: Automatic error correction of transactions or records that violate a detective control.

Example: A credit memo is automatically generated when customers overpay their account balances.

OUTPUT CONTROLS

Output controls are designed to check that input and processing resulted in valid output and that outputs are distributed properly. Typical output controls include the following items:

Reconciliation: An identification and analysis of differences between the values contained in two substantially identical files or between a detail file and a control total. Errors are identified according to the nature of the reconciling items rather than the existence of a difference between the balances.

Example: The bank reconciliation identifies service charges and fees on the monthly bank statement that have not yet been recorded in the company's accounts.

Aging: Identification of unprocessed or retained items in files according to their date, usually the transaction date. The aging classifies items according to various ranges of duties.

Example: The aging of accounts receivable balances to identify delinquent accounts.

Suspense File: A file containing unprocessed or partially processed items awaiting further action.

Example: A file of back-ordered items awaiting shipment to customers.

Suspense Account: A control total for items awaiting further processing.

Example: The total of the accounts receivable subsidiary ledger should equal the balance of the general ledger control account.

Periodic Audit: Periodic verification of a file or process to detect control problems.

Example: All customers are mailed monthly statements of account to confirm their balances.

Discrepancy Reports: A listing of items that have violated some detective control and require further investigation.

Example: A list of customer accounts that have exceeded their credit limit is sent to the credit manager for review.

Upstream Resubmission: The resubmission of corrected error transactions backwards (i.e., upstream) in the flow of transaction processing so that they pass through all or more of the detective controls that are exercised over normal transactions.

Example: Rejected transactions are resubmitted as a special batch as if they were new transactions.

PREVENTATIVE, DETECTIVE, AND CORRECTIVE CONTROLS

Transaction processing controls also may be classified as being primarily preventative, detective, or corrective in nature. **Preventative controls** act to prevent errors and fraud before they happen. **Detective controls** act to uncover errors and fraud after they have occurred. **Corrective controls** act to correct errors.

Many detective controls apply to both the input and processing stages of transaction processing. An example is the batch control total procedures used in an insurance company. Each day's incoming premium payments (checks) are grouped into batches of 50 checks; a clerk totals and records the dollar amount of the 50 checks. Then the batches of checks are given to a data conversion operator, who keys the check data into the computer by batch. A printout of the batch totals from the computer is then compared with the totals recorded by the clerk. Discrepancies are immediately uncovered and traced back, usually to mistakes by either the clerk or operator or both. This control procedure affects both the input and processing steps and is illustrated in a manual system in Figure 4.7.

The general ledger clerk compares the totals at point A in the figure with the totals at point B. Notice how the concept of segregation of duties is employed. An output detective control is simply a procedure to compare output totals with the control totals generated at the input and processing steps.

Classification of the general and application controls discussed here as preventative, detective, or corrective in nature is shown in the applications control matrix in Figure 4.9.

COMMUNICATING THE OBJECTIVES OF INTERNAL CONTROL

Internal control must be seen not as a process unto itself but as part of a larger process. It must fit in, or it may be totally ineffective or perhaps even harmful. One must not lose sight of what the purpose of internal control is.

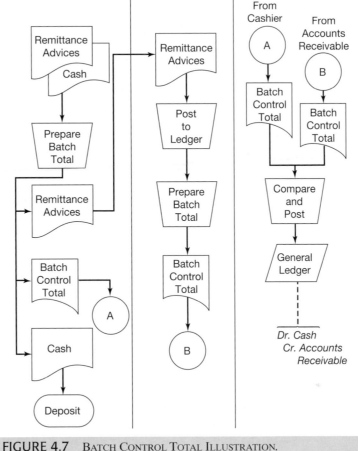

FIGURE 4.7   BATCH CONTROL TOTAL ILLUSTRATION.

People are an essential element in every internal control process. People are not perfect; they commit errors of omission and commission. If people were perfect, internal control would be an unnecessary waste of resources. Internal control is people. An internal control process consists of people checking the work of other people. The principal function of internal control is to influence the behavior of people in a business system.

There is a paradox inherent in a system of internal control. Controls such as rules and procedures are imposed on people who ideally, from a more humanistic view, should be responsible for their own self-control and self-direction. This inconsistency must be dealt with in every organizational control system.

Management's job is to ensure the efficiency of operations. Thus behaviors and activities need to be organized and controlled so that the organization's goals are attained. A system of internal control does interfere to some extent with an individual's self-control. By promoting the interests and safeguarding the assets of the overall organization, however, a system of internal control is really protecting the interest and integrity of each individual employee who is a part of that organization.

The objectives of internal control must be seen as relevant to the individuals who will comprise the control system. The system must be designed such that each employee is convinced that controls are meant to prevent difficulties or crises in the operation of the organization that otherwise could affect him or her very personally.

GOALS AND BEHAVIOR PATTERNS

An information system has several goals; chief among them is productivity. Reliability of information and the safeguarding of assets are also important goals. These goals are at times contradictory. Productivity in an information system is often constrained by the consideration of reliability. Controls are redundant. They constrain productivity but increase the reliability of resulting outputs. This conflict between internal controls and productivity must be acknowledged and carefully considered by the analyst because it may influence the behavior of people in a control system.

A common behavior caused by this goal conflict is the omission of an internal control duty (such as counting documents) in the interest of increasing production. Consider a clerk manually posting invoices. If the clerk double-checks each posting, the number of postings is approximately 50% of what would have been performed without double-checking. If the clerk's performance is evaluated by postings per time period, there will be a temptation to omit the double-checking for at least some items if the clerk falls behind schedule. Internal control duties typically require a tradeoff with production. The basic motivational problem is that productivity is usually measurable and forms the basis for performance evaluation, whereas reliability and degree of internal control are not as easily measured or incorporated into performance reviews. The systems analyst should keep this in mind in designing and evaluating internal controls.

The goals of an internal control system are achieved through the actions of the people in the system. The reliance on a formal plan of organization and related methods and measures to attain these goals entails important assumptions concerning collusion, reporting of irregularities, power relationships, and other behavior patterns within the organization. Organizational independence and segregation of duties are consistent with good internal control only if the probability of collusion between two or more duly segregated employees is low.

Collusion is agreement or conspiracy among two or more people to commit fraud. In a purchase procedure, control over acquisitions is obtained when duly segregated personnel from both receiving and stores acknowledge that the materials have been received by stores. Both must sign for the material, and neither could deceive the other without collusion or fraud. Of course, errors of omission are possible, such as both parties miscounting quantities. In fact, the same error (a shortage) could occur unintentionally as well as intentionally. However, if unintentional, the error would not be covered up, and other controls probably would uncover the discrepancy.

Justification for the assumption that the probability of collusion between two or more people will be low is found in the formal plan of organization. For one individual to suggest an irregularity to another person and be rejected would entail prohibitive costs to the first individual. He or she will be turned in by the second individual and hence lose his or her job or incur another punishment. This entails a related assumption that employees will always report irregularities to those higher up in the organization. This assumption, in turn, requires several others. One is that the formal plan of organization as denoted in procedures manuals and the like solely determines power relations in a system. A related assumption is that actions not specified by a system are dysfunctional or "wrong"; that is, deviations suggest irregularities that should be reported to those higher up.

Numerous factors influence an individual's behavior in a control system. One important influence is the formal plan of organization and the related methods and measures employed by an organization. Other factors do exist, however. Groups and other sources of informal pressure bear on an individual's behavior and may at times mitigate the desired, formally planned relationships between people in the system. For example, an individual with lengthy service may convince a young coworker that the omission of a control step is okay and need not be reported, because "it's been done that way in the past."

A receiving clerk transferring goods to inventory may convince the inventory clerk just to sign and not waste time counting the items she or he is receiving. A clerk performing a bank reconciliation may not examine several checks in detail because it is near quitting time.

What might be called "people failure" is the source of all theft and fraud in a system and is a prime contributor to serious errors of the production type and other ineffectiveness and inefficiency. In cases of defalcations, "the procedures did not fail, the people did." The variety and complexity of human behavior and the value constraints (principles of just, humane, compassionate conduct) we work within combine to make the production of "people-proof" procedures infeasible. As long as people have access to valuables, there will be the possibility of theft, sabotage, and serious error. These possibilities are minimized when employees fully understand, accept, and internalize the objectives of the internal control system of which they are the essential element.

ANALYSIS OF INTERNAL CONTROL PROCESSES

The analysis of an internal control process requires an understanding of the process both as it is designed and as it actually operates. The actual process may or may not conform to expectations. Documentation may be outdated, and the structure may be operating under new procedures. Procedures may have changed informally to adapt to circumstances not foreseen when the original system was designed and documented.

Internal control processes routinely collect information concerning fulfillment of duties, transfer of authority, approval, and verification. This documentation of internal control duties must be examined to evaluate the reliability of the system's operation.

Reliability depends on the people who administer internal control procedures. Designing an internal control process is only the first part of the problem; it is essential that internal control duties are actually performed as prescribed.

There are several reasons why internal control duties may not be administered. New employees or perhaps even experienced employees may not understand their duties. More common is the omission of an internal control duty (such as counting documents) in order to increase production.

ANALYTIC TECHNIQUES

The **internal control questionnaire** is a common analytic technique used in internal control analysis. Internal control questionnaires traditionally have been a central element in an audit program; accordingly, questionnaires are a standard form in public accounting firms, internal audit departments, and other organizations that are regularly involved in reviews of internal controls. Questionnaires are available for the review of specific application areas as well as for special reviews such as computer center audits. At times, the analyst may design a questionnaire specifically for a particular audit, or she or he may modify a standard questionnaire to better suit the needs or nature of a particular audit. Questionnaires usually are designed so that an affirmative answer to a question indicates an adequate degree of internal control, and a negative answer indicates the need for further information or a potential weakness in the structure.

However, a negative answer does not always indicate a weakness because other controls may compensate for the omission identified by the negative response. Questionnaires are essentially checklists to ensure that a review does not omit an area of major importance. Figure 4.8 illustrates a portion of a questionnaire for sales and shipping procedures.

Questionnaires are only tools; the manner in which they are used is extremely important. The questionnaire should be filled in on the basis of actual observations and

Sales and Shipping

1. Are sales orders adequately controlled?
2. Are all orders approved by the credit manager or department before shipment?
3. Is the credit department entirely independent of the sales department?
4. Are sales prices and credit terms based on approved standard price lists?
5. If so, are any deviations from standard approved
    a. by an officer?
    b. by another? Explain.
6. If not, are all sales prices and credit terms approved by the sales manager or in the sales department?
7. Are prenumbered shipping advices prepared for all goods shipped?
8. Are the quantities shown on the shipping advices double-checked in the shipping department?
9. Does the billing clerk or some other designated employee receive the shipping advices directly from the shipping department? (If so, identify this employee.)
10. Does this employee check the numerical sequence of shipping advices to assure that all are accounted for?
11. Are sales invoices checked
    a. as to prices?
    b. as to quantities?
    c. as to credit terms?
    d. as to extensions and footings?
    e. against customers' orders?
    f. against shipping advices?
    (Identify the department or individual responsible for the above.)
12. Are sales invoices prenumbered?
13. Is there a check on the arithmetical accuracy of total sales by means of a statistical or product analysis?
14. Are total sales for the respective accounting periods (e.g., monthly) reported directly to the general ledger bookkeeper independently of the work of the accounts receivable bookkeepers?
15. Are there adequate safeguards against understatement of sales through the suppression of sales invoices or shipping advices?
16. Are returned sales cleared through the receiving department (i.e., the department receiving incoming purchased materials and supplies)?
17. Are credit memos for returned sales supported by adequate data from the receiving department as to quantity, description, and condition?
18. Are the following classes of sales accounted for in substantially the same manner as regular credit sales of merchandise:
    a. Sales to employees?
    b. C.O.D. sales?
    c. Sales of property and equipment?
    d. Cash sales of merchandise?
    e. Scrap and waste?
    (If the answers are negative in any case, amplify by a concise description of the procedures.)
19. Is there an adequate check on freight allowances
    a. by reference to terms of sale?
    b. by checking against freight bills or established and up-to-date schedule of freight rates?
    c. Other? (If any, explain.)
    Comment on adequacy of internal control.

FIGURE 4.8 PORTION OF AN INTERNAL CONTROL QUESTIONNAIRE.

inquiries. But filling in the questionnaire is not the essence of the review. The essence of a review is the analyst's analysis of his or her findings. Questionnaires do serve as documentation that a review was undertaken; however, questionnaires are necessarily standardized and therefore are not equally applicable in all circumstances. Their use often must be supplemented with other forms of analysis, such as write-ups, flowcharts, or other charting techniques.

Analytic flowcharts might be used in internal control analysis, particularly if the analysis involves a computer system application. Flowcharting itself is not a form of structured analysis but rather a technique to organize data for analysis. An **application controls matrix** provides a structured form of analysis that is particularly relevant to internal control reviews of information systems. The rows of the matrix consist of various

Transaction/Process

Control Feature

Characteristics that Constitute Controls

PREVENTIVE CONTROLS

Reliability of personnel
Segregation of duties
Definition of responsibilities
Rotation of duties
Training of personnel
Competence of personnel
Secure custody
Dual access/dual controls
Standardization
Mechanization
Forms design
Prenumbered forms
Precoded forms
Authorization
Endorsement
Cancellation
Simultaneous preparation
Documentation
Formatted input

DETECTIVE CONTROLS

Accountability of Input

Anticipation
Transmittal documents
Batch serial numbers
Control register

Completeness of Input

Amount control total
Document control total
Line control count
Hash total
Batch totals
Batch balancing
Visual verification
Turnaround document
Passwords

Correctness of Input

Format
Completeness check

Check digits
Reasonableness
Limit check
Validity check
Read back
Dating
Expiration
Keystroke verification
Approval
Exception input
Default option
Labeling

Completeness of Processing

Run to run totals
Balancing
Reconciliation
Aging
Suspense file
Suspense account
Matching
Clearing account
Tickler file
Periodic audit
Activity log

Correctness of Processing

Redundant processing
Summary processing
Sequence checking
Overflow checks
Scan before distribution
Trailer label

CORRECTIVE CONTROLS

Discrepancy reports
Transaction trail
Error source statistics
Automatic error correction
Upstream resubmission
Backup and recovery

FIGURE 4.9 APPLICATION CONTROLS MATRIX.

control techniques. The columns of the matrix consist of activities or data values in the system under review. The matrix organization provides a structured method for the systematic evaluation of each activity or data item with respect to each type of control activity listed in the rows. Figure 4.9 illustrates an application controls matrix that is preprinted with a comprehensive list of controls. An application controls matrix can be designed as needed in any specific situation by providing one's own list of controls as the rows of the matrix.

To use the matrix, the analyst identifies the activities or data items that should be subject to control and lists them as the columns of the matrix. A matrix can be used systematically to evaluate an analytic or other type of flowchart by listing the sequence of operations shown in the chart as the columns of the matrix. Each row/column contribution of control/activity or control/data items can then be evaluated systematically. The analyst might enter an X or other symbol in each row/column box where a control existed and/or was performed, leaving blank those combinations that were absent. Another technique would be to rate the strength or relative reliability of each present control/activity combination by assigning numbers or letters to indicate relative strength or reliability. A 1 might indicate highly reliable, a 3 reliable, a 5 functioning but not reliable, and so on.

ILLUSTRATION OF AN INTERNAL CONTROL ANALYSIS

Many professional examinations, such as the Certificate in Public Accounting (CPA) examination and the Certified Internal Auditor (CIA) examination, test a candidate's knowledge of internal controls by requiring the candidate to evaluate potential control structure weaknesses that are evident in a narrative or graphic (flowchart) description of an application system. The candidate is usually required to do the control analysis solely on the basis of analytic reasoning. That is, questionnaires or other analytic aids, such as the applications controls matrix discussed previously, are not provided for the candidate's use. In such a case, the candidate must carefully evaluate the described system and, with the professional definition of internal control structures as a reference, identify potential control weaknesses through analytical reasoning.

As an illustration, following is a CPA examination question in which one is expected to evaluate internal controls in the manner just described. The published unofficial answer immediately follows the question.

> The Art Appreciation Society operates a museum for the benefit and enjoyment of the community. During hours when the museum is open to the public, two clerks who are positioned at the entrance collect a five dollar admission fee from each nonmember patron. Members of the Art Appreciation Society are permitted to enter free of charge upon presentation of their membership cards.
>
> At the end of each day one of the clerks delivers the proceeds to the treasurer. The treasurer counts the cash in the presence of the clerk and places it in a safe. Each Friday afternoon the treasurer and one of the clerks deliver all cash held in the safe to the bank, and receive an authenticated deposit slip which provides the basis for the weekly entry in the cash receipts journal.
>
> The Board of Directors of the Art Appreciation Society has identified a need to improve their system of internal control over cash admission fees. The Board had determined that the cost of installing turnstiles, sales booths, or otherwise altering the physical layout of the museum will greatly exceed any benefits that may be derived. However, the Board has agreed that the sale of admission tickets must be an integral part of its improvement efforts.
>
> Smith has been asked by the Board of Directors of the Art Appreciation Society to review the internal control over cash admission fees and provide suggestions for improvement.

Required   Indicate weaknesses in the existing system of internal control over cash admission fees, which Smith should identify, and recommend one improvement for each of the weaknesses identified.

Organize the answer as indicated in the following illustrative example:

Weaknesses	*Recommended Improvements*
1. There is no basis for establishing the documentation of the number of paying patrons.	1. Prenumbered admission tickets should be issued upon payment of the admission fee.

Unofficial Answer

Weaknesses	*Recommended Improvements*
1. There is no segregation of duties between persons responsible for collecting admission fees and persons responsible for authorizing admission.	1. One clerk (hereafter referred to as the collection clerk) should collect admission fees and issue prenumbered tickets. The other clerk (hereafter referred to as the admission clerk) should authorize admission upon receipt of the ticket or proof of membership.
2. An independent count of paying patrons is not made.	2. The admission clerk should retain a portion of the prenumbered admission ticket (admission ticket stub).
3. There is no proof of amounts collected by the clerks.	3. Admission ticket stubs should be reconciled with cash collected by the treasurer each day.
4. Cash receipts records are not promptly prepared.	4. The cash collections should be recorded by the collection clerk daily on a permanent record that will serve as the first record of accountability.
5. Cash receipts are not promptly deposited. Cash should not be left undeposited for a week.	5. Cash should be deposited at least once each day.
6. There is no proof of accuracy of amounts deposited.	6. Authenticated deposit slips should be compared with daily cash collection Discrepancies should be recorded, promptly investigated and resolved. In addition, the treasurer should establish a policy that includes an analytical review of cash collections.
7. There is no record of the internal accountability for cash.	7. The treasurer should issue a signed receipt for all proceeds received from the collection clerk. These receipts should be maintained and periodically checked against cash collection and deposit records.

(CPA)

❖ SUMMARY

Controls are needed to reduce exposures. An organization is subject to a variety of exposures that can have an adverse effect on its operations or even its very existence as a viable going concern. Many aspects of computer processing tend to significantly increase an organization's exposure to undesirable events. The analysis of exposures in an organization is often related to the transaction cycle concept. Management should develop detailed control objectives for each transaction cycle.

An entity's internal control process consists of the policies and procedures established to provide reasonable assurance that the following entity objectives will be achieved: (1) reliability of financial reporting, (2) effectiveness and efficiency of operations, and (3) compliance with applicable laws and regulations. An internal control process consists of five components: the control environment, risk assessment, control activities, information and communication, and monitoring. Controls can be classified as either general controls or application controls. A standard method of classifying application controls is by considering whether a given control applies to inputs, processing, or outputs. This chapter discussed and illustrated a variety of common control practices.

Ethical considerations must be addressed in the design of an internal control structure. People are an essential element in every internal control structure. It is important that the objectives of internal control be communicated and understood. The objectives of internal control must be seen as relevant to the individuals who will comprise the control system.

The analysis of an internal control structure requires an understanding of the structure both as it is designed and as it actually operates. The most common analytical technique used in internal control analysis is the internal control questionnaire. Analytic flowcharts are also useful in internal control analysis.

❖ GLOSSARY

accounting system: the methods and records established to identify, assemble, analyze, classify, record, and report the organization's transactions and to maintain accountability for the related assets and liabilities.

aging: identification of unprocessed or retained items in files according to their date, usually the transaction date.

amount control total: totals of homogeneous amounts for a group of transactions or records, usually dollars or quantities.

anticipation: the expectation of a given transaction or event at a particular time.

application controls: specific to individual applications.

application controls matrix: a structured form of analysis that utilizes a matrix of application controls.

approval: the acceptance of a transaction for processing after it is initiated.

audit committee: subcommittee of the board of directors that is charged with overall responsibility for the organization's financial reports.

audit trail: financial totals that appear in a general ledger account can be supported by evidence concerning all the individual transactions that comprise that total and vice versa.

authorization: limits the initiation of a transaction or performance of an activity to selected individuals.

batch control: any type of control total or count applied to a specific number of transaction documents or to the transaction documents that arrive within a specific period of time.

batch control log: synonym for control register.

batch control ticket: synonym for transmittal document.

batch sequence: synonym for batch serial numbers.

batch serial numbers: batches of transaction documents are numbered consecutively and accounted.

batch totals: synonym for batch control.

cancellation: identification of transaction documents in order to prevent their further or repeated use after they have performed their function.

clearing account: an amount that results from the processing of independent items of equivalent value. Net control value should equal zero.

collusion: agreement or conspiracy among two or more people to commit fraud.

control environment: the collective effect of various factors on establishing, enhancing, or mitigating the effectiveness of specific policies and procedures.

control procedures: the policies and procedures in addition to the control environment and accounting system that management has established to provide reasonable assurance that specific entity objectives will be achieved.

control register: a log or register indicating the disposition and control values of batches or transactions.

corporate crime: white-collar crime that benefits a company or organization, rather than the individuals who perpetrate the fraud.

corrective controls: act to correct errors.

detective controls: act to uncover errors and fraud after they have occurred.

document control total: a count of the number of individual documents.

dual control: the assignment of two individuals to perform the same work task in unison.

endorsement: the marking of a form or document so as to direct or restrict its further processing.

exposure: the potential financial effect of an event multiplied by its probability of occurrence.

fidelity bond: a contract with an insurance company that provides a financial guarantee of the honesty of the individual who is named in the bond contract.

forensic accounting: an activity concerned with preventing and detecting fraud.

fraudulent financial reporting: intentional or reckless conduct, whether by purposeful act or omission, that results in materially misleading financial statements.

general controls: affect all transaction processing.

hash total: a meaningless total that is useful for control purposes only.

input controls: designed to prevent or detect errors in the input stage of data processing.

internal accounting control: the plan of organization and the procedures and records that are concerned with the safeguarding of assets and reliability of financial statements.

internal control process: the policies and procedures established to provide reasonable assurance that the following entity objectives will be achieved: (a) effectiveness and efficiency of operations, (b) reliability of financial reporting, and (c) compliance with applicable laws and regulations.

internal control questionnaire: a set of questions pertaining to internal controls in an application area.

line control count: a count of the number of lines of data on one or more documents.

management audit: internal audit services to management that extend beyond the financial activities of the organization.

management fraud: diversion of assets or misrepresentation of assets by management.

operational audit: synonym for management audit.

output controls: designed to check that input and processing resulted in valid output and that outputs are properly distributed.

preventative controls: act to prevent errors and fraud before they happen.

processing controls: designed to provide assurances that processing has occurred according to intended specifications and that no transactions have been lost or incorrectly inserted into the processing stream.

reasonable assurance: principle that the costs of controls should not exceed their benefits.

responsibility: management and the board of directors are responsible for the internal control process.

risk: the probability of occurrence of an event.

run-to-run totals: the utilization of output control totals resulting from one process as input control totals over subsequent processing.

segregation of duties: responsibilities for authorization, custody, and record keeping for handling and processing of transactions are separated.

supervision: the direct monitoring of personnel performance by an employee who is so charged.

suspense account: a control total for items awaiting further processing.

suspense file: a file containing unprocessed or partially processed items awaiting further action.

tickler file: a control file consisting of items sequenced by age for processing or follow-up purposes.

transmittal document: the medium for communicating control totals over movement of data, particularly from source to processing point or between processing points.

upstream resubmission: the resubmission of corrected error transactions backward (i.e., upstream) in the flow of transaction processing so that they pass through all or more of the detective controls that are exercised over normal transactions.

white-collar crime: deceitful diversion of assets from proper use or deceitful misrepresentation of assets by an act or series of acts that are nonviolent in nature.

❖ CHAPTER QUIZ

Answers to the Chapter Quiz appear on page 154.

1. The potential negative financial effect of an event multiplied by its probability of occurrence is a(n) (_____).
   (a) control
   (b) exposure
   (c) hazard/
   (d) risk

2. Fraud that benefits a company or organization, rather than the individual(s) who perpetrate the fraud, is known as (_____).
   (a) white-collar crime
   (b) corporate crime
   (c) management fraud
   (d) fraudulent financial reporting

3. The responsibility for establishing and maintaining an internal control structure rests with (_____).
   (a) internal auditing
   (b) the treasurer
   (c) management
   (d) the controller

4. Which of the following is an element of an internal control process?
   (a) information and communication
   (b) reasonable assurance
   (c) internal audit function
   (d) management control methods

5. Which of the following limits the initiation of a transaction or performance of an activity to selected individuals?
   (a) authorization
   (b) approval
   (c) fidelity bond
   (d) audit trail

6. Computer master files and transaction files are maintained after the creation of an updated master file in case the current master file is corrupted. This is an example of (_____).
   (a) labeling procedures
   (b) recovery procedures
   (c) documentation procedures
   (d) secure custody

7. Marking bills as "paid" to prevent duplicate payment is an example of (_____).
   (a) cancellation
   (b) backup
   (c) approval
   (d) endorsement

8. A meaningless total that is useful for control purposes only is called a(n) (_____).
   (a) line control count
   (b) hash total
   (c) document control total
   (d) amount control total

9. An imprest payroll checking account has a zero balance after all paychecks have been cashed. This type of control practice is an example of a(n) (_____).
   (a) tickler file
   (b) upstream resubmission
   (c) redundant processing
   (d) clearing account

10. Agreement or conspiracy among two or more people to commit fraud is known as (_____).
    (a) dual control
    (b) complicity
    (c) intrigue
    (d) collusion

❖ REVIEW PROBLEM

The Fox Company, a client of your firm, has come to you with the following problem. It has three clerical employees who must perform the following functions:
(a) maintain general ledger
(b) maintain accounts payable ledger
(c) maintain accounts receivable ledger
(d) prepare checks for signature
(e) maintain cash disbursements journal
(f) issue credit memos on returns and allowances
(g) reconcile the bank account
(h) handle and deposit cash receipts

Assuming there is no problem as to the ability of any of the employees, the company requests that you assign these functions to the three employees to achieve the highest degree of internal control. Assume that these employees will perform no other accounting functions than the ones listed and that any accounting functions not listed will be performed by people other than these three employees.
(a) State how you would distribute these functions among the three employees. Assume that with the exception of the nominal jobs of the bank reconciliation and the issuance of credits on returns and allowances, all functions require an equal amount of time.
(b) List four possible unsatisfactory pairings of the listed functions.

(CPA)

❖ SOLUTION TO REVIEW PROBLEM

UNDESIRABLE COMBINATIONS ARE AS FOLLOWS:

1. Cash receipts and accounts receivable
2. Cash receipts and credit memos on sales returns and allowances
3. Cash disbursements and accounts payable
4. Cash receipts and bank reconciliation
5. Cash disbursements and bank reconciliation
6. Cash receipts and general ledger
7. Accounts receivable and credit memos on sales returns and allowances

ASSIGNMENT OF FUNCTIONS:

Employee no. 1:
(a) maintain general ledger
(f) issue credit memos on returns and allowances
(g) reconcile bank account

Employee no. 2:
(e) maintain cash disbursements journal
(d) prepare checks for signature
(h) handle and deposit cash receipts

Employee no. 3:
(b) maintain accounts payable ledger
(c) maintain accounts receivable ledger

❖ REVIEW QUESTIONS

1. Distinguish between risks and exposures.
2. Identify several common business exposures.
3. What is corporate crime?
4. What is management fraud?
5. Does computer processing increase an organization's exposure to undesirable events?
6. List the basic elements of an internal control process.
7. Distinguish between general controls and applications controls.
8. Why are written procedures manuals control tools?
9. Differentiate preventative, detective, and corrective controls. Give an example of each.
10. What is the purpose of a forced vacation policy?
11. What is batch control?
12. Why is collusion a problem in internal control design?
13. Why is it important that the purpose and nature of internal control be communicated to employees within an organization?
14. Discuss the statement "The procedures did not fail, the people did."
15. What role do physical security devices have in a system of internal control?
16. Why has the importance of the internal audit function continued to grow?
17. What are the functions of an audit committee?
18. Discuss the advantages and disadvantages of using a questionnaire or checklist in evaluating an internal control system.
19. Does filling out a questionnaire constitute an evaluation of internal controls?
20. What is an analytic flowchart? What is an applications control matrix?

❖ DISCUSSION QUESTIONS AND PROBLEMS

21. Internal accounting controls are not designed to provide reasonable assurance that
    (a) transactions are executed in accordance with management's authorization.
    (b) irregularities will be eliminated.
    (c) access to assets is permitted only in accordance with management's authorization.
    (d) the recorded accountability for assets is compared with the existing assets at reasonable intervals.

(CPA)

22. Internal control is a function of management, and effective control is based on the concept of charge and discharge of responsibility and duty. Which of the following is one of the overriding principles of internal control?
    (a) Responsibility for accounting and financial duties should be assigned to one responsible officer.
    (b) Responsibility for the performance of each duty must be fixed.
    (c) Responsibility for the accounting duties must be borne by the audit committee of the company.
    (d) Responsibility for accounting activities and duties must be assigned only to employees who are bonded.

    (CPA)

23. Effective internal control requires organizational independence of departments. Organizational independence would be impaired in which of the following situations?
    (a) The internal auditors report to the audit committee of the board of directors.
    (b) The controller reports to the vice president of production.
    (c) The payroll accounting department reports to the chief accountant.
    (d) The cashier reports to the treasurer.

    (CPA)

24. Transaction authorization within an organization may be either specific or general. An example of specific transaction authorization is the
    (a) setting of automatic reorder points for material or merchandise.
    (b) approval of a detailed construction budget for a warehouse.
    (c) establishment of requirements to be met in determining a customer's credit limits.
    (d) establishment of sales prices for products to be sold to any customer.

    (CPA)

25. A system of internal accounting control normally would include procedures that are designed to provide reasonable assurance that
    (a) employees act with integrity when performing their assigned tasks.
    (b) transactions are executed in accordance with management's general or specific authorization.
    (c) decision processes leading to management's authorization of transactions are sound.
    (d) collusive activities would be detected by segregation of employee duties.

    (CPA)

26. When considering internal control, an auditor must be aware of the concept of reasonable assurance that recognizes that
    (a) the employment of competent personnel provides assurance that the objectives of internal control will be achieved.
    (b) the establishment and maintenance of a system of internal control is an important responsibility of management, not of the auditor.
    (c) the cost of internal control should not exceed the benefits expected to be derived from internal control.
    (d) the segregation of incompatible functions is necessary to obtain assurance that the internal control is effective.

    (CPA)

27. Which of the following elements of an entity's internal control structure includes the development of personnel manuals documenting employee promotion and training policies?
    (a) control procedures
    (b) control environment
    (c) information and communication
    (d) quality control system

    (CPA adapted)

28. Which of the following statements about internal control structure is correct?
    (a) A properly maintained internal control process reasonably ensures that collusion among employees cannot occur.
    (b) The establishment and maintenance of the internal control structure is an important responsibility of the internal auditor.

(c) An exceptionally strong internal control structure is enough for the auditor to eliminate substantive tests on a significant account balance.

(d) The cost–benefit relationship is a primary criterion that should be considered in designing an internal control structure.

(CPA adapted)

29. Which of the following is not an element of an entity's internal control process?
    (a) control risk
    (b) control activities
    (c) information and communication
    (d) the control environment

(CPA adapted)

30. Employers bond employees who handle cash receipts because fidelity bonds reduce the possibility of employing dishonest individuals and
    (a) protect employees who make unintentional errors from possible monetary damages resulting from their errors.
    (b) deter dishonesty by making employees aware that insurance companies may investigate and prosecute dishonest acts.
    (c) facilitate an independent monitoring of the receiving and depositing of cash receipts.
    (d) force employees in positions of trust to take periodic vacations and rotate their assigned duties.

(CPA)

31. Proper segregation of functional responsibilities calls for separation of the
    (a) authorization, approval, and execution functions.
    (b) authorization, execution, and payment functions.
    (c) receiving, shipping, and custodial functions.
    (d) authorization, recording, and custodial functions.

(CPA)

32. A company holds bearer bonds as a short-term investment. Custody of these bonds and submission of coupons for interest payments normally is the responsibility of the
    (a) treasury function.
    (b) legal counsel.
    (c) general accounting function.
    (d) internal audit function.

(CPA)

33. Operating control of the check-signing machine normally should be the responsibility of the
    (a) general accounting function.
    (b) treasury function.
    (c) legal counsel.
    (d) internal audit function.

(CPA)

34. Internal control over cash receipts is weakened when an employee who receives customer mail receipts also
    (a) prepares initial cash receipts records.
    (b) records credits to individual accounts receivable.
    (c) prepares bank deposit slips for all mail receipts.
    (d) maintains a petty cash fund.

(CPA)

35. For good internal control, the monthly bank statements should be reconciled by someone under the direction of the
    (a) credit manager.
    (b) controller.
    (c) cashier.
    (d) treasurer.

(CPA)

36. For good internal control, the person who should sign checks is the
    (a) person preparing the checks.
    (b) purchasing agent.
    (c) accounts payable clerk.
    (d) treasurer.

    (CPA)

37. For good internal control, the credit manager should be responsible to the
    (a) sales manager.
    (b) customer service manager.
    (c) controller.
    (d) treasurer.

    (CPA)

38. The authorization for write-off of accounts receivable should be the responsibility of the
    (a) credit manager.
    (b) controller.
    (c) accounts receivable clerk.
    (d) treasurer.

    (CPA)

39. In general, material irregularities perpetrated by which of the following are *most* difficult to detect?
    (a) cashier
    (b) controller
    (c) internal auditor
    (d) data entry clerk

    (CPA)

40. A well-designed system of internal control that is functioning effectively is most likely to detect an irregularity arising from
    (a) the fraudulent action of several employees.
    (b) the fraudulent action of an individual employee.
    (c) informal deviations from the official organization chart.
    (d) management fraud.

    (CPA)

41. To provide for the greatest degree of independence in performing internal auditing functions, an internal auditor most likely should report to the
    (a) financial vice president.
    (b) corporate controller.
    (c) board of directors.
    (d) corporate stockholders.

    (CPA)

42. The use of fidelity bonds may indemnify a company from embezzlement losses. The use also
    (a) reduces the company's need to obtain expensive business interruption insurance.
    (b) protects employees who made unintentional errors from possible monetary damages resulting from such errors.
    (c) allows the company to substitute the fidelity bonds for various parts of internal accounting control.
    (d) reduces the possibility of employing people with dubious records in positions of trust.

    (CPA)

43. For good internal control, which of the following functions should *not* be the responsibility of the treasurer's department?
    (a) data processing
    (b) handling of cash
    (c) custody of securities
    (d) establishment of credit policies

    (CPA)

44. Which of the following sets of duties would ordinarily be considered basically incompatible in terms of good internal control?
    (a) preparation of monthly statements to customers and maintenance of the accounts receivable subsidiary ledger
    (b) posting to the general ledger and approval of additions and terminations relating to the payroll
    (c) custody of unmailed signed checks and maintenance of expense subsidiary ledgers
    (d) collection of receipts on account and maintaining accounts receivable records.

    (CPA)

45. The Foreign Corrupt Practices Act requires that
    (a) auditors engaged to examine the financial statements of publicly held companies report all illegal payments to the SEC.
    (b) publicly held companies establish independent audit committees to monitor the effectiveness of their system of internal control.
    (c) U.S. firms doing business abroad report sizable payments to non-U.S. citizens to the Justice Department.
    (d) publicly held companies devise and maintain an adequate system of internal accounting control.

    (CPA)

46. Establishing and maintaining a system of internal accounting control is the primary responsibility of
    (a) management and the board of directors.
    (b) the internal auditor.
    (c) the external auditor.
    (d) a financial analyst.
    (e) the data processing manager.

    (CMA adapted)

47. A certain business receives all payments of account by check. Checks are always received, so an analyst wants to use the checks themselves as posting media to the accounts receivable ledger rather than have to prepare and process remittance advices. Discuss the conflict between productivity and reliability that is inherent here.

48. What duties should not normally be performed by the same individual in each of the following procedures?
    (a) bad debt write-off
    (b) payroll preparation
    (c) sales returns
    (d) inventory purchases

49. The internal auditing department was told that two employees were terminated for falsifying their time records. The two employees had altered overtime hours on their time cards after their supervisors had approved the hours actually worked.

    Several years ago, the company discontinued the use of time clocks. Since then, the plant supervisors have been responsible for manually posting the time cards and approving the hours for which their employees should be paid. The postings are usually entered in pencil by the supervisors or their secretaries. After the postings for the week are complete, the time cards are approved and placed in the mail racks outside the supervisors' offices for pickup by the timekeepers. Sometimes the timekeepers do not pick up the time cards promptly.

    Required
    Assuming the company does not wish to return to using time clocks, give *three* recommendations to prevent recurrence of the situation described. For each recommendation, indicate how it will deter fraudulent reporting of hours worked.

    (IIA)

50. Discuss the purpose of the following questions that appear on an internal control questionnaire.
    (a) Does the company have an organization chart?
    (b) Are the duties of the principal accounting officer segregated from those of the treasurer?

   (c) Are employees in positions of trust bonded?

   (d) Are bank accounts reconciled regularly by the company?

   (e) Does the company maintain a ledger of its fixed assets?

   (f) Are journal entries approved by a responsible official?

   (g) Are aging schedules of accounts receivable prepared periodically and reviewed by a responsible person?

   (h) Does the company compare budgeted amounts with actual expenditures?

   (i) Are trial balances of the accounts receivable ledgers prepared and reconciled regularly?

   (j) Do the employees who maintain inventory records have physical access to the inventory?

   (k) Are the inventory records adjusted to physical counts at least once a year?

   (l) Are remittance advices that accompany receipts separated and given to the accounting department?

   (m) Are costs and expenses under budgetary control?

   (n) Is a postage meter used?

   (o) Are monthly statements of account mailed to all customers?

   (p) In reconciling bank accounts do employees examine endorsements?

   (q) Has the bank (or banks) been instructed not to cash checks payable to the company?

51. Mary's mother was dismayed. Her daughter had just been brought home by a city detective. Mary has been arrested at the bank where she had been working for three months.

    Mary's job had been in the cash receipts/payment processing operation. Mary's job was to operate a machine that would magnetically encode the amount of a customer's payment on the customer's remittance advice. Mary did not have access to the customer's payment. The amount that she was to encode was handwritten on each remittance advice. The magnetic encoding allowed the remittance advices to be processed by a computer.

    "I was only trying to help us, Mom," Mary explained. "with Dad laid off from the mill and all, I just figured that no one would notice if I took our utility bills in to work, encoded them with amounts as if payment had been made, and then inserted them with the other remittances I was working on. I didn't realize that my work was being checked. I guess I should have known better."

   Required

   Should Mary have known better? Does an organization, such as the bank where Mary worked, have any obligation to explain the control environment of a job to an employee?

52. Identify an internal accounting control or procedure that would detect the following errors or omissions in a transaction processing system.

   (a) A nonprofit organization regularly receives unsolicited cash donations in the mail. Clerks opening the mail routinely steal a sizable percentage of the cash sent as donations.

   (b) Employees in the mailroom routinely mail their own—as well as their friends'—letters at the company's expense.

   (c) A clerk accidentally posts a customer payment of $35 as $53 to the customer's account in the receivables ledger.

   (d) A clerk purposefully posts a payment of $35 received from a close friend as $53 to the friend's account in the receivables ledger.

   (e) A customer receives a bill for an item that was ordered but never shipped.

   (f) A vendor sends a company a bill for 50 copies of a report when only 25 copies of the report were ordered and received.

   (g) A clerk sends a check to a vendor to pay an invoice. The same invoice was paid by a check drawn last week by a different clerk.

   (h) Certain workers in a factory routinely request more materials than are needed for a job, taking the excess materials home for personal use.

   (i) A customer orders an item, which is requisitioned and shipped. The customer is never billed for the shipment.

   (j) A shipment received from a vendor is accepted by an employee in the receiving department. The employee forwards a receiving report to payables so that the vendor will receive payment. The shipment, however, is taken home for personal use.

53. The internal auditor of a manufacturer is reviewing order-entry and shipping procedures. Figure 4.10 represents the procedures in place. All documents used in the procedure are

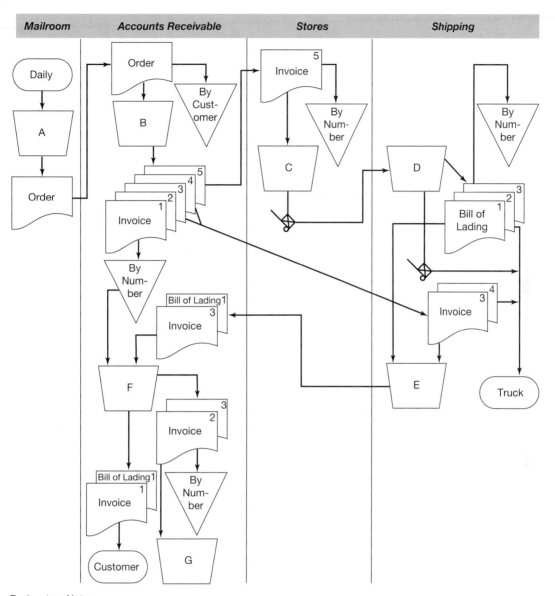

Explanatory Notes
A = Open Mail
B = Prepare Invoice from Customer Order and Distribute
C = Pick Goods to Extent Available and Forward to Shipping
D = Prepare Bill of Lading and Label Cartons for Shipment
E = Note Undershipments on Invoice #3 after Goods are Shipped
F = Complete Invoice Extensions Based on Actual Quantities Shipped
G = Post to Ledger and Prepare Daily Sales Journal
⊁ = Handtruck–Goods Movement

FIGURE 4.10 FLOWCHART FOR PROBLEM 53.

prenumbered. There are many undershipments on customers' orders, but goods not shipped are *not* automatically back-ordered.

Required
(a) Identify deficiencies and/or omissions in the control system for the order-entry and shipping functions.
(b) Suggest improvements in the control system to remove the deficiencies you noted.

Use the following format in responding to this question:
(a) Deficiency and/or omission
(b) Improvements suggested

(IIA)

54. Listed are 12 internal control procedures and requirements for the expenditure cycle (purchasing, payroll, accounts payable, and cash disbursements) for a manufacturing enterprise. Next to the list of controls is a list of reasons for the various controls.

Required
List the numbers 1 through 12, and then match each procedure or requirement with the most appropriate reason for implementing the control. Each reason can be used only once.

Procedures and Requirements	*Reasons for Controls*
1. Duties between the cash payments and cash receipts functions are segregated.	a. Prevents people from processing phony payables and diverting the signed checks to themselves.
2. Signature plates are kept under lock and key.	b. Prevents payroll checks for excessive amounts from being cashed.
3. The accounting department matches invoices to receiving reports or special authorizations prior to payment.	c. Ensures that people writing checks cannot cover a temporary "borrowing" of cash.
4. All checks are mailed by someone other than the person making out the check.	d. Prevents the abstraction of cash receipts from being concealed by the recording of fictitious payments.
5. The accounting department matches invoices to copies of purchase orders.	e. Helps guard against checks being forged.
6. The blank stock of checks is kept under lock and key.	f. Prevents the fraudulent use of properly signed checks.
7. Imprest accounts are used for payroll.	g. Helps prevent temporary "borrowing" from established cash funds.
8. Bank reconciliations are to be accomplished by someone other than the one who writes checks and handles cash.	h. Helps prevent unauthorized changes to very important documents.
9. A check protector is used.	i. Prevents payment for goods and services not actually received.
10. Surprise counts of cash funds are conducted periodically.	j. Prevents payments for purchases that have not been properly authorized.
11. Orders can be placed with approved vendors only.	k. Assures that purchases are "arm's-length" transactions.
12. All purchases must be made by the purchasing department.	l. Prevents inappropriate purchases by unauthorized people.

55. The cashier of the Easy Company intercepted Customer A's check payable to the company in the amount of $500 and deposited it in a bank account that was part of the company petty cash fund, of which he was custodian. He then drew a $500 check on the petty cash fund bank account payable to himself, signed it, and cashed it. At the end of the month while processing the monthly statements to customers, he changed the statement to Customer A so that it showed that A had received credit for the $500 check that had been intercepted. Ten days later he made an entry in the cash received book that purported to record receipt of a remittance of $500 from Customer A, thus restoring A's account to its proper balance but overstating the cash in the bank. He covered the overstatement by omitting from the list of outstanding checks in the bank reconcilement two checks, the aggregate amount of which was $500.

List what you regard as five important deficiencies in the system of internal control in this situation, and state the proper remedy for each deficiency.

(CPA)

56. As the internal auditor for a large company, you have been asked to consult with the operating management of a new division that consists of a chain of video game arcades. Specifically, management wants advice on the nature of accounting risks posed by the new operation and on the internal controls needed to reduce those risks. In reviewing the proposed video game arcade operation, you learn the following information.

The chain will consist of 40 locations, the most distant location being only 200 miles from the corporate offices. The 40 locations will be divided into two regions, each having a regional manager. Each location will contain an average of 35 machines, with some locations having as many as 60 machines and others having as few as 10 machines. Access to the game counter and coins in each machine will be by use of a master key.

To minimize cost, management insists on minimizing the number of operating and accounting personnel. However, management has agreed to hire sufficient maintenance personnel in-house to minimize downtime. Management also has agreed to provide a local manager for each operating location because of the cash nature of the business.

Management insists on daily collection and deposit of coins in a local bank by the resident manager. Validated deposit slips are to be mailed to the corporate offices. Bank statements will be mailed directly by the banks to corporate offices.

Required

The definition of internal accounting control addresses aspects of transaction execution, transaction recording, access to assets, and periodic comparisons of accountability. Based on these aspects and using the format that follows:

(a) Identify the risks for the major activities listed.
(b) Suggest internal accounting controls for the risks identified.

The required answer format is as shown:

Activity	Risk	Control
Transaction execution		
Transaction recording		
Access to assets		
Periodic comparisons of accountability		

57. The Luxnet division of the WSH Corporation publishes college textbooks. Luxnet employs about 20 senior editors, each of whom manages the production of several different textbooks.

In the production of a textbook, editors usually request several manuscript reviews from different college professors, with each professor being paid a fee for the service. Each senior editor is given a yearly budget that is to be spent for manuscript reviews.

Senior editors select professors whom they think will provide useful reviews. Requests for manuscript reviews are made by sending a letter that specifies the general terms and the fee to be paid. If the professor agrees to perform a review, a signed copy of the letter is returned to the editor. The editor then forwards the manuscript to the professor for review.

When the professor's review is received, the editor sends a memo to accounts payable indicating the account number charge, the professor's name and address, and the amount to be paid. Accounts payable prepares a check for the amount indicated and forwards it to the editor for delivery to the professor.

Required

(a) Identify deficiencies and/or weaknesses in the procedures described.
(b) Suggest an improvement to remove each weakness/deficiency you noted in part a.
Use the following format to answer this question.
(a) Deficiency/weakness
(b) Improvement suggested

58. You were recently appointed the internal auditor for a private college. Your first assignment is to appraise the adequacy and effectiveness of the student registration procedures. You

have completed your preliminary survey. Based on your interviews and a walk-through of the student registration operation, you prepared an informal flowchart.

Required

Examine the following informal flowchart and list five internal control weaknesses (such as omission of certain steps or measures) in the student registration procedures.

Admission—Processing of Registrations

(a) **Mailroom**

Opens all mail, prepares remittance advices and remittance listings.
Sends copies of advices and listings to

1. cashier (with cash and checks).
2. accounts receivable clerk.
3. general bookkeeper.

Destroys other copies of advices and listings.

(b) **Registration clerk**

Receives three copies of completed registration forms from students.
Checks for counselor's or similar approval.
Records appropriate fee from official class catalog.
If completed properly, approves forms and sends student with registration forms to cashier.
If not completed properly, returns forms to student for follow-up and reapplication.

(c) **Cashier**

Collects funds or forwards two copies of registration forms to billing clerk.
Records cash receipts in daily receipts record.
Prepares and makes daily deposits.
Forwards duplicate receipted deposit slips and daily receipt records to general bookkeeper.
Destroys copies of daily receipts records.

(d) **Billing clerk**

Receives two copies of registration form, prepares bill, and makes entries in registration (sales) journal.
Forwards copies of billings and registration forms to accounts receivable clerk and forwards copies of bill to general bookkeeper.

(e) **Accounts receivable clerk**

Posts accounts receivable subsidiary ledger detailed accounts from remittance listings.
Matches billings and registration forms and posts accounts receivable subsidiary ledger detailed accounts.

(f) **General bookkeeper**

Journalizes and posts cash receipts and applicable registrations to general ledger.
Enters registration (sales) journal data in general ledger.

(IIA)

59. Collateral Deposit (Part 2)[3]
(This is a continuation of Problem 27 in Chapter 2.)

Required

Part 1 Prepare an analytic flowchart and cross-reference it to the list of procedures that accompanies Problem 27 in Chapter 2.

Part 2 Prepare an application controls matrix for the process using the form shown in Figure 4.9. Cross-reference the controls to the matrix using the appropriate numbers from the list of procedures.

Identify any apparent weaknesses noted in the description of the collateral receipt process.

[3]Problems 59 and 60 were prepared by Frederick L. Neumann, Richard J. Boland, and Jeffrey Johnson; funded by the Touche Ross Foundation Aid to Accounting Education Program.

60. Collateral Withdrawal

Dan Matt drew up a flowchart for the depositing of collateral (Problem 59) and turned it over to his senior. The senior inquired if collateral was only deposited and never withdrawn. Dan realized he had not followed the collateral process through to its completion. He still had to investigate the withdrawal of collateral that resulted when the loan was paid.

Dan found that the customer initiates the withdrawal of collateral by presenting the pink receipt copy to the loan officer. The loan officer forwards the customer's request for return of the collateral to the collateral clerk, who prepares a prenumbered, four-part withdrawal form. Each copy of the form is a different color to facilitate its distribution. The original (pink) of the request is sent back to the loan officer, the second (blue) copy is sent to the vault custodian, and the third (white) copy is filed by the collateral clerk with the deposit form. Again, the yellow or fourth copy is discarded. The vault custodian takes the blue copy of the request to the vault attendant, and together they remove the collateral and match it against the request. If they match, both the vault custodian and the vault attendant sign the blue copy of the request. If they are not in agreement, the vault custodian contacts the loan officer to iron out the discrepancy. The signed blue copy is sent back to the loan officer, accompanied by the collateral. The loan officer verifies that everything is proper and then signs the blue copy and turns over the collateral to the customer. The customer, after verifying that the collateral is correct, signs the pink copy of the request, which had been on file with the loan officer. Then both the blue and the pink copies are returned to the collateral clerk. The collateral clerk matches the two copies of the request to the white copy in his file. If they are all in agreement, he records the return of the collateral in his log, staples the copies together, and files them in the completed file by number.

Required

(a) Prepare an analytic flowchart of the collateral withdrawal process using the description given in the case.
(b) Prepare the application controls matrix for the process, using the form shown in Figure 4.9.
(c) List any apparent weaknesses in the collateral withdrawal process as described.

61. An external auditor normally evaluates a client's system of internal control. The results of this assessment will directly affect the following:
(a) The extent of compliance testing
(b) The extent of substantive testing
(c) The extent of flowcharting
(d) All of the above
(e) None of the above

62. The proper design of forms is an important aspect of developing a system in which there is an adherence to control procedures and policies.

Required

(a) Specify the elements to be included in the design of an electronic form.
(b) Indicate the ways in which the elements of an electronic form might differ from those of a paper form.
(c) In what ways does good form design contribute to the internal control process.

63. The Whip-O Manufacturing Company manufactures neck braces for special orders. The firm hires 20 artisans who each work on a brace until completion. There are 8 to 10 operations performed on each custom brace, ranging from 1 to 6 hours each. At present, prescriptions and measurements are obtained from doctors by the sales representative. On receipt at the plant, the production agent prepares a production ticket and holds the information until an artisan is free.

Lists of materials needed for each job are compiled by the artisan and given to the production agent. The agent purchases the locally available items and orders the unavailable items from a medical supply catalog. Delivery of the ordered items usually takes less than a week.

When an employee finishes a job, he or she gives the brace, production ticket, and hours spent to the accountant, who adds the cost of materials and overhead and then calculates the price. The receivable is recorded and the brace and invoice are sent to the sales representative for delivery.

Each week the artisans turn in a time card to the general manager, who approves the cards and passes them to the accountant for payroll preparation and check distribution. The general manager has had several concerns:

(a) Doctors persistently call inquiring about cost and delivery date, and little information is available.

(b) Total time from receipt of order to delivery time seems excessive in most cases.

(c) Payroll costs do not appear to be in control.

Required

(a) Document in a flowchart the sales processing and payroll system.

(b) List the weaknesses and suggestions for improvement concerned with the general manager's comments. (Use the format below; you should have *at least six*.)

Weakness   Recommended Improvement

64. The following procedures relate to the sales-order system of the Tallahassee Sailboat Manufacturing Company.

All sales orders are received in the sales department. Customers deal directly with salespeople who write up specifications for custom-manufactured sailboats. Once an order is complete, it is sent to the production supervisor, who makes three additional copies of the sales order on the company's copying machine. The supervisor then numbers all four copies. The first copy is retained in an open file. Copy 2 is sent to the accountant. Copy 3 is returned to sales and is filed according to customer name. Copy 4 is attached to a job cost sheet for reference.

The accountant, on receiving her copy of the sales order, immediately checks the numerical sequence written in by the supervisor to ensure that it conforms to the company's scheme of prenumbering.

The job cost sheet is used to collect labor, material, and overhead costs. Materials are obtained from the stores supervisor, who reviews the specifications on the job cost sheet and estimates the materials required. He then pulls the appropriate materials and personally delivers them to the appropriate workers. He likes to do this personally because he feels that it minimizes errors and ensures that the workers do not enter the storeroom.

The company bills based on the stage-of-completion method. When the supervisor feels that a job is half complete, he notifies the accountant, who then bills the customer for 50% of the agreed-upon price. When the job is complete, the same procedure is followed.

The president's secretary opens the mail and separates checks and their accompanying invoices. The checks are rubber-stamped for deposit only. They are immediately forwarded to the cashier, who deposits them first thing the following workday. A copy of the deposit receipt is then forwarded to the accountant as a remittance advice. The invoices are sent to the accountant, who enters the amount received in the special journal for accounts receivable. Once a month she posts the journal entries to the accounts receivable subsidiary ledger and cash account. After posting to the control accounts, she makes up financial statements. These procedures are comprehensive and describe everything she does relating to sales and receipts.

Required

(a) Prepare an analytic flowchart relating to the procedures discussed above.

(b) Using a two-column approach, list internal control weaknesses and make suggestions for improvements.

65. The Watt Widget Company manufactures two principal types of widgets and purchases some products that are resold directly without further processing. The production processes are relatively straightforward, with low-technology processing and many manually controlled operations.

The purchasing agent uses various sources of information to determine when and how much to order. Three-part requisition forms are received from the various supervisors and other supervisory personnel, indicating when specific supplies are needed and how much of them.

Weekly open sales order and finished goods reports are used to evaluate current and future production plans in conjunction with a review of the raw materials on hand. The purchasing agent reviews the card file of stock on hand to ascertain use history and vendor lead times contained on the card files. When large and unusual orders are received by the sales manager, he notifies the purchasing agent so that she can evaluate the related raw materials requirements.

The purchasing agent prepares a three-part purchase order, reviews it with the office manager, and obtains his signature before distributing it. The purchasing agent distributes copies: Copy 1 goes to the vendor; copy 2 goes to the warehouse supervisor; and copy 3 is retained in alphabetical sequence by the vendor. The purchasing agent also prepares a purchase order log to control numerically all orders issued and to assure that they are subsequently received and reported on receiving reports.

When the material is received, the receiving dock personnel count the material and prepare a three-part prenumbered receiving form. They distribute copies: Copy 1 goes to the purchasing agent; copy 2 goes to the cost accountant; and copy 3 is retained and filed in numerical sequence. If the material received is a finished product, the receiving personnel sends the first copy of the receiving report to the sales manager, who makes a photocopy for updating the finished goods inventory records and then forwards the original copy to the purchasing agent. If the order is complete, the receiving personnel also send their copy of the purchase order to the purchasing agent, who will use it to denote the receipt of the material on her purchase order log. The cost accountant uses his copy of the receiving report to post the quantities received to the raw material card records. He then files the reports in numerical sequence, accounting for all numbers.

Production scheduling and control is based on a review of the weekly report of finished goods on hand and on order and on a walk-through review of work in process. There are no formal systems for evaluating the shop load or for tracking the flow of orders through the shop.

Following determination of production quantities required, the production supervisor verifies the availability of necessary raw materials with the warehouse supervisor.

While no formal priority system is established for releasing build orders to the shop floor, the production supervisor considers order requirements and releases items for production on the basis of his judgment of priorities.

Raw materials are issued from stock on the request of the production supervisor, and signatures are obtained from production personnel on material transfer forms. The forms are used to update raw material inventory files. Upon receipt of the raw materials, production on the required item begins. Occasionally, quantity checks are made at various workstations in the production process to verify piece counts; however, there is no formal production control over work-in-process.

The quantities and descriptions of raw materials transferred from the warehouse to the production area are recorded onto prenumbered transfer sheets. At the same time that these transfer sheets are posted to the perpetual inventory files, the actual unit cost of materials is obtained from the card records. The transfer sheets are extended and summarized for recording the monthly journal entry to credit raw materials and charge work in process.

Piecework quantities produced and payment rates per 100 units are recorded onto time sheets by the production workers. These amounts are extended and summarized for entry into the payroll system. The total of piecework dollars is charged to work-in-process. Wages paid on a day-rate basis for jobs that have no piece rate or for makeup pay (i.e., the per-job amount in excess of the piecework amount, in order that the individual earns a specified hourly rate) are included as part of factory overhead. Factory burden is charged to work in process at a standard rate of 200% of piecework dollars. There are no production order details or perpetual record controls maintained over the raw material, labor, or burden charged to work-in-process.

As work is completed and packaged for transfer into finished goods or for direct shipment, the quantities and descriptions are recorded onto prenumbered merchandise transfer sheets. Shipping department personnel are responsible for the accuracy of these sheets; they initial each line item as verification of the entries. Separate numerical series of transfer sheets are prepared by each production department. After obtaining shipping department approvals, transfer sheets are forwarded to the sales manager. The sales manager accounts for numerical control over all transfer sheets and enters the catalog numbers and quantities into a computer terminal for updating the finished goods stock on-hand file. At month end, an inventory summary report is prepared, containing the quantities and extended standard cost values of all transfers from work in process to finished goods. In order to compensate for unreasonably low unit standard costs, the standard value is increased by 30% for making the journal entry to relieve work in process and charge finished goods.

Hourly production employees are paid on a piece-rate basis with a guaranteed minimum hourly day rate for each job and for certain unrated jobs. Each employee is responsible for accounting for his or her units of production and hours worked on each job, recording the information onto weekly time sheets, and obtaining the approval of the department supervisors. Recently, individuals were assigned within several departments to verify the reported quantities on a test basis.

Both the clock cards and the time sheets are sent to the payroll clerk, who verifies the extensions of piece time rates, calculates makeup hours and pay, and calculates day work hours and pay. The clerk reviews the clock cards to determine whether any time sheets are missing but does not verify clock card hours with time sheet hours. The time sheets are then sent to a computer service bureau for preparation of checks and payroll journals. The transmittal sheets forwarded with the time sheets to the service bureau contain spaces for indicating batch totals of the gross wages within specified earnings categories. At present, these batch totals are not being calculated.

The checks prepared by the bank are forwarded to the office manager, who separates them by department. The checks and journals are then given to the controller for his review. If any errors are found, the check is cancelled, a new check is typed for the corrected amount, and the payroll records are corrected in the following period. The office manager distributes the checks to the employees.

The payroll journal provides subtotals of piecework, day work, overtime, vacation, sick, and bonus pay. At present, the totals of each of these breakdowns are recorded in the general ledger but with no details by department other than a separation between warehouse, shipping, and other wages. The payroll journal does not provide any product or job reporting.

The cost accountant has recently started to develop a computer program to accumulate and print product cost sheets using a time-sharing system. The program design has not been finished. The company is planning to mechanize the cost-sheet accumulation and printing process in order to expedite the revision of standard costs. Consideration is being given to mechanizing the raw-material perpetual inventory records and using this file in the standard cost program. However, before this can be done, the raw-material items must be numbered, and procedures and programs for updating these records must be designed and implemented.

Watt relies on an annual physical count of items to determine on-hand quantities. These counts are not directly reconciled to the perpetual inventory records because of difficulties in locating specific items. The current layout of the warehouse contains no logical organization as to part storage, bin space, or production work area. In addition, generally poor standards of orderliness (split and broken cartons, etc.) are prevalent. These factors create difficulties in locating desired items and contribute to inaccuracies in physical counts.

Required
Analyze the procedures relating to production and inventory control in effect at Watt.

66. WDI is an engineering and construction company that designs, fabricates, and erects various air-pollution control systems. Its customers consist of private industry as well as public utilities. The discussion below illustrates how a company, in this case WDI, can lose control of something as simple as postal cost through inadequate information systems, lack of management interest, and lack of communication.

BACKGROUND

WDI is structured in three major components: precontract operations, postcontract operations, and support groups. A brief description of each group's functions follows:

Precontract

Sales. This group performs the traditional function of any sales organization, namely, to locate prospective customers, promote WDI products, and develop long-term marketing strategies.

Application engineering. This section determines equipment selection, provides the estimate, and interacts with the sales department to provide technical input for various types of sales presentations.

Contracts. This department develops all nontechnical portions of the precontract effort. In addition, the group is responsible for all negotiations with potential customers.

Proposal administration. This department has the unenviable task of coordinating all of the above groups to ensure that concise, accurate proposals are issued. All outgoing proposals, letters, and so on are processed through this department.

POSTCONTRACTS

Engineering. Individuals in this group perform all detailed engineering and construction drawings required to execute a contract.

Construction. Field personnel who actually construct the air-pollution systems are in this group.

Project management. This department has complete control of and is responsible for coordinating all postcontract activities.

SUPPORT GROUPS

(*Note*: The labor costs of various departments designated as support groups are charged to overhead under WDI's accounting system.)

Finance. This department performs all cost-control functions normally associated with such a department.

Legal. This group provides legal consultation and handles all matters pertaining to litigation.

Administrative services. This department procures office supplies and operates the mailroom from which all outgoing mail is processed.

The late 1990s were prosperous times for WDI. Public utilities were converting their power-production facilities from oil to coal as a result of the oil shortages of that time, thus expanding the air-pollution control market. Smokestack industries were providing a steady market to supplement the large power-industry market.

In early 2000, the global recession resulted in the disappearance of the industrial marketplace, and the subsequent "oil glut" soon depressed the utility market. Like all companies during depressed economic conditions, WDI looked within to cut costs. This review of internal costs produced some interesting results, especially in the area of postal charges.

A group of individuals was given the task of finding areas of excess costs and recommending corrective action. The group was astounded at the huge increases in postal expenses starting in 2001. To determine why this startling increase developed, they questioned mailroom personnel. They were informed that proposal activity accounted for approximately 80% of documents processed through the mailroom. Hence, proposal activity for 1997–2003 was investigated.

These results further confused the situation. Not only did postal expenses soar beginning in 2001, but proposal activity (which comprises approximately 80% of postal expenses) dramatically decreased during this period.

The group's next step was to interview the vice president of finance and the controller. Surely they would have noted the increased expenses incurred and could provide some insight as to the cause. To the group's surprise, neither person was aware that any significant change in postal expense had taken place. Two problems were now obvious: (1) What caused the large increase? and (2) How could such a dramatic increase avoid the scrutiny of upper management?

One possibility immediately became apparent to all the members of the group. Was it possible that fraudulent postal expenses were being submitted? If so, management's ignorance of the problem could suggest complicity. Before alleging any wrongdoing, the group had to ensure that no other reasonable alternative existed.

On reviewing the quarterly expense reports, the group noticed that postal expense was not identified as a particular line item. Instead, it was included under the expense category miscellaneous administrative expenses, which consisted of postal expenses, office supplies, and printing costs. The group then researched the office supply and printing expenses from 1997–2003.

The office supply and printing expenses were directly proportional to the level of proposal activity, exactly as would be expected. It was apparent that the decreasing office supply and printing expenses offset the increases in the postal expenses. Thus the miscellaneous administrative expenses reported on the quarterly management expense summaries showed minimal changes.

The group still had no idea what caused the increased postal expense. Mailroom personnel were interviewed again. While one of the mailroom staff was discussing how the mailroom had changed over the years, he mentioned the dramatic increase in the use of express mail service. On reviewing the records, the group found that WDI had started using express mail services (other than those offered by the U.S. Postal Service) in May 2000.

In order to confirm their suspicions, the group reviewed a significant number of past proposals. They found that within two months of the establishment of express mail service at WDI, approximately 65% of all proposals were sent via this method; within six months this percentage had increased to 85%. Furthermore, the use of express mail service had proliferated to 50% of all written correspondence. The investigation was extended to the post-contract group, and it was found that nearly 90% of all engineering drawings required for contract execution were sent via express mail.

When various departments were asked why they had dramatically expanded their use of express mail service, the following responses were received:

"It is the most reliable and cost-efficient method to transmit a proposal, document, or such material that must be received across the country the following day."

"Utilizing express mail enables us to gain one or two days of in-house effort that would normally be wasted transmitting by regular mail."

"We feel express mail lessens the chances of correspondence getting lost in the mail."

Finally, one of the interviewees, who was hired after 2001, stated, "I thought it was standard procedure."

A complete review of the office records supported the group's hypothesis that the rampant use of this premium mail service had indeed caused the problem. For example, the cost of mailing a single-page letter in 2003 was 33 cents (postage only). That same letter mailed via express mail service costs $7.00. This cost differential is even greater when proposal packages, which weigh 5 to 10 pounds, are considered. The group's investigation indicated that if proposal activity again reached the levels of 1999, postal expenses could exceed $500,000. This would be an absurd amount of money to spend on postage for a company that employs only 225 people.

Required

(a) What caused the large increases in postal expense at WDI? How could such large increases have escaped management's scrutiny?

(b) Suggest changes in WDI's accounting system to prevent similar situations from occurring in the future.

(c) What steps should WDI take to bring postal expenses under management control?

❖ ANSWERS TO CHAPTER QUIZ

1. B	4. A	7. A	10. D
2. B	5. A	8. B	
3. C	6. B	9. D	

INFORMATION SYSTEMS SECURITY

LEARNING OBJECTIVES

Careful study of this chapter will enable you to:

❖ Describe general approaches to analyzing vulnerabilities and threats in information systems.

❖ Identify active and passive threats to information systems.

❖ Identify key aspects of an information security system.

❖ Discuss contingency planning and other disaster risk management practices.

AN OVERVIEW OF INFORMATION SYSTEMS SECURITY

The **information security system** is the subsystem of the organization that controls the special risks associated with computer-based information systems. The information security system has the basic elements of any information system, such as hardware, databases, procedures, and reports. For example, data concerning system usage and security violations might be collected in real time, stored in databases, and used to generate reports.

THE INFORMATION SECURITY SYSTEM LIFE CYCLE

The electronic security system is an information system, so its development requires application of the life-cycle approach. Computer security systems are developed by applying the established methods of systems analysis; design; implementation; and operation, evaluation, and control. The objective of each of these life-cycle phases is as follows:

Life-Cycle Phase	Objective
Systems analysis	Analyze system vulnerabilities in terms of relevant threats and their associated loss exposures.
Systems design	Design security measures and contingency plans to control the identified loss exposures.
Systems implementation	Implement the security measures as designed.
Systems operation, evaluation, and control	Operate the system and assess its effectiveness and efficiency. Make changes as circumstances require.

The objective of the first phase of the security system life cycle is to produce a vulnerability and threat analysis report. The objective of the second phase is to design a comprehensive set of risk-control measures, including both security measures to prevent losses and contingency plans to deal with losses should they occur. Collectively, all four phases are referred to as *information system risk management*. Information system risk management is the process of assessing and controlling computer system risks.

THE INFORMATION SECURITY SYSTEM IN THE ORGANIZATION

If the information security system is to be effective, it must be managed by a **chief security officer (CSO)**. This individual should report directly to the board of directors so as to maintain complete independence. A primary duty of the CSO should be to present reports to the board of directors for approval. These reports should cover each phase of the life cycle:

Life-Cycle Phase	Report to the Board of Directors
Systems analysis	A summary of all relevant loss exposures.
Systems design	Detailed plans for controlling and managing losses, including a complete security system budget.
Systems implementation, systems operation, evaluation, and control	Specifics on security system performance, including an itemization of losses and security breaches, an analysis of compliance, and costs of operating the security system.

ANALYZING VULNERABILITIES AND THREATS

There are two basic approaches to analyzing system vulnerabilities and threats. In the **quantitative approach to risk assessment**, each loss exposure is computed as the product of the cost of an individual loss times the likelihood of its occurrence. For example, assume that the likelihood of a loss can be represented by a risk factor between 0 and 1. Then a threat analysis report might look something like the one in Figure 5.1. In this example, data theft is the largest loss exposure, immediately followed by fraud and virus attacks (i.e., attacks that result from computer programs designed to sabotage important files). A significant benefit of an analysis such as this is that it often shows that the most likely threat to occur is not the threat with the largest loss exposure. For example, in Figure 5.1, the threat most likely to occur is equipment theft, but this threat represents one of the smallest loss exposures.

There are several difficulties in applying the quantitative approach to assessing loss exposures. First, identifying the relevant costs per loss and the associated likelihoods

THREAT ANALYSIS REPORT			
	Potential Loss ($)	Risk	Loss Exposure ($)
Data Theft	700,000,000	0.050	35,000,000
Fraud and Virus Attacks	1,200,000,000	0.025	30,000,000
Sabotage	2,500,000,000	0.010	25,000,000
File Alteration	400,000,000	0.050	20,000,000
Program Alteration	80,000,000	0.020	1,600,000
Equipment Theft	15,000,000	0.100	1,500,000
Natural Disaster	100,000,000	0.008	800,000

FIGURE 5.1 THREAT ANALYSIS REPORT.

can be difficult. The relevant cost of a loss is the decrease in the company's profitability as a result of the loss's occurrence. But this cost can be difficult to estimate because it might involve estimating unpredictable business interruption costs or estimating the replacement cost of computers that can only be replaced by noncomparable newer models. Second, estimating the likelihood of a given failure requires predicting the future, which is particularly difficult in a rapidly changing technological environment. For example, many managers fail to foresee problems with computer viruses. Furthermore, in assessing the likelihood of intentional attacks on the system, one must estimate the costs and benefits of such attacks to potential perpetrators. This estimate, however, requires assumptions about perpetrators' risk preferences. For example, one perpetrator might be willing to undergo substantially larger risks than another for the same dollar gain. An extremely **risk-seeking perpetrator** will take very large risks for a small reward.

A second method of risk assessment for computer security is the **qualitative approach**. This approach simply lists out the system's vulnerabilities and threats, subjectively ranking them in order of their contribution to the company's total loss exposures. Both the qualitative and quantitative approaches are used in practice, and many companies mix the two methods. Regardless of the method used, any analysis must include loss exposures for at least the following areas:

- Business interruption
- Loss of software
- Loss of data
- Loss of hardware
- Loss of facilities
- Loss of service and personnel

If the quantitative approach is used, costs might be estimated using one of many methods, including replacement cost, service denial, third-party liability (resulting from the company's inability to meet contracts), and business interruption.

VULNERABILITIES AND THREATS

A **vulnerability** is a weakness in a system, and a **threat** is a potential exploitation of a vulnerability. There are two categories of threats: active and passive. **Active threats** include information systems fraud and computer sabotage, and **passive threats** include system faults, as well as natural disasters, such as earthquakes, floods, fires, and hurricanes. **System faults** represent component equipment failures such as disk failures, power outages, and so on.

THE SERIOUSNESS OF INFORMATION SYSTEMS FRAUD

Computer-based crimes are part of the general problem of white-collar crime. The problem of white-collar crime is serious. Statistics have shown that corporate losses due to fraud and embezzlement exceed total losses due to bribery, burglary, and shoplifting by a wide margin. This might seem surprising because we seldom read about crimes such as embezzlement in the newspaper. This is so because, in the vast majority of cases, detected frauds are never brought to the attention of law enforcement people because this would lead to public disclosure of internal control weaknesses. Managers tend to shy away from the adverse negative publicity that would result from public prosecution.

Information system security is an international problem. Accordingly, many countries have laws directed at computer security (see Fig. 5.2). In the United States, various laws, regulations, and pronouncements address the problem of electronic crime. Most states have enacted specific criminal statutes directed against computer crimes.

FIGURE 5.2   INTERNATIONAL COMPUTER SECURITY LAWS.

INTERNATIONAL COMPUTER SECURITY LAWS	
 Canada	Criminal Code 301.2(1), Unauthorized Use of Computers, sets criminal penalties of up to 10 years for fraudulent use of computer service or interception of computer signals or functions.
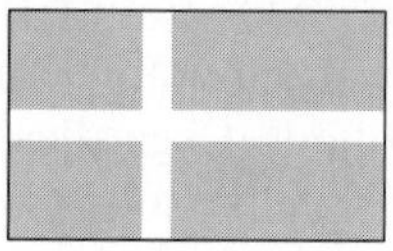 Denmark	Criminal Code Section 263, Access to Another Person's Information, sets criminal penalties of up to 2 years for unlawful access to another person's data processing information or programs.
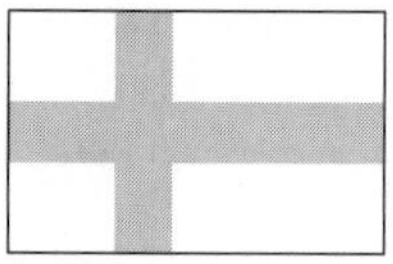 Finland	Penal Provisions of the Personal Registers Act, 1987, Section 45, Personal Register Trespass, sets criminal penalties of up to 6 months for use of another individual's user code or fraudulent means to access personal data maintained with automated data processing.
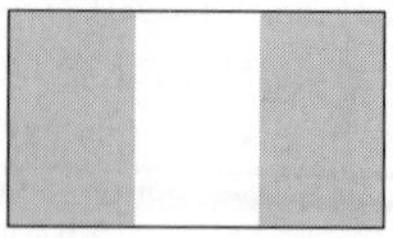 France	Law Number 88-19, Criminal Code, Chapter III, Article 462-2 through 9, sets criminal penalties of up to 3 years for unauthorized access to, falsification, modification, or deletion of data, or the use of such data from an automated data processing system.
 Switzerland	Criminal Code Section 147, Fraudulent Misuse of a Data Processing System, sets criminal penalties of up to 10 years for intentionally adding or deleting a data processing record for the intent of enrichment.

The **Computer Fraud and Abuse Act of 1986** makes it a federal crime to knowingly and with intent fraudulently gain unauthorized access to data stored in the computers of financial institutions, computers owned or used by the federal government, or computers operating in interstate commerce. Trafficking in computer access passwords is also prohibited. Felonies are determined by damage to $1,000 or more of software; the theft of actual goods, services, or money; or unauthorized access or alteration of medical records. Fines could range up to $250,000, or twice the value of stolen data, and first offenders could be sentenced to one to five years in prison.

The National Commission on Fraudulent Financial Reporting (Treadway Commission) linked management fraud to computer crime. Management fraud is deliberate fraud committed by managers with the intent of deceiving investors and creditors using materially misleading financial reports. This type of fraud is committed by those who are high enough in an organization to override accounting controls. Management might commit other types of errors or omissions that potentially could defraud employees or investors, but the term *management fraud* generally refers to financial statement manipulations.

The Treadway Commission defined fraudulent financial reporting as intentional or reckless conduct, whether by act or omission, that results in materially misleading financial statements. The commission studied 456 lawsuits brought against auditors. Management fraud was found to be present in about half these cases. The commission noted that computer-based information systems multiply the potential for misusing or manipulating information, thus increasing the risk of fraudulent financial reporting.

INDIVIDUALS POSING A THREAT TO THE INFORMATION SYSTEM

A successful attack on an information system requires access to hardware, sensitive data files, or critical programs. Three groups of individuals—systems personnel, users, and intruders—differ in their normal ability to access these things. Systems personnel often pose a potential threat because they are often given wide-ranging access privileges to sensitive data and programs. Users, on the other hand, are given much narrower access, but they still find ways to commit fraud. Intruders are given no access at all, but they are often highly determined individuals who are capable of inflicting great losses on the company.

COMPUTER SYSTEMS PERSONNEL

Systems personnel include computer maintenance persons, programmers, operators, information systems administrative personnel, and data control clerks.

Computer Maintenance Persons   Maintenance persons install hardware and software, repair hardware, and correct minor errors in software. In many cases these individuals must have high-level security access to do their jobs. For example, an individual installing a new version of an accounting program is often given complete access to the file catalog containing the accounting system and its related data files. In some cases such an individual might not even work for the company but rather for the vendor from whom the company bought the accounting software. In any case, maintenance persons typically possess the ability to illegally browse through and alter data and program files. Some maintenance persons may even be in the position to make undesirable modifications to the security portion of the operating system.

Programmers   Systems programmers often write programs to modify and extend the network operating system. Such individuals typically are given accounts with universal access to all the company's files. Application programmers might make undesirable modifications to existing programs or write new programs that do undesirable things.

Network Operators   Those individuals who oversee and monitor the immediate operation of the computer and communications network are called *network operators*. Typically, the operator is assigned a high level of security clearance, thus allowing him or her to secretly monitor all network communications (including individual users entering passwords), as well as access any file on the system.

Information Systems Administrative Personnel   The systems supervisor is in a position of great trust. This person normally has access to security secrets, files, programs, and so on. Account administrators have the ability to create fictitious accounts or to give away passwords to existing accounts.

Data Control Clerks   Those responsible for the manual and automated inputting of data into the computer are called *data control clerks*. These individuals are in the position to fraudulently manipulate the input data.

USERS

Users are composed of heterogeneous groups of people and can be distinguished from the others because their functional area does not lie in data processing. Many users have access to sensitive data that they can disclose to competitors. In some cases users may control important computer inputs such as credit memos, account credits, and so on.

INTRUDERS

Anyone who accesses equipment, electronic data, or files without proper authorization is an **intruder**. Intruders who attack information systems for fun and challenge are known as **hackers**. Other types of intruders include unnoticed intruders, wiretappers, piggybackers, impersonating intruders, and eavesdroppers.

Unnoticed Intruders   A customer might walk into an unguarded area and view sensitive data on an unattended personal computer. A hacker might break into and either pilfer or damage the company's Web site.

Wiretappers   A large portion of the information processed by the company's computers travels over wires and cables. Some information is transmitted only from one room to the next, and other information may be transmitted across the country via the Internet. These lines are vulnerable to wiretapping, which may be done with even inexpensive devices (e.g., a simple tape recorder and a short piece of wire) that are capable of performing the task without giving any clues that the wire is being tapped.

Piggybackers   The most sophisticated type of wire tapping is called **piggybacking**. With this method, the penetrator intercepts legitimate information and substitutes fraudulent information in its place.

Impersonating Intruders   Impersonating intruders are individuals who pose as someone else in order to defraud the company. One type of intruder uses an illegally obtained user ID and password to access the company's electronic resources. Many companies are very lax about security over user IDs and passwords. In some cases, an individual, through "social engineering," can obtain a user ID and password simply by calling the company's technology center on the telephone. Another type of intruder is the hacker (Fig. 5.3), who may gain access through the Internet by guessing someone's password. Guessing passwords is not as difficult as it might seem because hackers know that many individuals use the name of a close relative or pet for a password. Further, various password-guessing programs are publicly available on the Web. One such program contains a 300,000-word dictionary and operates very quickly. A third type of intruder is the professional industrial spy, who, for example, typically enters

---

**"Crackers" force universities
to shut down computer systems
and change their passwords**

Computer administrators around the world were racing last week to change users'
passwords in the wake of a warning that hackers had stealthily collected computer
passwords and were using them to infiltrate computers connected to the Internet. . . .

One site affected by the security breach was Rice University, where administrators
had brought back their systems to near-normal last week after an attack by hackers
forced the institution to cut off its links with the Internet and shut down a campus network
used by students. . . .

The shutdown at Rice was necessary because the "crackers"—a name given to
mean-spirited hackers who attempt to destroy data, pirate software, or obtain information
for financial gain—were roaming the system virtually unchecked and setting up numerous
entry points that they planned to exploit in the event their initial point of entry was sealed.

– –

Excerpts From *The Chronicle of Higher Education,* February 9, 1994.
Posted on ACADEME THIS WEEK

– –

FIGURE 5.3   HACKER ATTACK ON THE INTERNET.

through a rear door wearing a service or repair uniform. This individual knows from
experience that many companies have a rear door that employees often use for cigarette breaks. This door frequently is blocked open so that the employees can easily
reenter. It can be identified by the cigarette butts around it on the ground.

Eavesdroppers   Standard cathode-ray tubes (CRTs) used in common video display
units emit electromagnetic interference (EMI) on a frequency capable of being picked
up by an ordinary television set. Wim Van Eck, a Dutch electronics researcher, proved
to a number of banks that it was possible to read the information on their CRTs almost
a mile away using an ordinary television, a directional antenna, and an external sync
generator. Anyone with this equipment can monitor sensitive information as it appears
on the company's CRTs. Any information that passes through any public communication network is vulnerable to eavesdropping and piggybacking. For example, simply re-
moving one wire from a Tandy (Radio Shack) scanner will allow one to monitor analog
cellular telephone communications. There are clubs of individuals who make a regular
habit of recording telephone conversations involving celebrities and public figures.

ACTIVE THREATS TO INFORMATION SYSTEMS

We discuss six methods that an individual might use to perpetrate an information systems fraud. These methods are input manipulation, program alteration, direct file alteration, data theft, sabotage, and misappropriation or theft of information resources.

INPUT MANIPULATION

In most cases of computer fraud, manipulation of input is the method used. This
method requires the least amount of technical skill. One can alter input with almost no
knowledge of how a computer system operates.

- One individual hacked into a major corporate Web site and stole thousands of
  credit card numbers. He then went on a buying spree over the Web and engaged
  in hundreds of thousands of dollars of fraudulent transactions with a very large
  number of merchants.

- A teller employed by Union Dime Bank was discovered skimming money from bank accounts. This was accomplished by inputting fraudulent entries for computer processing. The crime was uncovered after police raided a bookie the teller was frequenting and discovered that the teller was betting over $30,000 per week. The bank lost more than $1 million.
- The bank Morgan Guaranty accepted a fraudulent telex from the Central Bank of Nigeria. Twenty million dollars in funds were to be electronically transferred to three different banks. However, when an attempt was made to transfer funds to a recently opened $50 account in Santa Ana, California, the transfer was refused. This led to the discovery of the fraud, with no loss to Morgan Guaranty.
- In one case four men who were involved in a complicated bank fraud scheme stole $1.3 million through manipulating deposit memos.
- In another case not only did a woman steal $200 a month for ten years by altering the input documents, she also paid herself an extra salary.
- The systems analyst in a department store purchased some items on his personal account, intercepted the documents, and lowered the prices.
- A data processing operator put flaws in some of the checks that were being processed. As a result of the errors, the checks were rejected by the computer and had to be processed manually. He then converted the checks to his own use.

PROGRAM ALTERATION

Program alteration is perhaps the least common method used to commit computer fraud. This is so because it requires programming skills that are possessed only by a limited number of people. Also, there are program testing methods available in most large companies that can be used to detect an altered program.

- Managers of Equity Funding Life Insurance Company created a program that generated over $100 million in fictitious insurance policies. The bogus policies were sold to other insurance companies, and the company's billing program was then altered to omit the billing of these policies. This was done by assigning fictitious policies to Department 99. When the computer came to a Department 99 policy, it would ignore the billing process.
- A programmer programmed the computer to ignore overdrafts in his account. He was caught when the computer broke down, and the records had to be processed manually.
- The data center manager of a brokerage firm stole $81,000 over several years based on a scheme relying on unauthorized program changes. He drew checks on his firm and then sent them to false accounts he had constructed.

A **trapdoor** is a portion of a computer program that allows someone to access the program while bypassing its normal security. Sometimes program developers place a trapdoor in a program to ensure that they will always have access to it. Trapdoors can exist in accounting systems, database programs, operating systems, and so on.

DIRECT FILE ALTERATION

In some cases individuals find ways to bypass the normal process for inputting data into computer programs. When this happens, the results can be disastrous.

- An employee of Waltson, one of the top 10 brokerage houses on Wall Street, allegedly stole $278,000 by transferring some of the firm's revenues to his personal account. The district attorney admitted that if the accused had not confessed, the prosecution would have had no evidence.

- One defrauder substituted his own version of a master file of accounts receivables for the real one.
- An operations officer at Wells Fargo used the bank's computerized interbranch account settlement process to withdraw funds from a different branch. Fraudulent credits were created to cover the withdrawals. The bank lost more than $20 million over a 3-year period.

DATA THEFT

Theft of important data is a serious problem in business today. In many highly competitive industries, both quantitative and qualitative information about one's competitors is constantly being sought.

The courts have long upheld that data stored in a company's computers are private and cannot be used without the company's permission. For example, in California, data theft can lead to conviction of violating a trade secret, punishable by a 10-year prison sentence. Similar trade secret laws apply in other states.

A considerable amount of information is transmitted between companies via the Internet. This information is vulnerable to theft while en route. It may be intercepted or tapped.

It also may be possible to steal an optical disk or diskette by smuggling it out of the firm in a pocket or briefcase. Bulkier items such as thick reports can be smuggled out in the trash.

- The Encyclopaedia Britannica Company allegedly accused the computer operators on its night shift of copying nearly three million names from the computer file containing the company's most valued customer list. Employees were accused of selling the list to a direct mail advertiser. Encyclopaedia Britannica claimed that the list was worth $3 million.
- A California man was accused of connecting directly into his competitor's computer network, bypassing the computer security system, and copying information as needed.

Further, individuals with access to e-mail simply might copy or attach proprietary information and then transmit it out over the Internet. Using this method, a perpetrator could steal very large amounts of information in only a few minutes' time.

SABOTAGE

Computer sabotage poses a very serious danger to any information system. The destruction of a computer or software can result in the bankruptcy of a firm. Disgruntled employees, especially fired ones, are common perpetrators of sabotage.

In some cases a defrauder may use sabotage to create confusion to cover up fraud. For example, an individual might alter the accounting databases and later try to cover up by sabotaging computer disks or other media.

There are many ways to cause serious damage to the computers. Magnets can be used to erase magnetic tapes and disks simply by placing the magnet (a common magnet will suffice) near the media. A radar beam can have a similar effect if it is pointed at a building containing magnetic media.

- The head of a data center of a leading credit card company, angry at top management, erased computer files containing hundreds of thousands of dollars worth of accounts receivable.
- A Cleveland manufacturer was put out of business when a disgruntled employee, left alone a few minutes in a data storage vault, erased many data files with a simple hand magnet.

- A Dow Chemical Company employee aided a group of radicals in erasing a thousand of the company's computer files.
- An editor who had been fired from Encyclopaedia Britannica Company sabotaged some of the company's computer files by rewriting history and substituting the names of Britannica employees for those of various historical figures.
- Some Internal Revenue Service (IRS) employees destroyed 27,000 tax returns and approximately 80,000 inquiry letters from taxpayers simply to avoid processing them.

Sabotage has become a major issue for Web commerce. Despite annual expenditures for electronic security that exceed $6 billion, successful hacker attacks on Web sites have increased steadily. Even the largest and most sophisticated organizations have suffered, and almost every day the financial press continues to report cases of hackers completely taking over corporate Web sites.

- One cyber gang hijacked the *New York Times* Web site for 3 hours. Other hackers have co-opted the Web sites for federal agencies such as the CIA, the FBI, NASA, and also the White House.

Sometimes computer programs are used to commit acts of sabotage. One of the oldest methods for committing such acts is the logic bomb. A **logic bomb** involves a dormant piece of code placed in a program for later activation by a specific event.

- A programmer for USPA, a Fort Worth–based insurance company, was fired for alleged misconduct. Two days later a logic bomb allegedly activated itself and erased approximately 160,000 vital records from the company's computers. Investigators concluded that the programmer had planted the logic bomb 2 years before he was fired.

A **Trojan horse** is a destructive program masquerading as a legitimate one.

- A Macintosh program lured victims with the promise of erotic pictures. Although it delivered on its unsavory promise, it also erased data on the computers that loaded it.
- Thousands of computer users received a professional-looking disk marked "AIDS Information, Introductory Diskette, Version 2.0." Users who loaded this program eventually found their hard disks locked, with the files encrypted. The program printed a message on the screen saying "The lease for a key software package has expired." Users were told to pay a "leasing fee" to unlock their hard disks by mailing a considerable amount of money to a post office box in Panama.

A **virus program** is similar to a Trojan horse but can spread itself to other programs, "infecting" them with the same virus. Viruses have become so prevalent that the majority of all companies now experience them daily.

- The Ambulance virus causes the image of an ambulance to move across the bottom of the display.
- The Ogre virus causes a sudden reformatting of the hard disk.
- The Ping-Pong virus causes images of Ping-Pong balls to bounce around the screen, erasing characters from the display.
- The Falling Letter virus causes letters in words to suddenly fall to the bottom of the display.
- The Yankee Doodle virus treats its victim to a daily playing of the tune "Yankee Doodle," right before 5:00 P.M. on the system clock.

Viruses can spread quickly through a company's computers, wreaking havoc.

- In one hospital, a virus destroyed nearly 40% of the patient records.

University computer laboratories have been especially vulnerable to viruses. In many cases student and faculty computers have been almost shut down by runaway infections.

A **worm** is a type of virus that spreads itself over a computer network. Because all the computers in a network are connected together, a worm actually grows in size as it infects more and more computers. The term *worm* arises from the different infected computers in the network being thought of as connected segments that resemble the buglike creature.

- The Melissa Macro virus attached itself to Microsoft Word files and spread over the Internet. It propagated itself by automatically sending out infected e-mail attachments to those in the user's e-mail address book. Recipients trusted the infected attachments because they appeared to come from someone they knew. The virus generated such a large volume of messages that it rapidly forced the shutdown of the e-mail servers for many large corporations.
- Robert Morris, Jr., a 22-year-old graduate student at Cornell University, developed a computer virus program that entered the Internet. The worm spread through the network very rapidly, temporarily disabling the operation of thousands of computers across the United States.

The word *virus* is sometimes used loosely to include all malicious programs, including logic bombs, Trojan horses, and worms. Some programs contain the essential features of more than one of these programs.

Another form of sabotage is the denial-of-service attack, in which one or more attackers flood the Web server (or other server) with very large numbers of requests within a short time interval. The resulting overload can clog the server until it can no longer respond to legitimate requests.

Finally, there is also the attack aimed at defacing a company's Web site. The hacker typically breaks into the Web site and modifies or replaces the home page. During the Iraq War, many hackers broke into Web sites and modified the home pages to contain antiwar messages.

MISAPPROPRIATION OR THEFT OF INFORMATION RESOURCES

One type of misappropriation of information resources exists when employees use company computers' resources for their own business:

- Five employees were accused of using their employer's mainframe computer during slack hours to operate their own data processing firm. The employees used the computer so heavily that their employer almost inadvertently upgraded the system to keep up with their demand.

The extent of this problem, like other types of computer fraud, is not well known. However, it is very likely that this problem occurs to some degree in many companies.

- Several employees stole their company's mainframe computer over a period of days, smuggling it out the back door a piece at a time!

THE INFORMATION SYSTEMS SECURITY SYSTEM

Controlling threats is accomplished by implementing security measures and contingency plans. Security measures focus on preventing and detecting threats; contingency plans focus on correcting the effects of threats. It is well-accepted doctrine in information system security that some active threats cannot be prevented without making the system so secure that it is unusable. Furthermore, no security system is of much value without a general atmosphere of honesty and security consciousness.

It should be emphasized that the computer security system must be part of the company's overall internal control structure. This means that the basic elements of internal control (adequate supervision, job rotation, batch control totals, validity checks, and so on) are all important to the computer security system. Information systems security is simply a particular application of established internal control principles to particular problems in the information system.

THE CONTROL ENVIRONMENT

The control environment is basic to effectiveness of the overall control system. Establishing a good control environment depends on eight factors. Each of these factors is discussed as it pertains to the computer security system.

MANAGEMENT PHILOSOPHY AND OPERATING STYLE

The first and most important activity in systems security is creating high morale and an atmosphere conducive to security. No matter how sophisticated a system is, there is always a way around it. Therefore, the primary line of defense should be an overall atmosphere of security consciousness. This can be accomplished in many ways.

All employees should receive education in security. The objective of security education is to obtain security by consent. Security should be taken seriously. All violations should result in immediate apprehension of the guilty. Those in charge should set a good example.

Security rules should be monitored. Otherwise, the system will soon be forgotten. Good relations must be kept with employees. Low morale may result in a higher probability of fraud. Good communication with employees may mitigate problems. For example, files should contain a statement to the effect that they are the property of the company and that their inappropriate use may constitute a criminal offense or a cause for dismissal.

ORGANIZATIONAL STRUCTURE

In many organizations, accounting, computing, and data processing are all organized under one chief information officer (CIO). Such a division, therefore, performs not only the traditional record-keeping functions of accounting but also various computing functions. This poses various problems for establishing and maintaining clearly defined patterns of authority and responsibility. For example, systems analysts and computer programmers may be called on to design, program, and implement an accounts receivable system. An accountant might be called on to make programming changes to an accounting package. The important thing is that clear organizational lines be drawn to designate who is responsible for making the decision directly pertaining to accounting software and accounting procedures. As was discussed, one individual must be in charge of the computer security system.

BOARD OF DIRECTORS AND ITS COMMITTEES

The board of directors must appoint an audit committee. The audit committee must, in turn, appoint or approve the appointment of an internal auditor. Ideally, the internal auditor should have a good background in computer security and serve as the chief computer security officer. In any case, this individual should report periodically to the audit committee on all phases of the computer security system. The audit committee should consult periodically with the external auditors and top management as to the performance of the chief security officer and the computer security system.

Methods of Assigning Authority and Responsibility   The responsibilities of all positions should be carefully documented using organization charts, policy manuals, job descriptions, and so on.

MANAGEMENT CONTROL ACTIVITIES

It is important to establish controls relating to the use and accountability of all resources relating to the computer and information system. Budgets should be established for the acquisition of equipment and software, for operating costs, and for usage. In all three categories, actual costs should be compared with budgeted amounts, and significant discrepancies should be investigated.

Budgetary control is especially important in the computer environment because there is often a tendency for companies to either overspend on information technology or spend on the wrong things. Employees often demand computing hardware, software, and services they really do not need. Buying the most recent model of a personal computer or the latest software package can be emotionally satisfying without producing any benefit to the company.

INTERNAL AUDIT FUNCTION

The computer security system must be audited constantly and then modified to meet changing needs. The chief security officer should establish security policies relevant to the existing system and changes to the system. All modifications to the system, either hardware, software, or personnel, should be implemented in accordance with the established security policies.

Security policies and procedures should be tested for both compliance and effectiveness. Some companies actually hire computer hackers to look for security system vulnerabilities. In more than one case a hacker's arrest and conviction have turned out to be good credentials in applying for a security job.

The system should be "challenged" periodically with hypothetical test transactions. Furthermore, changes to master files should be traced back to the relevant source documents. Such tracing is one way to detect unauthorized direct changes to master files. Another way to detect some such unauthorized changes is through batch control totals.

PERSONNEL POLICIES AND PRACTICES

Segregated duties, adequate supervision, job rotation, forced vacations, and double checks are all important personnel practices. Probably the most important rule is that the duties of computer users and computer systems personnel should be separated. This stems from the need to separate custody and record-keeping responsibilities. Users often have physical access to the company's assets, and computer systems personnel often have access to the data files containing the accounting records. Putting these two types of access privileges together is an invitation to commit fraud.

There also should be, if possible, a separation of duties regarding access to key accounting files. In many computer environments, having access to a file for an asset account might be very close to having access to the asset itself. For example, it might be possible to transfer cash out of a cash account using electronic transfer if the cash account is linked directly to an account in a financial institution.

Job rotation and mandatory vacations should apply to all systems-related personnel who have access to sensitive files. Many fraudulent schemes, even in a computer environment, require continued attention from the perpetrator. For example, an individual with access to both the cash and accounts receivable files might engage in electronic lapping. Such an activity would be very likely to be discovered by someone taking over the position either temporarily or permanently.

Personnel practices concerning hiring and firing are also important. Prospective employees should be screened carefully for the types of problems that might lead to fraud. Such problems include credit difficulties, various addictions (e.g., drugs, alcohol, and gambling), as well as previous employment problems. The more sensitive the position, the more extensive the background investigation should be. Remember, one deviant individual in a critical position might completely destroy the entire company.

Employees should be laid off and fired with the greatest care because terminated employees account for a significant portion of all sabotage incidents. When key employees are fired, all their access privileges to critical hardware, software, and data files should be revoked immediately.

EXTERNAL INFLUENCES

The company's information systems must be in compliance with all federal, state, and local laws and regulations. Among other things, these laws and regulations govern the security and privacy of many types of data, including those relating to customer and client credit, customer and client history, personnel, and government-classified records. They also govern the exportation of certain information to other countries. Failure to provide adequate security in any one of these areas could be a criminal offense.

It is also important to implement a well-documented internal policy to prevent **software piracy**, the illegal copying and distributing of copyrighted software. A company without such a policy might be subject to a variety of legal attacks.

CONTROLS FOR ACTIVE THREATS

The primary way to prevent active threats concerning fraud and sabotage is to implement successive layers of access controls. If all general organizational and data processing controls are in place and working, the primary consideration then becomes limiting unauthorized access to sensitive data and equipment. Just as it is impossible to start a fire without access to heat, it is impossible to commit computer fraud without access to sensitive data or equipment. Access controls separate the perpetrator from his or her potential target.

The philosophy behind the **layered approach to access control** involves erecting multiple layers of controls that separate the would-be perpetrator from his or her potential targets. Three such layers are site-access controls, system-access controls, and file-access controls.

The first step in establishing access controls is to classify all data and equipment according to their importance and vulnerability. Mission-critical equipment and data should be given the strictest controls. Of course, all controls must be applied on a cost-benefit basis within permissible legal constraints. Each group of controls is discussed.

SITE-ACCESS CONTROLS

The objective of **site-access controls** is to physically separate unauthorized individuals from computer resources. This physical separation must be applied especially to hardware, data entry areas, data output areas, data libraries, and communications wiring.

All users should be required to wear security identification badges (with photographs). All rooms containing computer devices or sensitive data should have locked doors. Preferably, the locks should be programmable so that they can reject the keys of those who have been transferred or fired. Many companies use card-key systems. **Biometric hardware authentication** systems also are readily available. These systems automatically identify individuals based on their fingerprints, hand sizes, retina patterns, voice patterns, and so on. Guards should patrol the premises. Operations should be monitored by closed-circuit television.

Data processing complexes should be located in isolated buildings surrounded by fences with gate access. No one except authorized employees should be permitted to enter the gate without having a prior appointment that is verified by security.

All concentrations of computer data (e.g., data libraries, network printers, data entry, and data output sites) and equipment should be located in hard-to-find places, behind doors with programmable locks. There should be no signs on how to find them, and their location should be kept as secret as possible, for there are many cases of highly visible data centers having been bombed.

Attacks on the data library and other mission-critical rooms can be minimized by a very strict entry system. One such system involves a double-door setup for a computer data storage vault, as shown in Figure 5.4. The person desiring admittance to the room must pass through two doors to gain entrance. The individual first uses the programmable lock to enter the outer door and then enters a small room where the intercom must be used to gain admittance to the vault. The vault may then call security, which checks the individual by way of the television monitor and informs the vault whether or not to admit the person. The room also can contain a magnet detector.

Centralized data entry centers should be highly protected areas and strictly off-limits to all nonessential persons. Network printers or other central printers, plotters, and facsimile machines, as well as their output, also must be protected. Highly sensitive output can be printed on hooded printers. The distribution of output should be controlled by a formal, secure delivery system.

Individual personal computers, terminals, disks, and tapes also must be protected. All these objects are subject to theft, malicious tampering, and destruction. Keeping everything under lock and key is the best protection. Personal computers should be locked to avoid internal tampering, should boot only from internal or network devices, and should be accessible only by password. Point-of-sale terminals should be locked when not in use. Finally, when possible, all computer devices should be located behind locked doors, and the walls should be shielded to prevent intrusions of undesirable electromagnetic radiation. Shielding, however, might not be sufficient to prevent EMI eavesdropping. This is best avoided by not displaying passwords and other critical information on CRT displays. Light-emitting diode (LED) and gas-plasma displays give off minimal EMI emissions and are relatively safe.

FIGURE 5.4 DATA STORAGE VAULT.

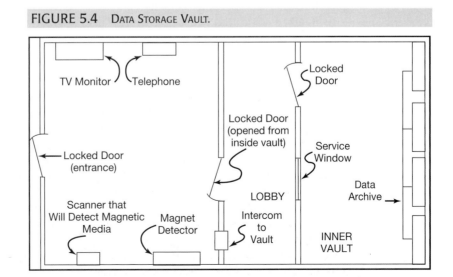

No software should be installed on any computer without prior approval of security. This is a difficult problem because viruses can enter the computer in so many ways. All software purchases should be required to pass through central purchasing and receiving. Any access to the Internet should be limited to those who can be trusted to not download programs from outside without approval. Any programs received in the mail or on the network from unsolicited sources should be destroyed, erased, or referred immediately to security for inspection.

There are other ways to physically limit the intrusion of viruses. One is to assign employees diskless workstations (i.e., that use network disks for storage). All software and data are stored on central file servers. This approach has the advantage of centralizing the installation of all software, as well as file backups. A second way to physically inhibit the intrusion of viruses is to use ROM-based operating systems. Many viruses alter key operating system files and routines. Putting the operating system in ROM therefore will provide some protection from virus threats.

Finally, all physical wiring should be unobtrusive, both indoors and outdoors. In some areas it might be advisable to add air shielding to the wiring that will sound an alarm if broken. Fiberoptic cable generally is considered reasonably safe from tapping and might be used. Wiring centers and communication devices should be located behind locked doors.

SYSTEM-ACCESS CONTROLS

System-access controls are software-oriented controls designed to keep unauthorized users from using the system. The objective of **system-access controls** is to authenticate users by using such means as user IDs, passwords, Internet Protocol (IP) addresses, and hardware devices.

Each internal user can be assigned a user ID number and password at nine levels: at the level of the workstation or personal computer, the network, the host computer, the file server, the file catalog, the program, the data file or database, the record, and the data field. Each of these levels provides a successive layer of protection, separating a would-be intruder from sensitive data. At the top level, the workstation level, the user must enter the correct identifying information before even being able to request access to the communications network. Then, after accessing the network, the user must enter more identifying information before accessing a host computer or file server. After that, additional identification is required before accessing a particular file catalog. This process of identification can continue on down to the individual data field in the database. The operating system(s) should automatically record the time, date, and user number associated with all accesses. This information can be used to investigate any illegal accesses after they occur.

All entries to master files and critical databases should automatically include the user's identification credentials and the time of the transaction entry. This makes it possible to audit all of an individual's transactions.

Passwords should be controlled carefully by a password management system. The system should initially assign passwords to users and then reassign them periodically. The most secure procedure is not to allow users to change their passwords. The reason for this procedure is that user-selected passwords are often very easy to guess because most users will select the name of a relative or pet or one of many well-known passwords such as *ABC, HELLO, APPLE, BANANA, IBM, PASSWORD*, or *TEST*.

The ideal password should consist of uppercase and lowercase letters, special symbols, and numbers. Connecting two unrelated words together with a special symbol is a good compromise between simplicity and security. An example of such a password would be *DOG&SKY*.

An additional layer of security can be introduced by using a sign-countersign system. The user first enters a user identification number. The system then responds with a sign (i.e., a code word). The user is then given a few seconds to enter the correct countersign. The strength of this system is that the same sign-countersign pair is never used twice. The user is periodically issued a list of the words to be used for this procedure.

Some systems allow users to select their own passwords subject to constraints. The passwords must be at least a minimum number of characters long, must not be certain easy-to-guess words, and must be changed periodically. By using this approach, passwords have expiration dates. Users who do not change their passwords by their expiration dates cannot access the system again until their accounts are reset by security.

Under some operating systems, the account limits for user accounts can be assigned a maximum number of attempted security violations within a given time interval. After this limit is exceeded, the account must be reset by security before it can be used again. Under such systems, entering a wrong password may be considered a security violation. A related operating system feature is the ability to automatically disconnect or block any remote communication device from which several consecutively wrong passwords are received.

Personnel should immediately notify security of any pending or actual termination or transfer of employees. Account numbers for these individuals should be cancelled immediately. Programmable locks also should be reprogrammed accordingly.

No password system is of much value unless the passwords themselves are protected. There are many reported cases of intruders finding passwords in the trash or obtaining them from the systems department over the telephone. All employees need to be educated in the proper handling of passwords.

Hardware also can be combined with software to authenticate individuals requesting access to some part of the system. The biometric devices mentioned earlier can be used. An additional precaution is to authenticate the communication device requesting access. Some data terminals and network adapters in personal computers contain unique codes in ROM that are transmitted automatically to the host computer. The operating system or communication software can be programmed to analyze these codes and reject unrecognized devices.

Firewalls (which are typically based on both hardware and software) can be programmed to reject any incoming packets of data that do not originate from preapproved IP addresses on the Internet. Still, a determined hacker can spoof a valid IP address, and for this reason, firewalls represent more of a deterrent than a total solution. A stronger solution combines the use of firewalls with encryption techniques. Outsiders may be required to present digital certificates to identify themselves, and then all exchanges of information can be made over encrypted channels.

Finally, it is often desirable to withhold administrative rights from individual PC users. This can prevent users from installing any software on their PCs, which can help prevent the PCs from becoming contaminated with viruses, Trojan horses, and so on.

FILE-ACCESS CONTROLS

The final layer of access controls is applied at the file level. **File-access controls** prevent unauthorized access to both data and program files.

The most fundamental file-access control is the establishment of authorization guidelines and procedures for accessing and altering files. Special restrictions should be placed on programmers who have the specific knowledge to make program changes. They should not be permitted access to any of the company's data files without written approval. Operators and supervisors should be told not to take instructions from programmers without written approval. And not even authorized program changes should be made without written approval. Programmers should make all properly authorized changes to a duplicate copy of the original program, not the original program itself, and the duplicate copy should be inspected before being substituted for the original.

All important programs should be kept in **locked files**. This means that the program can be run but not looked at or altered. Only security should know the code (password) to unlock the file. Security should keep a library of programs that are in operation. They should check the programs in operation periodically to determine if they are bit-for-bit identical to authorized versions in the library.

Programs also can be signed digitally (as discussed in Chap. 3) in the same way that electronic messages are signed, and verification of the digital signature can both positively authenticate the identity of the source of the program and verify that it has not been altered. For example, the XYZ Company might purchase a program for analyzing accounts receivables. To protect itself, XYZ would require the program to carry the digital signature of the vendor/developer. Furthermore, if XYZ does not know and trust the vendor/developer's public key, then XYZ also can require that the vendor/developer's public key be certified by a recognized certification authority.

It is possible to install resident programs that run constantly as background tasks and check for signs of viruses or altered files. Unfortunately, there are almost too many viruses in circulation to count, and there are new ones all the time that may outsmart existing virus detection programs. To give you an idea of the problem, consider what happened to an early version of one antivirus program. Someone distributed an unauthorized and bogus version of this program that contained a Trojan horse! Some virus detection programs (Fig. 5.5) also eradicate recognizable viruses from infected systems. The best way to avoid problems with viruses is to control the addition of new files to the system.

CONTROLS FOR PASSIVE THREATS

Passive threats include such problems as power and hardware failures. Controls for such threats can be either preventative or corrective.

FAULT-TOLERANT SYSTEMS

Most methods of dealing with system component failures rely on monitoring and redundancy. If one part of the system fails, a redundant part immediately takes over, and

FIGURE 5.5   PART OF THE VIRUS LIST IN A TYPICAL ANTIVIRUS PROGRAM.

Virus List	Type	Size	#
Beijing	File	1223	1
Best Wishes	File	1024	1
Best Wishes 2	File	970	1
Beta	File	1117	1
Bichi	File	1702	1
Big Joke	File	1068	1
Big Italian	Boot	1024	1
Black Death Necropolis	File	1951	1
Black Jack	File	247	3
Black Jack 3	File	231	1
Black Jack 5	File	267	1
Black Jack 5B	File	272	1
Black Jack 6	File	276	1

OK   Print

Search for: _____   Find Next   Info

the system continues operating with little or no interruption. Such systems are called **fault-tolerant systems**. Fault tolerance can be applied at five levels: to network communications, to CPU processors, to DASDs, to the power supply, and to individual transactions. Many companies have a high degree of fault tolerance in their systems because computer failures can corrupt data and completely disrupt operations. Some companies could not survive a few days without a high degree of operational capability in their computers.

Networks can be made fault-tolerant by introducing duplicate communication paths and communications processors. There are two main approaches to redundant CPU processing. Systems with **consensus-based protocols** contain an odd number of processors; if one processor disagrees with the others, it is thereafter ignored. Other systems use a second **watchdog processor** that takes over processing if something happens to the first processor.

DASDs are made fault-tolerant by several methods, including read-after-write checks, bad-sector lockouts, and disk mirroring. With **read-after-write checks**, the disk drive rereads a sector after writing it to disk, confirming that it was written without error. If the confirmation fails, the offending sector on the disk can be **flagged** and locked out so that it will not be used again. The data can then be written to a good sector. If the software program does not support bad-sector error recovery, it will abort the write process and return an error message. A utility program can then be used to lock out the offending sector, and the application program can be tried again. **Disk mirroring** or **disk shadowing** involves writing all data in parallel to two or more disks. If one disk fails, the application program can automatically continue, using the good disk(s). There are also software programs helpful in recovering data from damaged files or disks.

Fault tolerance for power failures can be achieved with an uninterruptable power supply. If the power fails, the backup system, sometimes battery-powered, takes over so fast that no loss of continuity in the processing activities occurs. Then there is plenty of time to either switch the system to a generator or shut it down in an orderly manner. In brief power outages, the power is restored before either of these measures is necessary. Finally, some devices smooth out voltage drops and surges, which can cause severe damage to some electronic components.

Fault tolerance applied at the transaction level involves **rollback processing** and **database shadowing**. With rollback processing, transactions are never written to disk until they are complete. If the power fails or another fault occurs while a transaction is being written, at its first opportunity the database program automatically rolls itself back to its prefault state. Database shadowing is similar to disk shadowing, except a duplicate of all transactions is made and possibly sent via communications to a remote location.

CORRECTING FAULTS: FILE BACKUPS

Some studies have suggested that over 50% of PC owners do not properly back up their files. For this reason, a system that centralizes the backing up of files is essential. Such systems are commonly used to back up critical disks. For example, Prudential Bache's system calls for files to be backed up every 2 to 5 minutes.

There are three types of backups: full backups, incremental backups, and differential backups. A **full backup** backs up all files on a given disk. In most systems, each file contains an **archive bit** that is set to 0 during the backup process. The operating system automatically sets this bit to 1 whenever a file is altered. An **incremental backup** backs up all files whose archive bit is set to 1. Each file's archive bit is then reset to 0 during the backup process. An incremental backup, therefore, backs up only those files that have been modified since the last full or incremental backup. Finally, a **differential backup** is the same as an incremental backup, only the archive bits are not reset to 0 during the backup process.

The simplest backup scheme is to periodically make full backups. After such backups, the backup sets (e.g., tapes or optical disks) should be removed immediately to an off-site storage area. Ideally, all full backups should be made in duplicate as an extra precautionary measure.

In many cases, if not most, taking continual backups of the entire disk or computer system throughout the business day is not practical. Many such systems do incremental or differential backups between full backups, only backing up the altered files. This procedure can save both time and storage media costs and is useful in many situations. In general, incremental backups require less storage media and are faster than differential backups. One problem, however, comes in restoring incremental backups. The procedure to restore incremental backups involves first restoring the last full backup set and then restoring all incremental backup sets, one after the other, in chronological order. The problem with this procedure is that it can result in files being restored that were erased from the system sometime between the full backup and the last incremental backup. Of course, this is only a problem if files are erased. The differential backup, on the other hand, avoids this problem altogether.

Backing up files is not the same as archiving them. This is so because the media used for backup might not be reliable for long-term storage. For example, some optical disks are said to have an archival life of 10 years or less.

INTERNET SECURITY

The topic of Internet security deserves special attention because a company's connection to the Internet makes it a potential target for every hacker in the world. The Internet creates an electronic window to the outside world that eliminates the possibility of physically isolating the company's information resources, so it is not possible to completely implement the physical-separation layer of the layered-access approach to security. For example, the company might place a computer behind locked doors, but the computer is not really isolated if it is wired to the Internet.

Internet-related vulnerabilities may arise from weaknesses in five areas:

1. The operating system or its configuration
2. The Web server or its configuration
3. The private network and its configuration
4. Various server programs
5. General security procedures

Each of these possible vulnerabilities is discussed.

OPERATING SYSTEM VULNERABILITIES

The Web server is essentially an extension of the operating system. The result is that any weakness in operating system security is also likely to create a related weakness in the Web server's security. For this reason, the security administrator must, first and foremost, secure the operating system.

The problem, however, is that no operating system is attack-proof, and hackers continually find new weaknesses in operating systems. Therefore, the administrator must constantly monitor security bulletins published by the operating system vendor and by third-party advisory services. For example, Microsoft keeps up-to-date security information for Windows on its Web site at *www.microsoft.com/*.

Even a correctly maintained operating system will fail if it is not configured properly. For example, by default, a recent version of Windows came preconfigured to include a "guest user" in its database of users authorized to access the system. The problem is, however, that this merely opened an unnecessary door for hackers.

WEB SERVER VULNERABILITIES

Web servers are similar to operating systems in that it is necessary to constantly monitor advisory bulletins for security updates and information on configuration issues. Such monitoring is especially important for Web servers because Web servers and Web browsers tend to be updated more frequently than operating systems, and updates always come with the possibility of new security weaknesses. Web servers also serve more on the front line of security because they are the portals through which outsiders often pass.

Web server security can be degraded seriously by configuration problems. One of the most common configuration problems is in the area of configuring permissions for directories and files relating to executable script programs. Executable script programs are a necessary component of almost any commercial Web site. For example, an executable program called a *forms handler* must be run anytime a customer enters a sales order into the company's Web site. Moreover, the forms handler must have write access to the disk to save the order information. Therefore, the anonymous customer must have both execute and write access, two privileges that together can form a very dangerous combination if applicable to the same file directory. This is so because a hacker could use the write privilege to upload a malicious program to a particular directory and then run the program in this directory using the execute privilege.

Therefore, write and execute access should never be granted to the same directory. In practice, however, this lethal combination of privileges is often granted by accident. For example, sometimes the administrator places the script files in the wrong directory, a directory that already has user-write privileges attached to it. Also, many Web administrators use Web authoring and design tools that automatically place files in particular directories unknown to the administrator and also automatically alter file permissions without any indication or warning. The file permission can get especially confused if more than one developer is working on the same Web site at the same time.

PRIVATE NETWORK VULNERABILITIES

Special risks are created when a Web server is placed on a host computer connected to other various users' computers via a local area network, and hackers may attack one computer through another. If the users' computers have access to the computer hosting the Web server, then the hacker can first break into one of the user's computers and then rely on the user's access rights to invade the host computer for the Web server.

This problem is very difficult because it may be virtually impossible for a server administrator to ensure adequate security on all users' machines. This is so because in many companies users typically access the Internet, run all kinds of strange and insecure programs, and improperly configure their operating systems.

One way hackers attack one computer through an alternate computer is by e-mailing (in the form of an attachment) a Trojan horse program to the alternate computer. The hacker typically tricks the recipient at the alternate computer into opening the e-mail attachment by spoofing a return address from someone familiar. (Hackers typically obtain e-mail lists from corporate directories available at many corporate Web sites.)

The Trojan horse program is automatically and secretly installed when the user/victim on the alternate computer opens the e-mail message. One such Trojan horse program, Back Orifice, permits the hacker to remotely take control of the victim's computer via the Internet and from there access the host computer for the Web server. The user of the alternate computer never sees or hears anything; the Trojan horse program runs quietly in the background.

Vulnerabilities from Various Server Programs

Many Web server host computers run not only the Web server but other servers as well, including FTP servers (for file transfers to and from other computers), e-mail servers, and remote control servers (that permit legitimate remote computers to take control of the host computer). The problem is that each additional server poses additional security risks, and a security flaw relating to any one server can open a door for hackers to attack all the other servers and all the files on the computer, even other computers that may be on the same local area network.

Sometimes FTP servers are much less secure than most Web servers. This is so because the basic File Transfer Protocol (FTP) sends passwords in the clear with no encryption. Despite this weakness, many organizations rely on FTP as a means of transferring sensitive files over the Internet. Finally, an advanced, encryption-based version of FTP also exists and should be used whenever possible.

In general, almost all server programs have the built-in capabilities to grant access privileges to remote users. This makes server programs very dangerous, for many server programs are based on extremely weak security models. For this reason, the administrator should not run any server programs not absolutely necessary.

General Security Procedures

A good overall security atmosphere is essential. The best security software in the world will not help if the system administrators do not enforce the policies. Further, all errors and exceptions must be logged to secure files, and these logs must be constantly monitored.

Securing log files is an especially important issue because hackers often try to "cover their tracks" by altering log files. One way to secure logs is to write them to a remote computer, where the file permissions on the remote computer are set so that new information can only be appended.

Finally, a word on firewalls; Firewalls are used commonly to restrict incoming access on network computers. Incoming access can be restricted to allow only particular incoming IP addresses and access to particular servers and to block incoming requests based on their content.

Firewalls also can block outgoing access or limit outgoing access to particular programs or servers. For example, the firewall might be set to allow outgoing access by the accounting program and the Web browser; any other program (such as a Trojan horse) would then be blocked automatically.

While firewalls are one important tool, it should be remembered that IP addresses can be spoofed, which in turn can permit illegitimate incoming or outgoing access. Thus, basic security training and procedures always must be given first consideration.

DISASTER RISK MANAGEMENT

Disasters happen. The destruction of the World Trade Center in New York City is just one example of an unexpected disaster that quickly and seriously interrupted normal business activity. Many organizations are critically dependent on computer systems to support daily operations. Consequently, if computer systems processing is delayed or interrupted, the organization may incur significant losses. Disaster risk management is essential to ensure continuity of operations in the event of a catastrophe.

Disaster **risk management** concerns prevention and contingency planning. In some cases, insurance might help control risks, but most insurers are reluctant to underwrite the costs of business interruptions for large companies, especially for those companies without disaster recovery plans. Both prevention and contingency planning are discussed in what follows.

PREVENTING DISASTERS

Disaster prevention is the first step in managing disaster risk. Studies have shown the following frequencies of disaster causes:

Natural disasters	30%
Deliberate actions	45%
Human error	25%

These data imply that a large percentage of disasters can be mitigated or avoided by good overall security policy.

Many disasters resulting from sabotage and errors can be prevented by good security policy and planning. Careful consideration should be given to natural-disaster risks associated with prospective building sites. Concentrations of computer equipment and data should be located in parts of buildings least exposed to storms, earthquakes, floods, and fire, as well as deliberate acts of sabotage.

Adequate electronic and mechanical systems for fire, flood, and intrusion are important. Water-based sprinkler systems can be harmful to electronic components. Many companies use fire-extinguishing systems that rely on something besides water, such as gas, foam, or powder.

CONTINGENCY PLANNING FOR DISASTERS

A **disaster recovery plan** must be implemented at the highest levels in the company. Ideally, it should be approved by a committee of the board of directors as part of the general computer security plan.

The first steps in developing a disaster recovery plan should be obtaining the support of senior management and setting up a planning committee. When completed, the disaster recovery plan should be thoroughly documented and approved by these same individuals. Overall, a life-cycle approach should be used to design, implement, operate, and evaluate the plan. Estimates suggest that the initial costs of implementing a disaster recovery plan can range from 2% to 10% of the overall information systems budget. The design of the plan should include three major components: an evaluation of the company's needs, a list of priorities for recovery based on these needs, and a set of recovery strategies and procedures.

ASSESS THE COMPANY'S CRITICAL NEEDS

All mission-critical resources should be identified. These include hardware, software, power and maintenance requirements, building space, vital records, and human resources.

LIST PRIORITIES FOR RECOVERY

Even with a good plan, fully recovering from a major disaster can take a long time. Therefore, priorities should be established that correspond to the company's critical needs. The priority list might indicate that certain mission-critical activities and services are to be reestablished within minutes or hours after the disaster. On the other hand, the plan might indicate that other activities and services are to be reestablished days, weeks, or months later.

RECOVERY STRATEGIES AND PROCEDURES

A complete set of recovery strategies and procedures is essential. The plan should include such detail so that when disaster strikes, the company immediately knows what to do, who should do it, how to do it, and how long it should take. These considerations are discussed in detail in what follows.

Emergency Response Center   When disaster strikes, all authority for data processing and computer operations is transferred to the **emergency response team**, headed by the emergency operations director. These individuals direct the execution of the recovery plan from the **emergency operations center**, a predesignated site.

Escalation Procedures   The **escalation procedures** state the conditions under which a disaster should be declared, who should declare it, and who that person should notify when executing the declaration.

Alternate Processing Arrangements   The most important part of a disaster recovery plan is the specification of a backup site to be used if the primary computing site is destroyed or unusable. Three types of backup sites are possible: cold sites, hot sites, and flying-start sites. A **cold site** is an alternate computing site that contains the wiring for computers but no equipment. A **hot site** is an alternate site that contains the wiring and the equipment as well. A **flying-start site** is an alternate site that contains the wiring, the equipment, and also very up-to-date backup data and software. A cold site is capable of assuming full operation in a matter of days, a hot site in a matter of hours, and a flying-start site in a matter of seconds or minutes. In practice, the type of backup site used must be determined for each company on a cost-benefit basis, although few companies find the high cost of owning a flying-start site justifiable.

One way to maintain up-to-date data at a flying-start site is to mirror all transactions at the primary site and then immediately transmit them via communications to the backup site. Such data could be transmitted at high speed through the use of fiberoptic channel extenders. In some cases, a nearby backup site might be acceptable.

There are, however, alternatives besides actually purchasing an alternate site. Three such alternatives involve contracting with a computing service bureau, a commercial vendor of disaster services, or with another ordinary company, one possibly in the same industry.

A **service bureau** specializes in providing data processing services to companies who choose not to process their own data. In some cases it may be useful to establish a contingency plan based on a contract with a service bureau. This option may be viable for relatively small companies with simple data processing needs. However, the service bureau is unlikely to be a workable solution for a company with complex computing needs. The computing needs of most large companies are too complex to be satisfied by the limited data processing services offered by typical service bureaus. Further, most service bureaus will not put computers on employees' desks, something that might be needed.

Several vendors provide disaster recovery services, including Comdisco, IBM, and Sungard. Comdisco, for example, specializes in leasing hot sites for a monthly fee. This company supports an international disaster recovery network of hot sites linked together by satellite.

The third type of arrangement is a contract with another ordinary company. Some companies have enough excess computing power to temporarily assume the needs of others. A **shared contingency agreement** or **reciprocal disaster agreement** is an agreement between two companies in which each company agrees to help the other if the need arises. In a variation on this agreement, the two companies share a common hot site through joint ownership.

The Personnel Relocation Plan   Contingency plans need to be made for the possibility of having to suddenly relocate employees to a backup site. Careful planning is needed in this regard, because many employees might have difficulty in relocating on short notice.

The Personnel Replacement Plan   The possibility of losing employees to the disaster must be considered. Replacing highly skilled employees can be difficult, and the replacement employees may require extensive training.

The Salvage Plan   In some disasters it is possible to recover equipment and valuable records if quick action is taken. For example, a building that loses its roof in a hurricane will be exposed to rain. Losses in such a situation might be minimized if salvage efforts get under way immediately.

The Plan for Testing and Maintaining the System   Companies' computing needs often change rapidly. For this reason, any disaster recovery plan should be tested every 6 months. Outdated or untested plans might not work in a crisis.

❖ SUMMARY

The information system security system is the subsystem of the organization that controls the special risks associated with computerized information systems. Security systems are developed by applying the traditional life-cycle approach of systems analysis, design, implementation and operation, evaluation, and control.

There are two major approaches to analyzing system vulnerabilities and threats in computer security planning. In the quantitative approach to risk assessment, each loss exposure is computed as the product of the cost of an individual loss times the likelihood of its occurrence. In the qualitative approach to risk assessment, the system's vulnerabilities and threats are listed and subjectively ranked in order of their contribution to the company's total loss exposures.

A vulnerability is a weakness in a computer system, and a threat is a potential exploitation of a vulnerability. Various laws, regulations, and pronouncements address the problem of computer crime. A successful attack on a computer system requires some sort of access to the hardware, sensitive data files, or critical programs. Anyone who accesses equipment, computer data, or files without proper authorization is an intruder. There are many types of intruders, such as unnoticed intruders, impersonating intruders, wiretappers, piggybackers, and eavesdroppers. There are at least six different methods that an individual might use to perpetrate a computer fraud. These are input manipulation, program alteration, direct file alteration data theft, sabotage, and misappropriation or theft of computer resources.

Sabotage poses a very serious danger to any installation. There are many ways to cause serious damage to the installation. Computer programs might be used to commit acts of sabotage. Potential problems include logic bombs, Trojan horses, virus programs, and worms. Controlling threats is accomplished by implementing security measures and contingency plans. Security measures focus on preventing and detecting threats; contingency plans focus on correcting the effects of threats. The organization's control environment is basic to effectiveness of the overall control system.

The primary way to prevent fraud and sabotage is to implement successive layers of access controls. A layered approach to access control involves erecting multiple layers of control that separate the would-be perpetrator from potential targets. Three such layers are site-access controls, system-access controls, and file-access controls.

Most methods of dealing with system component failures rely on monitoring and redundancy. If one part of the system fails, a redundant part immediately takes over, and the system continues operating with little or no interruption. Such systems are called fault-tolerant systems. Fault tolerance can be applied at five levels: to network communications, CPU processors, DASDs, the power supply, and to individual transactions. Many companies have a high degree of fault tolerance in their systems because computer failures can corrupt data and completely disrupt operations.

Disaster risk management includes prevention and contingency planning. Disaster prevention is the first step in managing disaster risk. A disaster recovery plan must be implemented at the highest level in the company. It should be approved by a committee of the board of directors as part of the general computer security plan.

❖ GLOSSARY

active threats: computer fraud and computer sabotage.

archive bit: a bit used to determine whether or not a file has been altered.

biometric hardware authentication: systems that automatically identify individuals based on their fingerprints, hand sizes, retina patterns, voice patterns, and other personal features.

chief security officer (CSO):   individual charged with management of the computer security system.

cold site: an alternate computing site that contains the wiring for computers but no equipment.

Computer Fraud and Abuse Act of 1986:   makes it a federal crime to knowingly and with intent fraudulently gain unauthorized access to data stored in the computers of financial institutions, the federal government, or computers operating in interstate or foreign commerce.

consensus-based protocols: systems that contain an odd number of CPU processors; if one processor disagrees with the others, it is thereafter ignored.

database shadowing: a duplicate of all transactions is automatically recorded.

differential backup: an incremental backup in which the file archive bits are not reset to 0 during the backup process.

disaster recovery plan: a contingency plan for recovering from disasters.

disk mirroring: fault-tolerant processing control that involves writing all data in parallel to two disks.

disk shadowing: synonym for disk mirroring.

emergency operations center: a predesignated site designed to assist in disaster recovery.

emergency response team: individuals who direct the execution of a disaster recovery plan.

escalation procedures: state the conditions under which a disaster should be declared, who should declare it, and who that person should notify when executing the declaration.

fault-tolerant systems: use of redundant components such that if one part of the system fails, a redundant part immediately takes over, and the system continues operating with little or no interruption.

file-access controls: prevent unauthorized access to both data and program files.

flagged: marking and locking out a disk or DASD sector so that it will not be used again after it has been found to be unreliable.

flying-start site: an alternate processing site that contains the necessary wiring and equipment, and also up-to-date backup data and software.

full backup: all files on a given disk are backed up.

hackers: individuals who attack computer systems for fun and challenge.

hot site: an alternate computer processing site that contains the wiring and the equipment as well.

incremental backup: all files whose archive bit is set to 1 are backed up.

information security system: the subsystem of the organization that controls these risks.

intruder: anyone who accesses computer equipment, data, or files without proper authorization.

layered approach to access control: erecting multiple layers of access control that separate a would-be perpetrator from potential targets.

locked files: a program can be run but not looked at or altered.

logic bomb: a dormant piece of code placed in a computer program for later activation by a specific event.

passive threats: system faults and natural disasters.

piggybacking: the interception of legitimate information and substitution of fraudulent information in its place.

qualitative approach to risk assessment: a system's vulnerabilities and threats are listed and subjectively ranked in order of their contribution to the company's total loss exposures.

quantitative approach to risk assessment: each loss exposure is computed as the product of the cost of an individual loss times the likelihood of its occurrence.

read-after-write checks: a DASD (e.g., disk drive) rereads a sector after writing it to disk, confirming that it was written without error.

reciprocal disaster agreement: synonym for shared contingency agreement.

risk management: the process of assessing and controlling computer system risks.

risk-seeking perpetrator: one who will take very big risks for a small reward.

rollback processing: transactions are not written to disk until they are complete so that if power fails or another fault occurs while a transaction is being written, the database program may automatically roll itself back to its prefault state.

service bureau: provides data processing services to companies who choose not to process their own data.

shared contingency agreement: an agreement between two companies in which each company agrees to help the other with disaster recovery should the need arise.

site-access controls: controls that physically separate unauthorized individuals from computer resources.

software piracy: the copying and distributing of copyrighted software without permission.

system-access controls: software-oriented controls designed to keep unauthorized users from using the system by such means as account numbers, passwords, and hardware devices.

system faults: system component failures, such as disk failures or power outages.

threat: a potential exploitation of a system vulnerability.

trapdoor: a portion of a computer program that allows someone to access the program while by-passing its normal security.

Trojan horse: a destructive program masquerading as a legitimate one.

virus program: similar to a Trojan horse but can spread itself to other programs, "infecting" them with the same virus.

vulnerability: a weakness in a system.

watchdog processor: a second CPU processor that takes over processing if something happens to the first CPU processor.

worm: a type of virus program that spreads itself over a computer network.

❖ CHAPTER QUIZ

Answers to the Chapter Quiz appear on page 194.

1. Collusion appears to be (_____) in a computerized versus a manual system.
   (a) less likely
   (b) more likely
   (c) equally likely

2. Which of the following is an active threat to computer security?
   (a) computer sabotage
   (b) earthquake
   (c) equipment failures
   (d) power outages

3. Individuals who attack computer systems for fun and challenge are sometimes called (_____).
   (a) duffers
   (b) geeks
   (c) hackers
   (d) flaggers

4. The interception of legitimate information and substitution of fraudulent information in its place is called (_____).
   (a) EMI eavesdropping
   (b) flagging
   (c) hacking
   (d) piggybacking

5. In most cases of computer fraud, (_____) is the method used.
   (a) program alteration
   (b) input manipulation
   (c) direct file alteration
   (d) misappropriation or theft of computer resources

6. A destructive computer program masquerading as a legitimate one is called a (_____).
   (a) trapdoor
   (b) logic bomb
   (c) Trojan horse
   (d) worm

7. Five employees were accused of using their employer's mainframe computer during slack hours to operate their own data processing firm. This is an example of (_____).
   (a) program alteration
   (b) input manipulation
   (c) direct file alteration
   (d) misappropriation or theft of computer resources

8. An alternate computer processing site that contains the necessary wiring and computer equipment for operation, but not data files, is called a (_____).
   (a) hot site
   (b) cold site
   (c) flying-start site
   (d) fault-tolerant site

9. Marking and locking out a disk or DASD sector so that it will not be used again after it has been found to be unreliable is called (_____).
   (a) hacking
   (b) flagging
   (c) disk shadowing
   (d) disk mirroring

10. A dormant piece of code placed in a computer program for later activation by a specific event is a (_____).
   (a) trapdoor
   (b) logic bomb
   (c) Trojan horse
   (d) worm

❖ REVIEW PROBLEM

Hart Manufacturing has a large computer department. Barbara May is in charge of the internal audit staff. A routine investigation revealed that several customer accounts are phony and that several accounts with balances in excess of $1,000 each could not be traced to the names and addresses listed on the accounts. For example, one account was listed as belonging to an individual named John Day. When she tried to contact this individual, she found that the address was that of her local cemetery. In addition, the telephone number was not a working number. Furthermore, there was no individual in the telephone directory listed as John Day. Additional investigations revealed that there was no credit application on file for this individual.

To make things more complicated, it was found that all these accounts were 12 months overdue. For some reason that had not yet been ascertained, none of these accounts appeared on the accounts receivable aging reports.

Required
What type of fraud has probably been committed here? Which individuals are the ones most likely to have been involved?

❖ SOLUTION TO REVIEW PROBLEM

Program alteration is the most likely cause of this problem:
A. It is very likely that someone has altered the accounts receivables program to allow transactions by individuals not on the approved credit list. This individual has covered up by fixing the aging program to omit these accounts. There is also the possibility of collusion between a programmer and someone in the credit department. This would explain the fact that there was not adequate supporting documentation on file supporting credit approval. Of course, the programmer might have put a trapdoor in the program that would allow credit to certain individuals, even though they were not in the approved customers database. This could have been done without the help of someone in the credit department.
   (1) It should be noted that the program alteration might have been done by a system operator. System operators sometimes have access to all files on the computer system. The operator might have replaced the legitimate version of the accounts receivables program with an altered one.
B. The solution to this type of problem is to have a formal system for installing and maintaining software.
   (1) All changes to software should be supported by documentation, including complete review and approval.

(2) Programmers should not have access to the working versions of software. They should be restricted to making changes, on an approved basis, to copies of working software. The modified copies should be reviewed before formal installation.

(3) Master copies of software should be kept in a secure place. These master copies should be periodically compared, using readily available file comparison utilities, to the operating versions.

❖ REVIEW QUESTIONS

1. Identify several unique problems and risks associated with computerized information networks.
2. What elements are included in a computer security system?
3. Does the development of a computer security system require application of the life-cycle approach? Discuss.
4. What is risk management?
5. Distinguish between the qualitative and the quantitative approaches to analyzing system vulnerabilities and threats.
6. Identify some of the general types of threats that affect computer systems.
7. Is it possible to rigorously identify characteristics of the white-collar criminal?
8. What types of individuals pose a threat to a computer system?
9. Identify several different types of intruders.
10. Identify and discuss six different methods that an individual might use to perpetrate a computer fraud.
11. How might computer programs be used to commit acts of sabotage?
12. What is a virus program? Give several examples.
13. What role does an organization's control environment play in information system security? Give several specific examples.
14. Describe the layered approach to access control. What specific layers of access control might be implemented?
15. What are fault-tolerant systems? Illustrate the application of fault tolerance to the following areas:
    (a) network communications
    (b) CPU processors
    (c) DASDs
    (d) power supply
    (e) individual transactions
16. Distinguish between full backups, incremental backups, and differential backups of files.
17. What steps should be taken in the development of a disaster recovery plan?
18. Identify several recovery strategies and procedures that might be included in a disaster recovery plan.
19. Identify several alternate processing arrangements that might be included in a disaster recovery plan.

❖ DISCUSSION QUESTIONS AND PROBLEMS

20. XYZ Hardware Retailing Company runs a batch system for accounts receivable. On the first Monday of each month, the operations specialist runs an accounts receivable update. The procedure is as follows: The accountant prepares a list of all updates on a disk file; this disk file is then transferred to the account of a systems specialist; the operations specialist then carefully edits the data and then generates the batch job.

    Required
    Evaluate this procedure from a control standpoint.

21. The Randell Company is a medium-sized toy manufacturer. The information services division of this company is composed of user services, systems programming, and systems maintenance. In addition, the company has a batch-oriented accounts receivable system. All the databases related to accounts receivable are maintained by the systems programmer.

Recently, a minor bug was detected in the accounts receivable program. The procedure to correct the bug was as follows: First, it was reported to the systems programmer by a member of the accounting staff; next, the systems programmer discussed the problem with the head of systems programming and agreed to an appropriate change; then the individual who reported the problem was notified that appropriate corrective action was being taken.

Required
Evaluate the procedures used in the Randell Company for program modification.

22. Barbara Carson is a high-ranking officer in the Marines. She has recently been placed in charge of computer-assisted design and manufacturing for a highly classified project relating to a new high-technology aircraft. The project is so secret that she has been assigned to develop it in an abandoned base high in the mountains of California. Project resources included are a mainframe computer, 100 military personnel (including programmers, operations specialists, and so on), and 50 nonmilitary support staff. Most of the support staff do not have security clearances. The problem is that their skills lie primarily in programming, computer operations, and hardware maintenance.

Required
Develop an overall security system that maintains appropriate security regarding outsiders and effectively uses the nonmilitary support staff without violating security.

23. Renco Manufacturing has had a problem with unauthorized access to its accounts receivable database. The chief accountant suspects that one of the systems operators is somehow making changes to the accounts receivable database in an unauthorized manner. The accountant, however, is uncertain about the methods being used. It is possible that an operator has made changes to the accounting program. Another possibility is that the operator is accessing the accounting program without proper authorization.

Required
Discuss appropriate methods for resolving this problem.

24. Rauls Retailing has a high turnover rate among its employees. It maintains a very large computer system that supports approximately 200 networked PCs. The company maintains fairly extensive databases regarding its customers. These include customer profiles, past purchasing patterns, and prices charged.

Recently the company has been having major problems with competitors. It appears that one competitor seems to be very effective at taking away Rauls' customers. Most of the company's customers have been visited by this competitor, and identical products have been offered at lower prices in every case.

Required
What is the possible security problem? What can be done about it?

25. Green Manufacturing maintains a large computer systems division. The company recently has faced a major problem with its software. It seems that ever since one of the computer programmers has been fired, disk files are mysteriously being erased. The chief analyst suspects that the fired programmer had placed a logic bomb in the operating system somewhere so that disk files would be erased in the event that his Social Security Number was no longer in the accounting database.

Required
Discuss the methods for the detection of this logic bomb. What methods could be used to prevent this type of problem?

26. Finco Merchandising specializes in purchasing bankrupt firms and disposing of their assets by direct mail. It maintains about 30 sales offices around the United States. Each of these sales offices does the actual direct-mail work within its own region. The central office in Atlanta maintains the customer database, and customers' names are transferred from this office to the individual sales offices on a weekly basis. The transfer is presently being done through one of the major public packet-switched networks. It is suspected that customers' names are somehow leaking out to competitors as a result of their being transmitted through the public network.

Required
Discuss at least two alternatives that might be used to ensure greater security.

27. Hart Manufacturing Company is relatively small, with approximately 100 employees. The company's minicomputer is run by two individuals. One individual is responsible for the physical operation of the computer. This includes maintaining the company's magnetic tape library. At present, the tape library includes master files for most of the important accounting systems databases. Although the company has plenty of disk space, the accounting master files are maintained on tapes. The system is primarily batch-oriented, and updates are run only once a month. Currently, the tape library is adjacent to the computer room and can be entered either through the computer room or via another outside door. Because this individual is very busy, most employees enter the tape room and log their tapes in and out as needed.

    ### Required
    Given the limited resources of this company, discuss an appropriate security system for the tape library.

28. Bundy Retailing sells building supply materials. It is located in a medium-sized midwestern town and has four sales offices there. Each sales office has its own computer terminal that is hardwired to the company's main computer through a dedicated line. These terminals are used to authorize sales transactions. Given that an appropriate credit check has been made, the salesperson simply types in the sales order on one of the computer terminals, and authorization to release the goods is immediately printed out at the company's central warehouse. Recently, however, the company has detected a security problem. There are several salespeople working in each office and sharing the same terminal. It appears that one of the salespeople has been entering sales transactions and charging them to Brown Contracting Company. The problem is that Brown Contracting has never received any of these goods. In fact, all the goods have been released to an impostor. This is a very serious problem because the total amount of goods released cost the company approximately $20,000. The chief of security is perplexed because she does not know which salesperson is responsible. There is even some discussion about the possibility that an unauthorized intruder may have accessed the terminal.

    ### Required
    Discuss appropriate security measures that could have been taken to prevent this problem from occurring.

29. Waldo Company has had a problem with one of its employees using the computer network to play games. In the past the company has not been very strict about controlling the use of the company's network because employees often have slack time during the off-season. Recently, however, a serious problem has occurred. It appears that one of the game programs run on the network contained a virus. The virus is a special type of computer program that can cause considerable damage to a network when run with other computer programs in the system concurrently. The virus "looks around" the network and checks to see if other computer programs in the network are infected with the virus. If not, the virus program will then infect them. Part of the infection process involves making certain random changes to the other programs. These random changes are such that the infected program will produce unpredictable or invalid results at some specified date subsequent to the infection. For example, an accounting program might be modified so that it will scramble all the accounting databases exactly 6 months after its infection. The nature of the virus is particularly bad because a program, once infected, has the ability to spread the infection to other programs. Therefore, once a virus is introduced into a computer network, all programs in the network might be infected in a matter of a couple of weeks. To make things worse, the infection process may carry to all the company's backup copies as well. This is particularly true if the virus program lies dormant for a long period of time before producing its disastrous results.

    On June 15 this company went into a major state of disaster. The virus had evidently invaded all major portions of the computer network. The network database manager looked with great horror to find that all the databases were completely scrambled. To make things worse, backup copies were scrambled as well. Inspection of the backup copies of databases revealed that they were completely worthless. As a result, the company was unable to do its accounts receivable billing. Two months later it filed for Chapter 11 bankruptcy.

Required

Discuss the means by which this problem should have been prevented.

30. The Morgan Department Store has approximately 1,000 customer accounts. Each month a special clerk opens the mail and prepares a remittance list of all monies received on account. The checks are then sent to a cashier for further processing. In addition, copies of the remittances are sent to accounting and computer services. At the computer services office, an operator keys the remittances directly onto a disk file. The disk file is then used to update the accounts receivable master file.

The computer operator has devised an interesting scheme for defrauding the company. The operator keys in approximately a $100 credit to a friend's account each month. The operator and the friend agree in advance about the amount to be keyed in. The friend will then make purchases exactly in this amount. Normally, the error entered into the system by this procedure would be detected by the batch control totals; however, the operator decreases the amount credited to a number of other accounts. In each case, the amount of the decrease is only $1 or $2. Because the error is very small, most customers let it go unnoticed. However, in a relatively small number of cases where they do detect the error, corrections are made on an authorized basis without further comment. For example, in the previous month, a total of $10 worth of corrections were made because of the complaints. However, these corrections were all processed semiautomatically by the system, and no one realized that it was part of a cover-up.

Required

What can be done to detect and prevent this problem relating to input manipulation?

31. The Mid City Sales Company manages a discount store that sells most department store items at a discount. The entire accounting system is computerized. Barbara West is in charge of computer operations and oversees a medium-sized minicomputer with ten support personnel. The present system is based on on-line input and on-line accounting processing. All accounting updates are keyed directly into the system and processed immediately.

The company's accounts payable program works as follows: Customer invoices are matched with purchase orders and receiving reports. Assuming that these documents are in order, the chief accountant enters the appropriate information into the accounts payable program. Entering this information results in a computer-generated check (to pay the supplier) and updates the accounts payable. The check is processed by the finance manager, who signs it and then mails it out. To ensure against unauthorized access to the system, both an identification number and a password are required before the accountant can request the computer to make a payment on an account.

The company's computer system is such that the operator can access any account from the operator's console. Over a period of several months, the operator has been accessing the accounts payable system and ordering the computer to make payments to fictitious vendors.

Required

What security measures can be taken to prevent and detect this type of problem?

32. A programmer in the Ace Bottle Company installs a patch in one of the computer's billing routines that skips over the billing of a friend's account. The program allows the account balance to increase without bounds. Another patch was put into the program to ensure that the friend's account balance never appeared in an aging report.

Required

Discuss the appropriate security measures that could detect and prevent this problem.

33. West Manufacturing's computer division is quite large, consisting of over 200 employees. Relations among the employees within the company are quite good. Although the accounting department is a separate group, the accountants and computer people eat lunch together and socialize regularly. This has led to some problems. Recently, two accountants, a systems programmer, systems analyst, and computer operator worked together to divert the deposit of funds from the company's bank account to their individual personal accounts. The defalcation involved the forging of source documents by the accountants and cover-up by the systems programmers and operators. The systems analyst designed the entire scheme. The whole thing was discovered by accident when the accountant was forced to take time off

from work for a surgical operation. The replacement accountant suspected that something was wrong when she noticed that a number of deposit slips were missing.

As it turns out, the total loss to the company was only a couple of thousand dollars. However, if it had not been for the accidental discovery by the temporary accountant, the fraud could have grown to the extent that it could have bankrupted the company.

Required

What could have been done to prevent the problem that occurred?

34. Manchester Sales Company is a medium-sized retail operation with a computer staff of 10 employees. The computer staff effectively maintains all accounting functions as well as computer operations. The overall internal control and security system is quite good. However, there are a number of problems. First, all the computer employees know the passwords to each others' accounts. Although this is a breach of the security system, most employees feel that the other employees are basically honest and that there is no need to worry. Second, employees are lax about document distribution procedures. Almost anybody can come into the computer room and pick up a printout without an entry being logged into the records. Security has repeatedly complained to these employees about the problem but to no avail.

Required

Discuss the problem of lax security in this company. What are its implications? What can be done about it?

35. Beard Manufacturing is extremely security conscious, especially in the area of its computer. Because of this, the director of the computer center has installed a sophisticated computer security system costing the company over $1 million. The system is so sophisticated that all communications terminals require positive voice identification. In addition, each user is assigned a security-level clearance by the operating system. All systems application and data files require specific levels of security for access. For example, individuals running accounting reports are assigned a low-level classification that will allow them to access the data files that they need but will not allow them to make any changes to these files. In addition, a large number of other measures are part of the system, including security guards and closed-circuit television.

Despite this sophisticated system, a very intelligent systems programmer managed to break through the company's security and alter the accounts receivable files. He managed to find a trapdoor in the operating system that allowed him to operate with a level 8 security clearance. In addition, he was able to access the system update log to instruct the computer to completely forget that he accessed the data files. In other words, he was able to make changes to the data files without any trace being left of the transaction.

In this case the company was very lucky because the systems programmer was honest and took his scheme to the director of computer security. Needless to say, the director of security was flabbergasted. As a result of what the programmer did, the director of security is considering replacing the entire security system with a more sophisticated $2 million system.

Required

What response should the director of security make regarding the systems programmer? What measures could have been taken to prevent the problem from occurring? Is a more expensive security system a good idea?

36. Equity Financing Life Insurance Company is headquartered in Miami, Florida. The company is very large, so it operates an enormous mainframe computer system. Recently, a group of political radicals threw a small bomb through the window (breaking the glass) in the main computer room. Because this happened late at night, there were no human injuries. However, the damage was extensive, and the central processing unit and three major disk drives were completely destroyed.

Required

Is what happened in any way the company's fault? Why or why not?

37. Eagle Airlines is headquartered in Chicago. The corporate administrative offices consist of 10 buildings in a complex that spreads over 4 square miles. The main computer system is

centrally located. All the buildings in the complex contain computer users and, therefore, are connected to the main computer center by way of telephone cables.

Recently, the company's computer system was violated by the following scheme: A couple of college students from a nearby university purchased an inexpensive magnetic cassette tape recorder with a plug-in microphone and line-powered modem. The modem does not require any power supply because it derives its power needs directly from the telephone line to which it is connected. Using this equipment and a PC, the two students removed the microphone and connected the bare wires directly to one of the telephone lines coming out of the computer center. They then proceeded to record onto cassette everything that came across the telephone line. After trying this procedure a couple of times, they found that the cassette player was unnecessary and learned to capture the communications information directly onto the PC's disks. Later, they connected the PC to a printer and printed the contents of the disk.

To their amazement, the listings included the sign-on procedures and passwords for access to all the company's major databases, including accounts payable and accounts receivable. To exploit this information, it was necessary for the students to obtain access to the company's computer through a data terminal. This posed a problem, however, because most of the company's data terminals were carefully guarded. To get around this, one of the students suggested that the company might have a dial-up port into the company's computer. The biggest problem, however, was finding the correct telephone number of the computer. They reasoned that the company's computer dial-up telephone number was probably very similar to the telephone number for the administrative offices. Therefore, they wrote a computer program that simply dialed one telephone number after another looking for a computer modem carrier signal. The program was set to try all numbers that matched administrative telephone numbers in the first four digits. Therefore, the program was set to test 999 different telephone numbers. This procedure worked out very well, and the company's computer was discovered on about the twentieth try. As it turned out, the computer's number differed from the administrative number in only the last two digits.

Once into the company's computer, it then became necessary to try a scheme to try to defraud the company. After much discussion, they finally decided to order the computer's accounts payable program to issue checks to a post office box registered under a fictitious name. Finally, the illegally obtained checks were deposited to the bank account registered to the fictitious name.

The students might have gotten away with their scheme if they had not gotten greedy. They had requested a large number of small checks totaling $100,000. This would have gone unnoticed; however, the checks requested bounced because there was not enough money in the company's bank account to pay them. Once the checks bounced, the accountant immediately figured out that the checks were not supported by adequate documentation. The authorities were notified, and the students were caught while checking their post office box for mail.

Required

Discuss the specific security measures that could have been taken to prevent this scheme.

38. The Base Level National Bank of Washington, D.C., has used computers to process cash deposits made by its customers for more than 20 years. The bank's computer system for customer deposit accounting is a batch processing system. Customers fill out a deposit slip when they deposit cash. The cashier validates the deposit slip, collects the cash, and then issues a dated receipt to the customer to evidence the deposit. The batches of deposit slips are processed overnight in a computer batch processing run to update the customer account records.

Two different types of deposit slips might be used by a customer. One type is a blank-form deposit slip that the customer obtains at the bank. Typically, large quantities of blank-form deposit slips are left on counters in the bank's lobby for the customers' convenience. A blank-form deposit slip does not contain any preentered data. In particular, the customer or the cashier must manually enter the customer's account number on this form. The other type of deposit slip is contained in a customer's checkbook. In the case of a checkbook deposit slip, the customer's account number has already been entered on the form in computer-readable form. Each checkbook deposit slip contains the customer's account number in magnetic-ink character recognition (MICR) format to facilitate computer processing.

The two types of deposit slips look similar but are distinguishable. When batches of deposit slips are processed in the computer department, one of the first steps is to enter, using a special machine, both the customer's account number and the amount of the deposit in MICR format at the bottom of each deposit slip. MICR input is used because of the large volume of transactions. Because each checkbook-type slip already has the customer's account number in MICR, it is only necessary to MICR-encode the amount of the deposit. Both the customer's account number and the amount of the deposit must be MICR-encoded on the blank-form deposit slips.

Several months ago Base Level National Bank was the victim of a clever fraud. It seems that some person entered the busy bank and left a stack of fraudulent blank deposit slips on one of the bank's counters. These deposit slips were exact duplicates of those normally placed on the counters, with one important difference. Each fraudulent blank deposit slip had been MICR-encoded with the account number of a checking account that apparently had been opened under a false name. Recall that MICR-encoded account numbers are normally entered on the blank-form deposit slips after the deposit has been accepted by a cashier. During the day, the fraudulent deposit slips were used by many people making deposits at the bank. Most or all of these deposits were incorrectly credited to the fraudulent checking account in the overnight computer batch processing run of the day's deposit slips. Within a few minutes of opening the next morning, this person returned to the bank, inquired as to his checking account balance, and withdrew 90% of the balance in cash. To date the identity of the person is unknown, and the cash, more than $150,000, has not been recovered.

Required

(a) What factors contributed to the success of this clever fraud? What role did Base Level's computer system play in the perpetration of this fraud?

(b) Suggest control procedures that could prevent the occurrence of this type of fraud.

39. Grand Bank Corporation (GBC)—Case A

Grand Bank Corporation (GBC) operates a communications network that supports data processing for its subsidiary banks and their branches. The corporate database is centralized at the GBC Network Communication Command Center (NCCC). About 100,000 transactions are processed against the database each day.

GBC's NCCC consists of 2 coupled mainframe processors, 16 magnetic disk drive units, 12 tape drives, and other equipment. The communication network uses dedicated lines leased from a PBX. The system supports processing for demand deposit (checking), savings, commercial and personal loans, and general ledger.

Processing Controls

Control procedures exist to prevent unauthorized access to the communication network and unauthorized use of files. Transactions are entered by tellers using intelligent data terminals. In the case of communication interruptions, the terminals can do limited off-line processing. At the end of each day, the terminals print transaction totals for balancing the cash drawer. A log of all transactions received during the day is reprocessed off-line that evening and reconciled to the day's on-line processing. These totals along with an updated general ledger are transmitted to the network members each morning.

Each terminal's identification code is hardwired. Each transaction is identified by the terminal identification code, along with the employee identification code and time of day. The central computers recognize only authorized terminal identifications and requests to use the system.

Software controls are used to ensure that users access only their own data files and the application programs authorized for them. All files and programs are protected by frequently changed codes and passwords.

Access Controls

All visitors sign in and out in a log indicating the time of day, whom they represent, and whom they are visiting. Visitors are issued badges and are required to wear them in plain view while on the premises.

Access to the data processing area is restricted to authorized management and operating personnel. Access is controlled by doors activated with magnetic card readers attached on-line to a separate computer security system. Codes in the magnetic cards issued to each authorized employee designate which doors are available for access. A log is maintained of the card number and all access attempts.

Access to the computer room is restricted to the operations staff and equipment vendors only. A building security guard is on duty at all times.

Environmental Controls

An electronic heat, fire, and smoke detection alarm system has been installed at NCCC. A halon gas fire extinguishing system is incorporated into the system to put out any fire in the computer area. The fire alarm system is connected to an automatic power-off trip switch and to the building's manned engineer console.

Portable carbon dioxide fire extinguishers are readily accessible in and around the computer facility. These are periodically weighed and kept charged, and computer operators are trained to use them. All electrical equipment is approved by Underwriters' Laboratories (UL).

Flammable material in or around the data processing center is removed daily to avoid potential fire hazards. Waste containers are designed to retain and smother fires. Paper and other combustible supplies are not stored in the computer room. The computer room construction material is noncombustible. Exterior computer room walls have a 2-hour fire rating. A no-smoking rule is enforced in the computer room.

There are several independently controlled air-conditioning modules distributed between two independently fused power panels. The failure of any module can be compensated for by the other modules. All air-conditioning modules are inspected monthly when filters are changed. There is a backup system for pumping water to the air-conditioning system. If one motor fails, that motor will be bypassed and pumping capacity maintained by a second motor and pump. The water softening system utilizes a dual filter to prevent clogging of water intake systems. A separate electrical power supply for the air-conditioning systems is maintained.

Maintenance Procedures

Proper maintenance procedures concerning hardware help NCCC prevent failures. The maintenance technicians perform preventative maintenance on the equipment daily, and on every Sunday, they thoroughly check the mainframe processors.

The operations manager, in order to locate problems, reviews the engineer's weekly report of preventative and remedial maintenance. The operations manager also closely supervises the work being done to ensure a prompt and proper solution.

File Security

The library of data files is physically controlled by a librarian who maintains the file usage records. Periodically, file media are checked and their operating condition certified. The librarian is the only person authorized to erase file media.

The librarian controls all files in the library and in the off-site storage location. Each file has retention instructions printed on it. All file media that are necessary for recovery and restart are stored in a heat-resistant, fireproof, locked vault.

The locked computer center vault holds the first-generation backup files, which can be used for immediate backup. The files in the vault include program object files, transaction backup files, and account master files. Operating system backup is ensured by periodically copying the object code and related data files from the system residence device directly to cartridge tape. A copy of the source code for each application is also kept on cartridge tape.

Each day, two copies of the daily transactions are prepared and put on cartridge tape. One tape is placed in the computer room vault and the other one is sent to an off-site storage location. On-line and off-line month-end master files, month-to-date history, and object and source programs are sent to off-site storage twice a week and after each end-of-month processing.

Hardware Controls

Either of the two coupled processors can be used individually for running all on-line and off-line processing. If hardware problems should develop in one machine, the other is available for backup.

All peripheral equipment, which includes tape drives, disk drives, printers, and communication equipment, can be switched to either computer.

Backup telephone lines connect the telephone center to the computer room. If a restart is needed, the on-line system files from the beginning of the day can be processed against the network transactions entered during the day.

Recovery and Restart

Procedures that are necessary for computer operators to restart and recover from a business interruption are fully documented. The run manual documents all necessary recovery and restart procedures for the network communications system together with their priorities.

The tape library retains all necessary system files and transaction files so that the network communications processing for any of the last 30 days can be recreated.

In the event of the destruction of files at NCCC, the present system provides the capability to be operational with up-to-date files in 24 hours. To achieve this type of recovery, files would be removed from off-site storage and the most recent master files would be processed off-line with the 1 to 3 days of daily transactions required to recreate current master files.

There is a 20-page set of detailed procedures and guidelines to be followed in the case of a disaster. These procedures indicate who is to be notified, what tasks they are to perform, and in what order.

NCCC has letters of support from suppliers of the center's equipment and related elements that indicate that in case of a disaster, support will be offered on a timely basis. These letters are from the suppliers of business forms, the air-conditioning company, the computer manufacturer, the suppliers of the peripheral equipment, and the PBX company.

Required

(a) Identify major areas that should be considered in a security review to determine the potential for loss of data or the ability to process it. Identify some controls in each of these areas.

(b) Evaluate the general security and recovery procedures as described at NCCC. What other areas might warrant consideration in a review of security and recovery procedures?

40. Grand Bank Corporation (GBC)—Case B

Management of GBC commissioned a security review task force to review compliance with corporate security policies and procedures at NCCC. The following observations were made during several on-site visits to NCCC and the off-site file backup storage location.

1. Frequent visitors, such as equipment technicians or important management personnel, often do not have to sign the visitor's log.
2. The computer room door is often left unlocked by employees who are "running out for something and will be right back."
3. The back door to the computer room is sometimes opened on very hot days to help reduce the load placed on the air conditioners.
4. Several holiday banners were noticed hanging from a fire detector and a halon gas register.
5. Several computer programmers were observed playing video games on the data terminals at their desks.
6. Several unlabeled data files were observed in the computer room. Several files that should have been destroyed several days previous were found in the library.
7. Several persons have "extra" keys to the file storage vault.
8. An outside vendor provides cleaning services on Sundays during off-hours. Often no NCCC employees are at the center during this weekly cleaning.
9. The company that picks up and transports data files to the remote storage location is often late picking up the files for off-site storage.

10. Several programmers were observed walking directly into the file library and picking up data files for usage.
11. The off-site file storage location, a very old warehouse building, lacks adequate temperature and humidity controls and also has inadequate fire detection and prevention systems.
12. Records maintained at the off-site storage location—which is used by several different companies as well as GBC—were inadequate and not up-to-date. The physical storage of the backup files was in locked closets labeled only by numbers.
13. Letters sent to confirm the backup support promised to NCCC in letters obtained before equipment was actually purchased received lukewarm and sometimes contradictory responses from vendors. In several cases, the claim was made that existing NCCC equipment is quite different and somewhat incompatible with the products now offered and supported by the vendor.

Required

1. Discuss the security problems indicated by the items noted.
2. What do these data suggest about the evaluation of general security and recovery procedures such as those in effect at GBC's NCCC?

41. The ABC Company has suffered from repeated attacks on its Web site. In the most recent attack, the server was suddenly bombarded by requests to view Web pages. The number of requests was so large that it caused an overflow in the activity log after the first hour. The Web manager estimated that the total number of requests exceeded 4 million, but she would never know for sure because the entire Web server crashed after 45 minutes.

   One of the analysts inspected the remains of the activity log and quickly discovered that all the requests came from a small group of IP addresses.

Required

Describe what types of measures might be taken to protect the ABC Company against subsequent attacks of this nature.

42. Ace Pencil, the Web manager of the XYZ Company, was horrified when he received a call one night around midnight from Bob Drake, one of the salespersons.

   "Our entire Web site has been replaced by cartoon characters," said Bob Drake. Ace jumped out of bed and stepped into his home office, where he nervously signed on to the Internet and viewed the company Web pages. Sure enough, the story was true. There, in front of him, he was staring at all the cartoon characters that his children watched on Saturday mornings.

   Further investigation revealed that in fact there was absolutely nothing wrong with his Web site. All the files on the server were exactly as they were supposed to be. Yet, when he went to the Web, to *www.xyzandonlyxyz.com*, the company's URL, he only saw cartoon characters.

Required

(a) Describe what has happened to the XYZ Company.
(b) What can be done to correct the problem?

43. The Greenwood Worm Company sells earthworms over the Web. You have been hired as a consultant to help Greenwood set up a completely new Web site, and the owner of the company tells you that she wants all the best in security.

Required

(a) What would be your top priorities in developing a secure Web site?

44. The Nelm Company has discovered through experience that somehow Erm, its major competitor, seems to discover its every secret. For example, when Nelm launches a new advertising campaign, Erm always immediately launches an advertising campaign that appears to be specifically designed to nullify the effects of Nelm's advertisements.

   Barbara Woods, the head of Nelm's security department, is convinced that somehow Erm is invading its computer network and browsing secret files at will.

   Nelm's network is set up as follows:

(a) One large Web server machine that also supports applications for 15 users in the sales department.

(b) The Web server is on a local area network, and the files for the 15 users in the sales department are shared with users in engineering and production.

(c) Nelm supports Internet-based e-mail services for all its employees.

Required

(a) Describe security flaws in Nelm's system.

(b) Make suggestions for improving Nelm's security system.

(c) How might Erm be invading Nelm's network?

45. The RWD company has three Web servers, A, B, and C, connected together over a local area network. Server A is the "sacrificial lamb," the only server outside the firewall. In other words, from outside the company it is only possible to reach server A and not servers B and C.

There has been a debate among the company's IS security staff about the desirability of local area network links between the three servers. Jane Doe argues that there should be no links between server A and the other two servers. "It's just too dangerous," she said.

The other employees feel that there is no need to worry about the other two computers, as they are safe behind the firewall.

Required

(a) Do you agree with Jane Doe? Why or why not?

(b) What risks, if any, would be caused by connecting server A to the other two servers via the local area network?

46. The GGY company is debating the issue of who should be in charge of managing its private keys that it uses for its digital signatures. Some argue that the keys should fall under control of management, others argue that the job should belong to finance, and still others feel that it should belong to accounting.

Required

(a) In general, which of the above-mentioned groups is in the best position, from a control standpoint, to manage the company's private keys?

(b) Does your answer depend on which particular keys are in question? Explain.

47. The North Palm Company sells its own brand of shoes via its Web site. The company is owned and operated by a small family consisting of Maria and Henry Rodriguez, the husband and wife, and their 25-year-old son Jeremy Rodriguez.

Jeremy has some understanding of Web development but not enough to do things himself. So the Rodriguez family contracted with a local company who provides turnkey Web-based storefronts.

The Web site had been working well for several months, and every week the number of orders continued to grow. Both Maria and Henry were ecstatic with all the money they were making. They were continually amazed how with a tiny office and an inexpensive computer they make enough money to live comfortably.

Things changed, however, one Monday morning when Maria tried to access the orders that had arrived over the weekend. The problem was that there was not one single order in the system.

Jeremy Rodriguez investigated, and by noon he had to come to realize that their home page had been replaced by a picture of a crazy-looking stuffed duck and a banner message that said "Hackers Unite. Free the Web."

Desperate, Maria Rodriguez called their Web developer, who was out of the office for unexplained reasons. She left a message for him to return the call and that it was very urgent.

The whole afternoon went by, and still no more orders, and no call back from the Web developer. Henry called the developer six times, until the developer's secretary became angry. Finally, Henry Rodriguez became so agitated that he drove to the developer's office and caused a minor scene, but the developer was still nowhere to be found.

At 9:00 A.M. the next morning the developer returned the call and said, "I'll give it my highest priority this morning."

The whole morning went by without word from the developer. So Henry called the man's office again, and to his surprise the developer himself answered on the first ring.

"Have you figured out the problem?" asked Henry Rodriguez.

"To make a long story short, no," said the developer.

Henry was mortified. "This is killing us," he said. "We'll lose all our customers, and we have not one penny in sales now."

"I understand," said the developer. "The only problem is that about 30 of my customers have the same problem as you. I've been trying to repair some of their sites today, but it seems that the hackers managed to infect the Web servers with some terrible new virus. It is going to take two to four weeks to get everyone going again."

Things got even worse, and by Wednesday several other merchants had filed lawsuits against the developer. Maria Rodriguez heard about the lawsuits late that day from a friend who worked at the newspaper office, and she called the developer the first thing Thursday morning, only to find that the telephone was disconnected.

In a panic she went to another Web developer, who promptly told her that she had been the victim of a sophisticated multilevel marketing scam. The people involved had all been selling the same prepackaged Web storefront, which they had actually stolen from a legitimate company. To make things worse, they had installed every customer's Web site on an insecure server, with almost no access restrictions. Anyone could modify anyone else's Web site without even entering any account and password information.

Reluctantly, Maria wrote the new developer a check for $5,000 for him to get started on creating a new Web site, but the developer cautioned them it would take at least two days because he had to transfer North Palm's domain name, *www.northpalmshoes1.com*, to his server.

Maria and Henry signed a contract with the new developer and went home feeling better. "That took every penny from our bank account," said Maria. "Now I don't even have enough cash to pay the mortgage on our house or any of the bills this month."

"Don't worry," said Henry, "the money will start coming in again in a couple of days, as soon as we get our new site up and running."

Two days later they got a call from the new developer. "Bad news," he said. "I can't transfer your domain name because it is registered in the name of your previous developer. So technically the name belongs to him and not you."

"What can we do?" asked Maria.

The developer sighed. "There's only one thing you can do to get things moving quickly. Start over. You can e-mail all your old customers about your Web site."

Henry and Maria thought for a few seconds. Then Maria realized that all the customer files were stored on the server. The developer had convinced them that the server was the safest place to keep all the files, because the developer did tape backups of the server several times a day.

The Rodriguez family ended up in personal bankruptcy and lost everything, including their house and car. In the end, they were forced to move in with Maria's parents in Miami.

Required

(a) Could the Rodriguez family have prevented all their problems? How?

(b) Prepare a list of all the mistakes that the Rodriguez family made.

(c) For each mistake, make a positive suggestion as to what should have been done instead.

❖ **ANSWERS TO CHAPTER QUIZ**

1. b	4. d	7. d	10. b
2. a	5. b	8. a	
3. c	6. c	9. b	

CHAPTER 6

ELECTRONIC DATA PROCESSING SYSTEMS

LEARNING OBJECTIVES

Careful study of this chapter will enable you to:

❖ Describe how application controls are used in data processing systems to ensure accuracy and integrity.

❖ Characterize the various types of electronic systems used for transaction processing.

❖ Describe the basic functions and operation of a computerized accounting application.

THE INPUT SYSTEM

PAPER-BASED INPUT SYSTEMS

In some computerized accounting systems, inputs to the accounting system are based on handwritten or typed source documents. These documents are then collected and forwarded to computer operations for error checking and processing. Each phase of input processing is discussed below.

PREPARATION AND COMPLETION OF THE SOURCE DOCUMENT
The source documents, such as sales orders, are prepared manually. Errors that might occur at this stage can be minimized if the source document is well designed and easy to understand. Completed source documents are collected periodically and transferred to the data processing department for entry into the computer system.

TRANSFER OF SOURCE DOCUMENTS TO DATA PROCESSING
Batch control totals and data transfer registers are fundamental controls over data transfer between user departments and data processing. The absence or inadequacy of procedures for the control of data transmitted between user departments and the data processing department could represent a significant weakness because it presents an opportunity for unauthorized and/or fraudulent transactions to be introduced into the processing system.

[Prenumbered]
150

Batch Control Form

Originating Department ____________________
Date ____________________
Preparer's Signature ____________________

Control Totals

Batch Number |_|_|_|_|_|_|_|
Number of Documents |_|_|_|_|
Field Totals (list):

Field Number	*Name*	*Total*

FIGURE 6.1 INPUT DOCUMENT CONTROL FORM.

The use of batch control over the entire data processing input-process-output sequence is fundamental to organizational independence. Proof and control functions should be performed outside the data entry department. Original source documents should be retained for a period of time sufficient to facilitate error correction. Procedures should be designed to ensure that source documents are not processed more than once. Control practices such as the use of prenumbered forms, supervision, and approval apply to electronic data processing (EDP) applications as well as others.

Submission of input data should be accompanied by the completion of an **input document control form** similar to the one shown in Figure 6.1. Document counts are a simple form of batch control. In addition to document and/or record counts, batch totals may be taken for all or several numeric fields in the original data file. These totals may be used throughout the data processing cycle to monitor the completeness of processing.

The data entry group should not accept data unless an input document control form is present to evidence and reference the transfer of these data. The input document control form may be dated and time-stamped, and the batch should be checked to ensure that it is complete and consistent with control procedures. Information in the input document control form typically is entered in a *data transfer log* (register) to provide a control over the disposition and use of these data. Batch control totals are fundamental to this process.

Figure 6.2 illustrates the development and use of batch control totals in a data processing application. User departments develop control totals over batches of input and then forward the batches of documents along with an input document control form to the data processing department. The input document control form is logged in the data processing department and then balanced to the output control totals that are developed during the processing of the batch of input. The output is returned to the user department, where it is batch-balanced to the batch totals on the input document control form.

Data Entry After the source documents such as invoices are received by data processing, they are manually key-transcribed or keyed (i.e., typed) using a data terminal or personal computer (PC) and then stored on disk. Next, the input file is key-verified. **Key verification** is a control procedure that detects errors in the keying operation. An error might occur, for example, when a customer account number is mistyped because the data entry clerk presses the wrong key or misinterprets a character on a source document. In key verification, each source document is key-transcribed a second time.

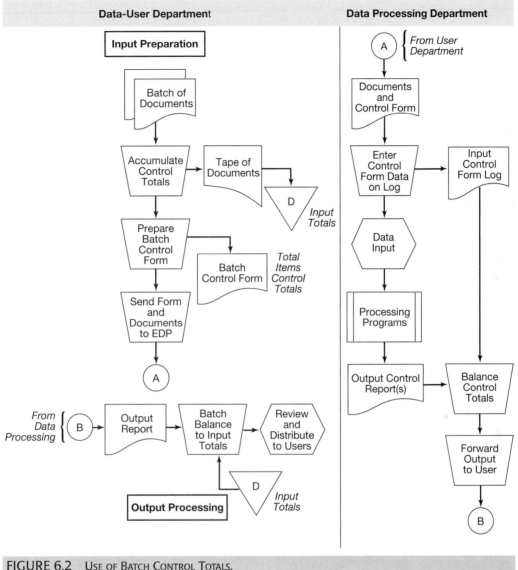

Data-User Department   **Data Processing Department**

FIGURE 6.2   USE OF BATCH CONTROL TOTALS.

The key-verification software compares the retranscribed data as they are being entered, key by key, with the input data already on the disk file. If these are the same, nothing happens, and the operator proceeds with the next character of data. In the case of a mismatch, the operator is notified and may then correct the error. To reduce the costs associated with key-verifying input data, nonessential fields, such as a customer's name and street address (as opposed to account number or ZIP code), are often not verified. A second but less effective way to detect data entry error is *visual verification*. With this approach, someone compares the source documents with a printout of the key-transcribed file.

Program Data Editing   Since verification does not edit data, it is essential that data be thoroughly edited after entry to ensure valid content. **Program data editing** is a software technique used to screen data for errors prior to processing. It should be used in addition to verification for several reasons. First, input errors can occur that will pass verification. Incorrect recognition of a character on a source document is one possibility; another is the simple omission of a necessary input item by the individual preparing the source document. As this second example illustrates, data editing at the programming level is a control over the initial verification function. Last, the volume of data in EDP operations, coupled with the fact that once data are entered in the system they may be used without reconversion, necessitates a methodologic screening of all input data.

Program Data Editing Techniques   Data editing routines may be applied to each of the basic data structures—characters, fields, records, and files. The most basic editing technique ensures that all data fields contain only valid characters. For example, numeric data items should contain only digits, and alphabetic data items should not contain any digits.

After data items have been edited at the character level, they can be checked for reasonableness. One way to edit for reasonableness is to establish a table file that contains a list of acceptable values for each field. The edit program then compares the actual value of each field with the acceptable values in the table. This is called a **table lookup**. For example, an actual value of the customer account field might be compared with a master list of customer account numbers stored in a table.

Numeric data values, as opposed to numeric codes, in general should fall within certain ranges; thus, checking numeric data as being within certain limits requires a check only against extreme values of the range. This is called a **limit test**. For example, the field payroll hours typically may not be less than zero or more than, say, 100 for a 2-week pay period. Sales in a certain department generally should be within a range of zero to some upper limit based on historical data.

It is possible to edit numeric data with respect to being outside acceptable ranges; in such cases, the data are rejected. At times, it may be desirable to discriminate further among acceptable items as well. For example, a payroll field may contain a value that is acceptable but so high or low as to warrant investigation. This item may be accepted for processing but flagged for a subsequent audit. Alternatively, such items may be held in suspense of processing until the data are reverified. The use of programmed edit tests to discriminate among acceptable data so that some items are either held in suspense of processing until audited or collected for audit after processing is called **continuous operations auditing**.

Numeric codes can be verified by using a check digit. A **check digit** is an extra, redundant digit added to a code number much as a parity bit is added to a byte. The check digit is computed when a code is initially assigned to a data element. Check digits are computed by applying mathematical calculations to the individual digits in a code number in such a way as to generate a result that is a single digit. This digit becomes the check digit and is added to the original code. In subsequent processing, this same mathematical operation can be performed to ensure that the code has not been recorded incorrectly.

There are numerous check-digit procedures. The following illustration is one version of a technique known as *Modulus 11*:

The use of check digits is very common because of the high reliability of this procedure. Commercial check-digit packages catch 100% of transposition errors and a very high percentage of random errors. However, check digits do not guard against all possible input errors.

Account number:	1	2	4	0
Multiply each digit separately by the corresponding digit in the sequence 5 4 3 2:	×	×	×	×
	5	4	3	2
Add results of digit multiplication digit by digit:	5 + 8 + (1 +·2) + 0 = 16			
Subtract results from next highest multiple of 11:	22 − 16 = 6			
Check digit = 6				
Complete account number:	1 2 4 0 6			

TABLE 6.1   Data Edit Illustration

Data Edit	Description	Example
Completeness check	Check that entries exist in fields that cannot be processed blank.	Each field in a record is checked to assure the presence of data.
Field format check	Check that each character in a field is in proper mode (e.g., alpha or numeric).	Each character of a vendor number field is checked to assure it is numeric.
Field length check	Check the entry in a field for a specific number of characters.	A date field in a month-day-year format is checked that it contains six digits.
Field sign check	Check the sign (positive/negative) of a numeric field for the correct value.	The amount due field of a bill is checked that the sign is positive.
Limit check	The value of a numeric field is checked against a predetermined upper and/or lower limit.	The value of the hours worked field in a time card record is checked that it does not exceed a predetermined limit of 60 hours.
Reasonableness check	The value of a numeric field is compared to another numeric field in the same record.	Overhead costs in a work-in-process record are checked that they do not exceed 200% of the labor cost field.
Valid code check	Match the value of a code to a table file of acceptable code values.	A vendor code field is validated by matching it to a table file of valid vendor codes.
Check digit	Validate a numeric code through the use of a check digit algorithm.	A point-of-sale system validates a credit card by recomputing the check digit in the customer's account number.
Combination field check	The value of one field is compared or related to another field to establish validity.	A transaction code field is compared to a department code field. Certain transaction codes are only valid for certain departments.
Internal label check	An internal file label is read to validate the characteristics of a file.	The file code on an internal label is checked by a payroll program to assure that it is the payroll file.
Sequence check	A field in a series of records is checked for ascending or descending sequence.	The sequence of invoice numbers is verified as the invoice file is processed.
Record count check	The number of records in a file is counted during processing and balanced to input controls.	The record count of time cards processed is balanced to input totals from the payroll department.
Hash total check	The hash total of a field in a file is computed during processing and balanced to input controls.	The hash total of employee numbers is computed during processing and balanced to input controls from the payroll department.
Financial total check	The financial total of a field in a file is computed during processing and balanced to input controls.	The total dollar amount of invoices processed is computed and balanced to a total from the billing department.

Data Editing Terminology   The data edits just discussed, as well as several other types of data edits, are illustrated with examples in Table 6.1. The terminology illustrated in Table 6.1 is typical, but many other terms are used to describe the same type of data edit. A **valid code check**, for example, is a particular type of table lookup in which the table file consists of valid codes. Other authors use terms such as *validity check* or *existence check* in describing the same type of data edit.

PAPERLESS INPUT SYSTEMS

In *paperless input systems*, sometimes called *on-line input systems*, transactions are input directly into the computer network, and the need for keying in source documents is eliminated. Paperless systems therefore provide a higher degree of automation than do paper-based systems. Still, there are various degrees of automation in different paper-based systems. Users might initiate transactions by manually keying them into the computer. This type of input has become very common because it occurs when users enter data into forms displayed as Web pages. On the other hand, a computer might originate transactions automatically and then process them with no human intervention. For example, an electronic data interchange (EDI) purchase order originating from a vendor's computer might be received automatically and processed with no human intervention.

One problem with paperless systems is the possible loss of segregation of duties and audit trail. In paper-based input systems, source document preparation and data entry are normally segregated, as they are in a manual system. In paperless input systems, however, these functions are performed by the same person, or no person is involved directly. Therefore, the concentration of functions in paperless data entry eliminates controls associated with a segregation of duties. These controls—review and batch control of source documents and controls related to source document preparation, such as prenumbering, authorization, and review—are important to the integrity of the audit trail and must be compensated for in paperless systems.

The loss of paper-based internal controls can be compensated for by using transaction logs. *Transaction logs* or *transaction registers* are created by logging all inputs to a special file that automatically contains tags to identify transactions. **Tagging** means that additional audit-oriented information is included with original transaction data. Such information as date and user authorization codes can be included to provide an extensive audit trail. Transaction logs also provide an important backup, as well as a source for control totals.

PAPERLESS INPUT SYSTEMS REQUIRING HUMAN INTERVENTION

There are many types of paperless input systems in which users enter transactions directly into the computer. These systems include, for example, on-line manual data entry systems and automatic identification systems such as point-of-sales (POS) systems.

In on-line *manual data entry systems*, users manually type transactions into the computer system. For example, a plant manager (possessing appropriate access codes) might manually type a purchase requisition into a data terminal. The requisition would then be forwarded automatically to purchasing for additional processing. The purchase order would be generated with no rekeying in of data. In *automatic identification systems*, merchandise and other items are tagged with machine-readable codes. One example of automatic identification is the *automated POS system*, in which salespersons use an optical scanner to scan the bar-coded merchandise for sale, as well as the customer's credit card. The transaction information is then forwarded automatically to the billing and inventory systems for additional processing, and no additional human intervention may be required. Another application of automatic identification involves the electronic tagging of containers in the shipping industry.

Automatic identification can be especially useful if two trading partners agree on a standard method of tagging cartons and boxes. The tags on incoming cartons can be scanned, facilitating their identification and matching with the related purchase order.

Transactions in paperless input systems involving human intervention typically proceed through two phases: (1) data entry and data editing and (2) transfer to the host application system. Both these phases are discussed.

Data Entry and Data Editing   In paperless input systems, complete program data editing is often performed when the transaction is entered. Once the transaction is accepted, it might be processed either immediately or at a later time. If it is processed at a later time, additional data editing may be performed.

Transfer to the Host Application System   In centralized paperless systems, transactions usually are input directly into the central computer through some type of remote data terminal. In decentralized and distributed systems, transactions might be entered into one computer and then either immediately or later transferred to another computer for processing.

PAPERLESS SYSTEMS REQUIRING NO HUMAN INTERVENTION

In some systems, transactions are processed from beginning to end without any human intervention: completely automated transaction processing. One application of this technology is the *networked vending machine* (NVM). The POS gasoline pump is a good example of NVM technology. With this system, the customer inserts a credit card or automatic teller machine (ATM) card into the gas pump. The pump then delivers the gas, and the customer's credit card company or bank is billed electronically. Another interesting application is the automated slot machine. The customer inserts an ATM card into the POS slot machine, enters a personal identification number (PIN) code, and pulls the handle. Losses and gains are charged or credited immediately to the customer's bank account!

Another important application of completely automated transaction processing is electronic data interchange (EDI). With EDI and the appropriate database servers, incoming purchase orders and outgoing sales orders can be handled with no human intervention. For example, when inventories are low, the inventory server sends a purchase order message to the EDI translation server. The translation server then translates the message into ANSI X.12 format and sends it to the communications server. The communications server then forwards it electronically to the desired vendor. The remainder of the entire transaction cycle, including payment, also can be automated with EDI, electronic funds transfer (EFT), and automatic identification.

THE PROCESSING SYSTEM

PAPER-BASED PROCESSING SYSTEMS

Virtually all paper-based systems for processing transactions are batch-oriented. In *batch-oriented processing systems*, transactions are entered into the computer (as was discussed previously) in batches. These batches are then processed periodically. Examples of batch processing include processing weekly time reports to produce paychecks, processing groups of checks to update accounts payable master files, and processing invoices to update an accounts receivable master file.

Batch processing is economical when large numbers of transactions must be processed. It is best suited to situations in which files do not need to be updated immediately to reflect transactions and reports are required only periodically. Payroll is a good example. Payroll is prepared periodically. It is not calculated every day. The major disadvantage of batch processing is that files and reports might be out of date between periodic processing. A good example of this is an inventory file. If the inventory file must be used frequently to determine the availability of product for sale, the file often will be out of date if sales are processed only periodically in batches. It is primarily for this reason that many companies use real-time processing systems. Batch processing is still used widely, however, because there are still many situations in which it is a very efficient method of processing data.

Batch processing can be performed with either sequential or random-access (i.e., direct or indexed) file updating. Both approaches are discussed below.

BATCH PROCESSING WITH SEQUENTIAL FILE UPDATING

Many paper-based, batch-oriented systems use *sequential file processing* to update the master file. Processing in such a system usually involves the following steps:

- *Preparing the transaction file.* First, any additional data editing and validation are performed. Then the records in the transaction file are sorted into the same sequence as the master file.
- *Updating the master file.* The records in both the transaction and master files (i.e., subsidiary ledgers) are read one by one, matched, and written to a new master file that reflects the desired updates.
- *Updating the general ledger.* The general ledger is updated to reflect changes in the master files.
- *Preparing general ledger reports.* Trial balances and other reports are produced.

Figure 6.3 outlines the processing of transaction data in a typical paper-based batch processing accounting system. Each business process generates batches of transactions for processing. Examples are sales transactions generated by the customer order management business process and purchasing transactions generated by the procurement business process. Batches of transactions from each business process are

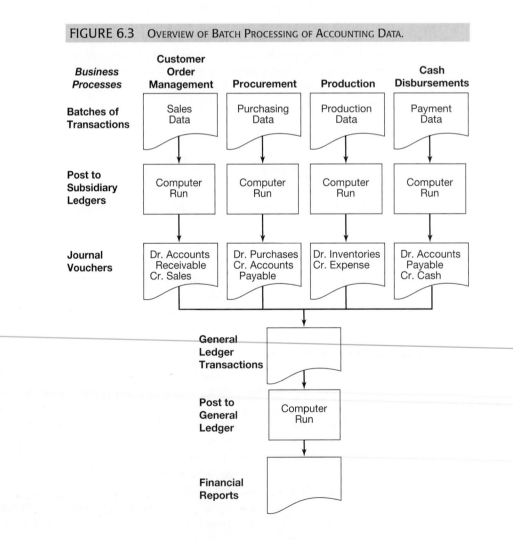

FIGURE 6.3 OVERVIEW OF BATCH PROCESSING OF ACCOUNTING DATA.

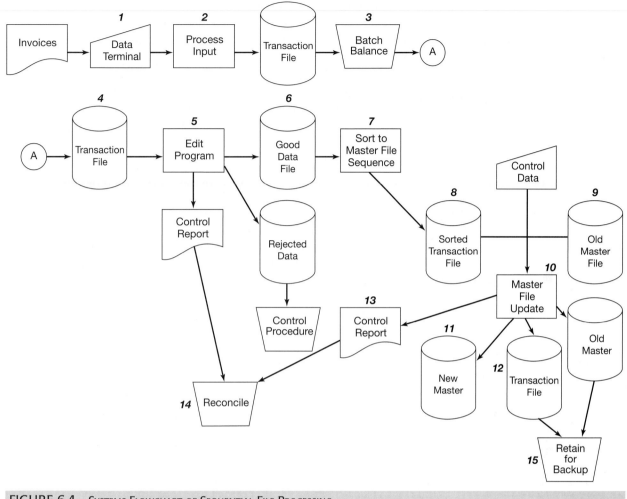

FIGURE 6.4 SYSTEMS FLOWCHART OF SEQUENTIAL FILE PROCESSING.

processed against the relevant application files in separate computer runs. The computer runs post the transactions to subsidiary ledgers and also generate the information necessary to prepare journal entries (journal vouchers) for posting to the general ledger. The journal vouchers are accumulated and processed as a batch against the general ledger in a separate computer run.

As indicated earlier, batch processing often involves maintaining a sequentially organized master file. This file—an accounts receivable master file for illustration—commonly resides on a direct-access storage device. Sales transactions affect the information on the accounts receivable file. These transactions and others—such as new accounts and payments on account—must be reflected in the master file. Figure 6.4 outlines the procedural steps in paper-based batch processing with sequentially organized files, beginning with data input. The numbers in this figure are keyed to the following discussion.

Preparing the Transaction File   As Figure 6.4 illustrates, batches of documents are input (1), processed to build a transaction file (2), and subjected to batch balancing procedures (3) to ensure that all documents are accounted for prior to computer processing. The batch control totals normally would be supplied by the user along with the input data and reconciled by the data-entry function prior to further processing. The resulting file of transactions is on disk (4). This file is processed with an edit program (5) to screen the data before further processing. Data editing of the source documents prior to input is essential to ensure the reliability of the data processed.

In addition to screening data, the edit program (5) must accumulate revised batch control totals for the input data. This is necessary, as the figure shows, because the input data have been divided into good data—those that have passed the edit program—and rejected data. The rejected data must be held in suspense until they are corrected. To facilitate processing, the rejected data usually are reentered for processing as a separate batch at a later date. The control report that is output by the edit program provides the data necessary to reconcile the results of the edit program to user-supplied batch control totals.

The file of edited transactional data (6) is sorted to master file sequence (7) to facilitate the matching process necessary for efficient sequential file processing. It should be noted that Figure 6.4 shows data editing performed at the earliest possible point in the flow of processing, that is, before the transactions are sorted. At times, however, depending on the particular circumstances, data editing may be performed after the transactional data have been sorted to master file sequence. This allows input editing to detect duplicate transactions or to check the sequence of records to be processed. Therefore, either sequence, "edit and sort" or "sort and edit," is possible, with the best sequence determined by the particular circumstances surrounding the application (Fig. 6.5).

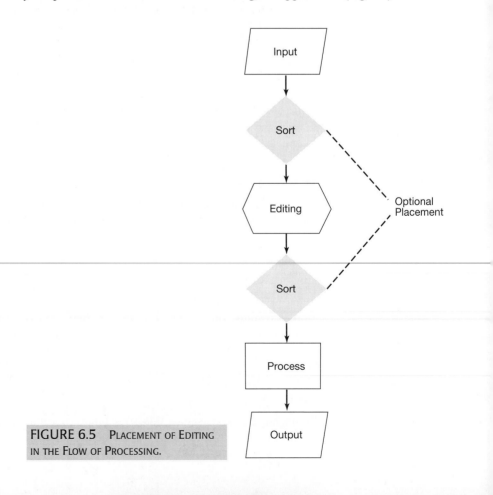

FIGURE 6.5   PLACEMENT OF EDITING IN THE FLOW OF PROCESSING.

Updating the Master File   Once the transaction data have been edited and sorted (8), they are processed against the old master file (9) in the accounts receivable application program(s) run (10). This master file update program (or set of programs) posts the detail of accounts receivable transactions to the accounts receivable master file. The new updated master file (11) is the basis for generating reports and other detailed information. This master file is a subsidiary ledger, the accounts receivable subsidiary ledger in this illustration. The transaction data (12) and the old master file are retained for backup control, as illustrated in Figure 6.4. The control report (13), which is printed at completion of the processing, is reconciled (14) with the batch totals/control report produced by the edit program. These control totals must be reconciled with user-supplied batch control totals before any output is returned to the user. Reconciliation must allow for any transactions that were rejected by data editing. This reconciliation of input to output control totals is performed by the user department, a special control unit, or the internal audit function. The control report (13) normally would include a detailed listing of transactions processed against the master file. This transaction register is the equivalent of a journal produced in a manual system.

As Figure 6.4 shows, the old master and the transaction files should be retained for backup (15). If the new master file is lost or found to be in error, the processing run may be repeated using the old master file and the transaction file. This concept is often referred to as **son-father-grandfather retention**, with each version of the master file being a *generation*. As Figure 6.6 shows, the old master file that is used as input to a file update is the "father." The processing yields a "son"—the new master file. The new master is another generation of information. The "son" file then becomes the input master for the next file update. Thus, the "son" file becomes a "father," there is a new "son," and the old master file that is the backup master from the previous file update becomes a "grandfather" file, that is, a file that is at least two processing cycles old. Several generations of backup files may be kept, depending on the control objectives.

Updating the General Ledger   Every organization must maintain some type of general ledger accounting system. Data must be collected, recorded, classified properly, and

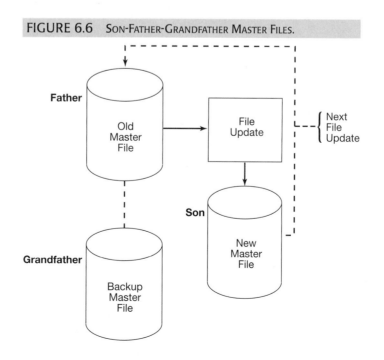

FIGURE 6.6   SON-FATHER-GRANDFATHER MASTER FILES.

entered into the appropriate records for further financial report summations. A general ledger system is the cornerstone of an accounting system.

There are two major aspects to the operation of a computerized general ledger system. One concerns the direct processing of the general ledger programs, most of which takes place on a monthly basis. The second aspect concerns the processing in other computer application systems to prepare the inputs to the general ledger system. One of the tasks to be undertaken in designing a general ledger system is the creation of a pro forma set of journal entries providing for the collection and updating of all data needed for financial reports. The typical approach is to have each relevant application system (such as payroll or accounts payable) generate general ledger transactions (standard journal entry data) to be used as input at the proper time. Doing this implies the use of a separate transaction file in the general ledger system.

The processing procedure described in detail earlier posts transactions to subsidiary ledgers maintained for accounts receivable. The general ledger has not yet been updated. The summary information needed to prepare journal entries may be printed at the completion of processing the subsidiary ledgers and used to update a manual general ledger, or subsequently, this information may be input for processing against a computerized general ledger system. Alternatively, the standard journal entries may be output initially in machine-readable form.

All entries into the general ledger should be documented with journal vouchers. Responsible departments originate the input data to the general ledger system. This may entail the manual preparation of journal vouchers or, in cases where these data are provided by other application programs, the review and adjustment (if required) of these data into journal voucher format.

The journal voucher format (Fig. 6.7) is similar in most organizations and includes the journal voucher number and date, the control and subaccounts (as applicable), and the debit and credit amounts. One or several accounts may be entered on one journal voucher, depending on the complexity of the transaction and the system design. Journal voucher numbers are established to code the type of transaction (cash, receivables, sales, and the like). The column headed by ID designates that the journal is an original entry or the reversal of a prior entry. The account and debit/credit amounts are self-explanatory. This basic format may be expanded to include other information relevant to a particular system. Examples of such data are detailed cost ledger information (to support a subsidiary cost file) and details of expenses by organizational unit for responsibility reports.

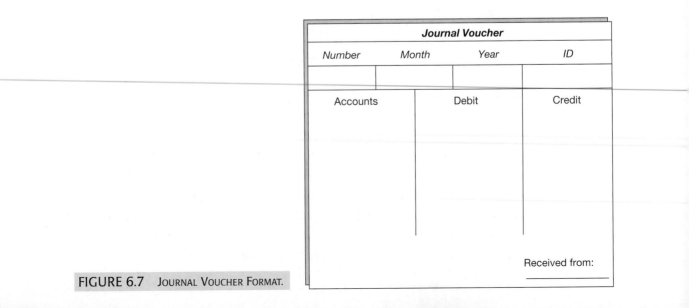

FIGURE 6.7   JOURNAL VOUCHER FORMAT.

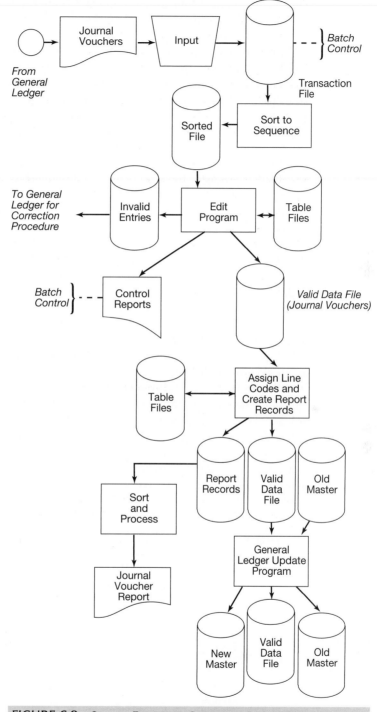

FIGURE 6.8   SYSTEMS FLOWCHART SHOWING A GENERAL LEDGER UPDATE.

Either of these data items might be used in conjunction with a separate master budget file to produce reports showing "budget versus year-to-date" and so forth.

General Ledger File Update   Figure 6.8 provides a systems flowchart overview of a typical general ledger file update. As they are released by the general ledger department, journal vouchers are used to build a journal voucher file (the transaction file).

This file is program data edited to check for the proper journal and account numbers and to determine whether the accounts are correctly associated with their related journals. Invalid data are reported as exceptions and returned to their originating sources for correction and reentry. The edited journal voucher file may be sorted and structured to produce a variety of reports. The current journal voucher transactions are processed against the previous month's general ledger master file (the old master) in order to update that file and produce the current period's general ledger register.

Computer processing of accounting data typically is a two-step procedure. The first step produces preliminary reports, which are forwarded to the accounting department for review and audit relative to the journal voucher listings and general ledger listing. After the audit and submission of corrections and any additional data, the second step is a run that produces the final listings and financial schedules. Numerous reports may be prepared.

Preparing reports requires a link between the general ledger accounts and the report(s) in which they appear. This process is called *line coding*.

Line coding is a procedural step typically accomplished by a table-lookup (matching) process between the updated general ledger file and a line-coding table file. Table files function as reference files. Table files contain items or records that are not a part of data files but are an integral part of the processing function. Tax tables and line-coding assignments are examples of table files stored on direct-access storage devices in accounting applications. The result of the line-coding procedure is several report files that ultimately are printed and distributed to users.

Figure 6.9 illustrates a line-coding assignment. A specific general ledger account, such as "marketable securities," is located in the line-coding file. The line code is then used to structure the report. In Figure 6.9, the first field (one digit) indicates the type of schedule—a financial one in this illustration. The second field identifies the specific report—a balance sheet in our example. The third and fourth fields locate the item in the report structure. Marketable securities is the third line item on the balance sheet, and this account value is placed in column 2. A balance sheet typically has four columns of data: (1) actual this period, (2) beginning-of-year balance, (3) budget, and (4) variance between (1) and (3). As an alternative to the procedure just described, line codes could be stored within the general ledger file itself. The line code for the marketable securities account could be stored as a separate field within the marketable securities record structure.

Common General Ledger Reports   In addition to financial reports and schedules, common reports from a general ledger system would include the following five items:

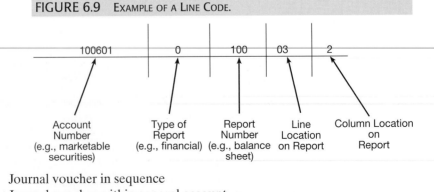

FIGURE 6.9   Example of a Line Code.

- Journal voucher in sequence
- Journal voucher within general account
- General ledger by account
- General ledger summary
- Working trial balance

The general ledger by account is a summary of this month's activity in the general ledger, the general ledger summary is a year-to-date summary, and the working trial balance is a sort/summarization of the year-to-date general ledger in trial balance format. Typically, financial statements and trial balances contain details summarized from the general ledger rather than a listing of all the individual accounts. Detailed reports for lower levels of management may be prepared from the relevant subsidiary ledger files.

BATCH PROCESSING WITH RANDOM-ACCESS FILE UPDATING

Although the updating in the preceding example is done with sequential file updating, random-access updating is also possible, even desirable, with batch processing. In many systems [especially database management system (DBMS)–oriented accounting systems as opposed to file-oriented accounting systems], indexes are maintained for both the subsidiary and general ledger files. Maintaining these indexes serves the primary need of allowing users to quickly access a particular account. For example, an interactive query program might use an index file to help the end user to quickly locate a customer's account. Given that an index is present, however, it also can be used for file updating.

Random-access file updating is simpler than sequential-access updating. With random-access updating, it is not necessary to sort the transaction file into the same order as the master file, and there is no need to generate a new master file. Instead, individual records are read one by one from the transaction file and used to update the related records in the master file *in place*. The following steps are followed:

- A record is read from the transaction file.
- The key value of the transaction record is used to randomly access (by using the index) the related record in the master file.
- The record in the master file is updated in memory and then rewritten back to the data file.

Of course, a backup of the master file should exist before the updating begins, and a transaction register must be generated as the update proceeds.

ILLUSTRATION OF BATCH PROCESSING WITH RANDOM-ACCESS FILE UPDATING

This section depicts an on-line cash receipts application. Batches of customer remittances on account are entered via data terminals and posted with random-access file updating directly to the accounts receivable file. Figure 6.10 presents a system flowchart of the on-line cash receipts application.

New Invoice Application   The application maintains an open-item accounts receivable file. New invoices are posted periodically to the open-item accounts receivable file. A control file is updated to reflect the addition of the new batch of invoices to the accounts receivable file. The control file is a summary of the accounts receivable file by type of account (such as installment or net 30 days). A file-control summary report is generated, reviewed, and approved by management prior to the processing of daily cash remittances. This procedure ensures that the accounts receivable file and the control file are in balance after the new billing data are added.

Cash Remittance Processing   Customer payments are remitted to a special post office box number. This approach separates the checks from other mail received by the organization, thus eliminating manual sorting of the checks and reducing the number of individuals handling them when they are received.

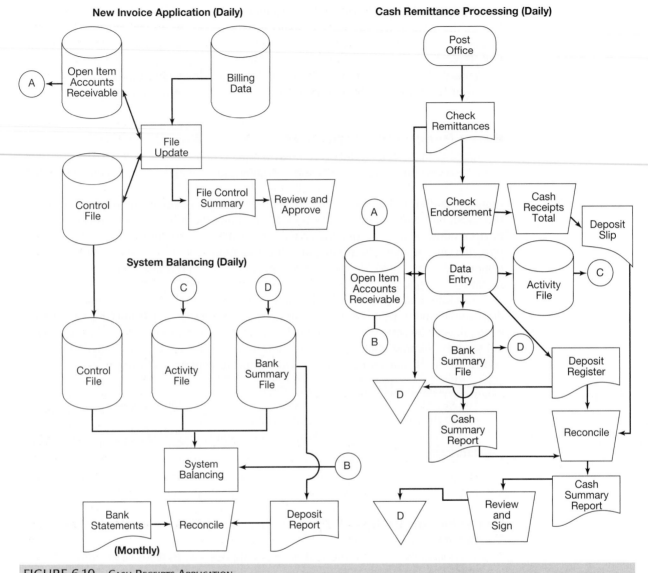

FIGURE 6.10   CASH RECEIPTS APPLICATION.

When the checks are brought from the post office, they are given to a control desk, where a clerk restrictively endorses them. This stamped endorsement prevents the deposit of the remittance to any unauthorized bank account. The clerk then totals all checks by adding machine and prepares a deposit slip. This ensures the accountability of checks received and their subsequent disposition. When the checks are deposited, the bank-validated deposit slip and adding machine tape are filed to be reconciled later to a cash summary report.

For ease of handling, controlling, and reconciling, the payments are batched into groups of 30 or fewer checks. When the checks are ready to be processed, a terminal operator requests access to the accounts receivable system through a network terminal. The operator keys into the terminal a unique security code and employee number and identifies the type of transaction to be processed.

A security application, which controls access to all applications, verifies that the operator is an authorized user of the system and that his or her personal profile of clearances includes the transaction he or she has requested. Accounts receivable management may delegate or remove authority to process transactions, but the security application limits management to the delegation of transactions within the scope of its authority (as defined by a similar type of manager's security profile) and to transactions that will not compromise good separation of duties when processed in combination with existing transaction authorities.

The terminal operator enters from the remittance advice the invoice number and check amount as an individual line item for as many lines as the terminal is capable of displaying. The accounts receivable system then compares the individual line items against the records in the accounts receivable file. For those line items where an invoice number and check amount match a corresponding record in the file, the check amount is applied using random-access file updating. If there are line items that do not completely match an invoice number and check amount, or if the accounts receivable system notes that an entered invoice number was cleared previously, an error message is immediately transmitted back to the input terminal indicating the line item in error and the reason for rejection (e.g., no unpaid invoice number on file or the check amount entered is under or over the invoice amount of the file).

As payments are applied against the unpaid invoice records on the accounts receivable file, the invoice records are updated to reflect the payment date, activity code (e.g., check payment, invoice adjustment), and a sequential check number generated by the system. The paid customer invoice records are retained on-line for 1 year and are available for inquiries.

The terminal operator is restricted by application controls within the system to applying cash remittances to a single customer account. The terminal can access only one customer account for each check remittance. The entire check remittance amount must be applied to that customer account. The terminal operator cannot apply the remaining check amount of one customer's payment to another customer's account. If a terminal operator is unable to apply a customer remittance because the customer's account is not on the file (usually the result of a check misrouted by the customer), then accounts receivable management follows up with the customer. If it is appropriate to do so, the check amount is subtracted from the batch total, and the check is returned to the customer.

All check remittances within a batch must be applied except those that were sent erroneously to the company. If a check remittance for some reason is not entered into the system and not subtracted from the batch control totals, the discrepancy will be highlighted by the cash balancing procedure employed at the end of the daily application of remittances.

System Balancing   All cash remittance activity is logged on an activity file to provide an audit trail of all cash transactions processed. The activity file is used in the daily balancing of the accounts receivable system and for preparing, on request, listings that assist data processing personnel in tracing any lost activity that may have resulted from a system error.

After a batch of checks has been applied, the system updates a bank summary file for the dollar amount of the batch of checks. Also, a deposit register detailing and totaling the invoice numbers and invoice amounts in the batch is printed.

Daily, on completion of the application of cash remittances, the accounts receivable system prints a cash summary report from the bank summary file. This report lists the total number of checks and total dollars applied during that day. The deposit register is compared with the cash summary report to ensure that the cash applied to the system is in balance. In addition, the bank-validated deposit slip is reconciled with the cash summary report. This reconciliation ensures that the cash deposited was applied by the accounts receivable system. After the deposit register and the cash summary report are balanced, the cash summary report is given to management for review and signature and is filed for future reference. The deposit register is filed with the day's customer remittance advices for future reference or reconciliation.

Daily, the activity file is summarized and compared with the totals in the bank summary file. Also, the activity file totals by type of accounts receivable are subtracted from the control file totals, which reflect the previous day's accounts receivable file data by type of accounts. Finally, the current accounts receivable file is accumulated by type of account. These accounts receivable system processing steps are made daily before the accounts receivable file is updated with new billing data or invoice adjustment data.

Comparing the activity file and the bank summary file ensures that all cash that has been deposited has been applied and recorded on the activity file. The total derived from subtracting the activity file from the control file should equal the sum of the totals by type of the current accounts receivable file. This system balancing imposes a three-way check to ensure that each file within the accounts receivable system is in balance. As a result, any out-of-balance condition is readily identified, and appropriate corrective action is initiated prior to proceeding with the next day's accounts receivable processing procedures.

Bank statements are received each month and reconciled with reports prepared from the bank summary file. Also, at the end of each month, the total amount of cash activity on the activity file is summarized and forwarded to the general ledger application system. This information, which is used as a standard journal entry, is output in machine-readable form and as such is directly entered into the month's journal voucher file for posting to the general ledger.

PAPERLESS PROCESSING SYSTEMS

In paperless processing systems, either batch or real-time processing is possible. With **real-time processing**, sometimes called *on-line real-time processing*, transactions are processed as they are input into the system. Both batch and real-time processing are discussed in the context of paperless processing systems.

BATCH PROCESSING IN PAPERLESS PROCESSING SYSTEMS

Batch processing in paperless systems is similar to batch processing in paper-based systems. The main difference is that journal vouchers are replaced by their electronic equivalents, and the general ledger is updated automatically in periodic batch runs. Either sequential or random-access file updating is possible.

REAL-TIME PROCESSING IN PAPERLESS PROCESSING SYSTEMS

A primary advantage of paperless systems is that they make possible real-time processing. **On-line, real-time systems (OLRS)** process transactions immediately after they are input and can provide immediate output to users. Transactions are not accumulated into batches, but rather, on input they are applied immediately to updating the master file using random-access file updating. The processing of individual transactions as opposed to groups of transactions is called *immediate, direct*, or *real-time processing*. Immediate processing is the primary characteristic of OLRS. Master files are always up to date because they are updated as soon as transaction data are input. Responses to user inquiries are immediate because information in randomly accessible files can be retrieved quickly.

Types of Real-Time Processing in OLRS   Many types of real-time processing are possible in OLRS. In *inquiry/response systems*, users do not input data for processing; rather, they only request information. Inquiry/response systems are designed to provide users with quick responses to their requests for information. A common example is when a bank clerk wishes to find out if a customer has a sufficient balance to cover the check he or she wishes to cash.

In *data entry systems*, users interactively input data. The data are stored by the OLRS but are processed periodically in batches. For example, stores may capture sales transactions in real time during the day and then process them at night in batches.

In file processing systems, users also interactively input data as they do in data entry systems. However, *file processing systems* differ from data entry systems in that they go one step further and immediately process the data against the relevant master files. For example, a retail store might collect and process sales transactions immediately, charging the customer's account within moments of the sale. The transaction, however, would be incomplete until the customer is billed at the end of the month.

In *full processing systems*, or **transaction processing systems**, users also interactively input transactions. However, full processing systems differ from file processing systems in that they go even further and complete the entire transaction when it is input. For example, in the case of the retail store example in the preceding paragraph, the customer also would be billed immediately, thus completing the transaction. Sometimes in practice, however, the terms *file processing system* and *full processing system* are used interchangeably.

The Economics of OLRS   Most of the attributes of OLRS, such as immediate processing of transactions and quick response to inquiries, are relative advantages when compared with batch processing systems. OLRS are desirable in many situations. On-line reservation systems, inventory control in retail stores, and customer account files in a bank are some familiar examples. The relative disadvantages of OLRS stem from the increased costs and complexity of systems operation. In particular, OLRS are more sensitive to hardware and software errors and are much more susceptible to processing errors that arise from erroneous or fraudulent input. Whereas a hardware or software malfunction in a batch system might have little or no effect on users because they are not directly using the system, a hardware or software malfunction in an OLRS immediately affects users. An incorrect transaction in a batch processing system might be corrected prior to processing or detected in a review of the results of processing. In an OLRS, however, an incorrect transaction is processed immediately and might contaminate several different files that are updated at the same time. In addition, the results of processing an incorrect transaction are available immediately to users of the OLRS.

Control of transaction processing is much more involved in OLRS than in batch-oriented systems. Application system files are integrated, and transactions are entered directly by users through remote network terminals (e.g., POS terminals) or PCs for immediate processing. Application system interfaces are handled automatically; once a transaction has been input, it may be posted immediately to several different files. Printed output concerning transaction processing usually is not produced because transactions are processed individually in real time rather than as a batch. As a result, a transaction may generate no directly human-verifiable evidence of its processing. The audit trail must be considered carefully in the design of such systems. The high degree of concentration of functions characteristic of on-line systems necessitates the use of special control techniques to ensure that data are processed accurately and reliably.

REAL-TIME SALES SYSTEMS

Real-time sales systems use contemporary information technology to maximize system performance. In real-time sales systems, purchase orders for inventory items are made on a *demand-pull* basis rather than a fixed interval (e.g., monthly or weekly) push basis to restock inventory levels. New goods arrive when they are needed, that is to say, just in time (JIT). Orders to vendors are placed on the basis of actual sales to quickly replenish stocks of items that are selling. Current sales demand pulls (i.e., automatically generates) orders for inventory. Retailers order on the basis of current buying trends. This is critical in retailing, where fads (i.e., customer demand for certain products) can and do change rapidly. What sold last year, last month, or maybe even last week may no longer be what the customer wants.

Real-time sales systems are central to the competitive strategy of mass retailers such as Sears, Wal-Mart, and J.C. Penney. These systems are also central to the competitive strategy of major vendors to mass retailers, such as Levi, Haggar, and Wrangler (all brand-name suppliers of men's clothing for retail outlets). This is so because major vendors to mass retailers are themselves operating sales systems, and they face exactly the same problems. If Levi, for example, is out of stock of a popular item when it is ordered, the delay or inability to satisfy the order is lost revenue. In a competitive market, this revenue is lost forever. Sears will buy similar merchandise from a competitor who can fill the order when it is needed. The customer, in turn, will purchase a competitor's product.

Levi, Haggar, and Wrangler in their turn must issue purchase orders to their vendors to stock the items that they in turn manufacture and/or resell to retailers. The suppliers face the same situation in their sales systems. If they are out of stock when items are ordered, the delay or inability to satisfy the order is lost revenue. And so on, the situation repeats for each trading partner. If a major competitor participates in a real-time retail sales system, then one is likely to be in a position of competitive disadvantage unless one also participates.

A significant degree of cooperation among trading partners is required to implement real-time sales systems. Companies, their suppliers, and buyers often enter into close, noncompetitive trade partnership agreements. In some cases, customers and suppliers coordinate their production schedules so that goods can be manufactured just in time. Prior to real-time systems, trading partners customarily have worked at arm's length from each other, sharing the minimum information required to make a deal. Reveal more information, and your trading partners might take advantage of you. The development of mutual trust among trading partners is essential to the operation of real-time retail sales systems. The retailer must trust the supplier to whom he or she supplies current data from his or her POS terminals. The retailer trusts that the supplier will use these data to ship the right product to the right store at the right time. The supplier must, in turn, trust that the retailer is providing accurate data and that the retailer will accept shipments when they arrive. All trading partners must trust that their data are being used solely for the intended purposes and are not being sold or supplied to direct competitors.

COMPONENTS OF REAL-TIME SALES SYSTEMS

Three technologies make real-time retail sales systems feasible: the point-of-sale (POS) system, bar coding for automatic identification, and the electronic data interchange (EDI) ordering system. Each of these technologies is discussed below.

The POS System   The uniform product code (UPC) bar code scanned by POS technology at the checkout counter of a retail store is the initial event in a chain of events that ends with the right item being quickly replenished in the store's inventory so that it can be sold again.

A consideration of the type of information useful to the management of a retail store would include numerous summaries of sales transaction data, such as total sales, total cash sales, total sales on credit, sales returns, total purchases, and current inventory status. Further consideration of a retailing store would indicate that a large percentage of transactions originate at the cash registers—the point of sale in the merchandising cycle. Enhancing of the traditional cash register to allow it to function as a source data-entry device for sales transactions is the essence of a POS system.

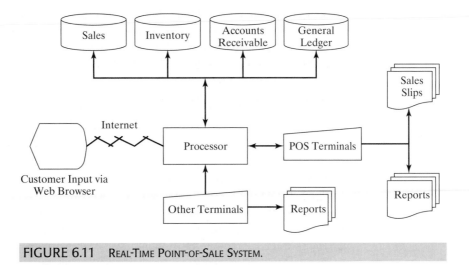

FIGURE 6.11   REAL-TIME POINT-OF-SALE SYSTEM.

A system that collects data on retail sales in this fashion is referred to as a **point-of-sale (POS) system** because data are collected at the point where the sale is completed (Fig. 6.11) The specially designed cash registers are called *point-of-sale retail terminals*. Data may be entered manually through a keying operation by the sales clerk or automatically using special codes and sensing devices. Sensing devices include wands and scanners for UPC bar-code recognition.

POS terminals record both cash and charge sales. Data relating to either type of sale are transmitted to a computer network, where it may be processed immediately. In a cash sale, the customer pays cash and receives the goods. In addition, a sales slip is printed by the terminal. Data relating to the transaction—such as the inventory codes for the items purchased, the number of items purchased, the cost of each item, the date, the total sales amount, and any sales taxes—are recorded via the terminal and made available to the store's computer network for immediate processing. Inventory records can be updated immediately in real time to reflect the goods purchased by the customer. The sales tax, cost of the items sold, and total sales price will be posted to daily sales records.

Sales on account require that a customer's charge account number and credit standing be verified prior to releasing the goods. The customer's charge account number is input to the POS terminal, allowing the computer system to access the customer's record, examine it, and determine the status of the account. If the charge sale is authorized, the system automatically completes the transaction. The sale on credit will be posted automatically against the appropriate records in the same manner as a cash sale. The status of the customer's charge account also will be updated to a new charge balance, and an update of the credit available to the customer and a record of the items purchased will be made.

The Internet has enhanced the real-time sales system by extending it to customers who are off-site. Using their Web browser, customers may input sales transaction data into the system to make purchases. The design of the browser interface guides the customer during input. The resulting information that is collected for the retail sale can be identical to that which would have been collected had the customer physically been in the retailer's store and made the transaction at a POS terminal. Internet sales can be made 24/7, that is, 24 hours a day, 7 days a week.

POS systems have a major impact on the management of a retail firm, providing a variety of timely and detailed reports concerning operations. Various reports may pinpoint areas of responsibility and accountability. Typical reports that may be obtained include checker settlement, deposits and receipts, checker cash list, department sales, store dollars, hourly activity, price lookup file, and check authorization file.

An hourly activity report offers management detailed statistics about customer activity, average sale per customer, average number of items sold per customer, and total items sold within a specified period of time. Such a report summarizes sales data by hourly time intervals and enables store management to monitor customer traffic patterns throughout the store and at checkout lanes. POS systems provide detailed information on stock turnover that is useful to management in assessing profitability.

Bar-Coding Technology Automatic identification of sales input is essential to a real-time system; thus machine-readable bar codes and scanner technology are critical components of real-time retail sales systems. Maximum benefit is obtained when the standard, widely used UPC bar-code system is used. Originally used in grocery retailing, UPC coding is now commonplace on consumer products. When UPC coding is used, all participants in the real-time system chain share and process the same basic data. Without code standardization, each agent in the chain uses his or her own codes, which must be cross-referenced to everyone else's codes. While cross-referencing codes is possible, it is both time-consuming and error-prone. Neither of these attributes facilitates real time.

Using UPC as a base, all agents use the same product code, eliminating cross-referencing problems. However, this is a relatively minor consideration when compared with the other benefits obtained from UPC standardization. The UPC product identification code can be scanned and used for automatic identification throughout the chain of real-time events. Cartons or other containers in transit or in inventory can be coded and scanned as well as individual items at the POS checkout counter. Cartons are UPC-coded when shipped by the vendor. Cartons are scanned when received by the retailer, and the data are input to the store information system. Cartons can be scanned when in inventory to easily identify the items contained within. UPC coding also lets the vendor code individual products for sale in the retailer's store. A retailer no longer has to code its own inventory; it arrives precoded with UPC.

The EDI Ordering System EDI is the direct computer-to-computer exchange of business documents via a communications network. The EDI link between the retailer's computer system and the vendor's computer system allows near instantaneous placing and processing of the purchase order, facilitating quick shipment. The vendor also could invoice the retailer using EDI. In some cases EFT payment might be made by the retailer to the vendor's account. All these events, including the picking of the order from the vendor's inventory, might take place without any human intervention.

Public EDI standards, in particular ANSI X.12, also provide maximum benefit when used in real-time systems. Without standardization, each agent in the chain must cross-reference everyone else's codes. Public EDI standards provide a common architecture for data interchange and thus eliminate costly and error-prone cross-referencing. Many early users of EDI started with their own proprietary codes for EDI and then switched to the ANSI X.12 standard.

In addition to purchase order and invoicing data, EDI also can be used to transmit retail sales data captured from the retail store to vendors. These data can then be analyzed by the vendor and input directly to purchasing and production applications to provide maximum inventory planning and control. This is feasible because both the retailer and vendor use the UPC product code. Actual retail sales data at the size and color level may be known instantaneously by the vendor due to the integration of UPC coding, scanner technology, and EDI.

EDI also might be used by vendors to electronically transmit catalogs with current price information to retailers.

TRANSACTION PROCESSING IN REAL-TIME SALES SYSTEMS

Although the exact sequence of events will vary somewhat from system to system, the processing of an order typically will involve seven steps. These include sending the customer an electronic catalog, forecasting the customer's sales order, receiving and translating the incoming order, sending an acknowledgment, sending the order to inventory or production (as applicable), generating and transmitting an advance shipping notice, and shipping the goods (see Fig. 6.12). Each of these events is discussed in turn.

Sending the Customer an Electronic Catalog   The customer is periodically sent (via EDI) an electronic catalog of the company's products. A special version of this catalog might be made for each customer to reflect any possible contract prices agreed on through competitive bidding.

Sending the catalog electronically has three major advantages over sending it in paper form. First, the information in the electronic catalog can be used by the customer to generate an EDI purchase order. This minimizes errors that might arise from the manual keying of data that otherwise would be required. Second, the catalog allows

FIGURE 6.12   TRANSACTION PROCESSING IN REAL-TIME SALES SYSTEMS.

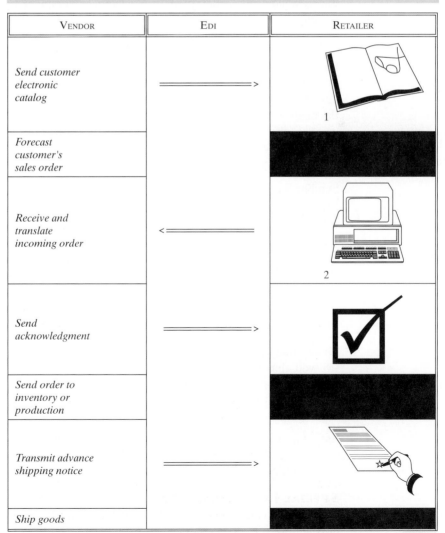

VENDOR	EDI	RETAILER
Send customer electronic catalog	===>	1
Forecast customer's sales order		
Receive and translate incoming order	<===	2
Send acknowledgment	===>	
Send order to inventory or production		
Transmit advance shipping notice	===>	
Ship goods		

the company to almost instantly bring the customer up to date with new prices and other information order lead times. Third, the electronic catalog can contain UPC product codes that can be used subsequently by both companies for automatic identification and tracking.

Forecasting the Customer's Sales Order   In many cases the company will analyze the customer's sales trends and predict future needs. Even in a JIT system, predicting demand can facilitate production planning.

Receiving and Translating the Incoming Order   The initial processing of the incoming EDI order involves several phases. These include the physical receipt of the order, validation and authentication, and decryption and translation. Each phase is discussed.

Physical Receipt of the Order.   There are several ways that an order may arrive, depending on the system. It can arrive as an electronic-mail message either in the company's internal mail system or in a third-party mail/EDI system. Alternatively, the company might have its own dedicated EDI communications server.

Validation, Decryption, and Authentication.   Regardless of how the incoming message physically arrives, it must be validated, decrypted, and authenticated. Even if the message itself is encrypted, its electronic envelope generally will not be. As an initial check, the return address in this envelope will be checked to see if the message originated from a recognized customer. Next, the message will be decrypted (if necessary) and authenticated. Authentication is accomplished through the use of authentication codes that ensure the message has not been altered in transit.

Once decrypted, the message is checked for internal consistency and completeness. EDI documents typically contain dual control numbers, one control number at the beginning of the message and another at the end. The correctness of internal passwords is also verified. Then the message is translated into a format recognized by the company's accounting system, and finally, the document is assigned an internal sequence number.

Sending an Acknowledgment   Next, the sender of the message is sent an acknowledgment. Three types of acknowledgments are possible. A transmission acknowledgment simply indicates that a message was received. A functional acknowledgment not only acknowledges receipt of the message but also reports in detail the items in the received message. Finally, a transactional acknowledgment provides full verification of all data (e.g., the correctness of the part numbers) in the message.

Sending the Order to Production/Inventory   The order is sent to production or inventory for processing. Transaction processing in the production and/or inventory department is discussed below.

Generating and Transmitting an Advance Shipping Notice   The advance shipping notice will alert the customer to the planned delivery date. This notice typically will include the customer's purchase order number, the quantities being shipped, and bar codes for automatic identification. In many companies the advance shipping notice also serves as an invoice.

Shipping the Goods   The shipping department scans items as they are packed. This permits automatic matching of the bar codes on the packed items against those in the advance shipping notice. The packing slip is then generated automatically.

SPECIAL INTERNAL CONTROL CONSIDERATIONS
Certain internal control problems particularly pertain to real-time sales systems. First, customer orders may be processed without human intervention or approval. In effect,

the customer may have the ability to generate his or her own sales order because generation of the sales order is performed automatically when a valid EDI purchase order is received. Second, the traditional separation of duties in transactions is completely obliterated. The computer handles the transaction from beginning to end. Finally, many traditional documents may be eliminated in EDI-based systems. For example, as was discussed earlier, in such systems it is common practice to dispense with invoices. The various special control problems in real-time systems can be compensated for by careful program data editing checks and transaction logs, as well as by good computer security.

THE OUTPUT SYSTEM

The output system can be paper-based, paperless, or something in between. Most paper-based batch-oriented systems with sequential file processing produce very large volumes of output. Since such systems do not provide random-access user queries, they typically generate printouts or microfiche copies of all files for reference. For example, a printout of the accounts receivable file might be used to look up individual customer balances.

On the other hand, on-line, real-time paperless systems tend to produce very little output. Such systems are almost imperative in very large companies for this reason because it would be impractical to continually print what may be hundreds of thousands or even millions of records.

Output controls are designed to check that processing results in valid output and that outputs are distributed properly. Reports should be reviewed critically by supervisory personnel in user departments for general reasonableness and quality in relation to previous reports. Control totals should be balanced to control totals generated independently of the data processing operation, as discussed earlier. Further, program data editing checks should be performed on all outputs. This can prevent problems such as those that once occurred in the Social Security system when Social Security Numbers were printed accidentally in the amount fields on Social Security benefits checks.

A separate *EDP control group* is often established to monitor EDP operations. The EDP control group is frequently part of the internal audit function. Procedures should be established to provide assurance that errors are reported to the EDP control group. These procedures must ensure that such errors are entered into controls, corrected, and reentered properly into the system for further processing. Corrections should be subject to the same testing as original data. The distribution of output should be controlled so as to minimize the danger of unauthorized access to confidential data. Output distribution is controlled through documentation and supervision. Typically, an **output distribution register** is maintained to control the disposition of reports. This register and its attendant documentation should be reviewed periodically in the internal audit function.

❖ SUMMARY

Data processing systems vary in the degree to which they are computerized. Some systems, although computerized, rely heavily on paper documents. Other systems can process transactions from beginning to end without a shred of paper. A number of application controls might be used in a data processing system, including batch controls, programmed data editing, and transaction logs.

Batch processing of transactions is a common approach to data processing. Representative examples of batch processing include processing weekly time reports to produce paychecks, processing groups of checks to update accounts payable files, and processing invoices to update an accounts receivable file. In a paper-based batch processing accounting system, batches of transactions from each application system are processed against the relevant application files in separate computer runs. The computer runs post the transactions to subsidiary ledgers and also generate the information necessary to prepare journal entries (journal vouchers) for posting to the general ledger. The journal vouchers are accumulated and processed as a batch against the general ledger in a separate computer run. Computer processing of accounting data typically is a two-step procedure. The first step produces preliminary reports, which are forwarded to the accounting department for review and audit relative to the journal voucher listings and general ledger listing. After the audit and submission of corrections or additional data, the second step is a run that produces the final listings and financial schedules.

Many EDP systems maintain indexes for both subsidiary and general ledger files. These indexes allow users to quickly access particular accounts. When an index is present, it also can be used for random-access file updating. With random-access updating it is not necessary to sort the transaction file into the same order as the master file, and there is no need to generate a new master file. Individual records are read one by one from the transaction file and used to update the related records in the master file in place. Batch processing with random-access file updating was illustrated in the context of an on-line cash receipts application.

On-line, real-time processing systems are transaction-oriented rather than file-oriented. Individual transactions may be input for processing by users through network terminals rather than being batched and submitted to a processing center as a group of source documents. Extensive control and audit trails may be implemented in such systems, but these features must be included within the design of the system during development. Standard application controls over system inputs and processing in an on-line, real-time processing system were discussed in the context of a purchasing application.

❖ GLOSSARY

batch processing: accumulating source documents into groups for processing on a periodic basis.

check digit: an extra digit added to a code number that is verified by applying mathematical calculations to the individual digits in the code number.

continuous operations auditing: the use of programmed edit tests to discriminate between acceptable and nonacceptable data values so that some items are either held in suspense of processing until audited or collected for audit after processing.

input document control form: documents batch control totals for batches of input data transmitted between user departments and the data processing department.

key verification: a control procedure to ensure the accuracy of key-transcribed input data.

limit test: an edit program checks the value of a numeric data field as being within a range of certain predefined limits.

line coding: assigning codes to items in the general ledger that indicate the item's use and placement in financial statements.

on-line, real-time systems (OLRS): computer systems that process input data immediately after they are input and can provide immediate output to users.

output controls: designed to check that processing results in valid output and that outputs are distributed properly to users.

output distribution register: a log maintained to control the disposition of output and reports.

point-of-sale (POS) system: technology that enhances the traditional cash register to allow it to function as a source data entry device for sales transactions.

program data editing: a software technique used to screen data prior to computer processing.

real-time processing: immediate or fast-response processing.

son-father-grandfather retention: retaining the old master (i.e., father) and the transaction file for backup over the new master file (i.e., son).

table lookup: an edit program compares the value of a field with the acceptable values contained in a table file.

tagging: audit-oriented information that is included with original transaction data when they are recorded.

transaction processing system: a system that collects and processes transactions and provides immediate output concerning processing.

valid code check: a table-lookup procedure in which the table file consists of valid data codes.

❖ CHAPTER QUIZ

Answers to the chapter quiz appear on page 236.

1. Which of the following is (are) a typical example of batch processing?
   (a) processing weekly time reports to produce paychecks
   (b) processing groups of checks to update accounts payable files
   (c) both a and b
   (d) neither a nor b

2. Accumulating source documents into groups prior to processing is a characteristic of (_____).
   (a) batch processing
   (b) on-line, real-time processing
   (c) both a and b
   (d) neither a nor b

3. Which of the following errors probably would be corrected by key verification of data input?
   (a) A salesperson manually enters an incorrect product number on a sales invoice, which is subsequently given to a data entry operator in the information systems department for key transcription to machine-readable format.
   (b) A data entry operator in the information systems department mistypes a product number on a sales invoice when keying the document to machine-readable format.
   (c) Both a and b.
   (d) Neither a nor b.

4. Which of the following controls would prevent the following situation? A worker's paycheck was processed incorrectly because he had transposed letters in his department identification code, having entered *ABC*, an invalid code, instead of *CAB*.
   (a) control total
   (b) limit test
   (c) internal label check
   (d) table-lookup procedure

5. The son-father-grandfather concept of backing up master files can be used when master files are stored on (_____).
   (a) magnetic tape
   (b) magnetic disk
   (c) both a and b
   (d) neither a nor b

6. A review of an EDP system reveals the following items. Which of these is a potential internal control weakness?
   (a) Backup master files are stored in a remote location.
   (b) Users must verbally approve all changes to be made to application programs.
   (c) Computer operators have restricted access to system programs and data files.
   (d) Computer operators are required to take vacations.

7. For control purposes, data clerks total up the employee Social Security numbers in each batch of payroll transactions. Which of the following terms best describes the resulting total?
   (a) hash total
   (b) financial total
   (c) parity total
   (d) record count

8. In an on-line computer system, which of the following may be used to ensure that users have proper authorization to perform a task?
   (a) check digits
   (b) passwords
   (c) control totals
   (d) limit tests

9. For control purposes, data clerks total up the employee gross pay amounts in each batch of payroll transactions. Which of the following terms best describes the resulting total?
   (a) hash total
   (b) financial total
   (c) parity total
   (d) record count

10. A customer inadvertently orders part number 1234-8 instead of 1243-8. Which of the following controls would detect this error during processing?
   (a) hash total
   (b) financial total
   (c) limit check
   (d) check digit

❖ REVIEW PROBLEM

The computer system most likely to be used by a large savings bank for customers' accounts would be (_____).
(a) an on-line, real-time system
(b) a batch processing system
(c) a generalized utility system
(d) direct-access database system

❖ SOLUTION TO REVIEW PROBLEM

Answer a.
(a) An on-line, real-time system is characterized by data that are assembled from more than one location and records that are updated immediately. A large savings bank likely would have several different branches from which transactions on customer accounts are to be entered, and it is desirable that records be processed immediately in order that customer account data reflect their current financial positions.
(b) A batch processing system is characterized by data that are assembled at a centralized location and processed against records periodically as batches of sufficient size are accumulated. A large savings bank could use a batch processing system to post transactions on customer accounts, but it is desirable that such records be processed immediately rather than periodically as a batch in order that customer account data reflect their current financial positions.
(c) A generalized utility system is not a defined term in data processing.
(d) A direct-access database system sounds good, but this is not a defined term in data processing, as is an on-line, real-time system.

❖ REVIEW QUESTIONS

1. Identify and describe several controls over data transfer between user departments and data processing. Why are such controls necessary?
2. Describe key verification of input data. What types of errors does key verification control?
3. Describe program data editing. Is program data editing necessary if input data have been key-verified? Explain.
4. Identify and describe several program data editing techniques.
5. Describe how the loss of paper-based internal controls can be compensated for in paperless input systems.
6. Give an example of automatic identification in a paperless input system that requires human intervention.
7. Give an example of a paperless input system that requires no human intervention.
8. Describe batch processing of transactions in a paper-based processing system. When is batch processing most economical?
9. Identify several points where reconciliation of control totals should occur in the batch processing of transactions against a master file.
10. Explain son-father-grandfather file retention.

11. What is a journal voucher? Describe how computer batch processing of journal vouchers may be used to update the general ledger.
12. Identify several general ledger reports that might be prepared after updating the general ledger with computer batch processing.
13. Explain how random-access file updating differs from sequential-access updating.
14. Characterize several different types of real-time processing in OLRS.
15. Identify and describe several output controls. Why are such controls necessary?

❖ DISCUSSION QUESTIONS AND PROBLEMS

16. What type of EDP system is characterized by data that are assembled from more than one location and records that are updated immediately?
    (a) microcomputer system
    (b) minicomputer system
    (c) batch processing system
    (d) on-line, real-time system
    (CPA)
17. An EDP technique that collects data into groups to permit convenient and efficient processing is known as
    (a) document-count processing.
    (b) multiprogramming.
    (c) batch processing.
    (d) generalized-audit processing.
    (CPA)
18. Which of the following is not a characteristic of a batch-processed computer system?
    (a) The collection of like transactions that are sorted and processed sequentially against a master file
    (b) Key transcription of transactions, followed by machine processing
    (c) The production of numerous printouts
    (d) The posting of a transaction, as it occurs, to several files without intermediate printouts
    (CPA)
19. What is the computer process called when data processing is performed concurrently with a particular activity, and the results are available soon enough to influence the particular course of action being taken or the decision being made?
    (a) real-time processing
    (b) batch processing
    (c) random-access processing
    (d) integrated data processing
    (CPA)
20. The real-time feature normally would be least useful when applied to accounting for a firm's
    (a) bank account balances.
    (b) property and depreciation.
    (c) customer accounts receivable.
    (d) merchandise inventory.
    (CPA)
21. An EDP input control is designed to ensure that
    (a) machine processing is accurate.
    (b) only authorized personnel have access to the computer area.
    (c) data received for processing are properly authorized and converted to machine-readable form.
    (d) electronic data processing has been performed as intended for the particular application.
    (CPA)
22. When erroneous data are detected by computer program controls, such data may be excluded from processing and printed on an error report. This error report should be reviewed and followed up by the
    (a) computer operator.
    (b) systems analyst.

    (c) EDP control group.

    (d) computer programmer.

(CPA)

23. Which of the following would lessen internal control in an EDP system?
    (a) The computer librarian maintains custody of computer program instructions and detailed program listings.
    (b) Computer operators have access to operator instructions and detailed program listings.
    (c) The control group maintains sole custody of all computer output.
    (d) Computer programmers write and debug programs that perform routines designed by the systems analyst.

(CPA)

24. An internal administrative control sometimes used in connection with procedures to detect unauthorized or unexplained computer usage is
    (a) maintenance of a computer tape library.
    (b) use of file controls.
    (c) maintenance of a computer console log.
    (d) control over program tapes.

(CPA)

25. A procedural control used in the management of a computer center to minimize the possibility of data or program file destruction through operator error includes
    (a) control figures.
    (b) crossfooting tests.
    (c) limit checks.
    (d) external labels.

(CPA)

26. If a control total were to be computed on each of the following data items, which would best be identified as a hash total for a payroll EDP application?
    (a) net pay
    (b) department numbers
    (c) hours worked
    (d) total debits and total credits

(CPA)

27. In designing a payroll system, it is known that no individual's paycheck can amount to more than $300 for a single week. As a result, the payroll program has been written to bypass writing a check and will print out an error message if any payroll calculation results in more than $300. This type of control is called
    (a) a limit or reasonableness test.
    (b) error review.
    (c) a data validity test.
    (d) a logic sequence test.

(CPA)

28. Where disk files are used, the grandfather-father-son updating backup concept is relatively difficult to implement because the
    (a) location of information points on disks is an extremely time-consuming task.
    (b) magnetic fields and other environmental factors cause off-site storage to be impractical.
    (c) information must be dumped in the form of hard copy if it is to be reviewed before being used in updating.
    (d) process of updating old records is destructive.

(CPA)

29. A customer inadvertently ordered part number 12368 rather than part number 12638. In processing this order, the error would be detected by the vendor with which of the following controls?
    (a) batch total
    (b) key verifying
    (c) self-checking digit
    (d) an internal consistency check

(CPA)

30. In the weekly computer run to prepare payroll checks, a check was printed for an employee who had been terminated the previous week. Which of the following controls, if used properly, would have been most effective in preventing the error or ensuring its prompt detection?
    (a) A control total for hours worked, prepared from time cards collected by the timekeeping department
    (b) Requiring the treasurer's office to account for the numbers of the prenumbered checks issued to the EDP department for the processing of the payroll
    (c) Use of a check digit for employee numbers
    (d) Use of a header label for the payroll input sheet
(CPA)

31. Accounting functions that normally are considered incompatible in a manual system often are combined in an EDP system by using an EDP program or a series of programs. This necessitates an accounting control that prevents unapproved
    (a) access to the magnetic tape library.
    (b) revisions to existing computer programs.
    (c) use of computer program tapes.
    (d) testing of modified computer programs.
(CPA)

32. Totals of amounts in computer-record data fields that are not usually added for other purposes but are used only for data processing control purposes are called
    (a) record totals.
    (b) hash totals.
    (c) processing data totals.
    (d) field totals.
(CPA)

33. The use of a header label in conjunction with magnetic tape is most likely to prevent errors by the
    (a) computer operator.
    (b) data entry clerk.
    (c) computer programmer.
    (d) maintenance technician.
(CPA)

34. Where computers are used, the effectiveness of internal accounting control depends in part on whether the organizational structure includes any incompatible combinations. Such a combination would exist when there is no separation of the duties between the
    (a) documentation librarian and the manager of programming.
    (b) programmer and the console operator.
    (c) systems analyst and the programmer.
    (d) processing control clerk and the data entry supervisor.
(CPA)

35. The basic form of backup used in magnetic tape operations is called
    (a) odd parity check.
    (b) dual-head processing.
    (c) file protection rings.
    (d) the son-father-grandfather concept.
(CPA)

36. When an on-line, real-time (OLRT) EDP system is in use, internal control can be strengthened by
    (a) providing for the separation of duties between data entry and error-listing operations.
    (b) attaching plastic file protection rings to reels of magnetic tape before new data can be entered on the file.
    (c) preparing batch totals to provide assurance that file updates are made for the entire input.
    (d) making a validity check of an identification number before a user can obtain access to the computer files.
(CPA)

37. Which of the following most likely constitutes a weakness in the internal accounting control of an EDP system?
    (a) The control clerk establishes control over data received by the EDP department and reconciles control totals after processing.
    (b) The application programmer identifies programs required by the systems design and flowcharts the logic of these programs.
    (c) The systems analyst reviews output and controls the distribution of output from the EDP department.
    (d) The accounts payable clerk prepares data for computer processing and enters the data into the computer.

    (CPA)

38. An effective control designed to provide reasonable assurance that hourly payroll information has been entered accurately into the computer system is to
    (a) establish the use of batch control totals for total hours to be processed.
    (b) review the contents of the computer master file.
    (c) limit access to the on-line terminals.
    (d) circulate to user departments periodic reports containing the contents of the master file.

    (IIA)

39. Which of the following activities most likely would be performed in the EDP department?
    (a) initiation of changes to master records
    (b) conversion of information to machine-readable form
    (c) correction of transactional errors
    (d) initiation of changes to existing applications

    (CPA)

40. Carmela Department Stores has a fully integrated EDP accounting system and is planning to issue credit cards to creditworthy customers. To strengthen internal control by making it difficult for one to create a valid customer account number, the company's independent auditor has suggested the inclusion of a check digit that should be placed
    (a) at the beginning of a valid account number only.
    (b) in the middle of a valid account number only.
    (c) at the end of a valid account number only.
    (d) consistently in any position.

    (CPA)

41. One of the major problems in an EDP system is that incompatible functions may be performed by the same individual. One compensating control for this is use of
    (a) a tape library.
    (b) a self-checking digit system.
    (c) computer-generated hash totals.
    (d) a computer log.

    (CPA)

42. The primary documentation on which a company should rely for an explanation of how a particular program operates is the
    (a) run manual.
    (b) periodic memory dump.
    (c) maintenance of three generations of master files.
    (d) echo check printout.

    (CPA)

43. The use of external labels in conjunction with magnetic tape storage is most likely to prevent errors that might be made by which of the following?
    (a) a computer programmer
    (b) a systems analyst
    (c) a data entry clerk
    (d) a computer operator

    (CPA)

44. An on-line sales order processing system most likely would have an advantage over a batch sales order processing system by
    (a) detecting errors in the data entry process more easily by the use of edit programs.

(b) enabling shipment of customer orders to be initiated as soon as the orders are received.

(c) recording more secure backup copies of the database on magnetic tape files.

(d) maintaining more accurate records of customer accounts and finished goods inventories.

(CPA)

45. Which of the following is a general control that most likely would assist an entity whose systems analyst left in the middle of a major project?

(a) grandfather-father-son record retention

(b) input and output validation routines

(c) systems documentation

(d) check-digit verification

(CPA)

46. This question requires using the check-digit formula presented in this chapter (page 198).

(a) Calculate check digits for the following hypothetical account numbers: 4388, 5100, and 9106.

(b) Verify the following codes (which include a check digit): 10307, 50008, and 22222.

47. Consider the following numerical input data used in an accounts receivable application:

Account Number, 4 digits	Invoice Number, 4 digits	Gross Amount, 7 digits	Discount, 5 digits	Net Amount, 7 digits
4012	1003	265000	15000	250000
4810	1007	321550	27130	294420
7188	1008	108010	11500	96510

Required

(a) For the preceding data, calculate an example of each of the following: hash total, financial total, record count.

(b) You are to design an edit program that will be used to screen the preceding data before they are processed against a sequentially organized accounts receivable master file. Assuming that the input data the edit program receives will be sorted in ascending order by account number, what detailed editing procedures would you include in the design of the edit program?

48. The Foxx Company is designing a standard postings file to be used in the editing of transactions to be posted to the general ledger. The file (relation) as designed has the following format:

```
STANDARD-ENTRIES (CODE#, DESCRIPTION, DR-or-CR,
ACCOUNT#, ACCOUNT-NAME)
```

Is this relation a flat file? If not, how would you normalize this relation?

49. Indicate the objective of the following questions, which are abstracted from an EDP internal control questionnaire. What error or weakness might exist if the answer to a specific question is "No?"

(a) Do management and user departments review and approve all new systems design work?

(b) Have backup procedures been documented, and are the arrangements up to date?

(c) Is there an organizational chart of the EDP function?

(d) Are computer operators required to take vacations?

(e) Does more than one programmer or a supervisor have a working knowledge of each specific program?

(f) Are internal file labels tested by computer programs to validate file setup?

(g) Are check digits used where appropriate?

(h) Are changes to master files, such as pay rates or price changes, properly authorized, and is their posting to the file verified by the originating department?

(i) Are output reports reviewed critically by supervisory personnel in user departments for general reasonableness and quality in relation to prior periods?

50. What control or controls would you recommend in a computer processing system to prevent the following situations?

   (a) Working through the main control console, the night-shift computer operator made a change in a payroll program to alter his rate of pay in his favor.

   (b) A customer payment recorded on a remittance advice as $55.05 was entered into the computer from a data terminal as $550.50.

   (c) A new program to process accounts receivable was unreliable and would not handle common exceptions. The programmer who wrote the program recently quit the organization because he was repeatedly asked to document this program (which he never did do).

   (d) The payroll master file was loaded incorrectly on a disk drive that was supposed to hold the accounts receivable master file. The accounts receivable program was nevertheless run, destroying the payroll master file.

   (e) A weekly payroll check issued to an hourly employee was based on 96 hours rather than 46.

   (f) The master inventory file, contained on a removable magnetic disk, was destroyed by a small fire next to the area where it was stored. The company had to take a special complete inventory to reestablish the file.

   (g) The magnetic tape containing accounts receivable transactions could not be located. A data processing supervisor said that it could have been put among the scratch tapes available for use in processing.

   (h) In preparing payroll checks, the computer omitted 12 of a total of 1,570 checks that should have been processed. The error was not detected until the supervisors distributed the checks.

   (i) A sales transaction document was coded with an invalid customer account code (seven digits rather than eight). The error was not detected until the updating run, when it was found that there was no such account to which the transaction could be posted.

   (j) During data entry of customer payments, the digit 0 in a payment of $123.40 was mistakenly entered as the letter O. As a result, the transaction was not processed correctly.

   (k) A systems analyst entered a special routine one evening after work. The next day she obtained the program that calculates interest payments on customer accounts and processed it to add her routine to the program's logic. Her routine adds the fraction of a cent of each customer's interest, which otherwise would be rounded off, to her own account at the bank.

   (l) A salesman entering a customer order from a portable data entry terminal entered an incorrect but valid product number. As a result, the customer received a delivery of 100,000 kilograms of industrial salt rather than industrial sugar.

   (m) A customer called to inquire as to why he received a bill for 5 cents amount due when postage cost is more than a quarter.

51. The Western Savings and Loan Association, a client of yours, recently installed an new on-line, real-time computer system. Each teller in the association's main office and seven branch offices has an on-line input/output terminal. Customers' mortgage payments and savings account deposits and withdrawals are recorded in the accounts by the computer from data input by the teller at the time of the transaction. The teller keys the proper account by account number and enters the information in the terminal keyboard to record the transaction. The accounting department at the main office also has input/output devices. The computer is housed at the main office.

    In addition to servicing its own mortgage loans, the association acts as a mortgage servicing agency for three life insurance companies. In this latter activity, the association maintains mortgage records and serves as the collection and escrow agent for the mortgagees (the insurance companies), who pay a fee to the association for these services.

Required

You would expect the association to have certain internal controls in effect because an on-line, real-time computer system is employed. List the internal controls that should be in effect solely because this system is employed, classifying them as

   (a) those controls pertaining to input of information.

   (b) all other types of computer controls.

                                                      (CPA)

52. The inventory of Molly Company, a wholesaler of softgoods, is composed of approximately 3,500 different items. The company employs a computerized batch processing system to maintain its perpetual inventory records. The system is run each weekend so that the inventory reports are available on Monday morning for management use. The system has been functioning satisfactorily for the past 15 months, providing the company with accurate records and timely reports.

    The preparation of purchase orders has been automatic as a part of the inventory system to ensure that the company will maintain enough inventory to meet customer demand. When an item of inventory falls below a predetermined level, a record of the inventory item is written. This record is used in conjunction with the vendor file to prepare the purchase orders.

    Exception reports are prepared during updating of the inventory and preparation of the purchase orders. These reports identify any errors or exceptions identified during the processing. In addition, the system provides for management approval of all purchase orders exceeding a specified amount. Any exceptions or items requiring management approval are handled by supplemental runs on Monday morning and combined with the weekend results.

    Figure 6.13 presents a system flowchart of the inventory and purchase order procedure.

    Required
    (a) The illustrated system flowchart of Molly's inventory and purchase order system was prepared before the system was fully operational. Several steps that are important to successful operation of the system were omitted inadvertently from the chart. Now that the system is operating effectively, management wants the system documentation complete and would like the flowchart corrected. Describe steps that have been omitted, and indicate where the omissions have occurred. The flowchart does not need to be drawn.
    (b) In order for Molly Company's inventory purchase order system to function properly, control procedures would be included in the system. Describe the type of control procedures Molly Company would use in its system to ensure proper functioning, and indicate where these procedures would be placed in the system.

    (CMA)

53. Music Now is a large wholesaler of sheet music, music books, musical instruments, and other music-related supplies. The company acquired a midrange computer system last year, and an inventory control system has already been implemented. Now the systems department is developing a new accounts receivable system.

    Figure 6.14 is a diagram of the proposed accounts receivable system as designed by the systems department. The objectives of the new system are to produce current and timely information that can be used to control bad debts, to provide information to the sales department regarding customers whose accounts are delinquent, to produce monthly statements for customers, and to produce notices to customers regarding a change in the status of their charge privileges.

    Input data for the system are taken from four source documents—approved credit applications, sales invoices, cash payment remittances, and credit memoranda. The accounts receivable (A/R) file is maintained on magnetic disk by customer account number. The record for each customer contains identification information, last month's balance, current month's transactions (detailed), and current balance. Some of the output items generated from the system are identified and described briefly below.
    (1) Accounts receivable register (weekly)—a listing of all customers and account balances included on the accounts receivable file.
    (2) Aging schedule (monthly)—a schedule of all customers with outstanding balances, detailing the amount owed by age classifications—0–30 days, 30–60 days, 60–90 days, over 90 days old.
    (3) Delinquency and write-off registers (monthly)—(a) a listing of those accounts that are delinquent and (b) a listing of customers' accounts that have been closed and written off; related notices are prepared and sent to these customers.

    Required
    The systems department must develop the system controls for the new accounts receivable system. Identify and explain the system controls that should be instituted with the new system.

230

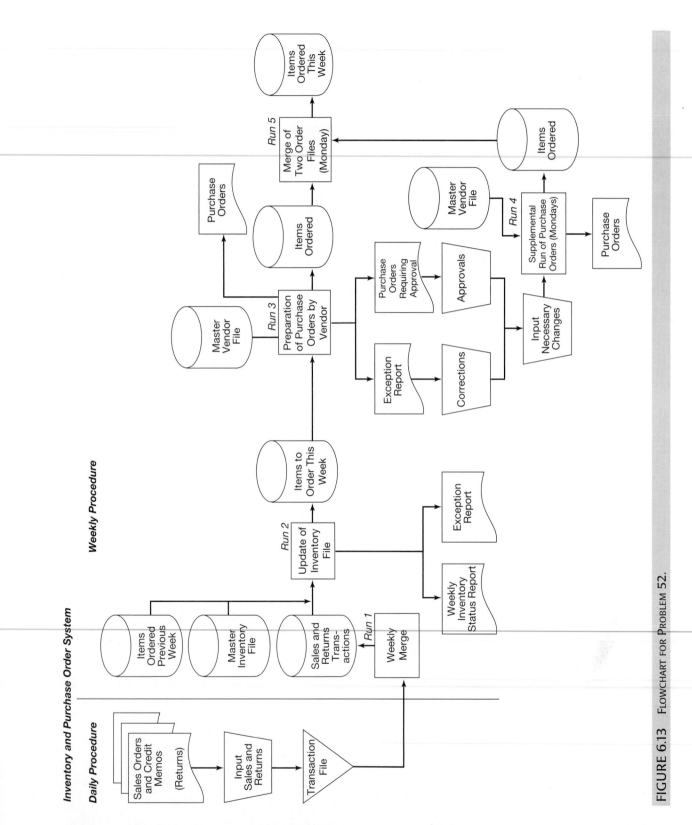

Inventory and Purchase Order System

Daily Procedure

Weekly Procedure

FIGURE 6.13 FLOWCHART FOR PROBLEM 52.

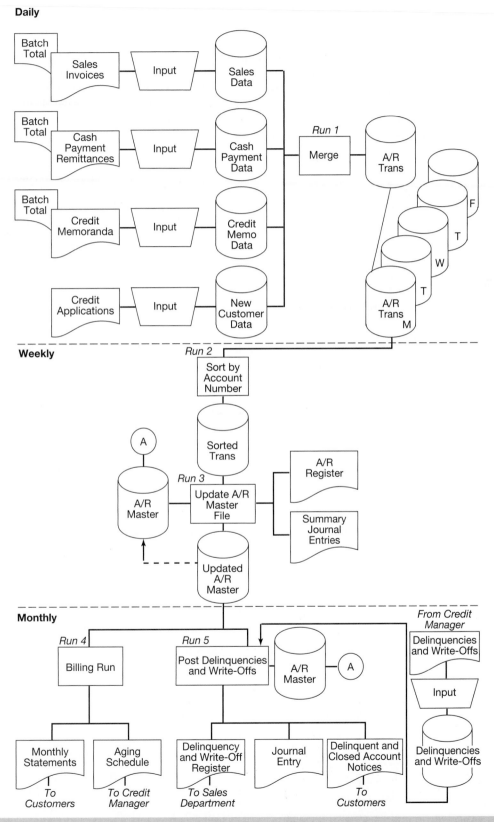

FIGURE 6.14   FLOWCHART FOR PROBLEM 53.

When appropriate, describe the location in the flowchart where the control should be introduced.

(CMA)

54. Consider the on-line cash receipts application discussed in this chapter. Modify the cash application procedure to allow the operator to process customer remittances with multiple payments or no payments (invoice numbers) referenced on them. Your comments should specify in detail the options that your procedure gives to the terminal operator.

55. Until recently, Amalgamated Gas employed a batch processing system for recording the receipt of customer payments. The following narrative and Figure 6.15 describe the procedures involved in this system.

The customer's payment and the remittance advice (an optically scanned turn-around document) are received in the treasurer's office. An accounts receivable clerk in the treasurer's office enters the cash receipt onto the remittance advice and forwards the document to the EDP department. The cash receipt is added to a control tape listing and then filed for deposit later in the day. When the deposit slips are received from EDP later in the day (approximately 2:30 P.M. each day), the cash receipts are removed from the file and deposited with the original

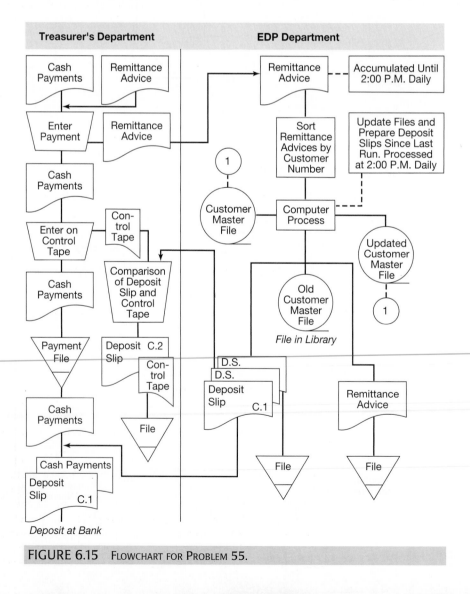

FIGURE 6.15   Flowchart for Problem 55.

deposit slip. The second copy of the deposit slip and the control tape are compared for accuracy before the deposit is made and then filed together.

In the EDP department, the remittance advices received from the treasurer's office are held until 2:00 P.M. daily. At that time the customer payments are processed to update the records on magnetic tape and to prepare a deposit slip in triplicate. During the update process, data are read, nondestructively, from the master accounts receivable tape, processed, and then recorded on a new master tape. The original and second copy of the deposit slip are forwarded to the treasurer's office. The old master tape (former accounts receivable file), the remittance advices (in customer-number order), and the third copy of the deposit slip are stored and filed in a secure place. The updated accounts receivable master tape is maintained in the system for processing the next day.

Amalgamated Gas has reviewed and redesigned its computer system so that it has on-line capabilities. The new cash receipts procedures, described below, are designed to take advantage of the new system.

The customer's payment and remittance advice are received in the treasurer's office as before. A terminal is located in the treasurer's office to enter the cash receipts. An operator keys in the customer's number and payment from the remittance advices and checks. The cash receipt is entered into the system once the operator has confirmed that the proper account and amount are displayed on the screen. The payment is then processed on-line against the accounts receivable file maintained on magnetic disk. The cash receipts are filed for deposit later in the day. The remittance advices are filed in the order in which they are processed; these documents will be kept until the next working day and then destroyed. The computer prints out a deposit slip in duplicate at 2:00 P.M. for all cash receipts since the last deposit. The deposit slips are forwarded to the treasurer's office. The cash receipts are removed from the file and deposited with the original deposit slip; the duplicate deposit slip is filed for further reference. At the close of business hours (5:00 P.M.) each day, the EDP department prepares a record of the current day's cash receipts activity on a magnetic tape. This tape is then stored in a secure place in the event of a systems malfunction; after 10 working days, the tape is released for further use.

Required
(a) Prepare a systems flowchart of Amalgamated Gas's new on-line cash receipt procedures.
(b) Have the new cash receipt procedures as designed and implemented by Amalgamated Gas created any internal and systems control problems for the company? Explain your answer.

(CMA)

56. The With-It Company, an Internet service provider, uses direct, on-line processing in its customer payments business process. Data entry terminals in the cashier's department allow direct entry of customer payments data into the computer system for processing.

Customer payments are delivered from the mailroom to the cashier's office for processing. Clerks working under the supervision of the customer payment supervisor open the customer payments to ensure that both a remittance advice and a check are enclosed. If either of these is missing, the payment is set aside in a batch that is subsequently delivered to the chief cashier for reconciliation. Payments containing both a remittance advice and a check are grouped into batches of about 50. The customer payment supervisor attaches a batch control form to each batch and assigns the batches to the data-entry operators for processing.

Data entry operators sign onto the computer system using their own unique password. Operators enter customer account numbers from the remittance advices. When an account number match is made, the system prompts the operator to key in the other information—such as check number and the amount of the payment—as required. These data are taken directly from the customer's check. In all cases where input is not possible, the remittance advices and customer payments are returned to the customer payment supervisor for resolution.

After each batch of payments has been entered, the operator terminates the session with a special command. The system then presents a summary report of terminal activity on the monitor. The operator copies the total amount of payments from the summary report onto the batch control form and then returns the batch to the supervisor. The supervisor keeps a cumulative total of payments applied by the operators; as each batch is returned, the total amount of payments shown on the batch control form is added to the running total. At the end of the shift, the customer payment supervisor prepares a payments received report (three copies). The customer payments and two copies of the payments received report are forwarded to the chief cashier for verification and deposit. The customer remittance advices, in batches, are filed with the payments received report by date.

Required

(a) Identify deficiencies and/or weaknesses in the data entry procedures described here.
(b) Suggest an improvement to remove each weakness/deficiency that you note in (a).
Use the following format to answer this question.
(a) Deficiency/weakness
(b) Improvement suggested

57. The Magic Rock Company of Houston, Texas, is implementing a computer-based inventory control system. The system will use a sequentially organized inventory master file and a transaction file. Transactions will be batched and processed at the end of each day. A description of the file structures and transaction processing logic follows.

INVENTORY MASTER FILE

This file contains fixed-length records. The file has a header label. The header label contains three fields:

Field 1   File identification number
Field 2   Record count (number of records in the file)
Field 3   Last posting date

The following data elements are in the detail inventory records:

Field 1   Product number
Field 2   Quantity on hand
Field 3   Unit cost
Field 4   Reorder point
Field 5   Quantity on order from vendor
Field 6   Reorder quantity
Field 7   Current shipping rate
Field 8   Current return rate

TRANSACTION FILE

The transaction file has a header label. The header label contains two fields:

Field 1   Hash total of field 3 of the transaction file
Field 2   Current processing date

There are four different types of detail transaction records. Each transaction record has five fields, but all five fields are not used for every transaction type. Field 1 of each transaction record is a code that indicates the type of transaction.

Transaction Code 1: Delivery from Vendor

Field 1   Transaction code
Field 2   Product number
Field 3   Quantity
Field 4   Vendor number
Field 5   Not used

Each delivery-from-vendor transaction causes an increase in the quantity-on-hand field in the associated inventory record and a reduction in the quantity-on-order-from-vendor field.

Transaction Code 2: Inventory Status Check

Field 1   Transaction code
Field 2   Product number
Field 3   Quantity
Field 4   Not used
Field 5   Not used

Each inventory status check transaction initiates a comparison of the actual quantity on hand and that which is recorded in the related inventory record. If a discrepancy is found, the inventory master record is changed to agree with the physical count quantity indicated on the transaction record.

Transaction Code 3: Customer Order

Field 1   Transaction code
Field 2   Product number
Field 3   Quantity
Field 4   Customer number
Field 5   Salesperson number

Each customer order transaction causes a check of the quantity on hand for the ordered product. If sufficient goods are on hand, a shipment notice is output, and the quantity-on-hand field is reduced in the associated inventory record. If insufficient product is on hand, a shipment notice is made for the amount of product available and the quantity-on-hand field is reduced by this amount. A notice is then output indicating the quantity still on order by the customer. The amount of the product ordered by the customer but not yet shipped (possibly zero) is then subtracted from the sum of the updated quantity-on-hand field plus the updated quantity-on-order-from-vendor field. If this result is less than the reorder-point field, a purchase notice is output for the product. The purchase amount is the reorder quantity field. The current shipment-rate field is then recalculated for each actual shipment made. The update formula is

$$\text{New value} = 0.99 \times \text{old value} + 0.01 \times \text{shipment amount}$$

The return-rate field also must be updated. The update formula is

$$\text{New value} = 0.99 \times \text{old value}$$

This inventory reorder policy is reasonably simple and effective. These formulas calculate an average shipment and return rate using a form of exponential smoothing.

Transaction Code 4: Sales Return

Field 1   Transaction code
Field 2   Product number
Field 3   Quantity
Field 4   Customer number
Field 5   Not used

Each sales return transaction causes an update of the quantity-on-hand field in the associated inventory record and also causes an update of the return-rate field. The updated formula is

$$\text{New value} = \text{old value} + 0.01 \times \text{return}$$

The transaction file will be sorted into ascending sequence on product number prior to processing against the inventory master file. Output from the processing run will include an updated master inventory file and a printed transaction register.

Required
(a) Identify data edits and application processing controls that you would recommend be included in this system.
(b) From a control viewpoint, do you see any significant differences among the fields of data contained in the master inventory file? Explain your answer.

58. Circle Company has asked you to submit a contract bid to render a professional opinion concerning the operation and control of the company's database system. A centralized database is maintained, and these data are shared by all users. Users access the database using remote data terminals. All access to the database is controlled by a database software system. The information technology (IT) department includes a manager of operations and a manager of computer programming. Both these managers report to the head of the IT department. The head of the IT department reports to the controller.

You visit the company to make a preliminary survey and review of the operation and control of the database system. During your visit to Circle, you review some of the database system documentation, observe some data terminal usage of the system, observe the operation of the IT department, and interview the head of the IT department. At the end of a very busy day, you return home with the following notes:

  (a) Access to on-line data terminals is not restricted. Any type of transaction may be input from any terminal.

  (b) Documentation of the database system is extensive. Complete system documentation is available to users and to IT personnel.

  (c) The database software maintains a user authorization table. User passwords and access codes are assigned by user management and approved by the manager of computer programming.

  (d) The database dictionary was established and is controlled by the manager of computer programming. Changes to data definitions are approved by users.

  (e) The database software maintains a transactions-conflict matrix. User requests for data are validated against this matrix to ensure that users receive only authorized data.

  (f) Users must enter their passwords when signing on the system. Terminal activity logs are maintained for backup and control purposes.

  (g) Terminal input is edited for reasonableness and completeness. Transaction control totals are developed, and transaction logs are maintained.

  (h) Processing control totals are developed and reconciled with changes in the database.

  (i) Output is reconciled with transaction and input control totals. Printed output is placed in a bin outside the IT room, where users pick it up at their convenience.

  (j) Backup copies of the database are made daily and stored in the file library area. Access to the file library area is restricted to IT personnel.

Required

Several days after your visit, you are reviewing your notes to prepare a written proposal to perform a controls review for Circle Company. What is your preliminary opinion concerning the operation of their database system?

❖ Answers to Chapter Quiz

1. c	4. d	7. a	10. d
2. a	5. c	8. b	
3. b	6. b	9. b	

CHAPTER

7

CUSTOMER ORDER AND ACCOUNT MANAGEMENT BUSINESS PROCESSES

LEARNING OBJECTIVES

Careful study of this chapter will enable you to:

❖ Describe the customer order management business process.

❖ Illustrate controls that apply to order processing.

❖ Describe the customer account management business process.

❖ Illustrate controls that apply to accounts receivable processing.

CUSTOMER ORDER MANAGEMENT BUSINESS PROCESS

OVERVIEW

The customer order management business process includes the following activities (Fig. 7.1):

- Inquiry (optional)
- Contract creation (optional)
- Order entry
- Shipping
- Billing

Inquiry and contract creation are optional activities. These sometimes may occur or even may be required in the customer order management business process of some organizations, but they are not necessary activities for many customers or organizations. Order entry, shipping, and billing activities are essential activities in all organizations.

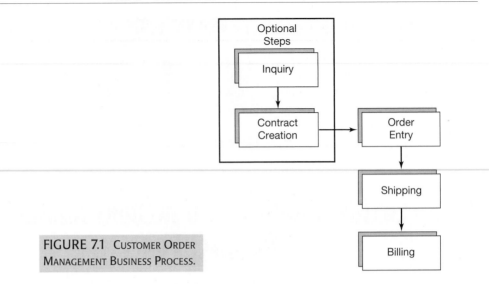

FIGURE 7.1 CUSTOMER ORDER
MANAGEMENT BUSINESS PROCESS.

Order fulfillment is the primary function of the customer order management business process. Orders are created when a customer—a *sold-to party*—requests goods or services from a firm. We shall describe a typical customer order business process in which customer orders are filled from an inventory of finished goods.

INQUIRY

The customer order management business process often begins when a potential customer makes an inquiry or requests a quotation. Some companies make quotations mandatory as a matter of company policy. Others do not. A **quotation** is a document[1] that is prepared and sent to a potential customer to inform him or her of product prices, product availability, and delivery information. A quotation is prepared when a potential customer has made a fairly specific request for details concerning a potential order. An **inquiry** is similar to a quotation, but an inquiry does not contain delivery information.

Customer information that is entered into the order-entry system to prepare the inquiry or quotation document is stored and can be reused subsequently if the customer places an order. A customer order management business process captures customer information as early as possible and reuses this information in subsequent activities.

CONTRACT CREATION

Some companies require that contracts (legal agreements) be prepared before selling to customers as a matter of company policy. Frequently, contract agreements are neither mandatory nor required as a matter of company policy. If contracts are required, then this is the next activity in the customer order management business process.

A *contract* is an outline agreement to provide goods or services to a customer. A contract usually specifies quantities and a general time frame for deliveries. Specific order details, such as delivery dates and perhaps even prices, are specified later, when the customer places an actual order that will be fulfilled according to the general conditions specified in the contract. A contract to provide goods over a period of time is sometimes called a **blanket order**.

---

[1]The term *document* is used generally to be inclusive of any physical medium used to store and transmit information pertaining to a specific business process activity. A document, such as a quotation or order, may be paper or electronic.

ORDER ENTRY

Order entry prepares the **sales order** document. The order-entry activity is essentially the same whether it is the first activity in the customer order management business process or occurs subsequent to either inquiry, contract preparation, or both. A different but similar document may be prepared when a customer is requesting delivery of goods that are detailed in a contract. For example, a document called a *release order* or *call-off* may be prepared rather than a sales order, but the information in these documents would be similar.

Order entry usually involves pricing and availability checking. Pricing an order involves knowing the current prices of products or services, any surcharges that may apply, any discounts that may apply, and shipping costs. Enterprise resource planning (ERP) information systems enable the implementation of sophisticated and flexible customer- and material-specific pricing procedures in the order-entry business process. Customer-specific procedures can be a significant competitive advantage in that the company can offer customers highly customized service. This is an essential aspect of the customer orientation that is central to ERP systems.

Many companies perform a credit limit check on the customer once pricing is complete and before the order is released for fulfillment. An order is usually blocked if it would cause the customer to exceed his or her credit limit. Blocked orders are listed for review by the credit department. The credit department is empowered to decide whether to release blocked orders for fulfillment.

If the customer's credit is satisfactory, then the availability of goods is checked to determine whether the items are either currently in stock or are expected to be in stock and available by the requested delivery date. Several options may exist in cases where the goods will not be available. The customer may wish to cancel the order. Partial delivery of the order is a possibility when the customer is willing to accept partial shipment. Another option is to hold the order until all the goods are available if the customer is willing to extend the requested delivery date.

SHIPPING

Shipping activity is initiated with the preparation of a shipping document called a *delivery*. A delivery document is created to arrange for the delivery of goods to the customer. All the information that is required to prepare and deliver the goods to the customer is contained in the delivery. The delivery is usually prepared at the production or distribution location.

The sales order contains much of the information that is necessary in a delivery. The ERP automatically copies this information into the delivery. The ERP might perform additional checks at this point to ensure quality. For example, the availability of goods may be rechecked to ensure that delivery is immediately possible.

Delivery documents are processed to prepare a schedule (i.e., work list) for shipping. The schedule is based on customers' requested delivery dates. Actual shipment of goods out of inventory requires picking the order, packing the order, and posting the shipment. Picking fills the order and involves the selection of goods from the plant or warehouse to be prepared for shipment. Packing involves packaging of the goods in the order for shipment and loading the shipment onto vehicles for transportation to the customer. The complexity of picking and packing differs significantly for different products. Some products are ready to pick and ship "as is," whereas others may require assembly or special equipment to be used during picking and packing.

Several other documents are prepared during shipping activities. A picking list is prepared to guide picking activities. A packing list is prepared for each shipment, and a copy usually is included in the shipment to document what has been shipped. A **bill of lading** is prepared to document the loading of goods onto vehicles for transportation to the customer. The ERP can copy much of the information contained in these documents from either the sales order document or the delivery document.

Shipping personnel post a **goods issue notice** when goods have been shipped. This posting updates the relevant delivery document. The ERP uses this information to update inventory as necessary based on the shipment. The posting of a goods issue notice also initiates the billing process. **Shipping advice** is a synonym for a goods issue notice.

BILLING

Deliveries are included in the billing work schedule and are invoiced. The ERP copies much of the data used in billing from the customer's sales order or from the customer's delivery document. An **invoice** (Fig. 7.2) for the shipment is prepared and issued to the customer. The issuing of the invoice is the end of the customer order management business process.

In many cases the goods are shipped before the customer is invoiced. In some cases it may be appropriate to invoice customers after the sales order has been prepared but before the goods have been shipped. Invoices are forwarded to accounts receivable processing to await payment by the customer.

ERP ILLUSTRATION

ERP systems are capable of storing and processing a vast amount of information pertaining to the customer order management business process. This section provides an overview of the data that is stored and processed in the customer order management business process by SAP R/3.[2] The customer order management business process is part of SAP's sales and distribution module.

FIGURE 7.2   INVOICE.

					INVOICE		
SOLD TO:	CITRUS SUPPLY CO. 1467 CLAY STREET PETERSBURG, WISCONSIN 44444				**Burroughs** Ⓑ		
SHIP TO:	CITRUS SUPPLY CO. 1467 CLAY STREET PETERSBURG, WISCONSIN 44444						

TERMS	ORDER NO.	CUSTOMER NO.	SOLD BY	SHIP VIA	DATE	INVOICE NO.
2-10 NET 30	P87654	102,912	7	OUR TRUCK	NOV. 15	12,347

CODE	QUANTITY	DESCRIPTION	PRICE	UNIT	GROSS	DISCOUNT	NET
13414522	10	CUTTING TIP TT-3	2.80	EA	28.00	.00	28.00
12415710	10	SCREWDRIVER 6"	1.90	EA	19.00	.38	18.62
15611410	5	WELDING GLOVE #10	1.50	PR	7.50	.15	7.35
12488806	10	DSK	1.00	EA	10.00	.00	10.00
							63.97
					TAX	5.0%	3.20
					HANDLING		25.00
							92.17

---

[2]SAP R/3 is a registered trademark of SAP Aktiengesellschaft, Systems, Applications, and Products in Data Processing, Neurottstrasse 16, 69190 Walldorf, Germany. *(www.sap.com)*. The material in this section is based on "SAP R/3 3.0 in a Box," © 1999 CBT Systems, published and © 1999 by Prentice-Hall, Inc.

CUSTOMER MASTER RECORDS

Customer master records contain all the information that pertains to a customer. Customer master records have to be created before processing sales orders in R/3 because the information in customer master records is used in sales order processing.

SAP R/3 requires four types of master records:

- Sold-to-customer records
- Ship-to-customer records
- Bill-to-customer records
- Payee customer records

When a new sold-to-customer master record is created, the other three master records are created automatically using the same information. When a customer has different locations for receiving, shipment, and/or payment, the information in these records can be changed as necessary. Additional records can be created as necessary. For example, a customer may have several ship-to addresses. Such records must be linked to the sold-to-customer master records. This is known as *partnering*.

Customer master records should be unique. Thus, it is necessary to check that a customer is not already in the system before the creation of a new customer master record. R/3 requires that a customer's hierarchy assignment be known prior to the creation of a master record. The customer's hierarchy assignment is a representation of the customer's organization structure that determines pricing information used in R/3. For example, a chain of stores inherits pricing agreements from its main office. Hierarchy assignment includes a distribution channel, type of industry, and geographic location. R/3 also requires that a customer has been approved for sales prior to the creation of master records.

DATA FIELDS

Customer master records are created by inputting information into R/3. R/3 guides the input process by displaying a series of screens on a video monitor that prompt the user to input the necessary data. Each screen collects a category of data pertaining to a customer. Most input is coded as numbers. The user hits the "Return" key when a screen is completed, which causes the next screen to display. The Create Customer input screens in R/3 facilitate input through the use of list boxes and search facilities. List boxes allow the user to choose an item from a list. The items usually are displayed as text, and the input is coded as a number by R/3 when the user selects an item in the list. Search facilities allow the user to enter a word or phrase, and R/3 finds the required code. The Create Customer screens and some of the data that are input into these screens are described below (Fig. 7.3).

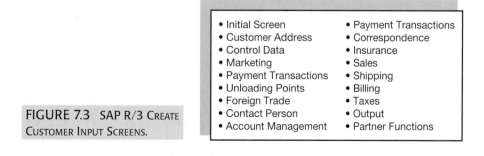

- Initial Screen
- Customer Address
- Control Data
- Marketing
- Payment Transactions
- Unloading Points
- Foreign Trade
- Contact Person
- Account Management

- Payment Transactions
- Correspondence
- Insurance
- Sales
- Shipping
- Billing
- Taxes
- Output
- Partner Functions

FIGURE 7.3   SAP R/3 CREATE CUSTOMER INPUT SCREENS.

Create Customer: Initial Screen   The initial screen prompts for a customer number that is used to uniquely identify the customer master record. This number can be assigned externally or internally. Customer numbers are assigned externally when the person who is inputting the data selects the number. Internal assignment is performed automatically by R/3, which assigns the next number in a sequence.

Additional input is required for a company code and organizational data that identify the sales area. A sales area is identified by three required fields: sales organization, distribution channel, and division. Sales organization is the company unit that is responsible for the sale. Distribution channel includes direct sales, retail, and wholesale. Division is a code that identifies a subgroup in the sales organization. These items can be selected from drop-down list boxes. An account group field is filled automatically by default.

Create Customer: Address Screen   This screen prompts for the customer's address information, which is primarily text. The company's name is entered into the name field. The search term field is used to input a phrase that can be used to search for the company when the company number is required for input. For example, the search term for Candy Maker Corporation might be *candymaker*.

Input fields are provided for street, post office box, city, region (or state), postal code (or ZIP code), and country. Input is required for the city, postal code, and country fields. A code indicating the language to be used must be entered in the communication section of the create customer address screen. For example, "E" indicates English. Optional fields are provided for telephone, telex, and fax numbers.

Create Customer: Control Data Screen   The fields entered in this screen depend on a company's specific needs. The transport zone field is the only required field. It identifies the regional zone where the ship-to party is located. Zone is coded and is entered by selecting from a list box. Some of the other fields that may be entered to provide transport information are a location number, industry, train station, express station, and location code. The account control section provides fields for vendor, trading partner, authorization, and group key. The tax information section provides fields for tax code, fiscal address, county code, city code, equalization tax, sole proprietor, tax on sales/purchase, VAT registration number, and tax jurisdiction code. A company defines it own tax codes. For example, tax code field 1 could be used to enter a customer's taxpayer ID number for a customer who resides in the United States.

Create Customer: Marketing Screen   The marketing screen is used to input statistical and demographic data concerning the customer. The Nielson ID field (which may be required) specifies a regional division according to marketing categories created by the A. C. Nielson Company and is used for marketing analysis. Other fields collect codes for customer classification, industry, and region. Customer classification is freely definable according to a company's needs. The Operating Figures section collects statistics such as the annual sales of the customer and its number of employees.

Create Customer: Payment Transactions Screen   This screen is used to input the customer's banking information. Fields are provided for a bank country code, bank key, bank account number, reference details, and several other details. Data may be input for several different banks.

Create Customer: Unloading Points Screen   This screen is used to input where the customer unloads received goods and the customer's *factory calendar*, which specifies what days and hours the customer accepts deliveries. Each unloading point has a factory calendar that is stored and available as a menu selection. If the customer has multiple unloading points, one can be designated as the default. Receiving hours by day of the week are entered for each unloading point. Specific hours (as start and stop times) can be entered, or one can choose from a list of predefined delivery times. The input can be extremely detailed as to hours and dates for each unloading point.

Create Customer: Foreign Trade Screen   This screen is used to input data relating to export controls.

Create Customer: Contact Person Screen   This screen is used to input data relating to a contact person or persons. Fields are provided for name, telephone number, form of address (e.g., "Mr."), and department code. The department code field is filled by choosing from a list that has entries such as "0001 managing director," "0002 purchasing," and "0003 sales." There is also a department function field, which is a code identifying the contact's function. This is selected from a list box that has entries such as "01 executive board" and "02 head of purchasing." Once a code is selected, the accompanying description is displayed next to the code on the input screen.

Create Customer: Account Management Screen   This screen is used to specify account reconciliation data. A reconciliation account is a general ledger account that is updated parallel to accounts receivable postings. It is a control account used for reconciliation. The account is selected from a menu list. A sort key is selected to specify how line items will be sorted in the customer's account listing. For example, posting date, document date, local currency amount, or some other field may be selected as the sort key. Several other optional fields may be input, such as head office and planning group.

Create Customer: Payment Transactions Screen   This screen collects data for payment transactions, including automatic payment transactions. The Payment terms field specifies cash discount terms and payment periods that comprise overall terms of payment. One can specify that a payment history should be maintained by checking a specific field. One can input a lock-box number. Several fields collect data concerning payment methods used for automatic payment transactions as necessary. The account number of an alternate payer, if any, can be specified. If open items are to be paid separately during automatic payment, this is specified by selecting (checking) a specific field.

Create Customer: Correspondence Screen   This screen can be used to establish a dunning procedure and other correspondence with the customer. A *dunning procedure* is the action taken to collect payments from customers who are late in making payments on their accounts. A dunning procedure code is input by selecting from a list box. One can specify the customer's representative who will receive dunning notices, as well as the customer's accounting clerk who handles invoices and dunnings (if a dunning recipient is not specified in the dunning recipient field).

Additional input can specify how frequently account statements are mailed to the customer and whether a customer's payment notice should display cleared items or not. If the customer's payment notice must be created for the legal department, then the legal department field on the entry screen should be selected. The sales field or accounting field is selected if the customer's payment notice must be created for either of these departments.

Create Customer: Insurance Screen   This screen can be used to input data relating to export credit insurance. Fields are provided for policy numbers, amounts insured, insurance company, lead months, and deductible percent.

Create Customer: Sales Screen   This screen is used to identify areas within the company that are responsible to the customer. As necessary, data are entered for geographic sales region or district, sales office, sales group, and customer group (wholesale or retail). One must specify a currency for the settlement of accounts. One can specify a *pricing procedure,* which is an R/3 term for the type and sequence of pricing conditions used to price a sales order. One also can specify a price list type—wholesale or retail.

The product proposal number field is used for defaulting products into the customer's orders if the customer routinely orders the same products. One can enter the company's vendor account number—what the customer uses to identify the company in the customer's information system. One also can enter a code that identifies how to determine the currency exchange rate.

Create Customer: Shipping Screen   This screen is used to specify shipping details. The order combination field is selected by default. It should be deselected if the customer does not accept partial shipments. A shipping conditions code is input to select a general shipping strategy from those that have been defined by the company. Fields are provided for a shipping plant code and a delivery priority (low, normal, or high). The complete delivery field is selected if deliveries to the customer must be delivered all together. If individual items can be delivered partially, this is indicated with the appropriate code in another field. The maximum number of partial deliveries (up to nine per item) is entered into another field.

Create Customer: Billing Screen   This screen is used to input data concerning billing. The incoterms field identifies international trading terms. A corresponding text description is required. For example, if "FOB" is entered in the incoterms field, then San Francisco could be entered as the corresponding required text to indicate the shipping location. Fields specify whether manual invoicing is required and if the customer is eligible for rebates. Input specifies the billing schedule, which defines the dates on which customers are billed. An invoice list schedule is input. This is a calendar used to place the customer's invoice on a collection list. An input field collects the account assignment group, which is used for integration with the accounts receivable module of R/3.

Create Customer: Taxes Screen   This screen is used to input data concerning the customer's tax liability. The categories displayed will vary depending on the countries in which the company does business. Tax classification fields are completed for each tax category that is listed. Data that are entered include tax exemption certificates, license number, date valid from, and date valid to.

Create Customer: Output Screen   This input screen is used to change the default output specifications for various documents that can be produced for the customer. Fields collect data concerning details such as output type (quote, invoice, etc.), language, transmission medium (paper, fax, EDI), send time (immediately or next batch run), and number of copies produced. Items can be changed, added, or deleted.

Create Customer: Partner Functions Screen   When a sold-to-customer record is created, R/3 automatically creates bill-to, payer, and ship-to master records for the same customer using the same information. These master records are partnered on this input screen. If a sold-to customer has multiple or different partners for billing, paying, or shipping, then the customer numbers of those partners are entered. However, if these partners do not have master records, then such records must be created before the partners' numbers can be entered in this screen.

The customer master record can now be saved because this is the final create customer screen.

ONE-TIME CUSTOMERS

Due to complexity of this process for creating customer master records, R/3 allows for the creation of a single master record *dummy* for one-time or infrequent customers. All these customers are passed through this one-time record. The master record has minimal information. Only the Address, Sales, Shipping, Billing, Taxes, and Output Create Customer screens are completed. For these screens, only fields that will apply to all of the customers who use this record are input. Additional specific information for shipping is added when orders by specific customers are placed. This process saves the trouble of creating detailed records for one-time customers.

STANDARD ORDER PROCESSING IN SAP R/3

OVERVIEW

This section provides an overview of standard order processing in SAP R/3. *Standard order processing* is a term that describes the customer order management business process in which customer orders are filled from an inventory of finished goods. Standard orders usually are received by telephone, mail, fax, sales representative, or voice mail.

A quotation may first be issued to the customer. If there is no quotation, then an order is created when a customer requests delivery of goods or services. A standard sales order contains information about prices, quantities, and dates (requested delivery date, shipping date, etc.).

After an order has been created and processed, a delivery document is created. R/3 calculates the expected shipping date using the requested delivery date and the transit time to the customer. These data are available in the customer master record.

CREATING A SALES ORDER

A customer master record has to exist before a sales order can be created. R/3 can copy information from the master record into the sales order as necessary.

Create Sales Order: Initial Screen   This screen is used to input information for the sales area. There are three mandatory fields. The sales organization field identifies the unit responsible for the sale. The distribution channel field classifies the order as direct sales, retail, or wholesale. The division code field is used to identify a subgroup in the sales organization. For every division, customer-specific agreements concerning partial deliveries, pricing, payments, and so on can be defined. Optionally, an area also may contain a sales office and a sales group. These are the personnel responsible for processing sales. Fields are available to input these items if they are used. The order type field differentiates orders as to their purpose. Some examples of the many codes provided are "CR," credit memo request; "DL" delivery (without order); "DR" debit memo request; and "OR," standard order.

Create Sales Order Screen   This screen has two parts: a document header and an area for item data. The document header contains fields for items that describe the entire order. The sold-to-party field collects the customer's code. The customer's purchase order number is entered into the purchase order number field. The purchase order date field is used for the date the customer's purchase order was received. Usually this date is the same as the order date, but not always. The requested delivery date field is used to enter the delivery date requested by the customer or a date that is proposed automatically by SAP R/3. The pricing date field is used to price material and to calculate foreign exchange rates. The order field number is assigned externally, or SAP R/3 will automatically enter an order number. For example, if the order-entry system is down (i.e., not operating on-line) and a customer needs an order confirmation number immediately, the user can give the customer an externally assigned order number and then later enter it as the order number.

The item data section contains the product numbers and order quantities. Search features help the user to find product numbers. SAP R/3 does an automatic availability check as items are entered. If an item is not available, it proposes options, such as partial delivery. SAP also enters some default data, such as parts descriptions. The total value of the order is calculated.

The preceding describes the minimum number of data-entry fields necessary for an order. Several optional screens allow detailed editing of an order.

The optional pricing screen allows editing of pricing conditions, such as gross price, discount, rebate, units (how an item is priced: each, dozen, etc.), and currencies. The optional scheduling screen allows editing of individual items in the order. One can edit when an item will be available and schedule it for delivery. One also can edit shipping dates by item. Individual dates for each step in the shipping process are available, such as loading and goods issue. These dates can differ for products that are complicated to pack and ship.

The optional business data header screen allows editing of shipping and billing data for the entire order. One can edit the order combination field, which indicates whether the customer allows orders to be combined into one shipment. One can edit the complete delivery field, which indicates whether the customer accepts partial orders. The default value in both these fields defaults from the customer master record.

The delivery block field is used to block an order from further processing. For example, SAP R/3 automatically places a block order if the customer's credit limit is exceeded. The billing block field is used to block an order from being invoiced. For example, there may be a need to verify or change pricing on the order before billing. One can edit business data concerning material, sales, shipping, and billing for specific line items. For example, one could block billing of a specific item if pricing information for that item is incomplete.

DATABASE FEATURES

Each activity in the customer order management business process—quotation, order, delivery, invoice, etc.—generates a document. SAP R/3's document flow feature lets one track and view these documents.

A *query* is a request for information in a database. SAP R/3 features powerful query capabilities. One can display an order by inputting the order number. One can display a list of documents according to a specific criteria. For example, one can list all the orders for a particular customer or for a particular product number. The system allows one to drill down to more detail, for example, to display more detailed information concerning a line item on an order.

SAP R/3 provides a Standard Order: Overview screen. One can list and display all the documents related to a particular sales order. A "Status Overview" button provides a summary of the processing status of the order.

TRANSACTION CYCLE CONTROLS IN ORDER PROCESSING

Figure 7.4 illustrates an analytic flowchart of a standard sales order business process where customer orders are filled from an inventory of finished goods. Transaction cycle controls are based on a separation of functions within a business process. As shown in Figure 7.4, these functions are order entry, credit, finished goods, shipping, billing, accounts receivable, and general ledger.

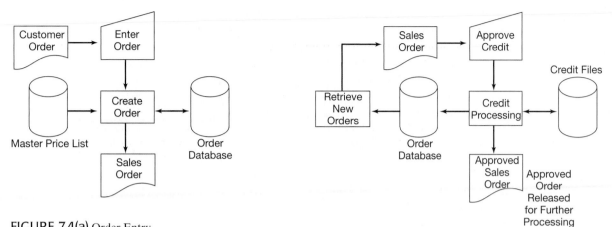

FIGURE 7.4(a) Order Entry.

FIGURE 7.4(b) Credit.

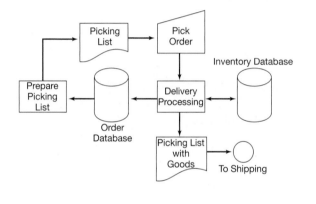

FIGURE 7.4(c) Finished Goods.

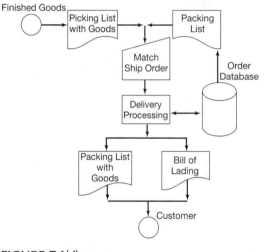

FIGURE 7.4(d) Shipping.

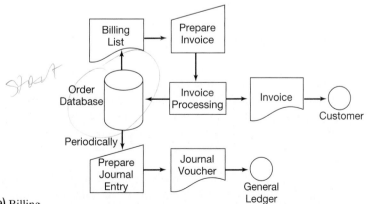

FIGURE 7.4(e) Billing.

FIGURE 7.4 CUSTOMER ORDER MANAGEMENT BUSINESS PROCESS.

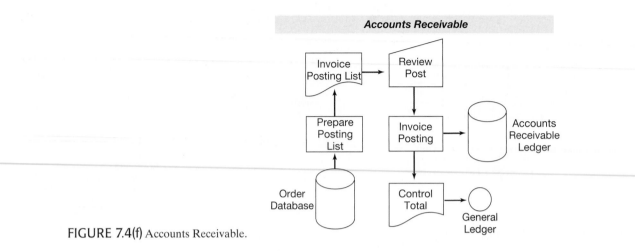

FIGURE 7.4(f) Accounts Receivable.

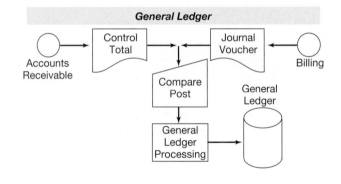

FIGURE 7.4(g) General Ledger.

FIGURE 7.4   (CONTINUED).

ORDER ENTRY

The order-entry function initiates the processing of customer orders with the preparation of the sales order document. The sales order contains descriptions of the products ordered, their prices, and descriptive data concerning the customer, such as name, shipping address, and if necessary, billing address. If the time between receiving an order and actual shipment of the order is significant, an acknowledgment notice may be sent to the customer to inform the customer that the order has been received and is being processed.

Prices entered on sales orders should be approved by management or an organizational function that is independent of the sales order function. The master price list shown in Figure 7.4 emphasizes this control. An independently prepared master price list contains the prices authorized by management and in effect at a particular date and is the source of prices used in the preparation of sales orders.

The sales order is primarily an internal document. The invoice, or bill, is a separate document that usually is prepared after the goods have been shipped and notice of shipment is forwarded to billing.

CREDIT

A customer's credit standing should be verified prior to the shipment of goods. For regular customers, the credit check involves determining that the total amount of credit granted does not exceed management's general or specific authorization. For new customers, a credit check is necessary to establish the terms of sale to the customer. As Figure 7.4 illustrates, the order-entry function should be subject to the control of an independent credit function to maintain a separation of duties within the business process. Once credit has been approved, the order is released for processing.

FINISHED GOODS

Finished goods picks the order as described on a picking list. The picking list is prepared from the delivery document that is prepared by the order database to process the approved order. Picking information is input to update delivery information in the order database. Inventory records are updated to reflect the actual quantities picked and to be forwarded to shipping. The goods are forwarded to shipping. Shipping should acknowledge receipt of the goods transferred.

SHIPPING

Shipping accepts the order for shipment after matching the order as described on the picking list that accompanies the goods to the order as it is described on the packing work list. The order information contained in the packing work list is prepared independently because it is based on the orders prepared by the order-entry function and approved by the credit function.

Shipping documentation is prepared, and the order database is updated for the shipment. Shipping typically prepares a bill of lading (Fig. 7.5) for the delivery. A bill of lading is the documentation exchanged between a shipper and a carrier such as a trucking company. The bill of lading documents freight charges and the transfer of goods from the shipping company to the transportation company. Frequently, freight charges are paid by the shipper but billed to the customer on the sales invoice. Copies of the packing list and the bill of lading usually are included with the customer's order when it is shipped.

BILLING

Billing completes the order process by preparing invoices for orders that appear on the billing work list. Billing verifies the order and then prepares the invoice. The invoice contains charges for the actual quantities shipped, freight charges (if any), and taxes (if any). Invoices are mailed to customers. Invoices are recorded in the sales journal, and notice is sent to accounts receivable. Periodically, a journal voucher is prepared and forwarded to the general ledger function for posting to the general ledger.

ACCOUNTS RECEIVABLE AND GENERAL LEDGER

The distinction between billing and accounts receivable is important to maintain separation of functions. Billing is responsible for invoicing individual orders, and accounts receivable maintains customer-accounts information and sends periodic statements of account to customers. Billing does not have access to the financial

SHIPPER'S NO.	CARRIER'S NO.

STRAIGHT BILL OF LADING—SHORT FORM—ORIGINAL—Not Negotiable

RECEIVED, subject to the classifications and tariffs in effect on the date of the issue of this Bill of Lading

the property, described below, in apparent good order, except as noted (contents and condition of contents of packages unknown), marked, consigned, and destined as indicated below, which said carrier (the word carrier being understood throughout this contract as meaning any person or corporation in possession of the property under the contract) agrees to carry to its usual place of delivery at said destination, if on its route, otherwise to deliver to another carrier on the route to said destination, it is mutually agreed, as to each carrier of all or any of said property over all or any portion of said route to destination, and as to each party at any time interested in all or any of said property, that every service to be performed hereunder shall be subject to all the terms and conditions of the Uniform Domestic Straight Bill of Lading set forth (1) in Uniform Freight Classification in effect on the date hereof, if this is a rail or a rail-water shipment, or (2) in the applicable motor carrier classification or tariff if this is a motor carrier shipment.

Shipper hereby certifies that he is familiar with all the terms and conditions of the said bill of lading, including those on the back thereof, set forth in the classification or tariff which governs the transportation of this shipment, and the said terms and conditions are hereby agreed to by the shipper and accepted for himself and his assigns.

FROM:			CONSIGNED TO:		DATE SHIPPED
NAME			NAME		
ADDRESS:			DELIVERY ADDRESS:		
CITY	STATE	ZIP CODE	CITY	COUNTY	STATE
					ZIP CODE

Number Packages	KIND OF PACKAGE, DESCRIPTION OF ARTICLES, SPECIAL MARKS, AND EXCEPTIONS	*WEIGHT (Subject to Correction)	Class or Rate	Ck. Col.

Subject to Section 7 of conditions, of applicable bill of lading, if this shipment is to be delivered to the consignee without recourse on the consigner, the consigner shall sign the following statement:
The carrier shall not make a delivery of this shipment without payment of freight and all other lawful charges.

(Signature of consigner.)

If charges are to be prepaid, write or stamp here, "To be Prepaid."

Rec'd $ to

apply in prepayment of the charges on the property described hereon.

Agent or Cashier.

Per

(The signature here acknowledges only the amount prepaid.)

Charges advanced:

$

*If the shipment moves between two ports by a carrier by water, the law requires that the bill of lading shall state whether it is "carrier's or shipper's weight." NOTE—Where the rate is dependent on value, shippers are required to state specifically in writing the agreed or declared value of the property.

The agreed or declared value of the property is hereby specifically stated by the shipper to be not exceeding per

Shipper, Per Agent

Permanent post office address of shipper. per

†"The fibre containers used for this shipment conform to the specifications set forth in the box maker's certificate thereon, and all other requirements of Rule 41 of the Uniform Freight Classification and Rule 5 of the National Meter Freight Classification."
†Shipper's imprint in lieu of stamp; not a part of bill of lading approved by the Interstate Commerce Commission.

FIGURE 7.5 BILL OF LADING.

records (the accounts receivable ledger), and the financial records are independent of the invoicing operation. Note in Figure 7.4 that the control total of postings to the accounts receivable ledger that is sent to the general ledger by accounts receivable is compared with the journal voucher sent from billing to validate postings to the general ledger. In this same fashion, the distinction between shipping and finished goods functions is important to the establishment of accountability for the release of finished goods from inventory. Shipping only accepts goods that are identified on the independently prepared packing list.

CUSTOMER ACCOUNT MANAGEMENT BUSINESS PROCESS

The customer account management business process includes accounts receivable processing through the collection of customer payments on account. We include a brief discussion of the cash sales business process because it is often integrated with the process for the collection of customer payments on account.

ACCOUNTS RECEIVABLE

Accounts receivable represents the money owed by customers for merchandise sold or services rendered on account. Because most business is done on credit, accounts receivable often represents the majority of an organization's working capital. Accounts receivable also maintains customer credit and payment history information, which is essential in the customer order management business process.

Conceptually, the accounts receivable procedure is straightforward. A subsidiary ledger of individual accounts is maintained, with a control account in the general ledger. Remittance advices are routed from the cash receipts function; credit memos and other invoice adjustments are routed to the accounts receivable department from the billing department. Debits and credits are posted to the individual accounts; periodically, statements are prepared and sent to customers. Aging schedules are prepared as a by-product of sending statements. Special credit reports also may be prepared.

There are two basic approaches to an accounts receivable application: open-item and balance-forward processing. In **open-item processing**, a separate record is maintained in the accounts receivable system for each of the customer's unpaid invoices. As customer remittances are received, they are matched to the unpaid invoices. In **balance-forward processing**, a customer's remittances are applied against the customer's total outstanding balance rather than against the customer's individual invoices.

Data processing of accounts receivable can be complicated owing to the volume of transactions and number of accounts that may exist. Even with computer processing, mailing all statements at month's end may be impossible. Many businesses use a **cycle billing plan**, in which the accounts receivable file is subdivided by alphabet or account number. The idea is to distribute the preparation of statements over the working days of the month. For example, accounts A through H may be billed on the tenth, I through P on the twentieth, and so on. Cycle billing plans often have a beneficial effect on a company's cash flow because consumers generally pay bills shortly after receiving them. Some companies sell their accounts receivable at a discount to collection agencies. This process, called **factoring**, avoids record-keeping costs. This alternative should be considered, but one should carefully consider the potential negative effects of factoring on customer relations. Some customers may be unhappy when they discover that their accounts are owed to a collection agency rather than to the company with which they did business.

TRANSACTION CONTROLS IN THE ACCOUNTS RECEIVABLE BUSINESS PROCESS

Figure 7.6 illustrates a document flowchart of an accounts receivable business process. The main feature in the illustration is the separation of the following functions within the business process.

CASH RECEIPTS

Customer remittance slips are forwarded to accounts receivable for posting from cash receipts. Accounts receivable does not have access to the cash or checks that accompany customer remittances.

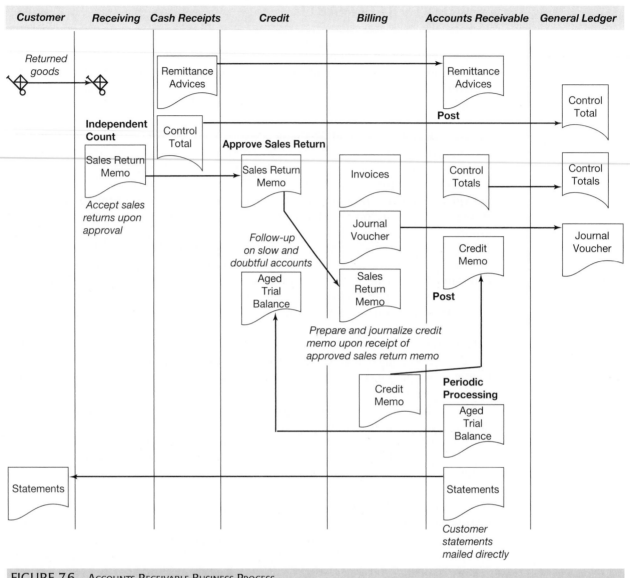

FIGURE 7.6   ACCOUNTS RECEIVABLE BUSINESS PROCESS.

BILLING

Invoices, credit memos, and other invoice adjustments are routed to accounts receivable for posting to the customer accounts. This maintains a separation of functions. Billing does not have direct access to the accounts receivable records.

ACCOUNTS RECEIVABLE

Accounts receivable is responsible for maintaining the subsidiary accounts receivable ledger. A control account is maintained by the general ledger department. Debits and credits are posted to the customer accounts from the remittance advices, invoices, and other documents received from billing and cash receipts. This maintains a separation of functions. Periodically, customer statements are mailed directly to customers by the accounts receivable department. Periodic processing also includes the preparation of an aged trial balance of the accounts receivable subsidiary ledger for review by the credit department. Other types of customer credit reports may be prepared based on the needs of the company. Such reports often are prepared as a by-product of the processing required to send customers their statements.

CREDIT

Credit department functions include the approval of sales returns and allowances and other adjustments to customer accounts, the review and approval of the aged trial balance to ascertain the creditworthiness of customers, and the initiation of write-off memos (documents) to charge accounts to bad-debt expense. These functions are discussed in what follows.

GENERAL LEDGER

General ledger maintains the accounts receivable control account. Debits and credits are posted to the accounts receivable control account from the journal vouchers and matching control totals that are received from billing and cash receipts. These amounts are reconciled to the control totals sent to the general ledger directly from accounts receivable. This reconciliation is an important transaction cycle control in the accounts receivable business process.

SALES RETURNS AND ALLOWANCES

Sales returns and allowances require careful control. Allowances occur when, because of damaged merchandise, shortages in shipments, clerical errors, or the like, the customer and the seller agree to reduce the amount owed by the customer. Generally, the merchandise is retained or destroyed by the customer. The amount of the allowance is negotiated between the customer and the sales order department (or salesperson). The allowance should be reviewed and approved by an independent party (usually the credit department). After an allowance has been authorized and approved, billing issues a **credit memo** to document the reduction to the customer's account.

A sales return occurs when a customer actually returns goods that have been shipped. Full credit usually is granted for the goods returned. As illustrated in Figure 7.6, sales return procedures are initiated by the receiving department. Once goods are received from the customer and returned to inventory for proper control, receiving forwards a sales return memo or similar document to the credit department. Credit approves the sales return memo and forwards it to billing. The approved sales return memo authorizes billing to issue a credit memo for the return. Note that as described for both returns and allowances, two independent functions approve a transaction, and a third independent function maintains the records.

WRITE-OFF OF ACCOUNTS RECEIVABLE

A separation of functions is essential in a business process to write off accounts receivable. The central feature in a write-off process is an analysis of past-due accounts. This is usually done with an aged trial balance report. A number of techniques are available to attempt to collect past-due accounts. These include dunning procedures such as sending the customer a series of follow-up letters and the use of collection agencies to approach the customer for payment. However, some accounts ultimately are worthless and have to be written off.

Figure 7.7 illustrates a separation of functions in a business process to write off accounts receivable. The credit department initiates a write-off by preparing a write-off memo (or similar document) that is approved by the treasurer or some other independent

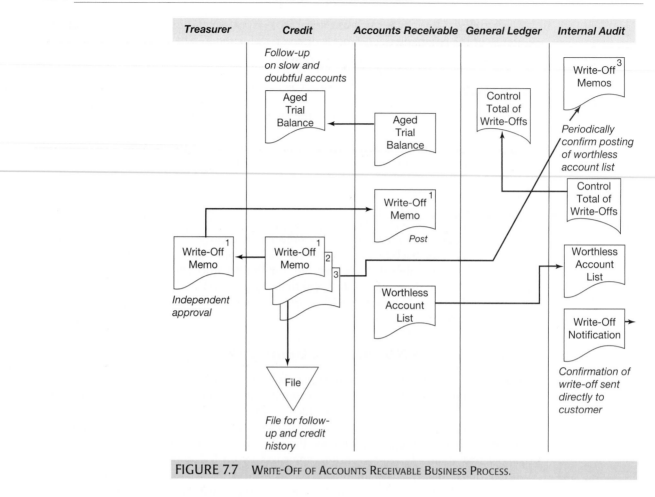

FIGURE 7.7 WRITE-OFF OF ACCOUNTS RECEIVABLE BUSINESS PROCESS.

function. Accounts receivable is authorized to write off the account on receipt of the approved write-off memo. A copy of the approved write-off memo is also sent to an independent third party (internal audit in Fig. 7.7) for purposes of record keeping. This is necessary because after the write-off, accounts receivable no longer has an active record of the account. Figure 7.7 details the role of the independent third party. Note that internal audit confirms write-offs directly with the customer to ensure that no collections have been made on written-off customer accounts. An employee might intercept a customer's payment on account and then arrange for the account to be written off so that the customer does not continue to be billed for the amount.

CASH-RECEIVED-ON-ACCOUNT BUSINESS PROCESS

OVERVIEW

A cash-received-on-account business process is used when there is an existing customer account balance. Cash received on account typically comes into a business through the mail or is paid in person to a central cashier or cash window. Customer payments always should be acknowledged. Customers should receive receipts and monthly statements showing amounts paid. Acknowledgment of payments is an important control. The recorded receivable that exists prior to the payment enhances control over payments received. In the event that a customer's payment is not acknowledged on his or her next statement, the customer likely will notify the company and inquire as to the reason.

Figure 7.8 is an analytic flowchart of a cash-received-on-account business process. The major feature illustrated is the separation of the following functions.

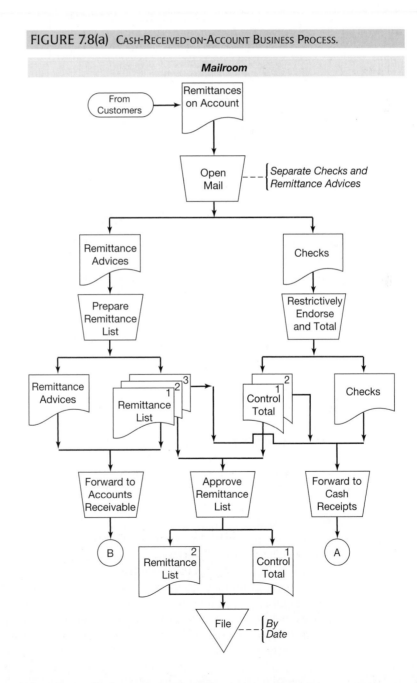

FIGURE 7.8(a)   CASH-RECEIVED-ON-ACCOUNT BUSINESS PROCESS.

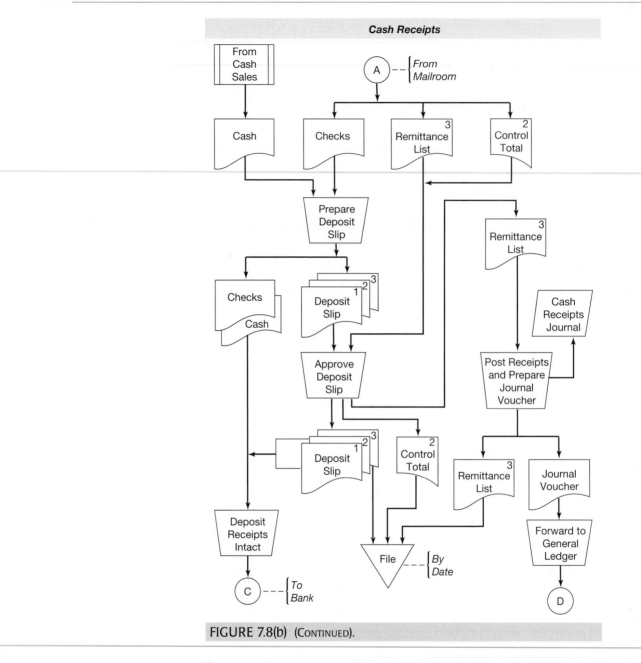

FIGURE 7.8(b)   (CONTINUED).

MAILROOM

Customer remittances on account are received in the mailroom. The mail is opened, and the checks and remittance advices are separated. Checks are restrictively endorsed and totaled. A **remittance list** that documents the payments received is prepared. The remittance list is balanced to the total of the checks received, and the agreement of these amounts is approved. Copies of the remittance list and the remittance advices are forwarded to accounts receivable. The checks and a control total are forwarded to cash receipts for deposit. Copies of the remittance list and the control total are filed by date.

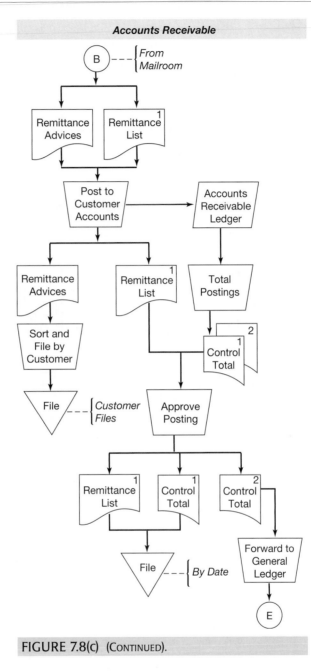

FIGURE 7.8(c) (CONTINUED).

CASH RECEIPTS

Checks received from the mailroom are combined with cash receipts from cash sales (if any), and a deposit slip is prepared. The remittance list and control total received from the mailroom are balanced with the deposit slip, and the agreement of these amounts is approved. The remittance list is then used to post the amount of the payments received from the mailroom into the cash receipts journal. A journal voucher is prepared and forwarded to the general ledger. The remittance list, control total, and a copy of the deposit slip are filed by date. The deposit is forwarded intact to the bank.

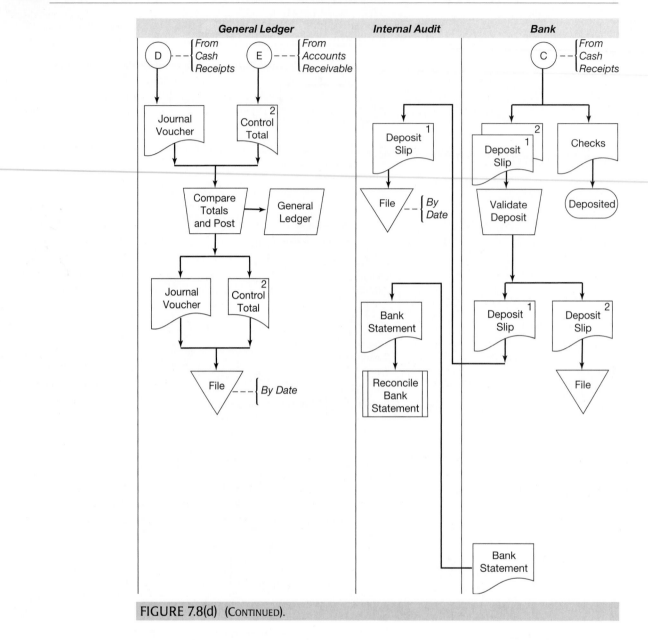

FIGURE 7.8(d) (CONTINUED).

ACCOUNTS RECEIVABLE

The remittance advices are posted to the accounts receivable ledger. The postings to the ledger are totaled. The control total is balanced to the remittance list. The agreement of these amounts is approved. The remittance advices are sorted and filed by customer. The remittance list and a copy of the control total of postings are filed by date. A copy of the control total is forwarded to the general ledger.

GENERAL LEDGER

The journal voucher from cash receipts and the control total received from accounts receivable are compared. The amounts are then posted to the general ledger. The source of posting to the general ledger is the cashier's journal voucher notification of the amount of the deposit of the payments received. This amount must reconcile with the total of items posted to the accounts receivable ledger. The journal voucher and the control total are filed by date.

BANK

The bank accepts the deposit and validates a copy of the deposit slip. The validated copy of the deposit slip is returned to internal audit. The validated deposit slip is filed by date.

INTERNAL AUDIT

Internal audit receives the periodic bank statement. An independent bank reconciliation is an important control in a cash-received-on-account business process.

SUMMARY

To control incoming cash received through the mail, it is important that no one in the mailroom (where the correspondence is opened), in cash receipts (where the money is summarized and a deposit prepared), or in accounts receivable (where the asset reduction is recorded) has complete control over the transaction. Often invoices or statements sent to customers are prepared such that the portion with the name and address of the customer is returned with the payment as a remittance advice. This is common with telephone, utility, and department store invoices and provides good documentation for the payment (Fig. 7.9).

As illustrated in Figure 7.8, the source of posting to the general ledger is the journal voucher notification issued by the cashier indicating the amount of the deposit of cash receipts. This amount must reconcile with the total of the items posted to the subsidiary receivable file. Validated copies of the deposit slip go to the internal auditor, who uses them when reconciling the bank account. The control of actual cash (as opposed to checks) received by mail relies largely on direct supervision.

LOCK-BOX COLLECTION SYSTEMS

In collecting accounts receivable, time is money. Even if a firm cannot persuade its customers to pay their accounts more rapidly, using a **lock-box deposit system** usually can reduce **float**—the time between the signing of the payment check by the customer and

---

FIGURE 7.9   REMITTANCE ADVICE.

Circle Utility Company

NOV 28, 1999   123   _____ _____

PLEASE MAIL THIS ADVICE WITH YOUR PAYMENT
BRING ENTIRE BILL FOR RECEIPT IF PAYING IN PERSON   _____

CUSTOMER NAME

CUSTOMER ADDRESS

CIRCLE UTILITY COMPANY
BOX 1000
ANYWHERE, USA

4025170000005476

MAKE CHECKS PAYABLE TO "CIRCLE UTILITY"

TOTAL AMOUNT DUE   54.76

the moment the firm has use of the funds. A lock-box system reduces float that usually occurs because the bank does not allow the firm to have use of out-of-state checks until they have been cleared through the customer's bank. This process can take up to a week. A lock-box system reduces float by having the checks deposited to a firm's account before the firm processes them. A firm in Los Angeles might have its eastern U.S. customers forward their payments to a lock box in a post office in New York City and arrange with a New York City bank to pick up these checks, credit them to the firm's account, and advise the firm as to the names of customers, check amounts, and other payment details. Payments can then be processed after the checks are on their way through the clearing process. Savings of lost interest can be considerable, especially when interest rates are high. A bank usually will require a fee plus a compensating deposit—one on which the firm cannot draw—to provide lock-box services. However, the value of net funds freed by float reduction and additional benefits, such as learning of dishonored checks sooner, generally will justify one or more lock-box regional collection systems for a firm whose customers are geographically widespread. An illustrative calculation is shown below assuming average daily collections of $500,000, 7 days' float without a regional lock box, and 2 days' float in a regional lock-box collection system.

Float in central system	$ 3,500,000
Less: Float in regional system	$ 1,000,000
Gross funds freed	$ 2,500,000
Less: Required compensating balance	$ 500,000
Net funds freed	$ 2,000,000
Fees and expenses = $150,000	
Cost of net funds freed =$150,000/$2,000,000 = 7.5%	

CASH-SALES BUSINESS PROCESS

The significant difference between a cash-sales business process and a cash-received-on-account business process is that there is no previous asset record (customer account balance) in a cash-sales business process. The generation of initial documentation of cash sales is thus the focal point of the control system. Once a record has been prepared, cash sales are subject to accounting control.

Cash sales are recorded in a cash register or other secure device to provide documentation. Sales receipts are prepared and issued to customers. Several techniques and devices are useful in establishing an initial record. **Customer audit** is a general term used to describe procedures in which the customer acts as a control over the initial documentation of a transaction. Pricing items at 99 cents rather than $1.00 is a customer audit technique as well as a marketing technique. This pricing forces the recording of a sale because the customer generally expects change. Techniques relating to sales invoices, such as awarding a customer a free gallon of ice cream if his or her receipt has a red star or other symbol, are intended to have the customer audit the recording of the sale. The possibility of receiving a prize increases the customer's interest in the invoice. Many cash registers sound a bell or buzzer when opened; it is hoped that the customer's attention is drawn to the amount actually being rung on the register. Sending monthly statements of account (to have the customer audit her or his own account) and providing customers with remittance advices (which they should return with their payments) are common examples of customer audit techniques.

Supervision involves having someone observe the work performance of others. Direct supervision over clerical work is common, such as in a mailroom where cash receipts are opened. Supervision techniques include the use of **professional shoppers**, people hired to purchase goods in a retail environment for the specific purpose of observing the recording of transactions. Supervision also includes the use of test packages. For example, a precounted amount of cash may be given to a teller or cash counter (with or without that person's knowledge) to ascertain the validity or error rate of the person's work.

Imprest techniques are used to control cash receipts in the same manner (but usually with less accuracy) that they are used to control petty cash disbursements. A clerk is given a precounted number of tickets and must account for either their retail value or the tickets themselves. Retail jobbers must account for the retail value of goods in their possession. Inventory control over sales that is applied through use of the gross profit method or retail sales analysis method of estimating inventory level is essentially an imprest technique. Although such controls cannot be effective enough to remove possibilities of manipulation completely, they can limit the size of potential defalcations.

❖ SUMMARY

The customer order management business process includes the following activities: inquiry, contract creation, order entry, shipping, and billing. ERP systems are capable of storing and processing a vast amount of information pertaining to the customer order management business process. The chapter provided an overview of the data that are stored and processed in the customer order management business process by SAP R/3. Transaction cycle controls over the customer order management business process includes a separation of the following functions: sales order processing, credit authorizations, custody of finished goods, shipping, billing, accounts receivable, and the general ledger.

The customer account management business process includes accounts receivable processing through the collection of customer payments on account. Transaction cycle controls include a separation of the following functions: cash receipts, credit authorizations, billing, accounts receivable, and the general ledger. Procedures that handle sales returns and allowances and procedures used to write off accounts receivable require careful design and control. The chapter included a brief discussion of the cash sales business process because it is often integrated with the process for the collection of customer payments on account.

❖ GLOSSARY

balance-forward processing: a customer's remittances are applied against a customer's outstanding balance rather than against individual invoices.

bill of lading: the invoice received from a carrier for shipments.

blanket order: a single order that calls for several shipments to the same customer over a specific time period.

credit memo: a form used to document reductions to a customer's account due to sales returns or sales allowances.

customer audit: procedure in which the customer acts as a control over the initial documentation of a transaction.

cycle billing plan: the processing of accounts receivable is subdivided by alphabet or account number in order to distribute the preparation of statements over the working days of the month.

factoring: the selling of accounts receivable at a discount to a collection agency.

float: the time between the signing of the payment check by the customer and the moment the firm has use of the funds.

goods issue notice: documentation that is forwarded to the billing function to evidence a shipment to a customer.

imprest techniques: a control technique in which an item is held accountable to a specified total amount.

inquiry: A document similar to a quotation that does not contain delivery information.

invoice: the document that informs a customer of charges for goods or services rendered.

lock-box deposit system: customer remittances are sent directly to a bank and are credited to a company's account before they are posted to customer accounts.

open-item processing: a customer's remittances are applied against individual invoices rather than against the customer's outstanding balance.

professional shoppers: people hired to purchase goods in a retail environment for the specific purpose of observing the recording of transactions.

quotation: a document sent to a potential customer to inform him or her of product prices, product availability, and delivery information.

remittance list: a listing of customer remittances that is prepared for control purposes.

sales order: a document prepared to initiate the shipment of goods to a customer.

shipping advice: synonym for goods issue notice.

❖ CHAPTER QUIZ

Answers to the chapter quiz appear on page 276.

1. Which of the following documents is used to post sales on account to customers in the accounts receivable ledger?
   (a) purchase orders
   (b) invoices
   (c) remittance advices
   (d) bills of lading

2. Which of the following departments should match shipping documents with open sales orders and prepare daily sales summaries?
   (a) billing
   (b) sales order
   (c) accounts receivable
   (d) shipping

3. The invoice is completed when (_____).
   (a) payment is received from the customer
   (b) the goods have been shipped
   (c) the sales order is approved by the credit department
   (d) the customer has acknowledged receipt of the shipment

4. The billing function normally should report to which of the following?
   (a) controller
   (b) treasurer
   (c) director of internal auditing
   (d) vice president of sales

5. Which of the following departments normally should be responsible for the preparation and journalizing of credit memos on the receipt of approved sales return memos to authorize a reduction in customer account balances because of returned goods?
   (a) receiving
   (b) accounts receivable
   (c) credit
   (d) billing

6. Which of the following steps in the customer order management business process is optional?
   (a) contract creation
   (b) order entry
   (c) shipping
   (d) billing

7. Pricing usually occurs during which step in the customer order management business process?
   (a) contract creation
   (b) order entry
   (c) shipping
   (d) billing

8. What has to exist before a sales order can be created in SAP R/3?
   (a) an invoice
   (b) a delivery document
   (c) a customer master record
   (d) a vendor master record

9. The remittance list prepared in the mailroom to document cash receipts should be forwarded directly to (_____).
   (a) finished goods
   (b) billing
   (c) accounts receivable
   (d) general ledger

10. Cash remittances received in the mailroom should be forwarded directly to (_____).
    (a) cash receipts
    (b) billing
    (c) accounts receivable
    (d) general ledger

❖ REVIEW PROBLEM

You are auditing the Alaska branch of Far Distributing Company. This branch has substantial annual sales, which are billed and collected locally. As a part of your audit, you find that the procedures for handling cash receipts are as follows:

> Cash collections on over-the-counter sales and COD sales are received from the customer or delivery service by the cashier. On receipt of cash, the cashier stamps the sales ticket "paid" and files a copy for future reference. The only record of COD sales is a copy of the sales ticket, which is given to the cashier to hold until the cash is received from the delivery service.
>
> Mail is opened by the secretary to the credit manager, and remittances are given to the credit manager for his review. The credit manager then places the remittances in a tray on the cashier's desk. At the daily deposit cutoff time the cashier delivers the checks and cash on hand to the assistant credit manager, who prepares remittance lists and makes up the bank deposit, which she also takes to the bank. The assistant credit manager also posts remittances to the accounts receivable ledger and verifies the cash discount allowable.

You also ascertain that the credit manager obtains approval from the executive office at Far Distributing, located in Chicago, to write off uncollectible accounts and that he has retained in his custody as of the end of the fiscal year some remittances that were received on various days during the last month.

Required

(a) Describe the irregularities that might occur under the procedures now in effect for handling cash collections and remittances.

(b) Give procedures that you would recommend to strengthen internal control over cash collections and remittances.

(CPA)

❖ SOLUTION TO REVIEW PROBLEM

(a) 1. The cashier could destroy cash or COD sales tickets and pocket the proceeds if sales tickets are not prenumbered or if accountability is not maintained for all sales ticket numbers.

2. Lapping might occur. This involves the withholding of cash receipts without an entry being made on the books. At a later date cash is collected and an entry is made for the first cash collected. The latest collection is held and used by the dishonest person. In the situation described, any of the four Alaska employees could lap the collections of accounts receivable.

3. Since the assistant credit manager had been told of doubtful accounts previously written off as uncollectible, she could appropriate cash collections to the extent of the remittances received on accounts previously written off.

4. The credit department personnel could enter discounts not taken by the customer or enter discounts on remittances made after the discount date. Those entries could cover the appropriation of an equivalent amount of cash for personal use.

5. Since no record is made of mail receipts until they have been handled by four people, any of the four could abstract funds without any covering action. On discovery of the theft, there would be no records to identify the thief.

6. The assistant credit manager could cover abstractions of cash by adding or destroying accounts receivable ledger records, by falsifying subsidiary ledger trial balances, by sending statements that differ from the accounts, and so on.

(b) The following procedures should be put into effect at the Alaska office to strengthen the internal control over cash receipts.

1. All sales tickets should be prenumbered, and all sales ticket numbers should be accounted for daily. All sales tickets stamped "paid" should be reconciled to the duplicate deposit slip receipted by the bank. This should be done by a responsible employee other than the cashier or a member of the credit department.

2. An employee other than the cashier or a member of the credit department should open the incoming mail and prepare daily a list in triplicate of remittances received that day. The original of the list should accompany the checks (and cash, if any) turned over directly to the cashier; one copy of the list of remittances should be routed to the responsible employee mentioned in number 1 above; one copy should be routed to the person responsible for posting to the accounts receivable ledger.

3. The responsible employee who received the copy of the list of remittances should compare the remittances shown thereon with the duplicate deposit ticket at the same time the cash sales tickets are reconciled to the deposit ticket. Any checks or cash not deposited the day received should be investigated.

4. Different forms (or colors) of sales tickets for cash, COD, and credit sales would facilitate the daily accounting for sales tickets used.

5. The cashier, who should have no duties connected with accounts receivable, should prepare bank deposits and forward the deposits to the bank. A responsible employee other than the cashier or a member of the credit department should establish agreement of the list of remittances and daily collections with the daily deposit ticket.

6. Remittances should not be held; those for each day or for each batch of mail, whichever is more practical, should be deposited intact. The credit department may make whatever record it needs for further follow-up on the remittances that are not in the correct amount.

7. The duty of posting remittances to the accounts receivable ledger may be left with the credit department. This operation normally should be performed subsequent to the receipt and control of cash; therefore, internal control over cash will not be weakened if credit department personnel perform the posting duty, provided they have no access to the cash represented by the remittance advices.

❖ REVIEW QUESTIONS

1. Identify the steps in the customer order management business process.
2. Identify several activities that usually occur during order entry.
3. Identify several documents that might be prepared during shipping activities.
4. List the four types of master records that are used in SAP R/3.
5. Describe some of the specifications that can be edited in the Create Customer: Output Screen section of the customer master record in SAP R/3.
6. What has to exist before a sales order can be created in SAP R/3?
7. Describe some of the basic database features available in SAP R/3 for processing information pertaining to the customer order management business process.
8. Distinguish between the billing and accounts receivable functions in a sales order procedure.

9. What accounting journal entry or entries summarize the activities of a sales order procedure?
10. When is it desirable to use an acknowledgment copy of a sales order?
11. How does the use of a master price list enhance control of the billing function?
12. What should be verified prior to the shipment of goods to customers?
13. What is cycle billing?
14. State two advantages of using cycle billing.
15. What is a dunning procedure?
16. What functions are served by periodic statements of account that are sent to customers?
17. Distinguish between open-item processing and balance-forward processing of accounts receivable.
18. Outline the major features of internal control in a sales return and allowance business process.
19. Why should write-offs of receivables be confirmed with the customer?
20. Identify the basic objective in a cash-receipts business process.
21. What is the most critical phase of a cash-receipts business process? Identify several controls that may be used to control this phase.
22. What is a remittance advice? What function do remittance advices play in a cash-receipts business process?
23. Identify the major features of control in a cash-receipts business process.
24. What is the potential advantage of using a lock-box collection system for customer remittances?
25. What is a professional shopper?

❖ DISCUSSION QUESTIONS AND PROBLEMS

26. The internal auditor is reviewing shipping procedures of a manufacturing company. The auditor should be greatly concerned when
    (a) merchandise is shipped without an approved customer's order.
    (b) invoiced prices on merchandise are not checked before orders are shipped.
    (c) the sales department is not notified promptly when merchandise is shipped.
    (d) only one quotation on transportation costs is obtained.
    (e) transportation tariffs are not checked before merchandise is shipped.

    (IIA)

27. Which of the following is an effective internal accounting control over accounts receivable?
    (a) Only people who handle cash receipts should be responsible for preparing documents that reduce accounts receivable balances.
    (b) Responsibility for approval of the write-off of uncollectible accounts receivable should be assigned to the cashier.
    (c) Balances in the subsidiary accounts receivable ledger should be reconciled to the general ledger control account once a year, preferably at year end.
    (d) The billing function should be assigned to people other than those responsible for maintaining accounts receivable subsidiary records.

    (CPA)

28. Which of the following would be the *best* protection for a company that wishes to prevent the lapping of trade accounts receivable?
    (a) Segregate duties so that the bookkeeper in charge of the general ledger has *no* access to incoming mail.
    (b) Segregate duties so that *no* employee has access to both checks from customers and currency from daily cash receipts.
    (c) Have customers send payments directly to the company's depository bank.
    (d) Request that customers' payment checks be made payable to the company and addressed to the treasurer.

    (CPA)

29. To determine whether the system of internal accounting control operated effectively to minimize errors of failure to invoice a shipment, the auditor would select a sample of transactions from the population represented by the
    (a) customer order file.

    (b) bill of lading file.
    (c) open invoice file.
    (d) sales invoice file.

(CPA)

30. For effective internal accounting control, employees maintaining the accounts receivable subsidiary ledger should *not* also approve
    (a) employee overtime wages.
    (b) credit granted to customers.
    (c) write-offs of customer accounts.
    (d) cash disbursements.

(CPA)

31. Which of the following control procedures may prevent the failure to bill customers for some shipments?
    (a) Each shipment should be supported by a prenumbered sales invoice that is accounted for.
    (b) Each sales order should be approved by authorized personnel.
    (c) Sales journal entries should be reconciled to daily sales summaries.
    (d) Each sales invoice should be supported by a shipping document.

(CPA)

32. To achieve good internal accounting control, which department should perform the activities of matching shipping documents with sales orders and preparing daily sales summaries?
    (a) billing
    (b) shipping
    (c) credit
    (d) sales order

(CPA)

33. Shipping documents should be compared with sales records or invoices to
    (a) determine whether payments are applied properly to customer accounts.
    (b) ensure that shipments are billed to customers.
    (c) determine whether unit prices billed are in accordance with sales contracts.
    (d) ascertain whether all sales are supported by shipping documents.

(IIA)

34. As payments are received, one mailroom employee is assigned the responsibility of prelisting receipts and preparing the deposit slip prior to forwarding the receipts, deposit slip, and remittance advices to accounts receivable for posting. Accounts receivable personnel refoot the deposit slip, stamp a restrictive endorsement on the back of each check, and then forward the receipts and deposit slip to the treasury department. Evaluate the internal control of the described process. Which of the following is a reasonable assessment of internal control in this process?
    (a) Adequate internal control
    (b) Inadequate internal control because mailroom employees should *not* have access to cash
    (c) Inadequate internal control because treasury employees should prepare the deposit slip
    (d) Inadequate internal control because of a lack of segregation of duties

(IIA)

35. Which of the following internal control procedures will *most likely* prevent the concealment of a cash shortage resulting from the improper write-off of a trade account receivable?
    (a) Write-offs must be approved by a responsible officer after review of credit department recommendations and supporting evidence.
    (b) Write-offs must be supported by an aging schedule showing that only receivables overdue several months have been written off.
    (c) Write-offs must be approved by the cashier who is in a position to know if the receivables have, in fact, been collected.
    (d) Write-offs must be authorized by company field sales employees who are in a position to determine the financial standing of the customers.

(CPA)

36. For the purpose of proper accounting control, postdated checks remitted by customers should be
    (a) restrictively endorsed.
    (b) returned to the customer.
    (c) recorded as a cash sale.
    (d) placed in the joint custody of two officers.

    (CPA)

37. A company policy should clearly indicate that defective merchandise returned by customers is to be delivered to the
    (a) sales clerk.
    (b) receiving clerk.
    (c) inventory control clerk.
    (d) accounts receivable clerk.

    (CPA)

38. To conceal defalcations involving receivables, the auditor would expect an experienced bookkeeper to charge which of the following accounts?
    (a) miscellaneous income
    (b) petty cash
    (c) miscellaneous expense
    (d) sales returns

    (CPA)

39. The most likely result of ineffective internal control policies and procedures in the revenue cycle is that
    (a) irregularities in recording transactions in the subsidiary accounts could result in a delay in goods shipped.
    (b) omission of shipping documents could go undetected, causing an understatement of inventory.
    (c) final authorization of credit memos by personnel in the sales department could permit an employee defalcation scheme.
    (d) fictitious transactions could be recorded, causing an understatement of revenues and overstatement of receivables.

    (CPA)

40. Proper authorization procedures in the revenue cycle usually provide for the approval of bad-debt write-offs by an employee in which of the following departments?
    (a) treasurer
    (b) sales
    (c) billing
    (d) accounts receivable

    (CPA)

41. Tracing bills of lading to sales invoices provides evidence that
    (a) shipments to customers were invoiced.
    (b) shipments to customers were recorded as sales.
    (c) recorded sales were shipped.
    (d) invoiced sales were shipped.

    (CPA)

42. A sales clerk at Schackne Company correctly prepared a sales invoice for $5,200, but the invoice was entered as $2,500 in the sales journal and similarly posted to the general ledger and accounts receivable ledger. The customer remitted only $2,500, the amount on his or her monthly statement. The most effective procedure for preventing this type of error is to
    (a) use predetermined totals to control posting routines.
    (b) have an independent check of sales invoice serial numbers, prices, discounts, extensions, and footings.
    (c) have the bookkeeper prepare monthly statements that are verified and mailed by a responsible person other than the bookkeeper.

(d) have a responsible person who is independent of the accounts receivable department promptly investigate unauthorized remittance deductions made by customers or other matters in dispute.

(CPA)

43. For good internal control, the billing department should be under the direction of the
    (a) controller.
    (b) credit manager.
    (c) sales manager.
    (d) treasurer.

(CPA)

44. Which of the following controls *most likely* would be effective in offsetting the tendency of sales personnel to maximize sales volume at the expense of high bad-debt write-offs?
    (a) Employees responsible for authorizing sales and bad-debt write-offs are denied access to cash.
    (b) Shipping documents and sales invoices are matched by an employee who does *not* have authority to write off bad debts.
    (c) Employees involved in the credit-granting function are separated from the sales function.
    (d) Subsidiary accounts receivable records are reconciled to the control account by an employee independent of the authorization of credit.

(CPA)

45. Which of the following controls *most likely* would help ensure that all credit sales transactions of an entity are recorded?
    (a) The billing department supervisor sends copies of approved sales orders to the credit department for comparison with authorized credit limits and current customer account balances.
    (b) The accounting department supervisor independently reconciles the accounts receivable subsidiary ledger with the accounts receivable control account monthly.
    (c) The accounting department supervisor controls the mailing of monthly statements to customers and investigates any differences reported by customers.
    (d) The billing department supervisor matches prenumbered shipping documents with entries in the sales journal.

(CPA)

46. An entity with a large volume of customer remittances by mail most likely could reduce the risk of employee misappropriation of cash by using
    (a) employee fidelity bonds.
    (b) independently prepared mailroom prelists.
    (c) daily check summaries.
    (d) a bank lock-box system.

(CPA)

47. Which of the following would the auditor consider to be an incompatible operation if the cashier receives remittances from the mailroom?
    (a) The cashier prepares the daily deposit.
    (b) The cashier makes the daily deposit at a local bank.
    (c) The cashier posts the receipts to the accounts receivable subsidiary ledger cards.
    (d) The cashier endorses the checks.

(CPA)

48. The most effective way to prevent an employee from misappropriating cash and then altering the accounting records to conceal the shortage is to
    (a) perform bank reconciliations on a timely basis.
    (b) deposit promptly all cash receipts in the company's bank account.
    (c) prenumber all cash-receipts documents.
    (d) enforce a segregation of duties between employees who have custody of cash receipts and those who account for them.

(IIA)

49. Which of the following is *not* a universal rule for achieving strong internal control over cash?
    (a) Separate the cash handling and record-keeping functions.
    (b) Decentralize the receiving of cash as much as possible.
    (c) Deposit each day's cash receipts by the end of the day.
    (d) Have bank reconciliations performed by employees independent with respect to handling cash.

    (CPA)

50. Cash receipts from sales on account have been misappropriated. Which of the following acts would conceal this defalcation and be *least likely* to be detected by an auditor?
    (a) Understating the sales journal
    (b) Overstating the accounts receivable control account
    (c) Overstating the accounts receivable subsidiary ledger
    (d) Understating the cash receipts journal

    (CPA)

51. Indicate the objective of each of the following controls.
    (a) Making surprise counts of imprest funds
    (b) Having registers read and cleared by internal auditors rather than cashiers
    (c) Comparing totals of mail receipts with duplicate bank deposit records (daily)
    (d) Providing multidrawer cash registers
    (e) Offering bonuses to customers for "red stars" or other special symbols on sales tickets

52. The customer billing and collection functions of the Misty Company, a small paint manufacturer, are attended to by a receptionist, an accounts receivable clerk, and a cashier who also serves as a secretary. The company's paint products are sold to wholesalers and retail stores.

    The following describes *all* the procedures performed by the employees of the Misty Company pertaining to customer billings and collections:
    (a) The mail is opened by the receptionist, who gives the customers' purchase orders to the accounts receivable clerk. Fifteen to twenty orders are received each day. Under instructions to expedite the shipment of orders, the accounts receivable clerk at once prepares a five-copy sales invoice form, which is distributed as follows:
        1. Copy 1 is the customer billing copy and is held by the accounts receivable clerk until notice of shipment is received.
        2. Copy 2 is the accounts receivable department copy and is held for ultimate posting of the accounts receivable records.
        3. Copies 3 and 4 are sent to the shipping department.
        4. Copy 5 is sent to the storeroom as authority for release of the goods to the shipping department.
    (b) After the paint order has been moved from the storeroom to the shipping department, the shipping department prepares the bill of lading and labels the cartons. Sales invoice copy 4 is inserted in the carton as a packing slip. After the trucker has picked up the shipment, the customer's copy of the bill of lading and copy 3, on which any undershipments are noted, are returned to the accounts receivable clerk. The company does not back order in the event of undershipments; customers are expected to reorder the merchandise. The company's copy of the bill of lading is filed by the shipping department.
    (c) When copy 3 and the customer's copy of the bill of lading are received by the accounts receivable clerk, copies 1 and 2 are completed by numbering them and inserting quantities shipped, unit prices, extensions, discounts, and totals. The accounts receivable clerk then mails copy 1 and the copy of the bill of lading to the customer. Copies 2 and 3 are stapled together.
    (d) The individual accounts receivable ledger cards are posted by the accounts receivable clerk using a one-write system whereby the sales register is prepared as a carbon copy of the postings. Postings are made from copy 2, which is then filed, along with staple-attached copy 3, in numerical order. Monthly, the general ledger clerk summarizes the sales register for posting to the general ledger accounts.
    (e) Since the company is short of cash, the deposit of receipts is also expedited. The receptionist turns over all mail receipts and related correspondence to the accounts

receivable clerk, who examines the checks and determines that the accompanying vouchers or correspondence contain enough detail to permit posting of the accounts. The accounts receivable clerk then endorses the checks and gives them to the cashier, who prepares the daily deposit. No currency is received in the mail, and no paint is sold over the counter at the factory.

(f) The accounts receivable clerk uses the vouchers or correspondence that accompanied the checks to post the accounts receivable ledger cards. The one-write system prepares a cash-receipts register as a carbon copy of the postings. Monthly, the general ledger clerk summarizes the cash-receipts register for posting to the general ledger accounts. The accounts receivable clerk also corresponds with customers about unauthorized deductions for discounts, freight or advertising allowances, returns, and so on and prepares the appropriate credit memos. Disputed items of large amounts are turned over to the sales manager for settlement. Each month the accounts receivable clerk prepares a trial balance of the open accounts receivable and compares the resulting total with the general ledger control account for accounts receivable.

Required

(a) Prepare a logical data flow diagram of the previous procedures.
(b) Discuss the internal control weaknesses in the Misty Company's procedures related to customer billings and remittances and the accounting for these transactions. In your discussion, in addition to identifying the weaknesses, explain what could happen as a result of each weakness.

(CPA)

53. After a shipment is prepared, the shipping department prepares a shipping order form in three copies. The first copy is included with the goods sent to the customer as a packing slip. The second copy is forwarded to the billing department. The third copy is sent to the accountant. When the billing department receives the second copy of the shipping order, it uses the information thereon to prepare a two-part sales invoice. The second copy of the shipping order is then filed in the billing department. The first copy of the sales invoice is sent to the customer. The second copy of the sales invoice is forwarded to the accountant. Periodically, the accountant matches the copy of the shipping order with the copy of the sales invoice and files them alphabetically by customer name. Before doing so, however, the accountant uses the copy of the sales invoice to post the sales entry in the subsidiary accounts receivable ledger.

Required

(a) For use in appraising internal control, prepare a flowchart covering the flow of documents reflected in the preceding situation.
(b) List those deficiencies and/or omissions revealed by the flowchart that lead you to question the internal control.

(IIA)

54. In a large manufacturing organization supplying goods and services, several departments may be involved in the processing of customer complaints and the issuance of any resulting credit memos. Following is a list of such departments:
(a) receiving
(b) sales
(c) production
(d) customer service
(e) accounts receivable

Required

Explain briefly the control function each of these departments performs when processing complaints and issuing credit memos.

(IIA)

55. The flowchart in Figure 7.10 depicts the activities relating to the shipping, billing, and collecting processes used by Pittsburgh Wood, Inc.

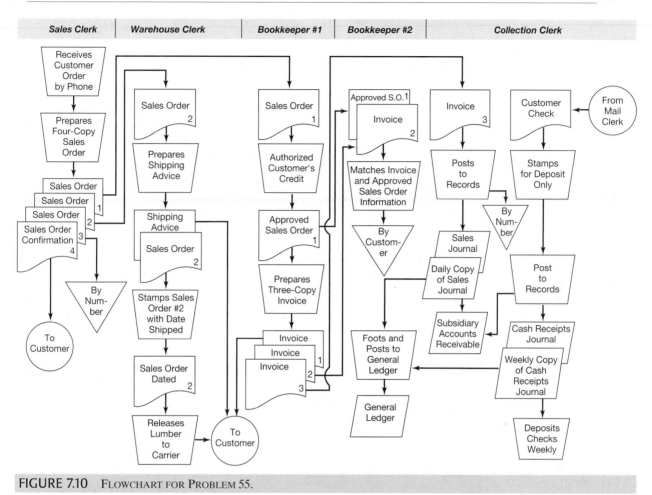

FIGURE 7.10 FLOWCHART FOR PROBLEM 55.

Required

Identify weaknesses in the system of internal accounting control relating to the activities of the

(a) warehouse clerk.
(b) bookkeeper 1.
(c) bookkeeper 2.
(d) collection clerk.

(CPA)

56. The Happiness Corporation of Boston is considering using a lock-box system for its customers in California. At present, its credit sales to that area amount to about $21,600,000. Establishing a lock box in San Francisco would enable the company to reduce its collection float from 8 days to 2 days. The bank in San Francisco will expect the company to maintain a minimum balance of $70,000. The net additional annual cost of adopting the system will be $1,200. Base calculations on a 360-day year.

(a) What is the net amount of cash that will be freed for use elsewhere in the business?
(b) What is the annual percentage cost of the funds released from the float?

57. Indicate the objective of the following questions taken from an internal control checklist.

(a) Are all disbursements, except petty cash, made by check?
(b) Are bank debit advices (such as NSF checks) delivered directly to a responsible employee (other than the cashier) for investigation?
(c) Is the credit department entirely independent of the sales department?

(d) Does the company record accruals of recurring income from rents, royalties, or other such items in advance of collection?

(e) Are requests for petty cash signed by the person who receives the cash?

58. A new audit client of yours processes its sales and cash receipts documents in the following manner:

(a) *Cash receipts.* The mail is opened each morning by a mail clerk in the sales department. The mail clerk prepares a remittance advice (showing customer and amount paid) if one is not received. The checks and remittance advices are then forwarded to the sales department supervisor, who reviews each check and forwards the checks and remittance advices to the accounting department supervisor. The accounting department supervisor, who also functions as the credit manager, reviews all checks for payments of past due accounts and then forwards the checks and remittance advices to the accounts receivable clerk, who arranges the advices in alphabetical order. The remittance advices are posted directly to the accounts receivable ledger. The checks are endorsed by stamp and totaled. The total is posted to the cash-receipts journal. The remittance advices are filed chronologically.

   After receiving the cash from the preceding day's cash sales, the accounts receivable clerk prepares the daily deposit slip in triplicate. The third copy of the deposit slip is filed by date, and the second copy and the original accompany the bank deposit.

(b) *Sales.* Salesclerks prepare the sales invoices in triplicate. The original and the second copy are presented to the cashier. The third copy is retained by the salesclerk in the sales book. When the sale is for cash, the customer pays the salesclerk, who presents the money to the cashier with the invoice copies.

   A credit sale is approved by the cashier from an approved credit list after the salesclerk prepares the three-part invoice. After receiving the cash or approved invoice, the cashier validates the original copy of the sales invoice and gives it to the customer. At the end of each day the cashier recaps the sales and cash received and forwards the cash and the second copy of all sales invoices to the accounts receivable clerk. The accounts receivable clerk balances the cash received with cash sales invoices and prepares a daily sales summary. The credit sales invoices are posted to the accounts receivable ledger, and then all invoices are sent to the inventory control clerk in the sales department for posting to the inventory control ledger. After posting, the inventory control clerk files all invoices numerically. The accounts receivable clerk posts the daily sales summary to the cash-receipts journal and sales journal and files the sales summaries by date.

   The cash from cash sales is combined with the cash received on account, and this constitutes the daily bank deposit.

(c) *Bank deposits.* The bank validates the deposit slip and returns the second copy to the accounting department, where it is filed by date by the accounts receivable clerk.

   Monthly, bank statements are reconciled promptly by the accounting department supervisor and filed by date.

Required

(a) Flowchart the sales and cash receipts application of your client.

(b) Identify potential internal control weaknesses in the client's procedures.

(CPA)

59. The town of Bellevue operates a private parking lot near the railroad station for the benefit of town residents. The guard on duty issues annual prenumbered parking stickers to residents who submit an application form and show evidence of residency. The sticker is affixed to the auto and allows the resident to park anywhere in the lot for 12 hours if four quarters are placed in the parking meter. Applications are maintained in the guard office at the lot. The guard checks to see that only residents are using the lot and that no resident has parked without paying the required meter fee.

   Once a week the guard on duty, who has a master key for all meters, takes the coins from the meters and places them in a locked steel box. The guard delivers the box to the town storage building, where it is opened and the coins manually counted by a storage department clerk who records the total cash counted on a weekly cash report. This report is sent to the town accounting department. The storage department clerk puts the cash in a safe, and on the following day the cash is picked up by the town's treasurer, who manually recounts the cash, prepares the bank deposit slip, and delivers the deposit to the bank. The deposit slip, authenticated by the bank teller, is sent to the accounting department, where it is filed with the weekly cash report.

Required

Describe weaknesses in the existing system, and recommend one or more improvements for each of the weaknesses to strengthen the internal control over the parking lot cash receipts. Organize your answer sheet as follows:

WEAKNESS	RECOMMENDED IMPROVEMENT

(CPA)

60. The Quill Electric Company recently has installed a new computer system that has on-line, real-time capability. Terminals are used for data entry and inquiry. A new cash receipts and accounts receivable file maintenance system has been designed and implemented for use with this new equipment. All programs have been written and tested, and the new system is being run in parallel with the old system. After 2 weeks of parallel operation, no differences have been observed between the two systems other than data entry errors on the old system.

Al Brand, data processing manager, is enthusiastic about the new equipment and system. He reveals that the system was designed, coded, compiled, debugged, and tested by programmers using an on-line terminal installed specifically for around-the-clock use by the programming staff; he claimed that this access to the computer saved one-third in programming elapsed time. All files, including accounts receivable, are on-line at all times as the firm moves toward a full database mode. All programs, new and old, are available at all times for recall into memory for scheduled operating use or for program maintenance. Program documentation and actual tests confirm that data-entry edits in the new system include all conventional data error and validity checks appropriate to the system.

Inquiries have confirmed that the new system conforms precisely to the flowcharts. A turnaround copy of the invoice is used as a remittance advice (R/A) by 99% of the customers; if the R/A is missing, the cashier applies the payment to a selected invoice. Sales terms are net 60 days, but payment patterns are sporadic. Statements are not mailed to customers. Late payments are commonplace and are not pursued vigorously. The company does not have a bad debt problem because bad debt losses average only 0.5% of sales.

Before authorizing the termination of the old system, Cal Darden, controller, has requested a review of the internal control features that have been designed for the new system. Security against unauthorized access and fraudulent actions, assurance of the integrity of the files, and protection of the firm's assets should be provided by the internal controls.

Required

(a) Describe how fraud by lapping of accounts receivable could be committed in the new system, and discuss how it could be prevented.
(b) Based on the description of the new system and the systems flowchart that has been presented in Figure 7.11,
    1. Describe any other defects that exist in the system.
    2. Suggest how each other defect you identified could be corrected.

(CMA)

61. The flowchart in Figure 7.12 depicts part of a client's revenue cycle. Some of the flowchart symbols are labeled to indicate control procedures and records. For each symbol numbered 1 through 13, select one response from the answer lists below. Each response in the lists may be selected once or not at all.

❖ ANSWER LISTS

Operations and control procedures
    (a) Enter shipping data.
    (b) Verify agreement of sales order and shipping document.
    (c) Write off accounts receivable.
    (d) Send to warehouse and shipping department.

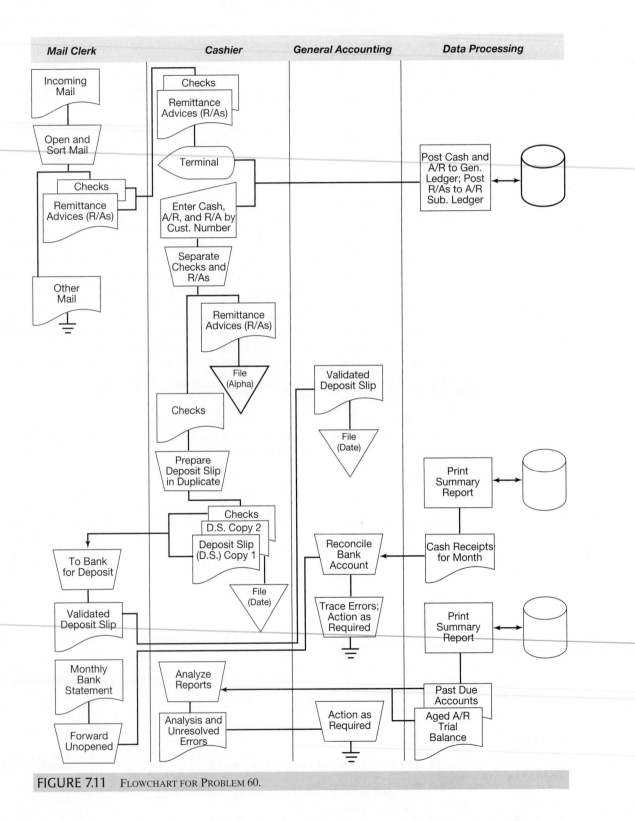

FIGURE 7.11   Flowchart for Problem 60.

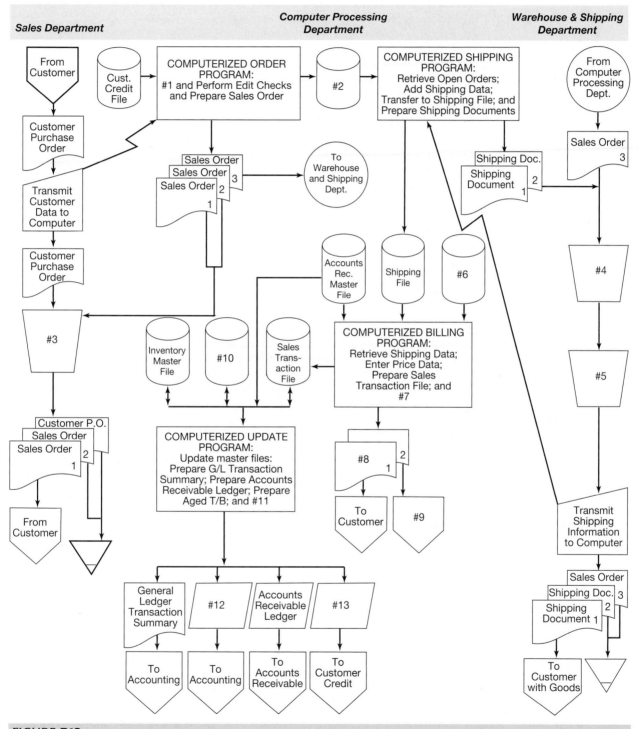

FIGURE 7.12 FLOWCHART FOR PROBLEM 61.

   (e) Authorize account receivable write-off.
   (f) Prepare aged trial balance.
   (g) Submit to sales department.
   (h) Release goods for shipment.
   (i) Submit to accounts receivable department.
   (j) Enter price data.
   (k) Determine that customer exists.
   (l) Match customer purchase order with sales order.
  (m) Perform customer credit check.
   (n) Prepare sales journal.
   (o) Prepare sales invoice.

Documents, journals, ledgers, and files
   (a) Shipping document
   (b) General ledger master file
   (c) General journal
   (d) Master price file
   (e) Sales journal
   (f) Sales invoice
   (g) Cash receipts journal
   (h) Uncollectible accounts file
   (i) Shipping file
   (j) Aged trial balance
   (k) Open order file

62. ERP systems are designed to accommodate companies that conduct business internationally. International transactions are more complex than domestic transactions because a foreign currency and perhaps other factors are involved.

    Consider the discussion of the SAP software for the customer order management business process in the text. Identify several order input data and/or customer master file fields that are necessary for international business transactions.

63. The process of creating customer master records in SAP R/3 is complex but results in information that is useful in the customer order management business process. However, the process of creating customer master records is not practical for one-time or infrequent customers. How does SAP R/3 accommodate the processing of sales to one-time or infrequent customers?

❖ ANSWERS TO CHAPTER QUIZ

1. b	4. a	7. b	10. a
2. a	5. d	8. c	
3. b	6. a	9. c	

CHAPTER 8

PROCUREMENT AND HUMAN RESOURCE BUSINESS PROCESSES

LEARNING OBJECTIVES

Careful study of this chapter will enable you to:

❖ Describe the procurement business process.

❖ Illustrate controls that apply to procurement.

❖ Describe the cash disbursements business process.

❖ Describe the human resource business process.

❖ Illustrate controls that apply to payroll processing.

THE PROCUREMENT BUSINESS PROCESS

OVERVIEW

Procurement is the business process of selecting a source, ordering, and acquiring goods or services. The goods or services might be obtained internally if the good is produced by another entity in the company. *Purchasing* is a synonym for procurement.

The general steps in the procurement process are (Fig. 8.1)

- Requirement determination
- Selection of source
- Request for quotation
- Selection of a vendor
- Issuing of a purchase order
- Receipt of the goods
- Invoice verification
- Vendor payment

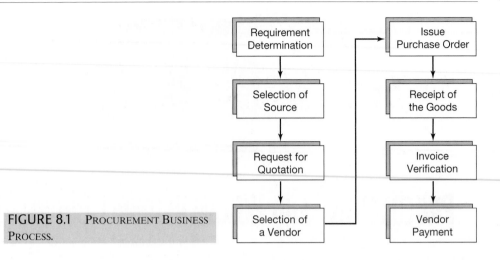

FIGURE 8.1   PROCUREMENT BUSINESS PROCESS.

Enterprise resource planning (ERP) systems are capable of storing and processing a vast amount of information pertaining to the procurement business process. This section provides an overview of the data that are stored and processed in the procurement process by SAP R/3.[1]

SAP R/3 supports procurement in its materials management module. R/3 provides an on-line, fully integrated system for the creation and exchange of the documents that are required in the procurement business process. The fully integrated nature of the system reduces errors and speeds the business process.

Documents in R/3 are on-line documents; they are created on-line and may be processed entirely as electronic documents. They also may be printed and exchanged manually. Procurement documents that are available in R/3 include

- Purchase requisition
- Request for quotation
- Quotation
- Purchase order
- Outline agreements
- Contracts
- Scheduling agreements
- Purchasing information records

These documents will each be discussed as they enter into the procurement process. In addition to the preceding documents, there are other documents that are used in invoice verification and goods receipt. Each document type is not used every time an item is purchased.

All procurement documents are assigned a document type code. This code determines the fields that are displayed on video screens and controls the range of unique numbers that are assigned to particular document types. Each document has a header area and an item (detail) area. The header area contains information relevant to the entire document, such as vendor number. The item area specifies the details of the individual items in the document, such as the product numbers of items to be ordered. Each new document that is created must be assigned a unique number. The number is

[1]SAP R/3 is a registered trademark of SAP Aktiengesellschaft, Systems, Applications, and Products in Data Processing, Neurottstrasse 16, 69190 Walldorf, Germany. (*www.sap.com*). Material pertaining to SAP R/3 in this chapter section is based on "SAP R/3 3.0 in a Box," © 1999 CBT Systems, published and © 1999 by Prentice-Hall, Inc.

an alphanumeric code. Usually this number is assigned automatically by R/3, but document numbers can be entered externally. Most documents usually can be prepared by referencing an existing document. R/3 can copy all relevant information from the existing document, thus speeding the process of creating the document and reducing error.

REQUIREMENT DETERMINATION

A **purchase requisition** is an internal document created to request the procurement of something so that it is available at a certain point in time. Purchase requisitions can be prepared manually. They also might be issued automatically by the materials requirements planning (MRP) system. The MRP system can perform sophisticated analyses to determine requirements based on customer demand for an item and the firm's production process. Purchase requisitions have an input field that indicates how they were created, that is, manually or automatically. A requisition tracking number is input when a large number of requisitions are issued for the same requirement. The requisition tracking number enables one to monitor progress of the group of requisitions. Purchase requisitions are processed line by line, so each line is, in effect, a separate requirement.

Once completed, the purchase requisition is forwarded electronically to a supervisor for approval. Approval typically involves determining that the purchase requisition is within cost limits. User profiles maintained in R/3 filter purchase requisitions and route them to the correct person for approval. A purchase requisition is an optional step in procurement in R/3.

SELECTION OF SOURCE(S)

The next step in the business process is to assign a source of supply to the purchase requisition. R/3 can check whether a contract exists with a vendor to supply an item that is requisitioned. If a contract exists, R/3 appropriates the required amount. If there is no contract for an item, then a request for quotation document is prepared.

R/3 provides support for the selection process in several ways. R/3 monitors outline agreements that exist with vendors. Outline agreements are contracts that specify long-term arrangements with vendors. If quota arrangements for an item have been contracted with vendors, R/3 automatically assigns a source of supply to a purchase requisition based on the quotas defined in the contract. R/3 maintains records for the vendor, validity period of the contract, and the quota amounts.

R/3 maintains lists of approved and disapproved sources of supply. R/3 also can select vendors that will be invited to bid on the requisition, basing its recommendations on data that have been saved concerning previous sourcing for the item.

REQUEST FOR QUOTATION

After vendors have been selected, R/3 is used to generate a **request for quotation** document. A request for quotation is created for high-cost items or services or for items or services for which bids are required as a matter of company policy. It is a document sent to vendors inviting them to confirm a price and payment terms for the supply of a product or service. The request for quotation might be sent as a paper document, as a fax, or electronically as an electronic data interchange (EDI). One can prepare a request for quotation document manually, but usually it can be prepared by referencing the purchase requisition. The request for quotation and the purchase requisition usually contain the same data except for the account assignments that are necessary on the purchase requisition. The request for quotation specifies closing dates for the application and bid-submission guidelines.

The issuing of a request for quotations results in one or more quotation documents being entered into R/3. Potential vendors' quotes for pricing and terms are entered into quotation documents. Quotation documents are used in the selection of a vendor.

SELECTION OF A VENDOR

R/3 compares procurement needs with vendors' quotes as they have been recorded in quotation documents and identifies the most suitable quotation for the requisition. R/3 sends rejection letters to vendors whose bids were not accepted.

Vendor evaluation often requires expertise or experience. R/3 offers an automatic vendor evaluation function to assist an organization in the procurement business process. R/3 scores vendors on the basis of 100 points that are assigned on different criteria such as delivery record on past orders, service, price, quality, and up to 99 user-defined criteria. There are also 5 system-defined subcriteria for each of the main criteria, and a user can define up to 20 subcriteria. The user also can weight each criterion. R/3 can display its vendor analysis sorted by total rank or sorted and ranked by a specific criterion. Quotes can be saved for future reference in purchase information records.

ISSUING OF A PURCHASE ORDER

A **purchase order** document identifies a vendor and confirms goods ordered, quantity, price, delivery date, terms of delivery, and payment terms. A purchase order can be created from scratch or by reference to an existing document. The purchase order can be sent as paper, as a fax, or electronically as an EDI document.

It is common for a company to configure its systems to issue a purchase order automatically for purchase requisitions that meet certain criteria. For example, a system might issue a purchase order automatically for purchase requisitions that do not exceed a specific price or amount.

R/3 processes several types of purchase orders. A standard purchase order is issued to order a good or service. A subcontract purchase order is issued when a vendor must receive parts (i.e., subassemblies) to produce an end product that will be delivered to the company. The subcontract purchase order specifies the end product and also the parts that the vendor must acquire. A consignment purchase order is issued for goods held in consignment. A third-party purchase order is issued when goods or services are to be delivered to a third party. Finally, a stock transport purchase order is issued to initiate a good movement between plants in the company.

Outline agreements are long-term arrangements with vendors. Terms and conditions usually are negotiated and maintained separately by each purchasing organization. An outline agreement has a header and items. The header specifies much the same data about terms and conditions as is done in a request for quotation and purchase order. Outline agreements also require specification of the time period to which the conditions apply. There are two types of outline agreements: contracts and scheduling agreements.

A *contract* is an outline agreement in which a vendor provides material for a period of time. A contract does not contain specific delivery dates or quantities. These are specified subsequently in release orders against the contract. A contract is either a value contract or quantity contract. A value contract is used when the total value of release orders is not to exceed a certain amount. A quantity contract is used when the total quantity to be ordered over a period of time is known.

Scheduling agreements are similar to contracts, but they also specify the price of items. A scheduling agreement has line items. A rolling delivery schedule is established for each scheduling agreement line item by creating a number of individual schedule times that are sent to the vendor in a scheduling agreement release document. Delivery dates and quantities are specified. Scheduling agreements reduce paperwork because a single schedule can replace many purchase orders or release orders. This helps reduce inventory because it enables just-in-time (JIT) delivery.

Using R/3, one also can set up a contract and/or a scheduling agreement at the same time that the purchase order is prepared. Because contracts are created in R/3, they can be referenced by R/3 when subsequent purchase orders are to be entered. A purchase order that is prepared under an existing contract or scheduling agreement is called a *release order*.

A purchase order can be changed after it has been sent to a vendor. R/3 generates a change document that is sent to the vendor identifying what has changed in the order. One also can cancel purchase orders, delete items, or block purchase orders to prevent receipt of the goods.

RECEIPT OF THE GOODS

When the vendor makes delivery, a goods-receipt document is prepared in R/3. This type of document is often called a **receiving report**. A goods-receipt document is issued whenever goods are inventoried, regardless of the source. Thus a goods receipt is prepared when an item is delivered from an in-house source as well as when an inventory transfer occurs that moves an item from one location to another.

If goods are damaged on delivery, they can be either entered as being returned or simply not accepted at delivery. If a vendor delivery is made in parts, then several goods-receipts entries must be made. R/3 monitors delivery and reports when an order has been fulfilled and may be closed. This ensures that payment for the goods occurs only after receipt. However, this feature can be overridden when necessary. For example, it would be necessary if a vendor could not fill an order completely but had made partial delivery.

A goods-receipt document can be prepared in three different ways. One way is by the inventory management system when the goods are assigned to temporary storage. After goods have been transferred and goods are checked and recorded, the goods receipt is complete. Another way that a goods-receipt document can be prepared is by reference to the purchase order. R/3 automatically fills the goods-receipt document using information in the purchase order and updates the purchase order for the goods receipt. A third way is that the goods receipt can be posted into quality inspection. Goods cannot be used until inspected and verified. If goods pass, a transfer posting is entered to move them from quality inspection to available inventory.

After a goods receipt is posted, R/3 makes an inventory document that documents the effect on inventory. It also produces an accounting document to show the general ledger transaction.

INVOICE VERIFICATION

Invoices must be checked against goods receipt documents and original purchase orders prior to payment. This business process—known as **invoice verification**—ensures that cost and quantity requirements have been met. R/3 has an invoice verification component. This component is not responsible for the actual payment of invoices. The accounts payable function pays invoices. Invoice verification links materials management and procurement with other R/3 modules such as financial accounting and controlling.

The purchase order number is entered along with other invoice details. R/3 copies information from the purchase order document into the invoice verification document.

One must enter the amount of the invoice and the quantity of goods or service that actually was invoiced.

When an invoice is posted, R/3 performs a three-way match that compares the purchase order with the goods receipt and with the invoice. This check ensures against inconsistent charges or incorrect amounts being delivered. As a result of posting the invoice, the purchase order is updated, and R/3 produces an accounting document to indicate the general ledger transaction.

VENDOR PAYMENT

Once an invoice is posted, payment can take place. Payment is made according to the payment terms and conditions specified in the purchase order or the vendor master record. Payment is processed through accounts payable in the financial accounting module.

MASTER RECORDS

Master records are created in R/3 for the objects that reflect the organizational structure and business processes of the company. Objects are identified by a code. The coding system for objects incorporates fields that identify company, plant, storage location, purchasing organization, and purchasing group.

The company code identifies an accounting unit that has a balance sheet and income statement. A consolidated company consists of several different companies, each of which is legally responsible for creating and maintaining its own accounting documents for legal purposes. The plant code identifies a separate location, such as a plant or warehouse. The storage location code identifies an area where goods are stored. The purchasing organization code identifies the unit responsible for negotiating purchases for one or several plants. A firm's purchasing organization may be decentralized or centralized. A plant can have several purchasing organizations assigned to it. Finally, the purchasing group code identifies the individual or team that is responsible for the procurement of a material or class of material. The purchasing group is the primary contact for the company's dealing with the vendor.

R/3 maintains a centralized database. Master records are created for each object. Each master record is accessible by every module in R/3, but every module can only "see" different areas of each master record. Procurement accesses vendor master records and material master records.

Vendor master data are maintained in the materials management module of R/3. Vendor master records are maintained centrally but are updated by users in many departments. There are three categories of information in vendor master records. General data consist of vendor number, name, address, telephone number, and similar items. Company code data (also called *accounting data*) are defined at the company code level and are linked to the financial accounting and general ledger modules in R/3. Company code data define agreed payment terms and the subledger reconciliation account number. Every vendor master record must have a reconciliation account number that links the vendor to the accounts payable subledger. Finally, purchasing data describe purchasing needs and are defined at the purchasing organization level. For example, purchasing data include information used for quotations, invoice verification, or inventory control. Each vendor master record has an account group field that determines how the vendor record is numbered and also determines which fields display on the vendor master screens.

Material master records contain information about materials that a company might procure, produce, or sell to customers. Material master records are used and shared by many departments. Material master records have a hierarchical structure. The organizational or client level is the highest level. It contains data that are relevant to all users, such as item description, unit of measure, and material group. At the plant level, a material master record can contain production or sales requirements. Sales and warehouse data can be maintained at other levels. Material master records contain so much data that they are organized as "views": Each department accesses and maintains its own view of the master record. Engineering, purchasing, inventory management, MRP, and accounting all use material master records. Procurement uses several views, including purchasing, accounting, production planning, and warehouse.

The inventory management (IM) component of R/3 records both the value and quantity of inventory. This allows one to enter and check goods movement, manage inventory stocks, and take a physical inventory. A *goods movement* is an internal or external event that causes a change in stock level. The issue of stock to production is an example of an internal event. A sale to a customer or receipt from a vendor is an external event. Current stock level is tracked by considering items in stock, on order, reserved, and in quality inspection. Consignment inventory is accounted for separately. Several values are updated when stock level changes. The stock value is charged internally to a cost center or project. The corresponding general ledger accounts are also updated. The IM component supports cycle counting and inventory sampling. In addition to these basic features, IM can be extended to incorporate warehouse management. IM is part of the materials management module and is integrated with other modules.

Purchasing information master records are used only by purchasing. They are used for *source allocation,* which is the process of vendor evaluation. These records contain performance information about a material, a vendor, and a plant, such as price and delivery times for the material from a vendor at a certain date. The vendor evaluation data include the planned delivery date and the corresponding actual delivery date for a material.

Contracts are transaction documents, but they function like master records for release orders.

TRANSACTION CYCLE CONTROLS OVER PROCUREMENT

Figure 8.2 illustrates an analytic flowchart of the document flow in a procurement (purchasing) business process. The main feature in the flowchart is the separation of the following functions: Requisitioning (e.g., stores), purchasing, receiving, accounts payable, cash disbursements, and general ledger.

REQUISITIONING (STORES)

Requests for purchases originate outside the purchasing department. In Figure 8.2, purchase requisitions originate in the stores department. Purchase requisitions also might originate in other departments within the firm. Purchase requisitions should be approved in the originating department.

PURCHASING

Regardless of how or where purchase requisitions originate, it is the function of the purchasing department to select a vendor and arrange for terms and delivery. How this is done depends on the relative degree of centralization in the company's purchasing

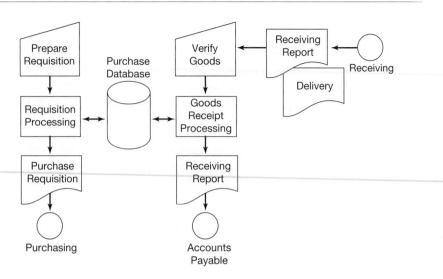

(a)   Stores (Requisitioning).

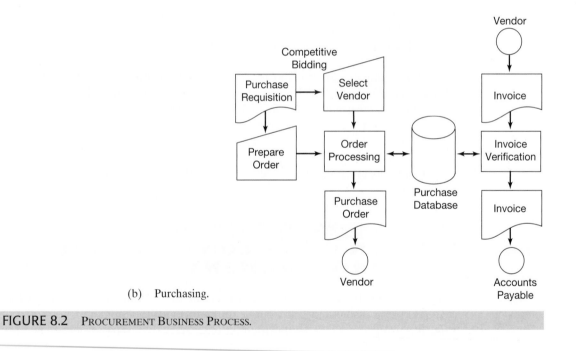

(b)   Purchasing.

FIGURE 8.2   PROCUREMENT BUSINESS PROCESS.

function. Purchasing may at times override a purchase requisition due to insufficient budget, lack of authorization, or some other reason. Purchase requisitions also might be altered or returned to the originating department for modification.

Purchasing selects a vendor and then prepares a purchase order for the requisition. A copy is sent to the vendor. Accounts payable, the requesting department (stores), and the receiving department each will access the purchase order in subsequent processing of the order. The vendor may return a copy of the purchase order to the customer to acknowledge receipt of the order. The requesting department should be notified that a purchase order has been issued, and it should review the order as necessary to verify its appropriateness for satisfying the needs identified in the purchase requisition.

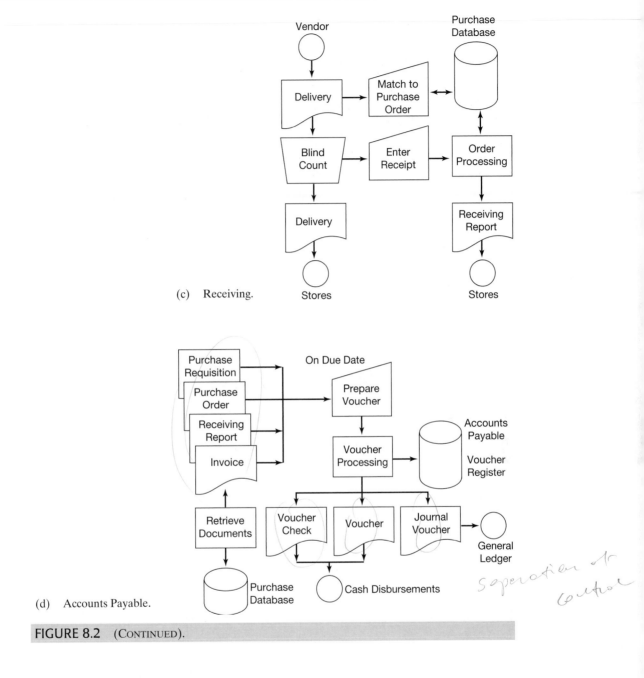

(c)   Receiving.

(d)   Accounts Payable.

FIGURE 8.2   (CONTINUED).

RECEIVING

The receiving function should be separate from and independent of the stores function. Receiving should access the purchase order and match it with the delivery from the vendor. The purchase order authorizes the receiving department to accept the delivery from the vendor when it is delivered. Receiving procedures should call for an independent count of the delivery and for the preparation of a receiving report.

An independent or **blind count** of a delivery may be obtained by not allowing the counters to have access to the quantities shown on the purchase order. This forces the counters to determine a quantity by counting, since it is not possible simply to copy the

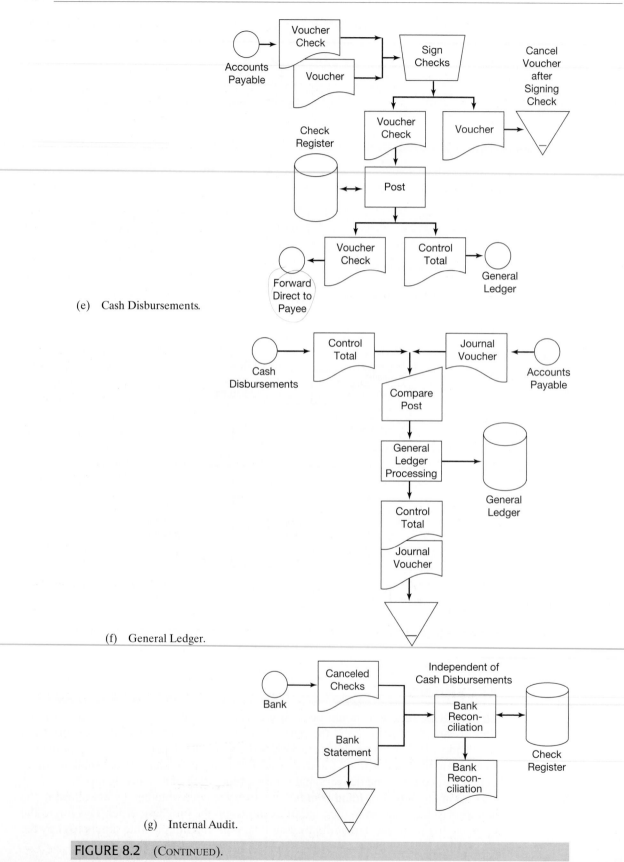

(e)   Cash Disbursements.

(f)   General Ledger.

(g)   Internal Audit.

FIGURE 8.2   (CONTINUED).

quantity number from the purchase order. A supervisor compares the quantities received as counted with those shown on the purchase order and then prepares a receiving report for the quantities received. A copy of the receiving report should accompany transfer of the delivery to stores, as shown in Figure 8.2.

In many cases only a person with technical ability can adequately inspect materials and give assurance to the requisitioning or using department. It may be desirable to have the quality of materials received tested before payment is made. An inspection function may be established for this purpose either as a part of the receiving department or as a separate department.

STORES

The stores department acknowledges receipt of the delivery from receiving by signing the receiving report and then forwarding it to accounts payable. If goods are delivered directly to the requisitioning department rather than to stores, a supervisor in the requesting department should acknowledge receipt on the receiving report and then forward the receiving report to account payable. This independent verification of receipt of the purchase is a central control feature in the procurement business process.

ACCOUNTS PAYABLE

Accounts payable is responsible for initiating payments to vendors. Four documents—purchase requisition, purchase order, receiving report, and invoice—are available to document a purchase transaction. The use of a voucher system to support payment is a major transaction cycle control over procurement. A voucher system is essentially a review technique to ensure that all appropriate documentation is assembled, verified, and reviewed prior to actual payment of an invoice. Approved vouchers are forwarded to cash disbursements for payment. Voucher systems are discussed in the context of the cash disbursements business process, which is the next topic discussed in this chapter.

There are several additional control features worth noting.

- Purchasing does not control the actual goods, nor does purchasing have complete control over the documentation that is required for payment.
- Receiving is separate from final custody of the delivery, which is stores in our illustration. Acknowledgment from both receiving and final custody is required before payment is authorized.
- Accounts payable handles only documents and is not able to obtain merchandise or cash independently.
- Purchase requisitions should be reviewed independently outside purchasing. This is often done by accounts payable. This review could verify the accounting charges shown on the requisition and also ensures that requisitions do not originate in purchasing.
- Invoices should be routed to purchasing for review and approval prior to being sent to accounts payable. This is particularly important if purchasing expertise is necessary to evaluate the propriety of the invoice.
- Purchase terms should be reviewed for propriety outside the purchasing department. This review is often done by accounts payable.
- Inventory records should be updated to reflect the receipt of goods.

INTEGRITY OF THE PROCUREMENT BUSINESS PROCESS

Purchase documentation simply ensures that individual orders are received as expected. Purchase orders and receiving reports control individual purchases, but they do not exercise control directly over the procurement business process. Control of the procurement business process centers on the integrity of the buyer-vendor relationship. Bribery, kickbacks, and conflicts of interest (such as buying from a relative or friend) are examples of improper buyer-vendor relationships that the procurement business process must address. Buyer-vendor relationships are more a matter of policy than procedure. Most companies have found it desirable and often necessary to have formal written policy and procedure manuals covering the procurement business process. Purchasing policies may require competitive bidding, which usually is implemented through the use of request for quotation documents.

Buyers must request competitive bids through request for quotation documents. These documents are filed and reviewed by purchasing management. Selecting the lowest-cost bid is not always an acceptable basis for selecting a vendor. Methods of evaluating and selecting bids based on vendor attributes, which are known as *vendor rating plans*, often are formalized, with evaluation decisions subject to review by a higher authority. A policy of rotating a buyer's responsibilities weakens buyer-vendor relationships but reduces the potential for buyer specialization. **Approved vendor lists**, prepared by an independent function, may be used to restrict a buyer's options to those vendors who have been found reliable, financially sound, and free of conflicts of interest. These examples are not exhaustive, but they indicate the types of controls that may be used to ensure the integrity of procurement business process. SAP R/3, as discussed earlier in this chapter, provides extensive support for vendor selection and evaluation.

THE ATTRIBUTE RATING APPROACH TO VENDOR SELECTION

The **attribute rating** approach to vendor selection is appropriate whenever an objective evaluation of the opinions of several independent evaluators is desired, that is, an amalgamation of evaluations of the same system. The following steps are involved:

- Identify and list the attributes to be included in the evaluation.
- Assign a weight to each attribute based on relative importance and objectivity.
- Have individual evaluators rank each vendor on each attribute, giving a numerical score on a range of 1 to 10 or some other scale.
- Total the individual evaluations by multiplying each attribute's numerical ranking by its weight; then total all evaluations by adding the scores together.

Given that the relevant costs, such as a vendor's prices or a system's cost, have been identified, a benefit-cost ratio can be computed for comparisons. While this method appears to be objective, both assignment of weights and numerical ranking are very subjective processes. Accordingly, attribute evaluation techniques are most useful for screening proposals and identifying vendors or systems that should be subject to final consideration. SAP R/3, as discussed earlier in this chapter, provides extensive computational support for the attribute rating approach to vendor selection.

CASH DISBURSEMENTS BUSINESS PROCESS

The cash disbursements business process controls check disbursements as well as actual cash disbursement. Typically, checks are used for the majority of disbursements, with currency disbursements restricted to small amounts drawn from and accountable to a petty cash imprest fund.

The imprest fund concept is not restricted to petty cash control. Imprest payroll funds and imprest charge or expense funds are common in systems design. An imprest fund is a fund maintained at a specified, predetermined amount. At all times the amount of cash on hand plus documented expenditures should equal the specified amount of the fund. Periodically, an imprest fund is replenished; documented expenditures (petty cash vouchers) are reviewed and approved, and a check is drawn to the fund or custodian of the fund for the amount necessary to bring the fund back to its specified amount. Separate imprest checking accounts may be maintained for payroll and other expense categories, such as dividend payments.

The major control features of a cash disbursements business process are the use of a voucher system to support the drawing of checks, the separation of approval from actual payment, and an independent bank reconciliation. These items are included in the following discussion and illustrated in Figure 8.2.

ACCOUNTS PAYABLE

The accounts payable department accesses the documents that are necessary to support a cash disbursement. As illustrated in Figure 8.2, these documents are a purchase requisition, purchase order, receiving report, and the vendor's invoice. These documents are reviewed, certified as to completeness, and processed to prepare a voucher. The voucher typically is prepared and processed for payment on the due date of the invoice.

Accounts payable initiates payment processing, which includes calculating the amount due, discount (if any), and other such items. A voucher check is prepared for each voucher. Voucher checks are posted to the voucher register. A total of these postings is prepared. Vouchers are posted to the accounts payable ledger. This posting is summarized on a journal voucher. Voucher processing includes processing the expense distribution. Vouchers are charged to the organizational units identified by account number on vouchers. The voucher checks and vouchers are approved and forwarded to the cash disbursements department. The journal voucher is forwarded to general ledger.

CASH DISBURSEMENTS

Voucher checks and vouchers are received from the accounts payable department. After the voucher checks and vouchers are reviewed, the checks are signed, and the vouchers are cancelled and filed by number. Vouchers, including the original documents, if possible, are cancelled to avoid the possibility of duplicate payments. The voucher checks are posted to the check register. A control total of the amount posted is prepared and reconciled with the vouchers received from accounts payable. Voucher checks are forwarded directly to the payees. The control total is forwarded to the general ledger.

GENERAL LEDGER

The journal voucher received from accounts payable and the control total from cash disbursements are reconciled, and the totals are posted to the general ledger. The journal voucher and the control total should be filed by date.

INTERNAL AUDIT

The cancelled checks are received from the bank along with the bank statement. An independent bank reconciliation is an important control in a cash disbursements business process.

VOUCHER SYSTEMS

A voucher system is essentially a review technique. The real control over disbursements is a final review of documents evidencing the entire transaction prior to authorization of payment. Authorization may take the form of physically signing off on a **voucher package**, preparing a document to authorize an entry in the voucher register, or entering data into a computer. This final review process evidences that procedures have been duly authorized and completed according to system specifications. It is the review process, not the actual signing of checks, that is the control. This is particularly evident in computer applications where checks are "signed" with a signature imprinter at the rate of hundreds of checks per minute.

An accounts payable system typically maintains a subsidiary ledger of creditors' accounts, posting invoices and payments on account to each individual creditor's account. Accounts payable generally refers to trade accounts, whereas a voucher payable system encompasses *all* expenditures, including trade accounts, payroll, capital expenditures, and so on. In a strict voucher payable system, individual accounts for creditors need not be kept. The voucher system maintains a voucher register or, alternatively, files of voucher packages in numerical or other order. Several vouchers may relate to the same creditor, as opposed to a single account in an accounts payable system. If information on individual creditors is desired, copies of vouchers may be used to generate this information. Numerous voucher payable files are maintained in most systems because payable information is essential to short-run financial planning.

A **voucher system** centers around vouchers. **Vouchers** themselves can take several forms, ranging from a simple form or envelope to a voucher-check combination (Fig. 8.3).

FIGURE 8.3 VOUCHER CHECK.

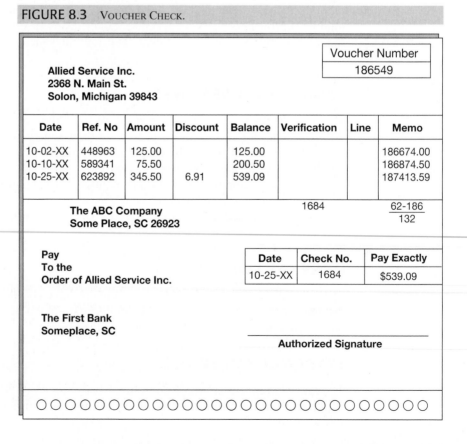

Allied Service Inc.
2368 N. Main St.
Solon, Michigan 39843

	Voucher Number
	186549

Date	Ref. No	Amount	Discount	Balance	Verification	Line	Memo
10-02-XX	448963	125.00		125.00			186674.00
10-10-XX	589341	75.50		200.50			186874.50
10-25-XX	623892	345.50	6.91	539.09			187413.59

The ABC Company
Some Place, SC 26923

1684

$\frac{62\text{-}186}{132}$

Pay
To the
Order of Allied Service Inc.

Date	Check No.	Pay Exactly
10-25-XX	1684	$539.09

The First Bank
Someplace, SC

_____

Authorized Signature

A voucher shows, among other things, the name and address of the vendor, a description of the invoice, total or net amount due, and the accounts to be charged (distribution). In a computer application, most of the documents included in the voucher are coded and processed by the computer. A voucher system may be implemented by rubber-stamping an invoice or purchase order with a voucher stamp and documenting the voucher on this original document. The voucher stamp creates an area on the document for authorizing signatures, document numbers, dates, and so on.

The form of the voucher itself is not significant. A voucher system may operate without a human-readable voucher. In this case the "voucher" is an approved entry in the voucher register, some type of computer file. References to documents rather than the documents themselves are provided in the register, and voucher entries are under strict numerical control.

POSTING OF PAYABLES

A basic question in the design of a voucher system concerns when invoices are to be posted to vouchers payable. Specifically, when are liabilities "booked" (excluding end-of-period accruals)? After invoices have been approved for payment, they may be held until the due date and formally posted at that time; alternatively, they may be booked at the time of approval (which is generally different from the due date). Because most firms attempt to pay invoices on the due date to maximize working capital, this question relates to whether there is a formal record of amounts owed to creditors. If invoices are booked on the due date, there is no formal record of unpaid invoices because the liability is immediately cancelled by payment. If invoices are booked on the date of approval, a formal record of liabilities exists. This advantage is gained at a cost: The voucher register (or file of vouchers) now must be searched or sorted by due date to facilitate payments. Typically, a voucher register is used for numerical control when invoices are booked at the time of approval.

Preparing vouchers for individual invoices when several invoices refer to the same vendor in the same time period would result in the drawing of several checks to the same vendor in the same month. This is generally inefficient. Accordingly, many firms use built-up voucher systems. **Built-up voucher systems** accumulate several invoices from the same vendor and pay these invoices with a single check.

A built-up voucher system functions essentially as an accounts payable system. After invoices are approved, they are sorted and accumulated by vendor or voucher number. Payments are made at month end or due date. A built-up voucher procedure as just described is a full accrual system; vouchers payable replace accounts payable in the general ledger.

Three files are necessary to maintain useful information: (1) a file of approved but unpaid invoices, with access to due date for payment, (2) a file of paid invoices, usually in numerical order, and (3) a vendor file showing both paid and unpaid amounts, ordered by vendor ID. In a manual system, these files are obtained by filing copies of vouchers. In a computer system, separate files may be maintained, or database processing may yield similar results without having three separate files.

The voucher concept is helpful in the disbursement procedure of any organization when a basic record is desired and proper authorization and control over disbursements are important. Requiring signatures before disbursement documents knowledge and approval of the disbursement. Paid vouchers can be filed in strict numerical sequence to provide documentation for every amount paid. Such a procedure provides orderly records and good documentation and is advantageous in establishing good stewardship of cash.

HUMAN RESOURCE MANAGEMENT BUSINESS PROCESS

The business process that involves management of human resources is concerned with establishing and maintaining an information system that processes human resources (HR) information. The HR system should provide tools for the setup and maintenance of information pertaining to the organizational structure. A listing of jobs that exist in an organization, a listing of job descriptions, and a listing of any qualifications that are required for a job are examples of HR information pertaining to the organizational structure. The HR system also should provide tools for the processing of employee data, such as employee address, payroll, and employment history. We will illustrate these HR business process concepts by examining some of the basic features of the human resources component of SAP R/3.

HR PROCESSING IN SAP R/3

The HR module in SAP R/3 includes components that address the objectives stated earlier in an integrated, on-line environment. HR data are available immediately to anyone who has authorization to use them because all HR data are on-line. The HR component can be implemented stand-alone or can be integrated with other modules, such as the production planning and control module or the plant maintenance module.

SAP R/3 contains two HR modules. The personnel administration module (HR-PA) is concerned with the maintenance of employee data, such as personnel details, salary data, and performance appraisal data. The personnel planning and development module (HR-PD) provides tools for the setup and maintenance of organizational structure information. Organizational structure is represented as an administrative hierarchy in which each unit in a company reports to a parent organization unit. This type of hierarchy relationship is known as a *parent-child* or *parent-subordinate relationship*. A unit can be a subsidiary, a division, a department, a project team, and so on. Each unit is assigned a manager, and each unit is allocated positions to which individual employees are assigned. Other functions in HR-PD include workplace and job descriptions, career planning information, and shift planning.

The time management component is one of the most important and most often used HR modules. It performs time recording and time evaluation to record employee absences and attendance information. This module usually is implemented in a manufacturing or service environment where employees work in shifts and attendance monitoring is critical to the management of operations. The component can be implemented to use either negative or positive time recording. Negative time recording is less complex because only exceptions need to be recorded. In positive time recording, all attendance and absence information must be entered. This requires a system such as time cards or electronic swipe cards to record the required information.

The payroll component can calculate pay based on attendance information accumulated in the time component or based on a fixed amount per pay period. Deductions for taxes, medical payments, and so on are made based on a variety of predefined wage types. The use of predefined data types or *blueprints* is an important characteristic of ERP systems such as SAP R/3.

The travel expense component of HR-PA is used to process any employee expenses. One can enter and authorize expenses and pay the correct amount into employees bank accounts. The module supports recruitment. It can track job vacancies and the applicants that are being considered to fill those vacancies. Any positions marked vacant in the HR-PD module are automatically accessible in the recruitment component of

HR-PA. The module can record details of applicants and progress that has been made with processing their applications. The module can link applicants to the source that caused them to apply, such as advertisements in a newspaper. This allows HR management to evaluate the relative efficiency of different recruitment methods.

HR DATA STRUCTURE

A data structure provides the basis for the storage and manipulation of data. The HR data structure contains three elements:

- HR master data
- HR data organization
- HR objects

MASTER DATA

Master data records in the HR-PA and HR-PD modules are created and maintained for organizational units, job profiles, employees, and training. In many business processes, the data in master records are referenced often but seldom changed. However, some HR master records are subject to frequent change. For example, employee master data change frequently as the lives and careers of the employees change. As this example illustrates, HR information systems are focused on maintaining master data records rather than processing transactions.

DATA ORGANIZATION

Data are organized and presented to users in R/3 by *infotypes* and personnel *events*. An infotype is a SAP term that denotes a collection of data fields that are grouped together for display. In database terminology, an infotype is a segment. Employee personnel data, employee pay data, employee appraisal data, and a work schedule are common infotypes in HR. New or custom infotypes can be defined as necessary. SAP R/3 offers a number of standard infotypes that are specific to the tax and benefit systems of different nations. These blueprint infotypes may be included in the implementation of the HR module as appropriate. Each of these nation-specific supplements adds a suite of infotypes to the employee management component of the HR-PA module.

Infotypes change over time, and it is usually important to retain old versions in order to track changes in HR organization and personnel records over time. Validity data are assigned to each infotype to make each unique and to prevent overwriting when an infotype is updated. Date fields are added to infotypes to indicate the beginning and end dates of the period for which the infotype is considered valid. Thus several infotypes for the same object exist at the same time, but only one is valid. A *delimited* infotype is one whose validity end date is past.

The system has functions to create and manipulate infotypes as well as display them. The create function adds a new blank infotype with a default validity date from current date to "end of time." In R/3 terms, the end of time is 12/31/9999. If a current infotype already exists when one is being created, it is delimited automatically. Copy, delete, and list functions are supported.

A personnel *event* is a group of infotypes. Events are created to simplify HR transaction entry. Personnel events are specifically designed for use in a company and are easily customized in R/3. For example, a hiring event would be recorded as a transaction by inputting all the infotypes necessary to create a new employee. The input screen would be designed to display and prompt for the infotypes. A "change of job" event would be input to a screen that displayed all the infotypes required to change an employee's job within the organization. The system can prompt for additional information and perform processing. For example, it might prompt for more information if a new employee is married. It might calculate the date of the end of a new employee's probationary period. It also might create a position vacancy if the employee in that position is transferred or leaves the organization.

HR OBJECTS

HR object types are identified with a one- or two-letter identifier. The code for the object employee is "P." Each employee also has a unique personnel number that identifies him or her throughout the information system. The code for the object job is "C." A job is a generic description. A job is not identical to the actual positions in the HR organization. The code for the object qualifications is "Q." A qualification is a skill required for a particular job, such as an educational degree, job experience, or capability. The code for organization unit is "O." An organization unit is a distinct area or section of the organization, such as the accounting department. The code for the object position is "S." A position is a specific work assignment within an organization unit. Each organization unit consists of one or more positions. Each position has a particular job and often one or more qualifications if these are needed to further define the job. The code for the object cost center is "K." Cost center data are used to capture and assign any HR costs that are incurred. For example, salary costs are often assigned to cost centers.

We illustrate the use of HR objects with an example. The organization unit marketing department has five positions. Each position has a job description. One of these positions is manager, one is supervisor, and three are sales associates. In addition, the manager position is qualified with the qualification "Japanese language skills" because the marketing department has frequent correspondence with a Japanese subsidiary.

TRANSACTION CYCLE CONTROLS IN PAYROLL PROCESSING

Payroll processing is extremely complex. In a large organization it is one of the most complex procedures in operation. All levels of government impose payroll taxes of one sort or another; regulations and rates are changed constantly, with the result that a payroll system usually requires constant modification. Payroll processing is one area in which the law imposes not only a fine but a jail sentence for willful negligence in maintaining adequate records. As with any law, ignorance is no excuse. The responsibility is on the systems analyst to keep current in this area.

Figure 8.4 illustrates a document flowchart of payroll processing. The main feature in the illustration is the separation of the following functions.

PERSONNEL

The personnel (employment) office is responsible for placing people on the company's payroll, specifying rates of pay, and authorizing all deductions from pay. All changes, such as adding or deleting employees, changing pay rates, or changing levels of deductions from pay must be authorized by the personnel office. The personnel function is distinct from timekeeping and from the payroll preparation function.

TIMEKEEPING

The timekeeping function is responsible for the preparation and control of time reports and job-time tickets. In a manufacturing firm, an hourly employee typically clocks on and off the job. At the end of a pay period, the employee's time card (or time report) indicates the amount of time the employee was on the job and the time for which he or she expects to receive pay.

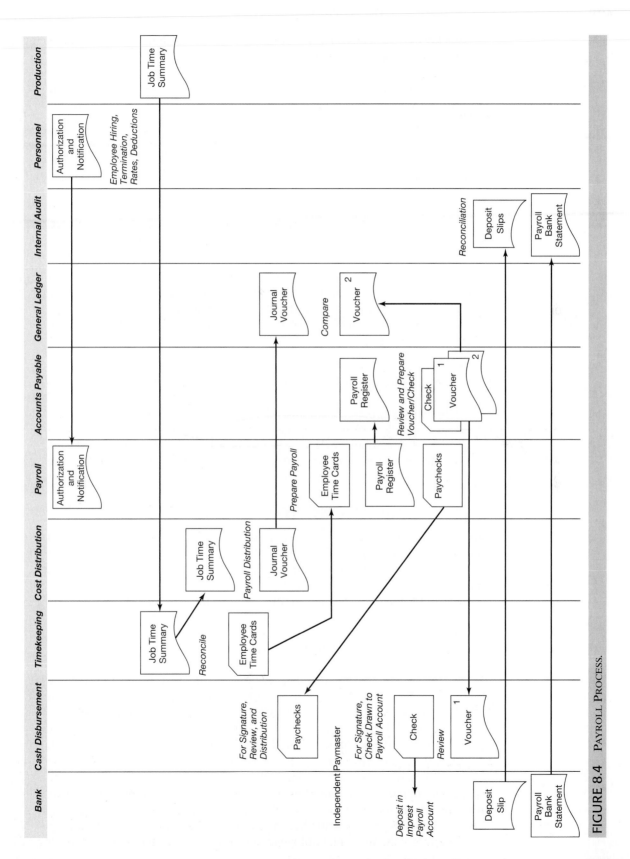

FIGURE 8.4 PAYROLL PROCESS.

Timekeeping is responsible for collecting and maintaining time cards or time reports, and reconciling these data with job time summary reports that are received from production. Job-time summary reports indicate the jobs employees were assigned to in production. Timekeeping reconciles time reports with the related job time summary report received from production and then forwards time cards to the payroll department.

Salaried employees typically do not clock on and off the job in the same manner as hourly employees. If no accounting for time is required, a supervisor's approval usually is required to initiate payroll processing. If salaried employees are required to submit time reports, the analogy to Figure 8.4 is straightforward.

PAYROLL

The payroll department is responsible for the actual computation and preparation of payroll. Note that preparing payroll is independent of the preparation of the input data on which pay is based—the time reports and personnel data. Personnel data are received from the personnel office. Time reports are received from timekeeping. The payroll register details the computation of net pay (gross pay less deductions from pay). Paychecks are sent to cash disbursements for signature, review, and distribution. A copy of the payroll register is sent to accounts payable to initiate the recording of a voucher for the payroll.

Several other features to note in Figure 8.4 include:

- The use of a separate imprest payroll account for paychecks to facilitate reconciliations.
- An independent reconciliation of the payroll-account bank statement.
- The use of an **independent paymaster**. The person who distributes the pay is independent of personnel, timekeeping, and payroll preparation. Neither the personnel office, the timekeeping department, nor the payroll department has access to the paychecks once they have been drawn.

PAYROLL PROCESSING REQUIREMENTS

Numerous files must be maintained in a payroll system. Basic employee information, such as name, address, rate of pay, and deductions, is necessary to prepare a payroll. A payroll register or journal must be maintained to document actual payments. Files pertaining to government reports, tax tables used in processing, pension plans, hospitalization plans, and similar plans are examples of information required to support a payroll procedure.

Social Security and other tax legislation imposes several taxes based on payrolls. The Federal Insurance Contributions Act (F.I.C.A.) provides that employees contribute equally to funds for old age, survivors', disability, and hospital insurance benefits for certain individuals and members of their families. The contribution is based on a tax rate applied to gross wages. The employer is required to deduct the amount of F.I.C.A. tax from each employee's pay each pay period. The employer is then required to match these deductions and deposit the entire amount in a government depository. A penalty is levied for failure, without reasonable cause, to make required deposits when due. Taxpayers who willfully claim credit on the record of federal tax deposits for deposits not made are subject to fine and/or other criminal penalties. The employer is responsible for the full amount of the tax even when he or she fails to withhold contributions from employees.

The Federal Social Security Act and the Federal Unemployment Tax Act provide for the establishment of unemployment insurance plans. Employers with covered workers employed in each of 20 weeks during a calendar year are affected. Payment to the federal government is required quarterly. Unemployment benefits are provided by the systems created by the individual states. Revenues of the federal government under the acts are used to meet the cost of administering state and federal unemployment plans, as well as to provide supplemental unemployment benefits.

Unemployment compensation laws are not the same in all states, but all states participate in the federal-state unemployment insurance program. In most states, laws provide for taxes only on employers. The federal legislation applies to all employers of one or more employees. Tax payment generally is required on or before the last day of the month following each calendar quarter. Most states have a merit-rating plan that permits a reduction in the tax rate for employers who establish a record of stable employment.

Federal income taxes on wages of an individual are collected in the period in which the wages are paid. Our "pay-as-you-go" system requires employers to withhold a portion of the earnings of their employees. The amount withheld depends on the amount of the earnings and on the number of exemptions allowed the employee. A withholding exemption certificate must be prepared by each employee. The certificate states the number of exemptions to which the employee is entitled. This certificate is given to the employer, who computes the proper amount of tax to be withheld. Current regulations provide a graduated system of withholding designed to make the amount of tax withheld closely approximate the rates used in computing the individual's tax liability at the end of the year.

Employers engaged in interstate commerce are required by the Federal Fair Labor Standards Act (also known as the Wages and Hours Law) to pay overtime at a minimum rate of one and one-half times the regular rate for hours worked in excess of 40 per week. Many companies also pay overtime premium rates for night shifts and for work on Sundays and holidays.

Employers must take care to deduct payroll taxes from all employees. A distinction is drawn between employees and independent contractors. Public accountants, architects, attorneys, and other people who render services to a business for a fee but are not controlled or directed by the client are not employees but independent contractors, and the amounts paid to them are not subject to payroll taxes.

At the close of each quarter an employer is required to file a quarterly return of Form 941 or 941E and pay the balance of undeposited taxes. If the taxes were deposited in full, ten additional days are allowed. This return covers income tax withheld and F.I.C.A. tax for all employees.

On or before January 31, each employer is required to give each employee a completed Form W-2 Wage and Tax Statement. The employer is required to forward a copy of these W-2 forms with a Form W-3 on or before February 28 to the government. Also on or before January 31 employers must file Form 940, Employer's Annual Federal Unemployment Tax Return.

The basic information about what the U.S. government requires with respect to payroll is outlined in the Department of Treasury Internal Revenue Service publication, *Circular E Employers Tax Guide*. This publication contains all the latest information on new laws and detailed information for employers. It tells how to fill out all the forms and reports required, how to compute employment taxes, and how and when to make deposits and payments, and it provides the invaluable tax tables. An employer who does not have this publication, or access to the information contained in it, will sooner or later make an error in payroll procedure that will cost a penalty.

Figure 8.5 contains a schedule of payroll-related deadlines that illustrates some of the processing and information a typical payroll system must provide.

DATE	EVENT
January 31	Form W-2 (Wage and Tax Statement) to be furnished to employees
January 31	Form 941 (Employer's Quarterly Federal Tax Return) due for 4th quarter of preceding calendar year
January 31	Form 1099-Misc. (U.S. Information Return for Recipients of Miscellaneous Income) to be furnished to consultants paid directly
February 28	Form W-3 (Transmittal of Wage and Tax Statements) due with Copy A of each Form W-2; Form 1096 (Transmittal) with each 1099-Misc.
February 28	Duplicate of Form 1096 due with State Copy of Form 1099-Misc.
March 15	File Form 1120 or 1120-S (Federal Corporate Income Tax Return for calendar year)
April 30	Form 941 due for 1st quarter
July 31	Form 941 due for 2nd quarter
October 31	Form 941 due for 3rd quarter

FIGURE 8.5   SAMPLE PAYROLL EVENTS TIMETABLE.

❖ SUMMARY

The procurement business process includes the following activities: requirement determination, selection of a source, request for quotation, selection of a vendor, issuing of a purchase order, receipt of the goods, invoice verification, and vendor payment. ERP systems are capable of storing and processing a vast amount of information pertaining to the procurement business process. This chapter provided an overview of the data stored and processed in the procurement business process by SAP R/3. Transaction cycle controls over the procurement business process includes a separation of the following functions: requisitioning, purchasing, receiving, stores, accounts payable, and the general ledger. Adequate vendor-selection procedures are an important factor in the overall integrity of a purchasing application system.

The cash disbursements business process is designed to control check disbursements as well as actual cash disbursements. Transaction cycle controls over cash disbursements include the use of a voucher system to support the drawing of checks, the separation of approval from actual payment, and an independent bank reconciliation. The design of the cash disbursements business process should include a separation of the following functions: cash disbursements, accounts payable, the expense ledger, and the general ledger.

The human resources business process establishes an information system that processes human resources (HR) information. The HR system should provide tools for the setup and maintenance of information pertaining to the organizational structure, as well as for the processing of employee data, such as employee address, payroll, and employment history data. Transaction cycle controls over payroll processing include a separation of the following functions: personnel (employment), timekeeping, payroll accounting, and the general ledger.

❖ GLOSSARY

approved vendor list: a list of vendors approved for use by the purchasing function.

attribute rating: an approach to vendor selection that identifies, lists, and evaluates several different aspects concerning a vendor.

blind count: counters in receiving do not have access to quantities shown on purchase orders.

built-up voucher system: the accumulation of several invoices from the same vendor and the payment of these invoices with a single check.

independent paymaster: the person who distributes pay is independent of the payroll preparation process.

invoice verification: the review of purchasing documentation prior to authorizing payment to vendors.

procurement: the business process of selecting a source, ordering, and acquiring goods or services.

purchase order: document issued to a vendor to initiate a purchase.

purchase requisition: document used to request a purchase.

receiving report: prepared to document the receipt of deliveries from vendors.

request for quotation: documents used to request competitive bids from vendors.

voucher: synonym for voucher package.

voucher package: a collection of documents that are reviewed and approved to authorize a disbursement.

voucher system: a system in which every organizational expenditure must be documented with an approved voucher.

❖ CHAPTER QUIZ

Answers to the chapter quiz appear on page 318.

1. In procurement, which of the following departments normally should be responsible for the preparation of purchase requisitions?
   - (a) cash disbursements
   - (b) purchasing
   - (c) receiving
   - (d) stores

2. In procurement, which of the following departments normally should be responsible for the preparation of purchase orders?
   - (a) cash disbursements
   - (b) purchasing
   - (c) accounts payable
   - (d) stores

3. In order to provide accountability for purchasing, purchase requisitions should be available to (_____).
   - (a) the vendor
   - (b) cash disbursements
   - (c) accounts payable
   - (d) receiving

4. Which of the following documents in the procurement business process is optional in SAP R/3?
   - (a) purchase requisition
   - (b) purchase order
   - (c) both are optional
   - (d) neither document is optional

5. For adequate internal control, the department responsible for preparing checks for signature should be (_____).
   - (a) the department that signs the checks
   - (b) the accounts payable department
   - (c) the purchasing department
   - (d) the treasury department

6. In a cash disbursements business process, the voucher package should be cancelled by (_____).
   - (a) cash disbursements
   - (b) accounts payable
   - (c) stores
   - (d) general ledger

7. Which of the following documents normally should be included in a voucher package?
   - (a) vendor invoice
   - (b) purchase order
   - (c) both a and b
   - (d) neither a nor b

8. Which of the following departments should directly forward to accounts payable the copy of the receiving report that is included in the voucher package?
   (a) purchasing
   (b) receiving
   (c) cash disbursements
   (d) stores

9. In payroll processing, which of the following should be responsible for preparation of the payroll register?
   (a) personnel department
   (b) payroll department
   (c) cash disbursements department
   (d) timekeeping department

10. In payroll processing, which of the following should be responsible for the authorization of pay rates for employees?
    (a) personnel department
    (b) payroll department
    (c) cash disbursements department
    (d) timekeeping department

❖ REVIEW PROBLEM

You have been engaged by the management of Alden, Inc., to review its internal control over the purchase, receipt, storage, and issue of raw materials. You have prepared the following comments that describe Alden's procedures.

> Raw materials, which consist mainly of high-cost electronic components, are kept in a locked storeroom. Storeroom personnel include a supervisor and four clerks. All are well trained, competent, and adequately bonded. Raw materials are removed from the storeroom only on written or oral authorization of one of the production foremen.
>
> No perpetual inventory records are kept; hence the storeroom clerks do not keep records of goods received or issued. To compensate for the lack of perpetual records, a physical inventory count is taken monthly by the storeroom clerks, who are well supervised. Appropriate procedures are followed in taking the inventory count.
>
> After the physical count, the storeroom supervisor matches quantities counted against a predetermined reorder level. If the count for a given part is below the reorder level, the supervisor enters the part number on a materials requisition list and sends this list to the accounts payable clerk. The accounts payable clerk prepares a purchase order for a predetermined reorder quantity for each part and mails the purchase order to the vendor from whom the part was last purchased.
>
> When ordered materials arrive at Alden, they are received by the storeroom clerks. The clerks count the merchandise and reconcile the counts with the shipper's bill of lading. All vendors' bills of lading are initialed, dated, and filed in the storeroom to serve as receiving reports.

Required
(a) Prepare a logical data flow diagram.
(b) Prepare an analytic flowchart.
(c) Describe the weaknesses in internal control, and recommend improvements of Alden's procedures for the purchase, receipt, storage, and issue of raw materials.

(CPA adapted)

❖ SOLUTION TO REVIEW PROBLEM

(a) See Figure 8.6.
(b) See Figure 8.6.
(c) As follows:

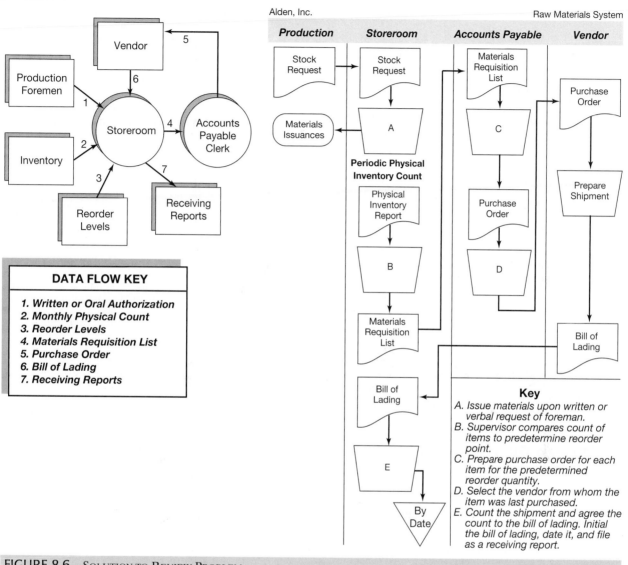

FIGURE 8.6   SOLUTION TO REVIEW PROBLEM.

Weaknesses	Recommended Improvements
1. Raw materials may be removed from the storeroom on oral authorization from one of the production foremen.	1. Raw materials should be removed from the storeroom only on written authorization from an authorized production foreman. The authorization forms should be prenumbered and accounted for, with quantities and job or production numbers listed, and they should be signed and dated.
2. Alden's practice of monthly physical inventory counts does not compensate for the lack of a perpetual inventory system. Quantities on hand at the end of one month may not be sufficient to last until the next month's count. If the company has taken this into account in establishing reorder levels, then it is carrying too large an investment in inventory.	2. A perpetual inventory system should be established under the control of someone other than the storekeepers. The system should include quantities and values for each item of raw material. Total inventory value per the perpetual records should be compared with the general ledger at reasonable intervals. When physical counts are taken, they should be compared with the perpetual records.

Where differences occur, they should be investigated, and if the perpetual records are in error, they should |

3. Raw materials are purchased at a predetermined reorder level and in predetermined quantities. Since production levels often may vary during the year, quantities ordered may be either too small or too great for the current production demands.

4. The accounts payable clerk handles both the purchasing function and the payment of invoices. This is not a satisfactory separation of duties.

5. Raw materials are always purchased from the same vendor.

6. There is no receiving department or receiving report. For proper separation of duties, the individuals responsible for receiving should be separate from the storeroom clerks.

7. There is no inspection department. Since high-cost electronic components usually are required to meet certain specifications, they should be tested for these requirements when received.

be adjusted. Also, controls should be established over obsolescence of stored materials.

3. Requests for purchases of raw materials should come from the production department management and be based on production schedules and quantities on hand per the perpetual records.

4. The purchasing function should be centralized in a separate department. Prenumbered purchase orders should originate from and be controlled by this department. A copy of the purchase order should be sent to the accounting and receiving departments. Consideration should be given to whether the receiving copy should show quantities.

5. The purchasing department should be required to obtain competitive bids on all purchases over a specified amount.

6. A receiving department should be established. Personnel in this department should count or weigh all goods received and prepare a prenumbered receiving report. These reports should be signed, dated, and controlled. Copies should be sent to the accounting department, purchasing department, and storeroom.

7. An inspection department should be established to inspect goods as they are received. Prenumbered inspection reports should be prepared and accounted for. A copy of these reports should be sent to the accounting department.

❖ REVIEW QUESTIONS

1. What is the nature of the procurement business process?
2. Identify the general steps in the procurement process.
3. How does a purchase requisition document differ from a purchase order document?
4. What accounting entry, if any, is necessitated by the issuance of a purchase order?
5. Briefly describe several types of purchase orders that are processed in SAP R/3.
6. Identify and describe three categories of information that SAP R/3 maintains in vendor master records.
7. Identify the two major aspects of the procurement business process.
8. What is the function of a receiving report?
9. What is the invoice verification process?
10. Identify several controls directed at ensuring the integrity of the procurement business process.
11. How might budgetary control be exercised over the procurement business process? Give specific examples.
12. What factors or qualifications might be considered in the implementation of an approved vendors' list?
13. Criticize the following statement: "The major control over cash disbursements is the actual signing of the checks."
14. Identify the major control features in a cash disbursements business process.
15. What is a voucher system?
16. Identify several files that might be kept in a voucher system to provide useful information.
17. What is the major difference between booking invoices on date of approval and booking them on date of payment?
18. Identify several objectives of the human resources business process.
19. Define the term *infotype* as it pertains to SAP R/3 human resources processing.

20. What is the meaning of the term *personnel event* in SAP R/3 human resources processing?
21. What is the basic source of information concerning federal requirements with respect to payroll processing?
22. Identify the major controls in a payroll business process.
23. Identify each of the following forms:
    (a) Form 941
    (b) Form W-2
    (c) Form W-3
    (d) Form 1099-Misc.
    (e) Earnings statement

❖ DISCUSSION QUESTIONS AND PROBLEMS

24. Which of the following procedures provides substantial assurance that invoices are paid for merchandise actually ordered and received in satisfactory condition?
    (a) The purchasing department sends copies of the purchase requisition to the accounts payable department and the supplier.
    (b) The receiving department counts all merchandise received.
    (c) The accounts payable department sends purchase requisitions to the purchasing department and the stores department.
    (d) The accounts payable department matches the purchase requisition, purchase order, receiving report, and invoice.
    (e) The stores department sends copies of the invoices to the receiving department and the insurance department.

    (IIA)

25. Which of the following in an internal control procedure that would prevent a paid disbursement voucher from being presented for payment a second time?
    (a) Vouchers should be prepared by individuals who are responsible for signing disbursement checks.
    (b) Disbursement vouchers should be approved by at least two responsible management officials.
    (c) The date on a disbursement voucher should be within a few days of the date the voucher is presented for payment.
    (d) The official signing the check should compare the check with the voucher and should deface the voucher documents.

    (CPA)

26. An effective internal accounting control measure that protects against the preparation of improper or inaccurate disbursements would be to require that all checks be
    (a) signed by an officer after necessary supporting evidence has been examined.
    (b) reviewed by the treasurer before mailing.
    (c) numbered sequentially and accounted for by internal auditors.
    (d) perforated or otherwise effectively cancelled when they are returned with the bank statement.

    (CPA)

27. Which of the following is an effective internal accounting control over cash payments?
    (a) Signed checks should be mailed under the supervision of the check signer.
    (b) Spoiled checks that have been voided should be disposed of immediately.
    (c) Checks should be prepared only by people responsible for cash receipts and cash disbursements.
    (d) A check-signing machine with two signatures should be used.

    (CPA)

28. In a properly designed accounts payable system, a voucher is prepared after the invoice, purchase order, requisition, and receiving report are verified. The next step in the system is to
    (a) cancel the supporting documents.
    (b) enter the check amount in the check register.
    (c) approve the voucher for payment.
    (d) post the voucher amount to the expense ledger.

    (CPA)

29. For the most effective internal accounting control, monthly bank statements should be received directly from the banks and reviewed by the
    (a) controller.
    (b) cash receipts accountant.
    (c) cash disbursements accountant.
    (d) internal auditor.
                                                                                    (CPA)

30. In a properly designed internal accounting control system, the same employee may be permitted to
    (a) receive and deposit checks and also approve write-offs of customer accounts.
    (b) approve vouchers for payment and also sign checks.
    (c) reconcile the bank statements and also receive and deposit cash.
    (d) sign checks and also cancel supporting documents.
                                                                                    (CPA)

31. In a properly designed internal accounting control system, the same employee should *not* be permitted to
    (a) sign checks and cancel supporting documents.
    (b) receive merchandise and prepare a receiving report.
    (c) prepare disbursement vouchers and sign checks.
    (d) initiate a request to order merchandise and approve merchandise received.
                                                                                    (CPA)

32. For effective internal accounting control, the accounts payable department should compare the information on each vendor's invoice with the
    (a) receiving report and the purchase order.
    (b) receiving report and the voucher.
    (c) vendor's packing slip and the purchase order.
    (d) vendor's packing slip and the voucher.
                                                                                    (CPA)

33. Which of the following is the most effective control procedure to detect vouchers that were prepared for the payment of goods that were *not* received?
    (a) Count goods on receipt in the storeroom.
    (b) Match purchase order, receiving report, and vendor's invoice for each voucher in the accounts payable department.
    (c) Compare goods received with goods requisitioned in the receiving department.
    (d) Verify vouchers for accuracy and approval in the internal audit department.
                                                                                    (CPA)

34. The mailing of disbursement checks and remittance advices should be controlled by the employee who
    (a) signed the checks last.
    (b) approved the vouchers for payment.
    (c) matched the receiving reports, purchase orders, and vendors' invoices.
    (d) verified the mathematical accuracy of the vouchers and remittance advices.
                                                                                    (CPA)

35. To determine whether accounts payable are complete, an auditor performs a test to verify that all merchandise received is recorded. The population of documents for this test consists of all
    (a) vendors' invoices.
    (b) purchase orders.
    (c) receiving reports.
    (d) cancelled checks.
                                                                                    (CPA)

36. Which of the following control procedures is *not* usually performed in the vouchers payable department?
    (a) Determining the mathematical accuracy of the vendor's invoice
    (b) Having an authorized person approve the voucher
    (c) Controlling the mailing of the check and remittance advice
    (d) Matching the receiving report with the purchase order
                                                                                    (CPA)

37. For effective internal control purposes, the vouchers payable department generally should
    (a) stamp, perforate, or otherwise cancel supporting documentation after payment is mailed.
    (b) ascertain that each requisition is approved as to price, quantity, and quality of an authorized employee.
    (c) obliterate the quantity ordered on the receiving department copy of the purchase order.
    (d) establish the agreement of the vendor's invoice with the receiving report and purchase order.

    (CPA)

38. Which of the following procedures in the cash disbursements cycle should *not* be performed by the accounts payable department?
    (a) Comparing the vendor's invoice with the receiving report
    (b) Cancelling supporting documentation after payment
    (c) Verifying the mathematical accuracy of the vendor's invoice
    (d) Signing the voucher for payment by an authorized person

    (CPA)

39. Mailing disbursement checks and remittance advices should be controlled by the employee who
    (a) approves the vouchers for payment.
    (b) matches the receiving reports, purchase orders, and vendors' invoices.
    (c) maintains possession of the mechanical check-signing device.
    (d) signs the checks last.

    (CPA)

40. Matching the supplier's invoice, the purchase order, and the receiving report normally should be the responsibility of the
    (a) warehouse receiving function.
    (b) purchasing function.
    (c) general accounting function.
    (d) treasury function.

    (CPA)

41. To avoid potential errors and irregularities, a well-designed system of internal accounting control in the accounts payable area should include a separation of which of the following functions?
    (a) Cash disbursements and vendor invoice verification
    (b) Vendor invoice verification and merchandise ordering
    (c) Physical handling of merchandise received and preparation of receiving reports
    (d) Check signing and cancellation of payment documentation

    (CPA)

42. It would be appropriate for the payroll accounting department to be responsible for which of the following functions?
    (a) Approving employee time records
    (b) Maintaining records of employment, discharges, and pay increases
    (c) Preparing periodic government reports as to employees' earnings and withholding taxes
    (d) Temporarily retaining unclaimed employee paychecks

    (CPA)

43. Jackson, the purchasing agent of Judd Hardware Wholesalers, has a relative who owns a retail hardware store. Jackson arranged for hardware to be delivered by manufacturers to the retail store on a COD basis, thereby enabling his relative to buy at Judd's wholesale prices. Jackson probably was able to accomplish this because of Judd's poor internal control over
    (a) purchase orders.
    (b) purchase requisitions.
    (c) cash receipts.
    (d) perpetual inventory records.

    (CPA)

44. Which of the following departments should have the responsibility for authorizing payroll rate changes?
    (a) personnel
    (b) payroll
    (c) treasurer
    (d) timekeeping

(CPA)

45. Which of the following constitutes the most significant risk within the purchasing cycle?
    (a) Receiving department personnel sign receiving documents without inspecting or counting the goods.
    (b) Large quantities of relatively inexpensive parts are stored in open areas near workstations to reduce production slowdowns.
    (c) Poor records of transfers between warehouses often result in unnecessary purchases and excess inventories.
    (d) Warehouse personnel do not compare quantities received to quantities shown on transfer tickets.

(IIA)

46. On receipt of a requisition, the stores manager initiates a three-part purchase order. Two copies go to the vendor, and one copy stays in the stores file. On receipt of goods, the stores manager matches the purchase order with the invoice and forwards them to accounts payable for payment. Which of the following statements best describes the internal control over purchasing?
    (a) Adequate internal control exists.
    (b) Inadequate separation of duties exists.
    (c) Inadequate control over accounts payable exists.
    (d) Inadequate control over the requisition process exists.

(IIA)

47. An appropriate compliance test to confirm that only valid employees are on the payroll is to ensure that
    (a) separate personnel folders are originated for each new employee.
    (b) payroll checks are delivered directly to each supervisor by the payroll clerk.
    (c) personnel places names on payroll only on the basis of written, prenumbered authorizations.
    (d) payroll bank accounts are reconciled monthly to appropriate personnel.

(IIA)

48. Which of the following would be the most appropriate test to determine whether purchase orders are being processed on a timely basis?
    (a) Determine the dates of unpaid accounts payable invoices.
    (b) Compare dates of selected purchase orders with those of purchase requisitions.
    (c) Select a block of used purchase order numbers and account for all numbers in the block.
    (d) Discuss processing procedures with operating personnel and observe actual processing of purchases.

(IIA)

49. Which of the following procedures, noted by an auditor during a preliminary survey of the payroll function, indicates inadequate control?
    (a) All changes to payroll data are documented by the personnel department on authorized change forms.
    (b) Prior to distribution, payroll checks are verified to a computer-produced payroll register.
    (c) A separate payroll bank account is used, and payroll checks are signed by the treasurer and distributed by personnel from the treasurer's office.
    (d) All unclaimed payroll checks are returned to the payroll clerk for disposition.

(IIA)

50. Proper internal control over the cash payroll function would mandate which of the following?
    (a) The payroll clerk should fill the envelopes with cash and a computation of the net wages.
    (b) Unclaimed pay envelopes should be retained by the paymaster.

    (c) Each employee should be asked to sign a receipt.

    (d) A separate checking account for payroll should be maintained.

(CPA)

51. A CPA reviews a client's payroll procedures. The CPA would consider internal control to be less than effective if a payroll department supervisor was assigned the responsibility for

    (a) reviewing and approving time reports for subordinate employees.

    (b) distributing payroll checks to employees.

    (c) hiring subordinate employees.

    (d) initiating requests for salary adjustments for subordinate employees.

(CPA)

52. Internal accounting control is strengthened when the quantity of merchandise ordered is omitted from the copy of the purchase order sent to the

    (a) department that initiated the requisition.

    (b) receiving department.

    (c) purchasing agent.

    (d) accounts payable department.

(CPA)

53. Which of the following controls would be most effective in ensuring that recorded purchases are free of material errors?

    (a) The receiving department compares the quantity ordered on purchase orders with the quantity received on receiving reports.

    (b) Vendors' invoices are compared with purchase orders by an employee who is independent of the receiving department.

    (c) Receiving reports require the signature of the individual who authorized the purchase.

    (d) Purchase orders, receiving reports, and vendors' invoices are matched independently in preparing vouchers.

(CPA)

54. The purpose of segregating the duties of hiring personnel and distributing payroll checks is to separate the

    (a) administrative controls from the internal accounting controls.

    (b) human resources function from the controllership function.

    (c) operational responsibility from the record-keeping responsibility.

    (d) authorization of transactions from the custody of related assets.

(CPA)

55. When goods are received, the receiving clerk should match the goods with the

    (a) purchase order and the requisition form.

    (b) vendor's invoice and the receiving report.

    (c) vendor's shipping document and the purchase order.

    (d) receiving report and the vendor's shipping document.

(CPA)

56. Effective internal control procedures over the payroll function may include

    (a) reconciliation of totals on job time tickets with job reports by employees responsible for those specific jobs.

    (b) verification of agreement of job time tickets with employee clock card hours by a payroll department employee.

    (c) preparation of payroll transaction journal entries by an employee who reports to the supervisor of the personnel department.

    (d) custody of rate authorization records by the supervisor of the payroll department.

(CPA)

57. For internal control purposes, which of the following individuals preferably should be responsible for the distribution of payroll checks?

    (a) bookkeeper

    (b) payroll clerk

    (c) cashier

    (d) receptionist

(CPA)

58. The authority to accept incoming goods in receiving should be based on a(an)
    (a) vendor's invoice.
    (b) materials requisition.
    (c) bill of lading.
    (d) approved purchase order.

(CPA)

59. Which of the following procedures most likely would be considered a weakness in an entity's internal controls over payroll?
    (a) A voucher for the amount of the payroll is prepared in the general accounting department based on the payroll department's payroll summary?
    (b) Payroll checks are prepared by the payroll department and signed by the treasurer.
    (c) The employee who distributes payroll checks returns unclaimed payroll checks to the payroll department.
    (d) The personnel department sends employees' termination notices to the payroll department.

(CPA)

60. Indicate the objective of each of the following controls.
    (a) Cancelling paid vouchers by perforating them at the time of payment
    (b) Simultaneously reconciling all bank accounts
    (c) Using prenumbered checks and carefully accounting for used and unused checks
    (d) Maintaining a record of numbers of all stock certificates and bonds
    (e) Periodically comparing personnel department rosters with payroll registers
    (f) Having checks mailed by people other than those causing them to be drawn

61. Indicate the objective of the following questions taken from an internal control checklist.
    (a) Are voided checks mutilated properly and held available for subsequent inspection?
    (b) Is the sequence of check numbers accounted for when reconciling bank accounts?
    (c) Are payroll checks drawn against a separate payroll bank account?
    (d) Are the names of employees hired reported in writing by the personnel office to the payroll department?
    (e) Are payroll checks distributed to employees by someone other than the supervisor?
    (f) Are salary payrolls approved by a responsible official prior to payment?

62. A treasurer insists that invoices be stamped "paid" prior to his actually signing the checks for payment. Discuss the merits of this policy.

63. Discuss the objectives of the following control procedures.
    (a) Purchasing policy manual
    (b) Approved vendors' list
    (c) Request for quotations form
    (d) Vendor rating plans (attribute evaluation)
    (e) Rotation of buyers

64. Identify the objective of distributing copies of a purchase order to the
    (a) requisitioning department.
    (b) receiving department.
    (c) accounting department.

65. What are the differences between approving vendor invoices covering services rendered and those for physical goods sent to an organization? Illustrate with several examples.

66. You have completed an audit of activities within the purchasing department of your company. The department employs 30 buyers, 7 supervisors, a manager, and clerical personnel. Purchases total about $500 million a year. Your audit disclosed the following conditions:
    (a) The company has no formal rules on conflicts of interest. Your analysis produced evidence that one of the 30 buyers in the department owns a substantial interest in a major supplier and that she procures supplies averaging $50,000 a year from that supplier. The prices charged by the supplier are competitive.
    (b) Buyers select proposed sources without submitting the lists of bidders for review. Your tests disclosed no evidence that higher costs were incurred as a result of that practice.
    (c) Buyers who originate written requests for quotations from suppliers receive the suppliers' bids directly from the mailroom. In your test of 100 purchases based on competitive bids, you found that in 75 of the 100 cases, the low bidders were awarded the purchase orders.

(d) Requests to purchase (requisitions) received in the purchasing department from other departments in the company must be signed by persons authorized to do so. Your examination of 200 such requests disclosed that 3, all for small amounts, were not signed properly. The buyer who had issued all three orders honored the requests because he misunderstood the applicable procedure. The clerical personnel charged with reviewing such requests had given them to the buyer in error.

Required

For each of the four conditions, state
(a) the risk, if any, incurred if each condition described above is permitted to continue.
(b) the control, if any, you would recommend to prevent continuation of the condition described.

(IIA)

67. The flowchart in Figure 8.7 was prepared by a CPA to portray the raw materials purchasing function of one of her clients, a medium-sized manufacturing company, from preparing initial documents through vouching for invoices for payment in accounts payable. The flowchart was a portion of the work performed on the audit engagement to evaluate internal control.

Required

Identify and explain the systems and control weaknesses evident from the flowchart. Include the internal control weaknesses resulting from activities performed or not performed. All documents are prenumbered.

(CPA)

68. A company employs about 50 production workers and has the following payroll procedures.

The factory foreman interviews applicants and, on the basis of the interview, either hires or rejects the applicants. When the applicant is hired, he or she prepares a W-4 Form (Employee's Withholding Exemption Certificate) and gives it to the foreman. The foreman writes the hourly rate of pay for the new employee in the corner of the W-4 Form and then gives the form to a payroll clerk as notice that the worker has been employed. The foreman verbally advises the payroll department of rate adjustments.

A supply of blank time cards is kept in a box near the entrance to the factory. Each worker takes a time card on Monday morning, fills in his or her name, and notes in pencil on the time card his or her daily arrival and departure times. At the end of the week, the workers drop the time cards in a box near the door to the factory.

The completed time cards are taken from the box on Monday morning by a payroll clerk. Two payroll clerks divide the cards alphabetically between them, one taking the A to L section of the payroll and the other taking the M to Z section. Each clerk is fully responsible for his or her section of the payroll. He or she computes the gross pay, deductions, and net pay; posts the details to the employee's earnings records; and prepares and numbers the payroll checks. Employees are removed automatically from the payroll when they fail to turn in a time card.

Payroll checks are signed manually by the chief accountant and given to the foreman. The foreman distributes the checks to the workers in the factory and arranges for delivery of the checks to the workers who are absent. The payroll bank account is reconciled by the chief accountant, who also prepares the various quarterly and annual payroll tax reports.

Required

(a) Draw a flowchart of these procedures.
(b) List your suggestions for improving the company's system of internal control for the factory hiring practices and payroll procedures.

(CPA)

69. A CPA's audit working papers contain a narrative description of a segment of the Croyden Factory, Inc., payroll system and an accompanying flowchart as follows:

The internal control system with respect to the personnel department is well functioning and is *not* included in the accompanying flowchart.

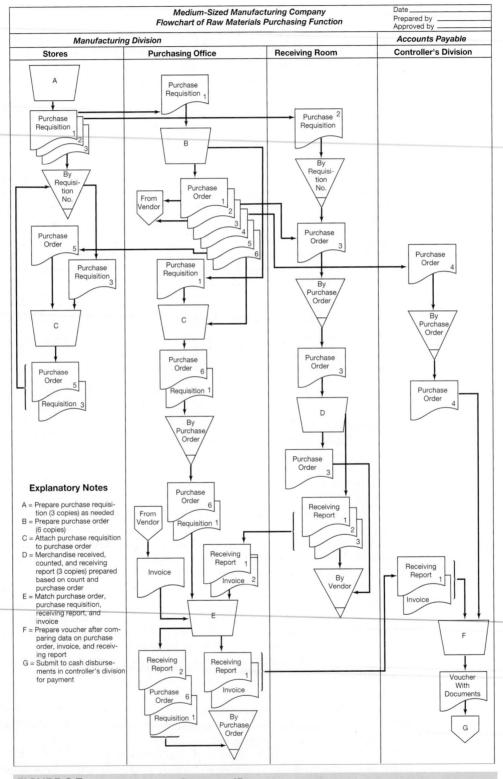

FIGURE 8.7   FLOWCHART FOR PROBLEM 67.

At the beginning of each work week, payroll clerk no. 1 reviews the payroll department files to determine the employment status of factory employees and then prepares time cards and distributes them as each individual arrives at work. This payroll clerk, who is also responsible for custody of the signature stamp machine, verifies the identity of each payee before delivering signed checks to the foreman.

At the end of each work week, the foreman distributes payroll checks for the preceding work week. Concurrent with this activity, the foreman reviews the current week's employee time cards, notes the regular and overtime hours worked on a summary form, and initials the aforementioned time cards. The foreman then delivers all time cards and unclaimed payroll checks to payroll clerk no. 2.

Required

(a) Based on the narrative and Figure 8.8, what are the weaknesses in the system of internal control?

(b) Based on the narrative and Figure 8.8, what inquiries should be made with respect to clarifying the existence of *possible additional weaknesses* in the system of internal control? (*Note:* Do not discuss the internal control system of the personnel department.)

(CPA)

70. The Poster Company is a beauty and barber supplies and equipment distributorship servicing a five-state area. Management generally has been pleased with the overall operations of the company to date. However, the present purchasing system has evolved through practice rather than having been formally designed. Consequently, it is inadequate and needs to be redesigned. A description of the present purchasing system is as follows:

Whenever the quantity of an item is low, the inventory supervisor phones the purchasing department with the item description and quantity to be ordered. A purchase order is prepared in duplicate in the purchasing department. The original is sent to the vendor, and the copy is retained in the purchasing department filed in numerical order. When the shipment arrives, the inventory supervisor sees that each item received is checked off on the packing slip that accompanies the shipment. The packing slip is then forwarded to the accounts payable department. When the invoice arrives, the packing slip is compared with the invoice in the accounts payable department. Once any differences between the packing slip and the invoice are reconciled, a check is drawn for the appropriate amount and is mailed to the vendor with a copy of the invoice. The packing slip is attached to the invoice and filed alphabetically in the paid invoice file.

Required

The Poster Company intends to redesign its purchasing system from the point in time when an item needs to be ordered until payment is made. The system should be designed to ensure that all the proper controls are incorporated into the system.

(a) Identify the internally and externally generated documents that would be required to satisfy the minimum requirements of a basic system, and indicate the number of copies of each document that would be needed.

(b) Explain how all these documents should interrelate and flow among the various departments, including the final destination or file for each copy.

(CMA)

71. The Moran Company is a discount tire dealer that operates 25 retail stores in a metropolitan area. Both private-brand and name-brand tires are sold. The company operates a centralized purchasing and warehousing facility and employs a perpetual inventory system. All purchases of tires and related supplies are placed through the company's central purchasing department to take advantage of quantity discounts. The tires and supplies are received at the central warehouse and distributed to the retail stores as needed. The perpetual inventory system at the central facility maintains current inventory records, designated reorder points, optimal order quantities, and continuous stocktakings for each type of tire and size and other related supplies.

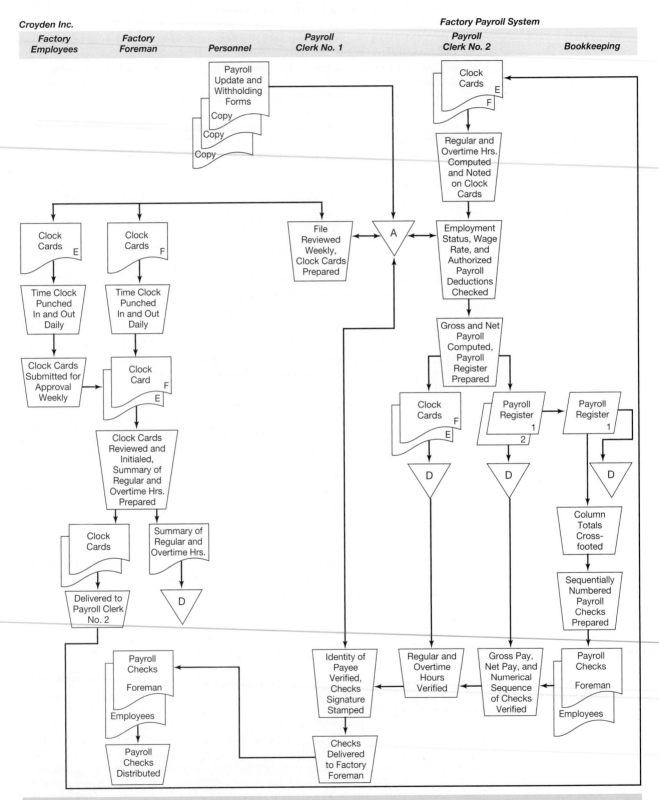

FIGURE 8.8   Flowchart for Problem 69.

The documents employed in the inventory control system and their use are presented below.

Retail stores requisition. This document is submitted by the retail stores to the central warehouse whenever tires or supplies are needed at the stores. The shipping clerks in the warehouse department fill the orders from inventory and have them delivered to the stores.

Purchase requisition. The inventory control clerk in the inventory control department prepares this document when the quantity on hand for an item falls below the designated reorder point. The document is forwarded to the Purchasing Department.

Purchase order. The purchasing department prepares this document when items need to be ordered. The document is submitted to an authorized vendor.

Receiving report. The warehouse department prepares this document when ordered items are received from vendors. The receiving clerk completes the document by indicating the vendor's name, the date the shipment is received, and the quantity of each item received.

Invoice. An invoice is received from vendors specifying the amounts owed by Moran.

The departments involved in Moran's inventory control system are described below.

Inventory control department. This department is responsible for maintaining all perpetual inventory records for all items carried in inventory. This includes current quantity on hand, reorder point, optimal order quantity, and quantity on order for each item carried.

Warehouse department. This department maintains the physical inventory of all items carried in inventory. All orders from vendors are received (receiving clerk) and all distributions to retail stores are filled (shipping clerks) in this department.

Purchasing department. The purchasing department places all orders for items needed by the company.

Accounts payable department. Accounts payable maintains all open accounts with vendors and other creditors. All payments are processed in this department.

Required

Prepare a flow diagram to show how these documents should be coordinated and used among the departments at the central facility of Moran Company to provide adequate internal control over the receipt, issuance, and replenishment of and payment for tires and supplies. Assume that the documents have a sufficient number of copies to ensure that the perpetual inventory system has the necessary basic internal controls.

(CMA)

72. The following is a description of purchasing and accounts payable procedures in effect at the Northwest Manufacturing Company:

> Using departments submit purchase requisitions on prenumbered requisition forms. Each requisition is approved by the using department head, who also indicates the accounting distribution on the requisition form. Two copies are forwarded to the purchasing department, and one copy is filed numerically.
>
> Purchasing accounts for the numerical sequence of requisition forms on receipt. Prenumbered purchase orders are prepared, approved, and distributed: one copy each to the requesting, receiving, and accounts payable departments. Two copies of the purchase order are sent to the vendor, and one copy is filed numerically with the requisition form attached to it. A copy of the requisition is also forwarded to accounts payable.
>
> In the receiving department, counters inspect shipments and record their counts on tally sheets. The counters do not have access to purchase orders. The tally sheets are forwarded to the head of the receiving department. She compares the tally sheets with the purchase orders and prepares a prenumbered receiving report. This report indicates the actual quantity received. Items that are returned to the vendor are indicated on the receiving report, and separate prenumbered debit memos are prepared. The department head accounts for the numerical sequence of receiving reports and debit memos. Goods are transferred to the stores department. Copies of receiving reports and debit memos are sent to the requesting, accounts payable, purchasing, and stores departments. Each of these departments files its copy numerically.

Invoices are routed from the mailroom to the accounts payable department. Clerks compare invoice details with those shown on the purchase order, requisition form, and receiving report and check for mathematical errors. The clerks also account for the numerical sequence of purchase orders and receiving reports.

The clerks withhold invoices until all the preceding documents are received and the matching process is complete. On completion, the clerks assemble the invoice, purchase order, receiving report, and any related debit memos into a voucher package, initial the package, and forward the package to the accounts payable supervisor. The supervisor reviews the package, initials it to indicate approval for payment, indicates the date payment should be made, and forwards the package to the cash disbursements clerk, who then forwards it to data processing. After processing for input, the voucher packages are returned to the accounts payable department.

Checks prepared by data processing are returned to accounts payable, attached to the corresponding voucher package, and submitted to the accounts payable supervisor for a final review before submission to the controller for signature. The controller reviews each voucher package and manually signs the checks. The checks and voucher packages are then sent to the treasurer, who also manually signs the checks. Two signatures are required on all checks. The treasurer's secretary cancels all supporting documents and returns the cancelled documents and the checks to the accounts payable supervisor. The voucher packages are filed by a clerk, who also prepares a data processing input sheet showing payee, check number, amount, and so on. The input sheets are processed to produce the cash disbursements records. The accounts payable supervisor forwards the signed checks to the mailroom.

Freight invoices, which are substantial in total amount, are routed from the mailroom to a clerk, who checks their mathematical accuracy. The freight invoices are then forwarded to the accounts payable supervisor for approval. The supervisor indicates the date payment should be made and then forwards the invoices for check preparation by data processing. At month's end, the cash disbursements book is totaled, and a journal entry is prepared by the cash disbursements clerk. It is approved by the accounts payable supervisor and given to the general ledger clerk for posting. The general ledger clerk is independent of all accounts payable and disbursement functions. Monthly bank statements are sent directly to the accounts payable supervisor, who performs the reconciliation.

Required

(a) Design a flowchart of the present system.
(b) Identify potential internal control weaknesses in the present procedures. Exclude the data processing department's operations in your review. Suggest modifications to present procedures to support your recommendations concerning potential weaknesses.

73. The accounting and internal control procedures relating to purchases of materials by the Branden Company, a medium-sized company that manufactures special machinery to order, have been described by your junior accountant in the following terms.

After approval by manufacturing department supervisors, materials purchase requisitions are forwarded to the purchasing department supervisor, who distributes such requisitions to the several employees under her control. These employees prepare prenumbered purchase orders in triplicate, account for all numbers, and send the original purchase order to the vendor. One copy of the purchase order is sent to the receiving department, where it is used as a receiving report. The other copy is filed in the purchasing department.

When the materials are received, they are moved directly to the storeroom and issued to the supervisors on informal requests. The receiving department sends a receiving report (with its copy of the purchase order attached) to the purchasing department and forwards copies of the receiving report to the storeroom and to the accounting department.

Vendors' invoices for material purchases, received in duplicate in the mailroom, are sent to the purchasing department and directed to the employee who placed the related order. The employee then compares the invoice with the copy of the purchase order on file in the purchasing department for price and terms and compares the invoice quantity received as reported by the shipping and receiving department on its copy of the purchase order. The purchasing department employees also check discounts, footings, and extensions, after which they initial the invoice to indicate approval for payment. The invoice is then submitted to the voucher section of the accounting department, where it is coded for account distribution, assigned a voucher number, entered in the voucher register, and filed according to payment due date.

On payment dates, prenumbered checks are requisitioned by the voucher section from the cashier and prepared except for signature. After the checks are prepared, they are returned to the cashier, who puts them through a check-signing machine, accounts for the sequence of numbers, and passes them to the cash disbursements bookkeeper for entry in the cash disbursements book. The cash disbursements bookkeeper then returns the checks to the voucher section, which then notes payment dates in the voucher register, places the checks in envelopes, and sends them to the mailroom. The vouchers are then filed in numerical sequence. At the end of each month, one of the voucher clerks prepares an adding machine tape of unpaid items in the voucher register and compares the total thereof with the general ledger balance and investigates any difference disclosed by such comparison.

Required

Discuss the weaknesses, if any, in the internal control of Branden's purchasing and subsequent procedures, and suggest supplementary or revised procedures for remedying each weakness with regard to

(a) requisition of materials.
(b) receipt and storage of materials.
(c) functions of the purchasing department.
(d) functions of the accounting department.

(CPA)

74. The mail is opened by an accounting clerk. Vendor invoices are stamped with a voucher stamp and forwarded to the purchasing agent. The purchasing agent matches the receiving report, purchase order, and vendor invoices. He then forwards the combined voucher set to the controller, who reviews the documents, approves them, and records the account coding within the voucher stamp. She then forwards the voucher set to the accounts payable clerk.

The accounts payable clerk records the approved invoices onto an accounts payable vendor card and a purchases journal using a one-write system. The clerk then initials the invoice and files it alphabetically by vendor. At month's end, the clerk prepares an accounts payable aging report and totals the columns in the purchases journal, which is used by the controller for preparing a monthly journal voucher.

The controller uses the accounts payable aging report to indicate those vendors to be paid. In addition, the accounts payable clerk files invoices that contain cash discount terms in a calendar according to due date. The accounts payable clerk manually writes the checks, posts the amounts to the vendor cards, and records the amount in the cash disbursements journal using a one-write system. The clerk then runs the checks through a check protector and forwards them to the check signers.

Two signatures are required. Normally, the controller signs the checks first, followed by the office manager. The checks occasionally are signed in advance by the office manager. Normally, the supporting invoice vouchers are not given to the check signers. The checks are then returned to the accounts payable clerk, who mails them along with any requested remittance advices to the vendors. The clerk then files the vouchers alphabetically in a paid bills file.

Each month the accounts payable clerk receives the bank statement and cancelled checks. Using the cash disbursements journal, the clerk prepares the bank reconciliation and forwards it to the controller for her review and approval.

Required

(a) Prepare a logical data flow diagram of these procedures.

(b) Prepare an analytic flowchart of these procedures.

(c) Identify potential internal control weaknesses in these procedures.

75. ConSport Corporation is a regional wholesaler of sporting goods. The systems flowchart in Figure 8.9 and the following description present ConSport's cash distribution system.

(a) The accounts payable department approves payment of all invoices (I) for the purchase of inventory. Invoices are matched with the purchase requisitions (PR), purchase orders (PO), and receiving reports (RR). The accounts payable clerks focus on vendor name and skim the documents when they are combined.

(b) When all the documents for an invoice are assembled, a two-copy disbursement voucher (DV) is prepared, and the transaction is recorded in the voucher register (VR). The DV and supporting documents are then filed alphabetically by vendor.

(c) A two-copy journal voucher (JV) that summarizes each day's entries in the VR is prepared daily. The first copy is sent to the general ledger department, and the second copy is filed in the accounts payable department by date.

(d) The vendor file is searched daily for the DVs of invoices that are due to be paid. Both copies of DVs that are due to be paid are sent to the treasury department along with the supporting documents. The cashier prepares a check for each vendor, signs the check, and records it in the check register (CR). Copy 1 of the DV is attached to the check copy and filed in check-number order in the treasury department. Copy 2 and the supporting documents are returned to the accounts payable department and filed alphabetically by vendor.

(e) A two-copy JV that summarizes each day's checks is prepared. Copy 1 is sent to the general ledger department, and copy 2 is filed in the treasury department by date.

(f) The cashier receives the monthly bank statement with cancelled checks and prepares the bank reconciliation (BR). If an adjustment is required as a consequence of the BR, a two-copy JV is prepared. Copy 1 is sent to the general ledger department. Copy 2 is attached to copy 1 of the BR and filed by month in the treasury department. Copy 2 of the BR is sent to the internal audit department.

Required

ConSport's cash disbursement system has some weaknesses. Review the cash disbursement system, and for each weakness in the system,

(a) identify where the weakness exists by using the reference number that appears to the left of each symbol.

(b) describe the nature of the weakness.

(c) make a recommendation on how to correct the weakness.

Use the following format in preparing your answer:

REFERENCE NUMBER	NATURE OF WEAKNESS	RECOMMENDATION TO CORRECT WEAKNESS

(CMA)

76. In 2001, XY Company purchased over $10 million of office equipment under its special ordering system, with individual orders ranging from $5,000 to $30,000. Special orders entail low-volume items that have been included in an authorized user's budget. Department heads include in their annual budget requests the types of equipment and their estimated cost. The budget, which limits the types and dollar amounts of office equipment a department head can requisition, is approved at the beginning of the year by the board of directors. Department heads prepare a purchase requisition form for equipment and forward the requisition to the purchasing department. XY's special ordering system functions as follows:

PURCHASING

On receiving a purchase requisition, one of five buyers verifies that the person requesting the equipment is a department head. The buyer then selects the appropriate vendor by searching the various vendor catalogs on file. The buyer then

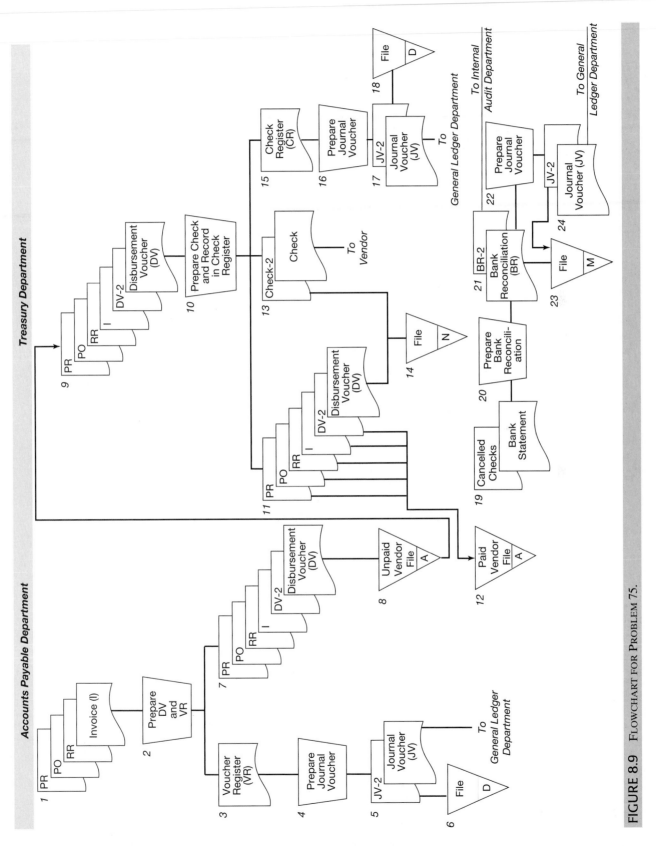

FIGURE 8.9 FLOWCHART FOR PROBLEM 75.

phones the vendor, requesting a price quotation, and gives the vendor a verbal order. A prenumbered purchase order is then processed, with the original sent to the vendor, a copy to the department head, a copy to receiving, a copy to accounts payable, and a copy filed in the open requisition file. When the buyer is orally informed by the receiving department that the item has been received, the buyer transfers the purchase order from the unfilled file to the filled file. Once a month the buyer reviews the unfilled file to follow up and expedite open orders.

RECEIVING

The receiving department receives a copy of the purchase order. When equipment is received, the receiving clerk stamps the purchase order with the date received and, if applicable, in red pen prints any differences between quantity on the purchase order and quantity received. The receiving clerk forwards the stamped purchase order and equipment to the requisitioning department head and orally notifies the purchasing department.

ACCOUNTS PAYABLE

On receipt of a purchase order, the accounts payable clerk files the purchase order in the open purchase order file. When a vendor invoice is received, the invoice is matched with the applicable purchase order, and a payable is set up by debiting the equipment account of the department requesting the items. Unpaid invoices are filed by due date, and at the due date a check is prepared. The invoice and purchase order are filed by purchase order number in a paid invoice file, and then the check is forwarded to the treasurer for signature.

TREASURER

Checks received daily from the accounts payable department are sorted into two groups: those over $10,000 and those of $10,000 and less. Checks for $10,000 or less are machine-signed. The cashier maintains the key and signature plate to the check-signing machine and maintains a record of use of the check-signing machine. All checks over $10,000 are signed by the treasurer or the controller.

Required
Describe the internal accounting control weaknesses relating to purchases and payments of special orders of XY Company for each of the following functions:
(a) purchasing
(b) receiving
(c) accounts payable
(d) treasurer

(CPA)

❖ ANSWERS TO CHAPTER QUIZ

1. d	4. a	7. c	10. a
2. b	5. b	8. d	
3. c	6. a	9. b	

The Production Business Process

LEARNING OBJECTIVES

Careful study of this chapter will enable you to:

❖ Describe transaction cycle controls that are used in the production business process.

❖ Describe the major features of a property accounting business process.

❖ Identify and describe key components of computer-integrated manufacturing (CIM) systems.

❖ Depict the flow of processing necessary to support manufacturing resource planning (MRP II) systems.

❖ Describe why activity-based costing is particularly relevant to CIM systems.

TRANSACTION CYCLE CONTROLS IN THE PRODUCTION BUSINESS PROCESS

Production control, inventory control, cost accounting, and property accounting are typical functions in the production business process of manufacturing firms. Few, if any, production activities exist as separate functions in nonmanufacturing firms, but to some extent most organizations hold some inventories and manage some type of productive activity, such as selling goods or services. Thus the principles of production control are relevant to most organizations.

This section provides an overview of the basic transaction cycle controls that support production control, inventory control, and cost accounting within a manufacturing firm. The discussion includes an overview of the transaction controls relevant to the property accounting business process.

PRODUCTION CONTROL

Cost accounting systems focus on the management of manufacturing inventories: materials, work in process (WIP), and finished goods. **Job costing** is a procedure in which costs are distributed to particular **jobs** or production orders. It requires a production order control system.

In **process costing**, costs are compiled in process or department accounts by periods (day, week, or month). At the end of each period, the cost of each process is divided by the units produced to determine the average cost per unit. Process costing is used where it is not possible or desirable to identify successive jobs or production lots. A classification of processes or departments may be set up for both cost distribution and production reporting purposes. This classification serves the purposes of process cost accounting and repetitive order production control. "Costs" in either job or process costing may be actual costs or standard costs.

Figure 9.1 is a document flowchart of the transaction flows essential to the production control business process. Cost accounting systems encompass both production and inventory control; both are closely related to order-entry, billing, payroll, shipping, and purchasing procedures.

Control over inventories and production is based on separation of functions and basic records and documentation, such as production orders, material requisition forms, and labor time cards. Protection of inventories from physical theft involves security and access provisions as well as periodic physical counts and tests against independent records.

FILES AND REPORTS

Production control involves planning which products to produce and scheduling production to make optimal use of resources. Basic production requirements are provided by the **bill of materials** and the **master operations list**. Detailed material specifications for a product are recorded on the bill of materials. The bill of materials lists all required parts and their descriptions in subassembly order. A master operations list is similar to a bill of materials: Detailed labor operations, their sequencing, and their related machine requirements are specified in the master operations list for a product. The bill of materials and the master operations list are used extensively in the production control function. In a standard cost system, the standard material and labor costs might be included on the bill of materials and master operations list.

Determining what products to manufacture requires an integration of the demand for a product, the product requirements, and the production resources available to the firm. Resources available for production are communicated to the production control function through **inventory status reports** and **factor availability reports**. A raw material status report details the material resources in inventory that are available for production. A factor availability report communicates the availability of labor and machine resources. Demand requirements for a product depend on whether it is custom manufactured per customer order or manufactured routinely for inventory. If the product is manufactured for inventory, production requirements depend on a sales forecast, which may be sent to production control from the sales or marketing department. Sales forecasts must be related to the amount of a product held in inventory. This information is provided in a finished goods status report, which lists the quantities of products in inventory. The integration of all these factors results in a production plan for the organization. The production plan is embodied in a production schedule and production order(s). These documents originate the flow of production data processing.

TRANSACTION FLOWS

The **production order** serves as authorization for the production departments to make certain products. **Materials requisitions** are issued for each production order to authorize the inventory department to release materials to the production departments. The items and quantities shown on a materials requisition are determined from the specifications in the product's bill of materials. Note the flow of the materials requisition and production order in Figure 9.1. The cost accounting function receives a copy of the production order directly from production control as well as from the production departments when

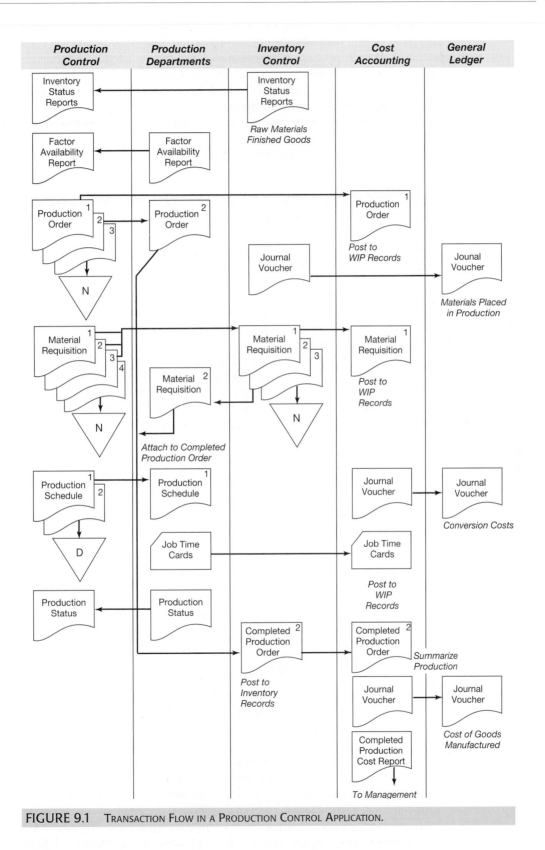

FIGURE 9.1 TRANSACTION FLOW IN A PRODUCTION CONTROL APPLICATION.

the production order is complete. In similar fashion, cost accounting receives copies of materials requisitions from both the inventory control function and the production departments. This distribution of documents implements an adequate segregation of duties and provides accountability for the production departments.

Labor operations are recorded on **job time cards**. These cards are posted to production orders and forwarded to the cost accounting department. The periodic reconciliation of time cards with production labor reports is an important internal control function.

Production status reports are sent periodically from the production departments to the production control function. A production status report details the work completed on individual production orders as they move through the production process. It is used to monitor the status of open production orders and to revise departmental production schedules as necessary.

The central document in the preceding process is the production order. A copy of the production order is used by the cost accounting function to establish a work-in-progress (WIP) record for each job.

COST ACCOUNTING

The cost accounting department is responsible for maintaining a file of WIP cost records. New records are added to this file on receipt of new production orders, initiated by production control. Materials costs are posted to this file from copies of materials requisitions. Direct labor costs are posted from job time tickets. Overhead costs often are applied on the basis of direct labor hours or direct labor costs and, therefore, are posted at the same time as labor costs. Cost accounting initiates a journal voucher reflecting each batch of job time tickets posted that contains a debit to WIP and credits to payroll and manufacturing overhead. This journal voucher is transmitted and posted to the general ledger.

As production orders are completed and goods are transferred to inventory, several documents must be updated. Production control removes the production order from its file of open production orders. Cost accounting closes the related WIP record, summarizes this activity, and communicates a completed production cost summary to various managers. The finished goods inventory records are updated to reflect availability of the product.

Control of production efficiency requires comparisons of actual production with scheduled production and an analysis of related variances. Production control also requires a comparison and analysis of other factors, including budgeted cost versus actual cost for individual production orders and/or departments and facility usage versus facility availability by department. The control of inventory loss and the maintenance of optimal inventory levels are also important to overall production control.

INVENTORY CONTROL

The control of inventories is accomplished through a series of inventory records and reports that provide such information as inventory use, inventory balances, and minimum and maximum levels of stock. Reorder points and procedures are established. A **reorder point** is the level of inventory at which it is desirable to order or produce additional items to avoid an out-of-stock condition. The development of reorder points requires an analysis of product demand, ordering or production setup costs, vendor or production lead time, inventory holding costs, and the costs associated with an out-of-stock condition such as lost sales or inefficient use of production facilities.

Because inventory control aims at minimizing total inventory costs, an important decision to be made is the size of each purchase order quantity, that is, the most

economic order quantity (*EOQ*). The reorder quantity must balance two system costs—total carrying costs and total ordering costs. A formula for calculating the EOQ is

$$\text{EOQ} = \sqrt{\frac{2RS}{PI}}$$

where

EOQ = economic order quantity (units)
R = requirements for the item this period (units)
S = purchasing cost per order
P = unit cost
I = inventory carrying cost per period, expressed as a percentage of the period inventory value

Once the *EOQ* has been calculated, the timing of the order must be decided; that is, the reorder point must be determined. If the order lead time and the inventory usage rate are known, determining the reorder point is straightforward. *Lead time* is the time between placing an order and the receipt of the goods. The *inventory usage rate* is the quantity of the goods used over a period of time. The reorder point should be where the inventory level reaches the number of units that would be consumed during the lead time. In formula form,

Reorder point = lead time $\times$ average inventory usage rate

Perpetual inventory records are the best source of the inventory information necessary to calculate the *EOQ*. The units in the beginning inventory, on order, receipts, issues, and balance on hand should be included in these records. Appropriate control over inventories requires periodic verification of items on hand. This can be done on a rotating basis when perpetual inventory records exist, or it can be done with a periodic physical count.

An important part of inventory control is the evaluation of inventory turnover to determine the age, condition, and status of stock. Special controls should be established to write down obsolete and slow-moving inventory items and to compare the balance with an appropriately established inventory level. A stock status report showing detailed use by period is especially helpful in maintaining the inventory at a proper level and controlling slow-moving items.

Control over inventory includes methods of storing and handling. Items need to be classified and identified properly so that they can be located appropriately and so that proper verification and reporting are possible. The storage and handling of items must provide security against embezzlement, protection against damage or spoilage, avoidance of obsolescence, and assurance of proper control.

Inventory is a substantial investment. An inventory control system should provide status reports on each active product so that the company can reasonably meet customer demands. Because of the large number of inventory items and the variety of transactions affecting them, it is difficult to keep inventory and production information up to date with manual systems. A computerized inventory control system can result in a substantial reduction in inventory investment; these savings include a reduction in inventory without a corresponding decrease in service, determination of economic order quantities and order points, establishment of adequate safety stocks, and forecasts of future demand based on current and past information. Usage records, turnover and obsolescence analyses, reorder points and quantities, and other statistics relevant to inventory control are difficult to generate in purely manual systems.

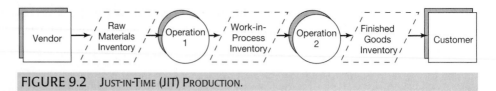

FIGURE 9.2   JUST-IN-TIME (JIT) PRODUCTION.

JUST-IN-TIME (JIT) PRODUCTION

Just-in-time (JIT) production is a term used to describe a production system in which parts are produced only as they are required in subsequent operations. JIT systems differ from conventional production systems in that inventories of work in process, raw materials, and finished goods are minimized or totally eliminated. The JIT concept is illustrated in Figure 9.2. The raw materials inventory, work-in-process inventory, and finished goods inventory are shown as dotted lines to indicate that they are eliminated to the extent possible in JIT production. The terms *minimum inventory production system* (MIPS), *material as needed* (MAN), and *zero inventory production system* (ZIPS) also describe this concept of minimizing inventories.

Inventories serve as a buffer between different operations. Inventories are eliminated by carefully analyzing operations to yield a constant production rate that will balance input and output at the various stages of production. JIT production also emphasizes quality control. Because inventories are minimized, defective production has to be corrected immediately if the constant flow of production is to be sustained. Vendors guarantee timely delivery of defective-free parts that may be placed immediately into production rather than first being placed into raw materials inventory.

The financial benefits of JIT production stem primarily from the overall reduction in inventory levels. This reduces a firm's total investment in inventories. Costs such as handling and storing materials, obsolescence, storage space, and financing charges on total inventory cost are reduced, perhaps significantly. Other benefits include possible lower labor costs as operations are redesigned for constant-flow production, quantity discounts from vendors who in return receive long-term contracts, and increased emphasis on quality production and the corresponding reduction in the cost of waste and spoilage.

PROPERTY ACCOUNTING APPLICATIONS

Property accounting applications concern an organization's fixed assets and investments. An important element of effective internal control is the accurate and timely processing of information relating to fixed assets and investments. Such processing is accomplished through the use of special accounting applications that provide for accounting, operational, and management information needs (see Fig. 9.3).

FIXED ASSETS

There are four objectives of fixed-asset or investment accounting applications:

- Maintain adequate records that identify assets with description, cost, and physical location
- Provide for appropriate depreciation and/or amortization calculations for book and tax purposes
- Provide for reevaluation for insurance and replacement-cost purposes
- Provide management with reports for planning and controlling the individual asset items

Fixed assets are tangible properties such as land, buildings, machinery, equipment, and furniture that are used in the normal conduct of a business. These items are

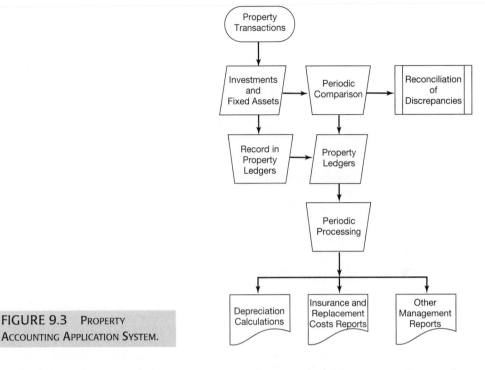

FIGURE 9.3   PROPERTY
ACCOUNTING APPLICATION SYSTEM.

relatively permanent and often represent a company's largest investment. Transactions that change the amount of investment in fixed assets tend to occur infrequently and usually involve relatively large amounts of money.

A company accumulates many assets over the life of the business, disposes of assets (by retirement, sale, or other means), moves assets from one location to another, and matches the costs (other than land) to revenues by means of periodic depreciation charges over the estimated useful life of the asset. To accomplish these tasks efficiently and to provide adequate control, an automated system frequently is required.

Every organization, including those that operate on a cash basis, should keep a ledger of fixed assets as an aid to effective control. A **fixed asset register** is a systematic listing of an organization's fixed assets. A separate section of the fixed-asset register usually is kept for each major category of asset. This categorization should be consistent with the general ledger account descriptions. For example, an organization may have separate ledger accounts for buildings, furniture and fixtures, and automobiles. There would be a separate section for each of these categories. Assets themselves should be labeled with identifiers linked to the fixed-asset register.

When each asset is acquired, it should be tagged and entered in the fixed-asset register. The total dollar amount shown in the register should agree with the general ledger control accounts. For this reason, entries must be made in the fixed-asset register not only to record additions but also to record asset sales or other dispositions.

Several entries must be made when an asset is disposed of. The first records the date of disposal. The second entry removes the original cost of the asset in the current period. A third entry removes the accumulated depreciation taken to date. A fixed-asset register functions as a subsidiary ledger to the corresponding general ledger control accounts.

INVESTMENTS

Investments, like fixed assets, require separate records; typically an investment register is used to provide accounting control over investments. As with all other assets, custody of investments should be separate and distinct from record keeping. The **investment**

register should contain all relevant information, such as certificate numbers and the par value of securities, to facilitate identification and control. All investment transactions should be duly authorized and documented. A common control practice with respect to the physical handling of investment securities is to require two people to be present when the firm's safe deposit box or other depository is entered.

INTERNAL ACCOUNTING CONTROL PRACTICES

The following questions suggest the internal accounting control procedures that would be expected in a property business process.

1. Do procedures require authorization by an official or committee for expenditures (possibly over certain amounts) for
   (a) Capital assets?
   (b) Repairs and maintenance?
2. Are actual expenditures compared with budgets and additional approvals required if budget authorization is exceeded?
3. Do written procedures exist that provide for distinguishing between capital additions and repair and maintenance?
4. Do procedures require formal authorization for the sale, retirement, or scrapping of capital assets?
5. Are property and equipment accounts supported by adequate detailed records?
6. Are these records maintained by people other than those who are responsible for the property?
7. Are the detailed records balanced at least annually with the general ledger controls?
8. Are physical inventories of property taken periodically under the supervision of employees who are not responsible for the custody or recording of such properties?
9. Are periodic appraisals of property made for insurance purposes?
10. Are significant discrepancies between book records and physical inventories reported to management?
11. With regard to small tools,
    (a) Are these physically safeguarded, and is responsibility for them clearly defined?
    (b) Are they issued only on written authorization?

QUICK-RESPONSE MANUFACTURING SYSTEMS

A **computer integrated manufacturing (CIM) system** integrates the physical manufacturing system and the manufacturing resource planning (MRP II) systems. A **quick-response manufacturing system** is a CIM system in which the physical manufacturing system and the manufacturing resource planning (MRP II) systems are integrated with advanced integration technologies (Fig. 9.4). **Advanced integration technologies** consist of electronic data interchange (EDI), automatic identification, and distributed processing.

COMPONENTS OF QUICK-RESPONSE MANUFACTURING SYSTEMS

THE PHYSICAL MANUFACTURING SYSTEM

Two subsystems directly support the physical manufacturing system. These are the **computer-aided design and drafting (CADD)** and the **computer-aided manufacturing (CAM)** systems.

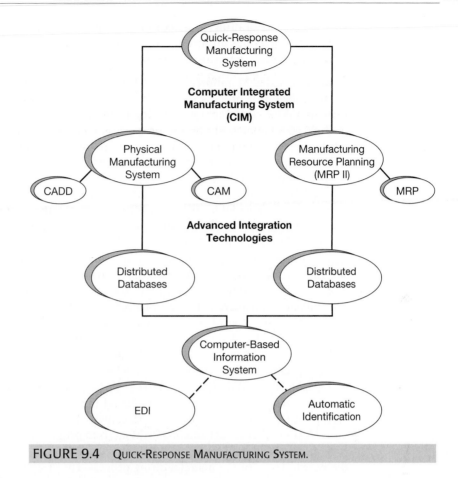

FIGURE 9.4   QUICK-RESPONSE MANUFACTURING SYSTEM.

Computer-Aided Design and Drafting (CADD)   CADD is the use of computer software to perform engineering functions, and it is intended principally to increase the design engineer's productivity. This productivity increase, in turn, allows the organization to be more responsive to market demands for new and improved product offerings. In addition, CADD systems allow the automation of repetitive design tasks, further increasing productivity, as well as accuracy.

Engineers, designers, and drafters work at CADD stations—electronic workstations dedicated to assisting in their jobs. A CADD station usually consists of a monitor with graphics capability, a light pen or mouse for placing lines and other details on the screen, and a plotter or printer for hard copy. Details on the product design are stored by the computer and can be recalled and manipulated by the user.

CADD systems provide several different types of support functions. **Solids modeling** is the mathematical representation of a part as a solid object in computer memory. These models are represented as volumes enclosed by surfaces. Part models can be used to predict properties of finished products, such as weight, stability, or moments of inertia. **Finite element analysis** is a mathematical method used to determine mechanical characteristics, such as stresses of structures under load. The structure is reduced to a network of simple geometric elements, such as rods, shells, or cubes. Each of these elements has stress characteristics that are obtained easily from well-established theory. The behavior of the structure is predicted by having a computer solve a resulting set of simultaneous equations for all elements.

Automated drafting produces engineering drawings and other hard-copy documentation. Drawings are produced by plotting various views of the geometric model previously created and stored in computer memory.

Computer-Aided Manufacturing (CAM)   CAM systems include software for defining the manufacturing process, tools to improve process productivity, decision support systems to aid in control and monitoring of the production process, and in some implementations elements of shop-floor process control such as robotics, programmable logic controllers, and machine vision systems. Such devices might be called *intelligent tools*. In robots or other intelligent tools, the sequence of instructions for guiding equipment through the steps of the manufacturing process is provided by a computer. An **industrial robot** is a device designed to move materials, parts, tools, or specialized devices through variable programmed motions for the performance of a variety of tasks. Industrial robots are flexible manipulators whose actions can be altered through programming rather than mechanical changes.

CAM systems typically include modules to facilitate process planning, line analysis, statistical process control, quality analysis, and maintenance monitoring. On-line process controllers are used to feed back process data to each of these systems for subsequent manipulation and analysis. Process planning considers the sequence of production steps required to make a part from start to finish, generally with successive operations on several machines. The plan that is developed describes the routing through the shop floor and the state of the part at each work center. Logic flow diagrams and information such as part specifications received from a CADD system, tooling requirements, assembling, and machining conditions are used to develop a production sequence for fabricating the part in the fastest, most economical manner. Line analysis for existing manufacturing operations can be used to predict the work centers that require improvement tools.

CAM systems collect and process data from programmable manufacturing processes to provide decision support. The data are used to generate reports and to analyze the performance of the manufacturing process. The system monitors status conditions and processing parameters from production machines, quality gauges, and in-process materials handling systems. The information collected from these systems includes machine status, fault alarms, part counts, machine efficiency, float counts, cycle times, quality levels, and part characteristics. This information is input to production monitoring, quality analysis, and maintenance monitoring systems.

Many CAM systems use statistical process control. **Statistical process control** is used to determine whether a manufacturing process is under control. The process outputs are compared with the engineering specifications. Usually, an average variation value and range from highest to lowest variation are calculated. These values are plotted on control charts and compared with statistical control limits. The process is considered under control when the points fall within the limits and are randomly located around the desired average.

Some CAM systems, called **flexible manufacturing systems (FMS)**, incorporate programmable production processes that can be reconfigured quickly to produce different types of products. An FMS can contribute significantly to the overall speed in which a system responds, for it can greatly speed up time-consuming retooling.

THE MANUFACTURING RESOURCE PLANNING (MRP II) SYSTEM

The **manufacturing resource planning (MRP II) system** consists of the **materials requirements planning (MRP) system** and the related systems for sales, billing, and purchasing. However, the MRP system is the heart of the MRP II system.

Initial applications of computers in manufacturing concentrated on materials control systems. The acronym *MRP* was coined to describe the use of computers in production planning and control systems. MRP systems use the computational ability of

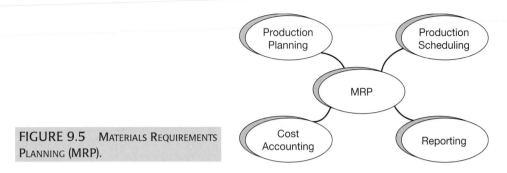

FIGURE 9.5   MATERIALS REQUIREMENTS PLANNING (MRP).

computers to process the vast amount of detailed data necessary to plan and schedule materials usage requirements. The *M* in MRP is used comprehensively to include all inventories—raw materials, work in process, and finished goods. Since work-in-process inventory includes direct labor and overhead costs in addition to raw materials, all manufacturing elements are included in MRP systems. MRP systems integrate four subsystems (Fig. 9.5): production planning, production scheduling, cost accounting, and reporting.

ADVANCED INTEGRATION TECHNOLOGIES

A manufacturing system's flexibility and speed of response depend largely on the degree to which its components are integrated. Automatic identification enhances integration because electronically tagging products and materials effectively makes them machine-readable and thus physically part of the organization's computer-based information system. EDI enhances integration because it effectively integrates the company's system with the systems of its suppliers and customers. Distributed processing enhances integration because it logically and physically combines geographically dispersed information resources into a single coherent system. Each of these integrating technologies is discussed.

Automatic Identification   Automatic identification of production activities is essential to factory automation; thus machine-readable bar codes and scanner technology are indispensable elements. If you look under the hood of a new car, you will see bar-code symbols on many parts, the bar symbol being similar to the bar code that is now commonplace on consumer products. A bar-code symbol for use in factories and warehouses has been developed and standardized, although some large firms use their own unique codes. The bar codes, which are as commonplace on factory goods as they are on consumer goods, allow a computer or robot to identify materials, process information, and initiate whatever procedures are necessary.

A manufacturer can obtain significant benefits by using the standard Uniform Product Code (UPC) bar-code system. UPC coding is as commonplace on commercial products as on consumer products. Products such as General Electric Information Services' *UPC*Express Catalog*, an electronic listing of UPC bar codes, facilitate UPC bar-code identification of products. Without UPC code standardization, one has supplier-assigned numbers for every product as well as customer-assigned numbers for every product. These codes must be cross-referenced during processing, which is both time-consuming and error-prone. With UPC coding, both customer and supplier use the same product code, eliminating cross-referencing problems. UPC coding is **vendor-based coding** that can be applied at any point. Problems with vendor-based coding usually result from different vendors using the same code for different items. UPC assigns a unique six-digit code to each vendor. Thus a duplication problem cannot occur as long as these six unique digits are included in the product code. Using

UPC coding, one no longer has to code one's own inventory because it arrives pre-coded with UPC codes.

EDI   In manufacturing as in most environments, a typical EDI application links a vendor and a customer electronically. EDI thus is a continuation of the integration of computerized applications inherent in CIM. EDI has an impact on manufacturing and inventory efficiency by simplifying the logistical chain of events in placing and filling orders and by making such systems more responsive to current needs. Inventory levels can be reduced simply by using EDI to shorten order filling and placement times. Errors are also reduced. While useful in any type of manufacturing environment, EDI can be a critical component of a JIT manufacturing environment.

UPC bar-code identification of products and scanning technology are essential to obtain maximum benefit from EDI. Commerce is moving toward common pools of information, based on scanned UPC bar codes, that manufacturers, shippers, retailers, banks, and other trading partners can use to track goods and create the necessary documentation. Documents such as invoices will become superfluous as this type of open-flow intercompany exchange of information becomes commonplace.

Distributed Processing   Distributed processing eliminates physical distances in information systems, thus increasing the overall system's responsiveness.

TRANSACTION PROCESSING IN QUICK-RESPONSE MANUFACTURING SYSTEMS

The discussion in this section focuses on transaction flow through the manufacturing process. We concentrate on production planning, production scheduling, cost accounting, and reporting. Activity-based costing and the relationships between JIT and CIM/MRP II are also discussed.

PRODUCTION PLANNING

Production planning involves the determination of which products to produce and the scheduling of production to make optimal use of production resources. The determination of which products to manufacture requires an integration of the demand for a product, its production requirements, and the production resources that are available to the firm.

Figure 9.6 is a diagram of the data flows involved in production planning. Demand requirements for a product depend on whether the item is manufactured per customer order or manufactured routinely for inventory. If the item is manufactured for inventory, production requirements depend on a sales forecast. The sales forecast (data flow 1 in Fig. 9.6) generally will be prepared by the sales or marketing department as part of the firm's budget preparation. On being authorized by management, the sales forecast is sent to the production planning function to indicate the expected demand for products.

The sales forecast must be related to the amount of each product that is currently held in inventory. Such information is provided in a finished goods status report (data flow 2 in Fig. 9.6). A finished goods status report is sent to production planning from inventory control. The finished goods status report lists the quantities of finished product that are in inventory. The amount of resources available for production is communicated to production planning through raw materials status reports (data flow 3 in Fig. 9.6) and factor availability reports (data flow 4 in Fig. 9.6). A raw materials status report details the amount of raw materials available for production. A factor availability report communicates the availability of labor and machine resources.

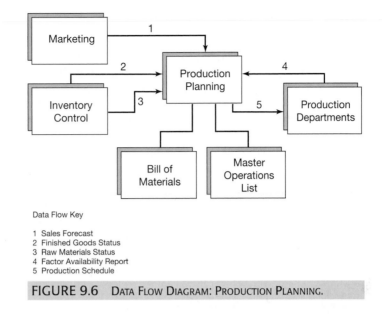

Data Flow Key

1 Sales Forecast
2 Finished Goods Status
3 Raw Materials Status
4 Factor Availability Report
5 Production Schedule

FIGURE 9.6   DATA FLOW DIAGRAM: PRODUCTION PLANNING.

The production requirements of products are specified in a bill-of-materials file and a master operations file. A bill of materials lists the raw materials necessary to produce a product and identifies the part number and quantity of each part used to make a product. A bill of materials provides a structured, level-by-level listing of the components of a product, including part number, part description, and quantity used and a linkage from each level of the assembly to subassemblies and components. In similar fashion, a master operations list identifies and specifies the sequencing of all labor operations and/or machine operations necessary to produce a product. The information contained in both the bill-of-materials file and the master operations file generally will be specified by the engineering or product planning department when a product is first designed.

The integration of all the preceding factors results in a master production plan for the firm. The master production plan is implemented through the issuance and subsequent accounting-for of production orders. Processing of production orders results in a master production schedule (data flow 5 in Fig. 9.6). Generation of the master production schedule is the focal point of MRP systems.

Implementing the Production Plan   Figure 9.7 illustrates the processing required to implement the master production plan. The master production plan is processed against the production status, bill-of-materials, and master operations files. This processing generates production order files, materials requisitions, and routings and also updates the production status file. The *production status file* contains both accounting data and operational data pertaining to the status of production orders. This file integrates production order data pertinent to the stage of completion of projects; the production status file is a major input to the scheduling and cost accounting applications.

The *bill-of-materials file* contains a record for each product manufactured. Each record contains the detailed material requirements and standard material cost of the product identified by the record's key field value. The *master operations file* contains similar data related to each product's detailed labor and machine operation requirements and their sequencing through the production process. Standard times and costs are also contained in the master operations file.

The production planning application program integrates data from the master production plan, bill-of-materials file, and master operations file and generates the necessary

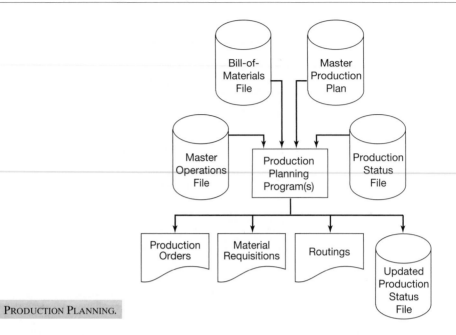

FIGURE 9.7   PRODUCTION PLANNING.

production order documents—detailed production orders, materials requisition forms, and **routings (RTGs)** to guide the flow of production. RTGs indicate the sequence of operations required to manufacture a product. RTGs contain information about the work center, length of time, and tooling required to perform each task. These documents are distributed to the factory departments along with up-to-date production schedules. The production planning application program also updates the production status file. This file contains information found on the production order and establishes a production status (work-in-process) record for each production order. This file is an essential input to the production scheduling and cost accounting applications discussed below.

PRODUCTION SCHEDULING

As Figure 9.7 illustrates, the production status file is updated by the production planning application. The production status file contains a record for each open production order. This file is also used to accumulate both cost and operational data pertinent to production status. It integrates functions relating to production order status and cost accounting. This integration results from use of the production status file in both the scheduling and cost accounting applications.

Production scheduling is detailed in Figure 9.8. RTG data concerning current production status are collected in the factory departments as work progresses. RTG data may be collected in different ways. RTGs may be output as turnaround documents by the production planning application. RTGs are filled in by the factory departments as work progresses on specific production orders. Each RTG contains a production order number and a format for specifying the work completed on an order. A separate RTG might be generated for each specific operation required on a production order. As each operation is completed, the corresponding RTG is completed by adding such information as units produced, scrap count, and actual time required. The RTGs are then forwarded to computer operations for input and processing. Alternatively, RTG data may be input directly from factory operations by having employees use data terminals to input RTG data at the completion of tasks. Employees might enter data such

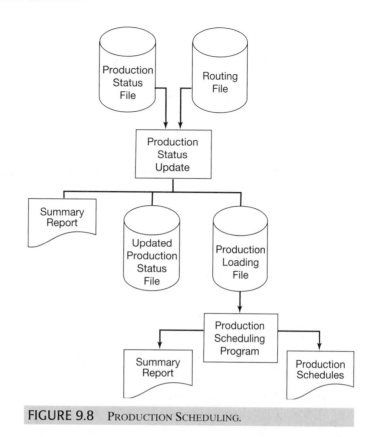

FIGURE 9.8 PRODUCTION SCHEDULING.

as production/work-order code, operation code, employee code, machine/department code, materials-used data, and time accumulated on the task.

CIM architectures provide the ability to tie factory floor machines directly to MRP systems. Automated data collection techniques may be used to electronically collect production data from the shop floor as production occurs. Sensors on production lines may be used to count production or identify completed operations, whereas data-entry stations are used by workers to manually enter codes indicating downtime and other production conditions.

RTG data received from the factory are used to update the production status file. RTG data are posted to the corresponding production order record in the production status file. Outputs of this operation include a summary report, the updated production status file, and a production loading file that details the production requirements associated with open production orders.

The production loading file is the major input to the production-scheduling application. This file is processed by the scheduling application program to produce production schedules. The scheduling application program simply may accumulate and print reports showing total labor and machine operation requirements for each department/work center. In MRP systems, the scheduling application program would include the use of linear programming or other decision support techniques to relate resource availabilities within each department or work center to overall production requirements to generate a schedule that represents an optimal assignment of available resources to production.

COST ACCOUNTING

Figure 9.9 presents a diagram of the cost accounting application within a MRP system. The central feature of the cost accounting application is the updating of the production status (work-in-process) file.

Materials requisitions data are transmitted from the inventory department for processing. Materials requisitions data document the issuance of materials to specific production orders. Job time data and machine time data are included in the RTGs forwarded from the production departments. RTG data show the distribution of labor and machine time to specific production orders within a production department or work center. Both materials requisitions data and RTG data are input to build a production data file. This transaction file is processed by the cost accounting application program, along with the production status file. This processing accumulates material and labor usage shown by materials requisitions data and RTG data and posts them to the work-in-process record maintained for each open production order. Overhead is applied to work in process on the basis of burden rates maintained in the cost accounting program. The program monitors the status of each production order and also prepares a file that summarizes the variances between standard cost and operational data maintained in the work-in-process record and the actual cost and operational data posted to each production order. As orders are completed, the related work-in-process record is closed, and a record is created to update the finished inventory file. The outputs of the cost accounting program include the following items:

- An updated production status file
- A completed production order file
- A resource usage file
- A summary report

The updated production status file contains current information on the status of all open production orders. This file is used in the next cycle of production planning and scheduling. The summary report includes batch and application control information, as

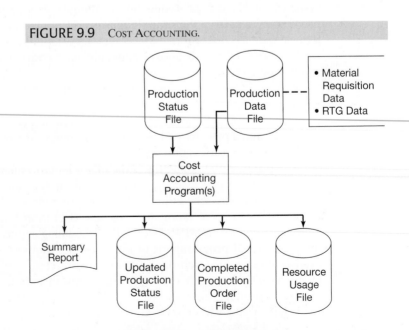

FIGURE 9.9   COST ACCOUNTING.

well as the summary journal-entry data debiting work in process for standard material, labor, and overhead costs; crediting stores, accrued payroll, and applied overhead; and debiting or crediting the necessary variance accounts. The completed production order file and the resource usage file are described in the next section.

REPORTING

The completed production order file lists all cost data for completed production orders. This file is used to update the finished goods inventory file, as shown in Figure 9.10. Outputs of this processing include an updated finished goods inventory file, a finished goods stock status report, a completed production order cost summary, and a summary report that includes batch and application control information as well as the summary journal-entry data debiting finished goods and crediting work in process for the standard cost of goods completed.

The resource usage file that is output from the cost accounting application contains both the actual and standard material, labor, and operation costs for work completed, as shown by the materials requisitions data and RTG data. The standard quantities, times, and costs are copied to this file from the production status file. This file is input to a computer application program that accumulates material and operation costs by department or work center and prints resource usage reports. These reports detail variances between standard and actual cost data. Resource usage reports are distributed to department supervisors to assist in the overall production control function.

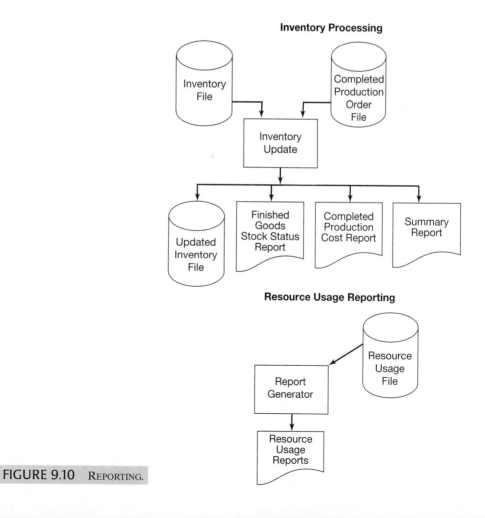

FIGURE 9.10 REPORTING.

ACTIVITY-BASED COSTING

Traditional cost accounting techniques may be inadequate in a CIM environment. Three major elements enter into the cost of manufacturing a product. These are direct materials, direct labor, and overhead. Overhead is best described as the portion of manufacturing cost that is neither direct materials nor direct labor. Overhead costs cannot be identified readily with the manufacturing of specific products; rather, overhead costs are identifiable to the production process itself. In addition to indirect materials and indirect labor, overhead includes such items as factory rent or depreciation, heat, power, insurance, maintenance, supervision, machinery costs, and material handling costs.

CIM Changes Cost-Behavior Patterns   The term *applied overhead* describes the familiar cost accounting technique in which the overhead charge to a product is calculated using a predetermined overhead application rate. Predetermined overhead rates traditionally have been based on either total expected direct labor hours or total expected direct labor cost. A predetermined overhead rate is computed as follows:

$$\text{Predetermined rate} = \frac{\text{budgeted overhead cost}}{\text{budgeted activity}}$$

For example, if overhead is budgeted as $200,000 and activity is budgeted as 5,000 direct labor hours, the predetermined overhead rate would be $200,000 divided by 5,000 hours, a rate of $40 per hour. Predetermined overhead rates may be computed on either a plantwide or a departmental basis. A plantwide rate is a rate that is used throughout the firm. That is, the rate does not differ from one department or division to another. A plantwide rate is usually inappropriate in a large firm that produces a variety of products or services and that has several distinct departments or divisions. In such cases, better control is achieved when overhead costs and activity are budgeted on a departmental or divisional basis.

CIM significantly alters a manufacturer's cost-behavior patterns by causing a substitution of capital equipment for direct labor. Direct labor is reduced, perhaps totally eliminated, as computer-controlled machinery manufactures products. Overhead costs increase, and direct labor costs decrease. The costs of computer-controlled machinery, like the costs of all other capital resources, are indirect rather than direct to production. They are primarily "fixed" relative to the volume of production. Thus CIM causes decreased variable costs by reducing direct labor cost and increasing the fixed costs of production (cost of CIM technology). In addition to equipment costs, many other overhead items may be increased significantly with CIM. Total supervision costs, for example, may increase even though there is less direct labor to supervise. The computer-controlled machinery that replaces workers needs to be "supervised" by skilled technicians, who likely earn significantly higher wages than the employee-oriented supervisors whom they replace.

Traditional cost accounting systems allocate overhead on a single base that all products have in common. This base typically has been direct labor hours or direct labor cost because direct labor was a critical manufacturing component common to all products. However, this method is deficient for a CIM environment because products manufactured with costly automated machinery, which contributes greatly to overhead costs, typically have the lowest number of direct labor hours associated with their production. If direct labor is used to allocate overhead, products that use relatively more manual labor will unfairly be charged more overhead than products that use relatively more automated, high-overhead machinery.

Activity-based costing (ABC) calculates several overhead rates, one for each manufacturing activity, and uses these rates to build product costs from the costs of

Traditional Cost Accounting (single overhead base)		
Overhead	$2,400,000	
Activity Base (labor hours)	100,000	
Rate per labor hour	$24	
	Product A	**Product B**
# Parts	50	100
# Labor Hours	25	20
Material cost	$800	$800
Labor cost ($20 per hour)	$500	$400
Overhead ($24 per hour)	$600	$480
Total cost	$1,900	$1,680

FIGURE 9.11   TRADITIONAL COST ACCOUNTING.

the specific activities undertaken during production. Activities might be machine centers, materials handling, inspection stations, or any other type of manufacturing operation. A single department might contain several different activities. For example, an assembly department where some products are assembled using robotics equipment and other products are assembled manually might have two activities, robotics and manual assembly. Different overhead bases then could be used to more accurately assign these different activity costs to products.

Figures 9.11 and 9.12 provide an illustration. Figure 9.11 shows the costing of products A and B in a traditional cost accounting system where all overhead is allocated to

Activity-Based Cost Accounting (several overhead bases)		
	Robotic Assembly	All Other
Overhead	$400,000	$2,000,000
Activity	40,000 (parts)	100,000 (hours)
Rates	$10 per part	$20 per hour
	Product A	**Product B**
# Parts	50	100
# Labor Hours	25	20
Material cost	$800	$800
Labor cost ($20 per hour)	$500	$400
Overhead ($10 per part)	$500	$1,000
Overhead ($20 per hour)	$500	$400
Total cost	$2,300	$2,600

FIGURE 9.12   ACTIVITY-BASED COST ACCOUNTING.

products on the basis of direct labor hours. Note that product A, which requires 5 more hours of direct labor, costs more to produce than product B. Product B, however, requires more parts than product A, which means that product B requires relatively more use of high-overhead robotics equipment during assembly.

Figure 9.12 shows the costing of the same two products in an activity-based cost accounting system where robotics equipment is identified as a separate activity. Several different overhead bases are used. Robotics equipment overhead is allocated to products on the basis of the number of parts in a product. All other overhead is allocated on the basis of direct labor hours. Note that product B, which requires 50 more parts, costs more to produce than product A according to the activity-based cost accounting system.

Cost Drivers   A **cost driver** is an element that influences the total cost of an activity. Typically, several cost drivers influence the total cost of an activity. Materials handling costs are influenced by the total number of items handled, the types of items handled (i.e., small, big and heavy, hazardous, etc.), the type of equipment used, and worker efficiency, to name just a few examples. Cost drivers might be measured by production volume, number of employees, number of forms completed, or number of parts in a product. Time-in-process measures, such as direct labor hours, machine hours, or clock time, are used frequently as cost drivers.

The significance of activity-based costing as a management tool depends largely on the accuracy of the cost drivers selected as the allocation bases for activity costs. The most benefit is obtained when the principal cost driver for an activity is selected as the overhead allocation base for that activity. This then links cost incurrence to product costing, and meaningful managerial decisions may be based on product cost information. Statistical regression analysis often is used as a means for identifying cost drivers.

MRP II versus MRP

An MRP II system includes the major processing modules of MRP (Fig. 9.13). The bill-of-materials module is used to communicate the structure of a product, as in MRP. Extensions to bill-of-materials processing in MRP II might include maintenance of engineering/product drawings from a CADD system. The routings file module indicates the sequence of operations required to manufacture a component or assembly, as in MRP. Extensions to routings file processing in MRP II might include expanded information concerning work center capacity data, maintenance of machine tooling data, and maintenance of numerical machine control data from the CADD system. The master production scheduling module maintains the assembly schedule for specific configurations, quantities, and dates based on product mix and material availability, much as in MRP. A production order module releases orders for manufacturing after evaluating materials, capacity, and tooling availability. If availability is adequate, a packet is prepared

FIGURE 9.13   Major Processing Modules in MRP II.

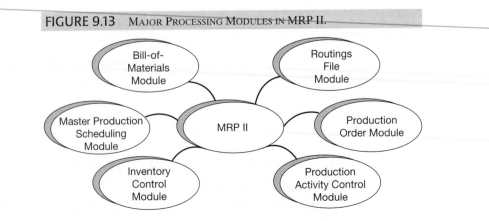

that contains the order, materials list, routing, and drawing information, much as in MRP. The packet is forwarded to the plant floor. Extensions to production order processing in MRP II might include the creation of transaction files and numerical machine control tapes for the plant floor. As in MRP, an inventory control module maintains accurate and timely status of on-hand balances. To maintain accuracy, techniques such as obsolescence analysis and cycle counting should be implemented to ensure accuracy on a continual basis. Finally, a production activity control module is used to implement the production plan developed in the master production scheduling module. As in MRP, this module reduces delays and waiting time by effective monitoring and feedback of production and shop-floor status data. Typical functions include attendance reporting, collecting direct labor and machine hours, and revising production status and priority data based on actual use of materials, labor, and machine resources.

IMPLEMENTING JIT IN A MRP II/CIM ENVIRONMENT

In a batch production environment, manufacture of specific products is sporadic. Batches of similar products are assembled periodically to satisfy present and planned future needs. Setup costs usually are incurred every time a batch is produced, and these costs are typically the same regardless of the proposed size of the batch production run. As the word *planned* indicates, a batch environment fosters a "push" concept of manufacturing efficiency. Economic (i.e., efficient) batch size is derived by using formulas (i.e., economic order quantity models) or is output from a computer simulation or computational model.

MRP II is directed at the synchronization and scheduling of the types of events that occur in batch environments. Batch size is determined from the production planning module. The scheduling module organizes and/or optimizes the timing of events necessary for production. The bill-of-materials module is used to forecast materials requirements and so on until the actual production orders are issued.

A JIT manufacturing environment is a continuous-flow environment. A JIT environment requires economical production of small lots—essentially the operation of production on a continuous basis—to minimize or totally eliminate inventories. JIT advocates the elimination of waste in the manufacturing process and stresses continuous improvement in operation. In a JIT environment, products are manufactured under a "pull" concept. Production occurs only when it is needed to fill a customer order. In contrast to a batch environment, there is no advance scheduling in a JIT environment. The customer order "pulls" product from the production line; in effect, demand schedules production. This type of operation requires rapid setups, high-quality production, continuous elimination of wasted motion, and inventory flow improvements.

As a manufacturer moves from a batch to a JIT continuous-flow manufacturing environment, less emphasis might be placed on a complete MRP II system. The de-emphasis on advanced scheduling in JIT and the associated reduction in inventories eliminate much data and computation toward which MRP II is directed. However, many aspects of MRP II might be used. Scheduling modules might generate level production schedules. Materials requirements planning might generate estimated procurement quantities to support the demand-pull system. CADD and CAM applications can support quality requirements by allowing greater amounts of process control technology on the plant floor. Adaptive, self-correcting decision support systems can become an integral part of the manufacturing process. Statistical process controls can monitor production to ensure that products are produced within quality control limits.

SPECIAL INTERNAL CONTROL CONSIDERATIONS

Quick-response manufacturing systems, similar to other totally computerized systems, intensify certain internal control problems. Transactions may be processed without human intervention or approval. This eliminates conventional controls associated with separation of duties in transactions. Thus a major consideration is to ensure that such controls, or their equivalents, are an integral part of a quick-response manufacturing system. Computer processing in general and EDI in particular eliminate human-oriented paper documents. However, challenging validation and authenticity problems are encountered in the operation of paperless processing systems, both within a firm (e.g., electronic production order) and in its exchanges with its trading partners (EDI and EFT).

Extensive control and audit trails may be implemented in quick-response manufacturing systems, but these features must be included within the design and development of the system. It is neither feasible nor desirable to install controls in a computer-based information system after it has been implemented. Programmed controls and audit trails can be highly effective, but their integrity must be established during system development. A control may look good on paper, but it will be ineffectual if its operation is programmed incorrectly. Also, a programmer might deliberately code a program incorrectly. Thus internal controls over system operation must be complemented with increased control over the systems development process. Audit trail and control techniques such as transaction logs and programmed edit checks require extra developmental resources and extra processing. The costs of their use must be balanced against overall system objectives. Because audit trails and controls require direct and obvious expenditures, underusage is perhaps more likely than overusage.

Systems development is a major concern in any computer-based system, but systems development is mission-critical in quick-response manufacturing systems. A major deterrent to the proliferation of automation in factories is the same one that has plagued the application of computers to other application areas—programming and software. The lack of *turnkey systems*—robots or other automated tools that can be bought and immediately turned on and used—has constrained the application of hardware technology that has been available for years. The same types of systems development problems that occur in information systems development occur in the application of computers to production processes. The cost of programming an industrial robot, which frequently involves extensive engineering or systems development, easily can exceed the purchase cost of the robot system.

❖ SUMMARY

Production control, inventory control, and property accounting are typical business processes in manufacturing firms. A production control business process plans and schedules production and issues production orders to authorize production activities. Materials requisition forms and job time cards are used to trace production costs to individual production orders. Transaction cycle controls in the production business process include a separation of the following functions: production control, the production departments, inventory control, cost accounting, and the general ledger.

Inventory control is accomplished through a series of records and reports that provide information concerning inventory use and inventory balances. Perpetual inventory records are the best source of inventory information. The storage and handling of inventory items must provide assurance of adequate control.

Property accounting business processes concern an organization's fixed assets and investments. Property accounting applications maintain records that identify an organization's fixed assets and investments, provide for appropriate depreciation and/or amortization for book and tax purposes, provide information for insurance purposes, and provide information to management concerning use and availability of an organization's fixed assets and investments.

Computer-integrated manufacturing (CIM) is an integrated approach to the use of information technology in manufacturing enterprises. Components of a CIM system typically include CADD workstations, real-time production monitoring and control systems, and order and inventory control systems. CIM components are connected by a network and equipped with software systems designed to support distributed operation. CIM can support product evolution from initial design and drafting through planning to manufacturing and assembly while also incorporating management accounting systems. CIM reduces information costs and, through EDI, brings the producer, the supplier, and the customer closer together.

❖ GLOSSARY

activity-based costing (ABC): a system that calculates several overhead rates, one for each manufacturing activity, and uses these rates to build product costs from the costs of the specific activities undertaken during production.

advanced integration technologies (AIT): consist of EDI, automatic identification, and distributed processing.

bill of materials: lists the raw materials necessary to produce a product.

computer-aided design and drafting (CADD): the use of computer software to perform engineering functions.

computer-aided manufacturing (CAM): includes software for defining the manufacturing process, tools to improve process productivity, and decision-support systems to aid in the control and monitoring of the production process.

computer-integrated manufacturing (CIM) system: integrates the physical manufacturing system and the manufacturing resource planning (MRP II) systems.

cost driver: an element that influences the total cost of an activity.

economic order quantity (EOQ): the order quantity that minimizes total inventory cost.

factor availability reports: report that communicate the availability of labor and machine resources.

finite element analysis: a mathematical method used to determine mechanical characteristics, such as stresses of structures under load.

fixed-asset register: a systematic list of fixed assets maintained for control purposes.

flexible manufacturing system (FMS): a CAM system that incorporates programmable production processes that can be reconfigured quickly to produce different types of products.

industrial robot: a device designed to move materials, parts, tools, or specialized devices through variable programmed motions for the performance of a variety of tasks.

inventory status reports: reports that detail the resources available in inventory.

investment register: a systematic list of investments maintained for control purposes.

job: synonym for production order.

job costing: production costs are assigned to production orders.

job time cards: used to document the amount of labor time spent working on each production order (job).

just-in-time (JIT) production: a system in which items are produced only as they are required in subsequent operations.

manufacturing resource planning (MRP II) system: comprises the materials requirements planning (MRP) system and the related systems for sales, billing, and purchasing.

master operations list: identifies and specifies the sequencing of all labor operations and/or machine operations necessary to produce a product.

materials requirements planning (MRP) system: the use of computers in production planning and control systems, particularly applications in materials control systems.

materials requisitions: documents that authorize the release of raw materials to the production departments.

process costing: production costs are compiled by department rather than by job.

production order: document that authorizes the production departments to make certain products.

quick-response manufacturing system: a CIM system in which the physical manufacturing system and the manufacturing resource planning (MRP II) systems are integrated with advanced integration technologies (AIT).

reorder point: the level of inventory at which it is desirable to order or produce additional items to avoid an out-of-stock condition.

routings (RTGs): documents that indicate the sequence of operations required to manufacture a product.

solids modeling: the mathematical representation of a part as a solid object in computer memory.

statistical process control: procedures used to determine whether a manufacturing process is under control, which involve comparing process outputs to engineering specifications.

vendor-based coding: having a purchaser (i.e., retailer) use a vendor's product codes as its own product codes for the same products.

❖ CHAPTER QUIZ

Answers to the chapter quiz appear on page 351.

1. In a production control application system, which of the following documents serves as authorization to release raw materials to the production departments?
    (a) production order
    (b) job time card
    (c) journal voucher
    (d) material requisition

2. In a production control application system, which of the following departments should receive copies of production orders?
    (a) inventory control
    (b) cost accounting
    (c) purchasing
    (d) general ledger

3. In a production control application system, which of the following documents serves as authorization to the production departments to make certain products?
    (a) production order
    (b) job time card
    (c) material requisition
    (d) journal voucher

4. Which of the following is a characteristic associated with just-in-time (JIT) production?
    (a) Parts are produced only as they are required in subsequent operations
    (b) A constant-flow production rate
    (c) Both a and b
    (d) Neither a nor b

5. Which of the following is an element of CADD technology?
    (a) solids modeling
    (b) statistical process control
    (c) both a and b
    (d) neither a nor b

6. (_____) integrates the physical manufacturing system and the manufacturing resource planning (MRP II) systems.
    (a) MRP
    (b) AIT
    (c) CIM
    (d) RTG

7. In a production planning system, the bill-of-materials file would be an input to which of the following?
    (a) production planning program(s)
    (b) cost accounting program(s)
    (c) both a and b
    (d) neither a nor b

8. In a production planning system, the production status file would be an input to which of the following?
    (a) production planning program(s)
    (b) inventory update program(s)
    (c) both a and b
    (d) neither a nor b

9. In a production planning system, the master operations file would be an input to which of the following?
    (a) cost accounting program(s)
    (b) inventory update program(s)
    (c) both a and b
    (d) neither a nor b

10. Cost drivers for activity-based costing might be identified with (_____).
    (a) solids modeling
    (b) finite element analysis
    (c) statistical regression
    (d) statistical process control

❖ REVIEW PROBLEM

CIM architectures provide the ability to tie factory-floor operations directly to computer-based information systems. Automated source data collection techniques may be used to electronically collect production data from the shop floor as production occurs. Sensors on production lines may be used to count production or identify completed operations, whereas data-entry stations are used by workers to manually enter data concerning completed operations.

Required
(a) What types of data might be entered by production workers concerning completed operations?
(b) Describe programmed edit checks that might be made on the data indicated in part a.
(c) Assume that all necessary files are direct-access organization. What on-line processing might result from a worker entering data on completed operations?

❖ SOLUTION TO REVIEW PROBLEM

(a) Workers might enter the following types of data at the completion of an operation:
    1. Production/work order code
    2. Operation code
    3. Worker code
    4. Machine/department code
    5. Materials used data
    6. Time accumulated on the task
(b) Possible edit checks include
    1. Label check on files
    2. Data access matrix to verify worker authorization
    3. Check-digit verification where appropriate
    4. Valid code checks
    5. Limit tests where appropriate
    6. Validity check on operation code entered relative to the production order file
(c) The following files might be updated to reflect the data entered:
    1. Raw materials inventory file
    2. Finished goods inventory file
    3. Production order (work-in-process) file
    4. Production scheduling file
    5. Employee data file (a production scheduling file for workers)
    6. Summary costing files

❖ REVIEW QUESTIONS

1. Distinguish between job-order costing and process costing.
2. Identify the accounting journal entries that summarize the activities involved in a manufacturing operation.
3. What is a bill of materials? A reorder point? A reorder quantity? A master operations list?
4. Identify the main features of control over inventories and production.
5. What information might be included on a production order? Identify the source(s) of this information. To whom should copies of production orders be distributed?
6. Identify the major features of just-in-time (JIT) production.
7. What are the objectives of a fixed-asset or investment accounting system?
8. Identify several controls relevant to fixed assets and investments.

9. What accounting entries are required when fixed assets are disposed of?
10. Identify and describe key components of computer-integrated manufacturing (CIM) systems.
11. Distinguish between MRP and MRP II.
12. Describe several different types of support functions that typically are provided by CADD.
13. Describe support functions that typically are provided by CAM.
14. Describe several uses of automatic identification in production activities.
15. Describe the flow of processing necessary to support manufacturing resource planning (MRP II) systems.
16. What is activity-based costing (ABC)? Why is ABC particularly relevant to CIM systems?

❖ DISCUSSION QUESTIONS AND PROBLEMS

17. For several years a client's physical inventory count has been lower than what was shown on the books at the time of the count, requiring downward adjustments to the inventory account. Contributing to the inventory problem could be weaknesses in internal control that led to the failure to record some
    (a) purchases returned to vendors.
    (b) sales returns received.
    (c) sales discounts allowed.
    (d) cash purchases.
                                                                                              (CPA)

18. Ball Company, which has no perpetual inventory records, takes a monthly physical inventory and reorders any item that is less than its reorder point. On February 5, 20XX, Ball ordered 5,000 units of item A. On February 6, 20XX, Ball received 5,000 units of item A, which had been ordered on January 3, 20XX. To prevent this excess ordering, Ball should
    (a) keep an adequate record of open purchase orders and review it before ordering.
    (b) use perpetual inventory records that indicate goods received, issued, and amounts on hand.
    (c) use prenumbered purchase orders.
    (d) prepare purchase orders only on the basis of purchase requisitions.
                                                                                              (CPA)

19. Sanbor Corporation has an inventory of parts consisting of thousands of different items of small value individually but significant in total. Sanbor could establish effective internal accounting control over the parts by requiring
    (a) approval of requisitions for inventory parts by a company officer.
    (b) maintenance of inventory records for all parts included in the inventory.
    (c) physical counts of the parts on a cycle basis rather than at year end.
    (d) separation of the store-keeping function from the production and inventory record-keeping functions.
                                                                                              (CPA)

20. To achieve effective internal accounting control over fixed-asset additions, a company should establish procedures that require
    (a) capitalization of the cost of fixed-asset additions in excess of a specific dollar amount.
    (b) performance of recurring fixed-asset maintenance work solely by maintenance department employees.
    (c) classifying as investments those fixed-asset additions that are not used in the business.
    (d) authorization and approval of major fixed-asset additions.
                                                                                              (CPA)

21. Which of the following is the *most important* internal control over acquisitions of property, plant, and equipment?
    (a) Establishing a written company policy distinguishing between capital and revenue expenditures
    (b) Using a budget to forecast and control acquisitions and retirements
    (c) Analyzing monthly variances between authorized expenditures and actual costs
    (d) Requiring acquisitions to be made by user departments
                                                                                              (CPA)

22. Which of the following is an internal accounting control weakness related to factory equipment?
    (a) Checks issued in payment of purchases of equipment are *not* signed by the controller.
    (b) All purchases of factory equipment are required to be made by the department in need of the equipment.
    (c) Factory equipment replacements generally are made when estimated useful lives, as indicated in depreciation schedules, have expired.
    (d) Proceeds from sales of fully depreciated equipment are credited to other income.

    (CPA)

23. Which of the following internal accounting control procedures could best prevent direct labor from being charged to manufacturing overhead?
    (a) Reconciliation of work-in-process inventory with cost records
    (b) Comparison of daily journal entries with the factory labor summary
    (c) Comparison of periodic cost budgets and time cards
    (d) Reconciliation of unfinished job summary and production cost records

    (CPA)

24. Which of the following is a question the auditor would expect to find on the production cycle section of an internal accounting control questionnaire?
    (a) Are vendors' invoices for raw materials approved for payment by an employee who is independent of the cash disbursements function?
    (b) Are signed checks for the purchase of raw materials mailed directly after signing without being returned to the person who authorized the invoice processing?
    (c) Are all releases by storekeepers of raw materials from storage based on approved requisition documents?
    (d) Are details of individual disbursements for raw materials balanced with the total to be posted to the appropriate general ledger account?

    (CPA)

25. Which of the following is the *most important* element of internal control relating to the raw materials inventory of a manufacturing company?
    (a) The physical inventory count should be made by personnel independent of the inventory custodians.
    (b) Materials from vendors should be received directly by the production department that will be using the materials.
    (c) Shortages in shipments from vendors should be reported immediately to the production department that will be using the materials.
    (d) Issues from inventory should be supported by sales invoices.

    (IIA)

26. A well-functioning system of internal control over the inventory/production functions would provide that finished goods are to be accepted for stock only after presentation of a completed production order and a(n)
    (a) shipping order.
    (b) materials requisition.
    (c) bill of lading.
    (d) inspection report.

    (CPA)

27. If preparation of a periodic scrap report is essential in order to maintain adequate control over the manufacturing process, the data for this report should be accumulated in the
    (a) accounting department.
    (b) production department.
    (c) warehousing department.
    (d) budget department.

    (CPA)

28. Which of the following control procedures *most likely* would be used to maintain accurate perpetual inventory records?
    (a) Independent storeroom count of goods received
    (b) Periodic independent reconciliation of control and subsidiary records

    (c) Periodic independent comparison of records with goods on hand

    (d) Independent matching of purchase orders, receiving reports, and vendors' invoices

(CPA)

29. Which of the following procedures is *most likely* to prevent the improper disposition of equipment?

    (a) A separation of duties between those authorized to dispose of equipment and those authorized to approve removal work orders

    (b) The use of serial numbers to identify equipment that could be sold

    (c) Periodic comparison of removal work orders to authorizing documentation

    (d) A periodic analysis of the scrap sales and the repairs and maintenance accounts

(CPA)

30. Which of the following controls would be *most effective* in ensuring that the proper custody of assets in the investing cycle is maintained?

    (a) Direct access to securities in the safety deposit box is limited to only one corporate officer.

    (b) Personnel who post investment transactions to the general ledger are *not* permitted to update the investment subsidiary ledger.

    (c) The purchase and sale of investments are executed on the specific authorization of the board of directors.

    (d) The recorded balances in the investment subsidiary ledger are compared periodically with the contents of the safety deposit box by independent personnel.

(CPA)

31. The objectives of the internal control structure for a production cycle are to provide assurance that transactions are executed and recorded properly and that

    (a) independent internal verification of activity reports is established.

    (b) transfers to finished goods are documented by a completed production report and a quality control report.

    (c) production orders are prenumbered and signed by a supervisor.

    (d) custody of work in process and of finished goods is properly maintained.

(CPA)

32. Independent internal verification of inventory occurs when employees who

    (a) issue raw materials obtain materials requisitions for each issue and prepare daily totals of materials issued.

    (b) compare records of goods on hand with physical quantities do *not* maintain the records or have custody of the inventory.

    (c) obtain receipts for the transfer of completed work to finished goods prepare a completed production report.

    (d) are independent of issuing production orders update records from completed job cost sheets and production cost reports on a timely basis.

(CPA)

33. Hermit Company manufactures a line of walnut office products. Hermit executives estimate the demand for the double walnut letter tray, one of the company's products, at 6,000 units. The letter tray sells for $80 per unit. The costs relating to the letter tray are estimated to be as follows for 20XX:

    (a) Standard manufacturing cost per letter tray unit—$50

    (b) Costs to initiate production run—$300

    (c) Annual cost of carrying the letter tray in inventory—20 percent of standard manufacturing cost

    In prior years, Hermit Company has scheduled the production for the letter tray in two equal production runs. The company is aware that the economic order quantity (EOQ) model can be employed to determine optimal size for production runs. The EOQ formula as it applies to inventories for determining the optimal order quantity is as follows:

$$EOQ = \sqrt{\frac{2(\text{annual demand})(\text{cost per order})}{(\text{cost per unit})(\text{carrying cost})}}$$

Required

Calculate the expected annual cost savings Hermit Company could experience if it employed the economic order quantity model to determine the number of production runs that should be initiated during the year for the manufacture of the double walnut letter trays.

(CMA)

34. State why each of the following changes would affect (i) reorder point and (ii) economic order quantity, and state whether the effect would be an increase or a decrease in quantity.
    (a) Increase in demand for an inventory stock item.
    (b) Decrease in the cost of capital to the firm holding the inventory.
    (c) Increase in salaries in the purchasing and receiving departments.

(IIA)

35. Valpaige Company is an industrial machinery and equipment manufacturer with several production departments. The company employs automated and heavy equipment in its production departments. Consequently, Valpaige has a large repair and maintenance department (R&M) for servicing this equipment.

    The operating efficiency of R&M has deteriorated over the past 2 years. Further, R&M costs seem to be climbing more rapidly than other department costs. The assistant controller has reviewed the operations of R&M and has concluded that the administrative procedures used since the early days of the department are outmoded due in part to the growth of the company. The two major causes for the deterioration, in the opinion of the assistant controller, are an antiquated scheduling system for R&M work and the actual cost system to distribute R&M's costs to the production departments. The actual costs of R&M are allocated monthly to the production departments on the basis of the number of service calls made during each month.

    The assistant controller has proposed that a formal work order system be implemented for R&M. The production departments would submit a service request to R&M for the repairs and/or maintenance to be completed, including a suggested time for having the work done. The supervisor of R&M would prepare a cost estimate on the service request for the work required (labor and materials) and indicate a suggested time for completing the work on the service request. R&M's supervisor would return the request to the production department that initiated the request. Once the production department okays the work by returning a copy of the service request, R&M's supervisor would prepare an R&M work order and schedule the job. This work order provides the repair worker with the details of the work to be done and is used to record the actual repair/maintenance hours worked and the materials and supplies used.

    Producing departments would be charged for actual labor hours worked at a predetermined standard rate for the type of work required. The parts and supplies used would be charged to the production departments at cost.

    The assistant controller believes that only two documents would be required in this new system—a repair/maintenance service request initiated by the production departments and the repair/maintenance work order initiated by R&M.

Required

(a) For the repair/maintenance work order document,
   (1) Identify the data items that would be important to R&M and the production departments that should be incorporated into the work order.
   (2) Indicate how many copies of the work order would be required, and explain how each copy would be distributed.
(b) Prepare a document flow diagram to show how the repair/maintenance service request and the repair/maintenance work order should be coordinated and used among the departments of Valpaige to request and complete the R&M work, to provide the basis for charging the production departments for the cost of the completed work, and to evaluate the performance of R&M. Provide explanations to the flow diagram as appropriate.

(CMA)

36. The Wadswad Corporation manufactures both standard and customized electrical control boards for automated manufacturing machinery. The company was started by an electrical engineer and a salesman for a machinery company when they saw a demand for systems integration support by companies who were purchasing customized electrical control boards.

Since neither of their former employers seemed interested in providing systems integration support for customized electrical control boards, they started manufacturing control boards and offered complete systems integration support to companies desiring this service.

The firm was successful from the start and grew quickly. As the number of employees and sales increased, management began to computerize the firm's accounting system. First, payroll was computerized, and then accounts receivable and accounts payable. The company is now ready to implement a new computer system to control its work-in-process inventory. The firm uses a job costing system. Work-in-process numbers are established to control the manufacture of both standard and customized control boards. Boards usually are produced in batches of 10 to several hundred units.

Fred Beam, the controller of Wadswad, has just returned from a meeting with the programmer who is implementing the new computer system for work in process. The programmer explained the proposed structure of the master work-in-process file and the types of transactions that will be processed against the file. These structures are outlined below.

Each record in the master work-in-process file will contain the following data:

Field 1: Work-in-process number
Field 2: Units started
Field 3: Units spoiled
Field 4: Materials cost
Field 5: Direct labor cost
Field 6: Total cost
Field 7: Expected completion date

The work-in-process number, number of units started, and expected completion date will be entered into the computer when a job is authorized to begin production. The following four types of transactions will be processed:

(1) *Materials requisitions.*   The cost of materials requisitioned for each job will be posted to field 4 of the master work-in-process file, which accumulates the total materials cost of a job. The cost of materials requisitioned for each job also will be posted to field 6 of the master work-in-process file, which is used to accumulate the total cost of each job.

(2) *Job time tickets.*   The direct labor cost for each job will be posted to field 5 of the master work-in-process file, which accumulates the total labor cost of a job. The direct labor cost for each job also will be posted to field 6 of the master work-in-process file, which is used to accumulate the total cost of each job.

Applied overhead will be computed as a percentage of direct labor cost. Applied overhead will be posted to field 6 of the master work-in-process file, which is used to accumulate the total cost of each job.

(3) *Spoiled-production reports.*   Units spoiled in production for each job will be posted to field 3 of the master work-in-process file, which accumulates the total units spoiled in production for each job. Special messages will be printed during processing if the spoilage rate exceeds management's expectations.

(4) *Completed-production reports.*   When a job is complete, the computer system will report the total cost of the job and also the per-unit cost. The date of completion will be compared with the expected date of completion, field 7 in the master work-in-process file. Special messages will be printed during processing if a job is completed late.

Required
(a) The new computer-based work-in-process system will provide summary accounting data that must be posted periodically to the firm's general ledger. Prepare the standard journal entries that Fred Beam, the controller of Wadswad, could use to document how the expected outputs of the new system will affect the general ledger.
(b) Are accounting-related data the only type of output this system will provide? Discuss.

37. Deake Corporation is a medium-sized, diversified manufacturing company. Fred Richards has been promoted recently to manager, property accounting section. Richards has had difficulty responding to some of the requests from individuals in other departments of Deake for information about the company's fixed assets. Some of the requests and problems Richards has had to cope with are as follows:

(a) The controller has requested schedules of individual fixed assets to support the balances in the general ledger. Richards has furnished the necessary information, but he has always been late. The manner in which the records are organized makes it difficult to obtain information easily.

(b) The maintenance manager wished to verify the existence of a punch press that he thinks was repaired twice. He has asked Richards to confirm the asset number and location of the press.

(c) The insurance department wants data on the cost and book values of assets to include in its review of current insurance coverage.

(d) The tax department has requested data that can be used to determine when Deake should switch depreciation methods for tax purposes.

(e) The company's internal auditors have spent a significant amount of time in the property accounting section recently attempting to confirm the annual depreciation expense.

The property account records that are at Richards' disposal consist of a set of manual books. These records show the date the asset was acquired, the account number to which the asset applies, the dollar amount capitalized, and the estimated useful life of the asset for depreciation purposes.

After many frustrations, Richards has realized that his records are inadequate and that he cannot supply the data easily when they are requested. He has decided that he should discuss the problems with the controller, Julie Castle.

RICHARDS: "Julie, something has got to give. My people are working overtime and can't keep up. You worked in property accounting before you became controller. You know I can't tell the tax, insurance, and maintenance people everything they need to know from my records. Also, that internal auditing team is living in my area, and that slows down the work pace. The requests of these people are reasonable, and we should be able to answer these questions and provide the needed data. I think we need an automated property accounting system. I would like to talk to the information systems people to see if they can help me."

CASTLE: "Fred, I think you have a good idea, but be sure you are personally involved in the design of any system so that you get all the information you need."

Required
(a) Identify and justify four major objectives Deake Corporation's automated property accounting system should possess in order to provide the data necessary to respond to requests for information from company personnel.
(b) Identify the data that should be included in the computer record for each asset included in the property account.

(CMA)

38. Yard Company is a family-owned medium-sized manufacturing company that has been in operation for more than 30 years. The company makes moldings and related parts for other manufacturing firms. Yard Company's manufacturing operations include machining, welding, and assembly. The company has always employed skilled artisans and has been able to maintain a reputation for high-quality production.

Moldings are made to order and sold through contract with the purchasing party. The uniqueness of its product had allowed the company to avoid automating its production processes until just last year. Realizing that labor costs were going to escalate steadily for the foreseeable future, management purchased three numerically controlled machines to automate some of its production processes. A numerically controlled machine is a computer-operated workstation that is programmed to operate tools and to perform a sequence of manufacturing operations in conjunction with one or more human operators. For example, the machine might be programmed to drill several holes of specific sizes in a certain sequence. The human operator manipulates the part, pressing a button to let the machine know when to drill a hole.

Programming the numerically controlled machines requires skills that are obtained most readily by studying computer science in college or a trade school. Because none of the artisans employed by the Yard Company had the necessary background, it was necessary to hire two recent college graduates to program the machines. The two programmers were much younger than most of the artisans and had very different backgrounds and career objectives. It was very difficult for the two groups to communicate.

Relations between the artisans and the programmers deteriorated quickly because the numerically controlled machines operated very inefficiently, mostly due to programming errors. For example, a drill bit would withdraw several feet into the air so that an artisan could rotate a part, when it was only necessary for the drill bit to withdraw several inches. In addition to the time delay, errors of this type lessened the artisans' confidence in the programmers' work. This situation has existed for more than a year. One of the original programmers quit the company, and another was hired to take his place. Rumor has it that both programmers are currently seeking other positions.

The management of Yard Company is aware that there is a problem but does not know how it should proceed. The numerically controlled machines were a sizable investment for the company and were expected to make production more efficient. Management expected some start-up problems, but the problems that have been encountered have been much more severe than expected. Total production costs have increased rather than decreased, and management is aware that both the programmers and the artisans are blaming each other for the company's problems.

Required

(a) What factors have contributed to the problem Yard Company is experiencing in implementing numerically controlled machines in its production operations?

(b) Suggest a solution to Yard Company's problem.

39. Molly Company manufactures both standard and customized electrical control boards for automated manufacturing machinery. The company recently completed installation of a robotic assembly unit. This automated unit completely eliminates direct labor in the production of several types of standard electrical control boards.

Molly uses a job costing system. Boards usually are produced in batches of 10 to several hundred units. Overhead is applied to products based on direct labor hours.

Sally Seed, the controller of Molly Company, recently met with Sam Nut, the production supervisor, concerning the cost of producing several of the firm's products. The following discussion took place:

SAM: "Sally, I'm perplexed by your most recent cost figures for products X, Y, and Z, our big sellers. Before we installed the robotic assembly unit, the following data applied. Products X and Y had identical unit costs, and product Z was the cheapest to produce."

PRODUCT	X	Y	Z
Number of Parts	10	15	20
Labor Hours	4	4	2
Costs			
Material	$200	$200	$200
Labor ($30/hour)	120	120	60
Overhead	80	80	40
Total Cost	**$400**	**$400**	**$300**

SALLY: "That was correct, Sam. Our total budgeted overhead was $600,000. Given our expected 30,000 hours of direct labor, we had an applied overhead rate of $20 per direct labor hour. You can see, then, how these costs were calculated, as our direct labor costs were $30 per hour."

SAM: "According to your latest report, the first since we installed the new automated equipment, the following data apply."

PRODUCT	X	Y	Z
Number of Parts	10	15	20
Robot Hours	3	0	1
Labor Hours	0	4	2
Costs			
Material	$200	$200	$200
Labor ($30/hour)	0	120	60
Overhead	0	200	100
Total Cost	**$200**	**$520**	**$360**

"SALLY, I'm not so sure that these cost representations are believable. We purchased expensive automated equipment and overall eliminated almost a third of our labor cost, yet product Y, which does not use the new equipment, has increased more than 25 percent in cost. On the other hand, product X, which does use the new equipment, has decreased 50 percent in cost."

SALLY: "Well Sam, our total budgeted overhead has increased to $1,000,000. But our expected hours of direct labor drop from 30,000 to 20,000. This gives an applied overhead rate of $50 per direct labor hour. You can see, then, how these costs were calculated, as our direct labor costs were $30 per hour."

SAM: "Well, that may be, Sally, but something just doesn't make sense about using direct labor as the only allocation base for all overhead items. There are other things beside labor that increase production cost. Consider parts per product, for example. We spend a lot of effort in material handling, and it seems to me that more parts make more work, which means to me that it costs more."

SALLY: "Sam, you may be right. I wanted to investigate activity-based costing, and this conversation has convinced me to do so. I'm going to collect some data and recompute these cost figures using activity-based costing. I'll get back to you soon, and we can see if these new figures seem to make more sense."

Required
Sally collected the following data for activity-based costing.

	ACTIVITY		
	MATERIAL HANDLING	ROBOTIC ASSEMBLY	ALL OTHER OVERHEAD
Overhead	$200,000	$400,000	$400,000
Base	40,000	5,000	20,000
	(parts)	(robot hours)	(labor hours)
Rate	$5	$80	$20

(a) Compute product costs under activity-based costing using the three activities and their associated allocation bases shown here.
(b) How might allocation bases for activity costs be identified?

❖ ANSWERS TO CHAPTER QUIZ

1. d   4. c   7. a   10. c
2. b   5. a   8. a
3. a   6. c   9. d

Systems Planning and Analysis

LEARNING OBJECTIVES

Careful study of this chapter will enable you to:

❖ Describe the relationship of systems analysis to systems development as a whole.

❖ Describe the various stages of systems analysis.

❖ Discuss the major techniques for gathering and organizing data for systems analysis.

❖ Describe some of the human problems involved in systems analysis.

❖ Describe the various steps involved in specifying systems design alternatives.

❖ Discuss the various considerations relevant to preparing design specifications.

❖ Describe the content of a systems design proposal.

❖ Summarize several major design techniques.

❖ Discuss the usefulness of systems design packages.

GENERAL OVERVIEW

Systems development is the process of modifying or replacing a portion or all of an information system. This process requires a substantial commitment of time and resources and is an ongoing activity in many organizations.

Systems development normally is undertaken by a project team composed of system analysts, programmers, accountants, and other people in the organization who are knowledgeable about or affected by the project. Every systems development project goes through essentially the same **systems development life cycle**: planning and analysis, design, and implementation. Neglecting any portion of the life cycle may have serious consequences. The life-cycle concept provides a framework for planning and controlling the detailed developmental activities.

OVERVIEW OF SYSTEMS PLANNING AND ANALYSIS

Systems planning involves identifying subsystems within the information system that need special attention for development. The objective of systems planning is to identify problem areas that need to be dealt with either immediately or sometime in the future. **Systems analysis** begins after systems planning has identified subsystems for development. Its primary objectives (Fig. 10.1) are to understand the existing systems and problems, to describe information needs, and to establish priorities for further systems work.

Once a particular subsystem of the organization is targeted for development, systems analysis focuses on defining the information needs and system requirements necessary for the system to implement management's objectives. Therefore, systems analysis emphasizes the study of managers' decisions and their associated information requirements. These requirements are then translated into specific applications during the design and implementation phases of the systems development life cycle.

The importance of the systems analysis process can be seen in Figure 10.2. Most development-cycle costs are tied up in the design and implementation phases. This means that major errors in the analysis phase can become quite costly later. It is therefore very important that the systems analyst gain a thorough understanding of the situation in terms of management's problems and information needs.

FIGURE 10.1   OBJECTIVES OF SYSTEMS ANALYSIS.

Objectives

1. Gain an understanding of the existing system (if one exists).
2. Identify and understand problems.
3. Express identified problems in terms of information needs and system requirements.
4. Clearly identify subsystems to be given highest priority.

Focus
■ Identify critical success factors.
■ Give special attention to these factors.

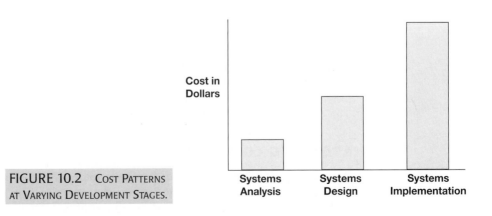

FIGURE 10.2   COST PATTERNS AT VARYING DEVELOPMENT STAGES.

SYSTEMS PLANNING AND FEASIBILITY ANALYSIS

It is essential that a top-down total systems approach be taken to systems development. Careful attention must be given to developing an overall systems plan and strategy. Such a plan must include the overall support and approval of top management. Without such an overall plan, the information system is likely to develop as a maze of patchwork. An overall plan seeks to ensure the following objectives:

- Resources will be targeted to the subsystems where the needs are greatest.
- Duplication and wasted effort will be minimized.
- Systems development in the organization will be consistent with the overall strategic plan of the organization.

Systems planning and feasibility analysis involve seven phases:

1. Discussing and planning on the part of top management
2. Establishing a systems planning steering committee
3. Establishing overall objectives and constraints
4. Developing a strategic information systems plan
5. Identifying and prioritizing specific areas within the organization for the systems development focus
6. Setting forth a systems proposal to serve as a basis of the analysis and preliminary design for a given subsystem
7. Assembling a team of individuals for purposes of the analysis and preliminary systems design

Notice that these seven steps operate in a top-down fashion. The planning effort begins with top management and ends with a specific team of individuals charged with the task of analyzing a particular system and coming up with a preliminary systems design. In the following sections, each of the seven phases is discussed individually.

SYSTEMS PLANNING AND TOP MANAGEMENT

It is crucial that all major systems development efforts have the support of top management. A major task of the systems developer is to discern the strategic plans, key success factors, and overall objectives of top management. The systems developer must do a lot more than simply ask top management what its problems are. The role of the systems developer is much like that of a doctor with regard to a patient. The patient is only able to describe symptoms of the problems; it is the doctor who must determine the underlying problem and its causes. Picture what a doctor would say if a patient said, "I have a bad headache, and I want you to give me a shot of penicillin." The doctor would take note of the patient's problems and suggested solution but would make an independent diagnosis and analysis of the underlying cause and the best treatment. The same approach must be taken by the systems developer.

STEERING COMMITTEE

A useful approach to guiding the overall systems development effort is to have a **steering committee** representing top management and all major functional areas within the organization. A primary responsibility of this committee should be to focus on the overall current and future information needs of the company. Such a committee must have representation by top management because it is essential that the information system fit within the overall strategic plan of the corporation. This entails taking a long-run view. Failure to take a long-run view can be very costly to the company. For example, if it is known that the company plans to launch a new product within the next 5 years, the information systems plan should allow for growth of the existing system in such a way that it can easily accommodate the new product. In fact, it might prove cost-effective to include plans for the new product in the current systems development effort instead of adding them later.

The steering committee should be responsible for overall planning and control of the systems development effort of the company. An ideal person to be in charge of such a committee would be a vice president of information systems. The steering committee should not, however, become involved in the details of specific development projects. Individual projects should be supervised and managed by an individual who reports periodically to the steering committee.

DEVELOPING OBJECTIVES AND SYSTEM CONSTRAINTS

Effective, overall sound planning calls for the development of general objectives for the company and specific objectives for individual subsystems within the company. General objectives include the overall strategic objectives relating to the company's long-run planning cycle. Subsidiary to the strategic objectives are tactical objectives. These correspond to tactical planning and typically relate to about a 1- to 3-year time horizon.

Also important are the company's **key success factors**. These factors are the characteristics that distinguish a company from its competitors and are the keys to its success. For example, some companies emphasize speed of service; others emphasize product quality; still others emphasize low prices. Whatever the key success factors are, they must be incorporated into the objectives for systems design. A company that has an overall key objective relating to fast delivery times would want to make information relating to late deliveries an important part of its shipping/delivery system.

DEVELOPING A STRATEGIC SYSTEMS PLAN

A major output of the steering committee or individual in charge of systems development should be a **strategic systems plan**. This plan should take the form of a written document that incorporates both the short- and long-run goals of the company's systems development effort. Key elements of a strategic systems plan include

- An overall statement relating to key success factors of the company and overall objectives
- A description of systems within the company for which development efforts are needed
- A statement of priorities indicating which areas are to be given the highest priority
- An outline of required resources, including costs, personnel, and equipment
- Tentative timetables for developing specific systems

IDENTIFYING INDIVIDUAL PROJECTS FOR PRIORITY

As stated previously, the strategic plan should identify specific areas to be given the highest priority. Setting priorities is crucial because financial resources are always limited. Prioritizing projects should be done in the same way as in capital budgeting. Specific benefits should be defined for projects, and their costs should be estimated as closely as possible and set forth in financial budgets. These financial budgets should be as accurate as possible.

Because the benefits of systems development are often difficult to quantify, it is easy to lose sight of financial considerations when prioritizing systems development projects. However, it is almost always possible to quantify the costs, and this should be done before commissioning a project. In addition, even though benefits may be difficult to quantify, they should be stated in formal written terms. For example, a company might consider a sales order system that would allow its salespeople to check on the status of incomplete orders. Such a system would allow salespeople to better deal with customers when there is a question about the status of a possibly overdue order. Such a system might allow a salesperson to immediately find the current or revised delivery date. This information could be conveyed to the customer, and the customer could plan accordingly. In this situation, it might be very easy to identify the costs. However, what are the financial benefits of being able to provide information to customers on short notice? There is an obvious benefit in terms of customer relations. This benefit might result in sales increases. If so, such increases should be estimated and incorporated into the formal system proposal.

COMMISSIONING THE SYSTEMS PROJECT

In many respects, commissioning the systems project is like constructing a building. A building project requires carpenters, plumbers, bricklayers, electricians, and metalworkers. Similarly, a systems development project requires individuals from several disciplines. The actual personnel requirements will depend on the specific project; however, it is common to require management, accountants, systems users, computer programmers, and various types of technical support individuals.

THE STEPS IN SYSTEMS ANALYSIS

Figure 10.3 depicts the major steps or phases of the systems analysis effort.

PHASE 1: SURVEY THE PRESENT SYSTEM

OBJECTIVES OF SURVEYING

The system survey has four objectives:

- Gain a fundamental understanding of the operational aspects of the system
- Establish a working relationship with the users of the system
- Collect important data that are useful in developing the systems design
- Identify specific problems that require focus in terms of subsequent design efforts

The systems development team must become very familiar with the workings of the system under consideration for change. It is dangerous to try to modify an existing

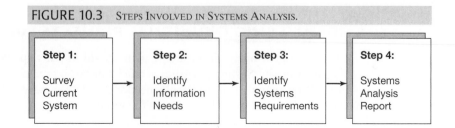

FIGURE 10.3 STEPS INVOLVED IN SYSTEMS ANALYSIS.

system that you do not understand thoroughly. In addition, developers must become familiar with the people who work in the system on a daily basis. This familiarity allows developers to gain an understanding of problems that top management may be completely unaware of.

The objective of establishing a relationship with individuals who work within the system under development is especially critical. *The success or failure of a development project will depend to a large extent on the quality of the relationship between the development team and the individuals working in the system.* A poor relationship can result in misunderstandings and misplaced design efforts. The individuals working in the system must live with the development results on a long-term basis. More specifically, it is a very real possibility that the new system can be rejected by the individuals for whom it is designed. If these individuals do not respect the development team, they may resist implementation of the completed design. Such resistance can come in many forms, including complaints to top management, strikes, or sabotage.

BEHAVIORAL CONSIDERATIONS

The human element is a key factor in conducting the system survey. The fact that systems development involves changing the existing system poses many problems. Most people do not like change. In many situations, an individual may have been at a certain job and routine that have not changed for many years. This individual is very likely to see you as a threat. Other individuals might be concerned about losing their jobs, possibly to a computer. Still other individuals might see you as a "front-office spy." Figure 10.4 depicts these problems in terms of a communication gap between the systems analyst and management. It is the responsibility of the systems analyst, not management, to bridge this communication gap. Therefore, the first task of the analyst conducting a systems survey should be to establish a good working relationship between the project team and management.

Certain approaches can help bridge this communication gap:

- Get to know as many people involved in the system as soon as possible.
- Communicate the benefits of the proposed system to the individuals involved.
- Provide assurances, to the degree possible, to all individuals that there will be no losses of jobs or major changes in job responsibilities.

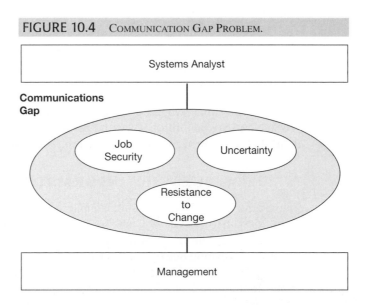

FIGURE 10.4   COMMUNICATION GAP PROBLEM.

- Provide assurances that you are genuinely concerned with making life better for those involved in the system.

SOURCES FOR GATHERING FACTS

A variety of techniques can be used to gather facts about the information subsystem under study. These include interviews, questionnaires, observations, and reviews of various types of documents such as corporate minutes, charts of accounts, organization charts, financial statements, procedure manuals, policy statements, job descriptions, and so on. In addition, sources of information outside the company should not be overlooked. These include industry and trade publications as well as professional journals. Finally, the customer should be viewed as a vital component of the system and included in any analysis.

ANALYSIS OF SURVEY FINDINGS

When the survey has been completed, the strengths and weaknesses of the subsystem under study should be thoroughly analyzed. The survey focuses on understanding the nature and operation of the system (with its associated problems), whereas the analysis of the survey findings focuses on strengths and weaknesses of the system. Some of the following questions might be asked in evaluating the present system:

- Is a given procedure necessary?
- Does the procedure involve unnecessary steps?
- Is the procedure cost-effective?
- Is a given report clear and easy to read?
- Are the source documents well designed?
- Are reports being generated that are not needed or used?
- What causes a particular problem?
- What additional reports might be useful to management?
- Is the system documentation adequate?

Overall, these questions should result in a report that summarizes the strengths and weaknesses of the existing system. In making such an evaluation, certain standards must be used as benchmarks. These standards relate to effectiveness and efficiency. *Effectiveness* here simply means that the system accomplishes the objectives set forth in the systems planning phase. *Efficiency* relates to whether these objectives are achieved at the lowest possible cost.

Evaluation of the effectiveness of the system's ability to achieve the overall planned objectives should focus on bottlenecks. **Bottlenecks** represent weaknesses in the system where small changes can result in major improvements. For example, a company may have difficulty delivering its goods to its customers within a reasonable time. An analysis of the situation might reveal that the job scheduling system is ineffective and that there are times when employees are idle, even though there is a backlog in the production schedule. In this case the results of the analysis would indicate a need to focus on the production scheduling system.

PHASE 2:   IDENTIFY INFORMATION NEEDS

The second major phase of systems analysis involves identifying information requirements for managerial decision making. In identifying information needs, the analyst studies specific decisions made by managers in terms of the information inputs. This process is called **information needs analysis**, and the heart of it is the study of decisions made.

How do you identify the decisions made by managers? You might think that it is good enough simply to ask managers what decisions they make. Unfortunately, managers often are unable to answer this question specifically. One reason for this is that managers often think in terms of getting certain jobs done. For example, a product engineer might view her job responsibility as being the designer of a particular new product. If you ask her what decisions she makes, she might respond, "I simply design new products." Your responsibility as a systems developer would be to ask more detailed questions that would get at the nature of some of the decisions the engineer makes in the process. For example, you might ask her, "What are some of the design considerations you have to take into account?" and "How do you make these considerations?" Answers to these questions might reveal that safety considerations are an important factor. From all this you might conclude that this particular individual might need certain product safety reports. In conclusion, you have to become intimately familiar with the problems of a particular manager in order to understand the decisions that he or she makes and the corresponding information needs.

Fortunately, some systematic techniques can be used to gain an understanding of decisions and information needs. Several basic approaches can be followed:

- Identify the manager's primary job responsibilities.
- Identify the means by which the manager is evaluated.
- Identify some of the major problems the manager faces.
- Identify the means by which the manager evaluates personal output.

The first two approaches suggest that you get an understanding of the manager's position and related responsibilities in a company. The means by which the manager is evaluated are especially important because they will determine, to a large extent, the approaches a manager takes in dealing with day-to-day problems. Another way of looking at this is that the criteria used to evaluate a manager should be based on a statement of the manager's performance goals. For example, an advertising manager might be evaluated on the responsiveness of customers to the company's advertising campaign. Therefore, such a manager would want specific reports relating to advertising expenditures and the associated customer responses.

While the approach of asking managers about their problems often can be very helpful, you cannot simply walk up to a manager and say, "What kind of problems do you have here?" First, managers are often reluctant to discuss their problems with someone they do not really know. Second, a given manager might feel that admitting a problem is somehow admitting failure. Therefore, it is often helpful to take an approach that involves asking the managers a lot of questions about what they do and then listening carefully. If you can get managers to talk long enough, their problems will come out. All this points to the importance of establishing a good working relationship with the manager.

PHASE 3:   IDENTIFY THE SYSTEMS REQUIREMENTS

The third phase of the system analysis project involves specifying systems requirements. Such requirements can be specified in terms of inputs and outputs. The input requirements for a given subsystem specify the specific needs that must be met in order for that subsystem to achieve its objectives.

For example, the information requirements of a production control system might include short-run sales forecasts, reports on the availability of materials, specifications of quality control and standard costs, and information needed to prioritize individual jobs. For the same system, the following might be considered as output requirements:

- Daily progress reports
- Daily finance reports

- Reports on defective units
- Reports on problems with raw materials

The input requirements for one subsystem will, in turn, specify output requirements for another subsystem. In this case, the input requirements of sales forecasts would be an output requirement for some other system within the company (such as marketing).

PHASE 4: DEVELOP A SYSTEMS ANALYSIS REPORT

The final output of the systems analysis project is a report. This report is extremely important because it often serves as a basis for further decision making on the part of top management. In addition, this report organizes and documents all the findings of the three phases of the systems analysis project. Without such careful documentation, a lot of information would be lost in the long run. If the analysis is not documented carefully at the time it is conducted, when the time rolls around for doing the design and implementation work, a lot can be forgotten. Also, to develop a design report, all the analysis findings must be organized carefully within some consistent framework.

Some of the key elements of the systems analysis report include

- A summary of the scope and purpose of the analysis project
- A reiteration of the relationship of the project to the overall strategic information systems plan
- A description of any overall problems in the specific subsystem being studied
- A summary of the decisions being made and their specific information requirements
- Specification of system performance requirements
- An overall cost budget and timetable for the project to date
- Recommendations for improving the existing system or for designing new systems
- Recommendations relating to modifying objectives for the subsystem under study

The systems analysis report, when completed, is presented to the vice president of information systems, the information systems steering committee, or if appropriate, directly to top management. The report is then reviewed and discussed by the individuals who decide whether a preliminary systems design should be undertaken. The preliminary systems design, if undertaken, provides a complete budget for the design and implementation parts of the development project.

FACT-GATHERING TECHNIQUES

A large portion of the systems analyst's job is to collect and organize facts. Fortunately, there are a number of techniques that help the analyst perform these difficult tasks. Table 10.1 summarizes some of the major tools used by analysts in fact gathering.

TECHNIQUES FOR ORGANIZING FACTS

The systems analyst needs formal techniques for organizing facts. Table 10.2 presents a number of techniques that are helpful in summarizing and organizing facts. Most of these techniques are discussed in Chapter 2. One additional technique, the Warnier-Orr methodology, is discussed here.

TABLE 10.1 Techniques for Gathering Facts for Analysis

Technique	*Objective*
Depth interview	Gain a fundamental understanding of the system.
Structured interview	Systematic follow-up based on depth interviews.
Open-ended questionnaire	Same as depth interview.
Closed-ended questionnaire	Same as structured interview.
Document reviews	Gain an understanding of the existing system.

Flowcharts
    Organization charts
    Procedure manuals
    Operations manuals
    Reference manuals
    Historical records
	(*Caution:* Sometimes the system does not operate as documented.) It is often helpful to review system documents before conducting interviews and distributing questionnaires.

Observation	Familiarity with the system.

TABLE 10.2 Techniques for Fact Organization

Technique	*Objective*
Work measurement	Summarize resources required for various tasks.
Work distribution	Summarize employee time utilization for tasks.

Flow charting
    General
    Decision flow
    Logical data flow
    Systems
    Detailed
	Graphically depict flows and relationships and process requirements, with a focus on modularity.

Decision analysis	Summarize decisions and needed information.
Functional analysis Hierarchical function	Summarize functions and related information.
Matrix analysis	Summarize related data inputs/outputs.
Narratives	Written summarization.
File/report summaries	

The **Warnier-Orr methodology** is based on analyzing the outputs of an application and factoring the application into a hierarchical structure of modules to accomplish the necessary processing. It uses a diagramming technique that is illustrated in Figure 10.5.

Warnier-Orr methodology uses brackets or braces to show hierarchy. The highest level is to the left of the figure, and the lowest level is to the right. The diagram is produced using only three basic constructs: sequence, selection, and repetition. The processes included in a sequence are enclosed in brackets and are executed from top to bottom. To compute the total amount due for a set of invoices, the following sequence is followed: First, determine the discount for an individual invoice, then determine the amount due as gross amount less discount, and then accumulate total amount due. Note that these three steps are enclosed in a single bracket. Selection is necessary when there are two or more alternatives. Mutually exclusive alternatives are enclosed in a bracket and separated by the exclusive symbol $\oplus$ (a plus sign enclosed in a circle). A discount is available if the due date is greater than or equal to today's date. There are two mutually exclusive alternatives, enclosed in a bracket and separated by the exclusive symbol. The discount calculation in either case is indicated by the next-lower bracket in the hierarchy. If no processing is required, the word *null* or *skip* is used to indicate this in the diagram. Repetition is indicated by subscripts. If a process is to be

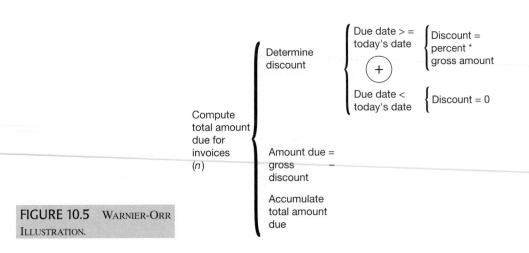

FIGURE 10.5   WARNIER-ORR ILLUSTRATION.

repeated only once, the subscript 1 would be used. In our illustration, we have an unknown number of invoices, so the subscript n is used.

Warnier-Orr methodology is easy to understand and use. It can be used to document any type of system, from a top-level overview to detailed program logic. Most significant, the left-to-right pattern forces a structured, top-down approach to analysis.

STRUCTURED SYSTEMS ANALYSIS

Thus far the discussion has focused on the general steps of systems analysis and the techniques for collecting and analyzing facts. In this section the focus is on the analysis of specific systems. **Structured systems analysis** is an approach to systems analysis that begins with a very general description of a particular system and then proceeds through a logically related set of steps, each increasing in detail, and ends with computer program code (and other details). Perhaps the best way to view structured systems analysis is as a system of documentation. This includes several levels of documentation, where each level is a logical blowup or "explosion" of the previous level. At the first level, logical data flow diagrams describe the system. They are then supported by additional logical flow diagrams that provide more detail. Other documentation describes the process logic and data components of these diagrams.

LOGICAL FLOW DIAGRAMS VERSUS FLOWCHARTS

The preceding description of structured systems analysis incorporates logical data flow diagrams as opposed to document or analytic flowcharts. In practice, either type of diagram might be used. Each approach has its unique advantages. The primary difference between the two approaches is that the flowchart gives a physical description of a system, whereas the logical data flow diagram gives a logical description of a system. Specifically, an analytic flowchart specifies input/output devices such as a data terminal or printer. It also specifies storage devices, such as magnetic tape or disk. The logical data flow diagram incorporates these same elements but leaves the exact physical description open.

In designing new systems, the logical data flow diagram is especially helpful because it does not require a commitment to a particular physical implementation. In addition, it is often useful to analyze an existing system without referring to physical input/output and storage devices. For example, an analyst might have to decide whether an existing accounts receivable system should be on-line or batch. The logical data flow diagram would be the same for either system, but the document flowcharts would vary considerably across the two situations. The logical data flow diagram would help the analyst conceptually separate the two problems of data flow and physical implementation.

Document and analytic flowcharts are indispensable tools. It is always necessary to document the physical implementation of a system. In addition, all other types of documentation, such as hierarchy plus input-process-output (HIPO) charts, file matrices, and so on, should be used as needed.

In summary, similar documentation is used for both design and analysis. In designing new systems or analyzing existing systems, logical data flow diagrams are especially helpful because they separate the problems of logical flow and physical implementation. On the other hand, document flowcharts are important in documenting physical implementation.

SYSTEMS DESIGN VERSUS SYSTEMS ANALYSIS

Structured systems analysis and structured systems design are very similar processes. Strictly speaking, *design* refers to the creation of a new or modified system, whereas *analysis* involves the critical evaluation of a particular problem or existing system. However, practically speaking, systems analysis and design are often indistinguishable. For example, in order to better understand and document a particular problem, the analyst often will develop logical data flow diagrams, document flowcharts, and specific process logic. All this documentation also can serve as the basis for a new system.

In conclusion, structured systems analysis must be studied simultaneously with structured systems design. The documentation and working steps of the two problems involve common elements.

THE STEPS IN STRUCTURED SYSTEMS ANALYSIS

DEVELOP LOGICAL DATA FLOW DIAGRAMS

The system is first described in general terms using a logical data flow diagram. Figure 10.6 gives a context diagram for a purchasing system. This diagram does not show the details of the logical processes or any error conditions. These types of details should be given in supporting diagrams. For example, Figure 10.7 provides additional details, exploding the "Purchasing System" process in Figure 10.6 into two subprocesses,

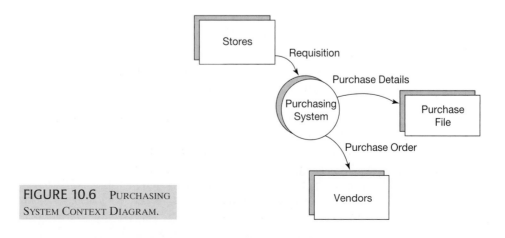

FIGURE 10.6   PURCHASING SYSTEM CONTEXT DIAGRAM.

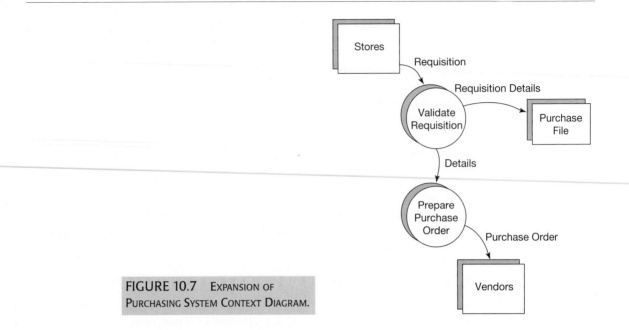

Stores
Requisition
Requisition Details
Validate
Requisition
Purchase
File
Details
Prepare
Purchase
Order
Purchase Order
Vendors

FIGURE 10.7 EXPANSION OF PURCHASING SYSTEM CONTEXT DIAGRAM.

"Validate Requisition" and "Prepare Purchase Order." It should be possible to provide even more detail in support of the original purchasing system context diagram by exploding the subprocess in Figure 10.7 into lower-level subprocesses. This procedure should continue until the system is adequately described.

DEFINE DATA DICTIONARIES

The next step is to define data dictionaries corresponding to the data stores referenced in the logical data flow diagrams. This involves giving a description of the data structure and data elements involved. For example, Figure 10.8 gives data dictionary details for the data store "Purchase File" in Figure 10.7. In this case, the data structure incorporates several categories, including "Account-Identifiers," "Validation-Information,"

	Purchase File Description	
Account-Identifiers		
account-no-1	. . .	primary account number
account-no-2	. . .	secondary account number
person-responsible	. . .	person in charge of account
expiration-date	. . .	account termination date
Validation-Information		
signature-required	. . .	name of required signer
maximum-charge	. . .	maximum limit per requisition
Financial-Information		
account-balance	. . .	current balance
last-purchase	. . .	most recent transaction
Vendor-Information		
vendor-1	. . .	list of approved vendors
vendor-2	. . .	
vendor-3	. . .	

FIGURE 10.8 DATA DICTIONARY FOR PURCHASE FILE.

FIGURE 10.9 STRUCTURED
ENGLISH FOR ACCOUNT VALIDATION
RELATED TO PURCHASE ROUTINE.

```
Access purchase file
For each purchase requisition
IF   account no. on requisition equals account-no-1
                      THEN   flag account-no-1 field
ELSE  IF   account no. on requisition equals account-no-2
                      THEN   flag account-no-2 field
ELSE  (none of the above)
SO   void the transaction and generate error code
```

"Financial-Information," and "Vendor-Information." Within each major category, individual data elements are listed. For example, the "Financial-Information" category includes the data items "account-balance" and "last-purchase."

Note that no physical detail is given at this point. At a subsequent time (the design and implementation stages), it would be necessary to provide specifics on forms layout, storage media, and so on.

DEFINE ACCESS METHODS

It is also necessary to specify how the data stores will be accessed. This typically involves defining primary and secondary access keys. For example, the purchase file in Figure 10.8 might have "account-no-1" as the primary key and "person-responsible" as the secondary key.

DEFINE PROCESS LOGIC

There are many approaches to documenting the process logic. These include various types of decision trees and decision diagrams, as well as structured English. The latter approach is discussed here because it is particularly easy to understand, flexible, and useful in the development of computer programs.

Structured English is a special language for describing process logic that uses several key words, including *IF, THEN, ELSE IF*, and *SO*. Figure 10.9 gives an example of structured English describing account number validation in the "Validate Requisition" subprocess in Figure 10.7. The logic is structured in a format that a nontechnical person can understand. This approach, therefore, has the additional benefit that it can be read and modified by system users.

Another very useful aspect of structured English is that it very closely resembles source code in structured programming languages such as COBOL and FORTRAN V. Therefore, structured English can greatly reduce the task of programming.

Structured English does not include provisions for error conditions and data file access. If these are added, the resulting documentation is sometimes referred to as **pseudocode**. It is sometimes desirable to develop pseudocode as a final step before program coding.

OVERVIEW OF SYSTEMS DESIGN

A systems design is very similar to the architectural layout of a house. In the planning phase, the architect determines the basic functions that the house should perform and formulates a general plan with regard to the overall layout. In the design stage, however, the architect prepares a specific blueprint of the house that can be used by electricians, plumbers, and carpenters. In a similar fashion, the systems designer prepares a blueprint that can be implemented by accountants, computer programmers, and management.

Small errors made at this stage can result in large amounts of wasted dollars and expenditures at later stages. Consider what would happen if, in building a house, an architect forgets to include plumbing in the kitchen. Further assume that such a house was built as designed. On discovering this error, the owners would have to pay to have the walls (and possibly the floors) ripped out to retrofit the omitted plumbing. Needless to say, this process would be quite painful and expensive. Similar problems can and often do occur in the design of accounting information systems. For example, a company might implement a systems design plan that calls for purchasing a particular computer and certain accounting software packages. After using this system for a year or two, the company might find that the software packages no longer meet the changing information needs of management. Furthermore, it might be impossible to modify these software packages, necessitating replacing the entire system after a short period of use.

There are other pitfalls. One of the most dangerous is user rejection of the system. Because of lack of adequate involvement of users in the design plan, the implemented system could become unpopular and ultimately be rejected by the individuals for whom the system was designed.

STEPS IN SYSTEMS DESIGN

Systems design can be defined as the formulation of a blueprint for a completed system. Systems design proceeds from the general to the specific. This is the nature of the top-down approach. The general functions and objectives that a specific system will accomplish must be identified first. Given these objectives, it is then possible to prepare detailed specifications, such as database structures, record layouts, and specific report forms. Therefore, systems design can be viewed as either preliminary or detailed. In most cases, the design effort actually begins during the systems planning and analysis phases of the development cycle. The design effort should be viewed as a process of continuously increasing detail that begins during the analysis and planning phases and ends with the beginning of the implementation phase of the development cycle. Furthermore, the entire development cycle, including the design phase, is a never-ending process. During implementation, problems are often encountered with the design specifications. When this happens, it is necessary to go back to the design process and make the necessary changes. Furthermore, the business environment is always changing, and as new system requirements arise, the systems design must be restructured as needed.

Figure 10.10 defines these major steps in systems design. The first is evaluation of various design alternatives, the second is preparation of design specifications, and the third is preparation of systems design specifications.

EVALUATING DESIGN ALTERNATIVES

In every case, the systems design project arises out of a specific need, as determined by the systems planning and analysis phases of the development cycle. The systems design should provide a solution to a specific problem. Systems design problems are much like many other problems in life; there is usually no single solution that perfectly solves the problem. The systems designer usually is faced with a number of solutions, all of which may appear very attractive on superficial examination. Therefore, a very important aspect of systems design is enumeration and consideration of the various major design alternatives.

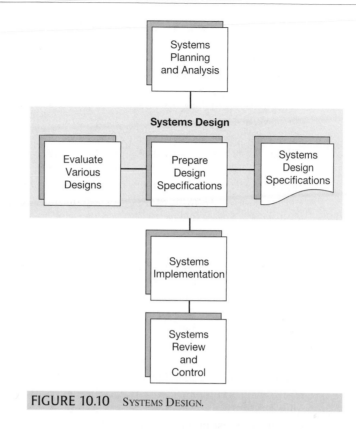

FIGURE 10.10   SYSTEMS DESIGN.

ENUMERATION OF DESIGN ALTERNATIVES

At the most general level, the designer is faced with the alternatives of either developing a completely new system or modifying the existing system. If the company has no existing system, the choice is easy. For example, if a company has no cost accounting system at all, it would not be necessary to consider various modifications to the existing system; the designer could build a new system from the ground up.

In designing a completely new system, there are two general approaches. One approach is to design the system completely from scratch. The other approach is to have the designer select and recommend a premade system. For example, a given company might find it very economical to purchase one of the many computerized accounting packages that are available. However, some software packages may be inappropriate for a given application. In addition, many packages give the user a wide range of alternatives for data items, report formats, and so on. It is often necessary to do a substantial amount of design work anyway because even predesigned packages do not solve design problems completely. This is an important point because there is a tendency on the part of managers to feel that either a computer or a computer package alone will solve their information needs.

Computer packages sometimes can meet the specific needs of an individual situation with minimal design work. This is particularly true where a computer package has been written for a specific industry. For example, a number of **turnkey systems** are available for lawyers, doctors, contractors, and so on. Such systems can very closely meet the needs of management. However, as firms increase in complexity and in the number of their products, it becomes increasingly difficult to find a predesigned system that adequately meets the needs of management.

A second situation often faced in systems design is an existing system that is not functioning adequately. In this case, it is necessary to design changes into the existing system. As a general rule, it is more difficult to modify an existing system than to implement a new one. This is especially true because of a tendency for individuals to resist change.

In modifying an existing system, several basic approaches can be taken. The first of these is that of simply modifying the data collected and reports generated. This is the simplest approach because it involves little or no redefining of individual job responsibilities. A second approach to redesigning existing systems involves reorganizing job responsibilities. This approach is substantially more drastic than the first and is much more likely to be resisted by employees. Employees usually feel comfortable in a particular job after working at it for several months. The possibility of changing job responsibilities can introduce considerable uncertainty into an employee's life. This uncertainty alone can make an individual uncomfortable, and the result could be resistance to the change. Therefore, systems designers should be careful to recommend organizational changes only in situations where changes are really needed. Although organizational changes should be recommended with caution, it is often desirable to either completely reassign employees or make dramatic changes in their job responsibilities. Such changes occur when clear-cut costs/benefits or internal control considerations are involved. In these situations, every effort should be made to alleviate employee uncertainty and discomfort.

Finally, a number of design alternatives might apply either to a new system or to a modification of an existing system. One general alternative might involve considering whether or not a particular system should be computerized. Another general alternative could involve deciding whether to create a centralized or decentralized system.

DESCRIBING THE ALTERNATIVES

Once a list of major alternatives has been made, each alternative should be documented and described. For example, a computer network for data collection and report distribution might be either centralized or decentralized. In a centralized design alternative, each division supplies accounting data to the central computer system. The central computer system then produces and distributes reports to each of the divisions. In a decentralized design alternative, each division has its own computer and collects its own data. The completed reports are transmitted to company headquarters. The description of each alternative should incorporate its relative advantages and disadvantages. Relevant cost information also should be provided so that cost/benefit comparisons can be made on design alternatives. For example, the centralized computer system might cost $1,000,000 and the decentralized computer system $1,250,000. On the surface, the centralized computer system appears cheaper. However, the decentralized system might provide a number of additional functions. Furthermore, the total capacity of the individual decentralized computers might exceed that of the centralized system substantially. This would be particularly important if there were a possibility that the capacity of the centralized system might be reached in the near future.

EVALUATING THE ALTERNATIVES

Once each alternative has been carefully laid out and documented, it is possible to compare alternatives. The primary criteria for selecting an alternative for implementation should be cost versus benefits. In addition, the selected alternative should satisfy all major systems objectives.

Another important factor that must be considered is **feasibility**. A given design proposal must be both technically and operationally feasible. It must be possible for a given company to actually implement the design specifications. For example, if a company is to acquire a sophisticated mainframe computer, it must be prepared to administer it. This may involve upgrading the job responsibilities of existing individuals. When such an approach is to be taken, the company must ensure that the targeted individual is capable of managing the new system. *It is very easy to underestimate the requirements of maintaining, managing, and operating sophisticated information systems.*

The best major design alternative is normally selected by top management. Furthermore, the major designs presented to top management typically are not highly detailed. Once management selects a design, the design team prepares detailed design specifications.

PREPARING DESIGN SPECIFICATIONS

The primary rule in developing design specifications is that the designer should work backward from outputs to inputs. Working with the system objectives, the designer should design all management reports and operational output documents as a first step in the process. Once all these outputs are specified, the data inputs and processing steps are determined automatically. Once these decisions have been made, the designer then builds in the appropriate controls. Figure 10.11 shows this process. In each phase of the design sequence, specific considerations must be made. In designing the reports and other outputs, such factors as the reporting frequency, the output medium, and the actual report format must be considered. In developing a database, design

FIGURE 10.11   DESIGN OF SYSTEM ELEMENTS.

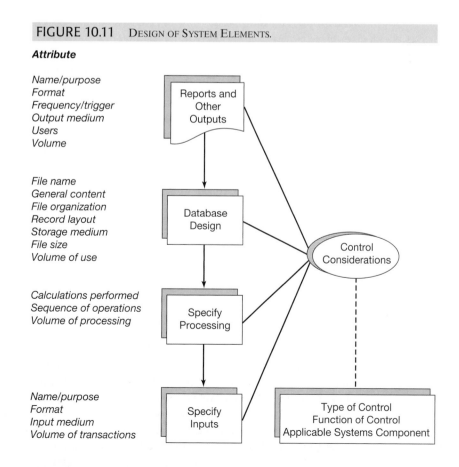

Attribute

Name/purpose
Format
Frequency/trigger
Output medium
Users
Volume

File name
General content
File organization
Record layout
Storage medium
File size
Volume of use

Calculations performed
Sequence of operations
Volume of processing

Name/purpose
Format
Input medium
Volume of transactions

Reports and Other Outputs

Database Design

Specify Processing

Specify Inputs

Control Considerations

Type of Control
Function of Control
Applicable Systems Component

considerations regarding file organization, record layout, storage media, and volume of usage must be made. For the processing phase, the exact calculations to be performed and the appropriate sequence of operations must be specified. Finally, in specifying the inputs, precise input formats, the input medium, and volume of transactions must be considered.

PREPARING AND SUBMITTING THE SYSTEMS DESIGN SPECIFICATIONS

The completed design specifications should take the form of a proposal. If the project is large, the proposal should be reviewed by top management before approval. However, proposals that are relatively inexpensive might be approved by a department or division manager. The **detailed design proposal** should include everything necessary to actually implement the design project. In general, it will include specific timetables for completion, a budget, and a description of personnel requirements, as well as flowcharts and other diagrams that describe the systems to be implemented. A copy of all proposed system outputs would be incorporated, as well as specifics on any databases to be created or modified. The database specifications would include the exact contents of specific data items, as well as file organization and file access methods. In addition, details relating to storage requirements, file size, and updating frequency should be provided.

With regard to data processing, details regarding required hardware and software should be provided. Hardware normally includes the computer itself, as well as communications equipment, printers, and input/output devices. On the software side, specifications regarding processing operations should be included. Furthermore, specific processing cycles and times should be given.

Next, specific details relating to the input of data in the system should be provided. These should include the method of input, procedures for screening input data, and the content of data inputs.

Finally, in all cases, specific volume and cost information should be provided. For example, if the system calls for manual entry of sales orders into a computer system, details regarding the personnel and cost and time requirements for data entry should be given. This information should be provided in terms of peak volume (e.g., during the busy season) and average volume.

It is also important that a detailed analysis of control and security measures be incorporated into the design proposal because a number of the design considerations may involve tradeoffs between internal control and efficiency. For example, a design might specify that a particular data item be entered into the system twice so that the computer can cross-compare the two entries for accuracy and consistency. In this case, the design proposal should clearly state that this is being done for internal control purposes.

BUSINESS PROCESS BLUEPRINTING

It is becoming increasingly popular to use prepackaged sets of blueprints for all a company's business processes. For example, those implementing the SAP Enterprise Resource Planning System begin the design effort with a complete set of SAP-supplied blueprints for all or almost all the company's business processes. The design team then focuses on adapting this initial set of blueprints to its own needs, focusing on the processes that are especially unique and important to the company's strategies and goals.

GENERAL DESIGN CONSIDERATIONS

The preceding section focused on specific factors to consider in developing a systems design proposal. This section considers objectives pertinent to each phase of the design process. Table 10.3 summarizes these general considerations for each major system element in the design phase.

OUTPUT DESIGN

The first and foremost consideration for output design is **cost-effectiveness**. The principle of cost-effectiveness should be applied to all elements of the system because an investment in the information system is like any capital budgeting expenditure—it should be evaluated on a cost/benefit basis. The intent is to maximize the ratio of the benefits to cost while satisfying the objectives for a given system.

   The properties of relevance, clarity, and timeliness are essential to managerial reports. Reports should include only information that is relevant to a particular decision maker. However, this principle cannot be strictly adhered to because some reports must be generated for more than one manager, and different managers have different preferences for information. Nevertheless, both unneeded or missing information can decrease the value of a report. A report that is cluttered with a lot of irrelevant information might be ignored by a manager who is unwilling to wade

TABLE 10.3   Design Considerations for System Elements

System Element	Design Consideration
Outputs (report or document)	Cost-effectiveness
	Relevance
	Clarity
	Timeliness
Database	Cost-effectiveness
	Integration
	Standardization
	Flexibility
	Security
	Accuracy
	Efficiency
	Organization
Data processing	Cost-effectiveness
	Uniformity
	Integration
	Accuracy
Data input	Cost-effectiveness
	Accuracy
	Uniformity
	Integration
Controls and security measures	Cost-effectiveness
	Comprehensiveness
	Appropriateness

through a lot of useless data. The inclusion of irrelevant information in a report also may result in excessive information costs.

One very important factor relating to clarity involves including appropriate titles and captions within a report. Far too often, information systems produce reports that are not titled and captioned adequately. The justification that managers know the contents of the reports and do not need detailed explanations is offered often. The danger in this line of reasoning is that many companies have a high rate of turnover in their management staff, which means that a new manager might either misinterpret a report or ignore it altogether because of its lack of clarity.

DATABASE DESIGN

Several important principles apply to database design. Of particular importance is that a company's databases be integrated. **Integration** means the avoidance of collecting and maintaining the same data items in more than one place in the company. In an integrated system, various phases of business operations can share the same data. For example, the sales department, shipping department, and billing department might all need a customer's name and address. In a fully integrated system, this information might be entered into the system once in the credit department. It could then be accessed by the sales department for generating orders and by the shipping department for shipping to the correct address. In a system without integration, this information might have to be typed three separate times. This not only would produce higher costs but also would result in a higher error rate.

Another important consideration in database design is that of **standardization**, which means that all data items are entered in a standard format and assigned a common name when used in more than one place. For example, if a departmental expense budget shows the item "Automobile Expense," it should be defined to mean the same thing throughout the entire company. It therefore would be undesirable to have "Automobile Expense" include depreciation in one department but not in another. Flexibility and security are other important features of a database design. Databases should be designed in such a manner that users can structure a wide variety of queries. For example, one manager might want sales broken down by district and then by product, whereas another manager might want sales broken down by product and then by district. A flexible database design would allow for either type of report.

DATA PROCESSING

One important consideration in data processing relates to uniformity and integration. It is important that the company's overall data processing system develop according to some general plan. For example, it might be undesirable for a given department to acquire microcomputers that would be incompatible with other microcomputers in the same company.

DATA INPUT

One often difficult consideration in designing the data input system is that of accuracy. The use of well-defined source documents can encourage employees to record data accurately without omissions. For example, if a customer's telephone number is a needed data input, the sales order document should have a specific line that is clearly labeled "Customer telephone number." A document that simply includes several lines with a label "Customer information" would be less desirable because some employees would leave out the telephone number.

CONTROLS AND SECURITY MEASURES

Implementing adequate controls is too often overlooked. Comprehensive, appropriate controls should be established for each phase of the system's design process. This is one area in which the accountant can play a critical role while working with a design team. In many cases the design team primarily may involve information systems specialists who might have an appreciation for controls but not detailed expertise in this area. In this case, the accountant can review the overall plan and discuss inadequacies in controls with the individual team members.

DESIGN TECHNIQUES

Designing a system is a creative activity. It is unlikely that two design teams will produce the same solution to a given problem. Therefore, systems design can be viewed somewhat as an art, although one in which various refined techniques have been developed. As an artist needs special tools for painting, the systems designer needs certain tools to assist in the design process. Many of these tools are also used in systems analysis. While all the systems analysis techniques pertain to systems design, certain special problems are more specific to information systems design. These are associated primarily with forms (document) and database design, which are discussed below.

FORMS DESIGN

The process of designing specific forms is called **forms design**. The area of forms design should be given very careful attention by the systems design team because forms are the interface between the users and the system itself. Therefore, forms design should focus on producing documents that provide effective interfaces between managers and the information system.

DATABASE DESIGN

A number of useful techniques are available for designing databases: data structure diagrams, record layouts, file analysis sheets, and file-related matrices. Data structure diagrams show the relationships between various kinds of records. For example, a manufacturing company may have several records in various databases relating to a given customer. One record may contain sales order information, another record production status information, and another information relating to billing. The data structure diagram defines the relationship among these different data records.

A record layout diagram shows the various data fields within a record. Both record layout and data structure diagrams are discussed in detail in Chapter 12, "File Processing and Data Management Concepts."

File analysis sheets provide the system designer with all major points of relevant information regarding the contents of a particular file. Such information would include record layouts, the purpose of the file, the expected number of records, and so on.

File-related matrices show the interrelationships between files, their contents, and their uses. File-related matrices can be helpful in determining the effective and efficient use of data items within files, eliminating unneeded or redundant data items, and optimizing file structure in general. For example, one file-related matrix might show a list of data items on one side versus a list of files in which these data items are used on the other side. Another example of a file-related matrix would be one that lists data items on one side and reports on the other side. This type of matrix would be helpful in assessing the use of particular data items in reports. If a data item does not appear in any of the reports, the company might consider eliminating it from the file.

SYSTEMS DESIGN PACKAGES

A number of prepackaged design methodologies are available to assist in the systems development cycle. The purpose of these packages is to assist the designer in systematically approaching a given problem. These packages help the designer structure the design problem and can result in considerable time savings.

Computer-aided software engineering (CASE) is computer software technology that supports an automated engineering discipline for software development and maintenance. CASE can produce data flow diagrams, narrative documentation, screen and report prototypes, and data dictionary descriptions. CASE can increase productivity, improve software quality though the introduction of rigorous standards and analysis, and decrease the cost of developing, documenting, and maintaining software. Most CASE products include some elements of prepackaged design methodologies.

Prepackaged design systems have the advantage of assisting the designer in structuring a particular problem; however, most design packages have certain shortcomings. In particular, the packages do not assist in specifying the desired outputs, nor do they deal adequately with the problem of system response time. The design packages may provide some assistance but not total solutions to all problems.

CHOOSING SOFTWARE AND HARDWARE

At some point the decision must be made as to whether the computer software is to be built from scratch or purchased. Although this seems to be a design decision, it should be made at the end of the analysis phase. Much of the design phase may be omitted if a purchase decision is made. Once the requirements of any new system have been specified, one can then look at available software packages to see which ones most closely fit a company's needs—all without actually "designing" that system.

On the other hand, nothing pleases computer professionals more than the freedom to design and build a new system from scratch. Since this is what they have been trained to do, they tend to ignore the multitude of good software packages already available on the market. It is economically more feasible for many businesses, especially smaller ones, to buy rather than build software.

Purchased software packages have several advantages:

- They are cheaper. The cost of development is carried by many purchasers rather than just the creator.
- They are already debugged. If several other organizations have been using the package for some months, it is reasonably safe to assume that most of the bugs have been found and exterminated.
- The company can try the product before investing a great deal of money. With in-house software, it is possible to put months of development time into a program only to discover that it does not produce the desired results when it is done.

The main disadvantage to **canned software packages** (i.e., purchased software packages) is that they rarely exactly meet a company's needs. It may be necessary to modify the software (which can be expensive, if not impossible) or to modify the company's procedures to match what the package requires.

A **dedicated software package** is intended for a narrow audience, such as retail stores or accounting firms. To find a good dedicated software package, talk to people who work for other companies in the same industry. Someone who works for another manufacturing organization, for example, may know of a good production control package. Trade magazines and Web sites for an industry also tell what is available (e.g., software packages for florists are advertised in *Florist's Review*).

When evaluating purchased software, it is helpful to use a decision-table format to consider the following:

- How close is the fit to what is needed? Will the programs or our procedures or both have to be modified?
- How stable is the software vendor? Will it still be in business in a year or two when problems arise? Does it give prompt support when problems arise? A toll-free, 24-hour telephone line is a good indicator.
- Is there a trial period, during which everything can be returned for a full refund after a month or so?
- How many other installations have used the software? For how long? Who are they? Some people get a list of users' names from the vendor but do not ask those users for evaluations because they know the evaluation will be good or the vendor would not have supplied them. Instead, ask them for second-level references—other organizations that they know are using the package but whom the vendor failed to mention. Here is where the skeletons can be uncovered.
- How flexible is the software? Can it change along with the changing business environment? Are there any growth limits on file size, number of transactions, or embedded tables?
- Is it user friendly? Does the software guide the operator through each program, with adequate explanations and error messages? Is the documentation clear, complete, and easy to read?
- Are source programs supplied? If not, the company will be forever dependent on the vendor for modifications at whatever price is named.

Only after collecting data on the various software packages available is it time to worry about choosing the hardware. Since the software is what determines how well the computer meets the company's needs, it is usually fairly safe to be content with the hardware on which that software runs. There are a few constraints in hardware selection that are much the same as those detailed in the preceding points. In addition, try to get machinery that is **upwardly compatible**—easily upgradable to a larger or faster model in the future without losing existing data or programs.

One last note on purchasing any computer hardware or software: It is a mistake to put off a purchase in the belief that either the price will drop shortly or a new version will be available soon. In most cases the price drop is negligible compared with the inconvenience caused by not having the computer in the meantime. And the state-of-the-art methods of the newer version usually are not required; mere adequacy has its merits. It might be better to buy the system now, when it is needed, than to try to outguess the computer market, which is so unpredictable that no one has a very good batting average for forecasting.

CONVENTIONAL WISDOM IN SYSTEMS DEVELOPMENT

Developing an information system is a creative and demanding task that can and should produce economic benefits for an organization. On the other hand, the systems development process can produce a disaster, with labor and financial resources being expended with no observable return and perhaps even a system that cannot be completed. In practice, the systems development process often has produced both these results. The history of systems development suggests that positive results are obtained more frequently if the systems development process is formally structured, documented, and subject to management control techniques. One of the most important control techniques is to actively involve the ultimate user in the development of information systems.

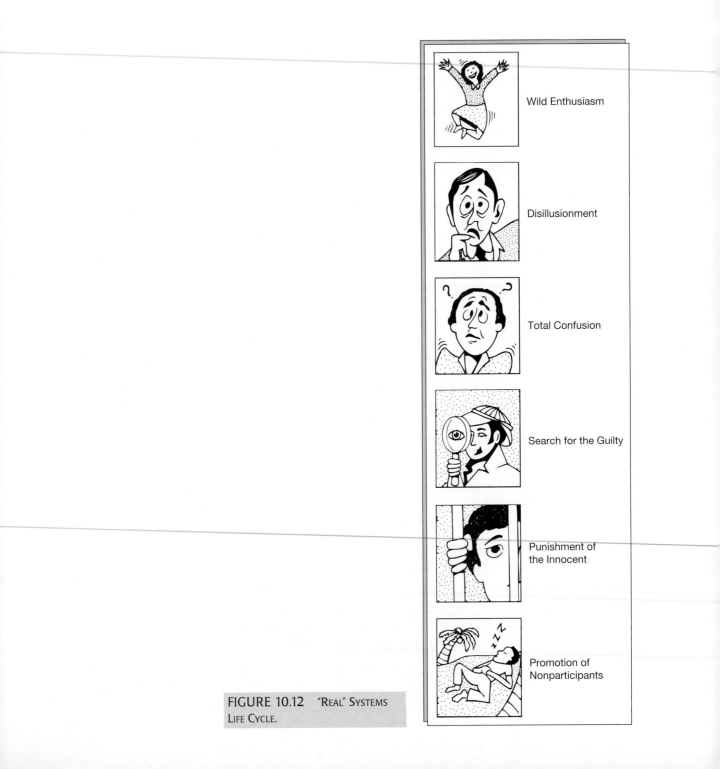

FIGURE 10.12 "REAL" SYSTEMS LIFE CYCLE.

The nature of the problems that historically have plagued systems development is humorously summarized in Figure 10.12. This figure shows the phases in a "real" systems development life cycle. The cycle begins with wild enthusiasm in the analysis phase, when all things seem possible and "all systems are go." Disillusionment and total confusion set in during the design phase as serious problems develop as the project group tries to design unrealistic or hopelessly vague requirements specified during the analysis phase. The result is a system that does not work technically, or operationally, in the sense of doing what it was supposed to do, or economically, in the sense of its return on costs, or some combination of these possibilities. Accordingly, the major phases of implementation consist of the search for the guilty, punishment of the innocent, and promotion of nonparticipants.

While perhaps a lesson in "how to survive life in a systems group," the figure is, more importantly, a demonstration of the likely outcome of an inadequately structured systems development effort. Management abdication of its responsibilities for the control of systems development is frequently cited as a major reason for such system failures in the past. The need for active involvement of all levels of management in systems development is widely and generally recognized as a major deterrent to systems development failure. The best way to ensure this involvement is through use of the life cycle concept.

Another type of problem that has plagued systems development concerns the quality of communication between the many parties in a systems development project. This problem can cause even a well-controlled project to generate a system that fails in the sense that the final user does not actually use it. The system works, is well documented, and is within budget and time controls, but it fails to provide the user with what he or she desires. This situation is shown pictorially in Figure 10.13, which illustrates a lack of communication between the many parties in the systems development process. Each party—user manager, steering committee, and so on—holds a different view of what was to be done. The lesson is that each party's perception of a system to be designed is influenced by his or her own functional specialty. Each functional specialty will see the project from its own viewpoint, preconceiving or assuming things based on its own knowledge. Great care must be taken to ensure that the chain of communication required in a project is effective and complete. Vagueness in communication leads to situations such as that shown in Figure 10.13. The solution to the communication problem is to actively involve the user in systems development.

❖ SUMMARY

Systems planning involves decisions on the part of top management with respect to prioritizing system development needs. The output of systems planning is a written document that states the overall information systems objectives for the company. In addition, the document specifies general areas of need for systems development work. A general plan is given for implementing these needs. The systems analysis plan is dynamic and must be revised continuously. Systems development is a never-ending process because the business environment and corporate information needs are constantly changing.

Systems analysis begins with a system or systems specified in the overall company information systems plan. The systems analysis effort involves three distinct phases: (1) surveying the current system, (2) identifying information needs, and (3) identifying systems requirements. After these steps are completed, a systems analysis report is written and conveyed to top management. This report should focus on particular problems discovered and should suggest general approaches to solving them. In addition, a specific proposal for developing a new system (or modifying an old system) should be included.

FIGURE 10.13   COMMUNICATION PROBLEMS IN SYSTEMS DEVELOPMENT.

The systems planning and analysis portions of the development cycle are extremely crucial because mistakes made at these levels can be extremely costly. Design and implementation costs often can run into millions of dollars. Therefore, the analysis phase should give management a clear picture of where it needs to go.

Many techniques can aid in the systems analyst's work, including questionnaires, interviews, and direct observation. The analyst also uses work measurement and work distribution techniques. These analyses are accompanied by narratives, input/output matrices, data flow diagrams, hierarchical function diagrams, and flowcharts.

A particularly useful approach is structured systems analysis. This approach begins with a general logical data flow diagram, which is then supported with detailed data flow diagrams, data dictionaries, access method descriptions, and specifics on process logic.

Systems design is an orderly process that begins at a very general level with the setting of objectives for a particular system. The process then proceeds to the more detailed level with the specification of file structures, processing operations, and forms design. The major steps in system design include evaluating design alternatives, preparing design specifications, and submitting a completed systems design report. Once a particular design alternative has been selected, it can be presented to top management. Top management then reviews the proposed design, along with its budget, and decides whether the project should proceed in more detail. If management does decide in favor of selecting a particular design project, the design team can specify the design details. Detailed design considerations would include things such as output design, database design, data processing operations, data inputs, and controls and security measures. The preferred procedure is to first design the system outputs and then work backward to define the inputs.

A number of systems design techniques are very helpful. These include standard systems design techniques, such as flowcharting, data flow diagrams, and input/output analysis. There are, however, a number of techniques that are particularly useful in systems design. These include forms analysis sheets, data hierarchy diagrams, forms layout charts, data structure diagrams, record layouts, file analysis sheets, and file-related input/output matrices. The first three techniques assist the systems designer in preparing and analyzing forms. The latter techniques are useful in the design and layout of databases.

Systems design packages provide a structured approach to systems design. The more sophisticated packages allow the designer to specify the desired inputs, outputs, and processing operations. The design package then generates a working database system. Such packages save the designer a considerable amount of time. Many decisions must be made, however, that the design package cannot help with. For example, the design package cannot tell the designer what the desired outputs should be. In addition, the design package may be inadequate with regard to specifying the optimal database structure and file access methods.

In conclusion, systems analysis and design are processes that involve a considerable amount of creativity. Success comes with good communication between the systems design team and management. All feasible alternatives should be considered carefully. Special emphasis should be given to system integration and security measures.

❖ GLOSSARY

bottlenecks: weaknesses in a system where small changes can result in major improvements in performance.

canned software packages: software packages purchased from a vendor.

cost-effectiveness: the benefits of a design should exceed its costs.

decision flow diagram: graphic technique that emphasizes the chain of decisions relating to a particular subsystem.

dedicated software package: a commercially available software package that is intended for a narrow audience.

detailed design proposal: everything necessary to actually implement a design project, including timetables, a budget, personnel requirements, and design documentation.

feasibility: design criterion that it must be possible to actually implement the design specifications.

forms design: the process of designing specific forms.

information needs analysis: analysis of specific decisions made by managers in terms of the information inputs.

integration: design criteria that mean the avoidance of collecting and maintaining the same data items in more than one place.

key success factors: characteristics that distinguish a company from its competitors and are the keys to its success.

pseudocode: structured-English type of system documentation that includes provisions for error conditions and data file access.

standardization: design criteria that all data items are to be entered in a standard format and assigned a common name when used in more than one place.

steering committee: committee representing top management and all major functional areas within the organization that is charged with guiding the overall systems development effort.

strategic systems plan: a written document that incorporates both short- and long-run goals relating to the company's systems development effort.

structured English: a special language for describing process logic that uses several key words, including *IF, THEN, ELSE IF,* and *SO.*

structured systems analysis: an approach to systems analysis that begins with a very general description of a particular system and then proceeds through a logically related set of steps, each increasing in detail.

systems analysis: the process of understanding existing systems and problems, describing information needs, and establishing priorities for further systems work.

systems development life cycle: the concept that every systems development project goes through essentially the same process or life cycle of systems analysis, systems design, and implementation.

systems planning: identifying subsystems within the information system that need special attention for development.

turnkey systems: computer packages that meet the specific needs of an individual situation with minimal design work.

upwardly compatible: computer hardware that is easily upgradable to a larger or faster model without losing existing data or programs.

Warnier-Orr methodology: a methodology and diagramming technique for analyzing the outputs of an application and factoring the application into a hierarchical structure of modules to accomplish the necessary processing.

❖ CHAPTER QUIZ

Answers to the chapter quiz appear on page 389.

1. It is crucial that all major systems development efforts have the support of (the) (_____).
    (a) steering committee
    (b) top management
    (c) chief systems analyst
    (d) controller

2. Which of the following should be responsible for the overall planning and control of the systems development effort of a company?
    (a) steering committee
    (b) top management
    (c) chief systems analyst
    (d) controller

3. Which of the following terms describes the analysis of specific decisions made by managers in terms of information inputs?
    (a) HIPO charts
    (b) work measurement
    (c) functional analysis
    (d) information needs analysis

4. The third phase of the systems analysis project involves specifying systems requirements. Such requirements are usually specified in terms of (_____).
    (a) reports
    (b) inputs and outputs
    (c) decisions
    (d) processes

5. Which of the following fact-gathering techniques best allows the systems analyst to establish a personal working relationship with a manager?
    (a) depth interviews
    (b) structured interviews
    (c) open-ended questionnaires
    (d) closed-ended questionnaires

6. Which of the following fact-gathering techniques often will provide the analyst with insight into system activities that can be obtained in no other way?
    (a) depth interviews
    (b) structured interviews

    (c) document reviews

    (d) observation

7. An overview logical data flow diagram, which shows only the basic entities and data flows in a system, is called a (_____).

    (a) decision flow diagram

    (b) sources and uses of information diagram

    (c) context diagram

    (d) HIPO chart

8. In a logical data flow diagram, which of the following symbols would be used to represent a file of data?

    (a) terminator

    (b) data flow

    (c) data store

    (d) process

9. In a logical data flow diagram, which of the following symbols is drawn either as a circle or as a rectangle with curved edges?

    (a) terminator

    (b) data flow

    (c) data store

    (d) process

10. Which of the following is *not* one of the three basic constructs used in creating a Warnier-Orr diagram?

    (a) redundancy

    (b) sequence

    (c) selection

    (d) repetition

11. Which of the following design criteria holds that the benefits of a design should exceed its costs?

    (a) feasibility

    (b) cost-effectiveness

    (c) standardization

    (d) integration

12. Which of the following design criteria holds that it must be possible to actually implement the design specifications?

    (a) feasibility

    (b) cost-effectiveness

    (c) standardization

    (d) integration

13. In a certain company, the data item "Automobile expense" includes depreciation in one department but not in another. This violates which of the following design criteria?

    (a) flexibility

    (b) security

    (c) standardization

    (d) integration

14. In a certain company, the data item "Customer address" is entered and maintained in separate databases by both the billing and sales departments. This violates which of the following design criteria?

    (a) flexibility

    (b) security

    (c) standardization

    (d) integration

15. Forms design should be given very careful attention by the systems design team because (_____).

    (a) forms are expensive to produce in volume

    (b) forms are the interface between users and the system

    (c) forms are the first step in detailed systems design

    (d) forms are the final step in detailed systems design

16. Computer packages that meet the specific needs of an individual situation with minimal design work are called (_____).

    (a) turnkey systems

    (b) CASE systems

    (c) integrated systems

    (d) database systems

17. Which of the following tools uses a grid on which each item in the grid corresponds to a particular location on a medium where a form is to be displayed?

    (a) input/output matrix

    (b) forms layout chart

    (c) data hierarchy diagram

    (d) forms analysis sheet

18. The main disadvantage to canned software packages is (_____).

    (a) they rarely exactly meet a company's needs

    (b) they are more expensive than developing software inhouse

    (c) they need to be debugged

    (d) they cannot be tried without investing a great deal of money

19. When evaluating purchased software, a good indicator of vendor support for the package is (_____).

    (a) a toll-free telephone number

    (b) the relative price of the package

    (c) the number of installations using the package

    (d) how user-friendly the package is

20. Computer hardware that is easily upgradable to a larger or faster model without losing existing data or programs is said to be (_____).

    (a) a superflexible system

    (b) an upwardly compatible system

    (c) a user-friendly system

    (d) a turnkey system

❖ REVIEW QUESTIONS

1. Define and explain each of the following terms.

    (a) systems planning

    (b) systems analysis

    (c) communications problem

    (d) information needs analysis

    (e) depth interview

    (f) open-ended questionnaire

    (g) closed-ended questionnaire

    (h) structured interview

    (i) work measurement

    (j) work distribution

    (k) hierarchical function diagram

    (l) input/output matrix

    (m) logical flow diagram

2. Is the systems analysis phase of systems development more expensive than the systems design phase?

3. Which individuals should be involved in systems planning?

4. What is the function of the systems steering committee?

5. What are the primary phases of systems analysis?

6. What are some of the major hurdles that the systems analyst must overcome?

7. Discuss the primary advantages of depth interviews.

8. Discuss the primary advantages of structured interviews.

9. Under what situations would a closed-ended questionnaire be appropriate?
10. What should be included in the contents of the systems analysis report?
11. What is the difference between work measurement analysis and work distribution analysis?
12. What is the primary advantage of hierarchical function analysis?
13. Where are the limitations of hierarchical function analysis?
14. What is a HIPO chart?
15. When would the use of a decision flow diagram be important?
16. What are the key elements of a logical data flow diagram?
17. Give three examples of matrix-oriented analysis.
18. Why is systems analysis an important first step preceding systems design?
19. What are some of the key behavioral considerations that are important in systems analysis?
20. Define each of the following terms.
    (a) design alternatives
    (b) forms analysis sheet
    (c) file-related matrices
    (d) operational feasibility
21. What are the major steps in the systems design process?
22. What are some of the major considerations that must be incorporated into the systems design process?
23. Which step in the design process is the most important?
24. In what ways can an accountant contribute the most to the systems design team?
25. Discuss the purpose of systems design packages.
26. Discuss the limitations of systems design packages.
27. At what stage should the systems design proposal be reviewed by top management?
28. Describe the major components of the systems design report.
29. Describe several major considerations involved in database design.
30. Describe several major considerations involved in output document design.

❖ DISCUSSION QUESTIONS AND PROBLEMS

31. Discuss some of the major problems often encountered in systems analysis. How can these problems be avoided?
32. Why is observation needed? Couldn't the analyst save a considerable amount of time simply by relying on the system as documented?
33. How do you deal with the situation in which a manager claims not to understand departmental information needs?
34. In a company too small for an information systems steering committee, which individual would be the most appropriate to oversee the systems development function?
35. For each of the following systems, develop a hierarchical function diagram.
    (a) purchasing system
    (b) production system
    (c) inventory management system
36. Assume that you have been hired as a consultant for a small company that has problems with its payroll system. Describe the steps you would take in developing a solution.
37. Discuss the major goals of systems analysis.
38. Discuss the importance of the systems analysis report.
39. Below is a list of problem situations. In each case, discuss some of the major steps you would follow in systems analysis.
    (a) A company has problems with raw material shortages.
    (b) A company has production bottlenecks and is not able to manage production according to a preset schedule.
    (c) A company has severe problems with credit losses.
    (d) Overall production employee morale is low.
    (e) Large quantities of units have been sitting in inventory for many years.
40. Describe several systems analysis techniques that would be helpful for purposes of gathering and organizing the facts needed in studying an accounts receivable system.

41. Which of the following systems analysis techniques—(i) work measurement analysis, (ii) work distribution analysis, (iii) questionnaire, (iv) logical data flow diagram, (v) interview, (vi) input/output diagram—would be the most appropriate for each case below?
    (a) Analyzing the information needs of a production manager
    (b) Analyzing the information flows within the sales department
    (c) Analyzing an inventory management system
    (d) Analyzing a purchase order system
42. Describe structured systems analysis.
43. Herman Manufacturing has been having many difficulties. This company manufactures caps and gowns used for graduation ceremonies in both high schools and colleges. Most of the company's problems have revolved around its inability to generate sufficient sales to maintain overall profitability. The president of the company, Barbara Novel, feels that this situation has been caused by poor relations between the company and its customers. Barbara has confided in some of the company's major customers about this matter, and they have advised her that they are very happy with the quality of the company's products. However, they mentioned a number of problems. Among the problems given were late deliveries and incomplete orders. Further discussion with some of the company's production employees has revealed that a wide range of production problems exist, including (i) low-quality raw materials, (ii) bottlenecks in production due to a general lack of coordination in job scheduling, and (iii) mixups in customer's orders.

    You have been called in as an independent consultant and have been asked to advise Barbara Novel.

    Required
    (a) Where do you begin dealing with this company's problem?
    (b) What type of systems analysis techniques would be useful in this situation?
44. Central Manufacturing produces custom-made kitchen cabinets. This is a medium-sized, family-owned corporation with approximately 150 employees. Joe Starr has been the president for the past 5 years. The company presently serves a wide range of customers in the Ft. Lauderdale–Miami area of south Florida. The organizational structure is reasonably simple. Under Joe Starr are three vice presidents (all of whom are major shareholders in the company): Mary Noddle (vice president of production), Ron Hill (vice president of sales), and Kim Debe (vice president of accounting).

    Under Ron Hill are seven sales managers, each of whom represents a particular segment of the Dade-Broward County areas. As sales orders are received, the production department processes a custom manufacturing order, which specifies the exact materials to be used. In the next phase, the raw materials are pulled, and the job is assigned to a team of workers. The size of this team depends on the size of the job.

    At present, Joe Starr is concerned with a number of problems but primarily with bad debt losses. A superficial analysis of accounts receivable indicated that a large number of accounts are more than 90 days overdue. Mr. Starr is sure that these will be collected eventually; however, Central Manufacturing has had difficulty in paying its bills due to these late collections.

    Joe Starr has asked the chief accountant, Jim Wdeve, for an explanation of the problem. Mr. Wdeve explained that he periodically reviews the accounts receivable records, making notes on overdue accounts, which he uses as a basis for telephoning customers and asking for explanations.

    Mr. Wdeve recommended that the problem be solved by implementing a network of microcomputers throughout the company. He suggested that with a microcomputer on each employee's desk, everyone would have instant access to any information needed.

    Required
    Comment on Mr. Wdeve's suggestion for installing a network of microcomputers.
45. John Needles has been hired as a systems consultant for Arco Manufacturing. The company's president, Barbara Arco, has told John that the company has been having numerous problems with late deliveries on customers' orders. The problem has been very acute because the competition has taken away a lot of business by offering faster delivery times.

John sets up an interview with the production supervisor to discuss the problem. The interview goes as follows:

JOHN: I have been hired to help alleviate any bottlenecks leading to late deliveries.

SUPERVISOR: I appreciate your offer to help, but I'm afraid that our problems can only be solved by someone with a considerable amount of experience doing this type of work.

JOHN: I agree. That's why I hope I can rely on you and your experience.

SUPERVISOR: I'm still afraid there isn't much I can do for you. Perhaps it would be better if you work directly with Ms Arco. I have an awful lot of work to do and need to make a production deadline this afternoon.

JOHN: Perhaps I can come back later this afternoon?

SUPERVISOR: You're welcome to come back, but again, I don't think I can help you.

Required

John Needles seems to be having trouble communicating with the production supervisor. Discuss some possible causes of this problem, and make suggestions for overcoming it.

46. The General Company has an accounting staff of five employees: a supervisor and four clerks. The daily tasks of each clerk are as follows:

Supervisor (Mary Wild)
Checking paperwork—5 hours
Filing documents—5 hours
Preparing invoices—4 hours
Other activities—1 hour

Accounts payable clerk (Joe Freedmire)
Preparing monthly statements—4 hours
Preparing aging report—3 hours
Checking invoices—4 hours

Helper clerk (Bob Stans)
Checking invoices—3 hours
Preparing aging report—2 hours
Account posting—5 hours

Document verification clerk (Margaret Lee)
Preparing disbursement vouchers—4 hours
Checking invoices—2 hours
Other activities—3 hours

Clerk-typist (Debbie Chase)
Typing invoices—4 hours
Assisting in verification of invoices—3 hours

Required

(a) Prepare a work distribution chart using tasks such as aging of accounts receivable, voucher preparation, and so on.

(b) Identify any weaknesses in the distribution of tasks. In addition, note any internal control problems.

47. Systems analyst Jack Blount has been hired as a consultant to a large national distributing company to develop a new system for inventory control. The company is extremely large and has manufacturing plants and offices throughout the country. Mr. Blount decided to focus his attention initially on the Chicago plant.

He first interviewed the plant manager. The discussion was very productive, and after several meetings, he felt that he was in a position to make suggestions for improving the system. Based on this, he prepared a systems analysis report for review by the company's chief accountant.

In his meeting with the chief accountant, a number of problems arose. The chief accountant told him that a number of employees had complained to him, "Mr. Blount said he was going to have a number of employees laid off." Several supervisors complained that they were being replaced by computers. The situation had got so out of hand that a number of employees were on the verge of striking. Such a strike could cost the company thousands of dollars in a very short time. For this reason, the chief accountant informed Mr. Blount that the company did not wish to proceed with systems design and implementation. Mr. Blount was very disappointed to hear this because he felt that a few simple changes to the existing system could be very helpful in terms of solving the company's problems.

Required

Has Mr. Blount made any mistakes? If so, what did he do wrong?

48. List several important data fields that would be found in a database design for accounts receivable.

49. In evaluating design alternatives, the costs versus the benefits of a particular design proposal should be weighed; however, it is often difficult to quantify the benefits associated with a particular proposal. Give several examples of systems design problems where the benefits would be difficult to quantify.

50. Consider a small manufacturing company that has taken on the project of designing databases for sales orders, inventory, and accounts receivable. List several data fields that these three databases might have in common.

51. A problem that sometimes can occur in systems design is that the final users of the system will fight its implementation. What can be done during the design phase to avoid this problem?

52. Assume that you have been assigned the job of designing a system for a medium-sized clothing manufacturing company. This company maintains raw material inventories for about 19 different fabrics. These fabrics are dyed and cut according to prespecified patterns. The plant manager has been advocating the introduction of a standard cost control system. Your job as the systems designer is to help the plant manager describe the various reports that would be required from a new system. The plant manager is specifically interested in reports for production cost control and inventory management.

Required

Describe at least three reports that could be produced by the new system.

53. A systems design team is considering the development of a system for sales orders. What members of management should this team communicate with throughout the design project?

54. Does the size of a company have any impact on the approach taken to the systems design project? If your answer is yes, explain.

55. What would be some unique problems associated with systems design in the automobile manufacturing industry?

56. You are in the process of designing an accounts receivable system for your company. A local computer retailer hears that you are designing a system and calls on you. He tells you that he can sell you a computer and software package that will solve all your problems. What is your response to the computer salesman?

57. You have been charged with the responsibility of heading up a design team. The team's responsibility will be to design a production control system. The team consists of you and four other members, including two systems analysts, a database designer, and the production manager. To initiate the project, you call a meeting of all individuals on the design team. At the first meeting, however, you find that the two systems analysts and the database designer have already made up their minds regarding the structure of the system under consideration. As head of the team, you feel that several major design alternatives should be considered before selecting a particular system. How do you deal with this problem?

58. A medium-sized grocery store has point-of-sale cash registers. The cash registers automatically summarize sales of all items sold in the store. One major problem facing the store is that of keeping adequate amounts of all grocery items on the shelves. Therefore, the store is searching for a way to monitor inventories and place daily orders for new goods, as needed.

Required

Give two major alternatives for the design of a system that accounts for and controls inventory for this grocery store.

59. The *Daily Times* newspaper company serves a small community. A considerable portion of the newspaper's revenues come from advertising. At present, all advertising orders are taken by salespeople, usually at the customers' places of business. At the end of every three days, all advertising orders are processed in a batch. Therefore, it normally takes four days between the time the orders are taken and the time the ad appears in the newspaper. Recently, however, a competitive newspaper has offered faster service to its customers.

Required

Present two major design alternatives for processing sales orders for the *Daily Times*.

60. The Good Burger Company owns and operates a chain of fast-food restaurants located throughout the southeastern portion of the United States. The company's main headquarters is in Atlanta. A major problem of the company is that of delivering food products to all the individual company stores. This involves loading up warehouse trucks and then stopping at individual stores on a weekly basis. Each store has a large refrigerator room where a considerable amount of food supply inventory can be maintained. Charles Hill, the general manager of food distribution, has noted that the company should develop a formal system for determining the amount of food to be delivered to each store. In addition, he has questioned whether it is necessary to deliver food to each store on a weekly basis. His rough calculations indicate that some stores might be visited less often. The major problem is that of communication between individual stores and the central office. At present, there is no way for the central office to know how much food to deliver to the individual stores.

Required

Design a system that would collect data on a daily basis at the central office regarding the need for food supplies by the individual stores. Your system should incorporate a database that keeps track of the sales and inventories of food supplies at individual stores. Your answer should be expressed in general terms. It is not necessary to develop a detailed database design.

61. Green Hardware Manufacturing produces and sells hardware products throughout the western portion of the United States. The primary source of revenue for the company comes from sales to individual hardware stores. The company has divided its sales territory into seven districts, with a sales manager in charge of each district. The individual sales managers try to travel around from store to store and take sales orders directly from store owners. The sales orders are then sent to company headquarters in Los Angeles, where they are processed. The present procedure is for the sales manager to write his or her own name on the sales order. At the end of each month, the company's accountant prepares a summary of sales by each district and for each product. This process, however, is extremely difficult and usually takes the accountant about 4 days to complete.

Required

Compose a general design alternative for collecting sales data and producing sales reports in a timely fashion.

62. Assume that you are the information systems manager for a medium-sized department store. At present, your company does all its customer billing manually. Your responsibility is to design a computerized database for customer accounts receivable.

Required

Exactly what data fields are needed for the accounts receivable database?

63. The Fund Travel Agency operates four offices in a medium-sized metropolitan area. Each office has several individuals who plan trips and make reservations for clients. In order to optimize the use of employee time, all reservationists are shifted from office to office as needed. The company's telephone system operates such that customers can dial a central number and then be connected to the office where a reservationist is then assigned to that particular customer. A problem in the system is that since the reservationists do not stay at

one office, they do not always have the customer's records when a customer calls in to review or change a reservation.

Required

Design a centralized reservation system for the Fund Travel Agency. Create a computerized system such that a customer's file can be accessed from any location.

64. Brown Chemical Manufacturing produces a single product called *CRX*. The company's product is sold mainly to food processing manufacturers who use it as a preservative. The production process for CRX is quite complicated. The product goes through four different stages, and each stage is carefully controlled with regard to temperature and moisture. At the first stage, two basic chemicals are mixed together and heated to 1,500 degrees. At stage two, the product is cooled, and an additional chemical is added when it reaches just the right temperature. At the third and fourth stages, the resulting chemical is refined successfully. Therefore, the company has to maintain raw materials inventory for three different chemicals. In addition, the finished-goods inventory for CRX has to be maintained. Almost all the cost of producing CRX is for raw materials and overhead. Since the process is fully automated, there is no direct labor cost. Another major cost, however, is that of storing the finished product. In order to increase the product's shelf life, the finished chemical is stored under specially controlled temperature conditions. These conditions require refrigeration to 0 degrees, with essentially no moisture. This refrigeration process is fairly expensive because the company manufactures a very large quantity of CRX.

Recently, management of the company has been evaluating the overall systems design. Several comments have been made with regard to the manufacturing and inventory systems:

(a) It has been determined that a large number of production batches of CRX have to be discarded due to inadequate environmental conditions during processing. At present, there is no management reporting for the costs of the lost materials or time.

(b) Management suspects that the company is incurring too high a cost in the refrigeration of finished goods. It would prefer that production batches be run as customer orders are placed. In this way, the finished CRX could be shipped directly to the customer without a need for refrigerated storage in inventory. However, the problem is that the company has never been able to successfully implement this type of system for several reasons: (1) delays in processing of customer orders, (2) difficulty with efficiently scheduling production, and (3) problems with distribution. It is often the case that when a production order is ready, the company's trucks are all out of state making deliveries. It would be disastrous if a production batch were completed and there was no truck to deliver it. This would result in the loss of the entire shipment.

Required

Present a systems design alternative for dealing with Brown Chemical's problems.

65. The Honest Law Firm is made up of five partners who specialize in various areas of law. The oldest partner, Bill Brown, founded the firm 30 years ago. His original practice consisted primarily of writing business contracts and helping businesses incorporate. In the early days, Mr. Brown had one secretary who did all the billing. Most of his work was done on a flat-fee basis, and there was no need to provide detailed accounting of time spent on individual clients. However, with the addition of the new partners, the business has become quite complicated. The newer partners specialize in areas such as criminal law, bankruptcy, real estate, and family law. The trend of the business has been such that most of the billing needs to be done on an hourly basis. At present, each partner submits a weekly billing report to the head partner's secretary. These reports are used as a basis for billing individual clients and providing weekly "salary" reports for the partnership.

The partnership's main problem is that most of the partners are having a difficult time recording all the necessary information to bill clients. As a result, it is estimated that only about 75 percent of the lawyers' actual time is billed to clients. Furthermore, it has been determined that a very weak area for collecting billing information is the telephone system. Several discussions among the partners revealed that the lawyers often spend a lot of time on the telephone with clients, but the information is not recorded into the system for appropriate measures of billing the client.

Required

Design a system that efficiently and effectively records and processes 100 percent of the firm's billing costs.

66. You are the partner in charge of management services for a medium-sized public accounting firm. You have contracted with a local manufacturing system to develop a specialized production control system. Several of your younger staff accountants have been involved in the actual systems design. A problem has arisen. They have reported to you that top management is very enthusiastic about the design of the new system. However, they are very confused about the response of the production managers and other key employees. The major problem is that the production manager and other employees keep missing meetings with the design team.

On one occasion the production manager told the design team that she liked what they were doing but just did not have time to work with them in detail.

Required

Discuss several possible causes for the problems encountered by the design team. What steps might have been taken to facilitate a better working relationship between the design team and management?

❖ ANSWERS TO CHAPTER QUIZ

1. b	5. a	9. d	13. c	17. b
2. a	6. d	10. a	14. d	18. a
3. d	7. c	11. b	15. b	19. a
4. b	8. c	12. a	16. a	20. b

APPENDIX[1]

SYSTEM MODELING

Systems designers use system models to test their ideas. As discussed in this chapter, it is cheaper to abandon a bad design than a finished system. Furthermore, the modeling process, briefly described in this appendix, leads systematically from the current system to a logical model of a new and improved one.

Before going further, a few critical terms must be defined. The *essence* of a system, or *essential activities*, means the parts that justify the very existence of the system and that will remain in any new version. For instance, in an invoice payment application, paying the invoice is an essential activity. Essential activities are the most logical part of the system because they need to be done regardless of the actual implementation of technology.

On the other hand, the *incarnation* of the system is the actual physical form, or implementation, that it takes. The essential activity of paying invoices could take one of several incarnations: Someone could write the checks manually, a computer could write them automatically, or the funds could be transferred directly from one bank account to another. Hence the essential activities are the most logical, whereas the incarnation is the actual physical form of the essential activities (see Fig. 10A.1).

---

[1]Adapted from Penny A. Kendall, *Introduction to Systems Analysis and Design: A Structured Approach* (Boston: Allyn and Bacon, 1987), Chap. 10. Copyright © 1987 by Allyn and Bacon, Inc. Reprinted with permission.

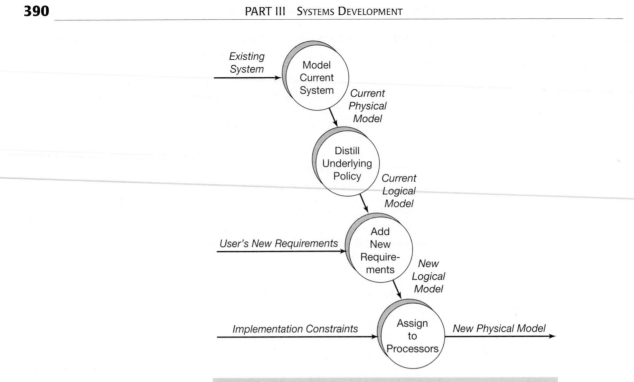

FIGURE 10A.1 MODELING THE SYSTEM.

Four system models are used to work from the old system to the new and from physical (incarnation) to logical (essential) and back to physical again. A data flow diagram (DFD) of the process is shown in Figure 10A.1. The four system models are

1. Current physical model (CPM), which shows the incarnation of the current system. Only by understanding the existing system can we attempt to better it.
2. Current logical model (CLM), which shows the essence of the current system. The essential functions are distilled from the CPM because those activities will remain the same in the new system.
3. New logical model (NLM), which shows the essence of the new system. Here, any new functions that the user requires are added to the essential parts of the old system (CLM).
4. New physical model (NPM), which shows the incarnation of the new system. This presents the actual physical form that the aggregate essential functions (the old plus the new of the NLM) will take in the new system.

In summary, the basic idea is to determine what currently exists (CPM), throw out anything unnecessary (CLM), add in any new functions the user wants (NLM), and finally, figure out how to implement the new design (NPM). The sections that follow discuss each model in depth.

CURRENT PHYSICAL MODEL

This model presumes the existence of a current system. If instead a new system is being created from scratch, as in the case of a brand-new business, bypass this and the following model and start with the new logical model.

Even if the current system is going to be discarded anyway, it still must be diagrammed because the process of researching and diagramming helps one understand the current system. A new system cannot be created without understanding the old.

The model of current procedures also starts the partitioning of the problem while still working with something that is concrete and verifiable. It is hard enough to partition without working in the abstract realm of essence at the same time.

Finally, the CPM serves as an excellent reference throughout the life of the project. It will be referred to many times to find out exactly how something is presently being done. In the actual model, DFDs reflect the system as it currently exists.

One common mistake is to overspecify the current physical model. It would be easy to spend months tracking down every last detail of the existing system, but there would be no time left for creating the new one. The intent is not to know every minute aspect but to understand the entirety in a reasonable amount of time.

When the current physical model is complete, walk through it with the user, who can spot errors and omissions while they are correctable with an eraser rather than with reprogramming. If the user is not familiar with DFDs, teach him or her how to read them. After all, a completed DFD is little more than a picture of the system. The only complicated part is in knowing the terminology and construction rules, and the user need not be concerned with all that.

CURRENT LOGICAL MODEL

The CLM still reflects the current way of doing business but shows only the essential functions. Remove all nonessential functions in order to reveal the underlying policy.

The nonessential functions, called *administrative activities*, are adjuncts to the essential activities. They are the more physical aspects of the system incarnation and usually change depending on the incarnation.

NEW LOGICAL MODEL

The NLM builds on the CLM, adding any new functions the user wants. For the first time, the process of design is entered, where it is decided what actually needs to be done, and a logical way of doing it is selected.

If a requested function is merely a modification of an existing activity, alter the overview diagram and the process's lower-level DFD to reflect the change. If, instead, the request reflects an entirely new activity, draw a lower-level DFD for it, and then add the new process to the overview. Either way, of course, the detailed system design and data dictionary must be changed to reflect any new access paths, entities, or data elements.

NEW PHYSICAL MODEL

The NPM shows the actual physical requirements, including such details as hardware and software specifications, for the new system. In returning to physical requirements, it is necessary to replace the administrative functions, particularly formats and writes, that were deleted back in the CPM. They should be put on the lower-level diagrams because, as trivial functions, they should not appear on the overview.

Then divide work among available *processors*. A processor is anything—human or machine—capable of performing work. If a system has eight people and one computer available, it has a total of nine processors.

Dividing the activities among processors is, at the same time, showing the *human-machine boundary*, indicating the automated and manual portions of the system.

Now that the processors have been allocated, it is necessary to specify a few more details about any processors that are computer hardware. Try to avoid getting into such detail as specifying the exact machinery, however. Instead of saying, "We need six Kluge 2s networked to a single Kluge hard disk, along with a Brightmodem and a Fastprint model B printer," say something more like, "We need six 32-bit microcomputers networked to a single 100-megabyte hard disk, along with an auto-dial auto-answer modem and a 300-character-per-second dot-matrix printer." This leaves the option of researching the exact equipment at a later time while still being able to come up with reasonable cost estimates now.

Part of the NPM includes an estimate of the costs and benefits inherent within the new system. Only then can management realistically evaluate any solution presented.

At this point, one of the options might be to buy a software package to handle all the computer's duties. If this turns out to be the final decision, most of the design phase, as such, will be eliminated, and the time will be spent evaluating packages instead.

The NPM has been discussed as if it were just one set of DFDs; in reality, it is multiple models. There is never just one "perfect" solution to a problem. In fact, there are many solutions, some better than others, to each problem encountered.

Complete models are developed for each alternative, including DFDs, data dictionary, data structure diagram, selected process specifications, and cost/benefit analysis. One handy way of summarizing the alternatives is to present them in a decision-table format, with benefits used as decision variables and costs used in the action rows so that one alternative occupies each vertical column.

Regardless of which solution seems to be the best, present all alternatives to management, and let it make the final decision. The systems analyst is far from objective as to which is the most appropriate—the analyst has been working with the system too closely. Only the people who will have to live with the system on a daily basis and who also have the most complete business experience should make the final decision.

CHAPTER 11

SYSTEMS IMPLEMENTATION, OPERATION, AND CONTROL

LEARNING OBJECTIVES

Careful study of this chapter will enable you to:

❖ Describe the major phases of systems implementation.

❖ Recognize some of the major human factors involved in systems implementation.

❖ Describe the major forms of documentation involved in the implementation of a new system.

❖ Understand how to plan and control a systems project.

❖ Describe several approaches for control over nonfinancial systems resources.

OVERVIEW

This chapter deals with implementation of the systems design plan. If the systems design process has been done carefully and thoughtfully, the systems implementation phase should proceed quite smoothly. It is impossible to anticipate all potential problems that might occur during the implementation phase. Because of this, delays and problems with implementation are routine. For example, a design plan might call for the installation of a new computer system. If the delivery of the new system is delayed beyond the delivery date specified in the general plan, the entire implementation project might be delayed.

Because of the many problems that can occur during systems implementation, formal plans and controls for the implementation phase should be established. Figure 11.1 shows the three major steps in systems implementation: (1) establishing plans and controls, (2) executing activities as planned, and (3) following up and evaluating the new system. Finally, the implemented system must be reviewed and controlled.

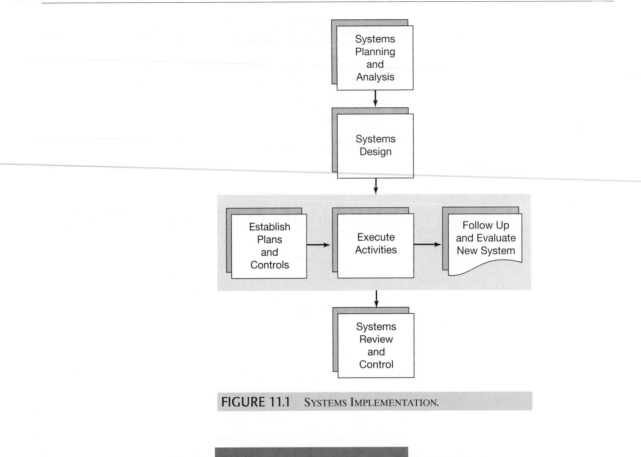

FIGURE 11.1 SYSTEMS IMPLEMENTATION.

SYSTEMS IMPLEMENTATION

ESTABLISHING PLANS AND CONTROLS FOR IMPLEMENTATION

Project management is a key concept in systems implementation. In order to manage the implementation project adequately, specific plans need to be developed. These plans should incorporate three major components: (1) a breakdown of the project into various phases, (2) specific budgets applicable to each phase, and (3) specific timetables applicable to each project phase. Various scheduling techniques might be used to control implementation.

Figure 11.2 shows a **Gantt chart**, which graphically depicts the major activities of a hypothetical systems implementation project. This chart shows both the actual and planned times for a given activity. Gantt charts can be very helpful; however, they are limited in that they cannot show the relationship between various project activities. They do not show the order in which the activities must be performed.

Figure 11.3 shows a **network diagram**, which depicts the order in which the activities must be performed. For example, notice that employees cannot be trained until the software is selected. The network diagram approach can be expanded to include estimated times for each of the individual activities. Given these times, it is possible to use the program evaluation and review technique (PERT) or the critical path method (CPM) to estimate the critical path for a project. The **critical path** is a list of activities that are critical to the project in the sense that if any one of them is delayed, the entire project will be delayed.

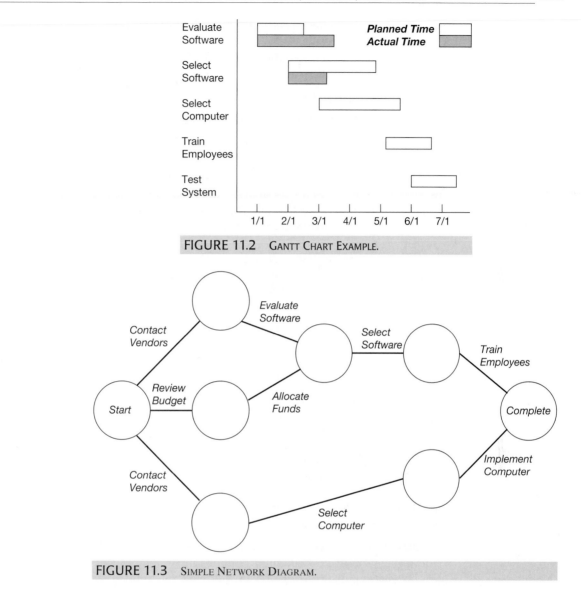

FIGURE 11.2   GANTT CHART EXAMPLE.

FIGURE 11.3   SIMPLE NETWORK DIAGRAM.

EXECUTING IMPLEMENTATION ACTIVITIES

Executing implementation activities involves the actual carrying out of the design plan. Typical activities during execution include selecting and training personnel, installing new computer equipment, detailed systems design, writing and testing computer programs, system testing, standards development, documentation, and file conversion. Each of these activities is discussed in detail in this section.

In carrying out the implementation plan, certain measures should be taken to provide a smooth transition and to ensure acceptance on the part of company employees. It is normally desirable for management and the systems team to make a formal announcement regarding execution of the project. Care should be taken to assure employees that the transition will be smooth, and when possible, employees should be assured that their jobs will be protected. A formal announcement process should have the benefit of minimizing rumors. This is important because rumors can generate a considerable amount of uncertainty and employee unrest.

Another important aspect of the execution phase is the organization of a special project team. Ideally, the team should consist of individuals who also participated in formulating the design specifications and plans for implementation. Affected managers also should participate.

EMPLOYEE TRAINING

Virtually any successful systems implementation requires that considerable attention be devoted to employee training. In some cases new employees must be hired and trained. In other cases, existing employees must be taught to work with new forms, reports, and procedures.

The importance of adequate training cannot be overemphasized. You should never assume that employees will learn to use the system by themselves. If employees are not trained adequately, it is likely that they will simply ignore the new system. Therefore, the success of the entire systems development project is affected by the adequacy of training.

The company typically will face a number of options relating to using and training employees. For example, management often has to decide whether the company should hire a new employee for a given position or retrain an existing employee. In many cases it is best to retrain an existing employee. There are several reasons for this:

- Recruiting costs relating to hiring a new employee are avoided.
- Existing employees are already familiar with the firm's operations.
- Employee morale is often enhanced, especially in cases where the new position would be a promotion for an existing employee.

In addition, a number of training approaches are available to the company, including

- Hiring outside training consultants
- Using training manuals
- Using videotape presentations
- Using audiotape presentations
- Using training seminars
- Using individualized hands-on instruction
- Using computer-assisted training

ACQUIRING AND INSTALLING NEW COMPUTER EQUIPMENT

The installation of new computer equipment sometimes can be a monumental task. For installations of any appreciable size, the computer manufacturer normally provides engineers and other personnel to assist in the installation. However, many problems can be encountered. First, adequate facilities must be available. Most large computers require controlled environments that keep humidity and temperature within specified ranges. In addition, these installations require rooms with false floors, where large bundles of wires can be run. Other requirements typically include specialized security measures, such as special fire extinguishing systems, video monitoring systems, or specialized door locks.

DETAILED SYSTEMS DESIGN

During the implementation phase, it is almost always necessary to do some additional design work. This might include the design of various kinds of forms or reports. Also, it is not uncommon for the implementation phase to reveal that certain parts of the design plan are unworkable; therefore, it is always necessary to do some last-minute fine-tuning of the systems design plan.

A very important part of detailed design execution during the implementation phase involves computer programming. In some cases the design plan might call for prepackaged computer programs; however, most large installations require custom programming. In addition, if the company is switching to a new computer system, it might be necessary to change existing programs so that they will run on the new system.

The design specifications for a computer program are determined by the design team, not the programmer. The programmer's primary function is to implement a specific plan; however, it is important for the programmer to work in conjunction with the design team. Finally, computer programs should be tested very carefully before being put into operation. One powerful means of testing computer programs involves processing test data. Test data either can be made up or can come from real data. In either case, the test data should include a large number of different kinds of errors. In addition, the test data should include a wide range of conditions, since a defective program often will work with no problems given that there are no errors in the input data file or where the test data represent the average operating conditions. Therefore, an attempt should be made to "break" the program; the individual doing the testing should do everything possible to find something wrong with the program.

Finally, all computer programs should be documented adequately, both internally and externally. Internal documentation includes various kinds of comments (embedded within the program) that describe different segments of the program code and define the various program variables. External documentation should be written both from the programmer's and users' points of view. Programmer's documentation would include structured English, flowcharts of the program logic, definitions of various subprograms, functions, and program variables. The documentation should be usable by a different programmer, working several years later, to modify the program. Programs without adequate documentation may be worthless when the programmer who wrote them leaves the company.

In addition to testing programs individually, it is also important to test related programs as a group. For example, a given system may have four programs that access the same data file. In this case, all four programs should be tested together. This type of testing would uncover integration errors. Such errors might occur when one program makes faulty assumptions regarding the tasks performed by another program.

DOCUMENTING THE NEW SYSTEM

Documentation is one of the most important parts of systems implementation, but it is often overlooked. One reason for the neglect in documenting systems adequately is that programmers typically receive substantial amounts of training in programming languages but little or no training in documentation. Of course, some educational institutions do an excellent job in teaching documentation skills; however, the opposite is too often true.

It has been said often that a good computer programmer will write several lines of program code per day. One reason for the small number is that a good programmer will spend a substantial portion of time developing plans and documentation. The development of computer software without documentation is an almost worthless exercise. Good documentation can serve a wide range of useful purposes, including (1) training new employees, (2) providing programmers and analysts with useful information for future program evaluation and modification activities, (3) providing auditors with useful information for evaluating internal controls, and (4) assisting in ensuring that systems design specifications are met.

FILE CONVERSION

A typical problem involved in systems implementation is that of data conversion. In many cases, files maintained manually must be converted to computer format. In addition, it is often necessary to convert from one computer medium to another. For example, a design plan might call for converting computer tape files to disk files.

Conversion can be an expensive, time-consuming process. This is especially true in the case of converting manual files to computerized files. In such cases it is often necessary to do a lot of data screening after entering the information into the computer because errors typically are made in the data input process.

TEST OPERATIONS

Before the system is actually implemented, it must be thoroughly tested as a whole. There are three basic approaches to the final testing of the system: (1) the direct approach, (2) parallel operation, and (3) modular conversion. The **direct approach** involves switching to the new system and abandoning the old system at a fixed point in time called the **cutover point**. The direct approach, while relatively inexpensive, has the distinct disadvantage of allowing for the possibility of major system problems that impair actual operation of the company. For example, it could be disastrous to find that a new accounts receivable system bills all the company's customers for incorrect amounts. The second approach, **parallel operation**, involves running the new and old systems simultaneously. All transactions are processed by both systems. The results of operations based on the two systems are compared. Any discrepancies probably indicate a problem in the new system. Parallel operation has the advantage of being extremely safe; however, it is very expensive and may not be cost effective in all applications. The final approach, **modular conversion**, involves phasing in the new system in segments. For example, the new accounting system might include modules for accounts receivable, accounts payable, inventories, and general ledger. A modular conversion approach might implement the inventory module itself. After the company feels comfortable with this module, other modules could be brought on line. A major drawback of the modular conversion process is that it can involve a greatly extended checkout period. This might delay final implementation of a new system far too long to be practical.

EVALUATING THE NEW SYSTEM

Once the new system has been implemented, more work remains. Follow-up is necessary to ensure that the new system operates as planned. There are many approaches that can assist in follow-up and evaluation, including observation, questionnaires, performance measures, and benchmarks. In summary, almost any system implementation will involve some problems and require adequate follow-up.

PLANNING AND ORGANIZING A SYSTEMS PROJECT

Operationally, project management techniques are the heart of a well-controlled systems development life cycle. The term *project* refers to a specific application that has been approved for development. Once approval has been obtained, **project management** begins and is concerned with the detailed analysis, design, programming, testing, implementation, operation, and maintenance of the project.

PROJECT SELECTION

If an organization's resources are limited, project development resources should be allocated to projects that yield the greatest benefits to the organization. Potential projects may be proposed directly by user departments or by a separate information system or corporate planning function or arise in response to an immediate problem—such as a change in federal reporting requirements. Typically, proposals arise in all these ways, and there are more project proposals that can be undertaken by the existing staff. Project selection is usually the responsibility of a steering committee or other organization-wide unit to ensure active user participation in the selection process. Project proposals are submitted to the steering committee in writing. A proposal should provide a statement of the expected benefits and costs, if possible. Frequently, costs and benefits can only be estimated subjectively owing to both the difficulties of costing information services and the difficulties of estimating the resources that will be necessary to complete the project. In large organizations, the project selection process may be highly formalized, with the project proposal document providing a detailed analysis of expected costs and benefits, both financial and nonfinancial. Expected return on investment (ROI) is frequently an important selection criterion in such cases. Once a project has been approved for development, a project team must be organized to begin work.

THE PROJECT TEAM

Labor is a basic resource in any systems project. One important task of project management is to assemble a suitable project team. For an applications system project, analysts, programmers, and other technicians are necessary, but representatives of the user department(s) for which the application is being developed usually should be included as well. One member must be selected as the project leader in order to focus control responsibilities for the project. Whether this project leader should come from the user department or the information systems department is a question best answered in the context of the specific project environment. If the project leader comes from a user department, then the user likely will be deeply involved and committed to the project's success. However, the quality of technical leadership may be weaker than if an information systems person is selected as the project leader.

PROJECT LEADER RESPONSIBILITIES

A diagram of a project team organization appears in Figure 11.4. The project leader has direct responsibility to the steering committee for project progress and completion. A steering committee or other such organizational unit is used to ensure a high level of user involvement in the work of the information systems department. The project team

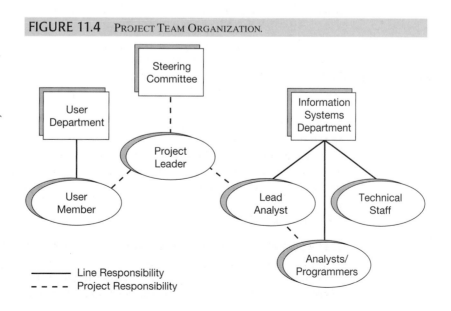

FIGURE 11.4   PROJECT TEAM ORGANIZATION.

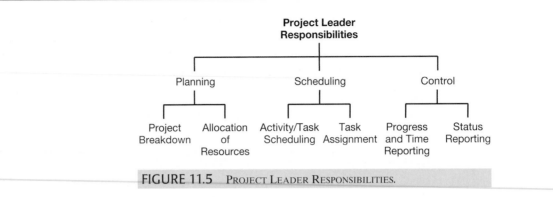

FIGURE 11.5   PROJECT LEADER RESPONSIBILITIES.

consists of the project leader, analysts, and programmers from the information systems department and one or more user participants from the organizational unit(s) for which the project is being undertaken. Each member of a project team maintains line responsibility to the manager/supervisor of his or her department. However, for project activities, each project team member reports to the project leader. On a large project, one or more lead or chief analysts and/or programmers are assigned to assist the project leader in supervising the technical staff.

The project leader must maintain contact with the principal user department manager who has responsibility for the project. The user manager is typically the person who must formally approve the project at its completion. The project leader also must be in contact with technical specialists, such as the database administrator, as required to complete the project successfully. In addition to project team organization, the primary responsibilities of the project leader are planning, scheduling, and controlling the project. These responsibilities are detailed in Figure 11.5. Planning involves project breakdown and allocation of resources. Scheduling is a successive refinement to the project plan; activities are scheduled chronologically, and detailed project responsibilities are assigned to team members. Project scheduling usually is done with the aid of Gantt charts or network charts such as PERT charts. Project control involves time and progress reporting as well as periodic project status reporting to upper-level management. A project accounting system is the means by which the project leader fulfills her or his project control responsibilities.

PROJECT UNCERTAINTY

The major problem faced by any project team is the uncertainty associated with an application systems project. The technicians have to work with the users to elicit the system's data requirements. Users often are unaware of the problem creating the need for the new project and may, in fact, be unaware of the specific data they use in their decision-making responsibilities. For these reasons, the user-designer interface is characterized by a high degree of uncertainty. Uncertainty also exists in the development of the system. Once the system design is set, programmers have to interpret the detailed specifications and write the necessary software. Software development—the total time required, whether or not the software is reliable, and whether or not the software conforms to system specifications—is also uncertain. The task of the project team is to reduce all these uncertainties, coordinate the activities of the diverse parties working on the project, and complete the project within a reasonable time and at a reasonable cost. The selection of an effective project leader is crucial to these tasks.

PROJECT BREAKDOWN INTO TASKS AND PHASES

To plan and control a project effectively, the required activities are broken down or factored into a detailed listing of tasks and phases. If a total project is suitably factored

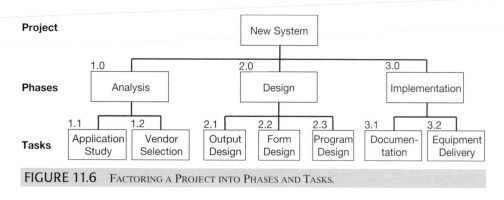

FIGURE 11.6   FACTORING A PROJECT INTO PHASES AND TASKS.

into the smaller components of a system life cycle, the project becomes easier to control and understand. There is no standard method for factoring a project into detailed activities, just as there is no standard listing of phases in the systems development life cycle. There are several reasons for this, including different opinions, different commercial project management packages, and different requirements for particular projects. The guiding philosophy is top-down design with successive refinement. The basic operational principle is that each specific task or phase should provide a *deliverable* at its completion, some type of tangible product (i.e., documentation) that can be reviewed and evaluated. The higher the degree of breakdown into specific tasks and phases, the higher is the certainty with which each task's or phase's requirements can be predicted. Figure 11.6 illustrates the concept of factoring a project into a set of phases and tasks and the use of a hierarchical (HIPO) chart to document this plan. The numbers assigned to the individual tasks and phases provide a basis for organizing the documentation generated during the course of the project.

The objective of project breakdown is to facilitate assignment and control of labor and other project resources. To the extent possible, tasks should be broken down to a level where task definition is sufficiently clear to enable individual personnel to be assigned to specific tasks. Task assignments should reflect the skills of individual personnel. Estimated time requirements for each specific task also must be included in the project breakdown.

TIME ESTIMATES

Estimating accurate task completion times for a systems project is difficult because of the uncertainties inherent in systems development. Poorly estimated task completion times severely limit the effectiveness of project management techniques. Accuracy depends partly on the previous project management experience within an organization. Experience from previous projects should increase the task time estimation skill of project personnel on each new project. However, estimates always will be inaccurate to some degree, and this fact must be accepted. Undue pressure to keep to unrealistic schedules may result in an unsatisfactory project outcome. The proper attitude toward time estimates is to accept them for what they are—estimates—and to be prepared to revise them frequently as a project is developed.

WORK MEASUREMENT TECHNIQUES

The simplest approach to estimation is to *guess*, meaning that no formal calculations are undertaken. The "guesstimate" is based on one's previous experience with similar projects or tasks. More rigorous approaches to estimation are based on the concept of

Standard Man-Days for Interviews

People to Be Interviewed	Number to Be Interviewed	Standard Man-Day Allowance	Total Man-Days
Managers	4	0.5	2
Supervisors	17	1.0	17
Technical Staff	18	1.5	27
Clerical Staff	8	0.5	4
Total	47	—	50

Complexity Factors

Simple	0.50–0.75
Average	1.00–1.50
Complex	2.00–2.50

Complexity judgment for the case in point is "somewhat above average"

Assign a factor of 1.30

Adjusted man-days = standard man-days times complexity factor
= 50 x 1.30
= 65 adjusted man-days

FIGURE 11.7 SAMPLE WORK MEASUREMENT CALCULATION.

work measurement, which was discussed in Chapter 2. Work measurement involves four basic steps:

- Identify the tasks to be estimated.
- For each task, estimate the total size or volume of the task in some suitable manner.
- Convert the size or volume estimate into a time estimate by multiplying the size or volume estimate by a standard or estimated processing rate.
- Adjust the estimated processing rate to include circumstantial considerations such as idle time, task complexity, or task newness.

Figure 11.7 illustrates this general approach. Note the adjustment of the initial estimate of 50 standard man-days for the interviews to 65 man-days to reflect the complexity of the task as "somewhat above average." A further refinement involves adjusting the estimated time for a task as just calculated by experience or competency factors, increasing or decreasing the total estimated time to reflect the relative capabilities of the specific individuals to be assigned to each task. Figure 11.8 illustrates this type of adjustment. Extending the final time estimates by suitable costing or charging rates provides the method for estimating the total budgeted project cost.

Although estimation for each different task in a project, such as analysis or programming, requires different basic data to describe its size or volume, the principles of work measurement are the same in each case. Because applications development projects are a regular activity in many organizations, standard task times or processing rates can be estimated and refined based on experience. Standards developed in house are likely to be more effective than standards or estimates available in the project management literature.

Personnel Factors

A. Competence and Experience

	Competence Level	
Experience	Low	High
Senior	1.0	0.7
Intermediate	1.8	1.1
Junior	2.8	1.9

B. Knowledge

	Knowledge Required		
Knowledge Available	Little	Average	Much
Much	0.0	0.1	0.3
Average	0.0	0.2	0.7
Little	0.1	0.5	1.0

Actual man-days = adjusted days x (personnel + knowledge)

Assume that a junior analyst of high competence will do the work. Average knowledge is available, and much knowledge is required.

Actual man-days = 65 x (1.9 + 0.7) = 169 man-days

FIGURE 11.8 COMPETENCY AND KNOWLEDGE ADJUSTMENTS.

ACCURACY OF ESTIMATES

The literature on project management is a source of estimation techniques as well as of detailed time estimates or standard processing rates for performing various project tasks. There are no commonly accepted standards largely because there is no general agreement of standard project phases and tasks. However, there is general agreement on several points related to the estimation process. The first point is that estimates are only estimates, no matter how carefully prepared. A second point of agreement is that the accuracy of estimation improves considerably as a project proceeds through its course of activities. That is, estimates of, say, the tenth phase of a project that are made at the completion of, say, the fourth phase are likely to be more accurate than estimates for the tenth phase that were made at the beginning of the project. It is commonly held that estimation errors of 100 percent are not unreasonable for the latter phases of a project when these estimates are made at a project's conception. This reinforces the importance of frequently revising estimates contained in the project plan to reflect actual project experience. Estimates made during the early phase of a project can be expected to be considerably inaccurate even if they were prepared carefully. For this reason, "guesstimates" are used frequently in the initial phases of a project rather than detailed calculations. These original estimates are revised successively as the project proceeds through its course of activities. This approach reflects the practical fact that as a project proceeds, it takes shape, meaning that what is left to be done is now based on everything else that has been completed and is now more predictable and hence subject to greater control.

Another area of consensus is that initial estimates frequently are made too low. Estimates that are made by personnel such as computer programmers who are subsequently the ones to perform the tasks for which they are providing time estimates tend to be overly optimistic. In consulting or contracting businesses, this type of behavior is known as **lowballing**—purposely or inadvertently submitting unreasonably low time or cost estimates to obtain a contract, knowing that once the contract is obtained, the work likely will be completed regardless of the actual amount of time or cost that is required. While lowballing is a possibility for in-house personnel as well, more common reasons for task time underestimation reside in job performance measurement factors such as a natural desire to be perceived as efficient in one's duties by one's superior. Underestimation also occurs when work measurement techniques are used to estimate task times. Often estimates of "productive hours per day," "work days," or similar work units fail realistically to consider idle or nonproductive time due to sickness, vacations, coffee breaks, washroom breaks, and other such factors. There are also considerable differences in the productive capabilities of different people. One person's day of output might be equivalent to another person's week of output. This is the reason for suggesting in the earlier discussion that basic work measurements should be adjusted with factors that compensate for the relative capabilities of different people or groups of people (e.g., senior programmers versus junior programmers). There also may be significant variation in the output of a single person over time, even when the same person works on similar tasks. Again, the best strategy is to revise estimates successively based on actual project experience.

Cost overruns are a frequent problem in systems development, but to the extent that costs are higher than predicted by estimates made during the early phases of a project, analysis of the cost overrun should be tempered by the problems of estimation just discussed. This is particularly true because a relatively larger percentage of total systems development costs are incurred during the later phases of a project (design and implementation), and it is these later project phases for which initial estimates are likely to be optimistic. Typically, 30% to 40% of total project *time* is spent in the analysis phase of the systems development life cycle, but 75% or more of total project *costs* is incurred during the design and implementation phases. Project resources tend to be spent at an increasing rate as a project proceeds to completion. Thus control of project costs in the early phases of the systems development life cycle is essential.

PROJECT ACCOUNTING

Project control is established by setting measurable goals for each phase and task in the overall project, reporting actual performance against these goals, and evaluating any significant deviations from the project plan. Measurable goal analysis is facilitated by the documentation or deliverable that is required of each phase or task to evidence its completion, as well as major milestones or project checkpoints, at which times the overall status of the project to date is subject to review by upper-level management. Well-established, clearly defined responsibilities for project personnel (which is facilitated by a detailed project breakdown) and some form of project accounting system to measure and report actual performance against responsibility are essential elements of a project control system.

OPERATION OF THE SYSTEM

A project accounting system is a cost accounting system in which costs are assigned to individual projects as the projects proceed through their development. Regardless of whether project costs are assigned to users in the context of a responsibility accounting system, effective project control requires a project accounting system that can keep track of costs incurred to date on a project and provide a summary cost report at a project's completion. Timely cost data are essential to making rational decisions about resource usage. Historical cost data from previous projects are an important source of information to use in estimating the time and cost components of new projects.

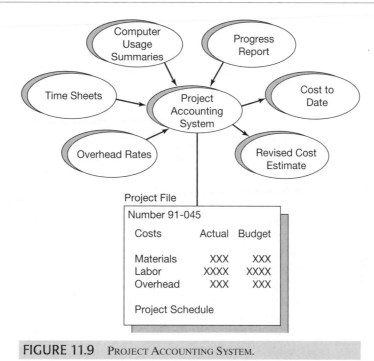

FIGURE 11.9   PROJECT ACCOUNTING SYSTEM.

The project accounting system might be manual or automated. A large firm that generally has several projects underway at the same time requires an automated system. Such a system probably would be run once a week. The important consideration is that status reports must be prepared on time. A weekly cost report that is available two weeks later is not likely to be effective for control purposes.

Figure 11.9 illustrates the components of a project accounting system. Projects must be numbered for identification purposes. The system operates much like a conventional cost accounting system: Materials, labor, and overhead charges are accumulated by project and compared periodically with budgeted costs, and reports are prepared. Materials in the case of application projects consist mostly of computer use charges for program development and testing. Labor costs are obtained from time sheets on which project personnel assign their chargeable hours to work in progress. Overhead consists of other charges that are only indirectly attributable to projects, such as the office space of personnel and the cost of running the project accounting system. Overhead charges usually are applied on the basis of an overhead rate. The final input that is needed on a regular basis is a report detailing the progress to date on each project. This is necessary if estimates of future costs to complete each project are to be revised successively. Progress frequently is measured in terms of earned hours—the equivalent of "standard earned hours" in a standard cost accounting system for manufactured products. Earned hours are used to represent the percentage of completion. For example, if a task time estimate is 40 hours and the task is estimated to be 30% complete, then the progress report would show 12 earned hours on the project task. Charging rates and the project budget are used in conjunction with the progress reports to provide revised cost estimates, project costs to date, and charges to users (if such charges are to be made). Periodically, special summary reports detailing the total cost of projects in process are prepared for supervisory management.

LEVEL OF DETAIL

The operation of a project accounting system as just discussed is quite similar to that of the production control system that was detailed in Chapter 8. As in any control system, if too much detail is required by the project accounting system, then the overhead cost of running the system will be too high, and project workers will be antagonized by the data required of them. If too little detail is provided, then the results will be ambiguous. The appropriate level of detail must be determined by project management. In most cases, weekly reports based on earned hours are sufficient for control purposes.

CONTROL OVER NONFINANCIAL INFORMATION SYSTEMS RESOURCES

A number of factors relating to information systems are important to management from a control point of view but are not measured in terms of dollars. These include performance measures for hardware, software, and personnel.

Measuring hardware performance involves system utilization, system downtime, and system responsiveness. Measures of systems utilization typically include ratios such as CPU time actually used to time available. Also, statistics can be derived for the individual components of the computer system, such as terminals, tape drives, and so on. Utilization statistics are very important because they can indicate bottlenecks or needs for systems expansion. In addition, utilization statistics reported for various times of the day can assist management in scheduling major computer runs at times when system utilization is low.

In many systems, downtime is a major concern. **Downtime** is the percentage of time that the machine is unavailable for use. Typically, the total number of hours in a given month that the machine is not available is reported. In addition, the mean time between failures and the mean time to repair the system are also reported. Downtime statistics are helpful in evaluating overall hardware effectiveness. A system that is down too much can cause a number of problems—including lost business.

A second major nonquantitative factor important to control is software performance. A very sound overall approach to evaluating software performance is to survey systems users, asking a large number of questions relating to ease of use, functionality, and user friendliness. Software performance must be monitored constantly because environmental changes can produce changes in the satisfaction of users.

Finally, it is necessary to apply controls relating to personnel. Therefore, reports need to be prepared for a large variety of factors. For example, programmers might be evaluated in terms of the quality of documentation written and the number of program lines written per day. Various other types of reports needed for evaluating personnel performance might include

- Performance reports for data-entry specialists. These reports might include statistics such as the number of keystrokes per hour or the number of data records entered per hour.
- Reports evaluating the efficiency of systems operators. These reports might include statistics relating to factors such as the length of time required for the processing of a tape mount or effectiveness in running prescheduled jobs on time.
- Reports relating to the efficiency of hardware repair persons. Such reports might include statistics on the number of repair jobs and the average length of time required for each repair job, broken down by various types of repair categories.

AUDITING THE INFORMATION SYSTEM

Most firms employ either internal or external auditors to audit the information system. The audit's focus should be on the information system itself and on the validity and accuracy of data as processed by the system. The accountants' interests in auditing the information system tend to focus on internal control. The general approach followed by the auditor is to first obtain a detailed description of the internal control system, typically using internal control questionnaires. Once a description of the internal control system has been obtained, the auditor then performs tests of compliance. During this process, the auditor ascertains the degree to which the company actually applies the internal controls as documented in the internal control evaluation. Finally, the auditor performs tests of specific transactions as they flow through the system. The amount of testing required depends on the degree to which an adequate set of internal controls exists and is in effective operation. In systems with a large number of internal controls, the auditor can rely on a statistical sampling of transactions.

MAINTAINING AND MODIFYING THE SYSTEM

In all operational systems it becomes necessary to make changes. One reason for changes is that it is not possible to foresee all contingencies during the design phase. In addition, environmental conditions and information needs change. Finally, almost any computer program contains some bugs. **Bugs** are computer programming errors that might not be detected until the system actually begins operation.

For control purposes, it is very important that all modifications to the system's software and data schema be formally reviewed and approved. Ideally, users should have the opportunity to make requests for systems modifications. These requests should be reviewed by a committee of managers and systems specialists. On approval, they should be referred to the appropriate systems or applications programmers for implementation. Systems and applications programmers should work according to a preestablished set of priorities. In addition, these programmers should not have access to the operational copy of software being modified. Instead, programmers should apply the modifications to a copy of the original software. This software, after being modified, should be reviewed very carefully and then installed by an independent person. All modifications of the system should be carefully documented. The documentation should include the reason for changes, the exact changes made, and the person approving the changes. In addition, normal documentation standards should apply. This means that user manuals and systems programming documentation should be updated.

❖ SUMMARY

Critical to success in systems implementation is the need to establish a systems implementation plan. This plan should include a detailed timetable and budget showing all key activities in the implementation plan. The implementation plan must then be monitored continuously, and any discrepancies relating to the timetable or budget should be reported.

Many implementation activities are required. These include personnel training, physical preparation, detailed systems design, program testing, standards development, documentation, file conversion, and systems cutover. In addition, the implemented system must be evaluated for ongoing control purposes.

Key concepts in systems project management include establishing a project team, dividing responsibilities (and tasks), dividing the project into phases, establishing time tables, and maintaining an accounting for project costs and compliance with time tables. Collectively, these steps work to ensure that the overall development effort produces systems that are cost-effective and meet the needs of the organization.

A number of factors relating to information systems are important to management from a control point of view but are not measured in terms of dollars. These include performance measures for hardware, software, and personnel. Formal procedures should be developed for maintaining and modifying the existing system.

❖ GLOSSARY

bug: a computer programming error that is not detected until the program is in use.

critical path: a list of activities that are critical in that if any one of them is delayed, the entire project will be delayed.

cutover point: the point in time under the direct approach to implementation where the switch to a new system is made.

direct approach: an approach to implementation that involves switching to a new system and abandoning the old system at a fixed point in time.

downtime: the percentage of time that equipment is unavailable for use.

Gantt chart: a scheduling technique that graphically depicts both the actual and the planned times for activities but does not show the relationships between various activities.

lowballing: purposely or inadvertently submitting unreasonably low time or cost estimates to obtain a contract.

modular conversion: an approach to implementation that involves phasing in a new system in segments.

network diagram: a scheduling technique that depicts the order in which activities must be performed.

parallel operation: an approach to implementation that involves running the new and old systems simultaneously before final conversion.

project management: tools used to track progress and manage resources for a systems development project.

❖ CHAPTER QUIZ

Answers to the chapter quiz appear on page 411.

1. Which concept is the most important to systems implementation?
   (a) Ashby's law of requisite variety
   (b) Grosch's law
   (c) project continuity
   (d) project management

2. The Gantt chart shows (_____).
   (a) planned activity times
   (b) relationships between activities
   (c) both a and b
   (d) neither a nor b

3. The conversion approach that is most risky to a company's operations is (_____).
   (a) the direct approach
   (b) parallel operation
   (c) modular conversion

4. The conversion approach that involves phasing in a new system in segments is (_____).
   (a) the direct approach
   (b) parallel operation
   (c) modular conversion

5. The least expensive conversion approach is (_____).
   (a) the direct approach
   (b) parallel operation
   (c) modular conversion

6. If a project activity on the (_____) is delayed, then the entire project will be delayed.
   (a) Gantt path
   (b) critical path
   (c) cutover point
   (d) flex point

7. A report specifying the events to occur in the implementation of a new system is called (_____).
   (a) a conversion plan
   (b) project acceptability
   (c) a feasibility study
   (d) information analysis

8. Time estimates should be (_____).
   (a) revised occasionally over the life of a project

(b) revised frequently over the life of a project

(c) not revised at all

9. The project team leader for a systems development project should have direct responsibility to the (_____).

(a) user department

(b) information systems department

(c) steering committee

(d) project lead analysts

10. Computer programming errors that are not detected until the system actually begins operation are called (_____).

(a) nuts

(b) bugs

(c) moths

(d) crackers

❖ REVIEW QUESTIONS

1. Define each of the following terms.

(a) PERT chart

(b) Gantt chart

(c) critical path

(d) parallel operation

(e) modular conversion

(f) test data

2. Identify the major steps in systems implementation.

3. Identify several key activities in systems operation. Briefly discuss the components of the systems implementation plan.

4. Why is detailed systems design work necessary during the systems implementation phase?

5. Contrast and compare the modular versus parallel operations approaches to conversion.

6. Discuss several functions of systems documentation.

7. What are some factors that should be considered when selecting a project leader?

8. What is the objective of project breakdown?

9. Identify several types of adjustments that might be made to basic time estimates in a project breakdown.

10. What is lowballing? What are some reasons that often make time estimates overly optimistic?

11. Identify the basic components of a project accounting system.

12. Do project costs always have to be charged to users? If not, why is a project accounting system necessary?

❖ DISCUSSION QUESTIONS AND PROBLEMS

13. The productivity of programmers is typically of concern to project management. Identify some factors that may affect the productivity of a programmer. How would you measure or evaluate the productivity of programmers assigned to a project team? What means might be used to increase the productivity of programmers?

14. A specific project task has been estimated to require 100 work hours to complete. Using the adjustment factors in Figures 11.7 and 11.8, adjust this estimate to reflect the following.

(a) The complexity is judged to be quite simple.

(b) The task is assigned to a "junior" whose competency level is low.

(c) Average knowledge is available, and average knowledge is required.

Required

What is the adjusted time estimate? Are adjustments of these types worthwhile?

15. If it is estimated that five programmers can complete a task in 50 workdays, is it likely that 50 programmers can complete the same task—such as coding programs for an application system—in 5 days? Would you expect diminishing returns in the addition of labor to project tasks? Why or why not?

16. How might a project accounting system assign overhead to individual projects? Does the assignment of overhead to individual projects enhance management control?

17. Wright Company employs a computer-based data processing system for maintaining all company records. The present system was developed in stages over the past 5 years and has been fully operational for the last 24 months.

    When the system was being designed, all department heads were asked to specify the types of information and reports they would need for planning and controlling operations. The systems department attempted to meet the specifications of each department head. Company management specified that certain other reports should be prepared for department heads. During the five years of systems development and operation, there have been several changes in the department head positions due to attrition and promotions. The new department heads often made requests for additional reports according to their specifications. The systems department complied with all these requests. Reports were discontinued only on request by a department head and then only if it was not a standard report required by top management. As a result, few reports were, in fact, discontinued. Consequently, the data processing system was generating a large number of reports each reporting period.

    Company management became concerned about the quantity of information that was being produced by the system. The internal audit department was asked to evaluate the effectiveness of the reports generated by the system. The audit staff determined early in the study that more information was being generated by the data processing system than could be used effectively. They noted the following reactions to this information overload:

    (i) Many department heads would not act on certain reports during periods of peak activity. The department head would let these reports accumulate with the hope of catching up during a subsequent lull.

    (ii) Some department heads had so many reports that they did not act at all on the information, or they made incorrect decisions because of misuse of the information.

    (iii) Frequently, action required by the nature of the report data was not taken until the department head was reminded by someone who needed the decision. These department heads did not appear to have developed a priority system for acting on the information produced by the data processing system.

    (iv) Department heads often would develop the information they needed from alternative, independent sources rather than using the reports generated by the data processing system. This often was easier than trying to search among the reports for the needed data.

    Required
    (a) For each of the observed reactions, indicate whether they are functional or dysfunctional behavioral responses. Explain your answer in each case.
    (b) Assuming that one or more of the preceding were dysfunctional, recommend procedures the company could employ to eliminate the dysfunctional behavior and to prevent its recurrence.

    (CMA)

18. You are assigned to review the documentation of a data processing function.

    Required
    (a) List three advantages of adequate documentation for a data processing function.
    (b) Following are two columns of information. The first column lists 6 categories of documentation, and the second column lists 18 elements of documentation related to the categories. Match each of the elements of documentation with the category in which it should be found. List letters *A* through *F* on your answer sheet. After each letter, list the numbers of the elements that best apply to that category. Use every element, but none more than once.

CATEGORIES
    (a) Systems documentation
    (b) Program documentation
    (c) Operations documentation

(d) User documentation
(e) Library documentation
(f) Data entry documentation

ELEMENTS

(1) Flow charts showing the flow of information
(2) Procedures needed to balance, reconcile, and maintain overall control
(3) Storage instructions
(4) Contents and format of data to be captured
(5) Constants, codes, and tables
(6) Verification procedures
(7) Logic diagrams and/or decision tables
(8) Report distribution instructions
(9) Messages and programmed halts
(10) Procedures for backup files
(11) Retention cycle
(12) Source statement listings
(13) Instructions to show proper use of each transaction
(14) A complete history from planning through installation
(15) Restart and recovery procedures
(16) Rules for handling blank spaces
(17) Instructions to ensure the proper completion of all input forms
(18) List of programs in a system

(IIA)

❖ ANSWERS TO CHAPTER QUIZ

1. d	4. c	7. a	10. b
2. a	5. a	8. b	
3. a	6. b	9. c	

FILE PROCESSING AND DATA MANAGEMENT CONCEPTS

LEARNING OBJECTIVES

Careful study of this chapter will enable you to:

❖ Define the basic terms used in database technology.

❖ Identify the three levels of database architecture.

❖ Compare and contrast the different logical models of databases.

❖ Explain the different methods of accessing files.

❖ Explain the benefits of database management systems.

❖ Describe the considerations that are appropriate to the design of computer-based files and databases.

INTRODUCTORY TERMINOLOGY

FIELDS, DATA ITEMS, ATTRIBUTES, AND ELEMENTS

The terms **field, data item, attribute**, and **element** are used interchangeably to denote the smallest block of data that will be stored and retrieved in an information system. If only some portion of the field may be needed by the users, then the field should be split into several separate data items. A field may be a single character or number, or it may be composed of many characters or numbers. Examples of fields include such items as

- Customer name
- Employee Social Security Number
- Purchase order number
- Customer account number

A field is usually logically associated with other fields; a logical groupings of fields is called a **record**. Records are groups of data items that concern a certain entity such

412

as an employee, a customer, a vendor, an invoice, and so forth. We will denote a record structure as follows:

```
RECORD-NAME(FIELD 1, FIELD 2, . . ., FIELD N)
```

RECORD-NAME is the name of the record, such as VENDOR or EMPLOYEE. The entries in parentheses are the names of individual fields in the record. The following examples explain:

```
CUSTOMER(ACCOUNT_NUMBER, NAME, ADDRESS, ACCOUNT_BALANCE)
EMPLOYEE(NAME, SSN, AGE)
PURCHASE_ORDER(PO_#, DATE, AMOUNT, VENDOR, QUANTITY, PRICE)
```

In the first example, CUSTOMER is the name of the record, and ACCOUNT_NUMBER, NAME, DDRESS, and ACCOUNT_BALANCE are the names of the fields.

DATA OCCURRENCES

A record structure has **occurrences**, also called **instances**. A record occurrence is a specific set of data values for the record. For example, for the record

```
EMPLOYEE(NAME, NUMBER, AGE)
```

we might have the occurrence

```
EMPLOYEE(Brown, 111222333,33),
```

and an occurrence for the CUSTOMER record just described might be

```
CUSTOMER(12122, ABC Hardware, 222 West Street, $1,050)
```

FIXED- AND VARIABLE-LENGTH RECORDS

Records within a file may be of either fixed or variable length. In a **fixed-length record**, both the number of fields and the length (character size) of each field are fixed. Fixed-length records are easier to manipulate in computer applications than variable-length records because the size of fixed-length records is standardized. Most records stored on direct-access storage devices (DASDs) are fixed-length.

The drawback of fixed-length records is that each field must be large enough to contain the maximum expected entry into the field. This typically results in wasted space, as in leaving 25 or so spaces for a name, whereas many names have 8 characters or fewer. In **variable-length records**, however, the width of the field can be adjusted for each data occurrence. Further, in variable-length records, the actual number of fields can vary from one data occurrence to another.

The end of a variable-length record must be indicated by a special symbol or a record-length field contained in the record itself. Variable-length records efficiently use available storage space, but manipulating such records is relatively difficult. Figure 12.1 illustrates several ways to implement variable-length records.

One approach to variable-length records that does not require programming system support for the variable-length structure is to use fixed-length trailer records. A **trailer record** is an extension of a master record. It is separate from the master record and written as required. Using an open-item accounts receivable file, for example, the master records contain information common to all accounts and the number of invoices sufficient for most of the accounts, whereas the trailer record contains more invoices. A master record may have as many trailer records associated with it as required. The trailer records may be written immediately after the associated master record.

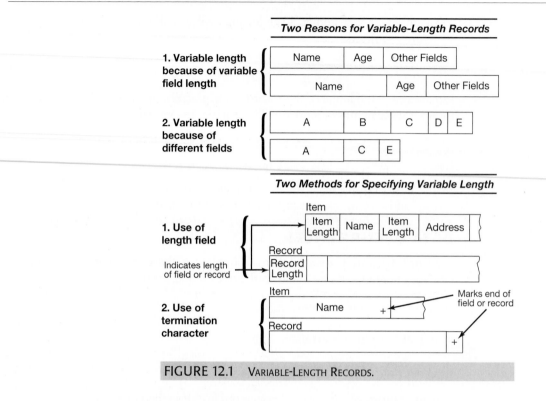

FIGURE 12.1   VARIABLE-LENGTH RECORDS.

Consider a hypothetical manufacturing company, Ace Tools, that maintains a raw materials inventory of hundreds of machine parts. Further, assume that Ace Tools purchases each part from one of several suppliers and then stores it in one of several warehouses. Any part can be purchased from any one or more of the suppliers and then stored in any one or more of the warehouses. The following data fields pertain to the parts inventory:

PART_NO	the part number
PNAME	the part name
TYPE	the type of part
COST	the standard cost per unit of the part
PVEND	the name of the vendor (supplier) from whom the part is purchased
WARHSE	the warehouse where the part is stored
LOC	the last two digits of the ZIP code of the warehouse where the part is stored

Note that it is not possible, in general, to store all information about a particular part in the following fixed-length record:

```
PART(PART_NO, PNAME, TYPE, COST, PVEND, WARHSE, LOC)
```

This is not possible, for example, because there may be more than one supplier for each part and because the record has room for only one supplier. The two-supplier case would require the following record format (assuming that there is only one storage location):

```
PART(PART_NO, PNAME, TYPE, COST, PVEND#1, WARHSE#1, LOC#1, PVEND#2, WARHSE#2, LOC#2)
```

where the suffix #1 applies to the part supplied by vendor number 1 and suffix #2 to the part supplied by vendor number 2. The record would need to be even longer if there

Variable-Length Record		
RECORD NAME	SUPPLIER (Repeated group 1)	LOCATION (Repeated group 2)
PART (PART_NO, PNAME, TYPE, COST,	PVEND # 01, PVEND # 02, PVEND # 03, PVEND # 04, • • • PVEND # 99,	WARHSE # 01, LOC # 01, WARHSE # 02, LOC # 02, WARHSE # 03, LOC # 03, WARHSE # 03, LOC # 03, • • • • • • WARHSE # 99, LOC # 99)

FIGURE 12.2 REPEATED GROUPS AS PART OF VARIABLE-LENGTH RECORDS.

were three suppliers, and in general, its length would depend on the number of vendors and storage locations associated with a given part. Such a record therefore would be a variable-length record.

Note that the variable record length arises because both the supplier (PVEND) and the storage locations (WARHSE and LOC) can occur more than once per record. That is, they are repeating (or repeated) groups of fields. (WARHSE and LOC are grouped together because they both relate to the storage location.) **Repeated groups** are related groups of fields that repeat themselves in variable-length records. This is shown in Figure 12.2. The first shaded block shows the SUPPLIER group, and the second shaded block shows the LOCATION group. Both these repeating groups belong to PART. This relationship is depicted in Figure 12.3 in a diagram that looks like a family tree. PART is shown to be the **parent** of SUPPLIER and LOCATION because each instance of PART may give rise to more than one supplier or location. In general, the highest level element in a tree diagram is the parent; lower-level elements in the tree diagram that are connected to (i.e., part of) the parent are called **children**.

PART itself might have a parent. For example, PART might be one of many children belonging to INVENTORY, with the other children being such things AS SUPPLIES and EQUIPMENT. For this reason, we shall refer to all the nodes in the tree, including PART, as *repeated groups*. In some cases we shall simply refer to them as **segments** or groups, or even **nodes**. Thus the terms *segment, group*, and *node* are shorthand for *repeated groups*. As we shall see in a later section of this chapter, segments are one of the fundamental building blocks used to construct databases.

Segments can be summarized in the same shorthand that is used for records. For example, PART, SUPPLIER, and LOCATION can be written as follows:

```
PART (PART_NO, PNAME, TYPE, COST)
SUPPLIER (PVEND)
LOCATION (WARHSE, LOC)
```

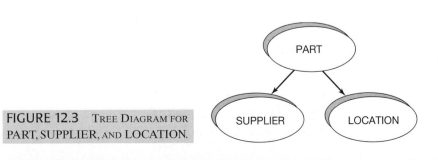

FIGURE 12.3 TREE DIAGRAM FOR PART, SUPPLIER, AND LOCATION.

Thus a record and a segment are in essence the same thing. Both are a collection of fields. In fact, there is nothing wrong with thinking of segments as records as long as it is remembered that segments, unlike simple records, have parents and children.

RECORD KEY AND FILE SEQUENCE

A **key** or **record key** is a data item or combination of data items that uniquely identifies a particular record in a file. Consider a file containing records of the format

```
PART(PART_NO, WARHSE)
```

where PART_NO is the part number of the part, and WARHSE is the warehouse number associated with its location. Further, assume that the file contains the following four records:

```
PART(101,1)
PART(102,2)
PART(103,1)
PART(106,1)
```

In this example, PART_NO is an acceptable key because it can be used to uniquely identify any one of the four records. This is not true, however, for WARHSE. For example, specifying a value of 1 for WARHSE does not uniquely identify one particular record; rather, it identifies three records, the first, third, and fourth ones.

In some cases it might be necessary to combine two fields to produce a key. Assume, for example, that one part can be stored in two warehouses. This would produce records such as

```
PART(101,2)
PART(101,1)
PART(102,1)
PART(103,1)
PART(103,2)
```

In this case, neither PART_NO nor WARHSE would in general uniquely identify an individual record. But both fields together would. Thus, combining the two fields into a single key would permit unique identification. For example, appending the value of WARHSE onto the value of PART_NO would work, giving key values of 1012, 1011, 1021, 1031, and 1032 for each of the five records, respectively.

It is sometimes useful to sort the records in a file so that they are in either ascending or descending order relative to the key. The four records in the first example are in ascending order by PART_NO. The five records in the second example could be ordered by the PART_NO + WARHSE key to produce the following:

```
PART(101,1)
PART(101,2)
PART(102,1)
PART(103,1)
PART(103,2)
```

In such cases, the first field (PART_NO) is called the **primary sort key** (or simply the **primary key**), and the second field (WARHSE) is called **secondary sort key** (or simply **secondary key**). Any additional fields required to uniquely identify and sort the records would be called **tertiary sort keys**. Therefore, a primary key is a field used to sort the records in a file, and a secondary key is used to determine relative position among a set of records when the primary key has the same value in each record of the set. In terms of the preceding example with five records, this means that when two records have the same value for PART_NO, the record with the smallest value for WARHSE will come first. In other words, the secondary key determines the order for records whose primary key values are all the same.

We shall denote key fields by underlining them. For example, QUANTITY is a key field in the following record:

PART(PART_NO, WARHSE, QUANTITY)

The term **relative random order** applies to a field on which the file is not sorted. Before sorting the preceding five records, the file is in random order relative to the WARHSE field. In the first record, WARHSE = 2; in the second record, WARHSE = 1; and in the fifth record, WARHSE = 2. Therefore, the file is not ordered by WARHSE.

Keys are important because they are necessary to process and locate records in files. These topics are discussed below.

DATABASE MANAGEMENT SYSTEMS AND THEIR ARCHITECTURE

As depicted in Figure 12.4, there are three levels of architecture relevant to databases and database management systems: the *conceptual level of architecture*, the *logical level of architecture*, and the *physical level of architecture*. At the conceptual level, databases are collections of various elements of information to be used for assorted purposes. Consider, for example, a sales-order database. Such a database might be defined at the conceptual level in terms of the kinds of information it includes (e.g., sales transactions, cash receipts, and customer information) and the purposes for which it is to be used (e.g., order entry and customer billing).

In order to implement a database defined at the conceptual level, specific data fields and records must be defined. It is also necessary to specify ways in which data records and fields will be viewed or reported, as well as related to each other. For example, it might be desirable to display the customer's account history with his or her open orders. This requires that the records and fields in the database be structured and

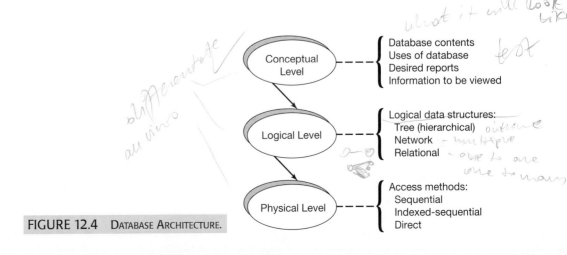

FIGURE 12.4   DATABASE ARCHITECTURE.

organized in some logical manner, thus giving rise to **logical data structures**. Three basic types of logical data structures can be used to accomplish this objective: *hierarchical, network*, and *relational*. Each of these data structures is discussed below.

The physical level of database architecture deals with specific implementation techniques and issues relating to methods for accessing data. The three most important data access methods (sequential, indexed sequential, and direct) are discussed in detail below.

CONCEPTUAL ARCHITECTURE

There is no one standard approach for developing a conceptual data model of a particular system. The **entity-relationship (E-R) data model** is one popular approach. The E-R model simply depicts the relationships between segments. In the E-R model, however, the term *entity* is used instead of segment, and the term *attribute* is used to refer to individual fields or data items. Graphically speaking, the E-R model uses square boxes for entities, ellipses for attributes, and diamond-shaped boxes for depicting relationships. Figure 12.5 shows an E-R diagram for the segments relating to the example record PART described previously. Note that two relationships are used, one indicating the relationship between the supplier and the part and the other indicating the relationship between the part and its storage location.

Other conceptual methods exist, including the **object-oriented modeling technique (OMT)**, originally developed for object-oriented programming and adapted for data modeling by Blaha, Premerlani, and Rumbaugh. This works by viewing the components of the system being modeled as object classes. In this method, an **object class** corresponds to a segment, and an **object** corresponds to a particular instance. Like the E-R model, the OMT defines relationships between segments. The most fundamental of these relationships is called **inheritance**. An inheritance relationship is created when an object class is divided into subclasses. For example, a general or parent class might

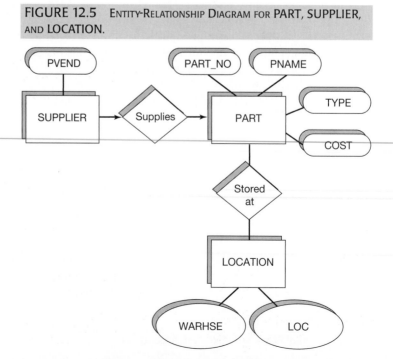

FIGURE 12.5   ENTITY-RELATIONSHIP DIAGRAM FOR PART, SUPPLIER, AND LOCATION.

be plant equipment, which might have subclasses such as hand tools, heavy machinery, repair equipment, and so on. The important thing is that the attributes of the general plant-equipment class are all inherited by each subclass. To further elaborate, we will define an object class as follows:

```
PLANT_EQUIPMENT(ACCOUNT_NO, COST, DEPRECIATION)
```

We also define the following two subclasses:

```
HEAVY_EQUIPMENT(ACCOUNT_NO, COST, DEPRECIATION, MAINTENANCE_FREQ, DATE_PURCHASED)
```

and

```
HAND_TOOLS(ACCOUNT_NO, COST, DEPRECIATION, USAGE)
```

Note that HAND_TOOLS and HEAVY_EQUIPMENT inherit all the attributes of PLANT_EQUIPMENT (i.e., ACCOUNT_NO, COST, and DEPRECIATION). The two subclasses, however, have their own unique attributes (i.e., USAGE for HAND_TOOLS and MAINTENANCE_FREQ, DATE_PURCHASED for HEAVY_EQUIPMENT). In general, subclasses have all the attributes of their parent class plus their own attributes. For our example, these relationships are depicted in Figure 12.6.

The subclasses might be further divided. For example, HEAVY_EQUIPMENT might be divided into grinding and cutting equipment, with both these subclasses having their own unique attributes.

In summary, there are a number of ways to conceptually model a system. All methods seek to gain a better understanding of the system and document what is learned. Ideally, one would like to derive a logical model from the conceptual model and then a physical model from the logical model. Conceptual modeling techniques, however, all share two common weaknesses. First, there are many ways to model an enterprise, so evaluating the results of a particular technique may be difficult. Second, there is a risk that the application of a particular technique might result in an incomplete picture of the system being modeled. The E-R model, however, also can lead directly to an implementable database. In fact, commercial software is available that takes the analyst's E-R model and automatically generates a working database system.

The OMT is perhaps the most promising modeling technique. It can be used with additional relationships besides inheritance (such as aggregation and association). Further, it can be implemented in successive levels of detail, leading directly to an implementable database.

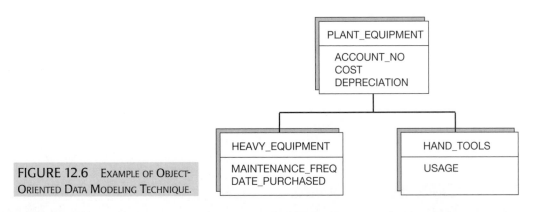

FIGURE 12.6   EXAMPLE OF OBJECT-ORIENTED DATA MODELING TECHNIQUE.

DATABASE ARCHITECTURE AT THE LOGICAL LEVEL: LOGICAL DATA STRUCTURES

The major task an analyst faces in designing a database is to identify and design systematic relationships between its segments. The database must be structured so that it is able to provide users with the information they need to make effective decisions. The relationships that exist between the segments in the database are determined by the **logical data structure**, also called the **schema** or **database model**.

Three major models of logical data structures appear in the literature: (1) tree or hierarchical models, (2) network models, and (3) relational models. Some authorities define as many as eight additional models, but the ones discussed below are of special importance to practice.

TREE OR HIERARCHICAL STRUCTURES

Tree structures are a direct representation of the segmenting process described earlier. In a **tree structure**, each node represents a set of fields (i.e., a segment), and a node is related to another node at the next-highest level of the tree. The latter is called the **parent** node. Every parent may have one or more **children**, and the connection between the children and parents is called a **branch**. The significant feature of the tree model is that a child node cannot have more than one parent. The tree model corresponds to the data structures supported by COBOL and other widely used programming languages and has been implemented in many commercial database management systems (DBMSs) such as IMS and IDMS. Figure 12.3 is a simple example of a tree structure, and Figure 12.7 depicts both tree and network structures in general.

NETWORK STRUCTURES

A **network structure** is one that allows a child segment to have more than one parent. A network, therefore, is a more general data structure than a tree. As

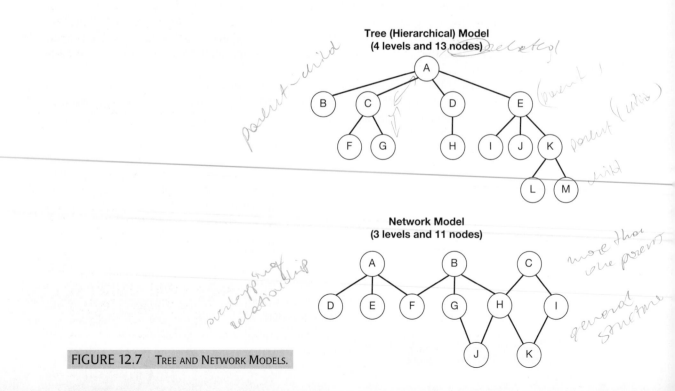

FIGURE 12.7   TREE AND NETWORK MODELS.

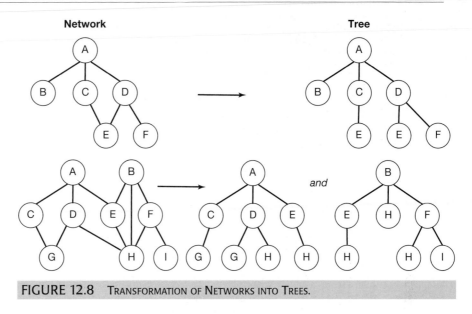

FIGURE 12.8   TRANSFORMATION OF NETWORKS INTO TREES.

Figure 12.8 shows, any network structure can be transformed to one or more tree structures by introducing a redundancy of nodes. Some DBMSs do not directly support network structures, but because any network may be transformed to a tree structure, it is possible to implement network structures in tree-oriented systems. The CODASYL model is a network model.

Both trees and networks are implemented with imbedded pointer fields, which cross-link segments, as discussed more thoroughly below. This creates a subtle intermingling of the logical structure of the data with the physical structure of pointers and chaining mechanisms needed to logically connect the segments together. Logical tree and network structures may become unduly complex because the logical description of the data tries to represent a complicated set of relationships between segments as a set of lines, physically representing the pointers in the logical diagram. Critics of tree and network approaches to database design have held that these models cause the analyst to be prematurely physical in database design.

Implementing Tree and Network Structures   The topic of implementing tree and network structures is more a part of the physical architecture of databases than it is of the logical architecture. Still, we discuss physical implementation here because, as discussed earlier, it is intertwined with the logical structures of the tree and network models.

There are various ways to implement tree and network structures. These include using lists and pointers. In a list organization, each record contains one or more pointers (fields) indicating the address of the next logical record with the same attribute(s). An invoice record may contain a field that contains (points to) the key of another invoice from the same vendor. A record may be part of several lists. This list is called **multilist organization**. A customer record, for example, may contain pointers for geographic location and customer type (industrial, etc.). By including a pointer in a record to point to the next logical record, the logical and physical structure can be completely different. Figure 12.9 illustrates a simple **list structure** and a **ring structure**. A ring structure differs from a list in that the last record in the ring list points back to the first record. In addition, all records in a ring may point backward as well as forward through the use and maintenance of additional pointer fields. In a **multiple-ring structure**, several rings pass through individual records.

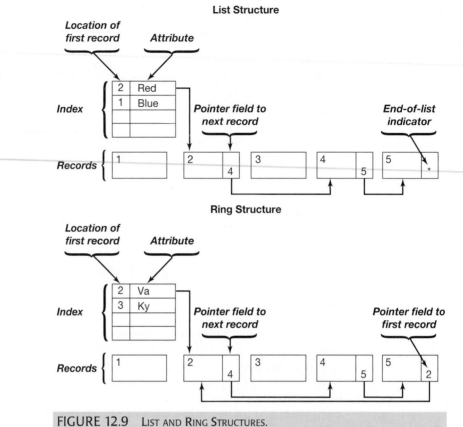

FIGURE 12.9   LIST AND RING STRUCTURES.

Designing and maintaining such structures are complicated, and pointers require additional disk space. Further, updating pointers is necessary every time a record is added or deleted. Nevertheless, using pointers in conjunction with hierarchical and tree structures is often a useful approach to data modeling, especially in cases when records are seldom added or deleted.

Hypertext systems are pointer-based systems that allow users to browse through databases in random fashion by selecting key words or objects. *Semantic data networks* are similar to hypertext systems. The only difference between the two is that in semantic networks the cross-linking of records is limited to text, whereas in hypertext systems the cross-linking can include multimedia objects such as photographs and other graphic forms.

RELATIONAL DATA STRUCTURES

The **relational model** views the database as a collection of two-dimensional tables rather than a hierarchical or network type of structure. Recall the variable-length PART record used in the preceding discussion on segments:

```
PART(PART_NO, PNAME, TYPE, COST, PVEND#1, WARHSE#1, LOC#1,
                                 PVEND#2, WARHSE#2, LOC#2
                                   ..        ..       ..
                                 PVEND#n, WARHSE#n, LOC#n)
```

This record can be segmented as follows:

```
PART (PART_NO, PNAME, TYPE, COST)
SUPPLIER (PART_NO, PVEND)
LOCATION (PART_NO, WARHSE, LOC)
```

PART						
PART_NO	PNAME	TYPE	COST	(SUPPLIER)	(LOCATION)	
				PVEND	WARHSE	LOC
101	wheel	A	1.40	ELFO	1	01
101	wheel	A	1.40	ELFO	2	72
101	wheel	A	1.40	GREEN	1	01
101	wheel	A	1.40	ACE	1	01
101	wheel	A	1.40	ACE	2	72
101	wheel	A	1.40	ACE	3	64
101	wheel	A	1.40	ACE	4	81
102	gear	D	6.60	ELFO	2	72
102	gear	D	6.60	ELFO	3	64
102	gear	D	6.60	ACE	2	72
103	cog	A	1.40	ELFO	2	72
104	wire	A	1.40	ELFO	1	01
105	pin	D	6.60	GREEN	3	64
105	pin	D	6.60	GREEN	4	81

FIGURE 12.10   PARTIAL LISTING OF PARTS INVENTORY FOR ACE TOOLS.

Note that unlike in the preceding example, we now assume that PART_NO, PVEND, and WARHSE are key fields. We also have added PART_NO to the SUPPLIER and LOCATION segments so that it is possible to identify the supplier and the storage location for each product.

Data (instances) for each of these three segments can be stored in a table, as shown in Figure 12.10. This is the essence of the relational model—representing segments in tables. The advantage of this logical data structure over trees and networks is immediately obvious: There are no complicated pointers or lists. Further, any information that can be extracted from a tree or network structure also can be extracted from relational tables. For these reasons, the relational model is the most popular data structure in today's business environment. However, despite its popularity, it is less efficient than trees and networks when the database is seldom updated and the relationships between nodes can be reasonably defined.

Information (e.g., a financial report) is extracted from tables using **relational algebra**, which can be summarized in three basic operations:

OPERATION	FUNCTION
Selection	Creates a new table from selected rows of existing tables. The rows are selected on the basis of their data values.
Join	Creates a new table from the rows of two existing tables. The rows are selected on the basis of their data values.
Projection	Creates a new table by deleting columns from an existing table.

Other operations also exist, but they are not discussed here because Selection, Join, and Projection represent the essence of the relational algebra. Using the three basic operations, it is possible to create a new table that contains any single occurrence of a data element or combinations of data elements.

Certain rules called **normal forms** govern the creation of tables. The process of applying these rules is called **normalization**. Tables that satisfy these rules are said to be *normalized*. Tables that do not satisfy these rules are *unnormalized*. Normalization is important because without it, updating the entries in the tables can cause problems. We will show this with an example.

Normalization is simply the process of converting the record structure from a tree or network format into the appropriate tables. This is not a difficult process because it is always possible to collapse a tree diagram into a single table, as is demonstrated for PART in Figure 12.11. This table is completely unnormalized, so it will serve as a good example of why normalization is necessary.

Note that part number 101 (as well as its name and cost) appears in each of the first seven rows. This is unnecessary duplication that not only wastes storage space but also makes it possible for the same part to have two different names in different rows. Thus a primary purpose of normalization is to eliminate unnecessary duplication.

The first step in normalization is to create a separate table for each repeating group. This is accomplished in Figure 12.11. Tables without repeating groups are said to be in **first normal form**. In the first normal form, no repeated groups (variable-length records) are allowed. There are also second and third normal forms, which can be obtained by eliminating redundancies from the tables in first normal form. The first of these additional redundancies can be seen in the LOCATION table. Note that LOC is always 01 when WARHSE is 1, 72 when WARHSE is 2, 64 when WARHSE is 3, and 81 when WARHSE is 4. It is therefore true that the value of WARHSE strictly determines the value of LOC. The value of LOC is therefore redundant. Again, as was the case with the first normal form, the redundancy not only wastes space but makes it possible

PART

PART_NO	PNAME	TYPE	COST
101	wheel	A	1.40
102	gear	D	6.60
103	cog	A	1.40
104	wire	A	1.40
105	pin	D	6.60

SUPPLIER

PROD_NO	PVEND
101	ELFO
101	GREEN
101	ACE
102	ELFO
102	ACE
103	ELFO
104	ELFO
105	GREEN

LOCATION

PROD_NO	WARHSE	LOC
101	1	01
101	2	72
101	3	64
101	4	81
102	2	72
102	3	64
103	2	72
104	1	01
105	3	64
105	4	81

FIGURE 12.11   PART, SUPPLIER, AND LOCATION DEPICTED AS RELATIONAL TABLES.

for the same warehouse (WARHSE) to have two different ZIP codes in two different rows. This problem occurs because the value of a key field (WARHSE) strictly determines the value of a nonkey field (LOC). In the **second normal form**, no key is allowed to determine the values of a nonkey field. The LOCATION table can be put in second normal form by dividing it into two tables, putting LOC in its own table away from PROD_NO:

LOCATION (<u>PROD_NO</u>, <u>WARHSE</u>)
WAREHOUSE (<u>WARHSE</u>, LOC)

In the **third normal form**, no nonkey field can determine the values on another nonkey field. This form is violated in the PART table. Both TYPE and COST are nonkey fields, and TYPE strictly determines COST. Again, this problem can be solved by splitting the table:

PART (<u>PROD_NO</u>, PNAME, TYPE)
COSTS (<u>TYPE</u>, COST)

In summary, the three normal forms are as follows:

NORMAL FORM	RULE
First normal form	Divide tables to eliminate repeated groups.
Second normal form	Divide tables so that no key determines the values of a nonkey field.
Third normal form	Divide tables so that no nonkey field determines the values of another nonkey field.

Finally, we note that in the terminology of relational databases, the term **relation** is synonymous with *table*, and **tuple** refers to a row in a table.

DATABASE ARCHITECTURE: THE PHYSICAL LEVEL

In discussing the physical level of database architecture, we will focus on the three file-access methods: sequential, indexed, and direct. DASDs are capable of supporting all these methods, and the choice of the best one will depend on the particular application.

SEQUENTIALLY ACCESSED FILES

In a **sequential-access file**, records can only be accessed in their predefined sequence. For example, if there are 100 records in a file, one must access the first 99 records before accessing the last record. The predefined sequence is normally a result of the records having been sorted on some record key. For example, instances of the record PART (<u>PROD_NO</u>, PNAME) would be sorted by PART_NO, and the record for part number 101 would appear in the file before the record for part number 102. In general, however, the sorting can be in either ascending or descending order.

Sequential file organization is not a useful means of storing data when only a small number of records need to be accessed in a file containing a large number of records. For example, accessing the last record in a file containing 1 million records would require 999,999 records to be accessed before reaching the desired record. This would produce an intolerable delay (perhaps several minutes) on a disk storage unit.

Sequential files are useful in batch processing, which normally accesses all the records in a file. The usual procedure is to first sort both the transaction and master files on the same key. A typical application might be updating customers' accounts receivable (in the master file) to reflect payments received (in the transaction file). First, the program sorts both files in ascending order by account number. Next, the program

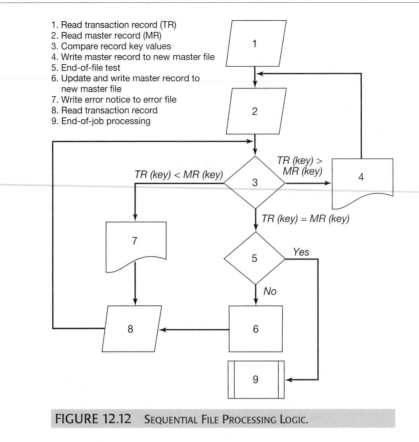

1. Read transaction record (TR)
2. Read master record (MR)
3. Compare record key values
4. Write master record to new master file
5. End-of-file test
6. Update and write master record to new master file
7. Write error notice to error file
8. Read transaction record
9. End-of-job processing

FIGURE 12.12 SEQUENTIAL FILE PROCESSING LOGIC.

reads one record from each file. If the account numbers on these two records match each other, then the information on the payment record is used to update the balance field on the accounts receivable record. The updated account record is then written to a new master file. This procedure continues according to the logic in Figure 12.12 until all records in both files are processed.

A careful study of Figure 12.12 will reveal that this sequential updating procedure will not work unless the files are sorted. For example, if the record in the transaction file with the highest key value is placed at the beginning of this file (instead of at the end, where it belongs if the file is sorted in ascending order), then the program will find and update the matching record at the end of the master file and then immediately terminate processing. In other words, the program will process only one transaction and quit. This happens because the program makes only one pass through each file and must go all the way to the end of the master file to find the record matching the first record in the transaction file. After that, there are no records left in the master file to process.

In conclusion, sequential file organization is useful when batch processing is required. Batch processing normally involves sorting and processing all the records in both the transaction and master files. In cases where only a small proportion of the records need to be accessed, one of the other file-access methods discussed below is more efficient.

INDEXED FILES

Any attribute can be extracted from the records in a primary file and used to build a new file whose purpose is to provide an index to the original file. Such a file is called an

indexed file or an **inverted file**. For example, assume that a customer invoice file exists with the record format

CUSTOMER(ACCOUNT_NO, <u>INVOICE NO</u>)

and the following instances followed by their disk addresses:

RECORD	RECORD'S ADDRESS ON THE DISK (CYLINDER #–SURFACE #–RECORD #)
CUSTOMER(141, 901)	1-2-1
CUSTOMER(164, 902)	9-5-2
CUSTOMER(175, 903)	6-1-6
CUSTOMER(141, 904)	7-4-4
CUSTOMER(182, 905)	2-3-7
CUSTOMER(164, 906)	2-2-8

An index for ACCOUNT_NO is given in Figure 12.13. In this example, the account number, 164, is typed into the computer, located in the index along with two related disk addresses, 9-5-2 pointing to invoice number 902 and 2-2-8 pointing to invoice number 906.

   This example shows that using the index to locate records on the disk is a two-step process. In the first step, the index is searched for the specified value of an attribute, and the desired disk addresses are retrieved. In the second step, the disk addresses are used to directly retrieve the desired records. This process can be considerably faster

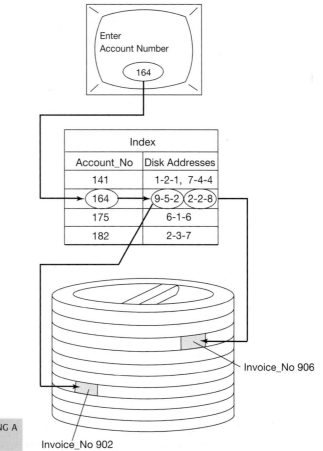

FIGURE 12.13   EXAMPLE OF USING A FILE INDEX.

than sequentially searching every record in the file, especially when the entire index can be loaded into primary memory before it is searched, for searching in primary memory is fast relative to searching on a disk. Still, if the index is very long and will not fit into primary memory, it may take an undue length of time to complete the search. This problem can be solved by factoring a long index into subindexes, but even this technique is impractical if the file is large enough.

Of course, it is possible to have more than one index for a given file. A file is said to be **fully inverted** when indexes exist for all its fields. The processing time required to maintain a fully inverted file can be high because the indexes must be updated whenever records are added, deleted, or modified. Further, each index requires additional disk storage, and the indexes can end up requiring more storage space than the data file itself.

Indexed-Sequential Files   One important type of indexed file is an indexed-sequential file. An **indexed-sequential file** is a sequential file that is stored on a DASD and is both indexed and physically sorted on the same field. Such files are commonly referred to as **ISAM** files, with ISAM being an acronym for *indexed-sequential access method*. ISAM is a powerful compromise between sequential and direct-access (discussed below) file organizations, providing the capabilities of both at a reasonable increase in cost.

The twin objectives of file usage—processing and inquiry—are both addressed by ISAM organization. The processing of a batch of records may be done sequentially, whereas individual inquiries to the file may be handled using the index. The more detailed the index, the quicker is the access; the tradeoff occurs in maintaining the index. Consider first a main file in sequence and an index (list of keys and record locations) to that file. If every record key is represented in the index (not normally necessary), then each time a main file record is added or deleted, the index must be changed. If, as is more likely, only every nth record or the first or last record in a major memory subdivision is represented in the index, then the index need not be changed so often, but it is always necessary to check to see whether this is the case. Most database programs automatically update the indexes as changes are made to the data file.

Structure of an ISAM File   An ISAM file structurally consists of three distinct areas: the index, the prime area, and the overflow area. The index is a map that relates the key fields of records to their corresponding addresses in the prime area. Each entry in the index gives the range of key fields on a particular track of the disk on which the file is stored. By searching the index, a program can locate the track containing the desired record. Although the track must then be searched sequentially, this search is very rapid.

Figure 12.14 illustrates the process by which a computer would locate a file record whose key is 1002. The computer reads the first record in the master index, which refers to records with key values between 0001 and 0500. Since 1002 is greater than 0500, the computer looks at the next index record, but this refers to file records with key numbers between 0501 and 1000. Then the machine checks the next master index record, which contains information about file record keys 1001 to 1500 and therefore includes 1002, the record key for which it is searching. The computer reads in the index that the next level of the index associated with this record is on track 0300. The computer goes to track 0300 and starts to read the records on that track. The first record indicates that it has information pertaining to records 1001 to 1005. Since 1002 is within this range, the computer notes that the record being sought is on track 0301 in the prime area. The computer goes to track 0301, searches sequentially until it finds record 1002, and retrieves the record called for. All this takes place in a fraction of a second.

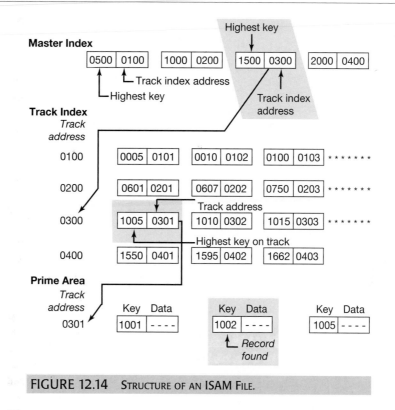

FIGURE 12.14   STRUCTURE OF AN ISAM FILE.

The *prime area* is the portion of the disk on which the actual records are written. The *overflow area* is a separate section of the disk that is allocated to the file to allow additions to be made without extensive processing of the initial file. The overflow area is originally empty. When a new record is to be added to the file, it must be placed in its correct position in the prime area to maintain the sequential organization of the file. Existing records in the prime area must be bumped to make room for the new record. If space is available on the track where the record must be inserted, the record is inserted in position, and the other records on the track are moved. Space may be available for the new record because some empty prime space was left originally in the file to facilitate additions or because prime space was made available by the deletion of one or more records. At times, however, the addition of a new record will bump an existing record off the track being updated. In this case, the bumped record is moved to the overflow area. Although records in the overflow area are not physically in key sequence, they can be accessed in key sequence by using the index. As before, the index is used to identify the track on which the record should be located. If the record is not found on the track referenced in the index, the overflow area is automatically checked sequentially until the record is found. Overflow lengthens the time needed to process an ISAM file; accordingly, an ISAM file should be reorganized periodically to make access more efficient. Reorganization consists of merging all the records so that the file is once again in physical sequential order in the prime area.

The index may be factored into a hierarchical set of master and subindexes—usually a cylinder index and a track index—to facilitate retrieval. This is shown in Figure 12.14. At times, a single-level index will be sufficient. Record key fields are listed sequentially in the index. In an ISAM file it is not normally possible for the record key field (e.g., account number or vendor number) to also serve as the address. The index links the record key to the address.

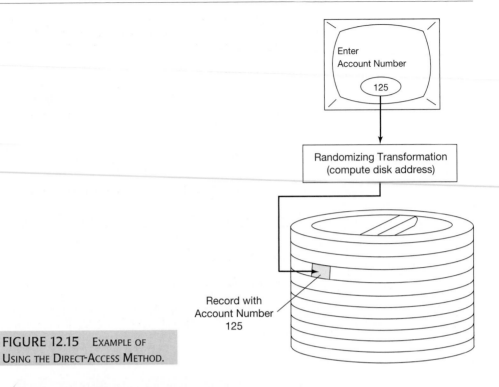

FIGURE 12.15   EXAMPLE OF
USING THE DIRECT-ACCESS METHOD.

DIRECTLY ACCESSED FILES

Direct-access files allow individual records to be retrieved almost instantly without the use of an index. This is accomplished by assigning each record to a storage location that bears some relationship to the record's key values. Therefore, with the direct-access method, the only thing needed to locate a record is its key value.

Several addressing methods are used to store and locate records in a direct-access file. One method is to have a record's key field correspond directly to the coding scheme used by the computer itself to identify the physical address on a DASD. A related method is to store physical device addresses as a field within a file's records. Neither of these methods requires any conversion of the key prior to access. However, neither of these methods is used widely because storage location addresses are rarely suitable as record identifiers, and security and systems management problems are associated with users knowing actual physical storage locations.

Most direct-access file systems convert a key to a storage location address using either an index (table) or a randomizing transformation. This means that it is possible to access any record on the disk almost instantly given its key value. The key value is converted to a disk address, and the record is accessed directly without any searching. This process is depicted in Figure 12.15.

A **randomizing transformation** is a widely used method of storing and locating records in a direct-access file. Figure 12.16 illustrates the use of a randomizing transformation to load a file on a disk. There are four records in the file; in turn, each record key is used in a mathematical calculation (divide by 7, note the remainder, and add a displacement factor). Once the file is loaded, any record may be accessed directly by passing the key through the randomizing calculation to determine its address; the device then accesses this particular record directly, bypassing all other records in the file.

Figure 12.16 illustrates several important concepts relating to direct-access file organization. The first is the use of a randomizing transformation to store and access

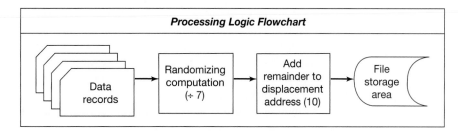

Processing Logic Flowchart

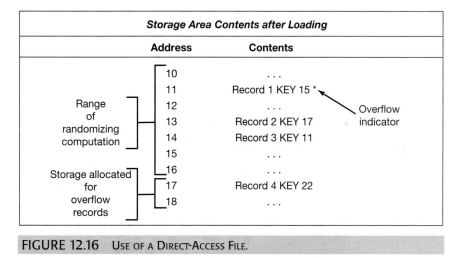

File Loading Illustration

Record	Key	Remainder after division by seven	+	Displacement factor (initial address of file area)	=	Record storage address	
1	15	1		10		11	*
2	17	3		10		13	Overflow
3	11	4		10		14	
4	22	1		10		11	*

Storage Area Contents after Loading

	Address	Contents
	10	. . .
	11	Record 1 KEY 15 *
Range of randomizing computation	12	. . .
	13	Record 2 KEY 17
	14	Record 3 KEY 11
	15	. . .
	16	. . .
Storage allocated for overflow records	17	Record 4 KEY 22
	18	. . .

Overflow indicator

FIGURE 12.16   USE OF A DIRECT-ACCESS FILE.

individual records. Note that dividing by 7 yields seven possible remainders (0 through 6); dividing by a prime number yields remainders that should tend to be uniformly and randomly distributed (thus the term **random access** is often used synonymously with *direct access*). In addition, it is very likely that several different records will randomize (*hash*) to the same physical address. Both these points are significant. The first point means that the storage space required for the file is largely determined by the range of the transformation results (0 to 7 in the example), even if the file is expected to be smaller than the range of the transformation. The second point is called *overflow* and means that some method of storing and retrieving overflow must be built into the system. In Figure 12.16, two records are hashed to the same address, requiring that one of them be stored in a different location. Overflow occurs when two or more records (called *synonyms*) yield the same address; in such cases, a special pointer field is used to indicate the addresses of the locations used to store overflow records. Note that overflow considerations require storage space in addition to that required by the randomizing transformation. The overall result is that storage efficiency typically is not high in direct-access files.

The drawbacks of vacant storage and overflow considerations typically are more than offset by the advantages of direct-access file organization. Direct access permits nonsequential updating—there is no need to sort and batch transactions. In fact, in a straight direct-access file update, nothing would be gained by batching and sorting transactions. Another major advantage of direct-access files is the speed of access to individual records. Records are accessed almost instantly. Often such speed is essential—as in an airline reservation system or a stock market quotation system. In addition, direct-access organization permits simultaneous updating of several related files. A sale affects both inventory and receivable files. If the inventory and receivable files are direct access, both may be updated in a single pass of an invoice by noting both inventory number and customer number, using each key to directly access and update the respective records. If both files were sequential, separate passes (and separate sorts) would be needed to accomplish this same task.

There is, however, a major limitation of the direct-access method. A record cannot be located if its key is not known. For example, it would not be possible to conveniently locate all sales transactions for product X with amounts greater than $1,000 because there is no common key to identify such transactions.

ECONOMIC RELATIONS BETWEEN FILE ORGANIZATION TECHNIQUES

The file-access techniques just discussed (sequential, indexed, and direct access) are appropriate in different circumstances. Figure 12.17 summarizes when to use each file organization technique. The basic economics of file processing are largely determined by the **activity ratio** (the number of accessed records divided by the number of records in the file) and the desired response time for processing and inquiries.

Figure 12.18 compares the average cost per transaction processed for these three techniques over a range of activity ratios. Sequential organization is a fixed-cost

FIGURE 12.17   WHEN TO USE EACH FILE ORGANIZATION TECHNIQUE.

File Organization Techniques	When Best to Use	Limitations
Sequential	High activity ratio, as in batch processing	Not possible to access quickly a single record
Indexed	Low activity ratio, moderate to large file size	File updates require indexes to be updated
Indexed-Sequential	File needs to be processed both in batch (high activity ratio) and nonbatch (low activity ratio) modes	Same as with indexed and sequential
Direct	Low activity ratio, very large files, networks, and trees	Need keys to locate records

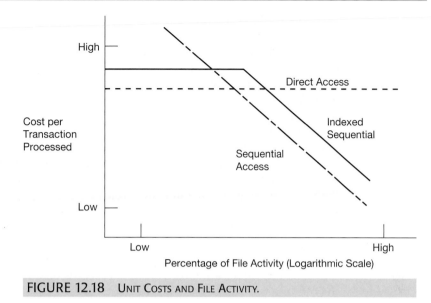

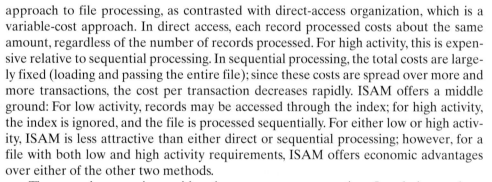

FIGURE 12.18   UNIT COSTS AND FILE ACTIVITY.

approach to file processing, as contrasted with direct-access organization, which is a variable-cost approach. In direct access, each record processed costs about the same amount, regardless of the number of records processed. For high activity, this is expensive relative to sequential processing. In sequential processing, the total costs are largely fixed (loading and passing the entire file); since these costs are spread over more and more transactions, the cost per transaction decreases rapidly. ISAM offers a middle ground: For low activity, records may be accessed through the index; for high activity, the index is ignored, and the file is processed sequentially. For either low or high activity, ISAM is less attractive than either direct or sequential processing; however, for a file with both low and high activity requirements, ISAM offers economic advantages over either of the other two methods.

The second economic consideration concerns response time. In relation to databases, *response time* is the length of time the user must wait for the system to complete an operation, such as a query. Direct-access files are necessary for very quick response times; longer response times (hours or more) can be handled economically by sequential files. When long response times can be tolerated, queries or file updates typically can be appended to batch processing runs. For example, a copy of customers' records can be obtained as a by-product of posting invoices to the accounts receivable file. ISAM again offers a middle ground. Short-response-time requests may be processed using the index; longer-response-time requests may be appended to any sequential processing runs against the file. Response times are also affected by hardware considerations, as discussed below.

PHYSICAL ARCHITECTURE, HARDWARE, AND RESPONSE TIME

Response time can become a major problem with large databases that might be accessed by hundreds or even thousands of users at the same time. If the database system and computer hardware are not suited for the demands placed on them, then users might find themselves waiting a hopelessly long time for responses to their queries. Therefore, the database system must be designed properly for the use to which it will be put, and the hardware must be fast enough to get the job done.

On the hardware side, response time is affected by physical access time. This is typically the time required for the CPU to retrieve a single block of data from the disk, called the **disk access time**. One problem is that the CPU operates much faster than the disk does, requiring the CPU to wait while disk input/output operations are being executed. This means that minimizing disk input and output can in some cases result in considerable increases in response time.

Another factor that can affect response time is how data records are distributed physically on the disk. If a group of records is to be accessed in sequence, then the response time will be faster if these records are contiguous (physically next to each other) on the disk. If they are contiguous, the read/write head on the disk drive will need to move only a small distance each time it accesses the next record in the list. If, on the other hand, the records are strewn all over the disk, then the read/write head will have to move a relatively long distance to access each new record, thus slowing things down.

On a hard disk, data on the same track or cylinder can be accessed without moving the read/write head. This means that in some cases it is possible to considerably speed up a database application by storing the records of a particular data file contiguously on one or more disk cylinders.

It should be emphasized that many database systems rely on operating system routines for their input/output operations. This means that it may be the operating system that determines where data will be placed on the disk. This is important because many operating systems have no provision to ensure that data will be stored contiguously. In fact, many operating systems will deliberately break up files and spread them all over a disk, putting their pieces into small empty spaces so that all areas of the disk are used and no space is wasted.

The need to store a file contiguously depends on the physical architecture of the database and its corresponding file access method. If the database uses the sequential-access method, then physically placing the records next to each other on the disk is desirable. For the indexed-access method, however, it is almost always desirable to place the indexes in contiguous storage because these files often are read sequentially and in their entirety. However, it may not be necessary to place the records in the related data files next to each other on the disk because records in these files are accessed randomly in the two-stage lookup process described earlier. Sometimes, however, it might be desirable to batch process all the records in an indexed file, (as is often done with ISAM files), and in such cases, contiguous storage for the primary file would be desirable. Finally, for the direct-access method, storing records next to each other would provide no improvement in response time. In fact, contiguous storage might be impossible due to the nature of the hashing approaches mentioned earlier.

DATABASE MANAGEMENT SYSTEMS AND DATABASES IN PRACTICE

WHAT DATABASE MANAGEMENT SYSTEMS DO

Database management systems (DBMSs) are computer programs that enable a user to create and update files, to select and retrieve data, and to generate various outputs and reports.

All DBMSs contain the following three common attributes for managing and organizing data.

DATA DESCRIPTION LANGUAGE (DDL)

The DDL allows the database administrator (DBA) to define the logical structure of the database, called the **schema**. Defining the schema normally involves defining each of the following:

- The name of the data element
- The type of data (numeric, alphabetic, date, etc.) and the number of decimal positions if the data element is numeric
- The number of positions (e.g., nine positions for Social Security Numbers)

The DDL also may be used to define **subschema**, which are individual user views of the database. For example, the sales order processing department might be able to view and edit the data elements DATE, CUSTOMER_NAME, ACCOUNT_NUMBER, QUANTITY, and PRICE. The production department might have a different view of the same database, seeing instead CUSTOMER_NAME, ACCOUNT_NUMBER, and SCHEDULED_ DATE_OF_COMPLETION. Further, the production department might be restricted from editing CUSTOMER_NAME and ACCOUNT_NUMBER. Note that in this example the application program (i.e., the accounting system) automatically generates the DDL statements required to create the subschemas.

The DDL also may be used to create, modify, and delete tables in a relational setting.

DATA MANIPULATION LANGUAGE (DML)

The DML consists of the commands for updating, editing, manipulating, and extracting data. In many cases the user does not need to know or use the DML. Rather, the application program (e.g., the payroll program or interactive accounting system) automatically generates the DML statements to accomplish the user's requests. Structured Query Language (SQL) is a common DML in relational settings.

DATA QUERY LANGUAGE (DQL)

The DQL is a user-friendly language or interface that allows the user to request information from the database. One such friendly interface is QBE (query by example), which allows the user to request information simply by filling in blanks. For example, a user might fill in the blanks in a form such as that shown in Figure 12.19 to request all records with account balances greater than $1,000.

There also exist natural-language interfaces, which allow users to make requests for information using ordinary, everyday English—for example, "May I please have a sales report for the month of June?" Such systems are capable of recognizing a variety of phrasings for the requests, and if the user makes an unintelligible or incomplete request, the system will ask the necessary questions to resolve the problem.

Figure 12.20 depicts the processing of a user query as it relates to the schema, the subschema, the DDL, and the DML.

SQL DATA MANIPULATION LANGUAGE

Structured Query Language (SQL) is the technology used to retrieve information from databases. SQL is a nonprocedural programming language. It allows the user to

FIGURE 12.19   SELECTING ACCOUNTS >$1,000 USING QBE.

Name	Account Number	Account Balance
		>1000

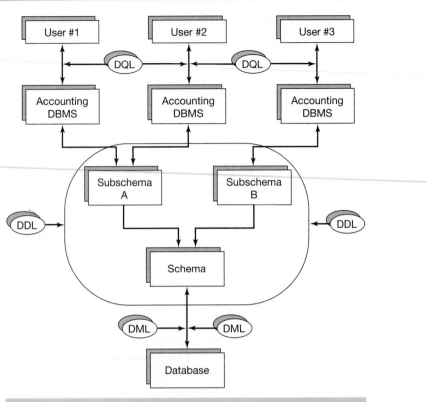

FIGURE 12.20   Logical Model for Processing User Queries.

focus on specifying what data are desired rather than focusing on how to get those data.

Four basic statement types comprise the DML (**data manipulation language**) component of SQL. These are

SELECT	Retrieves rows from tables
UPDATE	Modifies the rows of tables
DELETE	Removes rows from tables
INSERT	Adds new rows to tables

This section will discuss and provide specific examples for the SELECT statement type. The examples are designed for the Electric Books Company database described in the appendix to this chapter. These examples may be used in the Web SQL processor that is available to users of this textbook. The Web SQL processor functions to process SELECT queries against the Electric Books Company database. You may engage in active learning of basic SQL concepts by actually running the example queries to see their output from the Electric Book Company database.

The examples will illustrate several of the basic data retrieval capabilities of the SELECT statement. The examples also will introduce several of the more general features of SQL, such as arithmetic and logical expressions, which are also applicable to the UPDATE, DELETE, and INSERT statements. These latter statement types will be described only briefly herein. Only SELECT statements can be used in the Web SQL processor.

SELECT QUERIES

SELECT is usually the first word in an SQL statement that is intended to extract data from a database. SELECT specifies which fields (i.e., items in a database) or expressions based on fields that you want to retrieve. The FROM clause indicates which table(s) contain those items. FROM is required and follows SELECT.

SELECT Everything The * is a special query character that represents "all fields." This query selects all fields from the keywords table,

SELECT * FROM keywords

SELECT Fields SELECT specific fields (i.e., items) by name. If you wish to include more than one item, separate the items with commas. List the items in the order in which you want them to be retrieved.

SELECT name, country, currency FROM company

ORDER BY ORDER BY sorts the displayed data in the order specified in the clause. ORDER BY is optional. If you do not include it, the data appear unsorted. The default sort order is ascending (A–Z, 0–9).

This query adds the ORDER BY name clause to the previous query.

SELECT name, country, currency FROM company

ORDER BY name

You may specify ascending sort order for a data item by including the ASC keyword at the end the data item. To sort in reverse order (Z–A, 9–0), add DESC after each data item you want to sort in descending order.

WHERE Condition You can use WHERE to determine which records from the tables listed in the FROM clause will appear in the results of the SELECT statement. WHERE is optional, but when it is included, it follows FROM. If you do not include WHERE, all records are selected. The SQL statement selects only USA companies from the company table.

SELECT * FROM Company WHERE Country = 'USA'

String Functions The following SQL statement illustrates a word search. The word *goodwill* will be searched in the Notes. Topic field.

SELECT * FROM notes

WHERE Instr(1, topic, "goodwill") > 0

The Instr function searches a specific field ("topic" in the query) for a specific character string enclosed in quotes ("goodwill") starting at a specific position in the field (1 indicates the first position, the beginning, of the string).

Additional string functions include

- Left\$ (string, length): String is the expression from which the leftmost characters are returned. Length is the number of characters to return.
- Right\$ (string, length): String is the expression from which the rightmost characters are returned. Length is the number of characters to return.

Arithmetic Expressions SQL allows arithmetic expressions to be included in the SELECT clause. An arithmetic expression consists of a number of column names and values connected by any of the following operators:

+	Add
−	Subtract
*	Multiply
/	Divide

When included in the SELECT clause, the results of an expression are displayed as a calculated table column.

SELECT title, year1, year2, (year1 - year2) as dif
    FROM [balance sheet]
    WHERE company = "01"
    ORDER BY position

Comparison Operators   Any of the following comparison operators may be used:

=	equal to
<>	not equal to
>	greater than
<	less than
>=	greater than or equal to
<=	less than or equal to

Matching a Value in a List   The IN operator allows selection of rows with a column value that matches any value from a set of values.

SELECT * FROM company
WHERE company IN ("01", "22", "35")
Note again that string values must be enclosed in quotes.

Compound Expressions with Boolean Operators   Individual logical expressions may be combined in a WHERE clause with Boolean operators:

AND
OR

Aggregate Functions   You can select amounts that are calculated with aggregate functions. The function COUNT(*) AS tally illustrates how to count the number of occurrences in a table and name the result (AS tally).

SELECT COUNT(*) AS tally FROM keywords

The AS tally clause gives the aggregate function the name "tally," which will be used in the report. The AS clause is optional with aggregate functions. To see its effect, run this example; then click "New Report" on the SQL form, delete the "AS tally" part of the query, and then run the modified query.

Additional functions include

AVG(*column-name*)	Returns the average value
MAX(*column-name*)	Returns highest value
MIN(*column-name*)	Returns the lowest value
SUM(*column-name*)	Calculates the total of values

GROUP BY   The SQL statement COUNT(company.country) AS tally illustrates how to count the occurrences of the value of a field and name the result (AS tally).

GROUP BY combines records with identical values in the specified field list into a single record. A summary value is created for each record if you include an aggregate function, such as Sum or Count, in the SELECT statement. If the SQL statement includes a WHERE clause, records are grouped after applying the WHERE conditions to the records.

GROUP BY is optional, but when it is included, it follows FROM and WHERE. Summary values are omitted if there is no aggregate function in the SELECT statement. The example summarizes the count of companies by country.

SELECT company.country, count(company.country) AS tally FROM company
GROUP BY company.country

Inner Join   INNER JOIN combines fields from several tables. The example appends the company name for company 15 to each of its topics in the notes table.

SELECT company.name, notes.topic
FROM company INNER JOIN notes
ON company.company = notes.company
WHERE company.company = "20"

Nested Queries   One may specify a query within the WHERE clause that is executed *before* the outer query to return one or more rows that may then be compared with the rows returned by the outer query. The following example finds the name of the company that has the Max (i.e., largest) SIC code.

SELECT name
FROM Company
WHERE SIC = (SELECT MAX(SIC) FROM Company)

Note that the nested query SELECT MAX(SIC) FROM company is enclosed in parentheses.

UPDATE, INSERT, AND DELETE QUERIES

These types of queries modify a database. We provide brief descriptions of their use.
The UPDATE statement consists of three clauses:

UPDATE *tablename*
SET *column-assignment-list*
WHERE *conditional-expression*

In SET, *column-assignment-list* lists the columns to be updated and the values they are to be set to and takes the general form column-name1 = value1, column-name2 = value2, …
The WHERE clause is optional. When it is used, the WHERE clause specifies a condition for UPDATE to test when processing each row of the table.
The general form of the DELETE statement is

DELETE FROM *tablename*
WHERE *conditional-expression*

The DELETE statement removes rows from *tablename* that satisfy the condition specified in the WHERE clause.
The INSERT statement has two general forms. The simplest form is used to insert a single row into a table.

INSERT INTO *tablename*
VALUES (*constant-list*);

The INSERT statement also may be used in conjunction with a SELECT statement query to copy the rows of one table to another.

WHY DATABASE MANAGEMENT SYSTEMS ARE NEEDED

DBMSs *integrate*, *standardize*, and *provide security* for various accounting applications. In the absence of integration, each type of accounting application such as sales, payroll, and receivables will maintain separate, independent data files and computer programs for managing these files. Although maintaining independent files is simple, it has several disadvantages. First, the same data item may be used in several different application areas; with independent files, this data item has to be fed into each application file. A sale, for example, affects the inventory file, accounts receivable file, and various revenue and expense files. Inputting the same data element numerous times (once for each application it is used in) is time-consuming and potentially expensive; furthermore, there is a greater chance for errors and inconsistencies among the various representations of a piece of data in several independent files.

Second, because files must be rigidly defined early in the system implementation process, procedures may be constrained by the existing file structure rather than the evolving needs of applications. Finally, independence among files often leads to different structures for the same data, different coding systems, different abbreviations, and different field lengths, to name a few examples. Comparison and reconciliation of supposedly identical data may be difficult under these conditions. The result of inconsistent data is that inconsistent reports are produced from the various application programs. Such problems call into question the integrity of an information system.

In addition to the data management and storage problems just discussed, independent files each require their own processing and maintenance instructions because neither the content nor the structure of the files is standardized. Inquiry capability concerning nonkey information is restricted because each individual application program must specify detailed instructions concerning the physical handling of data.

DATA INDEPENDENCE

The solution to the problems with maintaining independent files lies in separation of the physical handling of data from their logical use. This requires two fundamental changes: First, data storage is integrated into a single database, and second, all access to the integrated set of files (database) is through a single software system designed to manage the physical aspects of data handling and storage. These are the essential characteristics of the database approach to data processing.

In a sense, the word *file* loses meaning in a database environment. A single master file may be logically subdivided into numerous subsystem files, and these files may be combined and recombined into numerous other files. Database software separates the physical and logical aspects of file use and in doing so opens up a broad spectrum of information processing capabilities simply not feasible without such software.

Figure 12.21 illustrates these concepts with two independent application files, each containing four fields per record. Note that two data items, X and Y, are common to both files. Below these files is a database—a single file that contains all the nonredundant

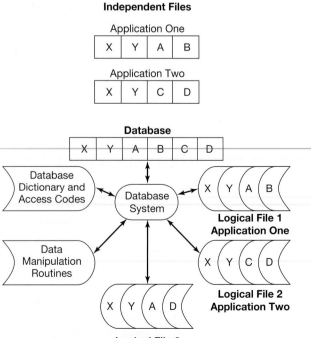

FIGURE 12.21   DATABASE MANAGEMENT CONCEPTS.

information previously found in the two physically independent files. This database file is structured and managed by a DBMS. On requests from user programs, the DBMS structures logical application files (subschema) through a database dictionary file. A **database dictionary** is a collection of all data item names in a database, along with a description of the standardized data representation form of these data items (e.g., their size, type of data—numeric, alphabetical, etc.). The database dictionary is defined and controlled by the database administrator.

Logical files 1 and 2 (see Fig. 12.21) are temporary files constructed by the DBMS for use by applications one and two. At completion of processing, the updated values in the logical files may be copied to the actual physical database. Logical file 3 is a new file created for a specific nonroutine use, such as a query (inquiry) or a special accounting data analysis. The ability to construct such special files quickly and efficiently is a major advantage of DBMSs. This ability is provided through the DBMS maintenance of inverted files, lists, rings, or other data structures designed to facilitate information retrieval by users.

SECURITY

Another advantage of DBMSs is their general ability to assign security codes to data items and their processing attributes. Part of the data dictionary file contains a list of authorized system users and their assigned security and access codes. Each of the six unique data elements in Figure 12.21 could be assigned a numerical priority code. These codes would specify which data items may be retrieved by each user of the DBMS; furthermore, such codes also may be used to restrict and define the processing a user may do to any data item.

Application one in Figure 12.21 could have authority to request only items X, Y, A, and B and authority to modify/update only fields A and B. Application two could request X, Y, C, and D and modify only C and D. Similarly, application three may have authority to access but not to modify any data items, and so on through a hierarchy of security or privacy coding applied to data items in the database.

DATABASE DOCUMENTATION AND ADMINISTRATION

Database dictionaries are used both alone and with DBMSs to centralize, document, control, and coordinate the use of data within an organization. The data dictionary is simply another file, a sort of file of files, whose record occurrences consist of data item descriptions. Figure 12.22 illustrates some likely data items for a data dictionary occurrence

Items in a Data Dictionary Occurrence

Specifications
- Name
- Definition
- Aliases

Characteristics
- Size
- Range of values
- Encoding
- Editing data

Utilization
- Owner
- Where used
- Security code
- Last update

FIGURE 12.22   DATA DICTIONARY FORMAT.

of a field. Most of the items shown in Figure 12.22 are self-explanatory or have been discussed previously. An **alias** arises when different users call the same field different names. For example, the warehouse may call "Requisition Number" the data item that purchasing calls "Order Number." Aliases also arise because the same data item is called different things in different programs written in different languages or by different programmers. *Encoding* refers to the physical form that the data item will be stored in, for example, BCD or EBCDIC. *Owner* refers to the user who has final responsibility or primary interest in the integrity of a data item occurrence.

The primary objectives of a data dictionary are to eliminate or at least control inconsistencies in usage that result from the processing of aliases and to eliminate data redundancies to the extent feasible. Responsibility for the data dictionary should be centralized in a **database administrator (DBA)**. Database administration is responsible for resolving incompatibilities and coordination and communication problems between groups of users sharing a database. A major task of the DBA is to establish standards, conventions, and documentation of the data resource. Administration of the data dictionary is the major means by which the DBA accomplishes this task. Effective control of data is central to the database approach to data processing. Incompatibilities and redundancies abound in a traditional file-oriented system in which users maintain and process their own data files. It might be impossible to centralize all data usage. Users may be unwilling to give up responsibility for their data elements. Many of the problems the DBA faces are political. The DBA has to be a diplomat in coordinating usage among various users and in dealing with users who might not obtain significant benefits from centralization and standardization of data. Accordingly, the DBA function needs to be sufficiently high in the organization or at least directly responsible to someone sufficiently high to be able to deal effectively with problems that cross organizational units.

The data dictionary might be maintained manually, but usually it is computerized and processed like other computer files. If the dictionary is used in conjunction with a DBMS, it can be maintained by the DBMS. In either case, it is the procedures surrounding use of the dictionary, as well as the dictionary itself, that make the concept an important element of database administration.

❖ SUMMARY

The architecture of database management systems (DBMSs) consists of three levels: the conceptual level, the logical level, and the physical level. The conceptual architecture involves defining in general terms the contents of the database and the required uses of the data. The logical architecture involves defining the logical data structure, which can follow either a hierarchical, network, or relational model. The physical architecture involves defining the file-access methods, which may be either sequential, indexed, or direct. In practice, the overall architecture will be structured around the users' needs for information. In today's business environment, the relational model is dominant among the logical models and is often implemented with either an indexed or direct-access physical architecture. Still, all models are being used.

Two conceptual modeling methods were discussed. In the entity-relationship model, segments (entities) are connected to each other by general relationships. In the object-oriented modeling technique, segments (object classes) are related through the concept of inheritance.

Three logical models were discussed. In hierarchical models, logical records are chained to each other by embedded pointer fields. Accessing one record allows accessing of the next record in the chain. A hierarchical model is formed by chaining the records together in such a way that a graph depicting their interrelationships forms a tree. All records are ultimately interconnected to one common record that forms the top of the tree. Network models are similar to hierarchical models, but there is no constraint that the records be chained in such a way as to form a tree. Finally, the relational model interrelates records sharing common attributes (fields) through the use of tables rather than embedded pointers.

Sequential file organization is the most basic physical architecture. In sequentially organized files, records are always accessed in the exact same sequence, from the first to the last. Such files are useful for batch processing, when a large percentage of the records need to be accessed. However, it is not an efficient file organization when, say, a single record needs to be accessed. A second type of physical architecture is an indexed file. An indexed, or inverted, file is used for faster access (relative to sequentially accessed files) to a single data record. To access an indexed file, the program first consults a directory (or index) and looks up the address of the desired record; it then retrieves this record directly. One special type of an indexed file is an ISAM (indexed sequential-access method) file. An ISAM file is a sequential file that is indexed and ordered physically on one key. Such a file can be processed either sequentially or through use of the index. A third physical architecture is direct-access file organization. Direct access is accomplished by physically placing each record on disk in such a way that it can be located by one or more of its data values.

Database management systems (DBMSs) are computer software programs that include a data definition language (DDL), a data manipulation language (DML), and a data query language (DQL). The database administrator (DBA) uses the DDL to define various fields and records and to create a data dictionary. Once data are input into the database, users can manipulate records and fields with a DML and then view data and extract reports with a DQL. DBMS, provide for standardization, integration, flexibility, and security.

❖ GLOSSARY

activity ratio: the number of active records divided by the number of records in the file.

alias: different users call the same field different names.

attribute: synonym for field.

branch: the connection between children and parent(s) in a tree structure.

children: lower-level elements in a tree diagram of a data structure that are connected to (i.e., part of) the parent element.

database administrator (DBA):   has overall responsibility for database administration.

database dictionary: a collection of all data item names in a database, along with a description of the standardized data representation form of these data items.

database management system (DBMS):   computer programs that enable a user to create and update files, to select and retrieve data, and to generate various outputs and reports.

database model: synonym for schema.

data description language (DDL):   the DDL is used to define the logical structure of the database (schema).

data item: synonym for field.

data manipulation language (DML):   the commands for updating, editing, manipulating, and extracting data from a database.

data query language (DQL):   a user-friendly language or interface that allows users to request information from a database.

direct-access file: each record has a storage location (address) that bears some relationship to the record's key field, allowing direct retrieval of each record in the file.

disk access time: the time required for the CPU to retrieve a single block of data from the disk.

element: synonym for field.

entity-relationship (E-R) data model: a conceptual model for depicting the relationships between segments in a database.

field: the smallest block of data that will be stored and retrieved in the information system.

first normal form: relational tables that do not contain any repeating groups.

fixed-length record: both the number of fields and the length (character size) of each field are fixed.

fully inverted: a file that is indexed for all its fields.

hypertext systems: systems that allow users to browse through databases in random fashion by selecting keywords or objects.

indexed file: one where an attribute has been extracted from the records and used to build a new file whose purpose is to provide an index to the original file.

indexed-sequential file: a sequential file that is stored on a DASD and is both indexed and physically sorted on the same field.

inheritance: a relationship created when an object class is divided into subclasses.

instance: synonym for occurrence.

inverted file: synonym for indexed file.

ISAM: indexed-sequential access method; synonym for indexed-sequential file organization.

key: synonym for record key.

list structure: each record contains one or more pointers (fields) indicating the address of the next logical record with the same attribute(s).

logical data structure: the logical manner in which records and fields in a database are structured and organized.

multilist organization: a record may be part of several list organizations.

multiple-ring structure: several ring organizations pass through individual records.

network structure: a logical data structure that allows a child segment to have more than one parent.

node: synonym for repeated group.

normal forms: rules that govern the creation of relational tables in the relational database model.

normalization: the process of applying normal form rules in the relational database model.

object: corresponds to an instance in the object-oriented modeling technique (OMT).

object class: corresponds to a segment in the object-oriented modeling technique (OMT).

object-oriented modeling technique (OMT):   a conceptual model for depicting the relationships between segments in a database that views the components of the system being modeled as object classes.

occurrence: a specific set of data values for a record.

parent: the highest-level element in a tree diagram of a data structure.

primary sort key: the first field used to sort the records in a file.

random access: synonym for direct access.

randomizing transformation: a widely used method of storing and locating records in a direct-access file.

record: a logical grouping of fields (data items) that concern a certain entity.

record key: a data item or combination of data items that uniquely identifies a particular record in a file.

relation: synonym for table in the relational model.

relational algebra: operations used to extract information from relational tables.

relational model: a logical data structure that views the database as a collection of two-dimensional tables.

relative random order: a field on which a file is not sorted.

repeated group: related groups of fields that repeat themselves in variable-length records.

ring structure: a list organization in which the last record in the ring list points back to the first record.

schema: synonym for logical data structure of a database.

secondary sort key: a field used to determine relative position among a set of records when the primary key has the same value in each record of the set.

second normal form: no key in a relational table is allowed to determine the values of a nonkey field.

segment: synonym for repeated group.

sequential-access file: records in the file can only be accessed in their predefined sequence.

subschema: individual, logical user views of the database.

tertiary sort keys: additional fields beyond primary and secondary keys required to uniquely identify and sort records in a file.

third normal form: no nonkey field in a relational table is allowed to determine the values on another nonkey field.

trailer record: a fixed-length extension of a master record.

tree structure: a logical data structure in which each node represents a segment, and each node is related to another node at the next-highest level of the tree.

tuple: a row in a relational table.

variable-length record: both the number of fields and the length (character size) of each field are variable.

❖ CHAPTER QUIZ

Answers to the chapter quiz appear on page 452.

1. Which of the following is(are) "fixed" in a fixed-length record?
   (a) the number of fields
   (b) the length of each field
   (c) both a and b
   (d) neither a nor b

2. Which of the following types of files might be stored on a direct-access storage device (DASD)?
   (a) a sequential-access file
   (b) a direct-access file
   (c) both a and b
   (d) neither a nor b

3. Which of the following terms is *not* a synonym?
   (a) field
   (b) instance
   (c) data item
   (d) element
4. Which of the following terms is a synonym with repeated group?
   (a) attribute
   (b) segment
   (c) field
   (d) record key
5. In a(n) (_____) system, a user may browse a database by selecting key words to retrieve information in a random fashion.
   (a) expert
   (b) object-oriented
   (c) segmented
   (d) hypertext
6. Which of the following conceptual database models views the components of the system being modeled as object classes?
   (a) object-oriented modeling technique
   (b) entity-relationship (E-R) data model
   (c) both a and b
   (d) neither a nor b
7. The (_____) should have overall responsibility for documentation and control of an organization's database.
   (a) database administrator
   (b) manager of programming
   (c) manager of operations
   (d) manager of systems analysis
8. Which of the following types of queries does not modify a database?
   (a) INSERT
   (b) UPDATE
   (c) SELECT
   (d) DELETE
9. Which of the following refers to the overall logical structure of a database?
   (a) alias
   (b) virtual data
   (c) schema
   (d) network
10. Which of the following would the database administrator use to define the overall logical structure of a database?
    (a) DBA
    (b) DDL
    (c) DML
    (d) DQL

❖ REVIEW PROBLEM

Consider the relation

   BOOK (<u>ISBN</u>, TITLE, AUTHOR, AUTHOR-AFFILIATION, PRICE)

The underlining of ISBN indicates that it is the record key.
(a) Is this relation normalized? If so, is it in first normal form, second normal form, or third normal form?
(b) If it is not already in third normal form, what is necessary to attain this?

❖ SOLUTION TO REVIEW PROBLEM

(a) Because the ISBN uniquely identifies each book, the relation is in first normal form. Since the key (ISBN) is a single key, the relation must be in second as well as first normal form. Is the relation in third normal form? That is, are all the nonkey fields mutually independent? No. AUTHOR-AFFILIATION clearly depends on AUTHOR.

(b) To attain third normal form, we must separate this relation, giving two separate third normal form relations:

BOOK (<u>ISBN</u>, TITLE, AUTHOR, PRICE)

and

AUTHOR-AFFILIATION (<u>AUTHOR</u>, AUTHOR-AFFILIATION).

❖ REVIEW QUESTIONS

1. Distinguish between fixed- and variable-length records.
2. Distinguish between primary and secondary sort keys.
3. What is a hypertext system?
4. Distinguish between the conceptual level, the logical level, and the physical level of database architecture.
5. Characterize each of the three major models of logical data structures.
   (a) Tree or hierarchical models
   (b) Network models
   (c) Relational models
6. What is list organization? How does it differ from a ring structure?
7. Identify the basic operations of relational algebra. What are they used for?
8. What is normalization? Distinguish between first, second, and third normal forms.
9. Distinguish between
   (a) sequentially accessed files.
   (b) indexed-sequential files.
   (c) directly accessed files.
10. What factors affect response time in database systems?
11. What are database management systems?
12. Distinguish between
    (a) data description language (DDL).
    (b) data manipulation language (DML).
    (c) data query language (DQL).
13. What is Structured Query Language?
14. What are the functions of the database administrator (DBA)?

❖ DISCUSSION QUESTIONS AND PROBLEMS

15. Discuss some of the differences between the traditional approach to data processing and the database approach.
16. Discuss the advantages and disadvantages of having an industry-wide standard to which all database software systems conform.
17. For each of the following applications, specify a file organization method (sequential, direct access, indexed sequential). Briefly justify your selection in terms of the anticipated activity ratio, processing time frame, file size, and response time to inquiries about file status.
    (a) General Motors stockholder file, updated weekly and used for mailing dividend checks, quarterly reports, and proxy requests.
    (b) A salesperson commission file, updated at the time of sale from a point-of-sale data entry terminal.

(c) A bank's customer account file, updated daily for deposits and withdrawals and used for mailing monthly statements of account.

(d) An inventory file, updated daily, that is also used to ascertain product availability and other related inquiries during daily operations.

(e) A master payroll file, used biweekly to process payroll and also quarterly to process various tax reports.

(f) A master scheduling file, used by a large airline to reserve seats on all its flights. The file is used heavily every day for scheduling and ad hoc inquiries concerning seat availability but is never processed to generate reports.

(g) A file of authors for a publishing company, processed quarterly to prepare royalty checks and once at year-end to prepare tax reports.

(h) A vendor file used by a large manufacturing company. The file is used heavily every day for ad hoc inquiries concerning orders and payments and is also processed once each week to generate payment checks for many of the company's 500 vendors.

(i) A master file of fixed assets for a small manufacturing firm, processed quarterly to produce depreciation for tax and accounting reports and once each year for insurance purposes.

18. The West Company maintains a master accounts receivable disk file. Approved applications for new charge accounts are keyed to disk. The resulting file is sorted and processed against the master file.

The current master disk file is strictly sequential. What are some advantages and disadvantages that might accrue from changing the file organization method to either a random or indexed-sequential structure?

19. For each of the following application files, discuss the relative merits of sequential, direct, and indexed-sequential file organization:

(a) Open-order file in a large manufacturing firm

(b) Accounts receivable file for a magazine publisher

(c) Inventory file for a large automobile dealership

(d) Accounts payable file for a retailing firm

(e) Fixed-assets file in a manufacturing firm

20. Identify an inquiry for (i) a specific record and (ii) a group of related records that might be made for each of the following files. Discuss how these inquiries might be satisfied if the file organization method was sequential, direct, or indexed sequential.

(a) An employee master file

(b) An accounts receivable file

(c) A work-in-process file

21. Use the flowchart in Figure 12.12 to solve this problem. Assume that the master file and the transaction file are composed of the record numbers shown below in the sequence given.

Master	11, 15, 31, 84, 87, 99
Transaction	11, 12, 31, 31, 15, 84, 99

Record number 99 in each file is used to indicate the logical end of the file.

Process these data, using the flowchart in Figure 12.12. Indicate

(a) which master records are updated.

(b) which master records are not updated.

(c) the disposition of each transaction record (i.e., posted to the master or an error condition).

22. Consider an open purchase order file in a manufacturing company. Identify several other files to which the purchase order file might be linked (chained) through the use of pointer fields.

23. A personnel file contains a record for each employee in an organization. Each record contains four fields: (a) name, (b) division, (c) specialty, and (d) age. Below are four sample records:

Storage Location	Name	Division	Specialty	Age
22	Ash	New York	Audit	30
28	Fox	New York	Audit	25
64	Luh	Chicago	Marketing	29
106	Smith	Los Angeles	Personnel	40

Each of the four fields is expected to be an important search parameter in the personnel application system. Design an index (directory) to invert the preceding file fully.

24. Discuss the relative advantages and disadvantages of inverted files and list or ring structures (pointer-field structures) in answering inquiries of the following types.
   (a) Are there any records that have both attribute 1 and attribute 2 (sales greater than $5,000 and location equal to the state of New York)?
   (b) How many records have attribute 1, attribute 2, ... attribute n?

25. Consider the following relation:

CLASS-LIST (STUDENT#, CLASS#, STUDENT-NAME, STUDENT-MAJOR, CLASS-TIME, CLASSROOM)

   Required
   (a) Suppose that we wish to add a new class time and room (i.e., a new section) for a particular class number (#). Is this possible? If not, what is necessary before we can add a new class time and room to the file?
   (b) Suppose that all students drop a particular class number (#) from their schedules. What effect would this have on the data stored in the CLASS-LIST relation?
   (c) Is CLASS-LIST in first, second, or third normal form?

26. An automobile manufacturer maintains a cumulative sales file in the following relation:

CUM-SALES (MAKE, BODY-STYLE, COLOR, SALES-REGION, SALES, OPEN-ORDERS)

An example (tuple) would be

CUM-SALES (Buick,Sedan,Red,West,123 400,4500)

Is this relation in third normal form?

27. Consider the two-record hierarchy

DEPARTMENT (DEPT#, DEPT-NAME, ..., PROFESSOR) PROFESSOR (PROF#, PROF-NAME, ...,)

in which professors are linked to their department by the field PROFESSOR in the DEPARTMENT record.

Does this relation have a repeating group? If so, how would you normalize this relation?

28. Organizing and maintaining a database are more complicated than organizing and maintaining independent files because a database provides more data retrieval functions and performs more operations. A DBMS may have three different types of languages associated with its use: a data manipulation language (DML), a data definition language (DDL), and a data query language (DQL). For each of the illustrations below, indicate which of these three languages probably would be used.
   (a) A programmer writes a COBOL program to update inventory records that are stored in the database.
   (b) The database administrator (DBA) documents the content and structure of the database.
   (c) A sales manager requests an ad hoc report on sales of a certain product over the past month.
   (d) The field for customer address in the accounts receivable segment of the database is expanded to allow for a 10-digit ZIP code.
   (e) The payroll manager requests a special report detailing those employees in the database who have college degrees.

(f) A programmer writes a COBOL program to prepare payroll checks for employees whose personnel records are stored in the database.

(g) A new field is added to employee personnel records in the database to allow for a new payroll deduction for health benefits.

(h) A programmer writes a COBOL program to update accounts receivable records that are stored in the database.

(i) The credit manager requests a special report detailing those customers in the database who have purchased more than $25,000 worth of goods in the past 3 months.

29. A data record is a collection of related fields or data elements. Record design is one of the fundamental problems of data management. A data record should include all the data elements that are essential to an application. In certain instances, however, a particular data element might be computed as needed on the basis of the other data elements stored in a record. In such cases it is not really necessary to store this type of data element in a data record because its value can be computed readily as needed. This type of data element is called *virtual data*.

For example, a payroll record might contain the following three data elements in addition to others:

Pay rate per hour
Hours worked
Gross pay

In this case, gross pay would be a virtual data element. Gross pay could be computed as needed based on the pay rate per hour and hours worked data elements.

Virtual data are an example of redundancy in data records. The elimination of virtual data has several advantages. One is to reduce the overall size of the data record and thus reduce the amount of storage space required. This would tend to reduce the total cost of storing a data record. Another advantage is that there are fewer data items in the data record that have to be maintained. This might lead to simpler application programs and would tend to reduce the possibility of having errors occur when the data record is modified. This becomes more important when a data element is contained in more than one data record. In such cases, a data element might be updated in one record but not in others. This results in inconsistent data in an information system.

Required

Consider the following data record for a work-in-process application system:

Work-in-process number
Materials cost
Direct labor cost
Applied overhead cost
Total cost
Units started
Units spoiled
Good units in process

Which of these data items is(are) virtual data? What types of advantages might be gained if virtual data elements are removed from the work-in-process record? Explain.

30. Ernst and Anderson is a manufacturer of power tools and other products used in the construction industry. The company was founded in the early 1900s as a manufacturer of quality hand tools such as hammers and screwdrivers, but such products have represented a decreasing percentage of total company sales for more than a decade. The company has been very successful in industrial power tools, which is its primary line of business. Several small companies were acquired in the late 1980s to broaden the company's product line to include a variety of commercial products such as small appliances and household cleaning equipment such as vacuum cleaners. Because their products are consumer-oriented and thus do not compete with industrial power tools, these acquisitions generally have been allowed to operate as independent companies.

The company operates several manufacturing facilities that produce power tools, but the largest and oldest plant, based in Pittsburgh, Pennsylvania, accounts for almost 80 percent of total production. The Pittsburgh plant employs more than 1,000 people and manufactures more than 250 different types of power tools. Much of the company's success in maintaining its position in the marketplace in the face of intense international competition can be attributed to its long-standing policies concerning good employee relations and adequate plant maintenance. Although old in years, the Pittsburgh plant has been well maintained, and the company has continuously invested in new manufacturing equipment.

A computer-based information system for production control has been used at the Pittsburgh plant since the early 1970s. Management of Ernst and Anderson was an early believer in the view that adequate information is an essential ingredient in the successful operation of a complex manufacturing operation. The production control system is organized into five major applications: production scheduling, materials management, labor cost reporting, work-in-process inventory, and finished goods inventory. These applications were developed separately and have been modified constantly over the years. The five different applications all use their own separate files and programs. Applications are linked together through separate batch processing runs. For example, periodically the work-in-process application is processed to generate a file of completed jobs. This transaction file of completed jobs is then reformatted as necessary and processed by the finished goods inventory application to update the finished goods inventory records. The reformatting is necessary because each application has been developed independently. This has resulted in some inconsistencies between identical data elements in the different applications.

These inconsistencies have become more and more bothersome as the company has expanded the role of its computer-based production control system. Management is convinced that the effectiveness of the information system can be increased significantly if the five separate, stand-alone applications are integrated in a DBMS. To this end, the company has established a project team to study the feasibility of using a DBMS. The company hired a large public accounting firm to assist in this project. On the advice of the consultants, the project team has begun a study of the inputs, file structures, and outputs of the five separate applications to determine the data-definition ambiguities that exist in the present systems. These ambiguities will have to be eliminated if the production scheduling, materials management, labor cost reporting, work-in-process inventory, and finished goods inventory applications are to be integrated in a DBMS.

To date, the project team has studied three of the five applications, and this has taken three times as long as the team had originally expected. More than 400 different data names were discovered, but analysis of these data names indicated that only about 150 different data variables really existed. The difference is due to data redundancy. For example, the number of units being produced in a job is referred to by the data name "Units started" in the production scheduling application but by "Quantity" in the work-in-process application and by "Units" in the finished goods inventory application. These three different data names in the three different applications refer to the same real data element. As another example, the economic production quantity for a product is referred to by the data name "Lot size" in the production scheduling application but by "Minimum level" in the finished goods inventory application. These examples indicate one reason why data have to be reformatted when they are transferred from one application to another. The project team found many other similar instances of data redundancy in the three applications it has studied so far.

The problem of data redundancy is also complicated by the fact that the different data names for the same data element usually have different physical representations in the different applications. For example, "Units started" in the production scheduling application has a length of 8 characters, but "Quantity" in the work-in-process application has a length of 10 characters.

Inconsistency is another type of data ambiguity the project team discovered. Inconsistency occurs when the same data name is used to mean different things in different applications. For example, the data name "Code" in the production scheduling application means department code, but "Code" means transaction code in the work-in-process application and product number in the finished goods inventory application. This is yet another reason why data have to be reformatted when they are transferred from one application to another. The project team found several other similar instances of data inconsistency in the three applications it studied.

The five applications cannot be integrated while data ambiguities exist. Yet the project is taking considerably more time than expected. The status of the DBMS project is currently being reviewed by the management of Ernst and Anderson.

Required

(a) If a user requested the data name "Lot size" in the production scheduling application, and the same user entered the data name "Minimum level" in the finished goods inventory application, what would be the result? If a user requested the data name "Units started" in the production scheduling application, then requested the data name "Quantity" in the work-in-process application, and then requested the data name "Units" in the finished goods inventory application, what would be the result? What additional consideration compounds this type of problem?

(b) If a user requested the data name "Code" in the production scheduling application, then requested "Code" in the work-in-process application, and then requested "Code" in the finished goods inventory application, what would be the result?

(c) Discuss the role of a data dictionary in analyzing data ambiguity. Indicate how specific sections of a data dictionary can help resolve data ambiguity.

(d) What action should the management of Ernst and Anderson take concerning the status of the DBMS project? Should the project team complete its study of data ambiguity even though the project has taken considerably more time than expected? Should the DBMS project proceed in view of the large amount of data ambiguity that has been discovered? If so, what is the first database that should be implemented?

31. The database administrator (DBA) is not necessarily a single individual. In a large organization, several individuals may share overall responsibility for the DBA function. Discuss each of the following.

(a) Why is the DBA function crucial to the concept of data management?

(b) What administrative responsibilities should be vested in the DBA?

(c) What responsibilities and duties should *not* be vested in or permitted to the DBA function?

(d) Where should the DBA function be placed in the organizational structure of a firm?

32. Consider the following relation in first normal form:

ORDER (<u>ORDER#, VENDOR#, PART#,</u> DESCRIPTION, QUANTITY, PRICE, TOTAL_AMOUNT)

The underlining indicates a combination key that consists of the concatenated fields ORDER#, VENDOR#, and PART#.

(a) What is needed to attain second normal form?

(b) What is needed to attain third normal form?

33. Consider the following relation:

CLASS-LIST (<u>COURSE#,</u> CLASS-ROOM, STUDENT#, STUDENT-MAJOR)

(a) Assuming that each student can have only one major, is this relation normalized? If so, is it in first, second, or third normal form? If it is not already in third normal form, what is necessary to attain this?

(b) Would your answer to part (a) be different if a student can have more than one major? Discuss.

34. The problems below are designed for the Electric Books Company database that is described in the appendix to this chapter. These problems may be used in the Web SQL processor that is available to users of this textbook. The Web SQL processor functions to process SELECT queries against the Electric Books Company database. You may engage in active learning of basic SQL concepts by actually running the queries that solve these problems to see their output from the Electric Books Company database.

(a) Design a query that selects everything from the SIC (Standard Industrial Classification) table.

(b) Design a query that selects the name and country of companies in the company table that are from countries other than the United States, which is indicated by the value "USA."

(c) Design a query that lists only foreign companies (i.e., not from the USA) and the caption of the line in their income statements that was used to indicate "gross profit" if it was in their income statement. Gross profit or the equivalent term is indicated by the code "+2" as the value for the Income.Term field.

(d) Design a query that lists all the instances of the word "contingent" in the balance sheet table.

(e) Design a query that lists the company name and the caption of the line in the company's balance sheet when the caption contains the word "contingent." Sort the output alphabetically by company name.

(f) Design a query that lists the company name and the caption of the line in the company's income statement sheet when the caption contains the word "restructuring." Sort the output alphabetically by company name.

(g) Design a query that lists all the topics in the Notes table that contain the word "goodwill."

(h) Design a query that shows a count of topics in the Notes table that is summarized by title.

(i) Design a query that shows which companies in the database report Treasury stock as an asset. Treasury stock is identified by the code "*9" (i.e., term = "*9"), and the balance sheet classification is determined by the expression LEFT$([balance sheet].ale,1), which will be "A" for a current asset or "B" for a noncurrent asset.

(j) The SIC table contains the two-digit major group codes of the SIC code and the related Group description. Design a query that lists each company name, its SIC major code, and its SIC major Group description, which is indicated by the left two digits of the SIC Field in the company table.

(k) Design a query that lists all the companies that are in the SIC major group "Communications," which is major code "48."

(l) Design a query that calculates the current ratio for company "54." (*Hint:* Search for the text "total current asset" and "total current liab" to find the numbers to compute the ratio.)

❖ ANSWERS TO CHAPTER QUIZ

1. c	4. b	7. a	10. b
2. c	5. d	8. c	
3. b	6. a	9. c	

APPENDIX

ELECTRIC BOOKS DATABASE DOCUMENTATION

Electric Books is a database of financial reports. The database has an income statement, two balance sheets, a cash flow statement, and selected text excerpts for each company in the database. The excerpts are from the Notes section of the company's report.

The Company table contains the basic data for each company.

Company Fields:

- Company: two-digit code
- Name: company name
- Country: country name
- Currency: reporting currency
- Amount: report units (e.g., thousands of dollars)
- Bsdate1: date of leftmost column in balance sheet
- Bsdate2: date of rightmost column in balance sheet

- Isdate1: date of income and cash flow statements
- Source: source of the data
- SIC: Four-digit Standard Industrial Classification (SIC) code

Company is a two-digit code that uniquely identifies each company's reports and provides the link to other tables in the database. The Name, Country, Currency, and Amount fields are self-explanatory. Each balance sheet contains two years of data. Bsdate1 and Bsdate2 follow the order used by each company. Bsdate1 might be 1995 and Bsdate2 1996 for Company ONE, but Company TWO might show Bsdate1 as 1996 and Bsdate2 as 1995. Isdate1 is the most recent year in the source.

The Source field indicates where the data were obtained. The source is usually Form 10-K or Form 20-F. In all cases where source is "Annual Report," the author has obtained written permission from the company prior to including their data in Electric Books.

SIC is obtained from the company's 10-K or 20-F filing. When SIC is not available, the field will contain "0000." The left-most two digits of SIC are a major group code. The SIC table contains SIC major group codes and their description. Use SIC to identify company industry and to identify companies in similar industries.

The Balance Sheet Table contains the body of the balance sheet for two consecutive years for each company in the database.
Balance Sheet Fields:

- Company: two-digit code (company in the Company table)
- Position: four-digit code (used to order balance sheet rows)
- Term: two-digit code (Termcode in the Keywords table)
- ALE: two-digit code
- -1st digit:
- A=Current Asset
- B=Non-Current Asset
- L=Current Liability
- M=Non-Current Liability
- E=Equity;
- -2nd digit: If "Q," the item appears in Quiz (an application under development).
- Title: text of the balance sheet row (e.g., Cash)
- Year1: the left-most amount column in the balance sheet.
- Year2: the right-most amount column in the balance sheet.

The Title field is sometimes blank because totals often are not labeled by companies. Year1 and Year2 follow the order used by each company. Year1 might be 1995 and Year2 1996 for Company A, but Company B might show Year1 as 1996 and Year2 as 1995.

The Balance Sheet for a company is constructed by obtaining header information from the Company table and joining this with the detail from the Balance Sheet Table. The two-digit code "Company" is used to obtain the matching data from the two tables.

The Income Table contains the body of the income statement for each company in the database.
Income Statement Fields:

- Company: two-digit code (company in the Company table)
- Position: four-digit code (used to order income statement rows)
- Term: two-digit code (Termcode in the Keywords table)
- Title: text of the income statement row (e.g., Sales)
- Year1: the amount column in the income statement

The Title field is sometimes blank because totals often are not labeled by companies.

The Income Statement is constructed by obtaining header information from the Company table and joining this with the detail from the Income Table. The two-digit code "Company" is used to obtain the matching data from the two tables.

The Cash Flow Table contains the body of the cash flow statement for each company in the database.
Cash Flow Fields:

- Company: two-digit code (company in the Company table)
- Position: four-digit code (used to order cash flow rows)

- Code: two-digit code used in Quiz
- Title: text of the cash flow statement row
- Year1: the amount column in the cash flow statement

The Title field is sometimes blank because totals often are not labeled by companies.

The Cash Flow Statement is constructed by obtaining header information from the Company table and joining this with the detail from the Cash Flow Table. The two-digit code "Company" is used to obtain the matching data from the two tables.

The Notes table contains descriptive data concerning the company's financial statements. The majority of these data are excerpted from the Notes to the financial statements, particularly sections that describe the company's accounting policies.

Notes Fields:

- Company: two-digit code (company in the Company table)
- Number: four-digit code used to order the table
- Topic: descriptive heading for the excerpt
- Chunk: the text of the excerpt (This field has been deleted in the working sample to reduce the size of the database.)

Topics are usually the heading used by the company for the excerpt, except when the company's heading is too lengthy or when a heading is necessary to describe an excerpt selected from a larger section of text.

The Keywords table contains the codes and related terms (i.e., "keywords") that can be used to classify or analyze selected financial report terminology in the reports of companies in the database. These items have been coded to facilitate queries concerning actual statement terminology.

Keywords Fields:

- Termcode: arbitrary two-character code used for a term
- Term: an accounting term, such as cash or common stock

You can use the Termcodes in the Keywords table in queries!

The SIC table contains the major groups of the Standard Industrial Classification (SIC) code and the related Group description. The SIC is the statistical classification standard underlying federal economic statistics classified by industry. Each company is assigned an industry code on the basis of its primary activity, which is determined by its principal product or group of products produced or distributed, or services rendered.

SIC Fields:

- Code: two-digit major group code used in the Standard Industrial Classification.
- Group: text description of major group.

You can use the left-most two digits of the SIC field in the Company table to identify the companies' major group classification and to identify companies in the same major SIC group.

This concludes the overview of the Electric Books database.

AUDITING INFORMATION TECHNOLOGY

LEARNING OBJECTIVES

Careful study of this chapter will enable you to:

❖ Distinguish between auditing through the computer and auditing with the computer.

❖ Describe and evaluate alternative information systems audit technologies.

❖ Characterize various types of information systems audits.

INFORMATION SYSTEMS AUDITING CONCEPTS

The term *information systems auditing* is used commonly to describe two different types of computer-related activity. One use of the term is to describe the process of reviewing and evaluating the internal controls in an electronic data processing system. This type of activity normally is undertaken by auditors during compliance testing and might be described as **auditing through the computer**. The other general use of the term is to describe use of the computer by an auditor to perform some audit work that otherwise would have to be done manually. This type of activity normally is undertaken during substantive testing of account balances and might be described as **auditing with the computer**. Many audits involve both compliance testing and substantive testing. Both types of information systems auditing might be undertaken by both internal auditors and external auditors.

STRUCTURE OF A FINANCIAL STATEMENT AUDIT

The primary objective and responsibility of the external auditor is to attest to the fairness of a firm's financial reports. Whereas the internal auditor serves a firm's management, the external auditor serves a firm's stockholders, the government, and the general public. Despite this clear difference of purpose, internal and external auditors do similar things in the area of information systems auditing. This is not to say that much audit work is duplicated. Generally, the opposite is true, due to the large degree

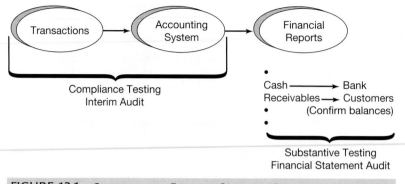

FIGURE 13.1   STRUCTURE OF A FINANCIAL STATEMENT AUDIT.

of cooperation and interaction that frequently exists between a firm's internal and external auditors. Internal auditors commonly undertake audits that are reviewed and relied on by external auditors as they audit a firm's financial statements.

In an audit directed toward the attestation of financial statements, the auditor could, in theory, ignore the system of internal control and still obtain sufficient evidence to justify a professional opinion of the financial statements. This approach is generally impractical because the cost of obtaining enough substantive evidence to be sufficient without using the internal control system is prohibitive. Total audit cost usually can be reduced significantly if some audit resources are directed at reviewing and verifying the internal controls in the system that generated the financial statements. Then, relying on the client's internal control system, a lesser degree of assurance is necessary in direct substantive tests of financial statement figures.

For this reason, an audit is almost universally divided into two basic components (Fig. 13.1). The first component, usually called the **interim audit**, has the objective of establishing the degree to which the internal control system can be relied on. This usually requires some type of **compliance testing**. The purpose of compliance testing is to confirm the existence, assess the effectiveness, and check the continuity of operation of those internal controls on which reliance is to be placed. The second component of an audit, usually called the **financial statement audit**, involves **substantive testing**. Substantive testing is the direct verification of financial statement figures, placing such reliance on internal control as the results of the interim audit warrant. For example, as shown in Figure 13.1, substantive testing of cash would involve direct confirmation of bank balances. Substantive testing of receivables would involve direct confirmation of balances with customers. In an audit directed at the attestation of financial statements, the direct purpose of the audit is served by substantive testing in the financial statement audit phase, whereas an indirect purpose (achieving overall economy through permitting reliance on internal control) is served by compliance testing in the interim audit phase.

AUDITING AROUND THE COMPUTER

During the early years of information systems development, computerized accounting systems provided auditors with very little need to significantly alter audit approaches and technology used in manual systems. Batch processing was the dominant method used in computers, and an around-the-computer approach provided for an adequate audit.

In general terms, an accounting system is comprised of input, processing, and output. In the **around-the-computer approach**, the processing portion is ignored. Instead, source documents supplying the input to the system are selected and summarized manually so that they can be compared with the output. As batches are processed through the system, totals are accumulated for accepted and rejected records. Auditors emphasize control over rejected transactions, their correction, and then resubmission.

Given advances in information technology, the around-the-computer approach is no longer used widely. This approach implicitly assumes that the computer does not exist. Assumptions about the system are drawn by examining the source documents and the output, comprised of error listings, reports, and so on. This approach also assumes that a computer cannot be used to falsify records without being detected by manual procedures.

AUDITING THROUGH THE COMPUTER

Auditing through the computer may be defined as the verification of controls in a computerized system. Consideration of the nature of information technology (IT) and internal control in an IT environment yields the framework shown in Figure 13.2. General controls are relevant to the information systems themselves, as well as to the systems development aspect of IT. Application controls are related to specific computer application systems. A thorough information systems audit involves verifying both general and application controls in a computerized system. More generally, an individual information systems audit would be directed at one of these areas, usually a specific application system such as accounts receivable.

Information systems audits to verify compliance with internal controls are performed by both internal and external auditors. The objectives of the external auditor usually are directed toward the attestation of financial statements. Frequently, internal auditors embrace the same objectives; at other times, internal auditors perform compliance audits that are responsive to the desires of top management and the particular needs of the company. The general conduct of an information systems audit is subject to the same professional standards relevant to any audit. For the external auditor, these standards are specified in AICPA's Statements of Auditing Standards. Internal auditors have professional auditing standards promulgated by the Institute of Internal Auditors that are similar to the AICPA standards. Basic auditing standards are not altered by the technology employed in the system to be audited.

AUDITING WITH THE COMPUTER

Auditing with the computer is the process of using IT in auditing. IT is used to perform some audit work that otherwise would have to be done manually. The use of IT by auditors is no longer optional. It is essential. Most of the data that auditors must evaluate are already in electronic format. It is senseless to convert electronic data to a

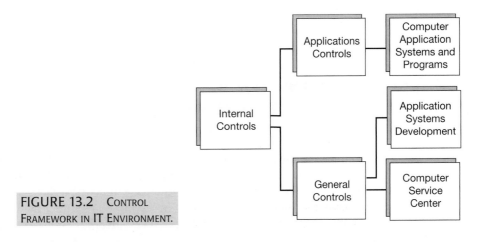

FIGURE 13.2   CONTROL
FRAMEWORK IN IT ENVIRONMENT.

paper format strictly for audit purposes. Furthermore, auditing itself is not immune to competitive pressures to be more productive. The use of IT is essential to increase the effectiveness and efficiency of auditing.

The potential benefits of using information systems technology in an audit include the following:

- Computer-generated working papers generally are more legible and consistent. Such working papers also may be stored, accessed, and revised easily.
- Time may be saved by eliminating manual footing, cross-footing, and other routine calculations.
- Calculations, comparisons, and other data manipulations are performed more accurately.
- Analytical review calculations may be performed more efficiently, and their scope may be broadened.
- Project information such as time budgets and the monitoring of actual time versus budgeted amounts may be generated and analyzed more easily.
- Standardized audit correspondence such as questionnaires and checklists, proposal letters, and report formats may be stored and modified easily.
- Morale and productivity may be improved by reducing the time spent on clerical tasks.
- Increased cost-effectiveness is obtained by reusing and extending existing electronic audit applications to subsequent audits.
- Increased independence from information systems personnel is obtained.

The benefits identified in the first four points accrue primarily to the individual auditor who is actually performing the audit. Clear and obvious benefits are obtained from the calculating and data analysis capability provided by IT. Properly programmed, totals and the like should be accurate. More complicated calculations such as statistical regressions are performed easily. The other benefits may be realized by management of the internal audit function. Management of internal audit, like managers in other organizational functions, has much to gain from the efficient application of IT. The ability to analyze time budget and other types of project control information facilitates managerial control, a quality necessary to the internal audit function as well as to all other organizational functions. The ability to standardize work papers, questionnaires, and other such documents used in audits performed by the audit staff also enhances managerial control and helps to ensure uniform and consistent application of practice by the audit staff. The reusability of electronic audit technology increases overall cost-effectiveness. And the potential positive effects on staff morale and subsequent productivity gains should make the use of IT a goal of every audit manager.

INFORMATION SYSTEMS AUDITING TECHNOLOGY

Information systems auditing technology has evolved along with computer system development. There is no one overall auditing technology (Table 13.1). Rather, there are a number of tools and techniques that may be used as appropriate to accomplish an audit's objectives. These technologies differ widely as to the amount of technical expertise required for their use. Several of the technologies entail significant costs to implement, whereas others may be implemented with relatively little cost.

TABLE 13.1   Information Systems Auditing Technologies

Technique	Description	Example
Test data	Test data are input containing both valid and invalid data.	Payroll transactions with both valid and invalid employee identification numbers.
Integrated test facility (ITF)	ITF involves both the use of test data and the creation of fictitious records (vendors, employees) on the master files of a computer system.	Payroll transactions for fictitious employees are processed concurrently with valid payroll transactions.
Parallel simulation	Processing real data through audit programs. The simulated output and the regular output are then compared.	Depreciation calculations are verified by processing the fixed-asset master file with an audit program.
Audit software	Computer programs that permit the computer to be used as an auditing tool.	An auditor uses a computer program to extract data records from a master file.
Generalized audit software (GAS)	GAS is audit software that has been specifically designed to allow auditors to perform audit-related data processing functions.	An auditor uses GAS to search computer files for unusual items.
PC software	Software that allows the auditor to use a PC to perform audit tasks.	A PC spreadsheet package is used to maintain audit working papers and audit schedules.
Embedded audit routines	Special auditing routines included in regular computer programs so that transaction data can be subjected to audit analysis.	Data items that are exceptions to auditor-specified edit tests included in a program are written to a special audit file.
Extended records	Modification of programs to collect and store data of audit interest.	A payroll program is modified to collect data pertaining to overtime pay.
Snapshot	Modification of programs to output data of audit interest.	A payroll program is modified to output data pertaining to overtime pay.
Tracing	Tracing provides a detailed audit trail of the instructions executed during the program's operation.	A payroll program is traced to determine if certain edit tests are performed in the correct order.
Review of system documentation	Extending system documentation such as program flowcharts are reviewed for audit purposes.	An auditor desk checks the processing logic of a payroll program.
Control flowcharting	Analytic flowcharts or other graphic techniques are used to describe the controls in a system.	An auditor prepares an analytic flowchart to review controls in the payroll application system.
Mapping	Special software is used to monitor the execution of a program.	The execution of a program with test data as input is mapped to indicate how extensively the input tested individual program statements.

TEST DATA

Test data are auditor-prepared input containing both valid and invalid data. Prior to processing the test data, the input is processed manually to determine what the output should look like. The auditor then compares the test output with the manually processed results (Fig. 13.3). If the results are not as expected, the auditor attempts to determine the cause of the discrepancy.

Historically, test data represented the first attempt to audit through the computer. While it might be impractical for an auditor to be able to understand the detailed logic of a computer program, he or she can understand the general specifications of a system and use this knowledge to determine whether or not the system works.

The test data technique is used widely by auditors as well as computer programmers to verify the processing accuracy of computer programs. Test data may be used to

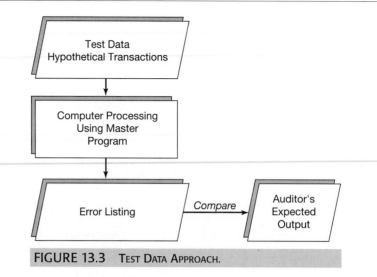

FIGURE 13.3   TEST DATA APPROACH.

verify input transaction validation routines, processing logic, and computational routines of computer programs and to verify the incorporation of program changes. The technique is particularly good for testing programs in which calculations such as interest or depreciation are involved. The technique requires minimal computer expertise and is usually inexpensive to implement because it requires no modification of existing computer applications.

With test data, regular live production programs are used, and it is essential to ensure that the test data do not affect the files maintained by the system. This requires coordination between the auditor and computer personnel. It would be ironic if an audit procedure designed to detect errors were to introduce its own errors. It is important to note that test data can only evaluate programs. Other tests of the integrity of input data and output files usually are needed as well.

Test data are prepared after the system to be audited has been reviewed and transactions (test data) are designed to test selected aspects of the system. The test data might be generated by completing input forms to generate fictitious test transactions or, alternatively, by reviewing actual input data and selecting several real transactions for processing as test data. A less common technique is to create test data using test data generators—specially designed computer programs that create comprehensive test data based on input parameters that describe the nature of the program to be tested.

As an audit technology, test data have several limitations. A test can be run only on a specific program at a specific point in time. The test data may become obsolete because of program changes. The use of test data must be announced; the data are processed in a test run rather than concurrently with actual live transactions. Thus an auditor cannot always ensure that the program being tested is the one that is used regularly. Finally, test data generally cannot cover all combinations of conditions that a computer program might encounter in use.

INTEGRATED-TEST-FACILITY APPROACH

Integrated test facility (ITF) involves the use of test data and also the creation of fictitious entities (e.g., vendors, employees, products, or accounts) on the master files of a computer system. The technique is integrated because the test data are processed concurrent with real transactions against live master files that contain the real as well as fictitious entities. Accordingly, audit checks are made as a part of the normal processing

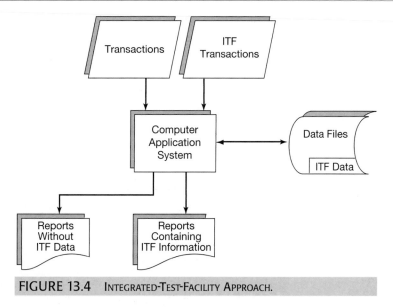

FIGURE 13.4   INTEGRATED-TEST-FACILITY APPROACH.

cycle, ensuring that the programs being checked are identical to the programs that process real data (Fig. 13.4).

Test data are identified by special codes and must be excluded from the normal system outputs either manually or by modifying or initially designing the application programs to perform this function. The need to exclude the fictitious data from normal output reports is the major disadvantage of ITF, but this is an unavoidable consequence of the objective of the technique, which is to process test data concurrent with real data. Careful planning is necessary to ensure that ITF data are segregated properly from the normal outputs.

ITF is a popular technique. If planned carefully, costs of using ITF are minimal. This is so because no special processing or other interruption of normal computer activity is involved. An ITF normally will be developed at the same time as the application system and will increase the normal cost of systems development. However, once implemented, operating costs are low. ITF is used commonly to audit large computer application systems that employ real-time processing technology. Concurrent testing is appropriate to concurrent real-time processing of transactions.

ITF is a powerful audit technology. Ironically, one of the earliest publicized computer fraud cases—the Equity Funding scandal—involved modification of computer programs to separately process thousands of bogus insurance policies, which is essentially the same concept used in ITF. The bogus policies were identified by a special code and were excluded routinely from reports provided to auditors but were included in all other reports. Similarly, test data differ from fraudulent data only in that test data are processed under controlled conditions by auditors.

PARALLEL SIMULATION

The test data and ITF methods both process test data through real programs. **Parallel simulation** processes real data through test or audit programs. The simulated output and the regular output are compared for control purposes. The amount of redundant processing undertaken by the test or audit program usually is limited to sections that are of major interest to the audit. For example, parallel simulation of a cost accounting program may be limited to the functions that update work-in-process records. Other

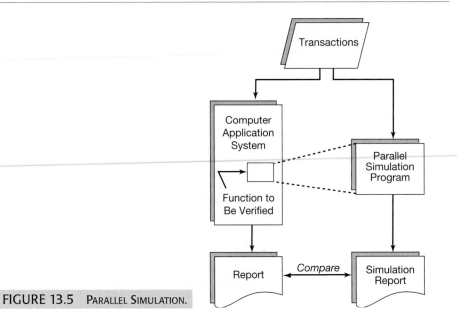

FIGURE 13.5 PARALLEL SIMULATION.

functions, such as scheduling or performance reporting, may not be included in the simulation program because they are not of direct interest to the audit. This is illustrated in Figure 13.5.

Parallel simulation—the redundant processing of all input data by a separate test program—permits comprehensive validation and is appropriate where transactions are sufficiently important to require a 100% audit. The audit program used in parallel simulation is typically some type of generalized audit program that processes data and produces output identical to the program being audited. The same actual data are processed by both programs and the results compared. This approach is expensive and time-consuming, but unlike the other approaches, it uses real data. Furthermore, it can be used off-site.

AUDIT SOFTWARE

Audit software includes computer programs that permit the computer to be used as an auditing tool. The computer is programmed to read, select, extract, and process sample data from computer files. There are many types of audit software that may be used to varying degrees in both mainframe and personal computer (PC) environments. Conventional software such as system utility programs, information retrieval programs, or high-level languages (e.g., COBOL) might be used. More common is the use of specially designed audit software packages, known as *generalized audit software* (GAS), and PC software packages. These are discussed separately.

GENERALIZED AUDIT SOFTWARE (GAS)

Generalized audit software (GAS) is software that has been designed specifically to facilitate the use of IT in auditing. GAS was developed originally by public accounting firms in the late 1960s and has a long history of use. GAS is designed specifically to allow auditors with little computer expertise to perform audit-related data processing functions. These packages can perform such tasks as selecting sample data from the files, checking computations, and searching the files for unusual items. They also incorporate many special features that are useful to auditors, such as the statistical selection of sample data and the preparation of confirmation requests.

PC SOFTWARE

The low cost of PCs, coupled with the wide variety of software packages available, has made the PC an important tool in administrating an audit. General-purpose **PC software** packages such as word processing and spreadsheet software have many audit applications. In addition, special-purpose audit-oriented software packages have been developed specifically for use in audit administration.

ACL, published by ACL Software, is one example of PC audit software. It allows the auditor to connect a PC to a client's mainframe or PC and then extract and analyze data. For example, using ACL, an auditor can directly access SAP R/3 data. ACL accesses files in their native format without any need to convert them. ACL provides a wide range of functions that allow the auditor to do such things as recalculate account balances for verification, age and analyze accounts receivable, and identify trends and exceptions.

EMBEDDED AUDIT ROUTINES

Embedded audit routines are an audit technology that involves modification of computer programs for audit purposes. This is accomplished by building special auditing routines into regular production programs so that transaction data or some subset of them can be subjected to audit analysis. One such technique has been termed *embedded audit data collection*. Embedded audit data collection uses one or more specially programmed modules embedded as **in-line code** within the regular program code to select and record data for subsequent analysis and evaluation (Fig. 13.6). The use of in-line code means that the application program performs the audit data collection function at the same time as it processes data for normal production purposes. Embedded routines are included more easily in a program as it is being developed than added as a modification later on.

Audit criteria for selecting and recording transactions by the embedded modules must be supplied by the auditor. This can be done in different ways. In an approach called the **system control audit review file (SCARF)**, auditor-determined programmed edit tests for limits or reasonableness are included in the program as it is developed

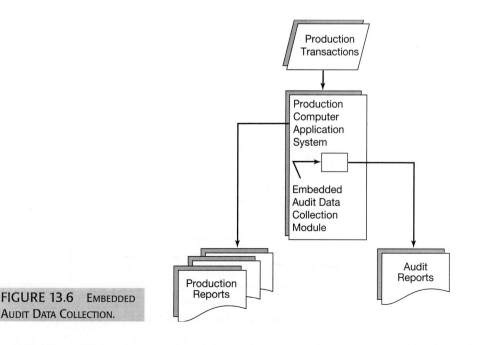

FIGURE 13.6 EMBEDDED AUDIT DATA COLLECTION.

initially. During normal operation of the program, data items that are exceptions to these edits are written on a file. This file of exceptions may be reviewed by the auditor, and any appropriate actions may be undertaken. Values used in such limit or reasonableness tests may be set when the module is developed; alternatively, the module may be programmed so that the test limits may be altered by the auditor as desired. Transactions might be selected randomly rather than as exceptions to programmed edit tests. The objective of this approach is to generate a statistical sample of transactions for later audit. This approach has been termed **sample audit review file (SARF)**.

EXTENDED RECORDS

Extended records involve the modification of computer programs to provide a comprehensive audit trail for selected transactions by collecting in one extended record additional data concerning processing that are normally not collected. Since many different processing steps may be combined within a single program, the intervening steps that make up the audit trail are often lost. Several different files might have to be reviewed to follow the processing of a specific transaction.

With the extended record technique, specific transactions are tagged, and the intervening processing steps that normally would not be saved are added to the extended record, permitting the audit trail to be reconstructed for these transactions. The extended record includes data from all the separate application programs that may process a transaction, thus providing a complete audit trail. Transactions might be identified by special codes, selected randomly, or selected as exceptions to edit tests.

SNAPSHOT

Snapshot, as the name implies, attempts to provide a comprehensive picture of the working of a program at particular points in time. Snapshot is a common program-debugging technique. Snapshot involves the addition of program code to cause the program to print out the contents of selected memory areas at the time, during processing, that the snapshot code is executed. This provides a hard copy of the operation of the program that otherwise would not be available and is very useful in locating bugs in a program. As an audit tool, snapshot code may be added to areas of the program that are of interest to the audit and executed only for transactions that are exceptions to predetermined edit tests. Snapshot and extended records are very similar technology, with snapshot generating a printed audit trail and extended records incorporating snapshot data in the extended record rather than on hard copy.

TRACING

Tracing is another audit technique that originated as a program-debugging aid. Tracing a program's execution provides a detailed audit trail of the instructions executed during the program's operation. Tracing normally is executed using an option in the program source code language (such as COBOL). The audit trail provided by the trace depends on the particular trace package. High-level languages are traced at the source-statement level; lower-level languages are traced at a more detailed level. Tracing provides a detailed listing of the sequence of program statement execution. A trace can produce thousands of output records, and care must be exercised that an excessive number of transactions are not tagged for tracing. For audit purposes, tracing might be used to verify that internal controls within an application program are executed as the program processes live or test data. A trace also may indicate sections of unexecuted program code, a situation that in some instances has resulted in the discovery of incorrect or unauthorized modifications to a program.

All embedded audit routine techniques require a high level of technical expertise when they are first set up and a moderate to high level of knowledge to use them effectively. They are far easier to implement when a program and/or files for an application are designed rather than after the system has begun operation. The degree of independence that auditors can maintain while developing such systems will depend largely on the level of technical expertise they possess. Even when the auditor possesses a high level of technical expertise, development still requires a good deal of cooperation between the auditor and systems personnel.

REVIEW-OF-SYSTEMS DOCUMENTATION

Review-of-systems documentation, such as narrative descriptions, flowcharts, and program listings, is probably the oldest information systems auditing technique and still a widely used one. This approach is particularly appropriate in the initial phases of an audit as preparation for the selection and use of other more direct audit technology.

Many types of reviews are possible. An auditor may request computer personnel to "dump" a computer file, that is, to provide the auditor with a complete listing of the file's contents. Alternatively, the auditor may request dumps of program source language listings. These listings may be reviewed manually by the auditor. Programs might be **desk checked** by the auditor. In desk checking, the auditor manually processes test or real data through the program logic. Program flowcharts might be reviewed in the same manner. A more sophisticated review of a program might be undertaken by requesting a dump of the object code, that is, machine-language version of a program. Review of this form of system documentation provides the greatest assurance that what is checked is actually what does the processing, but this form of review requires considerable technical expertise and patience. The auditor might review the manufacturer's blueprint of the software and compare it with the software in use. The auditor might verify a hash total of the object code of the software to detect modifications to the software.

Another type of documentation that may be examined is the operating documentation generated by many computer systems as a routine part of operations. Software that monitors the performance of computer operations is commonly available on large systems to provide technical statistics useful in tuning the system for efficient operation. While these statistics are oriented toward the operating functions of the system, such as channel and disk usage, they also might be used for specialized auditing purposes. Job accounting routines are frequently part of a computer's operating system. These routines collect and summarize statistics concerning program (job) resource use. Again, such statistics may be of interest to the auditor because they show who used the system, as well as when and which resources and programs were involved.

CONTROL FLOWCHARTING

In many cases, specific documentation for auditing purposes is reviewed and developed to show the nature of application controls in a system. This documentation has been termed **control flowcharting**. Analytic flowcharts, system flowcharts, and other graphic techniques are used to describe the controls in a system. A major advantage of flowcharts is that they are understandable to auditors, users, and computer personnel and thus facilitate communication between these different parties.

MAPPING

More direct audit evidence concerning programs may be obtained by monitoring the running of a program with a special software measurement package. This audit technique is termed **mapping**. Special software is used to monitor the execution of a program; in doing so, the software counts the number of times each program statement in the program is executed and provides summary statistics concerning resource use. Mapping originated as a technique to assist program design and testing. Auditors can use the same software to determine whether specific program statements have been executed. Mapping can help to ensure that program application control statements that appear in the source language listing of a program actually execute when the program runs and that they have not inadvertently or otherwise been bypassed by a logic not readily apparent in the source-code listing of the program. Although software measurement packages can ensure that certain program steps have been executed, they do not ensure that execution was performed in the proper sequence. Counts of the number of times each program statement was executed do not imply that the total program executes in accordance with the intent of the programmer (i.e., that the program does the right thing).

Mapping can be used effectively in conjunction with a test data technique. The execution of a program with test data as input can be mapped. Evaluation of the output of the software monitor can indicate how extensively the input tested individual program statements. Statements that have not executed have not been tested.

TYPES OF INFORMATION SYSTEMS AUDITS

GENERAL APPROACH TO AN INFORMATION SYSTEMS AUDIT

Most approaches to an information systems audit follow some variation of a three-phase structure. The first phase consists of an initial review and evaluation of the area to be audited and audit plan preparation. The second phase is a detailed review and evaluation of controls. The third phase involves compliance testing and is followed by analysis and reporting of results.

The initial review phase of an information systems audit determines the course of action the audit will take and includes decisions concerning specific areas to be investigated, the deployment of audit labor, the audit technology to be used, and the development of a time and/or cost budget for the audit. The primary control over the conduct of an information systems audit, like that of any other organized activity, centers on documentation and review of performance. Each general phase of an audit, as well as specific steps within each phase, should have as an objective the preparation of documentation. Such documentation provides a tangible output and goal for each audit step, allows effective supervision, and facilitates review.

Audit resources usually are limited, so it generally will not be possible to audit each application every year. Applications that are more subject to fraud or serious financial error are likely targets for audit. Frequently, a rotating system of selection is used to choose audit areas, with each application being audited according to some multiyear schedule.

Decisions concerning the deployment of auditing labor, the audit technology to be used, and the time/cost budget for the overall audit also should be made according to some systematic procedure. The outcome of all these decisions and the product of the initial review phase of an information systems audit is the audit program. An **audit program** is a detailed list of the audit procedures to be applied on a particular audit. Standardized audit programs for particular audit areas have been developed and are common in all types of auditing. The use of a standardized audit program is often possible, with modifications made to reflect the particular situation subject to audit.

The second general phase of an information systems audit is detailed review and evaluation. In this phase of the audit, effort is focused on fact finding in the area(s) selected for audit. Documentation of the application area is reviewed, and data concerning the operation of the system are collected by interviews, administration of internal control questionnaires, and direct observation. Transaction files, control logs, program listings, and other data are reviewed as necessary to confirm the scope of the audit set in the audit program and to design the test procedures to be used subsequently.

The third phase of the audit is testing. The testing phase of an audit produces evidence of compliance with procedures. Compliance tests are undertaken to provide reasonable assurance that internal controls exist and operate as prescribed in system documentation. The nature of compliance tests that might be included in an information systems audit are discussed in the following sections.

INFORMATION SYSTEMS APPLICATION AUDITS

Application controls are divided into three general areas; input, processing, and output. An application audit generally involves reviewing the controls in each of these areas. In addition to the usual manual tracing and vouching techniques, all the audit technologies discussed earlier are relevant. The specific technology used will depend on the ingenuity and resources of the auditor. Test data, ITF, or parallel simulation might be used to test processing controls. Transactions to be selected for audit might be generated by an embedded audit module or by a separate audit program. GAS might be used to review transaction and/or output files. The nature of an application audit will be heavily influenced by the amount of audit involvement in the systems development process. ITF and embedded audit modules can be used only if they already exist in the application.

APPLICATION SYSTEMS DEVELOPMENT AUDITS

Systems development audits are directed at the activities of systems analysts and programmers who develop and modify application programs, files, and related procedures. Controls governing the systems development process directly affect the reliability of the application programs that are developed. Three general areas of audit concern in the systems development process are systems development standards, project management, and program change control. The primary audit technique in each of these areas is a review and testing of the related documentation. This is accomplished by directly observing the documentation and by collecting relevant information through interviews and/or questionnaires.

Systems development standards are the documentation governing the design, development, and implementation of application systems. The existence of systems development standards is a major general control in computerized systems. Development standards ensure that appropriate application controls are considered, selected, and implemented in application systems, that an adequate audit trail is provided, and that suitable levels of operability and maintainability are achieved after implementation. The primary audit technique is to review such documentation, assess it for sufficiency, and then determine compliance with it. This is done by reviewing application system documentation. Application system documentation, such as flowcharts, system narratives, and test data, should conform to the specifications set forth in the organization's systems development standards.

Project management controls measure and control progress during application systems development. Project management consists of project planning and project supervision. A project plan is a formal statement of the project's detailed work plan.

Project supervision monitors the execution of project activities. Auditors can evaluate the adequacy of project management controls by comparing criteria available in the systems development literature. Compliance testing involves reviewing project planning and supervision documentation—such as PERT/CPM charts, Gantt charts, schedules, time reports, and status reports—and interviewing users and systems personnel.

Program change controls concern the maintenance of application programs. The objective of such controls is to prevent unauthorized and potentially fraudulent changes from being introduced into previously tested and accepted programs. Elements of control include documentation of change requests and a register of program changes with dates and appropriate approvals for authorization, programming the change, testing and certification of test results, and revision of the production program and its related documentation. Appropriate segregation of programmers, operations, and the program/tape library is necessary in the process. Program maintenance is more subject to error than normal program development and represents a major loss exposure in terms of both fraud and access to sensitive programs.

Compliance testing might involve the review of documentation of maintenance procedures, review of systems job accounting information, and source language and object code comparison techniques. The common technique for code comparison has the audit function retain custody of duplicate program copies and periodically compare its copies with the actual production programs. This is commonly done at the source-statement level; object-code comparison is less common. Any differences detected between the test program and the production program are reconciled by tracing back to the program change documentation file. Test data used in program maintenance also should be reviewed for completeness. If testing of program modifications is incomplete, the probability of introducing errors to an application program is increased.

Audits of the systems development process are more common to large organizations because many small organizations may not have a formal systems development process. The essence of a formal systems development process is documentation. If none exists, a potential audit is necessarily terminated because the audit consists primarily of review and testing of such documentation.

COMPUTER SERVICE CENTER AUDITS

Normally, an audit of the computer service center is undertaken before any application audits to ensure the general integrity of the environment in which the application will function. The general controls that govern computer service center operations complement application controls that are developed in specific application systems. The general controls that govern computer operations also help to ensure the uninterrupted availability of computer service center resources.

Audits might be undertaken in several areas. One area concerns environmental controls. Mainframe systems associated with large computer service centers generally have special temperature and humidity requirements that necessitate air conditioning. Another area that is closely related to environmental controls is physical security of the center. There are many concerns and thus many potential controls in this area. Controls are necessary to maintain a stable power source, as well as to provide for an alternative power source in the case of failure. Fire protection must be provided, and the center must be protected from water damage. Controls must ensure controlled physical access. Controls over the release of data, reports, and computer programs are also of concern. Provisions for casualty insurance and business interruption insurance might be reviewed.

The center's disaster recovery plan might be reviewed. A disaster recovery plan would include such items as management responsibility statements—specifying who is responsible for what in the event of a disaster—emergency action plans, facilities and data backup plans, and recovery process controls. Another area concerns controls over malfunction reporting and preventative maintenance. This area includes failure reporting and logging, preventative maintenance scheduling, and malfunction correction.

Management controls over operation of the computer service center are also an area of concern. This area includes techniques used to budget equipment load factors, project usage statistics, budget and plan staffing requirements, and plan equipment acquisitions. Job (i.e., computer resource) accounting systems are another general control over operations. Job accounting systems may contain user billing or charge-out procedures. Billing algorithms might be reviewed, and periodic user billing statements might be reconciled to usage.

The only compliance tests that would be used in all the preceding audit areas would be review of documentary evidence; corroborating interviews with users, management, and systems personnel; direct observation; and inquiry. Audits of computer service center operations require a higher degree of technical training and familiarity with information systems operations than do audits of computerized applications.

❖ SUMMARY

The term *information systems auditing* is used commonly to describe two different types of computer-related activity. One use of the term is to describe the process of reviewing and evaluating the internal controls in an electronic data processing system. This type of activity is described as auditing through the computer. The other general use of the term is to describe use of the computer by an auditor to perform some audit work that otherwise would have to be done manually. This type of activity is described as auditing with the computer.

Information systems audit technology has evolved along with computer system development. There is no one overall auditing technology. Rather, there are several technologies that may be used as appropriate to accomplish an audit's objectives. Technologies discussed include test data, integrated test facility (ITF), parallel simulation, and generalized audit software, among others. Information systems audit technologies differ widely as to the amount of technical expertise required for their use. Several of the technologies entail significant costs to implement, whereas others may be implemented with relatively little cost.

Most approaches to an information systems audit follow some variation of a three-phase structure. These phases are initial review and evaluation of the area to be audited, detailed review and evaluation, and testing. Three general types of information systems audits might be undertaken. These are application audits, application systems development audits, and computer service center audits.

❖ GLOSSARY

around-the-computer approach: information systems auditing approach in which the processing portion of a computer system is ignored.

auditing through the computer: the process of reviewing and evaluating the internal controls in an electronic data processing system.

audit program: a detailed list of the audit procedures to be applied on a particular audit.

audit software: computer programs that permit the computer to be used as an auditing tool.

auditing with the computer: use of the computer by an auditor to perform some audit work that otherwise would have to be done manually.

compliance testing: testing to confirm the existence, assess the effectiveness, and check the continuity of operation of internal controls.

control flowcharting: analytic flowcharts or other graphic techniques are used to describe the controls in a system.

desk checked: the auditor manually processes test or real data through the logic of a computer program.

embedded audit routines: special auditing routines included in regular computer programs so that transaction data can be subjected to audit analysis.

extended records: modification of programs to collect and store additional data of audit interest.

financial statement audit: the second stage of a financial statement audit that uses substantive testing for direct verification of financial statement figures.

generalized audit software (GAS): audit software that has been specifically designed to allow auditors to perform audit-related data processing functions.

in-line code: an application program performs an embedded audit routine function such as data collection at the same time as it processes data for normal purposes.

integrated test facility (ITF): concurrent information systems audit technology that involves the use of test data and also the creation of fictitious entities on the master files of a computer system.

interim audit: first stage of a financial statement audit that has the objective of establishing the degree to which the internal control system can be relied on.

mapping: special software is used to monitor the execution of a program.

PC software: software that allows the auditor to use PCs to perform audit tasks.

parallel simulation: the processing of real data through audit programs, with the simulated output and the regular output compared for control purposes.

review-of-systems documentation: existing systems documentation such as program flowcharts are reviewed for audit purposes.

sample audit review file (SARF): use of in-line code to randomly select transactions for audit analysis.

snapshot: modification of programs to output data of audit interest.

substantive testing: direct verification of balances contained in financial statements.

system control audit review file (SCARF): auditor-determined programmed edit tests for audit transaction analysis are included in a program as it is initially developed.

test data: auditor-prepared input containing both valid and invalid data.

tracing: provides a detailed audit trail of the instructions executed during the program's operation.

❖ CHAPTER QUIZ

Answers to the chapter quiz appear on page 481.

1. Which of the following is a potential problem when using test data?
   - (a) testing a program that is not the actual program used for processing
   - (b) introducing errors into the program being tested
   - (c) both a and b
   - (d) neither a nor b

2. Which of the following is a potential problem when using integrated test facility (ITF)?
   - (a) testing a program that is not the actual program used for processing
   - (b) introducing errors into the program being tested
   - (c) both a and b
   - (d) neither a nor b

3. Which of the following is a concurrent auditing technology?
   - (a) test data
   - (b) integrated test facility (ITF)
   - (c) both a and b
   - (d) neither a nor b

4. Which of the following is a concurrent auditing technology?
   - (a) parallel simulation
   - (b) generalized audit software
   - (c) both a and b
   - (d) neither a nor b

5. Which of the following is a concurrent auditing technology?
   - (a) embedded audit routines
   - (b) control flowcharting
   - (c) both a and b
   - (d) neither a nor b

6. Which of the following is used to test the functioning of computer programs?
   - (a) test data
   - (b) parallel simulation

    (c) both a and b

    (d) neither a nor b

7. Which of the following is used to select data for audit analysis?

    (a) generalized audit software

    (b) embedded audit routines

    (c) both a and b

    (d) neither a nor b

8. Which of the following most likely would be implemented with generalized audit software?

    (a) embedded audit routines

    (b) parallel simulation

    (c) both a and b

    (d) neither a nor b

9. Mapping is a technology that provides the auditor (_____).

    (a) assurance that program instructions are executing in proper sequence

    (b) summary information regarding which program instructions are executed

    (c) both a and b

    (d) neither a nor b

10. Normally an audit of the computer service center is undertaken (_____) any application audits.

    (a) during

    (b) before

    (c) after

    (d) instead of

❖ REVIEW PROBLEM

In the past, the records to be evaluated in an audit have been printed reports, listings, documents, and written papers, all of which are visible output. However, in fully computerized systems that employ daily updating of transaction files, output and files are frequently in machine-readable forms, such as tapes or disks. Thus they often present the auditor with an opportunity to use the computer in performing an audit.

Required

Discuss how the computer can be used to aid the auditor in examining accounts receivable in such a fully computerized system.

                (CPA)

❖ SOLUTION TO REVIEW PROBLEM

Testing Extension and Footings

The computer can be used to perform simple summations and other computations to test the correction of extensions and footings. The auditor may choose to perform tests on all records instead of just on samples because the speed and low cost per computation of the computer enable this at only a small extra amount of time and expense.

Selecting and Printing Confirmation Requests

The computer can select and print out confirmation requests on the basis of quantifiable selection criteria. The program can be written to select the accounts according to any set of criteria desired and using any sampling plan.

Examining Records for Quality (Completeness, Consistency, Valid Conditions, etc.)

The quality of visible records is readily apparent to the auditor. Sloppy record keeping, lack of completeness, and so on are observed by the auditor in the normal course of the audit. If machine-readable records are evaluated manually, however, a complete printout is needed to examine their quality. The auditor may choose to use the computer for examining these records for quality.

If the computer is to be used for the examination, a program is written to examine the record for completeness, consistency among different items, valid conditions, reasonable amounts, and so forth. For instance, customer file records might be examined to determine those for which no credit limit is specified, those for which account balances exceed credit limit, and those for which credit limits exceed a stipulated amount.

Summarizing Data and Performing Analyses Useful to the Auditor

The auditor frequently needs to have the client's data analyzed and/or summarized. Such procedures as aging accounts receivable or listing all credit balances in accounts receivable can be accomplished with a computer program.

Selecting and Printing Audit Samples

The computer may be programmed to select audit samples by the use of random numbers or by systematic selection techniques. The sample selection procedures may be programmed to use multiple criteria, such as the selection of a random sample of items under a certain dollar amount plus the selection of all items over a certain dollar amount. Other considerations can be included, such as unusual transactions, dormant accounts, and so forth.

(CPA)

❖ REVIEW QUESTIONS

1. What is meant by the expression *auditing around the computer*?
2. What are the two meanings of the term *information systems auditing*?
3. List and briefly describe the three phases of an information systems audit.
4. Distinguish between auditing through the computer and auditing with the computer.
5. What is a computer audit program?
6. What types of documents are examined in an information systems audit?
7. List five embedded audit routine techniques.
8. Compliance testing tests what?
9. How have PCs affected information systems auditing?
10. Identify the characteristics that are common to a typical information systems audit.
11. How would you select areas that should be audited in an information systems system?
12. Why do computer service center audits require the greatest expertise of an information systems auditor?

❖ DISCUSSION QUESTIONS AND PROBLEMS

13. Auditors' initial response to computer systems was to audit around the computer. This strategy is *least* likely to be successful in an audit of
    (a) a batch processing system for payroll.
    (b) a card-based system for inventory.
    (c) an on-line system for demand deposit accounts.
    (d) a mark-sense document system for utility billing.

(IIA)

14. Normally, auditors using the ITF technique enter immaterial transactions to minimize the effect on output. This is a disadvantage because
    (a) certain limit tests cannot be attempted.
    (b) the transaction will not appear normal.
    (c) a special routine will be required in the application system.
    (d) designing the test data can be difficult.

(IIA)

Use the following information to answer Questions 15, 16, and 17.

Management has requested a special audit of the recently established electronic controls systems division because the last three quarterly profit reports seem to be inconsistent with the division's cash flow. The division sells customized control systems on a contract basis. A work-in-process (WIP) record is established for each contract on the WIP master file, which is kept on magnetic disk. Contract charges for materials, labor, and overhead are processed by the WIP computer program to maintain the WIP master file and to provide billing information.

The preliminary audit has revealed that not all costs have been charged against the WIP records. Thus, when contracts are closed, reported profits have been overstated. It is now necessary to determine the reason(s) for this loss of control.

15. Which of the following information systems auditing techniques would be *most appropriate* to audit the processing accuracy of the WIP computer program in posting transactions to the master WIP file?
    (a) control flowcharting
    (b) test data
    (c) review of program documentation
    (d) embedded audit source code

16. Which of the following information systems auditing techniques would be *most appropriate* to audit the content of the WIP master file that is stored on magnetic disk?
    (a) control flowcharting
    (b) test data
    (c) generalized audit software
    (d) embedded audit source code

17. Which of the following information systems auditing techniques would be *most appropriate* to audit the overall business control context of the WIP computer processing system?
    (a) control flowcharting
    (b) test data
    (c) generalized audit software
    (d) embedded audit source code

(IIA)

18. Smith Corporation has numerous customers. A customer file is kept on disk storage. Each customer file contains name, address, credit limit, and account balance. The auditor wishes to test this file to determine whether credit limits are being exceeded. The best procedure for the auditor to follow would be to
    (a) develop test data that would cause some account balances to exceed the credit limit and determine if the system properly detects such situations.
    (b) develop a program to compare credit limits with account balances and print out the details of any account with a balance exceeding its credit limit.
    (c) request a printout of all account balances so that they can be checked manually against the credit limits.
    (d) request a printout of a sample of account balances so that they can be checked individually against the credit limits.

(CPA)

19. When an auditor tests a computerized accounting system, which of the following is true of the test data approach?
    (a) Test data are processed by the client's computer programs under the auditor's control.
    (b) Test data must consist of all possible valid and invalid conditions.
    (c) Testing a program at year-end provides assurance that the client's processing was accurate for the full year.
    (d) Several transactions of each type must be tested.

(CPA)

20. An auditor's objective is to verify the processing accuracy of an application. An information systems audit approach for achieving this objective that avoids contaminating client master files or requiring substantial additional application programming is the
    (a) embedded data collection technique.
    (b) integrated test facility.
    (c) test data method.
    (d) snapshot method.

(IIA)

21. Headquarters' auditors are reviewing a payroll application system via the ITF technique. Which of the following would be used by the auditors?
    (a) Fictitious names processed with the normal payroll application of the corporation to a dummy entity
    (b) Fictitious names processed in a separate run through the payroll application of the corporation
    (c) A sample of last month's payroll reprocessed through the audit software package to a dummy entity
    (d) Fictitious names processed through the generalized audit software package with the same company codes

                                                                                      (IIA)

22. Which of the following is true of generalized audit software packages?
    (a) They can be used only in auditing on-line computer systems.
    (b) They can be used on any computer without modification.
    (c) They each have their own characteristics, which the auditor must consider carefully before using in a given audit situation.
    (d) They enable the auditor to perform all manual compliance test procedures less expensively.

                                                                                      (CPA)

23. The most important function of generalized audit software is the capability to
    (a) access information stored on computer files.
    (b) select a sample of items for testing.
    (c) evaluate sample test results.
    (d) test the accuracy of the client's calculations.

                                                                                      (CPA)

24. When auditing around the computer, the independent auditor focuses solely on the source documents and
    (a) test data.
    (b) computer processing.
    (c) compliance techniques.
    (d) computer output.

                                                                                      (CPA)

25. In auditing through a computer, the test data method is used by auditors to test the
    (a) accuracy of input data.
    (b) validity of the output.
    (c) procedures contained within the program.
    (d) normalcy of distribution of test data.

                                                                                      (CPA)

26. Which of the following methods of testing application controls uses a generalized audit software package prepared by the auditors?
    (a) parallel simulation
    (b) integrated testing facility approach
    (c) test data approach
    (d) exception report tests

                                                                                      (CPA)

27. A primary advantage of using generalized audit software packages in auditing the financial statements of a client that uses a computer system is that the auditor may
    (a) substantiate the accuracy of data through self-checking digits and hash totals.
    (b) access information stored on computer files without a complete understanding of the client's hardware and software features.
    (c) reduce the level of required compliance testing to a relatively small amount.
    (d) gather and permanently store large quantities of supportive evidential matter in machine-readable form.

                                                                                      (CPA)

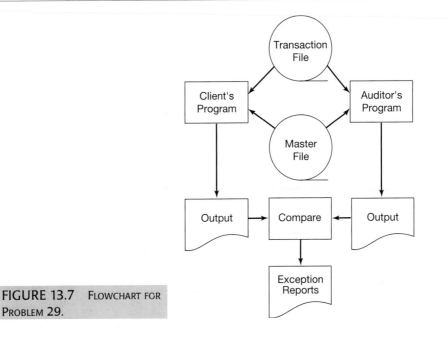

FIGURE 13.7 FLOWCHART FOR PROBLEM 29.

28. When testing a computerized accounting system, which of the following is *not* true of the test data approach?
    (a) Test data are processed by the client's computer programs under the auditor's control.
    (b) The test data must consist of all possible valid and invalid conditions.
    (c) The test data must consist of only those valid and invalid conditions in which the auditor is interested.
    (d) Only one transaction of each type need be tested.

    (CPA)

    Problem 29 is based on the flowchart in Figure 13.7.
29. The flowchart in Figure 13.7 depicts
    (a) program code checking.
    (b) parallel simulation.
    (c) integrated test facility.
    (d) controlled reprocessing.

    (CPA)

    Problem 30 is based on the flowchart in Figure 13.8.
30. In a credit sales and cash receipts system flowchart, the symbol X could represent
    (a) auditor's test data.
    (b) remittance advices.
    (c) error reports.
    (d) credit authorization forms.

    (CPA)

31. Which of the following computer-assisted auditing techniques allows fictitious and real transactions to be processed together without client operating personnel being aware of the testing process?
    (a) parallel simulation
    (b) generalized audit software programming
    (c) integrated test facility
    (d) test data approach

    (CPA)

32. An auditor who is testing information systems controls in a payroll system most likely would use test data that contain conditions such as
    (a) deductions *not* authorized by employees.
    (b) overtime *not* approved by supervisors.

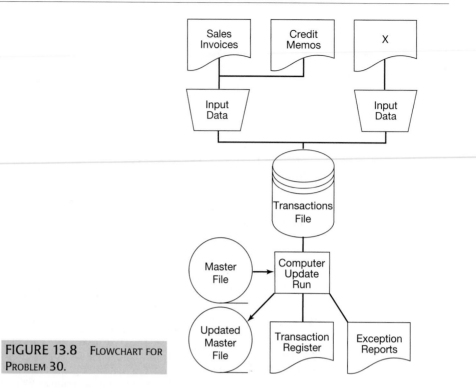

FIGURE 13.8 FLOWCHART FOR PROBLEM 30.

(c) time tickets with invalid job numbers.
(d) payroll checks with unauthorized signatures.

(CPA)

33. An auditor most likely would test for the presence of unauthorized systems program changes by running a
   (a) program with test data.
   (b) check-digit verification program.
   (c) source-code comparison program.
   (d) program that computes control totals.

(CPA)

34. You decided to use a newly acquired audit software package in auditing accounts payable. The accounts payable system has been computerized for several years, and the transaction records are recorded on magnetic disk.

Required
   (a) Briefly describe five of the major functions of the typical generalized audit software package.
   (b) List three important steps in auditing of accounts payable for which generalized audit software can be used.
   (c) Briefly describe how the generalized audit software should be used to perform these audit steps.

(IIA)

35. An auditor is conducting an examination of the financial statements of a wholesale cosmetics distributor with an inventory consisting of thousands of individual items. The distributor keeps its inventory in its own distribution center and in two public warehouses. An inventory computer file is maintained on a computer disk, and at the end of each business day, the file is updated. Each record of the inventory file contains the following data:
   Item number
   Location of item

Description of item
Quantity on hand
Cost per item
Date of last purchase
Date of last sale
Quantity sold during year

The auditor is planning to observe the distributor's physical count of inventories as of a given date. The auditor will have available a computer tape of the data on the inventory file on the date of the physical count and a general-purpose computer software package.

Required

The auditor is planning to perform basic inventory auditing procedures. Identify the basic inventory auditing procedures and describe how using the general-purpose software package and the tape of the inventory file data might be helpful to the auditor in performing such auditing procedures.

Organize your answer as follows:

BASIC INVENTORY AUDITING PROCEDURE	HOW GENERAL-PURPOSE COMPUTER SOFTWARE PACKAGE AND TAPE OF THE INVENTORY FILE DATA MIGHT BE HELPFUL
1. Observe the physical count, making and recording test counts where applicable.	Determine which items are to be test counted by selecting a random sample of a representative number of items from the inventory file as of the date of the physical counts.

(CPA)

36. Rayo Corporation: Completion of Systems and Programming Questionnaire.[1]

Mike Kess, a senior auditor for the regional accounting firm Sanders and McDonald, was assigned to audit the Rayo Corporation. He was to conduct a preliminary review of the general controls over systems and programming. He has already identified the current applications and the equipment used in the data processing system (Fig. 13.9) and is about to start on system maintenance.

Mike contacted Jim Stram, the manager of systems and programming in the EDP department. A summary of their conversation is presented below.

MIKE: "How are system maintenance projects initiated and developed?"

JIM: "All potential projects are sent to a member of my staff called an applications coordinator for analysis. We do all our systems and programming work in-house. If a programming change is required for a project, the applications coordinator prepares a revision request form. These revision request forms must be approved by both the manager of operations and myself. The director of data processing and the internal auditor receive copies of each revision request form for information purposes."

MIKE: "How does the applications coordinator keep track of the revision request form and any change that might be made to it?"

JIM: "The revision request forms are numbered in different series depending on the nature of the change requested. The applications coordinator assigns the next number in the sequence and records in a master log each request he prepares. Changes in revision requests, from whatever source, are prepared on request forms just as initial requests are. Each change request is given the same basic number with a suffix indicating that it is an amendment, and there is a place for recording amendments in the master log."

[1]Prepared by Frederick L. Neumann, Richard J. Boland, and Jeffrey Johnson; Funded by the Touche Ross Foundation Aid to Accounting Education Program.

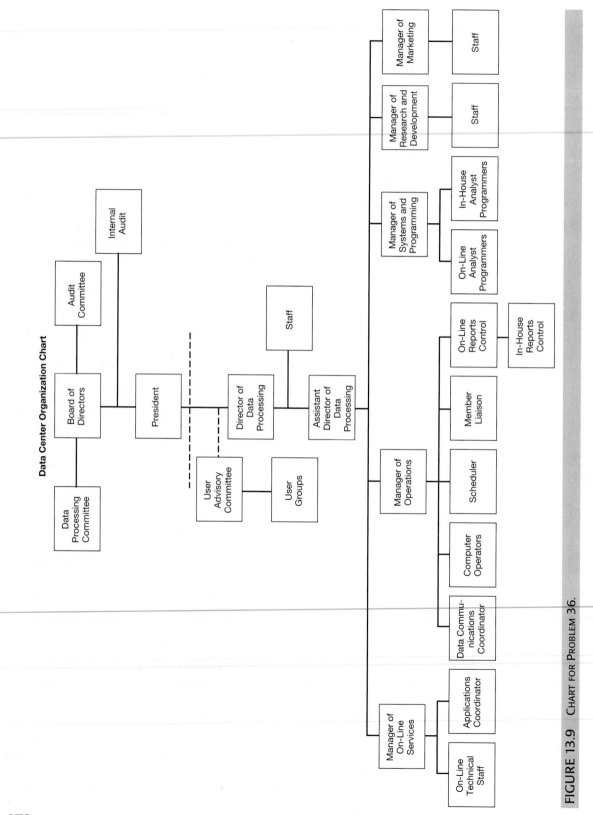

Data Center Organization Chart

FIGURE 13.9 Chart for Problem 36.

MIKE:	"What is the distribution of an approved request form?"
JIM:	"It goes to one of my systems supervisors for design, programming, and testing. The primary effort is usually performed by a programmer who has responsibility over the area of the application or the specific programs to be changed."
MIKE:	"But how are projects controlled?"
JIM:	"At the beginning of each programming project, an estimated start and completion date are assigned and entered on the request form and the master log. The system supervisor keeps on top of the projects assigned to him, and the applications coordinator also monitors the open requests. The system supervisor files a written status report with the applications coordinator twice a month, and he briefs me on any problems. However, I'm usually aware of any difficulties long before then.
	During the programming and testing phase, I think we have good control over the project. None of the compiles made during this phase changes any production source code for the existing computer programs. Also, all test object programs are identified by a strictly enforced naming convention that clearly distinguishes them from production programs. So far this has been successful in inhibiting their use in processing production. If a programmer has specific questions or problems on a project, his or her systems supervisor generally is available to give advice."
MIKE:	"Are there written guidelines to direct this activity? If so, how detailed are they?"
JIM:	"Only informal procedures exist to provide any uniformity to the programs and the coding changes that are made to a program. But formal standards do exist that define what documentation should be present for a system and for the programs within a system. These apply to program changes as well and again are strictly enforced. There is a periodic management review to see that we comply. We just had one about a month ago and got a clean bill of health."
MIKE:	"Are adequate tests and reviews made of changes before they are implemented?"
JIM:	"The applications coordinator, the systems supervisor, and the individual programmer informally discuss the necessary tests for a specific project. Sometimes I get involved too, but our guidelines are pretty good in this area and provide a fairly thorough approach to test design. After the tests have been completed to the systems supervisor's satisfaction, the applications coordinator reviews and approves the test results. This must be done on all revision requests before they are implemented into production. I usually review the programmer's work to see that all authorized changes are made correctly and are adequately tested and documented."
MIKE:	"How does implementation take place, and what controls are exercised over it?"
JIM:	"After the test results for a revision request have been approved by the applications coordinator, it is the responsibility of the programmer to implement the changes into production. In order for a programmer to put a program change into production, he or she must update the source code of the production program version. The programmer is required to provide program name and compile date information for all changed programs to his or her system supervisor. The programmer also has the responsibility of updating the systems and programming documentation. His or her system supervisor is supposed to review this and certify completion to the applications coordinator, who then completes the log entry."
MIKE:	"Are postimplementation reviews undertaken on system maintenance projects?"
JIM:	"Once the project is implemented, the applications coordinator reviews the output from the first few production runs of the changed program. He also questions users to see if any problem areas can be identified.
	A documented audit trail is provided by a completed project file that is maintained by the applications coordinator for each request number. This file

contains all the required documentation, including test results. A copy of the final summary goes to the department that originally submitted the request. A table in the computer is updated to provide listings of the most current compile dates for each set of production object code within the system. Before any program is implemented it is checked against the table."

Client _____ Audit Date _____

Systems and Programming Questionnaire

	Yes	No	N/A
1. Are there systems and programming standards in the following areas:			
a. Applications design?	____	____	____
b. Programming conventions and procedures?	____	____	____
c. Systems and program documentation?	____	____	____
d. Applications control?	____	____	____
e. Project planning and management?	____	____	____
2. Does the normal documentation for an application include the following:			
Application Documentation			
a. Narrative description?	____	____	____
b. Systems flowchart?	____	____	____
c. Definition of input data and source format?	____	____	____
d. Description of expected output data and format?	____	____	____
e. A listing of all valid transactions and other codes and abbreviations and master file fields affected?	____	____	____
f. File definition or layouts?	____	____	____
g. Instructions for preparing input?	____	____	____
h. Instructions for correcting errors?	____	____	____
i. Backup requirements?	____	____	____
j. Description of test data?	____	____	____
Program Documentation			
a. Program narrative?	____	____	____
b. Flowchart of each program?	____	____	____
c. Current source listing of each program?	____	____	____
Operations Documentation			
a. Data entry instructions, including verification?	____	____	____
b. Instructions for control personnel, including batching?	____	____	____
c. Instructions for the tape librarian?	____	____	____
d. Operator's run manual?	____	____	____
e. Reconstruction procedure?	____	____	____
3. Is there a periodic management review of documentation to ensure that it is current and accurate?	____	____	____
If yes, when and by whom was it last performed?_____			
_____			
4. Is all systems and programming work done in-house?	____	____	____
If not, is it done:			
a. By computer manufacturer's personnel?	____	____	____
b. By contract programming?	____	____	____
c. Other? Describe_____			
5. Are all changes programmed by persons other than those assigned to computer operations?	____	____	____
6. Are program changes documented in a manner that preserves an accurate chronological record of the applications?	____	____	____
If yes, describe _____			
7. Do the users participate in the development of new applications or modifications of existing applications through frequent reviews of work performed?			
If yes, are the results of reviews documented?	____	____	____
8. Are testing procedures and techniques standardized?	____	____	____
9. Are program revisions tested as stringently as new programs?	____	____	____
10. Are tests designed to uncover weaknesses in the links between programs, as well as within programs?	____	____	____
11. Are users involved in the testing process, i.e., do they use the application as it is intended during the testing process?	____	____	____
12. Do user departments perform the final review and sign off on projects before acceptance?	____	____	____
13. What departments and/or individuals have the authority to authorize an operator to put a new or modified program into production?_____			
14. What supervisory or management approval is necessary for the conversion of files? _____			
_____			

FIGURE 13.10   QUESTIONNAIRE FOR PROBLEM 36.

MIKE: "Well, that seems to be it. I think I have all that I need for now, but I'll probably be back to take a look at the files and records. I may have more questions
for you then. Thanks very much for your time and thoughtful answers. I really
appreciate your help."

JIM: "That's quite all right. If I can be of any more help, just let me know."

Required

(a) Keeping in mind that this is part of the preliminary phase of the review, are there any
additional questions you would have asked of Jim if you had been in Mike's place?

(b) Complete as much of the pages of the questionnaire shown in Figure 13.10 as you can
from the information Mike did collect in the interview.

(c) Make a list of weaknesses that you feel should be considered in the preliminary assessment of the internal control in this area.

❖ ANSWERS TO CHAPTER QUIZ

1. a	4. d	7. c	10. b
2. d	5. a	8. b	
3. b	6. c	9. b	